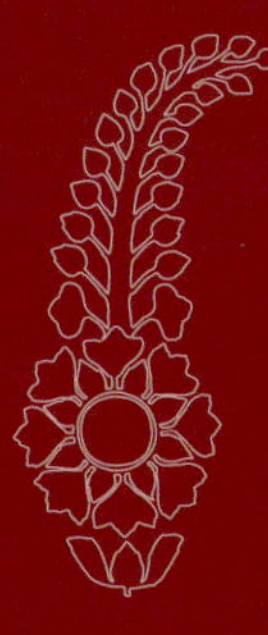

EAST MEETS WEST

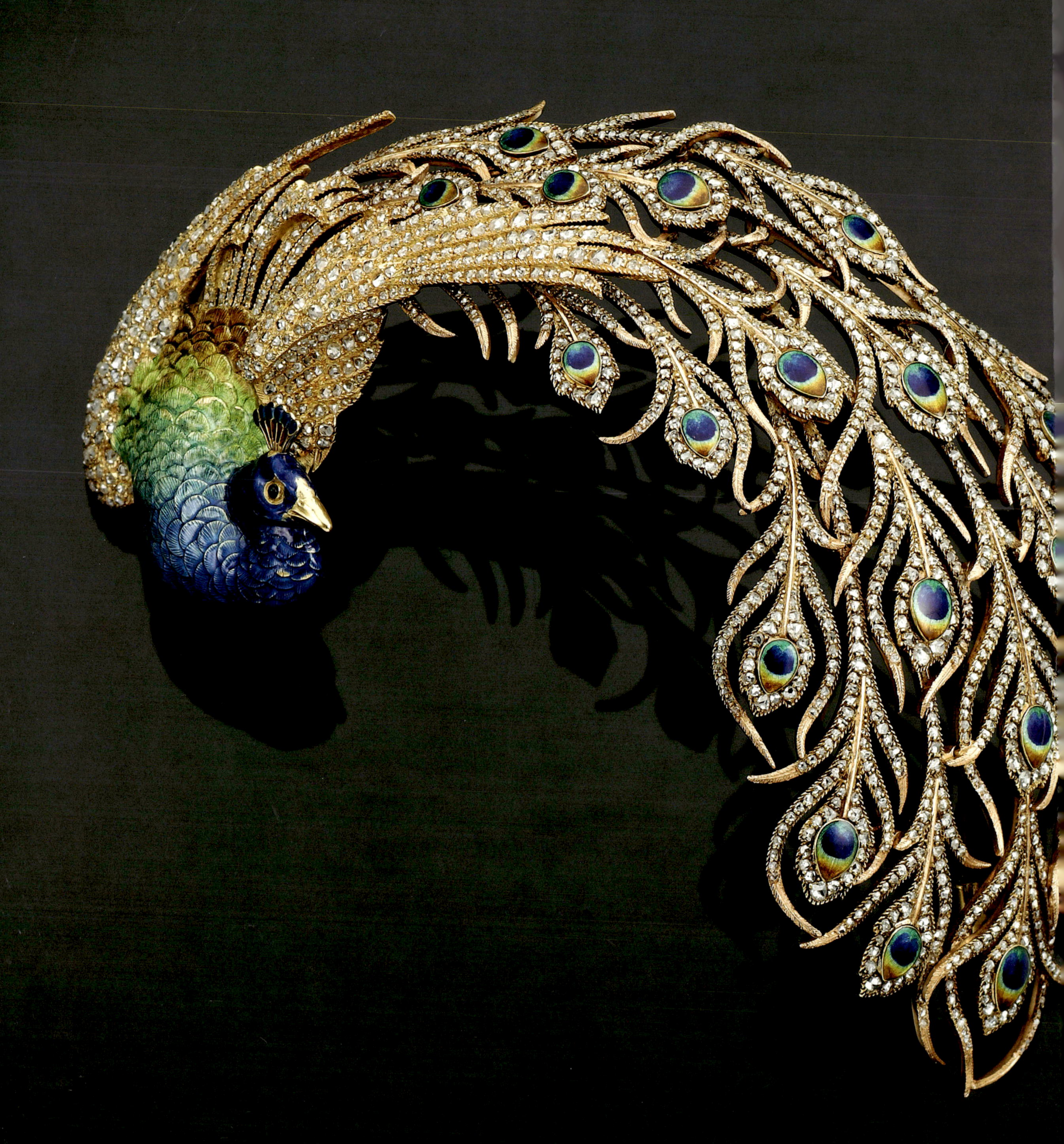

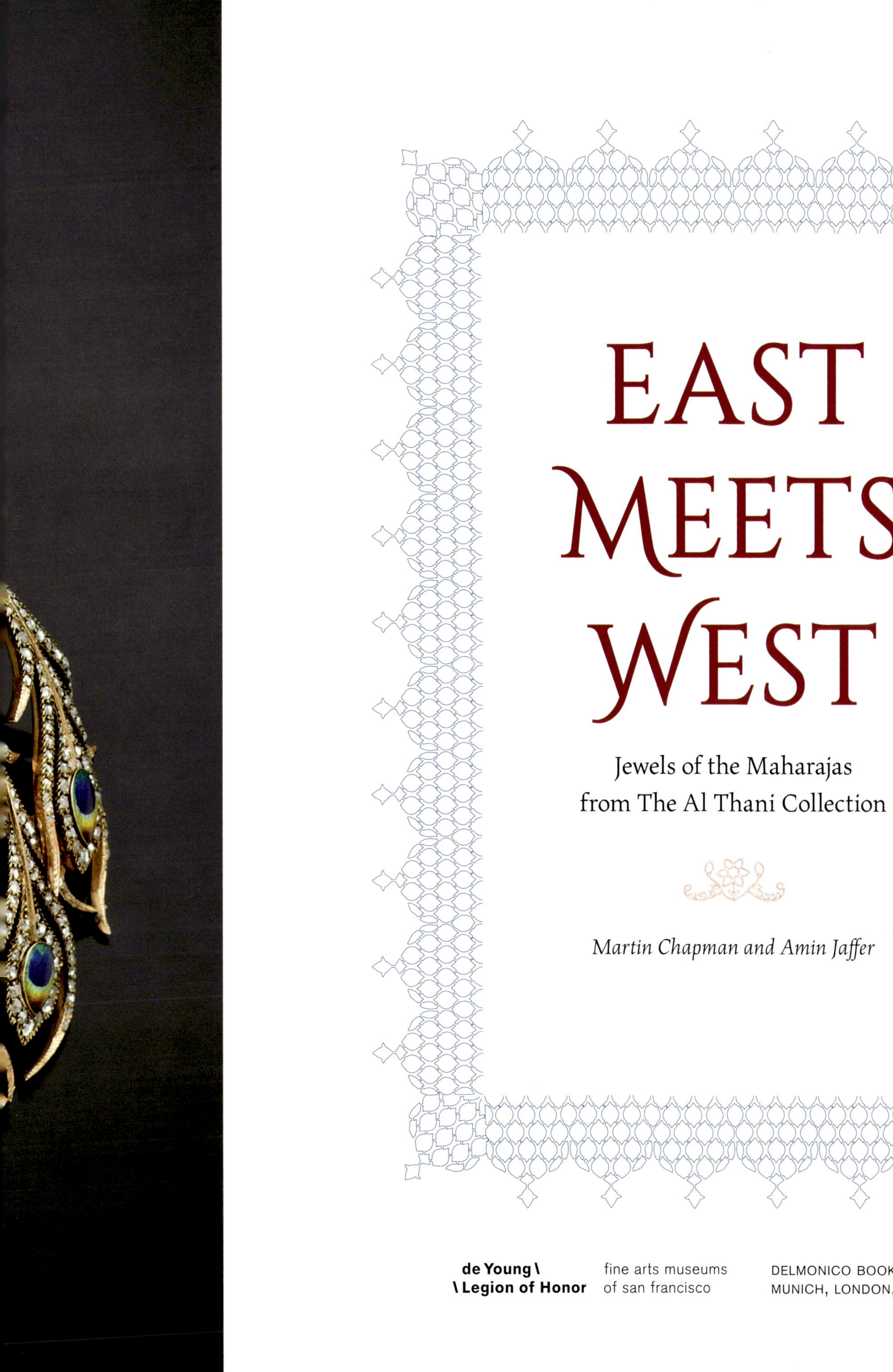

EAST MEETS WEST

Jewels of the Maharajas from The Al Thani Collection

Martin Chapman and Amin Jaffer

de Young \ \ Legion of Honor fine arts museums of san francisco

DELMONICO BOOKS • PRESTEL
MUNICH, LONDON, NEW YORK

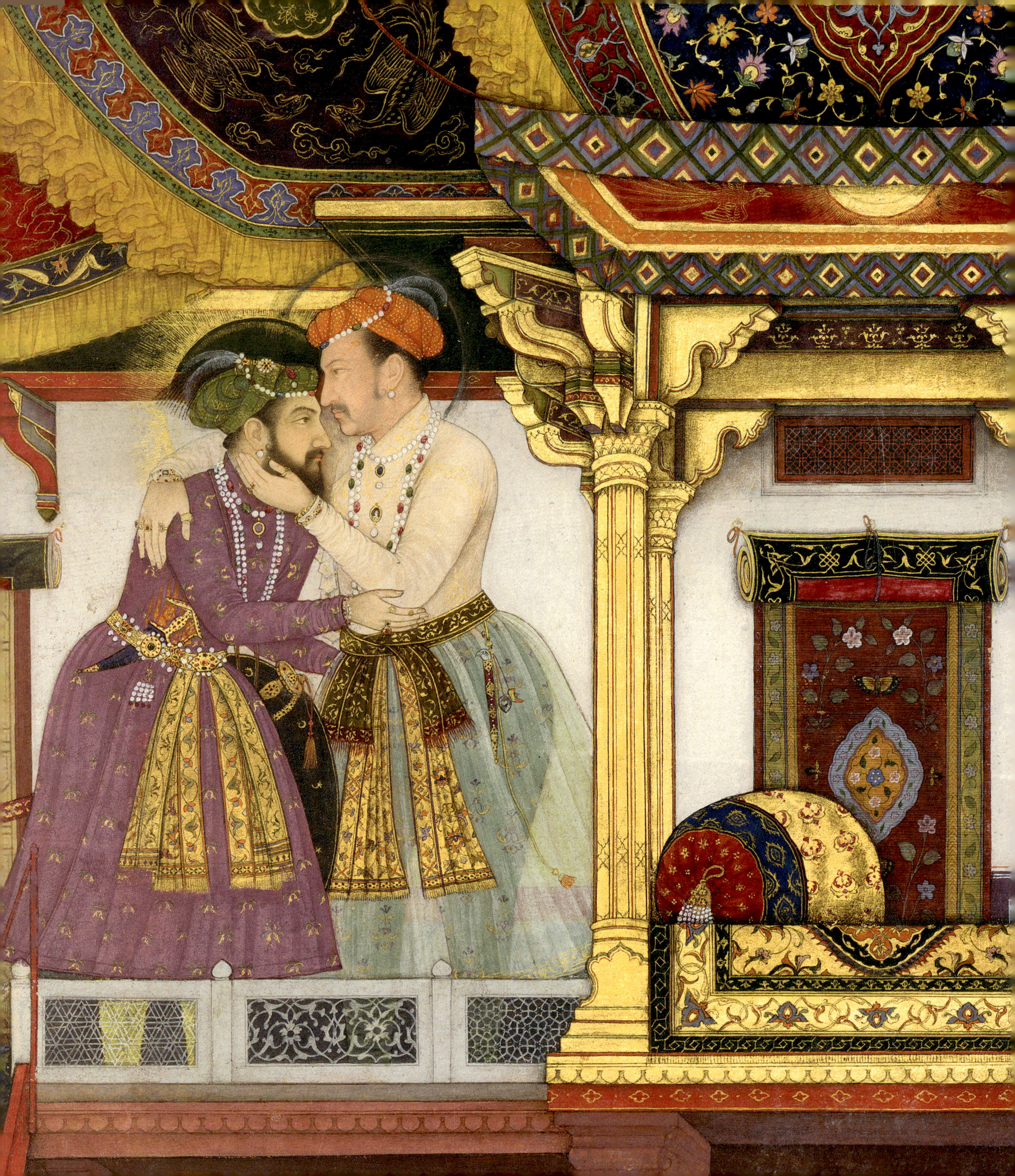

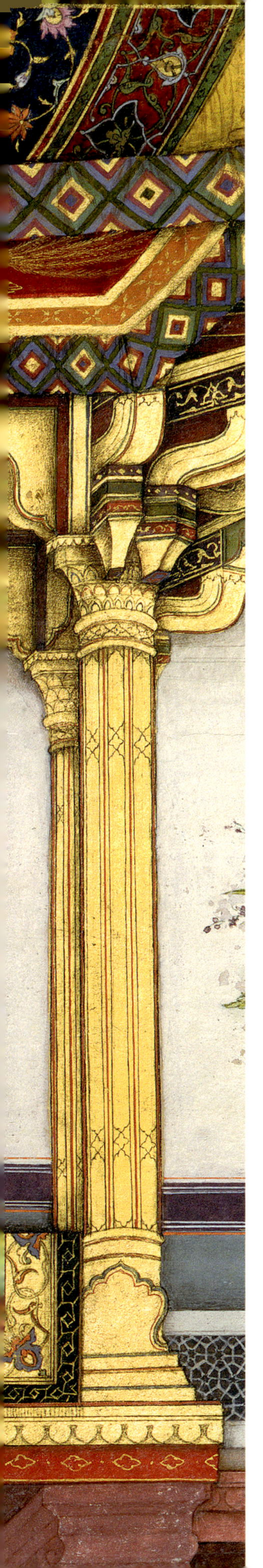

CONTENTS

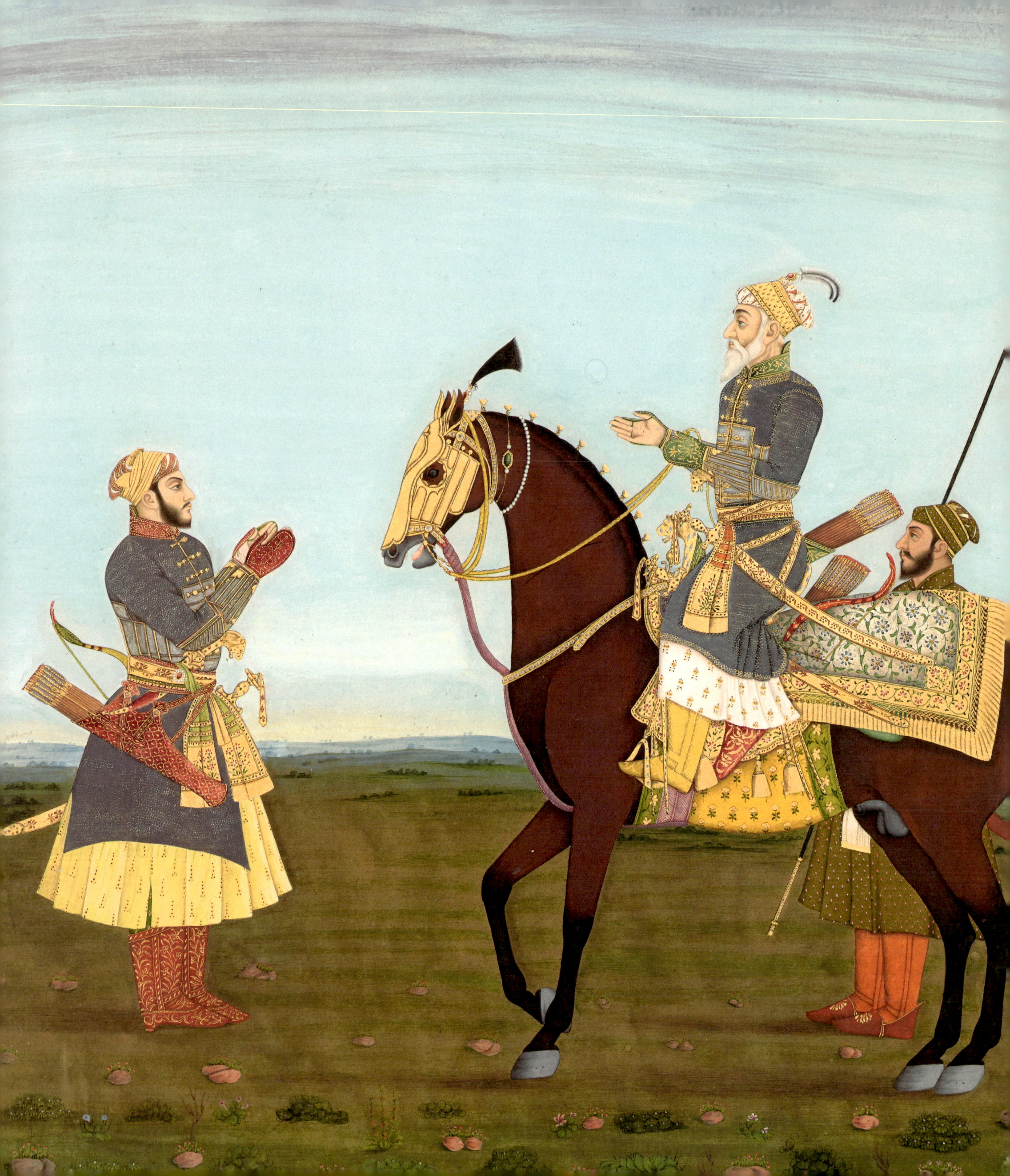

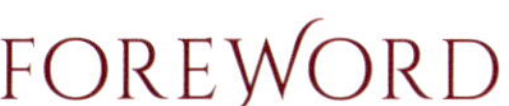

FOREWORD

MAX HOLLEIN
Director and CEO, Fine Arts Museums of San Francisco

The Fine Arts Museums of San Francisco are pleased to host *East Meets West: Jewels of the Maharajas from The Al Thani Collection* formed by His Highness Sheikh Hamad bin Abdullah Al Thani. Comprising Indian works of art and jewels from the time of the Mughal Empire in the sixteenth century to the present, the exhibition represents a wide cultural picture of luxury goods produced on the Indian subcontinent, and reflects the varied influences that were brought to bear by successive generations. India has been infiltrated by different cultures over the centuries, and the precious objects made there reflect this cultural domination while preserving their essentially Indian character.

For our viewing in San Francisco, we are concentrating on the influences of India on Western culture and the corresponding influences of Western culture on India. This has been the case ever since the Mughals invaded India and subsequently founded their empire in the sixteenth century, during which time Europeans already had trading posts on the subcontinent. The Mughal emperors were curious about the new European technology for warfare as well as the making of luxury objects such as jewelry and hardstone mosaics along with techniques such as gemstone cutting. In exchange for diamonds, textiles, and spices, the Europeans traded precious metals and emeralds from Colombia in addition to imparting some of their new technologies. This encounter grew from the simple trading posts run by the Portuguese to expand to the British taking over large parts of India in the eighteenth century, eventually resulting in the establishment of their empire in 1858.

Our exhibition also focuses on the question of gender. The wearing of sumptuous jewels is a long-standing tradition in India as a signifier of status and power. Unlike Europe and the West, where women are the principal wearers of jewelry, it is the men in India, specifically the male rulers—emperors and maharajas—who turn our expectations on their heads and disport the most extravagant programs of jewelry: elaborate bangles, bracelets, rings, necklaces, and earrings (as well as the most characteristic jewel, the turban ornament). There are some notable exceptions to this gender division among the male monarchs of Europe around 1700, such as King Louis XIV of France, who had a passion for acquiring large Indian diamonds and precious stones and who, like the Mughal emperors, wore them prominently as indicators of prestige. The maharajas, however, continued this tradition of bejeweled splendor up to 1947, just following the zenith in the 1920s and 1930s of Indian influence on jewelry design in Europe and America.

I would like to thank His Highness Sheikh Hamad for his generosity in lending his gorgeous array of precious objects, and for supporting the exhibition at the Legion of Honor. I would also like to thank his curator, Dr. Amin Jaffer, for his stalwart support and scholarship throughout this project, and Martin Chapman, curator in charge of European decorative arts and sculpture and interim curator in charge of European art at the Fine Arts Museums. This exhibition has been supported by our generous museum donors, and I would like to thank Diane B. Wilsey and Jamie and Philip Bowles for their donations to enhance the programming of this presentation. We are also grateful to our lenders who provided their important works for the exhibition, including Cartier Collection and a California private collection. Their generosity has allowed our audiences to more deeply understand Indian culture through many of its exquisitely beautiful jewels.

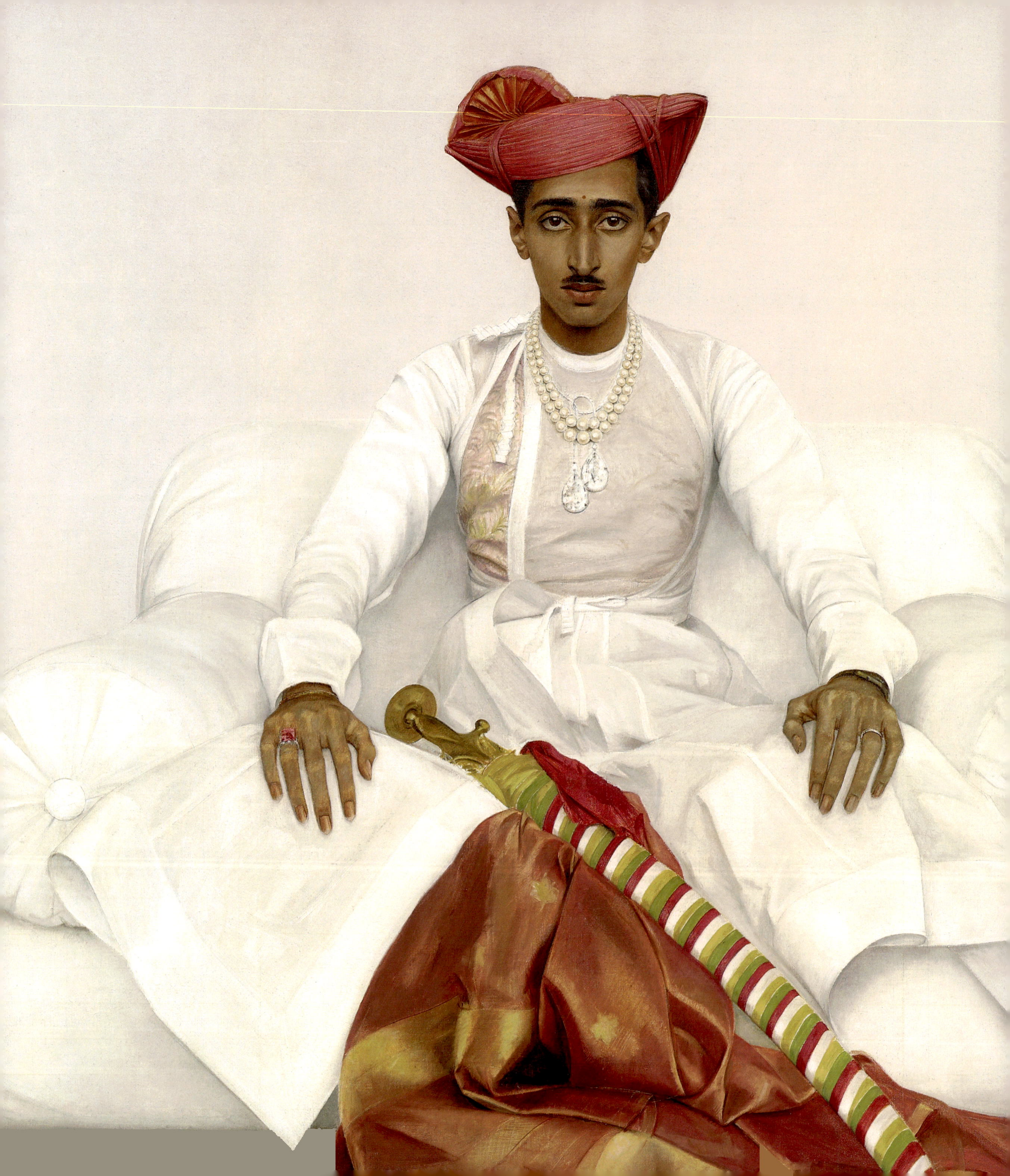

PREFACE

HIS HIGHNESS SHEIKH HAMAD BIN ABDULLAH AL THANI

It gives me great pleasure to see Indian gems and jewels from The Al Thani Collection displayed with such style at the Legion of Honor. The building is one of my favorites, having been modeled on the Palais de la Légion d'Honneur in Paris, where we first launched *Beyond Extravagance*, the catalogue of the Collection that now forms the subject of this book.

Spanning over five hundred years, the pieces on view represent the refined culture of Indian jeweled arts from the Mughal period and the age of the maharajas to the present day. The dialogue between the West and India in this sphere of jewelry forms a central component of the exhibition. Western jewelers and goldsmiths were present at the Mughal court, and the techniques and taste of European jewelry houses continued to exercise great appeal among Indian princes in the nineteenth and twentieth centuries. In later years it was to Europe that the maharajas flocked in order to reset gems in their treasuries, inspiring a fusion of Indian forms and tastes with Western settings that characterizes an apogee of twentieth-century jewelry design. The exhibition reflects this cultural exchange. Besides their aesthetic, cultural, and historic value, each and every piece in this exhibition has a profound personal meaning for me, and I am delighted to share this deep interest with a wider public.

East Meets West: Jewels of the Maharajas from The Al Thani Collection has been realized thanks to a collaborative effort of many people at the Legion of Honor and at The Al Thani Collection. I would like to convey my thanks to Colin B. Bailey, former director of the Fine Arts Museums of San Francisco, who initiated this project. Director Max Hollein has likewise supported the exhibition, which has been organized by Martin Chapman, curator in charge of European decorative arts and sculpture and interim curator in charge of European art. The designer Giuliano Spinelli has developed an elegant and original arrangement for showing the Collection within the magnificent galleries of the Legion of Honor. In addition, I would like to thank everyone at The Al Thani Collection for their work in presenting this exhibition.

I hope that this exhibition inspires visitors to the Legion of Honor with an interest in the gems and jewels of India, rightfully considered a high point in human creative endeavor.

ACKNOWLEDGMENTS

We are immensely grateful to His Highness Sheikh Hamad bin Abdullah Al Thani for his generosity and kindness in lending his rare and beautiful pieces to this exhibition and for supporting its installation at the Legion of Honor and its accompanying scholarly catalogue. Dr. Amin Jaffer, senior curator of The Al Thani Collection, has been the main conduit for the whole of this project, advising and directing its course, including his adroit contributions to the catalogue and the installation. We would also like to thank The Al Thani Collection staff for their assistance in making this project happen: Liv Constable-Maxwell, Richard Hart, Lisa Hockfield, Simon Jones, Anjali Kothari, Jennie Lord, and Laura Stuart. Previous contributors to Al Thani publications, Robert Skelton, Michael Spink, Judy Rudoe, Katherine Prior, Vivienne Becker, and Will Kwiatkowski, have provided scholarship that has informed so much of this book. Susan Stronge, senior curator of the South and South-East Asia collections at the Victoria and Albert Museum, London, has given much valuable advice. The beautiful design of the show has been conceived by the Italian theater designer Giuliano Spinelli.

We are especially grateful to lenders to this exhibition: Cartier Collection, Geneva and Paris, and its staff Pierre Rainero, Nadia Crétignier, Renée Frank, and Anne Lamarque; and a California private collection. Financial support for special programs has been generously provided by Diane B. Wilsey and Jamie and Philip Bowles.

At the Museums, Martin Chapman, curator in charge of European decorative arts and sculpture and interim curator in charge of European art, has guided the exhibition in its inception, as well as contributing to and overseeing the content of the catalogue. He has been assisted by many members of the Museums' staff. Krista Brugnara, director of exhibitions; Hilary Magowan, exhibitions manager; and Sarah Miller, exhibitions assistant, have led the show from concept to realization. For the layout of the show, associate exhibition designers Tristan Telander and Christopher Busch have ably executed the plans with Jesse Beckman, exhibitions graphics preparator, to produce the graphics. In registration, Nadia Ghani, museum registrar, has managed the complex details. Eve Rosekind, curatorial assistant of European decorative arts and sculpture, has provided much-needed administrative help.

Jane Williams, head of objects conservation, oversaw the task of mounting these delicate objects, and Ryan Butterfield, chief preparator, and his staff executed the installation.

This catalogue was produced under the elegant guidance of Leslie Dutcher, director of publications, who has ensured the design and production of this magnificent book. Trina Enriquez, associate editor, ably project managed the volume, keeping track of so many of its details, including the rights and reproductions necessary to realize its handsome imagery. Robert Carswell, digital assets and rights manager, secured image rights and reproductions for the exhibition materials, and José Jovel, publications assistant, offered valuable support at all stages of the book's creation. Outside the Museums, Jane Friedman gracefully edited much of the catalogue, and Yvonne Tsang is responsible for its lovely design. We are also grateful to Mary DelMonico and Karen Farquhar at DelMonico Books • Prestel, who helped with the myriad publishing aspects to make this book and distribute it in the trade.

Sheila Pressley, director of education, and Emily Stoller-Patterson, digital project manager, have edited and enhanced the gallery didactics and web materials. Rich Rice, director of events and exhibition technology, oversaw the audiovisual needs for the exhibition.

We thank our Board of Trustees, led by president Diane B. Wilsey, for their support. Furthermore, we acknowledge many individuals and their staffs who work behind the scenes to realize our many programs, including Megan Bourne, chief of staff; Melissa Buron, director, art division; Ed Prohaska, chief financial officer; Jason Seifer, director of finance; Patty Lacson, director of facilities; Tricia Robson, director of web and digital production; and Skot Jonz, manager of board relations. We thank our development team, headed by Amanda Riley, for organizing the opening events. Linda Butler, director of marketing, communications, and visitor experience, is thanked for supplying the publicity for the exhibition with the assistance of Amy Browne, director of graphic design; Miriam Newcomer, director of public relations; Wynter Martinez, associate director of marketing; and Helena Nordstrom, international public relations manager. We further extend our gratitude to Stuart Hata, director of retail operations, and Tim Niedert, book and media manager.

MAX HOLLEIN

Director and CEO, Fine Arts Museums of San Francisco

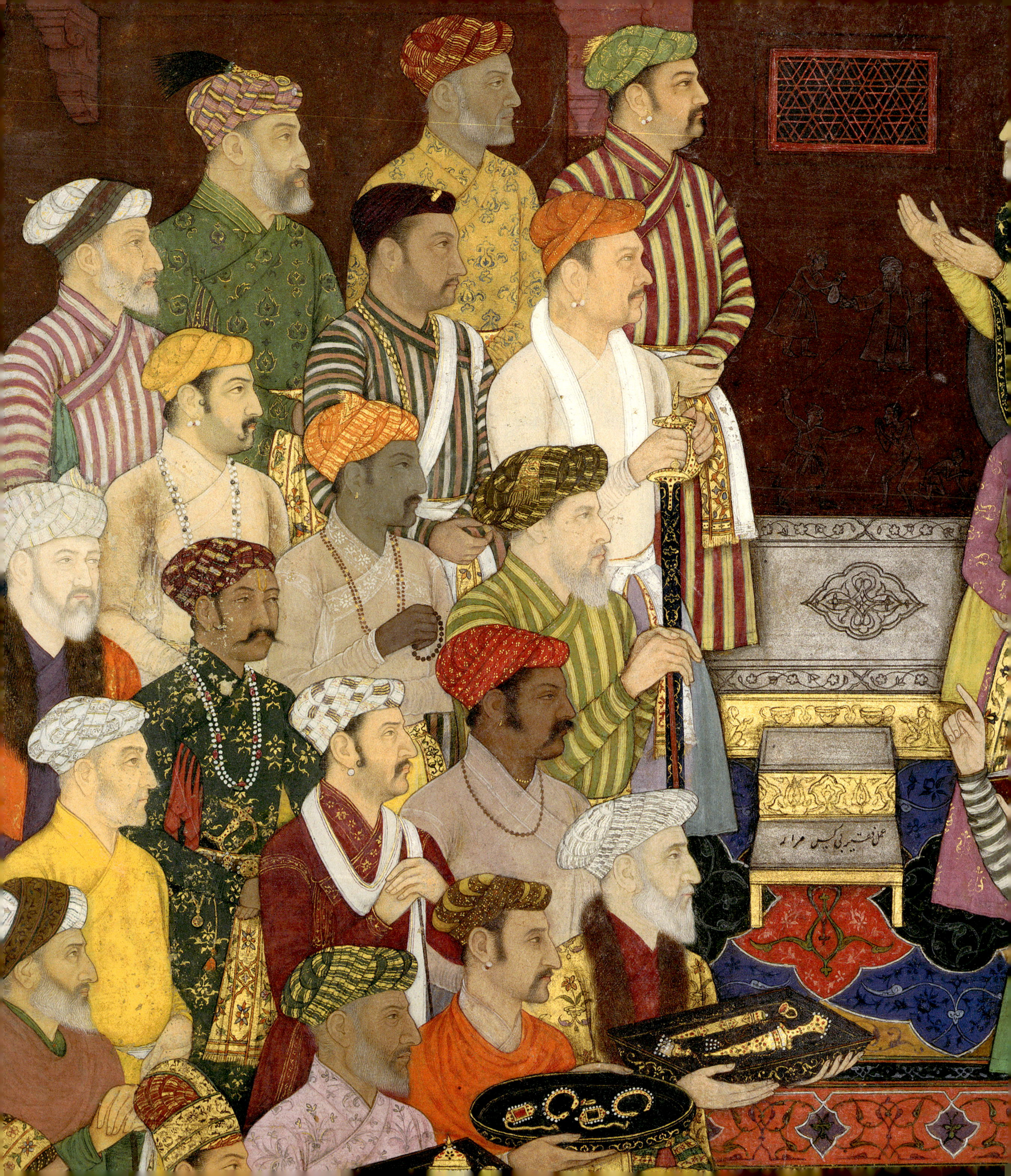

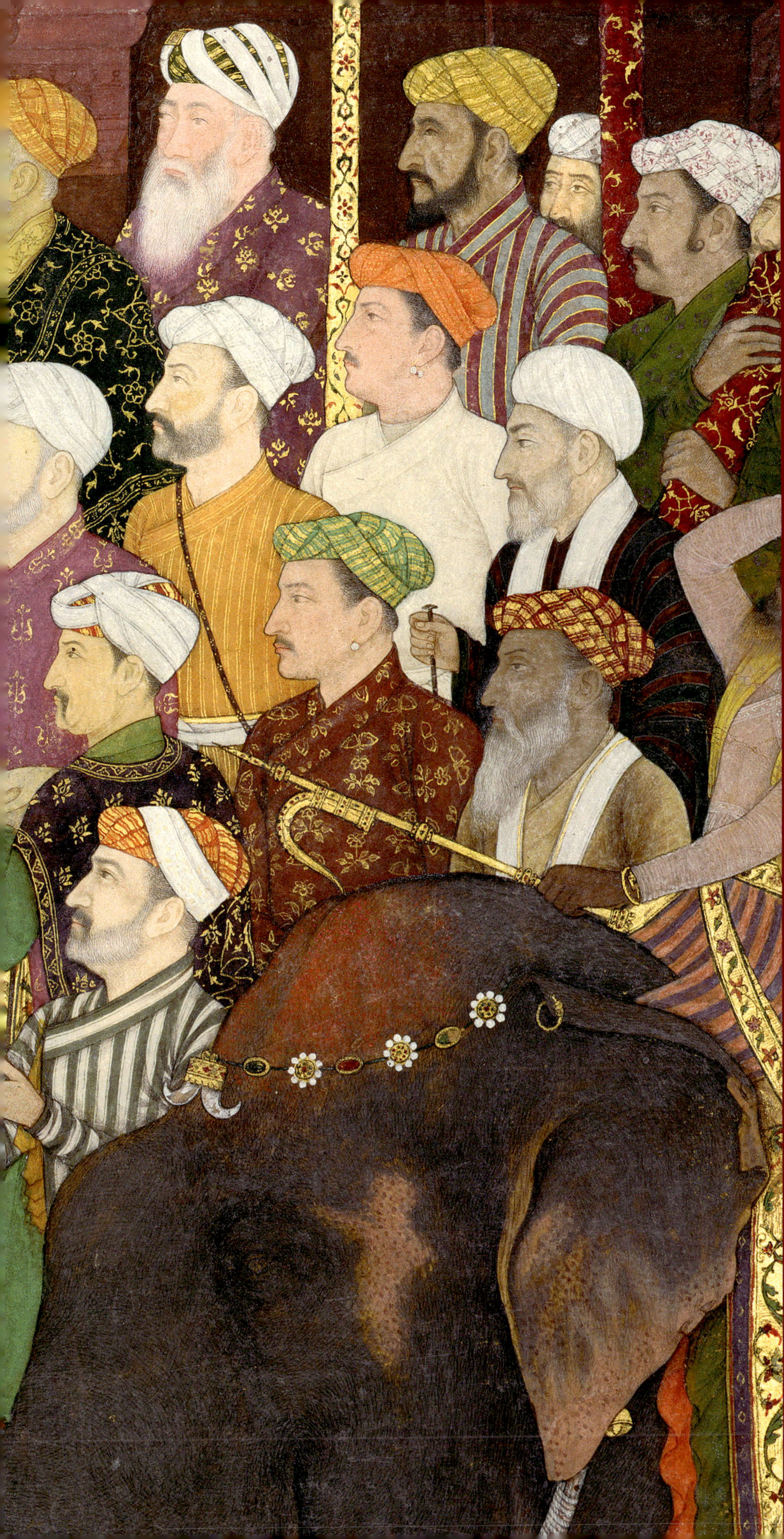

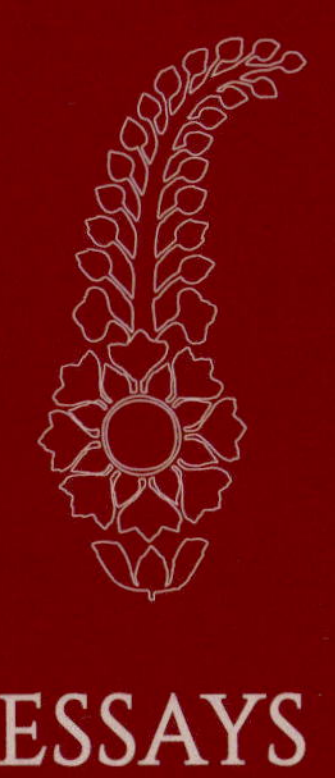

ESSAYS

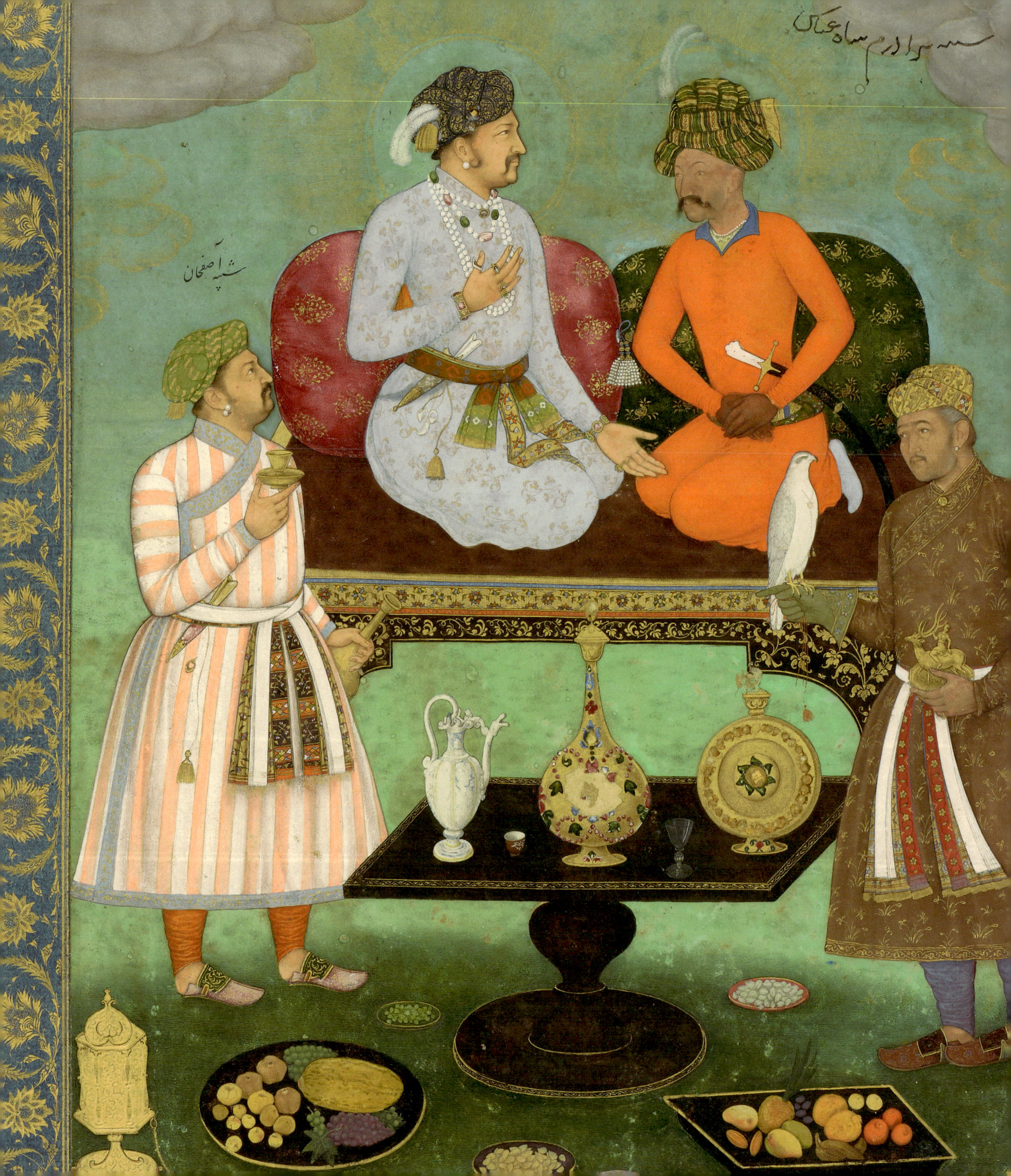
شبیه برادرم شاه عباس
شبیه آصفخان

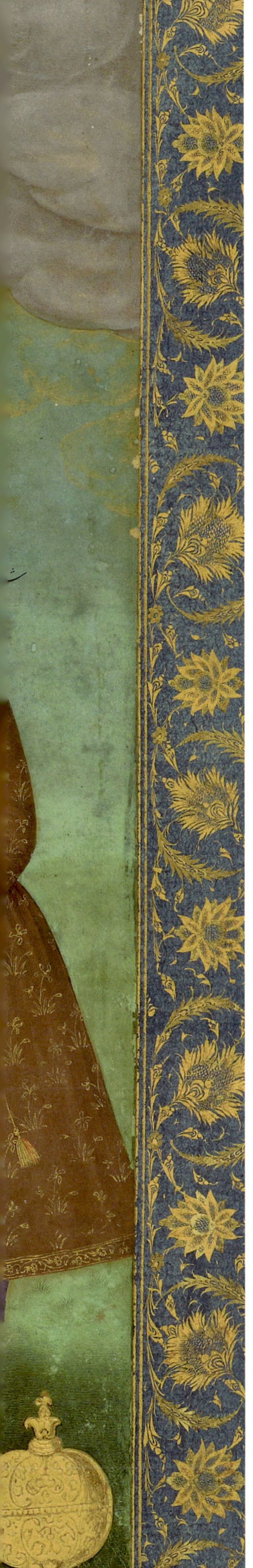

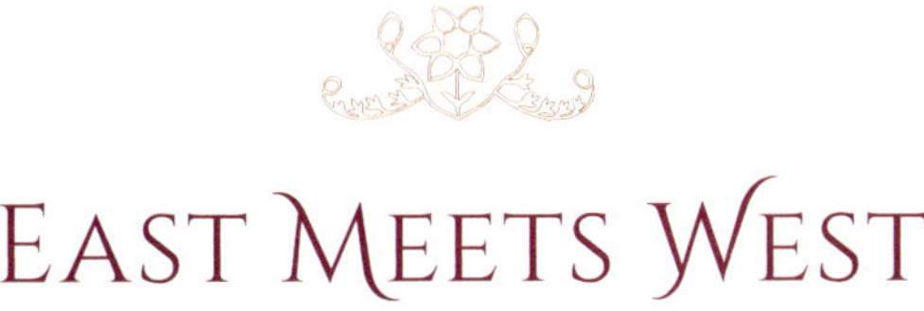

East Meets West

The Exchange between India and Europe for Jewelry and Precious Objects

MARTIN CHAPMAN

India has captivated the West since ancient times with its diamonds, gemstones, textiles, and spices—as well as the legendary exoticism of its culture. The modern-day interaction between India and Europe can be traced back to before the Mughal Empire (established 1526). The Mughal Empire was the largest in the world at that time, extending throughout India and into Afghanistan. Ruled by a Muslim dynasty from Central Asia, it was also the world's largest economic power, and Europeans were drawn to India for the trade chiefly in textiles and spices. Even prior to the Mughals' arrival in India, the Portuguese established their trading posts for spices, making their capital at Goa from 1510. The Portuguese presence, known as the Estado da Índia, would be effectively the main entrepôt for European trade for the next two hundred years. In the following century, the English founded the East India Company in 1600, also initially for trade in spices but later expanding to cotton, silk, indigo, gunpowder, tea, and even opium. The Dutch formed their East India Company (the Verenigde Oost-Indische Compagnie, abbreviated as the VOC) in 1602; the Danish founded theirs in 1620; and the French established their trading colony in 1668, having formed the Compagnie des Indes orientales in 1664. The primary aim for all these ventures was commerce, the fierce competition for which gave rise to conflicts both between the various European parties and with the Indians—conflicts that escalated into wars. With the waning power of the Mughal Empire in the eighteenth and nineteenth centuries, these European trading posts seized the opportunity to extend their interests and grew into sizable colonies. Following the initial dominance of the Portuguese, the English East India Company flourished to such an extent that its business eventually accounted for half the world's trade. In 1858 the British government co-opted the firm's role and established its Raj, or rule, under the crown, which ended only when India became independent in 1947.

The influences and commodities also flowed the other way. Gold and silver from Europe were exchanged for India's diamonds, spices, and textiles. Gold was mined in India, but with local demand exceeding the supply, this precious metal had to be imported.[1] In the sixteenth and seventeenth centuries, Europeans fashioned complex and expensive jewels set in highly colored enameled gold that arrived at the courts of the Mughal rulers as diplomatic gifts (fig. 1). On his visits to India between 1661 and 1666, the French traveler Jean-Baptiste Tavernier (1605–1689) is known to have taken with him European jewelry decorated with enamel that he would use to negotiate the purchase of large diamonds (fig. 2).[2]

The Mughals were so impressed by these luxurious European objects that they were inspired to create their own pieces in enameled gold, such as the jewelry and the ceremonial vessels for the table that became a significant part of formal Indian culture (see "The Royal Courts: Gold and Enamels," pages 94–115). The great Mughal emperor Jahangir (r. 1605–1627)

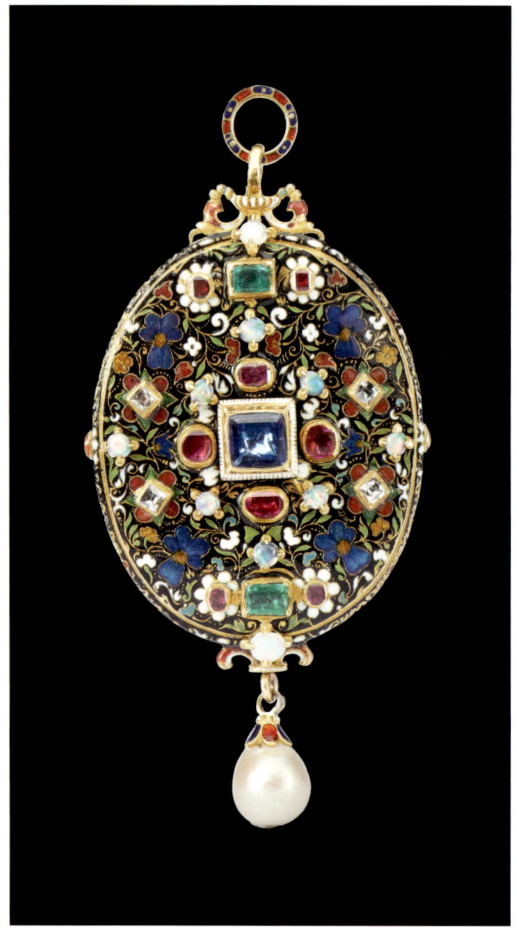

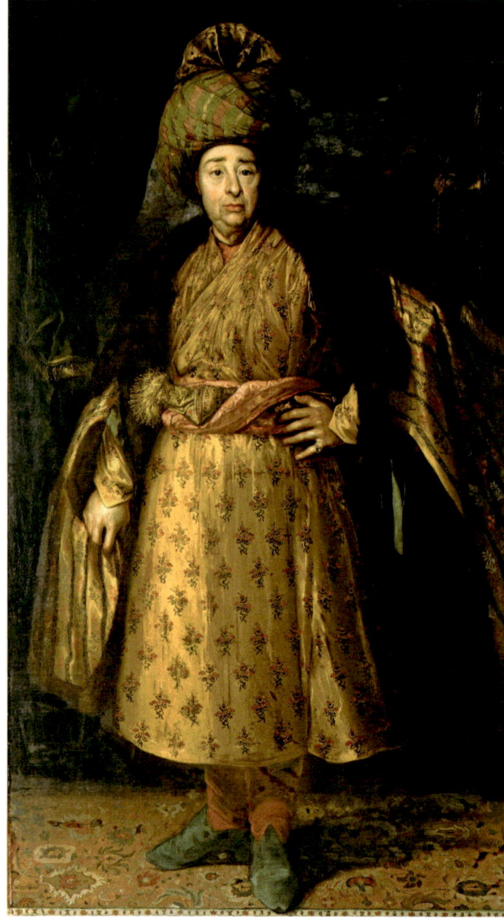

FIG. 1 (*far left*). The Grenville locket, England, ca. 1635–1640. Enameled gem-set gold, pearl, 4¼ × 1⅝ × 1¼ in. (10.9 × 4.2 × 3.2 cm). Waddesdon Bequest, British Museum, London, Bequest of Ferdinand Anselm Rothschild, WB.168

FIG. 2 (*left*). Nicolas Largillière, *Jean-Baptiste Tavernier in Oriental Costume*, ca. 1678. Oil on canvas, 83 × 47⅞ in. (210.9 × 121.7 cm). Herzog Anton Ulrich-Museum, Braunschweig, Germany, GG S20

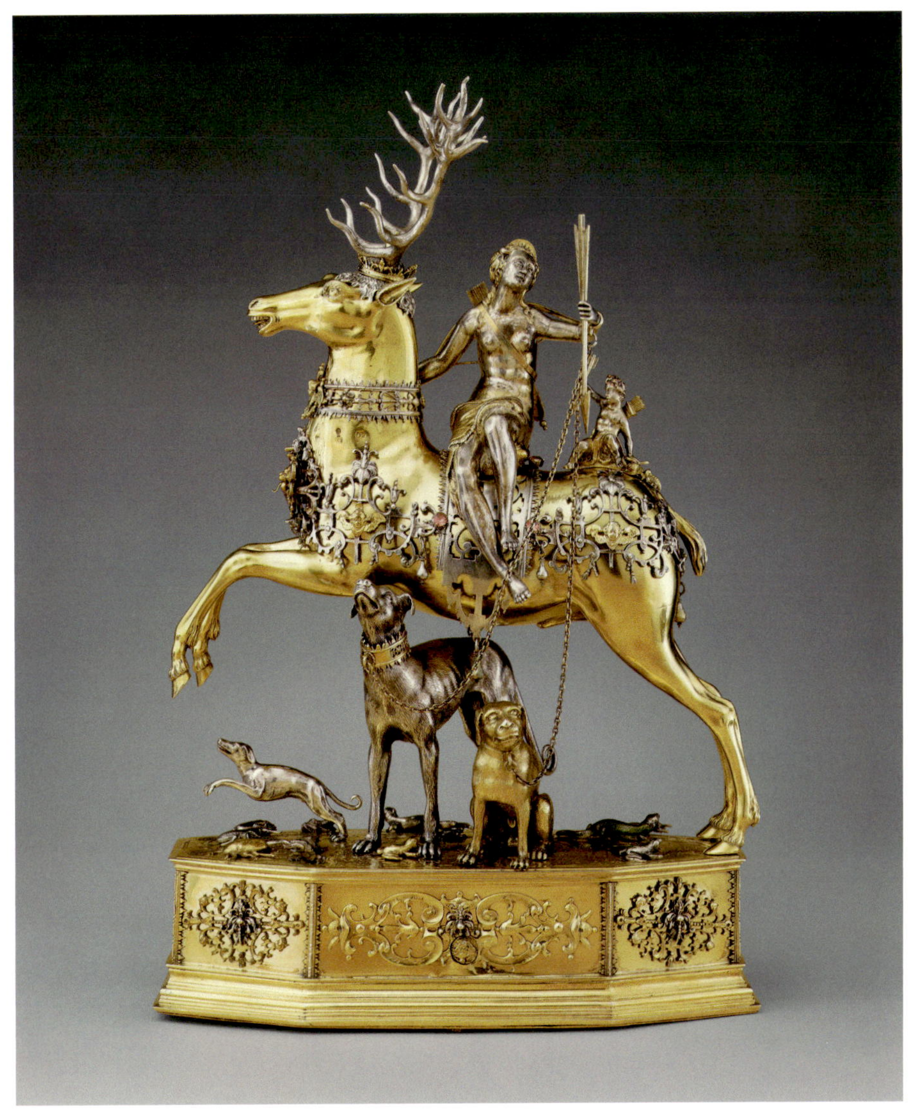

FIG. 3. Joachim Friess, *Diana and the Stag*, ca. 1620. Case: partially gilded silver, enamel, jewels; movement: iron, wood; 14¾ × 9½ in. (37.5 × 24.1 cm). The Metropolitan Museum of Art, New York, Gift of J. Pierpont Morgan, 1917, 17.190.746

was especially attracted by European art, design, and technology. A miniature showing a fictional meeting between him and Shah Abbas I of Persia depicts prized European luxury objects displayed in front of the two rulers that probably arrived at the Mughal court as diplomatic gifts. These objects include a European ewer of Mannerist design, appearing on the table before the emperors, and a sculpture of Diana and the Stag, cradled by the courtier Khan Alam, ambassador to the Iranian court, who is also holding a falcon.[3] The Diana figure is probably a silver-gilt automaton similar to those made by Augsburg goldsmith Joachim Friess (fig. 3).[4] Meticulously executed in minute detail and operating under clockwork, automata such as this were novelties that could be whizzed around the dining table for use in drinking games. They were often given as diplomatic gifts to delight their recipients, and this is the likely origin of this Diana figure at Jahangir's court.[5] A further, if unintended, dialogue between East and West can be observed in the same person of Khan Alam. In one hand he holds a falcon, symbolizing the most princely type of hunting at the Mughal (and Persian) court, while in the other he holds an allegorical depiction of stag hunting—the pursuit of European monarchs—in the form of the Diana figure.

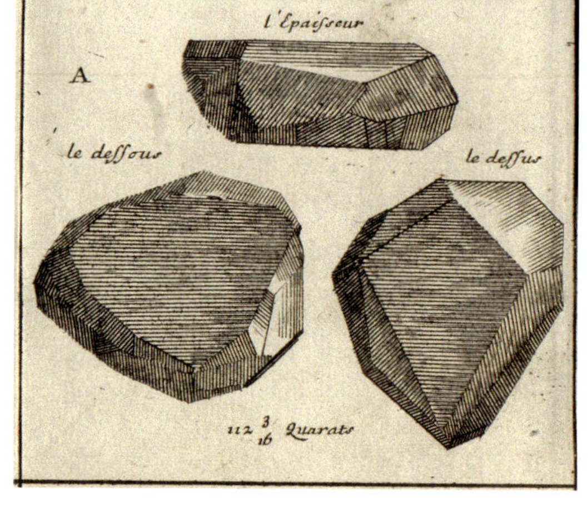

Gemstones also played an important role in the East-West exchange. The striking deep-green emeralds favored by the Mughal courts were mostly sourced from outside India, traded by the Spanish from Colombia, in South America, to Portuguese Goa. Green was sacred for Muslims as the "color of Paradise," and therefore emeralds were prized among the most important stones in the Mughal treasuries.[6] They were carved by lapidaries with the stylized floral and foliate patterns that gave Indian jewelry one of its highly recognizable features. The diamonds extracted from the riverbeds near Golconda in Southern India were the subcontinent's most valuable resource. They were then cut and traded in that city, which lent its name to this type of diamond that had a reputation for being the finest in the world for its quality as well as its size. Golconda diamonds were frequently traded to Europe, where the stones were recut to extract the greatest reflections, and therefore brilliance, out of the stones. In the late seventeenth century, Europeans developed the more scientific system of what is traditionally known as the brilliant cut (also called old mine or European cut), based on the principles of refraction that facilitated the production of "fire" from the gemstone. This cut produced symmetry and increased sparkle, but in the process resulted in a considerable loss of weight. This method departed from the traditional Indian approach to diamond cutting, in which the existing form was polished to preserve as much of the original stone's weight—and thus value—as possible (see figs. 4 and 20). Diamonds cut this way in Europe were often then traded back to India. Such was the desire of the Mughal emperors to have the most up-to-date gem cutting that they engaged Venetian and other European lapidaries to work at their courts, bringing with them Western techniques of the brilliant cut. The reputation of the Golconda stones for clarity and "water" was also such that diamonds found elsewhere were traded to India to lend them credibility. When the Portuguese discovered a new source of diamonds in Brazil around 1730, these stones were judged as somehow inferior in quality. So, in order to establish their credentials in a volatile market, the Portuguese shipped the gemstones from Brazil to Goa, where the stones were marketed as Indian diamonds.

Diamonds from India had been traded to Europe in ancient times, but a thriving export of these diamonds was revived only in the late sixteenth century. From this point on, European kings acquired Indian diamonds to demonstrate their power and wealth by wearing the stones in their crowns and regalia and on their dress as part of court ceremony. In this respect they were similar to the Mughal emperors, who also wore their diamonds and gemstones as a mark of their prestige, albeit in a different manner. Visitors to the imperial court

FIG. 4. Detail of the Blue diamond: "Vingt des plus beaux diamants rapports de l'Inde par Tavernier," from *Les six voyages de Jean-Baptiste Tavernier [. . .] en Turquie, en Perse et aux Indes* ("Twenty of the finest diamonds brought back from India by Tavernier," from *Six Voyages of Jean-Baptiste Tavernier [. . .] through Turky into Persia and the East-Indies*), Paris, P. Ribou, vol. 4, engraving between pages 60–61, 1713. Bibliothèque nationale de France

were dazzled by the splendor of the Mughal court, and English ambassador Sir Thomas Roe remarked on the profusion of jewels worn by Emperor Jahangir at court in 1617.[7]

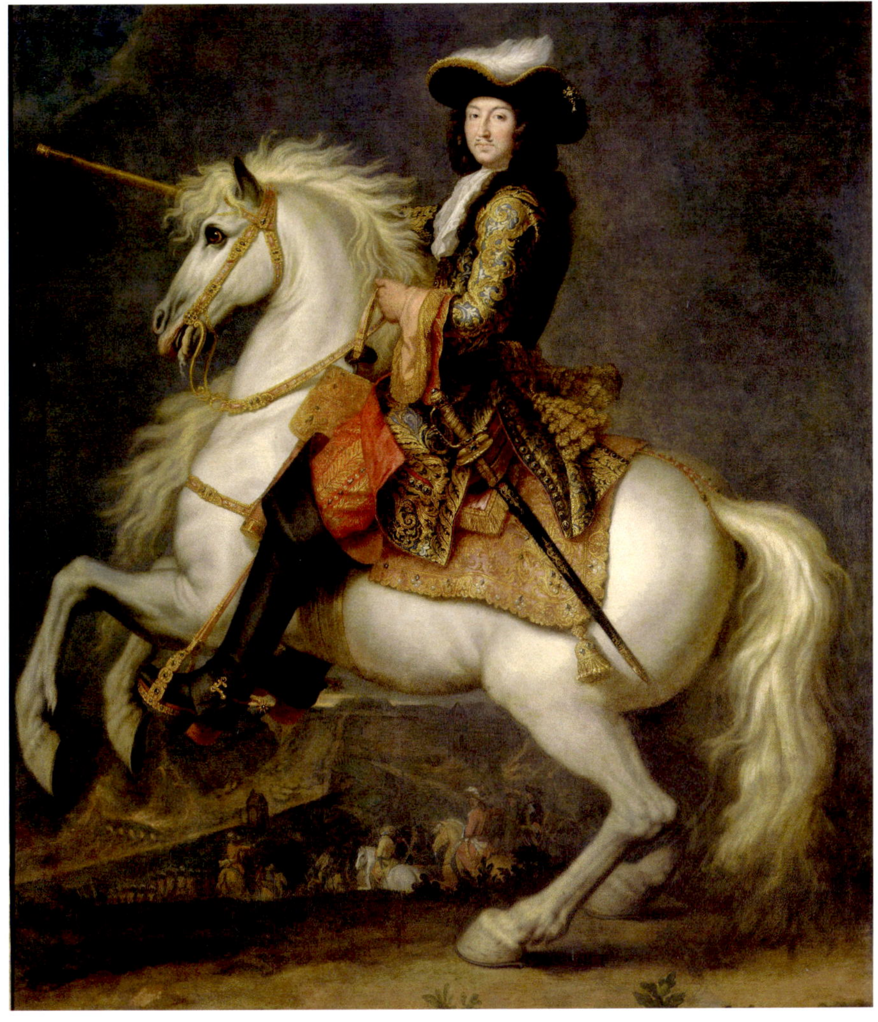

FIG. 5. René-Antoine Houasse, detail of *Equestrian Portrait of Louis XIV Wearing His Diamonds*, ca. 1679. Oil on canvas, 100 × 78¾ in. (255 × 200 cm). Château de Versailles et de Trianon, Versailles, France

In Europe the treasury of Louis XIV of France contained vast numbers of Indian diamonds on a scale not seen anywhere else in the West, some of which were acquired via Cardinal Mazarin from the former English crown jewels after the fall of the Stuart monarchy in 1649. These diamonds included the Mirror of Portugal and the famous Sancy, which in the seventeenth century was considered one of the biggest diamonds in Europe. Many of Louis XIV's large diamonds were later obtained from the dealer, traveler, and writer Jean-Baptiste Tavernier, who in his *Six Voyages* (1676) left an account of his journeys through India to acquire gemstones. In 1669 Tavernier sold the French monarch more than one thousand diamonds bought during these travels, including the huge French Blue, known to us today as the Hope Diamond (figs. 4 and 20). Like the Mughal rulers, Louis XIV displayed his diamonds in great profusion, but, in accordance with the prevailing European fashion of the day, wore them in suites, or parures, arranged in matching colors on his coat, as buttons, as cravat pins, in hat clasps, in orders of chivalry, and on his sword hilts (fig. 5). As the example of Louis XIV suggests, European monarchs were as anxious as their Indian counterparts to own and display diamonds as an outward symbol of power and prestige.

Although rulers in both India and Europe used jewelry to underscore their status, the form and function of gemstones varied greatly from East to West, especially in terms of gender. In India it was the male rulers who displayed the great jewels. The Mughal emperors and the maharajas were adorned with elaborate set pieces of jewelry—turban ornaments, necklaces, bracelets, and belts—items that in Europe, with a few subtle differences, would be donned only by royal and noble women. Although there are instances of European male rulers such as Louis XIV wearing prodigious amounts of jewelry, women were usually the ones bedecked in jewels at royal court events in the West, comprising whole parures of tiaras, necklaces, earrings, and bracelets, in matching sets. The turban ornament, intended to hold a heron's feather and worn by the maharajas as a symbol of their status, had close affinities with the European aigrette. But in the West the gender was again switched, with women, not men, generally sporting this stylized jeweled feather, or a jewel holding a feather (or feathers); examples include Marie Antoinette, who is portrayed wearing aigrettes in her high hairstyles of the 1770s (fig. 6).[8] As European aigrettes were documented as early as the start of the seventeenth century, it is a question of which type of head ornament influenced which.

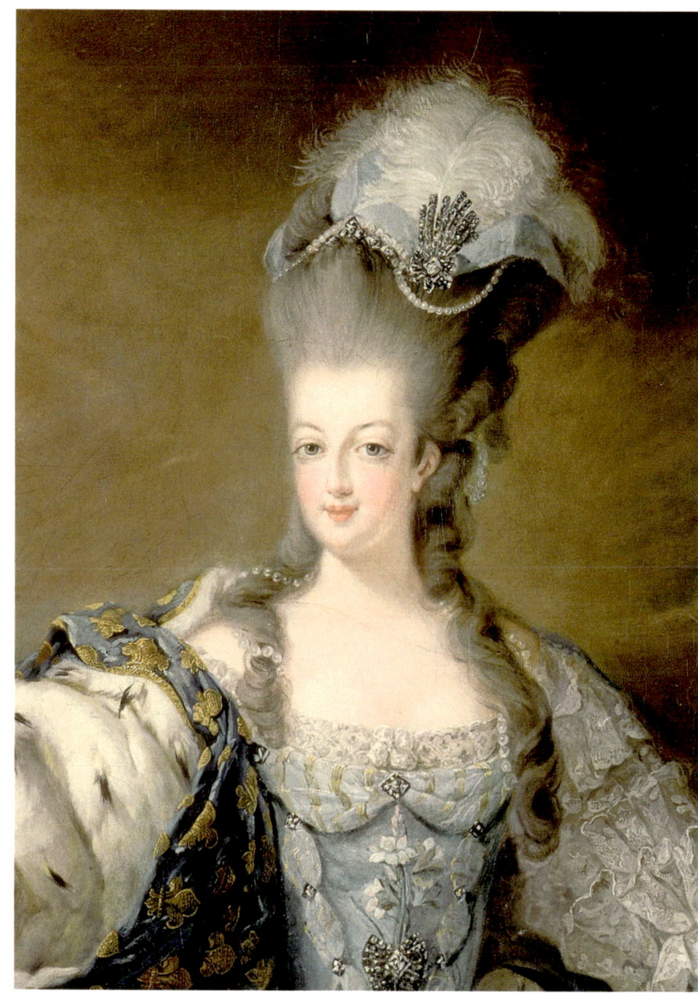

With this gender disparity between East and West over the wearing of jewels, a significant crossover occurred in the early twentieth century, when the queen consort of Great Britain, Alexandra of Denmark, paraded a spectacular array of jewels at her coronation in 1902 (fig. 7). The queen wore diamond necklaces and brooches, with ropes of pearls looped in seemingly endless layers, and in a profusion akin to that of a male maharaja. The message was intentional. Along with her dress, which was woven and embroidered in India, Queen Alexandra's costume and jewels conveyed her dual status as Queen consort of Great Britain and Empress of India. Alexandra had been fascinated with India since the 1870s, when her husband, Albert Edward, then Prince of Wales, visited the country in 1875–1876 in conjunction with the declaration of Queen Victoria as Empress of India. In a tradition dating back to the Mughal Empire, the Indian rulers gave the Prince of Wales large numbers of diamonds as tribute during this visit. Intended for male adornment, these gemstones were drafted into service for the queen's jewels for the coronation. New necklaces were fashioned for Alexandra, and, more important, a new crown was made that was set with the famous Koh-i-Noor diamond in the most prominent position, at the front. This historic stone had many different (male) owners in India, Pakistan, Iran, and Afghanistan before it was ceded to Queen Victoria under the Treaty of Lahore in 1849; thus, its appearance in the queen's crown made a dramatic statement about Britain's domination over India, as well as the diamond's switch from male to female use.[9]

From the Indian perspective, maharajas wore jewels originally made for European women without any qualms. The Maharaja of Patiala acquired the large diamond necklace of Empress Eugénie of France, for whom Paris jewelers created some of the most splendid suites and parures of diamonds during the Second Empire (1852–1870). These former French crown

FIG. 6. Jean-Baptiste Gautier-Dagoty, detail of *Marie Antoinette in 1775 Wearing Court Dress and with Her Hand on a Globe*, 1775. Oil on canvas, 63 × 50⅜ in. (160 × 128 cm). Châteaux de Versailles et de Trianon, Versailles, France, MV8061

jewels, comprising one of the largest assemblages of such jewels in the world, were later sold in 1887 in a fit of moral outrage by politicians during the Third Republic (1870–1940), thereby destroying the national collections of France's greatest diamonds and jewelry initially amassed by Louis XIV.[10] Such necklaces would never be worn by men in the West, but for the maharaja this type of sumptuous jewelry was grist to the mill for his splendor. The maharaja also wore a diamond pendant to the Eugénie necklace that has been identified as the Potemkin, formerly belonging to Catherine the Great of Russia and given to Empress Eugénie as a wedding present by Napoleon III in 1853 (fig. 8).[11] In addition, the Maharaja of Patiala had a tiara designed in the openwork, lacy design of the type that would only be worn in the West by women, but was greatly expanded in scale to fit the larger dimensions of the maharaja's turban.[12] The motif of a traditional turban ornament was included in the center, making this piece a true hybrid of Eastern and Western cultures (see fig. 46).

Sir Bhupinder Singh, Maharaja of Patiala (1891–1938), who acceded to the throne in 1900, would continue to augment his family's already sizable jewelry collection in subsequent decades. In the late 1920s, he visited Paris to have new suites made. An account of his appearance at the jeweler Boucheron captures the theatrical nature of the court that revolved around the ruler:

> The flamboyant Maharajah . . . arrived at Boucheron's in 1927 accompanied by a retinue of forty servants all wearing pink turbans, his twenty favorite dancing girls and, most important of all, six caskets filled with diamonds, emeralds, sapphires, rubies and pearls of incomparable beauty. Boucheron was commissioned to transform this mass of precious stones, then valued at about eighteen hundred million francs, into tiaras, aigrettes, belts and necklaces.[13]

Bhupinder Singh also went to Cartier Paris, which fashioned a choker (dog collar) of linked circles and circular brooches, again of a type only worn in the West by women (cat. 138/pl. 75). But his greatest moment in jewelry was commissioning Cartier to create a vast diamond-and-ruby necklace, completed in 1928, to house the maharaja's recently acquired enormous De Beers diamond (cat. 139/pl. 74). A cascade of diamond-set chains draped in layers, this necklace was the largest order the Parisian jeweler ever received. In its use of some 2,930 stones, the necklace can only be compared in European terms to the notorious *collier de la reine* (Queen's Necklace), fashioned in the 1770s. In both cases, such a massive accumulation of large diamonds was deemed too valuable to survive the passage of time. The so-called Queen's Necklace fomented a famous scandal that tarnished Marie Antoinette's reputation, after it was stolen in a dramatic heist and broken up for resale. Its composition of large diamonds that took the jeweler many years to assemble is known solely from engravings.[14] Similarly, the Patiala necklace disappeared after the fall of the Raj, in 1948. It was later found stripped of its

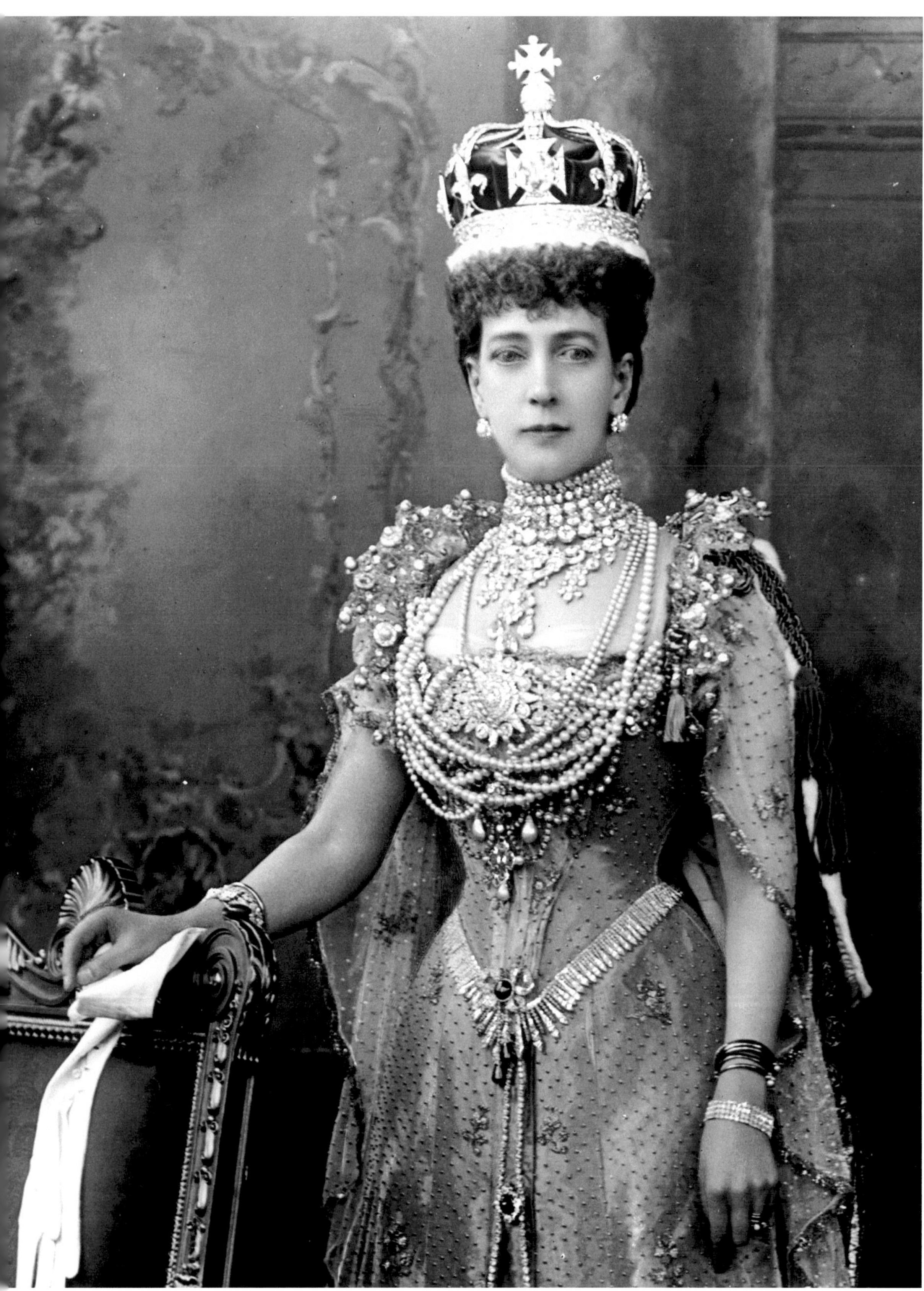

FIG. 7. Detail of Queen Alexandra, consort of King Edward VII, on the day of her husband's coronation, 1902. Hulton Royals Collection

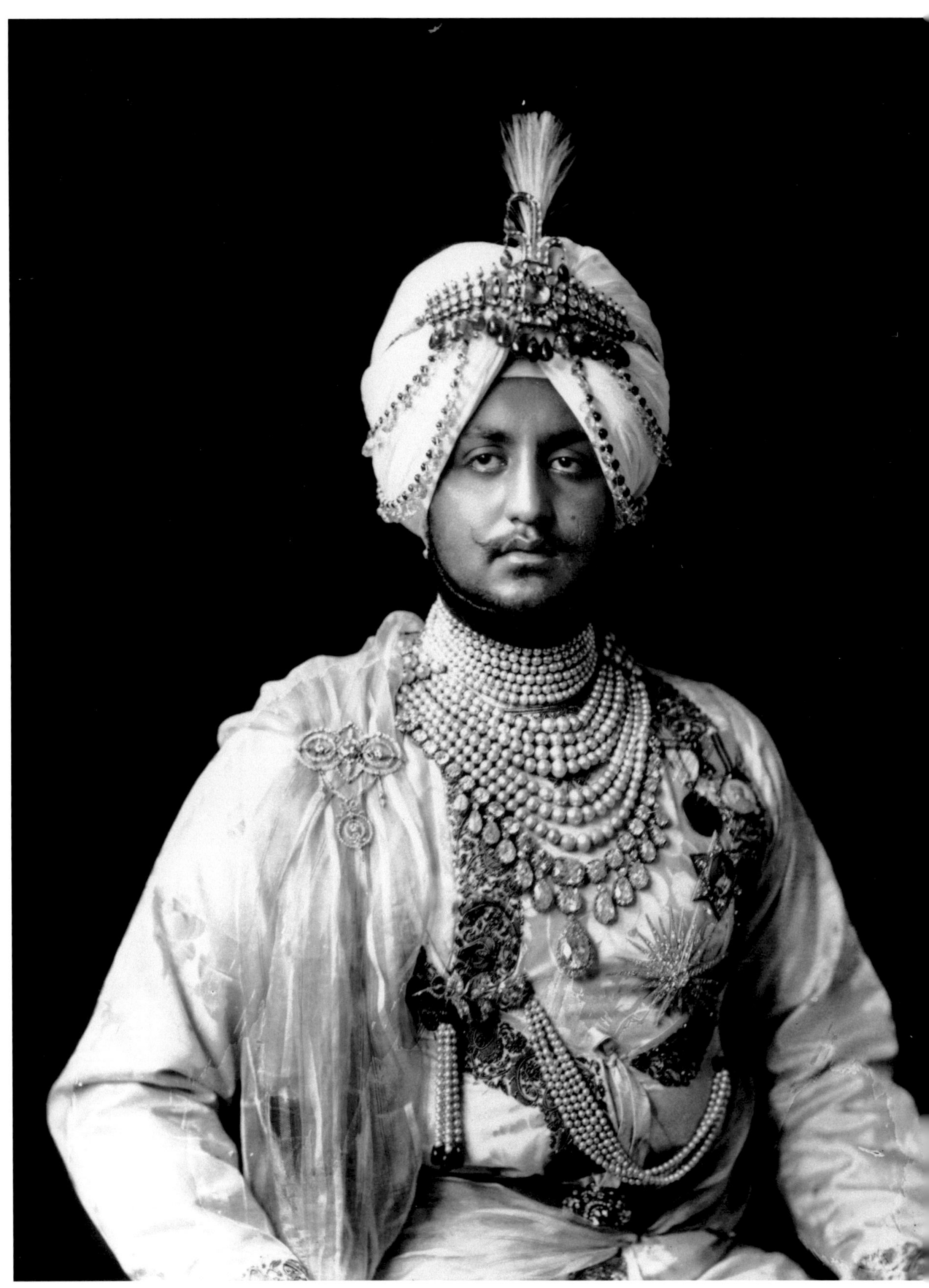

FIG. 8. Vandyk, detail of *Sir Bhupinder Singh, Maharaja of Patiala*, 1911. Glass plate negative, 12 × 10 in. (30.5 × 25.4 cm). National Portrait Gallery, London

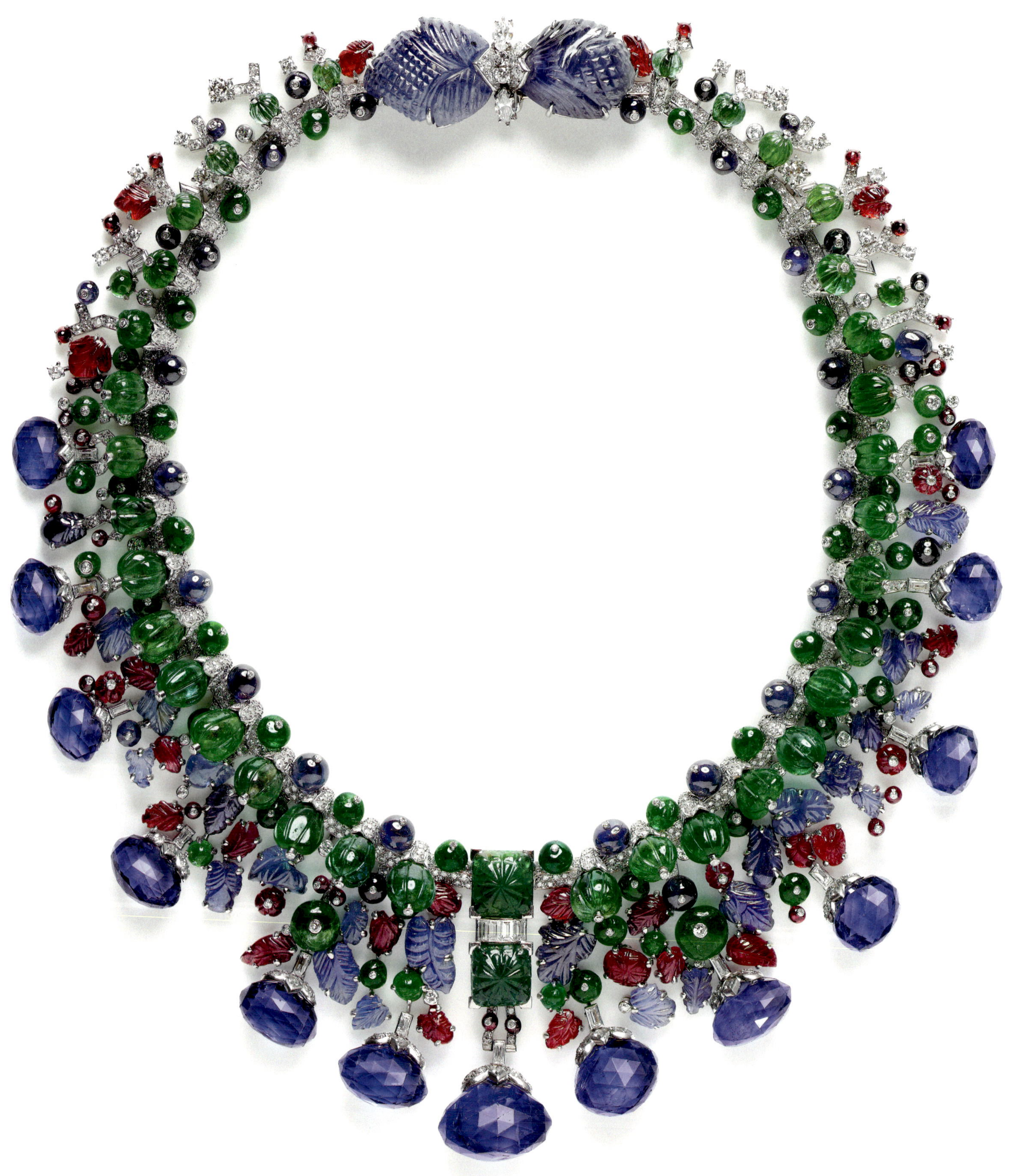

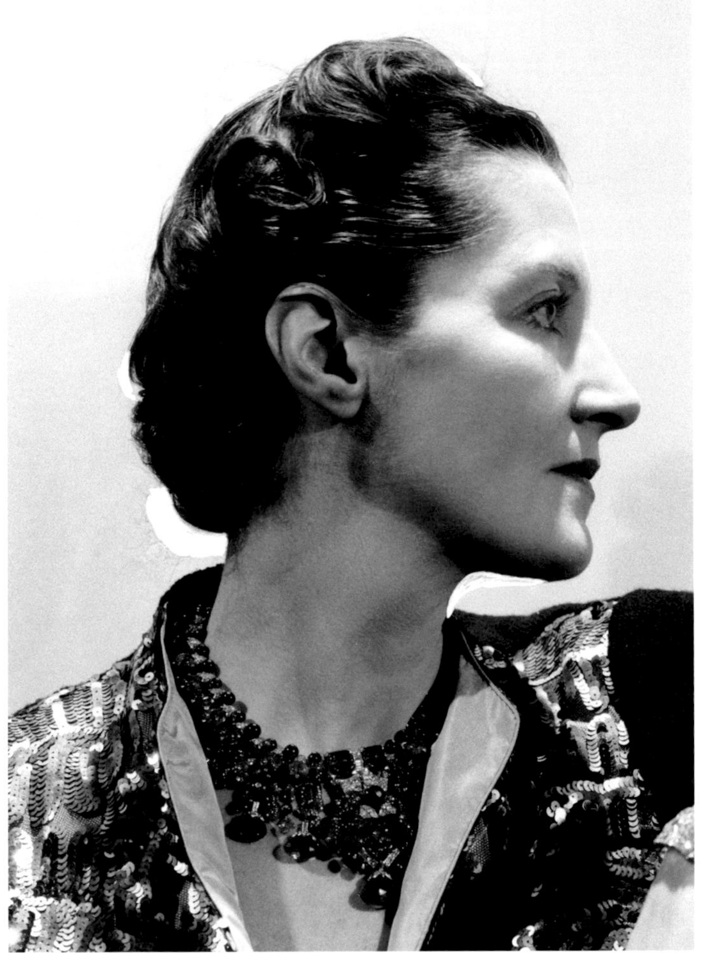

largest jewels and reconstituted as we see it today from the remaining platinum mount, with copies of the original large diamonds and rubies (cat. 139/pl. 74). In the end, the specific gender associated with jewelry mattered less for either the maharajas or the European monarchs than its magnificence in reflecting the status of the wearer.

In the nineteenth century, jewelry in India gradually assumed more Western aspects. Under the sway of the British, especially after the declaration of Queen Victoria as empress in 1876, the traditional ceremonial pieces, notably, the turban ornaments and necklaces made for the maharajas by Indian court jewelers, continued to draw on Mughal traditions but with increasing opulence. The settings could incorporate European designs with open backs and claws, rather than the closed and foiled settings of the traditional *kundan* type. Also in line with European models, Indian diamond jewelry was now mounted with silver-topped settings to enhance the size of the gems, rather than the yellow gold customarily used in traditional Indian pieces. The jewelry commissioned by the maharajas in the first half of the twentieth century coincided with the upsurge in jewelry making in the West, for both European and American clients. The jewelry sold to Indian maharajas was now made (or remade) by means of the more sophisticated techniques developed at this time by Parisian jewelry houses such as Cartier (founded 1847), with lighter settings in platinum (supplanting silver and gold) creating a meticulous finish and extraordinary delicacy.

Cartier reportedly had its first encounters with the Indian maharajas at the time of the coronation of Edward VII in 1902, when the king encouraged the firm to establish its first foreign branch in London. Jacques Cartier (1885–1942), who was eventually in charge of Cartier London, attended the Delhi Durbar in 1911, a huge event celebrating the coronation of King George V and Queen Mary, where he observed the splendor of jewels adorning Indian royalty and bought some emeralds that would have implications in succeeding decades. Cartier's London shop was positioned to attract maharajas, who often brought with them large numbers of diamonds and gemstones to be refashioned into new suites of jewelry during their visits to England. Cartier Paris and other French houses such as Boucheron and Van Cleef & Arpels competed with the London jewelers in supplying Indian maharajas, in particular Patiala in the late 1920s. But Cartier London continued to cater to the maharajas as well, creating and remaking substantial new pieces of jewelry for the Maharaja of Nawanagar at the time of

FIG. 9 *(opposite)*. "Hindu" necklace, 1936; Cartier Paris, altered 1963. Sapphires, emeralds, rubies, diamonds, platinum, white gold, 20 × 19 cm. Sold to Daisy Fellowes (Hon. Mrs. Reginald Fellowes), Cartier Collection, NE 28 A36

FIG. 10 *(above)*. Cecil Beaton, detail of The Hon. Mrs. Reginald Fellowes wearing the Cartier Tutti Frutti necklace [aka "Hindu" necklace], 1936

the 1937 coronation of King George VI and Queen Elizabeth (cat. 146/pl. 79 and cat. 147/pl. 81). The spectacular Tiger's Eye diamond turban ornament of 1937 follows traditional Mughal prototypes but seen through the lens of the prevailing hard-edged Art Deco style, with diamonds cut in rectangular baguettes and set in a highly stylized modernist form around a large brown diamond. The equally spectacular Nawanagar radiating ruby-and-diamond necklace (cat. 147/pl. 81) is more Western in its concept even though it is intended for a man. Ironically, it was later altered to be worn by a European woman (fig. 47),[15] and its design can be compared with a similar sapphire-and-diamond necklace fashioned by Cartier New York for a woman, Marjorie Merriweather Post, that same year.[16]

In the 1920s and 1930s, Cartier and other Western houses made much jewelry in the Indian style or using Indian gemstones for their European and American female clients. During this period—and even beyond—Indian influences are the most evident among the exotic styles featured by Parisian jewelers, which also embraced Chinese, Japanese, Persian, and ancient Egyptian sources. Cartier notably employed brilliantly colored carved Indian gemstones for its fashionable jewelry, creating a type that is now known as Tutti Frutti for the floral, fruit, and foliate shapes of its carved stones. Intended to be more relaxed than formal diamond suites, and often used for day wear, Tutti Frutti combined carved rubies, emeralds, and sapphires in bold settings. The best-known example of Tutti Frutti may be seen in the

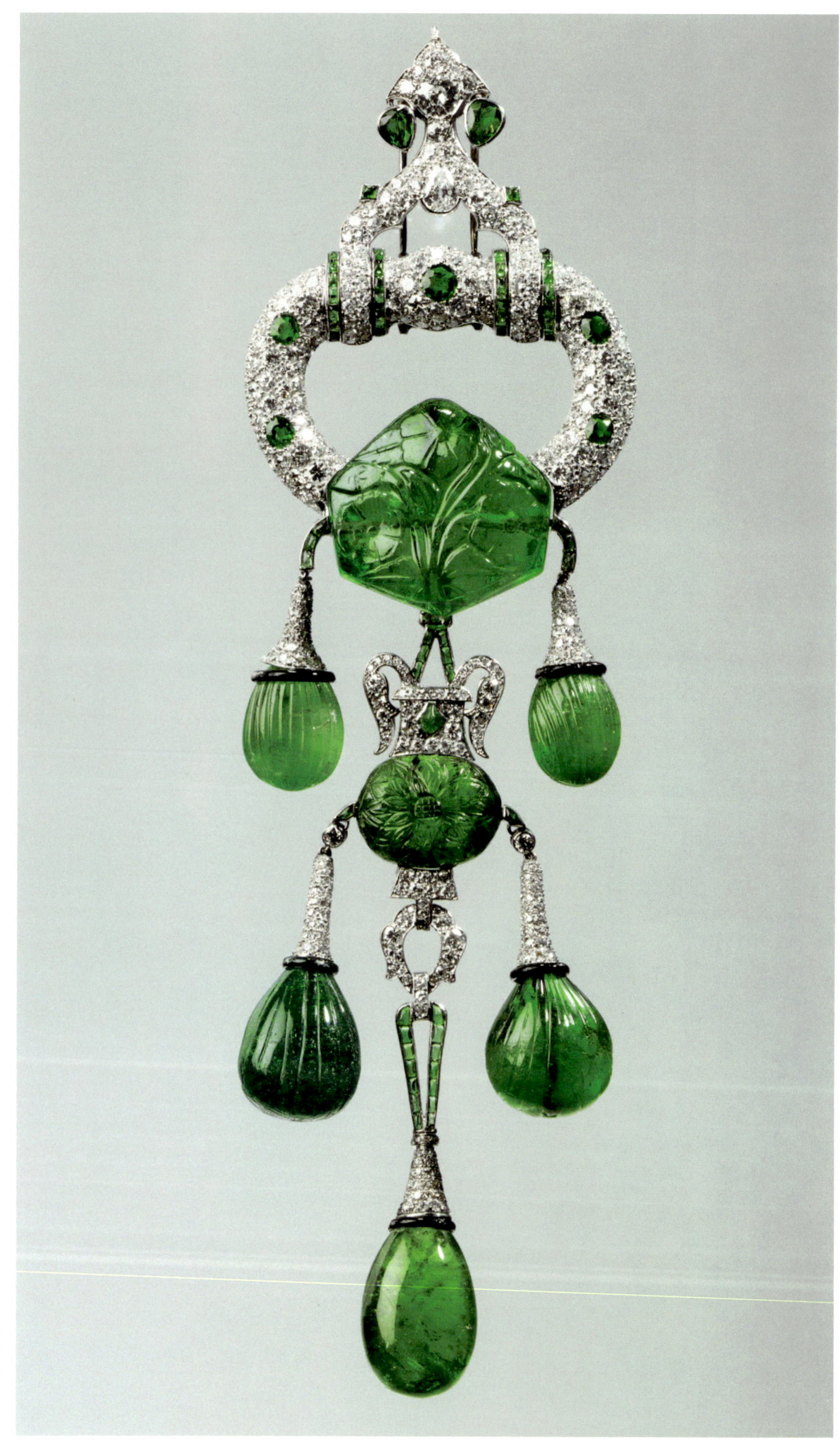

FIG. 11. Cartier London. Pendant shoulder brooch, 1923, altered 1928. Emeralds, diamonds, platinum, enamel, 8 × 2 in. (20.3 × 5.1 cm). Hillwood Estate, Museum & Gardens, Washington, DC, Bequest of Marjorie Merriweather Post, 1973, 17.75

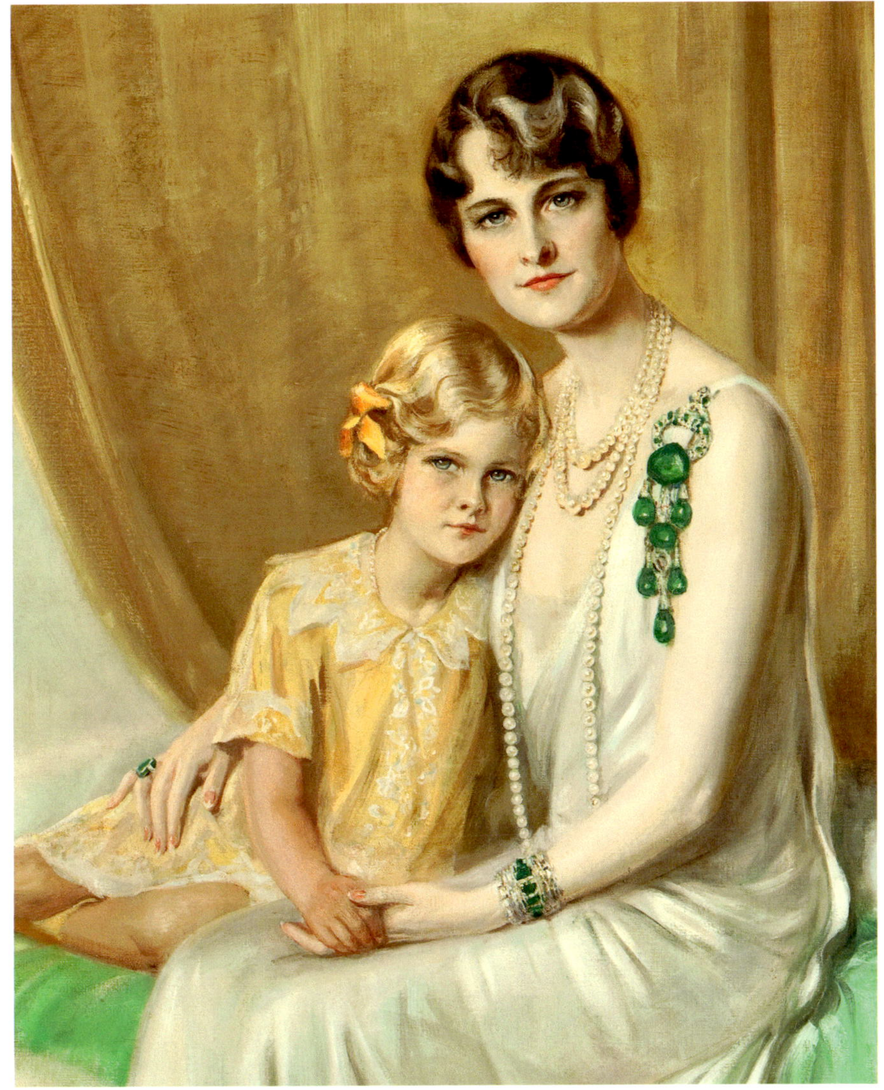

FIG. 12. Giulio de Blaas, *Portrait of Mrs. Hutton and Nedenia Hutton*, 1929. Oil on canvas, 59⅛ × 39⅛ in. (150 × 99 cm). Hillwood Estate, Museum & Gardens, Washington, DC, Bequest of Marjorie Merriweather Post, 1973, 51.146

"Hindu" necklace made by Cartier Paris in 1936 for Daisy Fellowes, who was at the forefront of European fashion in the interwar years and commissioned jewelry to suit her edgy style (figs. 9 and 10). Also for Fellowes, Van Cleef & Arpels crafted a dramatic pair of Indian-inspired Manchette bracelets in 1926 and 1928 (cat. 137/pl. 72). Based on traditional Indian anklets, these bracelets are made with the characteristic fringe of emerald drops (see cat. 107/pl. 60 for this type of Indian anklets), but with the equivalent of the anklet bands set with a mosaic of square and marquise-cut diamonds in the most high-style European Art Deco mode.

In the years between the wars, Cartier also had a business of remounting carved Indian emeralds in spectacular Art Deco settings for its Western female clientele. In 1928 Cartier New York altered a striking shoulder brooch, set with seven large carved Indian emeralds, for Marjorie Merriweather Post (figs. 11 and 12). The original brooch was made in London in 1923 with emeralds that were sourced by Jacques Cartier from India probably as far back as the Delhi Durbar in 1911. Cartier Paris also employed Indian emeralds as the centerpiece of a suite of jewels made in the most advanced style of the day for its display at the *Exposition internationale des arts décoratifs et industriels modernes* in Paris in 1925 (cat. 129/pl. 71).[17]

The main jewelry houses continued to draw inspiration from India into the 1950s. Cartier still embraced Indian styles in its necklaces made of beads or featuring leaflike sections, while the Roman jeweler Bulgari, famously beloved by Elizabeth Taylor, employed closely grouped cabochon (rounded) colored gemstones in its jewelry of the 1950s and 1960s, very much influenced by Indian examples.[18]

In the early twenty-first century, pieces made in India by Viren Bhagat and in Paris by the American jeweler JAR (Joel Arthur Rosenthal) stand as contemporary embodiments of the East-West dialogue. Fashioned in Mumbai, Bhagat's jewelry evokes the delicacy of Parisian jewelry of the early twentieth century but using traditional Indian forms in a new way. He employs many flat diamonds, native to India but largely eschewed by Western jewelers, and sets them in almost invisible mounts so they appear to float. He also includes traditional rose-cut diamonds, with their gentler sparkle. Although he prominently incorporates colored gemstones, the overall effect to which he aspires is an impression of white and silver produced by combinations of diamonds and light platinum settings in a manner reminiscent of formal European jewelry.

JAR has revolutionized Western jewelry by making pieces with unconventional settings, unusual assortments of stones, and utilizing a bold and vigorous approach that could be termed "sculpture as jewelry." Indian influences are frequently found in his highly original pieces. The Mughal brooch of 2002 is reminiscent of Indian architecture, with its cusped arch and back pierced in the form of a screen (cat. 156/pl. 88). The jabot or *cliquet* pin set, with large, elongated emeralds (cat. 159/pl. 90), is inspired by the turban ornament of Maharaja Sher Singh of Punjab (fig. 51). Hybrid in its design yet still redolent of Indian jewelry is a brooch (cat. 162) in which a carved jade camel is enfolded in a leaf consisting of an unorthodox combination of stones—chrysoberyls, green tourmalines, and green sapphires—from which a spray of feathers emerges very much as they would from a turban ornament. Another strongly sculptural brooch is modeled as the head of an elephant—a potent symbol of the magnificence of the courts and ceremonials of the Indian maharajas—its head and trunk fashioned in patinated titanium and its tusks in white cacholong, all topped by an explosive spray of diamonds in the mode of a turban ornament (cat. 163/pl. 93).

The exchange between India and the West in jewelry and luxury goods stretches back to the sixteenth century, starting with diplomatic gifts of European jewels and goldsmiths' work acquired by the Mughal emperors, and expanding to the taste for owning large Indian diamonds as a demonstration of power and prestige on the part of maharajas and European monarchs alike. The common thread shared by these rulers was their need for eye-catching display, resulting in increasingly splendid programs for jewelry by 1900. During the first half of the twentieth century, the maharajas distinguished themselves with the profusion and sumptuousness of their jewelry, eclipsing the brilliance of their Mughal forebears and (literally) outshining their Western counterparts. With the end of the British Raj in 1947 following the declaration of Indian independence, the maharajas who had ruled over some six hundred states in India lost the need to demonstrate their status through the conspicuous wearing of opulent jewelry. The exchange between East and West, however, continues today through the contemporary jewelry of Bhagat in India and JAR in Paris. The vigor of their work gives every indication that this cross-cultural fertilization will continue to flourish into the future.

NOTES

1. Gold is still mined in India today and remains an important material for jewelry.
2. Bernard Morel, *The French Crown Jewels* (Antwerp: Fonds Mercator, 1988), 158.
3. Nuno Vassallo e Silva, "Precious Stones, Jewels and Cameos; Jacques de Coutre's Journey to Goa and Agra," in *Goa and the Great Mughal* (Lisbon: Calouste Gulbenkian Foundation, 2004), 128.
4. See also Museum of Fine Arts, Boston, 2004.568, also marked by Joachim Friess.
5. A clockwork silver ship automaton was given to Jahangir by Jacques de Coutre on his visit to Agra in 1619. Vassallo e Silva, 128.
6. Kris Lane, *Colour of Paradise: The Emerald in the Age of Gunpowder Empires* (New Haven, CT: Yale University Press, 2010). Amin Jaffer, ed., *Beyond Extravagance: A Royal Collection of Gems and Jewels* (New York: Assouline, 2013), 94.
7. Jaffer, *Beyond Extravagance*, 36.
8. Although predominantly worn by women, aigrettes were also worn by European men from the early seventeenth century as hat ornaments. Male use was perpetuated as part of French military uniforms.
9. The Koh-i-Noor was worn by women in the British royal family, starting with Queen Victoria, because of the superstition that it could cause ill fortune to men but not to women: "He who owns this diamond will own the world, but will also know all its misfortunes. Only God, or a woman, can wear it with impunity."
10. This necklace was not part of the 1887 sale, as the empress brought it with her into exile after the fall of the Second Empire in 1870 and sold it shortly thereafter.
11. Katherine Prior, "Twentieth-Century Encounters between Indian and European Jewellery," in Jaffer, *Beyond Extravagance*, 286. This history is at variance with Ian Balfour's *Famous Diamonds*, 2nd ed. (Santa Monica, CA. GIA, 1992), 93, where he writes that this diamond was purchased by the Gaekwar of Baroda.
12. Ibid.
13. Alain Boucheron, "Boucheron," in A. Kenneth Snowman, ed., *The Master Jewelers* (London: Thames & Hudson, 1990), 89.
14. The Affair of the Diamond Necklace was an incident in the French court in 1785 involving Queen Marie Antoinette. The reputation of the queen, already tarnished by gossip, was ruined by the implication that she was involved in the theft of a large and very expensive diamond necklace. Spirited away by a woman posing as the queen, the necklace was broken up and sold in London. Although the queen had nothing to do with the necklace, she was wrongly blamed for its disappearance in the court of popular culture. The Affair is considered one of the events that precipitated the French Revolution. It has been the stuff of legend, engendering novels and even films.
15. The necklace was worn by Mrs. Loel (Gloria) Guinness at Truman Capote's famous Black and White Ball in New York City, November 28, 1966.
16. See Martin Chapman, *Cartier and America* (Munich, London, New York: Fine Arts Museums of San Francisco and DelMonico · Prestel, 2009), cat. 186.
17. The suite was so ahead of its time that it did not sell. It was deconstructed, and elements such as this brooch were recast to make them more appealing for sale.
18. Ibid., cats. 233, 238, 243. Margaret Young-Sánchez, *Cartier in the 20th Century* (Denver: Denver Art Museum and the Vendome Press, 2014), 216–217, fig. 235; necklace, bracelet, and pair of earrings made for Lady Deterding, Cartier Paris, 1951.

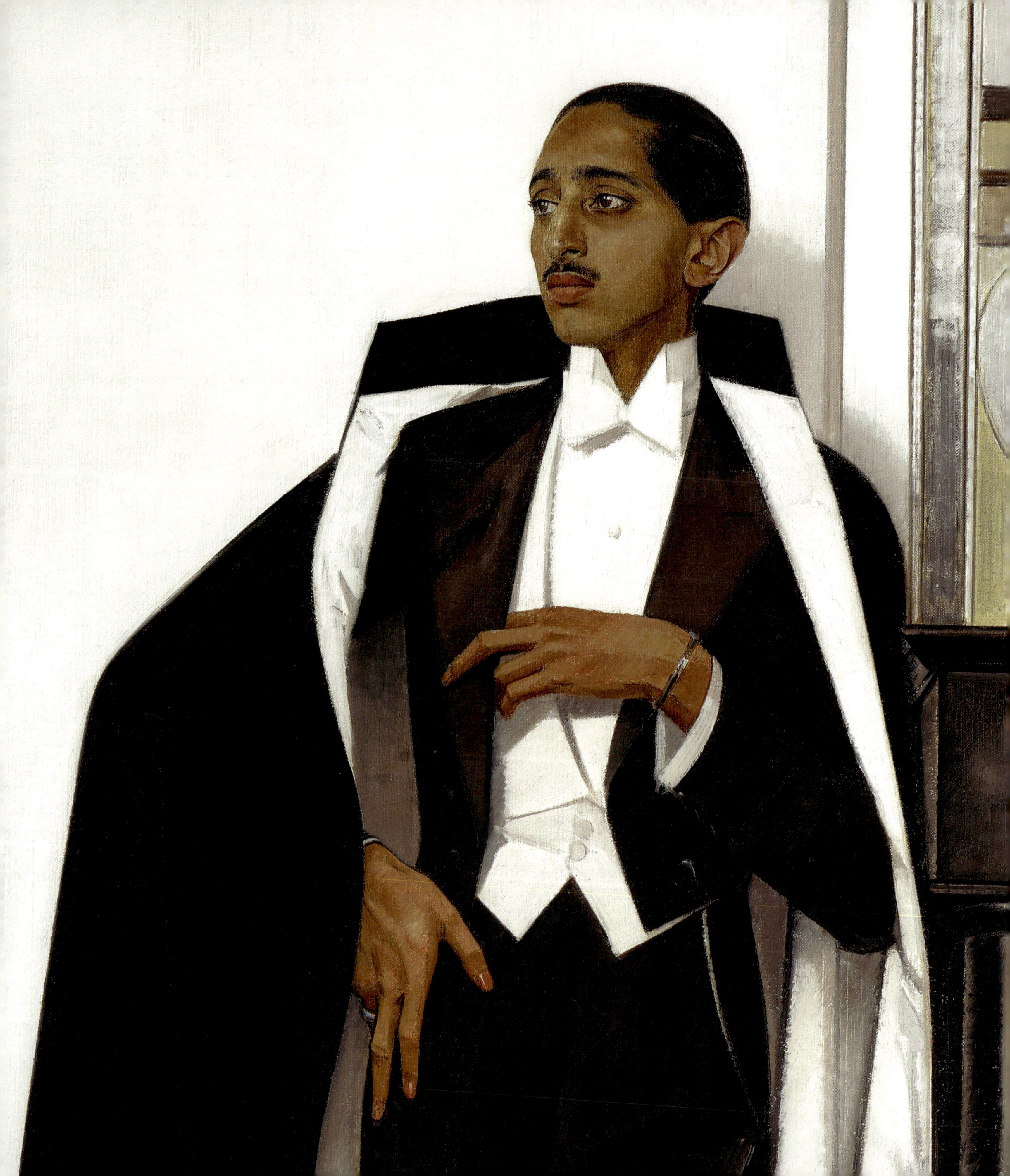

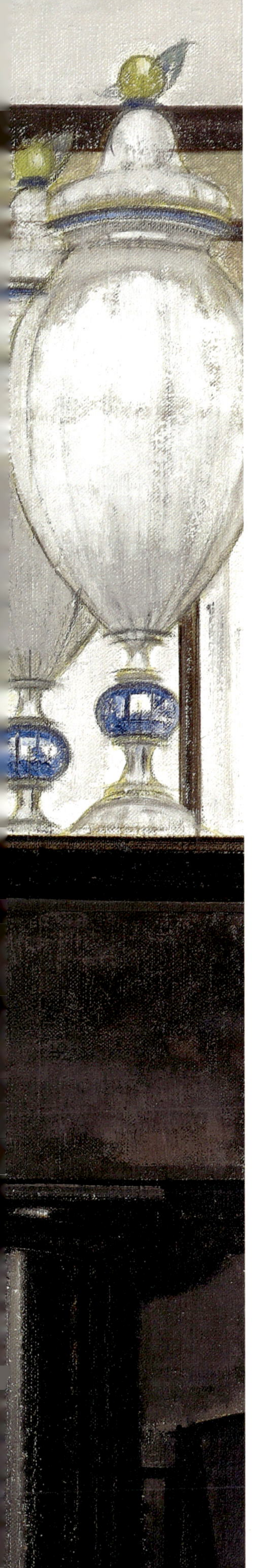

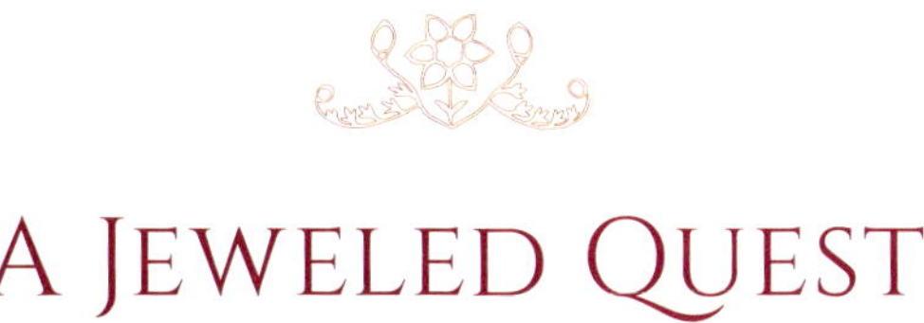

A Jeweled Quest

The Creation of The Al Thani Collection

AMIN JAFFER

From the ancient civilization of the Indus Valley to present times, the subcontinent of South Asia has enjoyed a uniquely sophisticated tradition of jewelry, in which gems and jewels—whether real or representational—have been an integral aspect of daily wear across classes and faiths. This rich culture is partly the result of natural circumstances. Throughout history, the region has been home to fine gemstones: the mines of Golconda yielded the highest grade of diamonds, Kashmir produced sapphires of the most beautiful hue, and Badakhshan was home to the most prized spinels. Sapphires and rubies were available from nearby Ceylon (Sri Lanka) or by trade with Burma (Myanmar), and monsoon winds brought to Indian shores pearls from the Persian Gulf. The greatest emeralds gravitated to India through commercial exchange, carried there by European merchants after the discovery of mines in Colombia. India had always supplemented its natural deposits of gold through a positive balance of trade; since antiquity, spices and textiles from the subcontinent were exported to East and West in exchange for bullion.

These precious materials were transformed through the ingenuity of Indian craftsmen, raised to fresh heights by a continuous tradition of patronage extending to the present day. Jewelry in India is not merely for adornment; for Hindus, every gem is pregnant with significance, reflecting a cosmic purpose or invoking a favorable horoscope. In popular culture, particular forms of jewelry reflect rank, caste, region, marital status, or, quite simply, wealth. Throughout the subcontinent, there exists a strong tradition of talismanic jewelry in which the wearing of particular gems, images, or inscriptions is seen as protection against illness or curse. Certain gems and materials are also seen to invoke good fortune and prosperity. Balancing one's fortune with gemstones represents a system of faith that is prevalent even today. The mythic origin, virtuous properties, and appropriate use of precious stones are articulated in early Sanskrit writings such as the *Ratnashastras* ("Treatise on Gems"). Over time, distinctions were made between the nine most significant stones (*navaratna*), which include diamond, pearl, ruby, sapphire, emerald, hyacinth (zircon), topaz, cat's eye, and coral, each symbolizing a different planet. Together these represent a microcosm of the universe and constitute a form of talismanic protection.

Evidence from sculpture and wall painting indicates that, since the earliest times, jewelry in India was worn in abundance. From crowns and hair ornaments to necklaces, armlets, bangles, waistbands, anklets, and toe rings, a number of forms were developed to adorn and beautify every part of the body. Little material evidence survives of ancient jewelry from the subcontinent, although particular forms and types have remained to the present day, in both sacred and secular contexts. Indigenous jewelry was also absorbed into the fashions of the Muslim invaders who first arrived in the eighth century and for whom the prospect of plundering Indian treasuries was a huge motivating factor for ventures into Hindustan. Surviving Indian jewelry belongs to the period following the defeat of the Lodi sultans by the Timurid prince Zahir al-Din Muhammad Babur in 1526. Once established as rulers of Northern India, his descendants emerged as committed patrons of the arts, with a passion for gems and jewels that arguably eclipses that of any court before or after.

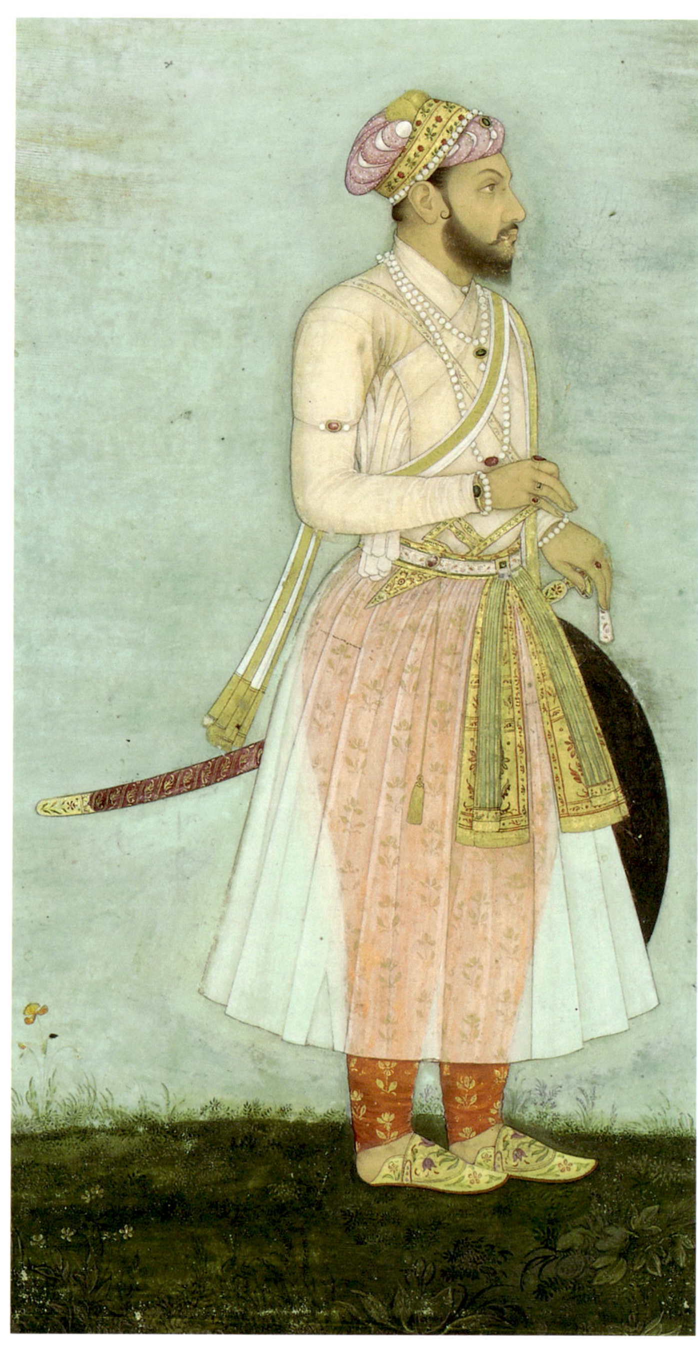

FIG. 13. A Mughal prince, probably Shah Shuja', detail of a folio from the Late Shah Jahan Album, India, ca. 1650 [Reverse with panel of calligraphy by (Mir) 'Ali al-Katib, Herat or Bukhara, 1500–1550]. Paper, opaque pigments, gold, 8⅝ × 5 in. (21.9 × 12.7 cm). The Al Thani Collection

Travelers' accounts, chronicles, and diaries from the height of the Mughal Empire reveal the extent to which rulers valued gems, whether for their rarity, physical properties, and provenance. The finest and largest gems unearthed in Mughal domains would be immediately offered to the ruler. These holdings were enhanced with a constant flow of presents and gifts from ambassadors, courtiers, and supplicants as well as by purchases from gem dealers who had come to court, from local lands and from as far away as Europe. Imperial fashions in jewelry and jeweled objects were subject to regional and external influence as regards form, material, technique, and design. A taste for Western exotica, for example, led to the appropriation of European imagery into Mughal ornament. In admiration of Western gem cutting and metalworking technologies likewise meant that highly skilled

European jewelers were welcomed at court, where some of them went on to play a role in the imperial workshops designing jeweled objects of great value and significance to the dynasty.

Much Indian jewelry is characterized by *kundan*, a technique by which gemstones are set in gold without the use of a conspicuous claw or prong. Instead, strips of extremely pure gold are used to fashion the mount around a gem. At room temperature, these strips form a molecular bond with one another while remaining malleable. Using an iron stylus, a goldsmith *(sonar)* is able to manipulate the gold to create a pliable but strong mount around a gem. The process has meant that in Indian jewelry, gemstones are typically closed-set, sometimes against gold or silver foil backing that creates a reflective glow, lending light and vivacity to the stone. Unlike in the West, where they were fashioned into symmetrical shapes, in India gemstones were cut in such a way as to retain their size as much as possible.

Enameling is also closely associated with Indian jewelry, particularly that from the north of the subcontinent. The technique first made its appearance in the Mughal period, probably inspired by an appreciation of the sophisticated enameled jewelry of Renaissance workshops, which arrived at the imperial court as gifts from Western ambassadors. The dominant role that this foreign technique has come to play in Indian jewelry is evidence of its ingenious assimilation into indigenous style. The Mughal approach to jewelry shaped tastes in the many regions that were subsumed within an empire that by the close of the seventeenth century covered most of the subcontinent.

The sack of Delhi perpetrated by the Iranian warrior Nadir Shah in 1739 and the subsequent collapse of Mughal imperial authority saw the dismemberment of provinces from the ailing empire. Yet imperial taste and forms of authority endured at the courts of Successor States, those new political entities that emerged following the collapse of the Mughal Empire, and to a certain measure in the liberated Rajput kingdoms, some of which had allied closely and intermarried with the Mughal dynasty. In an attempt to legitimize their power, newly emerging forces likewise appropriated aspects of imperial courtly culture, most evidently in the wearing of jewelry and the use of particular symbols of authority. The early rise of the various European trading companies in India had been dependent to an extent on the ability of governors and factors to engage with and assimilate local courtly customs, not only in expressing power but also in dress and manner. European officials had participated in the wearing and the giving of jewelry, which was an integral aspect of articulating authority in the Mughal tradition. The defeat of Tipu Sultan by British forces in 1799 and their gradual subjugation of India, however, firmly established Western norms as the dominant model for elite behavior.

Even if form and function remained constant, in the nineteenth century—especially after the establishment of the British Raj in 1858—fashionable Indian jewelry was increasingly shaped by Western influence. This was evident in design in the faceting of gems and in their setting, as the closed-back *kundan* mount indigenous to India gradually gave way to open, Western-style claw settings for holding precious stones. Although trends toward the revival of traditional Indian jewelry techniques persisted throughout the British period, from the late nineteenth century onward the princes who constituted India's ruling class veered in the opposite direction, replacing gold with platinum as the favored setting for their most important gems and eventually having their pieces remounted in the latest Western fashions by London and Paris firms. This appreciation for European taste was by no means unreciprocated: the early twentieth century witnessed a growing interest among leading Western houses for traditional Indian jewelry styles: with their gold mounts and stones of different colors, the latter offered a fresh approach that was so needed in the years following the First World War.

The creation of the collection by His Highness Sheikh Hamad bin Abdullah Al Thani was driven by his passion for the taste and style of Indian jewelry across various historical periods. Typically it is the jeweled arts of the Mughal court that have most excited enthusiasts of Indian jewelry. The scope of the present collection is wider in approach and attitude, driven by an underlying interest in the use of gems in Indian jewelry in different eras, reflecting indigenous tradition and the assimilation of foreign taste and technology. The direct inspiration behind the formation of this collection was the exhibition *Maharaja: The Splendour of India's Royal Courts*, held at the Victoria and Albert Museum in 2009–2010, which attempted to contextualize jewelry and luxury goods over many centuries, illustrating the impact on Indian royal taste of Mughal tradition, the British Raj, and the cultural encounter with Europe. This collection too derives particular meaning from this broad approach.

Over eight years, this collection has developed from a source of private pleasure into a leading group of jewelry worthy of publication and exhibition. Although this was not the intention at the start, the quality of the first acquisitions suggested immediately that this collection would be a serious one. Among the first acquisitions were two fine *jighas* (cat. 95 and cat. 96/pl. 53), a rare example in jade and one with a finely faceted central spinel. These were the first of what was to become an outstanding group of turban ornaments stretching from the Mughal period to the present day. Other early acquisitions included a fine, carved jade spoon (cat. 42), a sapphire *taweez*-shaped pendant (cat. 29), and a gem-set circular locket-pendant (cat. 73/pl. 37). But these were all eclipsed by a gem-encrusted imperial quality pen case (cat. 72/pl. 36), an exceptional and rare survival of a jeweled object with a very particular significance in Iranian and Mughal court culture.

Sheikh Hamad had long been an admirer of the work of the Parisian jeweler Joel Arthur Rosenthal (JAR), who shares a passion for India as he does for historic gems. With his eye now focused on Indian jewelry, the work of JAR assumed a new significance. Among the jeweler's most innovative works is a brooch conceived as a setting for an old-mine emerald, the front designed as a cusped arch and the reverse as a pierced lattice screen (cat. 156/pl. 88); the piece had been made in 2002, well before this collection was formed. The acquisition of the brooch opened a door to the work of contemporary designers in the collection. JAR went on to create an imposing pair of earrings with spinels and natural pearls—both gems closely associated

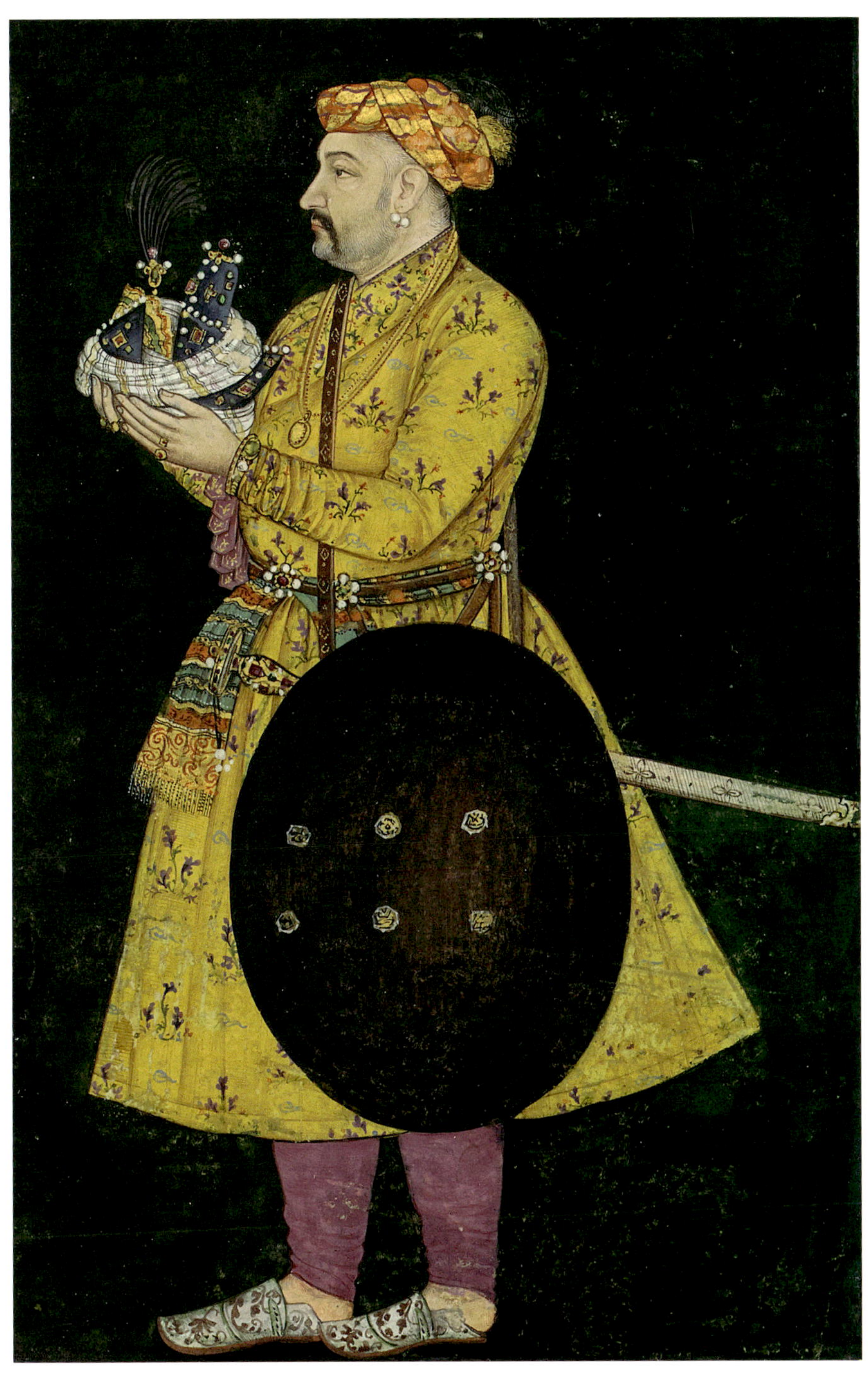

FIG. 14. Detail of Portrait of Asaf Khan holding a jeweled turban, India, ca. 1640. Paper, opaque pigments, gold, 5½ × 3¼ in. (14.2 × 8.4 cm). The Al Thani Collection

with Mughal jewelry, but in a style that is both unique and contemporary (cat. 157/pl. 89). Further examples of his ingenuity are a jabot brooch (cat. 159/pl. 90) incorporating three elongated emeralds of a type historically worn by Indian princes, and a pair of earrings in which natural pearls cascade as a waterfall (cat. 158).

A meeting with master jeweler Viren Bhagat enriched the contemporary holdings in the collection. Bhagat's work infuses a fresh delicacy and refinement into Indian jewelry, using old-cut gems with settings that disappear and seemingly suspend in midair transparent diamonds, laboriously shaped after petals, pointed leaves, and cusped cartouches. Among his most notable pieces in the collection is a diamond brooch with a pin of graduated pearls on which is suspended a substantial flat-cut diamond pendant lotus flower, closely associated with Indian culture as a symbol of purity and divinity (cat. 152/pl. 85).

Even before developing an interest in Indian jewelry or visiting India, Sheikh Hamad had acquired paintings of arresting beauty. The elegant marriage of modern design and Indian princely taste was therefore something to which he was sensitive even before considering Indian jewelry. As the collection grew, it became apparent that the extraordinary encounter between European jewelers and maharajas needed to be represented; equally fascinating was the role of Western firms in setting old Indian stones. Today the products of this cultural exchange between East and West constitute one of the strengths of the collection. Among the highlights is a brooch with a large carved Indian emerald, designed by Cartier for the 1925 Paris *Exposition internationale des arts décoratifs et industriels modernes* and modified in 1927 (cat. 129/

pl. 71), and a belt brooch created by the same firm using an old step-cut emerald of exceptional quality (cat. 134). The inspiration that Cartier found in traditional Indian jewelry is evident in a magnificent *cliquet* pin (cat. 127/pl. 69) drawing on eighteenth-century turban ornament forms and in a fine brooch that combines multicolored gems in a style called Tutti Frutti because of its visual similarity with hard candy (cat. 135/pl. 73). An early example of the reuse of old Indian gems and the juxtaposition of stones of different colors is found in this collection in a much published avant-garde aigrette, designed by Paul Iribe and executed by Robert Linzeler in 1910, in which sapphires, diamonds, and pearls complement a substantial carved emerald (cat. 126/pl. 68). This seminal piece, now in The Collection, belonged for many years to the Cartier brothers, suggesting that it inspired in some measure their bold Indian-style creations.

The Al Thani Collection holds a number of pieces designed in the West specifically for a royal Indian patron. Among these is the celebrated ruby bead choker (cat. 140/pl. 76) made by Cartier for Maharaja Bhupinder Singh of Patiala in 1931 as one of three necklaces that were conceived to be worn together to grand effect. The maharaja had famously reset many of his gems with Cartier and Boucheron in the 1920s and early 1930s and was a leading client for both firms. Another prince who patronized both of these houses was Maharaja Jagatjit Singh of Kapurthala, a polymath and statesman who felt naturally at home in France and became a leading patron of French luxury firms. Among his early jewelry acquisitions was a peacock-shaped aigrette made by Mellerio dits Meller (cat. 123/pl. 67), a Paris-based firm that had operated under French royal patronage since the time of Marie de' Medici and had enjoyed particular favor during the Second Empire. Western jewelry created for another leading Indian royal patron was found in the two rings owned by Maharaja Yeshwant Rao Holkar II of Indore (cats. 142 and 143), both of which are associated with Harry Winston, the legendary jeweler who became a close friend of the Indore royal family. The highlight among such creations is the magnificent Tiger's Eye turban ornament, designed for Maharaja Digvijaysinhji of Nawanagar by Cartier London in 1937 using a 61.5-carat golden-colored diamond acquired by his predecessor, the famous cricketer and gem collector Maharaja Ranjitsinhji of Nawanagar (cat. 146/pl. 79). Using rubies from the Royal Treasury, Cartier London also made a spectacular ruby necklace for the Nawanagar royal family, a true masterpiece of twentieth-century jewelry design that is now in The Al Thani Collection (cat. 147/pl. 81).

As a particular interest of Sheikh Hamad, gemstones—some with remarkable provenance—have come to form the backbone of the collection. Among these is the Arcot II (cat. 3/pl. 2), one of two pear-shaped diamonds given by the Nawab of Arcot, Muhammad Ali Wallajah, to Queen Charlotte, and later mounted in the Crown Jewels of George IV. Upon the king's death, the diamonds were sold to the 1st Marquess of Westminster; his descendant, the 3rd Duke of Westminster, sold them to pay taxes in 1959. The Idol's Eye (cat. 7/pl. 4) is another historical gem in the collection, prized as the largest cut

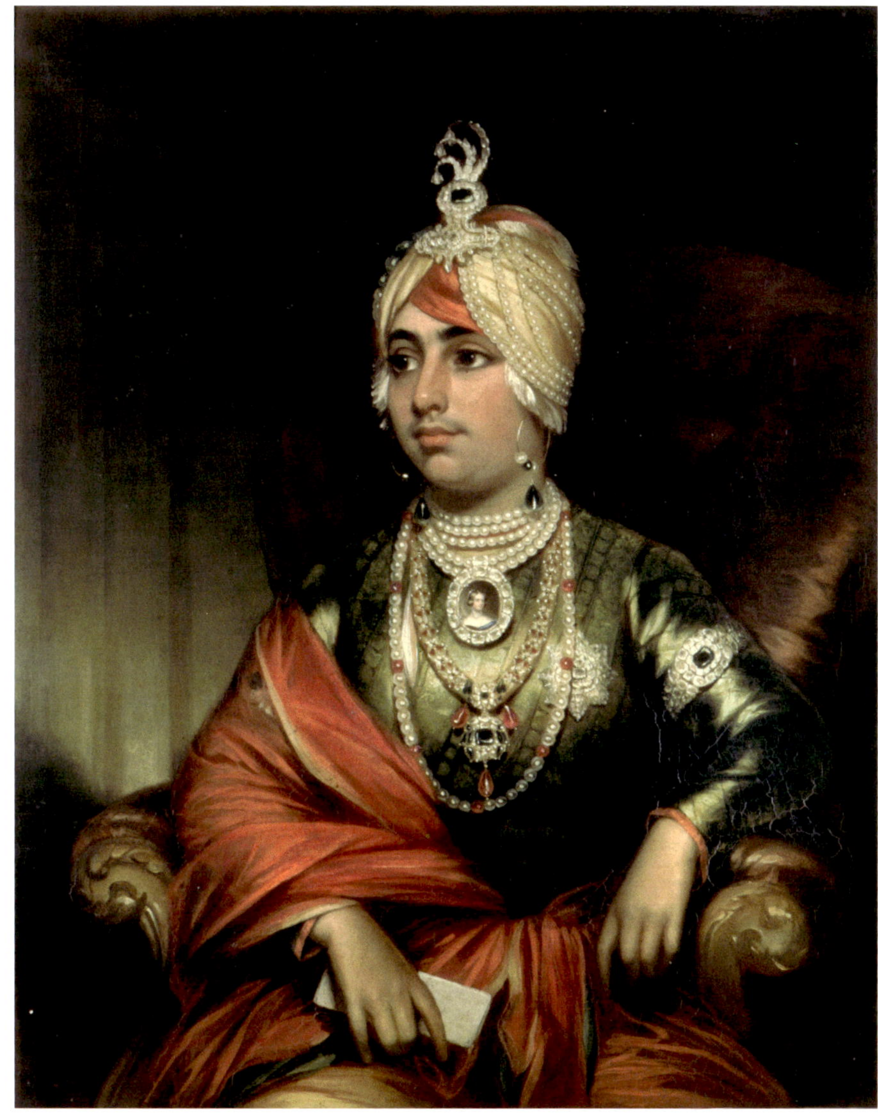

blue diamond in the world. The collection is particularly strong in its holdings of emeralds, both faceted and carved, dating from the Mughal period onward. As green was the favorite color of the Prophet Muhammad, emeralds found particular favor among Islamic rulers in the subcontinent and they were widely used in jewelry. Among the best-known examples in this collection is the Taj Mahal Emerald (cat. 14/pl. 7), set by Cartier in its legendary Collier Bérénice neckpiece made for the 1925 Paris Exposition. The holdings of emeralds are complemented by substantial numbers of spinels, some of which were considered dynastic gems and inscribed by successive royal owners with their names and titles (cat. 24/pl. 9, cat. 25/pl. 10, cat. 26, and cat. 27/pl. 11). Passed from father to son, from vanquished to victor, from dynasty to dynasty, today they find a fitting home in this collection.

Within an Indian context, diamonds were prized for their inimitable qualities, ranging from translucency to hardness: so much so that in Sanskrit the gem was called *vajra* (literally, "thunderbolt"). Their indestructible nature has meant that diamonds were traditionally considered masculine gems. For instance, the author of the sixth-century *Ratnapariksha* ("Appreciation of Gems") wrote that "the king, who according to what he has been told, wears a beautiful, light, sparkling diamond, possesses a power that triumphs over all other powers." It may actually surprise first-time students of Indian jewelry to learn that the great diamond necklaces in this collection were worn by men (cat. 112 and cat. 113/pl. 61), both for their supernatural properties and as a representation of the wealth of the State. Although subtler, women's jewelry is also represented in the collection, characterized by feminine scale and decorative palette. Among the pieces of particular interest is a pair of finely enameled anklets (cat. 107/pl. 60), nose rings (cats. 117 and 118), and hair ornaments (cat. 116/pl. 66 and cat. 119/pl. 65), all of which reflect the growing influence of Western taste and technology in the production of traditional jewelry.

FIG. 15. George Duncan Beechey, *Maharaja Duleep Singh of Punjab*, 1852. Oil on canvas, 36 × 29 in. (91.5 × 73.7 cm). Private collection

Each acquisition represents a different aspect of jewelry and the jeweled arts in South Asia. The fusion of traditional Indian jewelry with Western gem faceting and setting techniques during the British Raj is another peculiar area of interest, representing the taste of the high nineteenth century. Among the notable pieces of this group are spectacular diamond-and-emerald necklaces designed to be worn at durbar, the formal audience when an Indian ruler showed himself before the court (cat. 111, cat. 113/pl. 61, and cat. 114/pl. 62), diamond turban ornaments (cat. 100/pl. 55, cat. 101, and cat. 102/pl. 56), and a gem-encrusted State sword from Hyderabad (cat. 120/pl. 64). Ceremonial weapons had been part of Indian culture long before the arrival of Europeans and were often depicted in portraits of rulers; however, the style and shape of this sword reveals a clear debt to Western models.

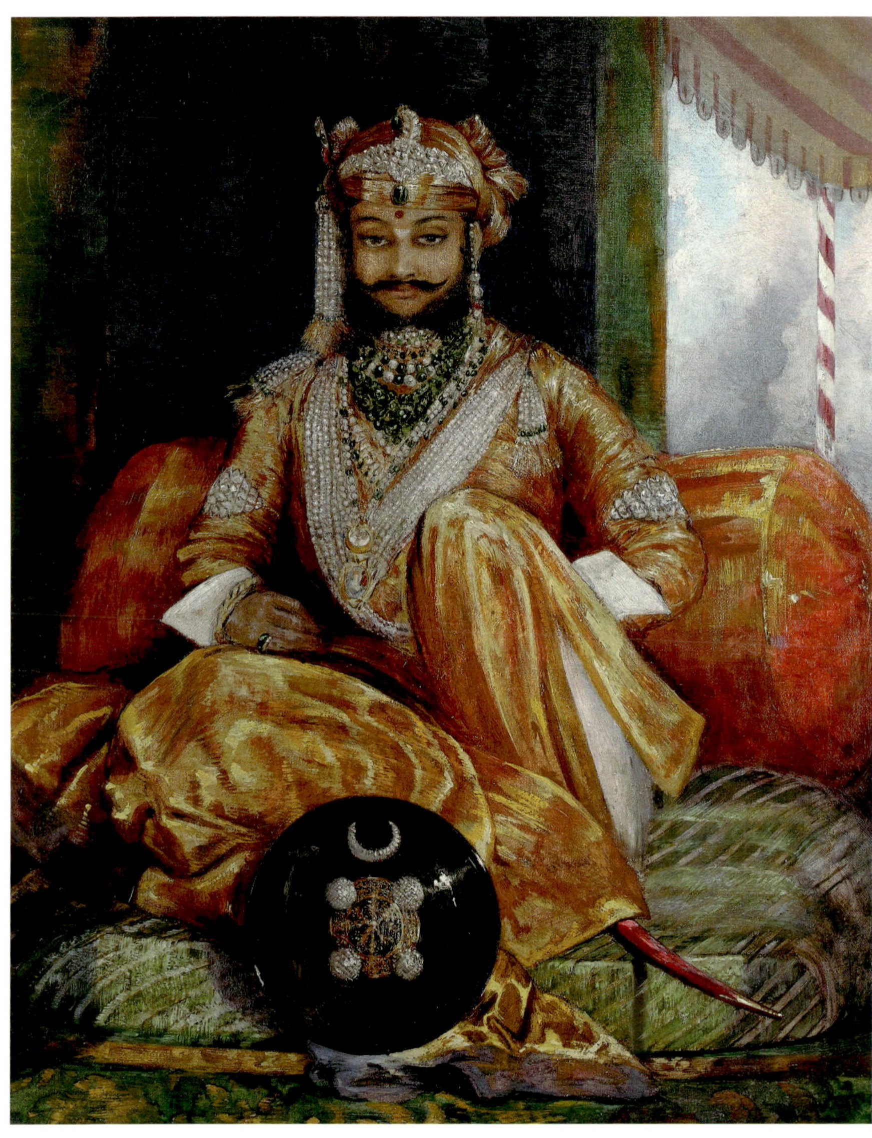

FIG. 16. George Landseer, detail of *Maharaja Tukoji Rao II of Indore*, 1861. Oil on canvas, 23⅜ × 17 in. (59.4 × 43.2 cm). The Al Thani Collection

FIG. 17 (*opposite*). Devare's Art Studio (photographer), *Maharaj Sajjin Singh (b. 1899)*, ca. 1906. Collodion silver print, 10¼ × 8¼ in. (26.2 × 21.1 cm). Fine Arts Museums of San Francisco, Achenbach Foundation for Graphic Arts, Gift of Dr. William K. Ehrenfeld, 2004.16.6

The paraphernalia of court culture has over time also been incorporated into the collection, as have objects associated with the pleasures of taking *paan* (cat. 91/pl. 51) and smoking the hookah. In this respect, the collection is fortunate to have an exceptionally rare ruby-inlaid spherical jade hookah base (cat. 46/pl. 19), which was acquired and subsequently found to have been exhibited in Delhi at the time of the 1903 Coronation Durbar by Maharana Fateh Singh of Udaipur. This is one of a group of objects whose provenance can be traced securely back to their original owner—a rarity in this field. A silver-gilt durbar set, an agate flywhisk, and a jade back scratcher in the collection all belonged to "Clive of India," the brilliant soldier and statesman who established British rule in South Asia, as found in family inventories (cat. 50, cat. 51, and cat. 84/pl. 42). Added to such pieces with impeccable provenance is a selection of enameled objects belonging to the Nizams of Hyderabad (cat. 57/pl. 27, cat. 88/pl. 49, cat. 89, cat. 90/pl. 50, cat. 91/pl. 51, and cat. 92), which reflect durbar rituals such as the sprinkling of rosewater and the presentation of *paan* and other delicacies to visitors at court. Among the other highlights in this category is a gem-encrusted gold finial from the

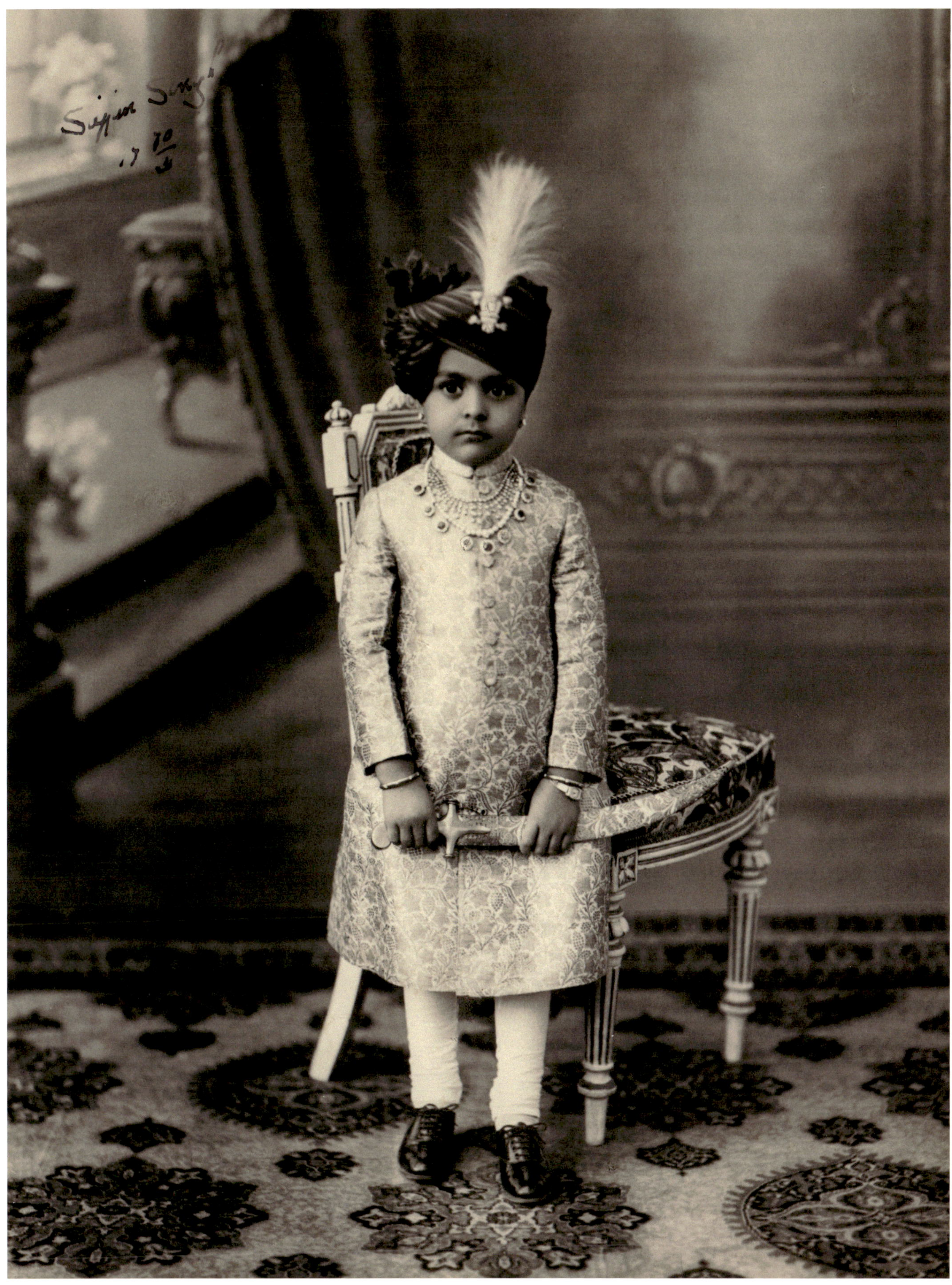

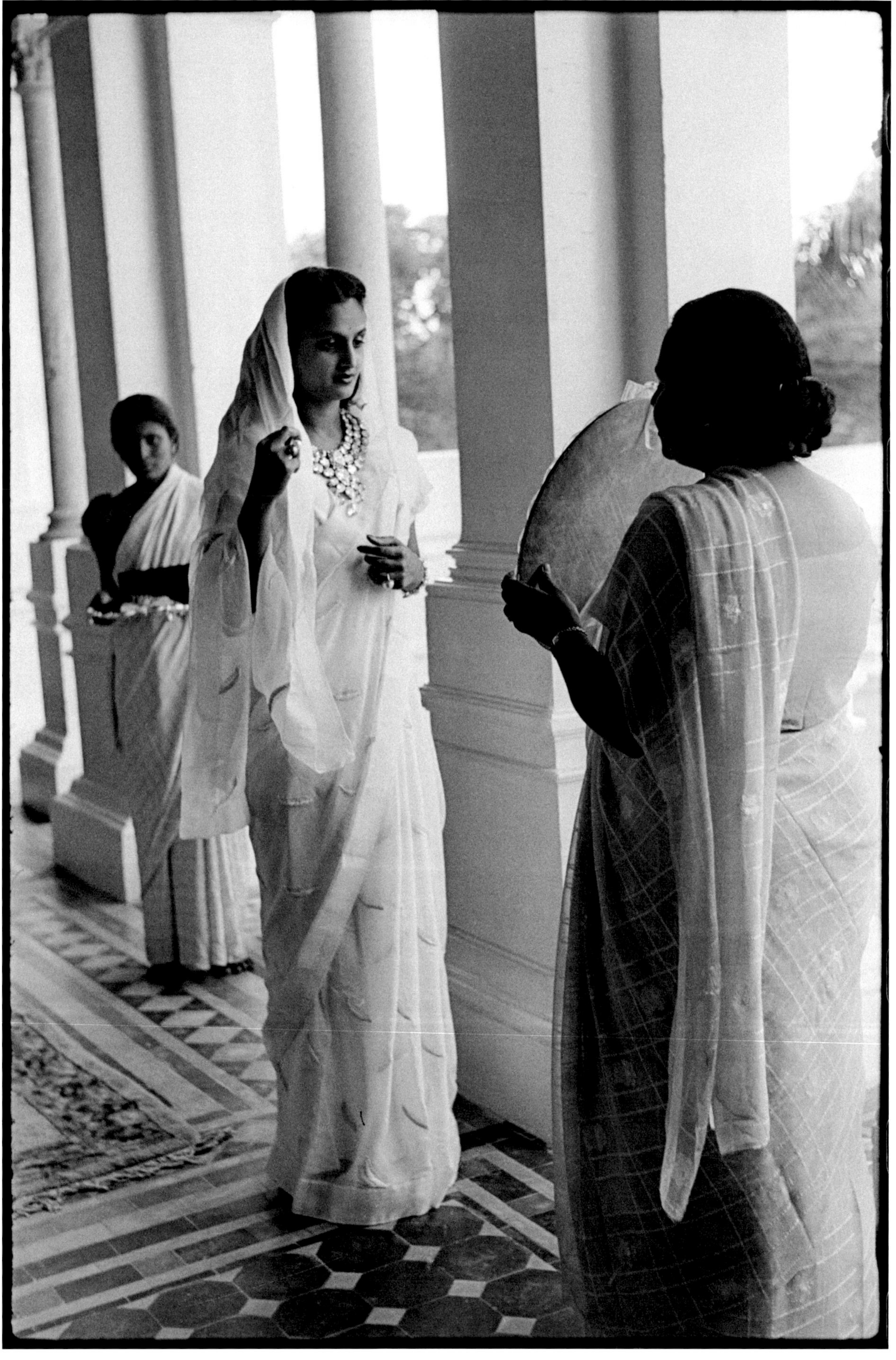

throne of Tipu Sultan, a gold box, and a hawking ring he owned are among the few fully documented examples of South Indian goldsmiths' work (cat. 85/pl. 47, cat. 86/pl. 48, and cat. 87) and reflect the refined taste of this great ruler.

Among the most prized pieces in the collection is a small dagger with a carved jade hilt that belonged to Shah Jahan and is depicted in portraits of this most refined gem-loving emperor (cat. 56/pl. 26). The pommel of this celebrated piece is carved with the head of an exotic youth clearly inspired by Renaissance depictions. The Mughal interest in Western art also finds expression in an exceptional pendant in the shape of a merman, but perhaps representing an Indian deity (cat. 74/pl. 38). Once again, the form finds direct inspiration in European jewelry, designed to incorporate the exceptional pearls that arrived at Western courts in the Age of the Discoveries, but the execution and iconography are chiefly Indian. Another example of cultural fusion is represented by a small enamel and gem-set figure whose depiction is a cross between a Christian saint and a Hindu deity (cat. 75/pl. 39).

Jade, rock crystal, and other hardstone objects form an aspect of the collection that is becoming increasingly significant. A major acquisition in this area is a jade cup made for the Mughal Emperor Jahangir that was formerly in the Guennol Collection (cat. 34/pl. 13). The cup is inscribed in exceptional quality with the ruler's titles along with two quatrains of Persian poetry. It is the earliest dated Mughal jade in existence and, along with the Shah Jahan dagger, provides a foundation for what has become a very significant holding of jades and hardstones from the Timurid period to the late Mughal Empire. These include containers, dishes and bowls, flywhisk handles, staffs, dagger hilts, and pieces of jewelry, such as pendants and rings (see chapters 2 and 3).

Acquisitions for the collection have been driven by personal passion and shaped by the idea of collecting for the sake of quality rather than quantity. As with any private holding, this group of objects represents a unique personal vision, inspired by taste, knowledge, and a deep passion that grows year on year. At the same time, a concerted effort has been made to represent leading schools of courtly jewelry from the Mughal period onward, revealing the full extent of the ingenuity of Indian jewelers and their impact in the wider world. From the elegant, restrained forms of early Mughal jades and jewelry to the wildly extravagant hybrid designs of the nineteenth century and the stylish, chic creations of the modern age, this exhibition of pieces from The Al Thani Collection will hopefully instill among visitors an understanding and appreciation of this subject, such as it exists in the collector himself and in the academic team that is privileged to work with objects of such aesthetic merit and cultural significance.

FIG. 18 *(opposite)*. Henri Cartier-Bresson, Maharani Sita Devi of Baroda, 1948, during the festivities for the thirty-ninth birthday of the maharaja

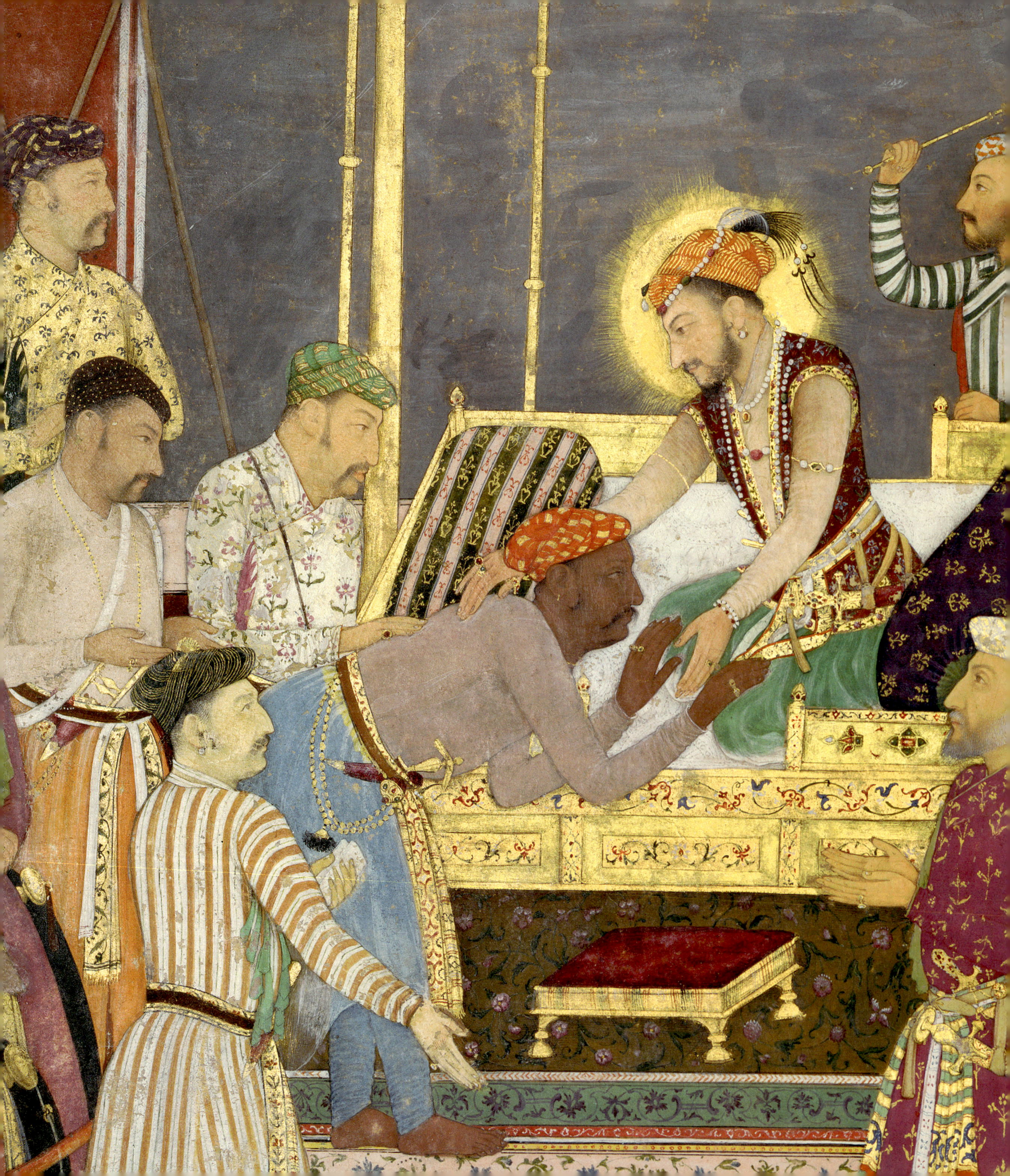

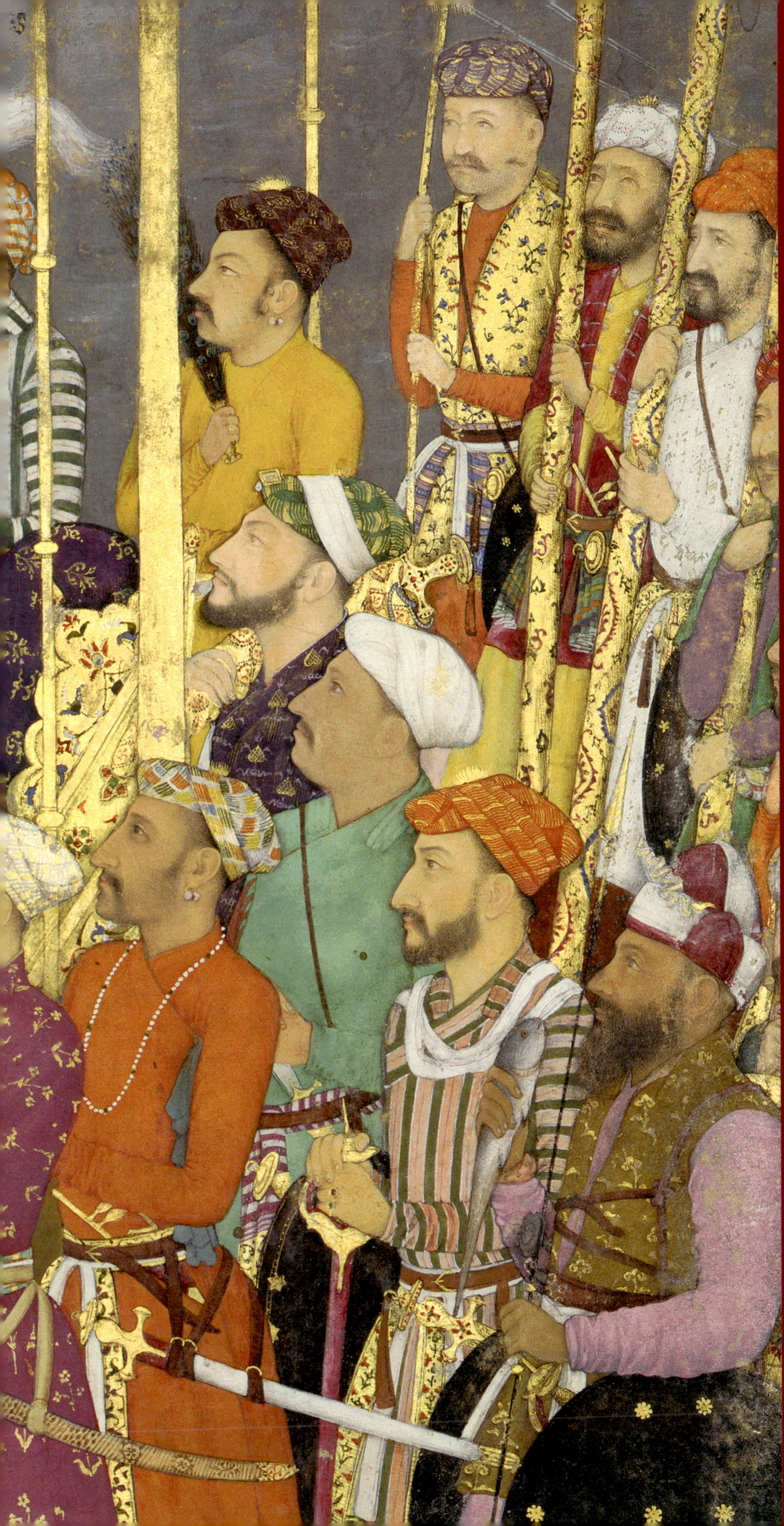

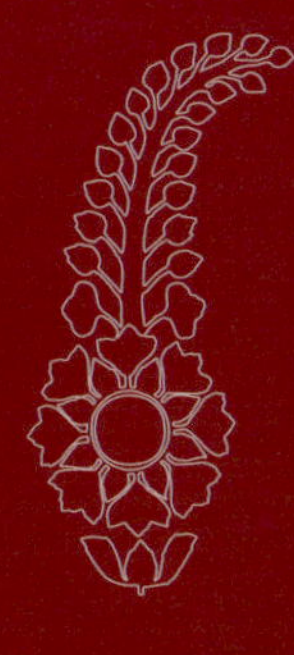

CATALOGUE

MARTIN CHAPMAN
AND AMIN JAFFER

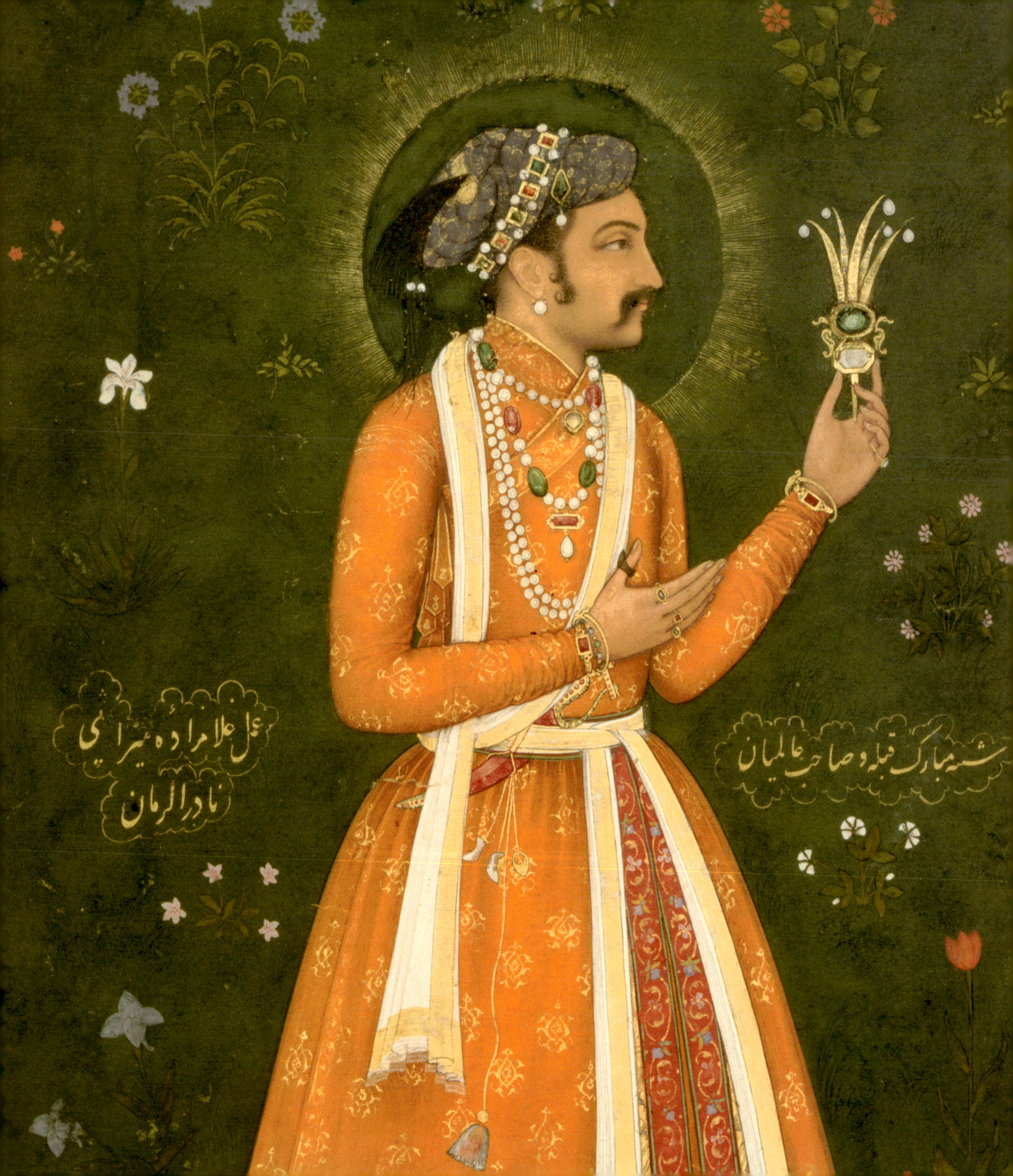
عمل غلامزاده بیریای
نادر الزمان
شبیه مبارک قبله و صاحب عالمیان

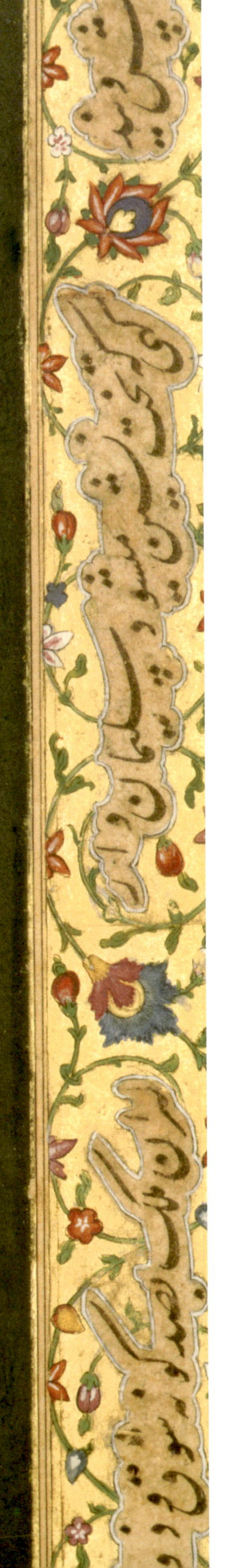

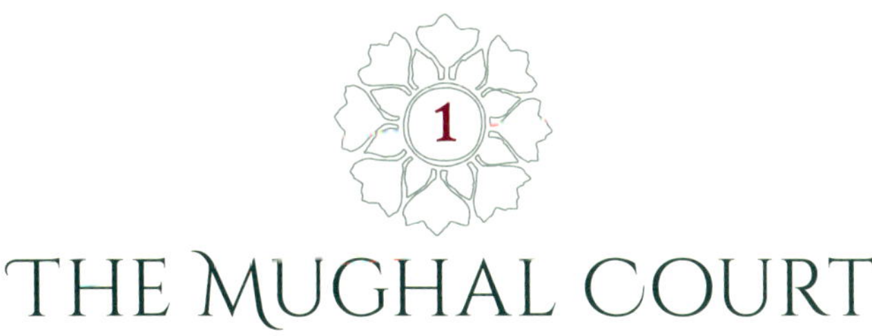

1 THE MUGHAL COURT

Gemstones and Jewelry

A descendant of both Timur (Tamerlane) and Genghis Khan, the Central Asian prince Zahir al-Din Babur invaded India in 1526, establishing a dynasty whose identity is inextricably linked with the possession of precious stones.

Indeed, when European visitors arrived at the Mughal court, they were dazzled by the richness of the Treasury, evident in the profusion of jewels on the emperor himself and on the ceremonial objects around him. The Mughals acquired a rich collection of gems as a result of conquest, as gifts, and through assiduous purchases.

Court chronicles and imperial memoirs reference the jewels in the Mughal Treasury and confirm that the emperors themselves were directly involved in assessing their quality and value. The Mughals inherited from their Timurid ancestors the custom of inscribing their names on the most precious gems and passing them from father to son as a dynastic heirloom. The culture of appreciating gemstones found its greatest expression during the reign of Shah Jahan, who not only wore and collected precious jewels but also commissioned a throne of unparalleled magnificence made of enameled gold encrusted with diamonds, emeralds, spinels, rubies, and pearls.

Along with vast holdings of precious stones and jeweled items from the Mughal Treasury, this spectacular Peacock Throne, as it came to be known, was removed from India by the Iranian warrior Nadir Shah. With the Sack of Delhi in 1739, Shah struck a blow that set the Mughal Empire in irreversible decline. Gemstones, however, were important symbols of authority in the Successor States and their maharajas. They were worn in increasing numbers in spectacular pieces of jewelry by the rulers of India in the nineteenth century and through to the end of the British Raj in 1947.

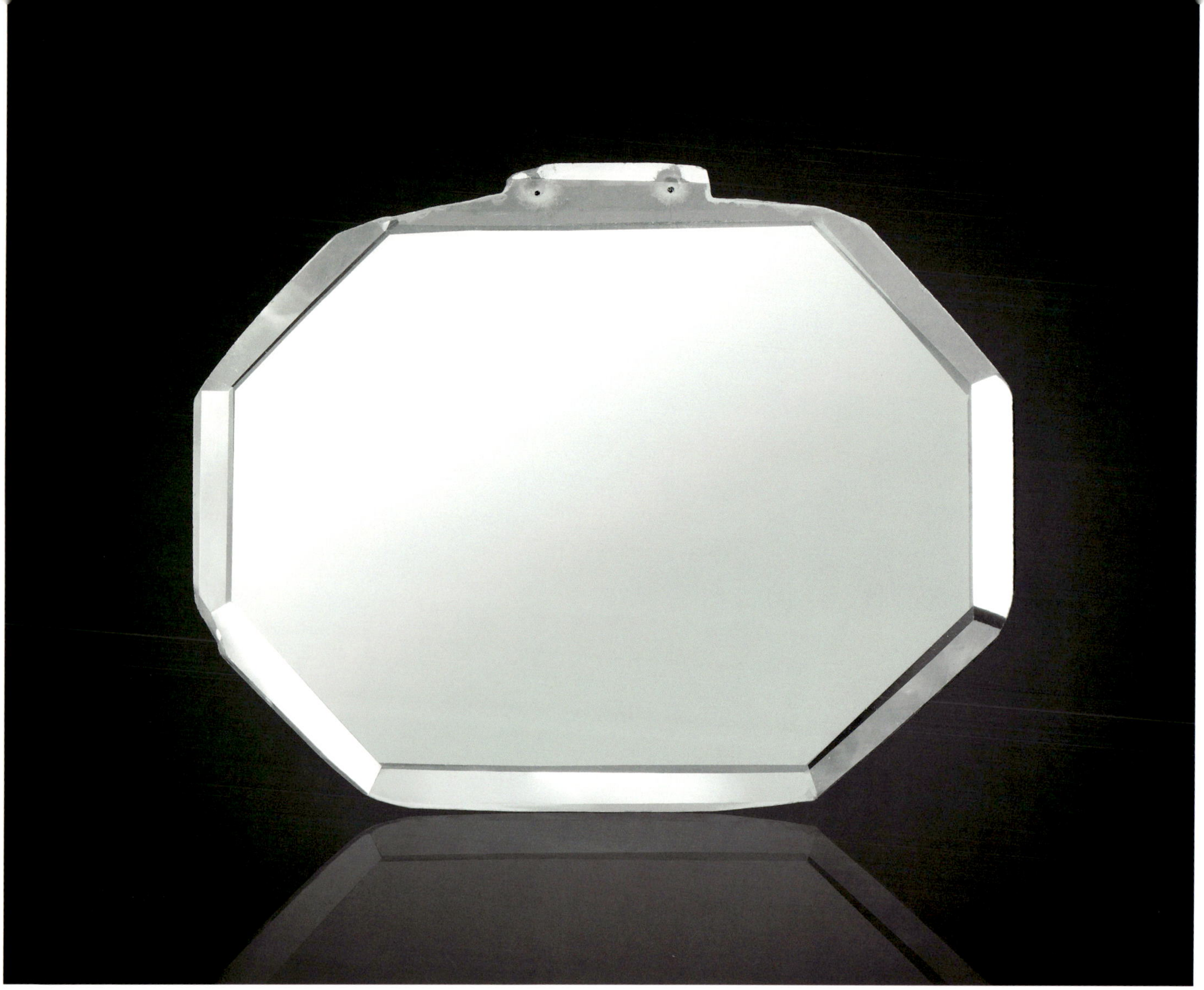

1

Portrait-cut diamond

India, 1650–1700. Cut-cornered, rectangular portrait-cut, grade J, type IIa. Weight 20.22 ct
CAT. 1

Flat-cut diamonds were favored at the Mughal court for wear as pendants as suggested by the two holes in the upper edge. Rarely used in the West, such flat-cut diamonds were employed as if glass to cover miniature portraits in pendants, rings, or bracelets, hence the term "portrait-cut."

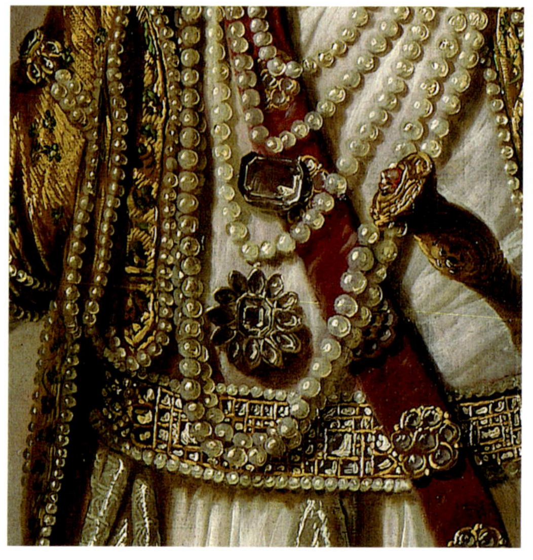

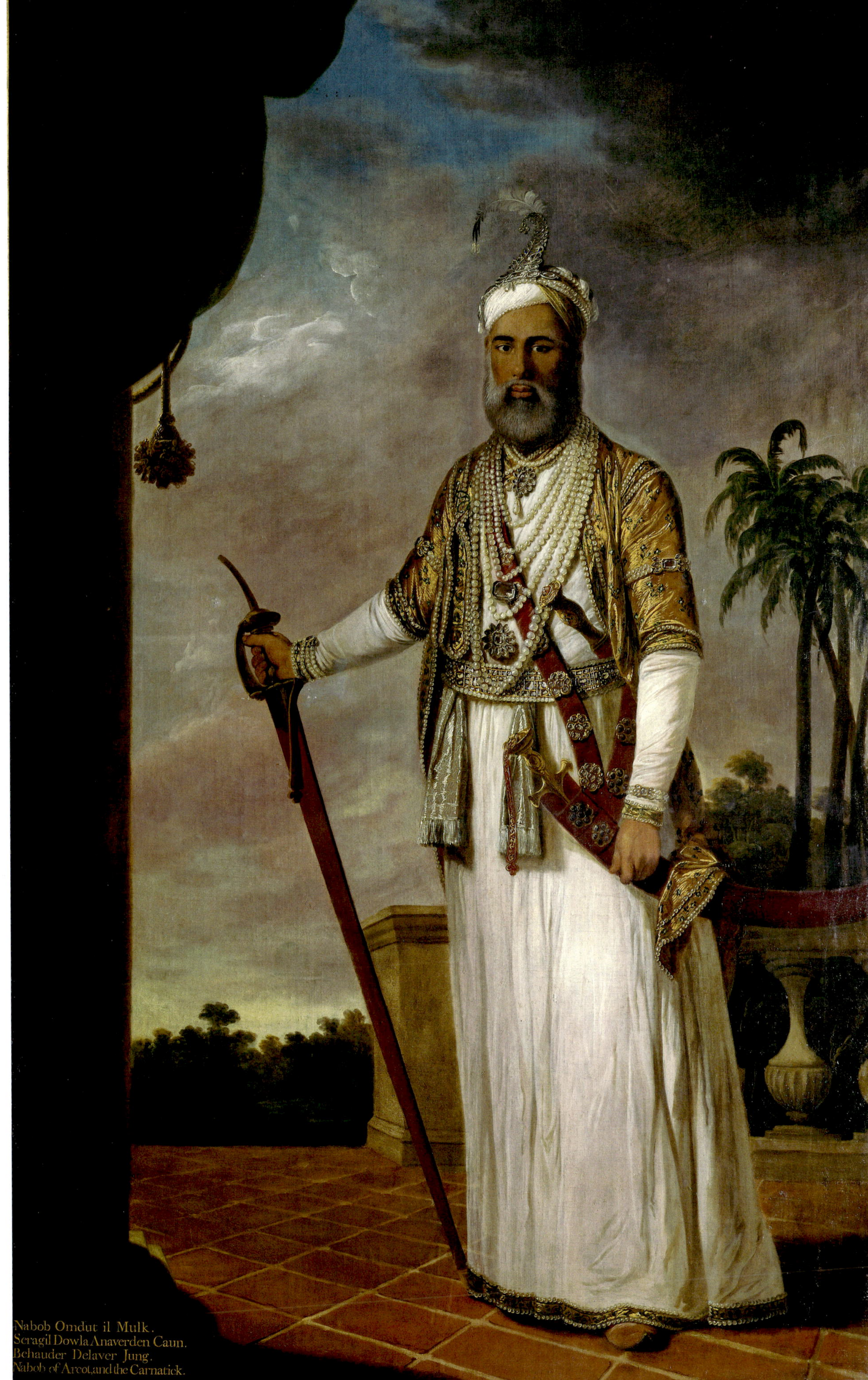

FIG. 19. Tilly Kettle, *Muhammad Ali Wallajah, Nawab of Arcot* (with detail, opposite), 1772–1776. Oil on canvas, 94 × 58¼ in. (239 × 148 cm). Victoria and Albert Museum, London, IM.124-1911

Diamonds

> *The jewels of the Mughals were equal to the wealth of all the monarchs of Europe combined.*
>
> Jacques de Coutre (1577–1640), Flemish gem trader and traveler

Until the 1730s, most of the world's diamonds were sourced from India. From the earliest times, diamonds were found in riverbeds in the plateau of the Deccan region in Southern India. Some of the world's most famous historical diamonds were obtained in the Kollur mines, then cut and traded at Golconda, near Hyderabad. They include the Koh-i-Noor (British crown jewels, now at the Tower of London); the Regent (French crown jewels, Musée du Louvre, Paris); the Hope (formerly French crown jewels, Smithsonian Institution, Washington, DC); and the Orlov (Diamond Fund, Moscow).

The Mughal emperors and the Indian princes had a passion for diamonds and gemstones, which they collected and wore in great profusion on state occasions. From the 1600s, European monarchs in the West similarly acquired large diamonds to reflect their prestige and power. While the Indians polished the existing facets of the diamonds to preserve precious weight, in the mid-1600s, the Europeans innovated the brilliant cut, which employed more scientific principles that maximized the refraction of light and created symmetry and fire. French monarch Louis XIV amassed the largest treasury of diamonds in Europe, all of which were sourced from India. In 1668 the king bought more than one thousand diamonds from the gemstone merchant, traveler, and writer Jean-Baptiste Tavernier (1605–1689), who published accounts of his voyages to India in 1676. This purchase included the enormous French Blue diamond, then weighing 115.28 metric carats, and which in 1678 Pitau recut to 67.125 carats to produce a symmetrical triangular stone. The king wore it prominently as a cravat pin. Stolen during the French Revolution, the stone was recut in London, and reemerged as what we know today as the Hope Diamond.

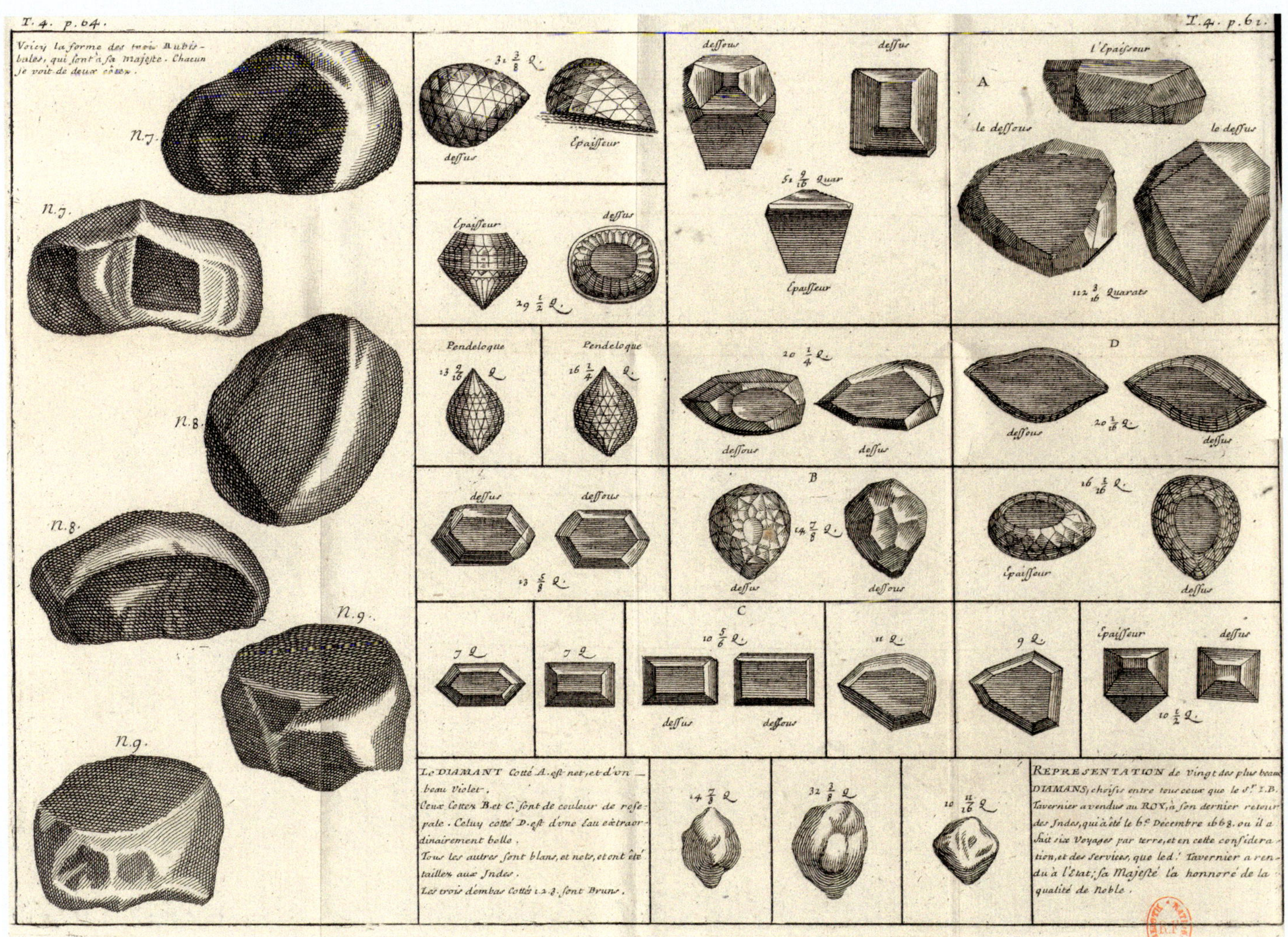

FIG. 20. "Vingt des plus beaux diamants rapports de l'Inde par Tavernier," from *Les six voyages de Jean-Baptiste Tavernier [. . .] en Turquie, en Perse et aux Indes* ("Twenty of the finest diamonds brought back from India by Tavernier," from *Six Voyages of Jean-Baptiste Tavernier [. . .] through Turky into Persia and the East-Indies*), Paris, P. Ribou, vol. 4, engraving between pages 60–61, 1713. Bibliothèque nationale de France

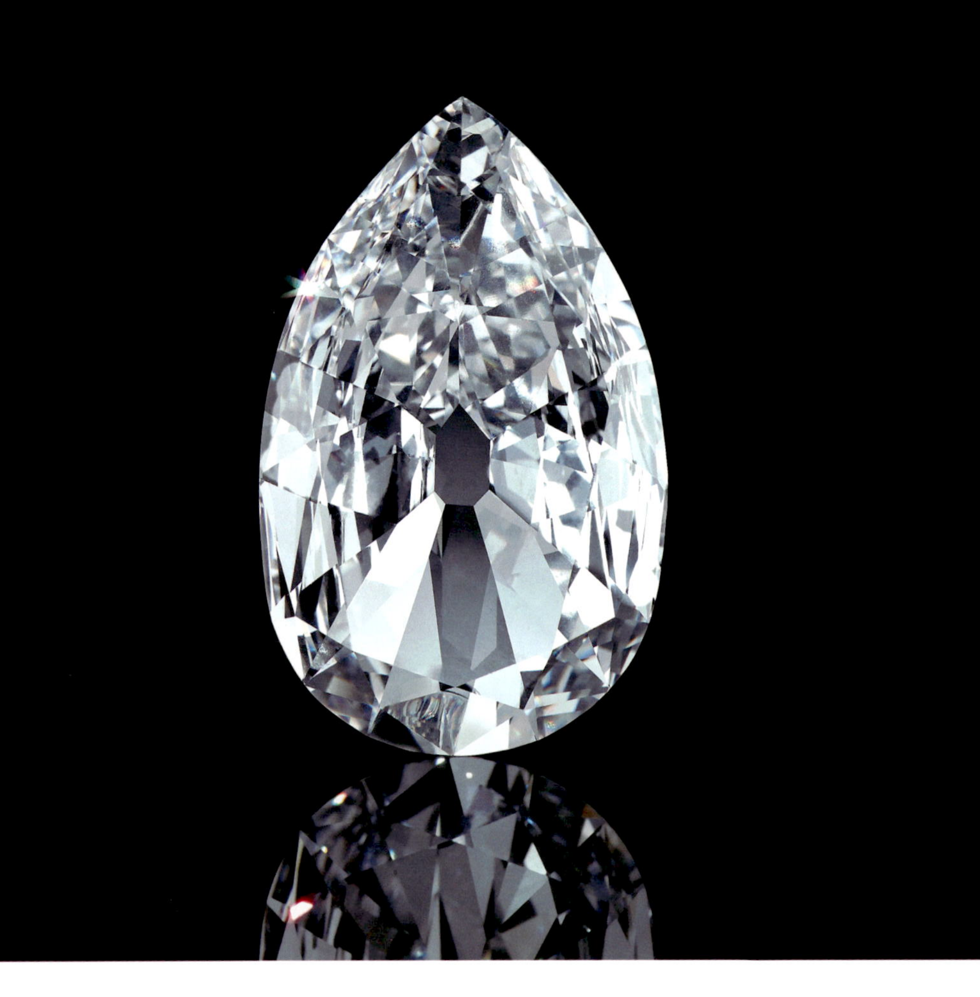

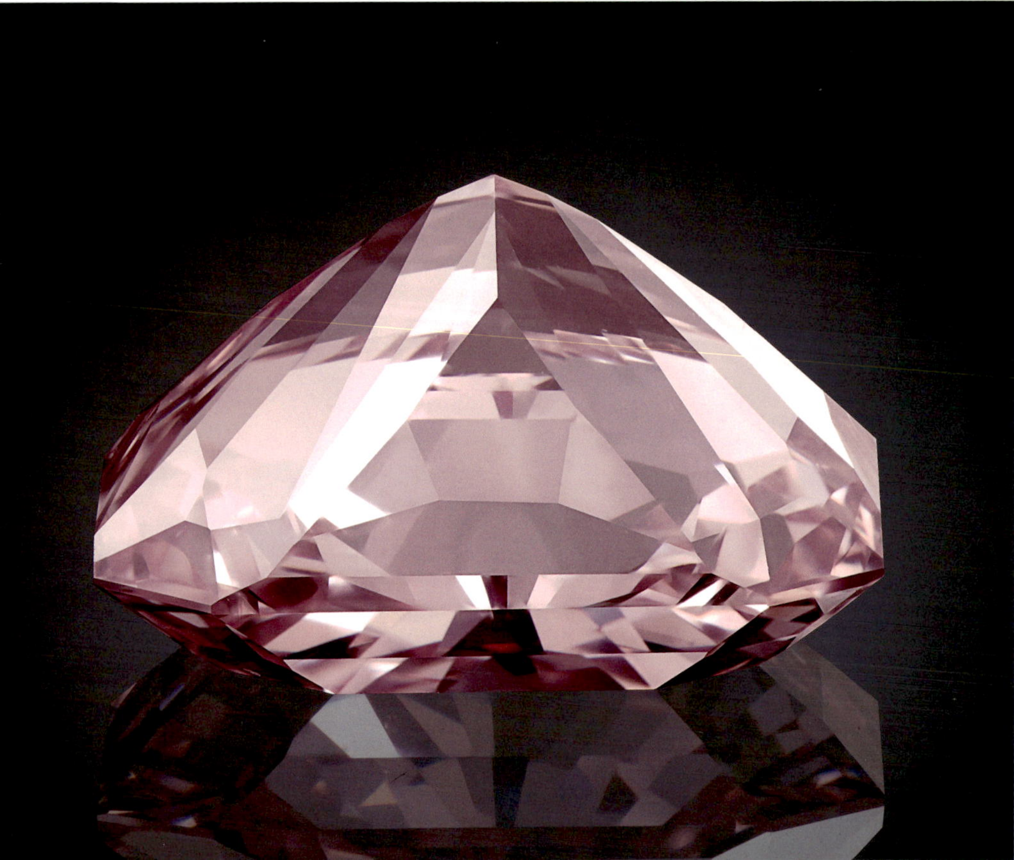

2

The Arcot II Diamond

India, ca. 1760; modified 1959 and 2011.
Brilliant-cut, pear-shaped, grade D internally flawless, type IIa. Weight 17.21 ct
CAT. 3

Muhammad Ali Wallajah, Nawab of Arcot, was a firm British ally during the Anglo-French conflicts of the mid-eighteenth century. He gave two pear-shaped diamonds to Queen Charlotte, wife of George III, who had them set as pendant earrings. She bequeathed the Arcots—as they came to be known—to her four unmarried daughters, who would have received little funding from the British crown. At the time of her death in 1818, however, they were taken by her son, the Prince Regent, who mounted them in his crown when in 1821 he ascended to the throne as George IV. Only in 1837 were they sold as directed by the former queen. The Arcots were acquired by the Marquess of Westminster, set in a family tiara, and later sold by a descendant in 1959.

3

The Agra Diamond

India, before 1526; reworked 1880 and 1990.
Cut-cornered, rectangular mixed-cut, fancy intense pink. Weight 28.15 ct
CAT. 2

An extraordinary pink diamond, this gem takes its name from a legend claiming that it came into the possession of Emperor Babur (r. 1526–1530)—the founder of the Mughal Empire—when conquering Agra in 1526. It was given by a raja of Gwalior as tribute for having saved his life to the new master of Hindustan. It is more securely documented as being bought by the Duke of Brunswick in London in the 1840s when it weighed 41 carats.

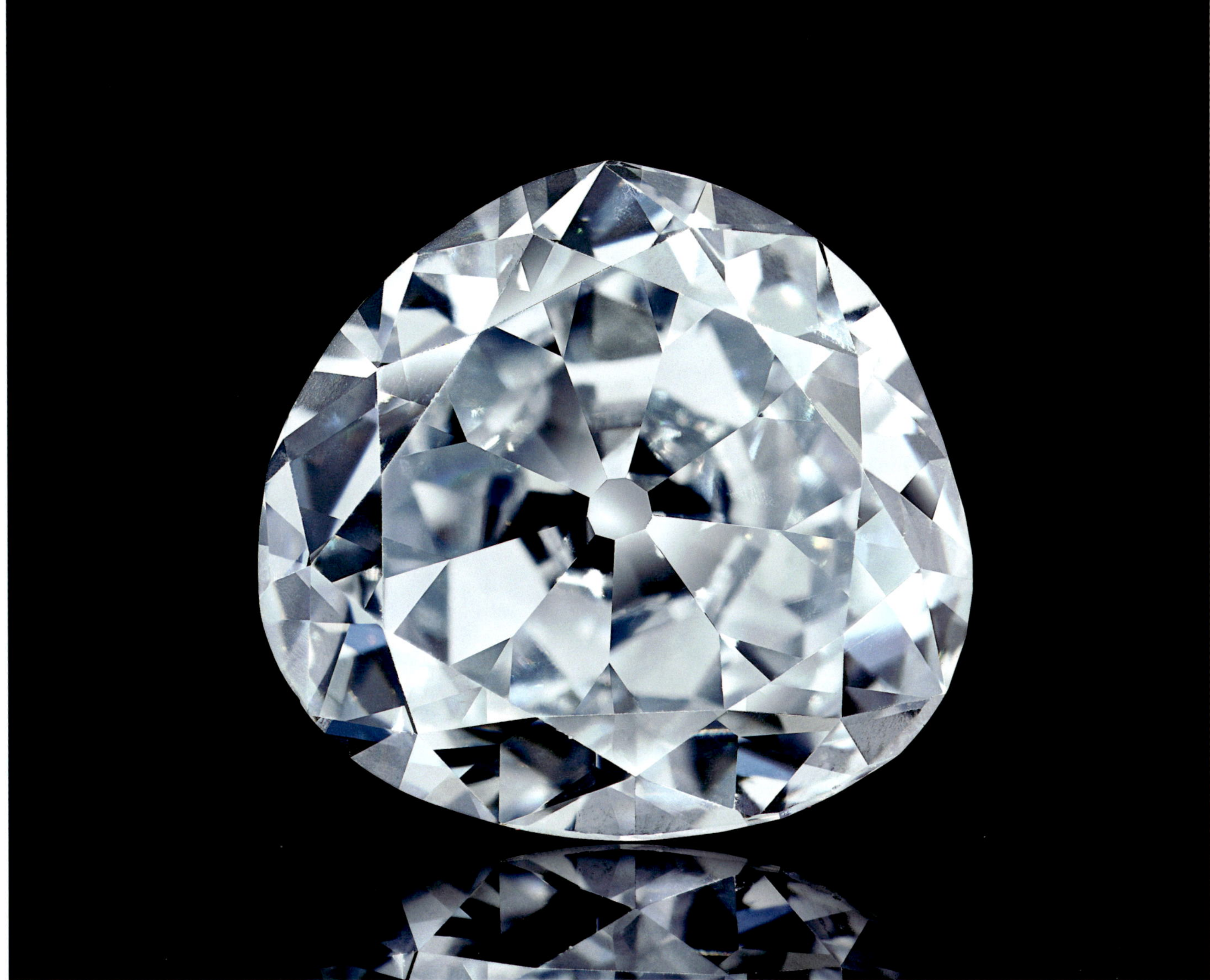

4

The Idol's Eye Diamond

India. Modified brilliant-cut light blue, VVS2 clarity. Weight 70.21 ct

CAT. 7

The largest cut blue diamond in the world, this gem was so named because it was said to have been taken from the eye of a Hindu deity in India. The diamond is first documented around the time of the publication of Wilkie Collins's novel *The Moonstone* (1868), in which a celebrated diamond likewise looted from an Indian temple is featured. The rarity of its pale blue color and the provenance of this diamond attests to its importance through history.

EMERALDS

Colour of Paradise

Main title of a book by Kris Lane subtitled
The Emerald in the Age of Gunpowder Empires, 2010

Emeralds were highly regarded by the Mughal emperors for their intense green hue. Green was sacred for Muslims, and, as such, emeralds took pride of place in Mughal jewelry. They were often worn as pendants carved with stylized floral and foliate designs or with inscriptions. Either religious or dynastic, the inscriptions were usually worn turned toward the skin, while the carved faces of emeralds were turned outward. Emeralds were also featured as beads for turban ornaments and necklaces.

Emeralds were sourced in India since ancient times and constitute one of the nine auspicious stones in Hindu gemology and horoscopes, representing the planet Mercury. It was thought that serpents and demons could be blinded by looking at emeralds. By the period of the Mughal Empire, the finest emeralds were imported from distant Colombia in South America via the Spanish trade to Europe and then by the Portuguese to Goa in India. A huge treasury of emeralds was maintained by the Mughal emperors, much of which was taken as loot to Iran after the Sack of Delhi in 1739.

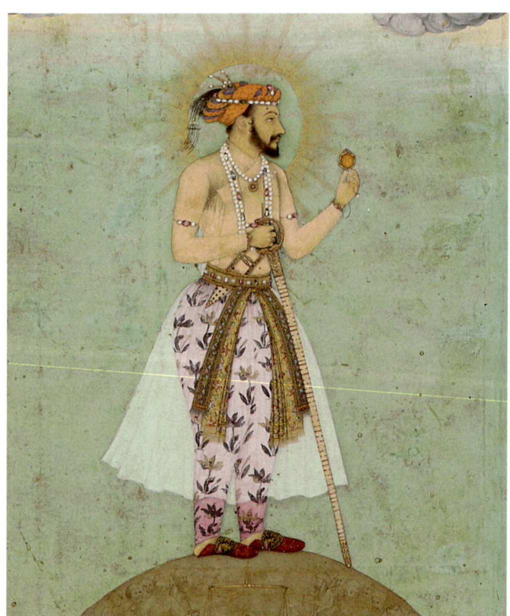

FIG. 21. Hashim, Shah Jahan standing on a globe, detail of a folio from the Shah Jahan Album, ca. 1630–1640. Opaque watercolor, ink, gold on paper, 9⅞ × 6¼ in. (25.1 × 15.8 cm). Freer Gallery of Art, Smithsonian Institution, Washington, DC, Purchase F1939.49a

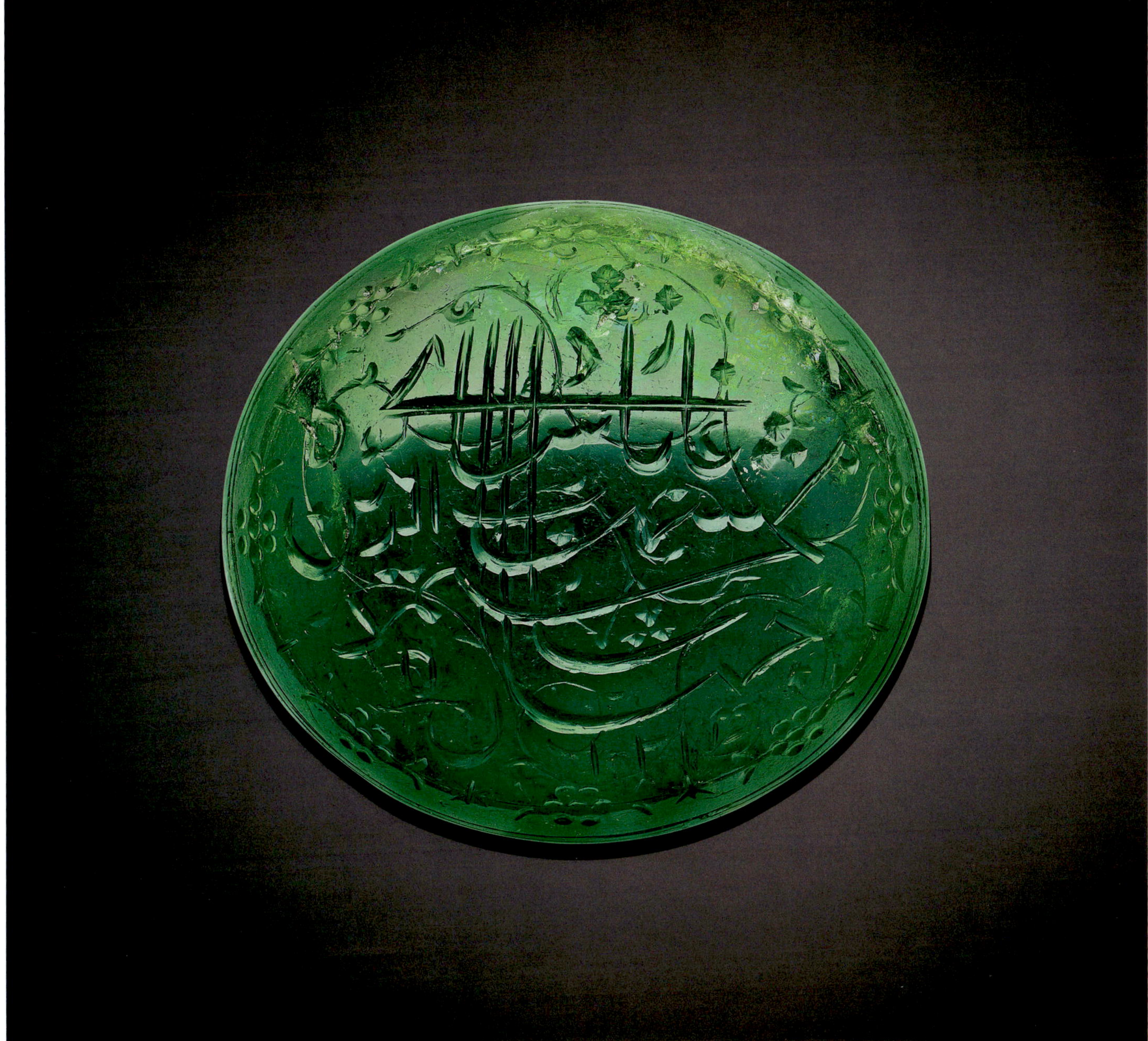

5

The Shah Jahan Emerald

North India or Deccan, 1621–1622. Weight 30.31 ct
Inscribed in Persian: *Shihab al-Din Muhammad Shah Jahan Warrior Emperor 1031*
CAT. 10

When inscribed, Mughal emeralds are more usually adorned with spiritual texts than with royal titles. This rare cabochon-cut emerald bears the name of Shah Jahan as emperor but is dated before the prince's accession to the throne. This indicates that the stone would have been inscribed at the time he rebelled against his father. This attempt to seize the throne failed, and Shah Jahan succeeded his father only some years later, in 1628.

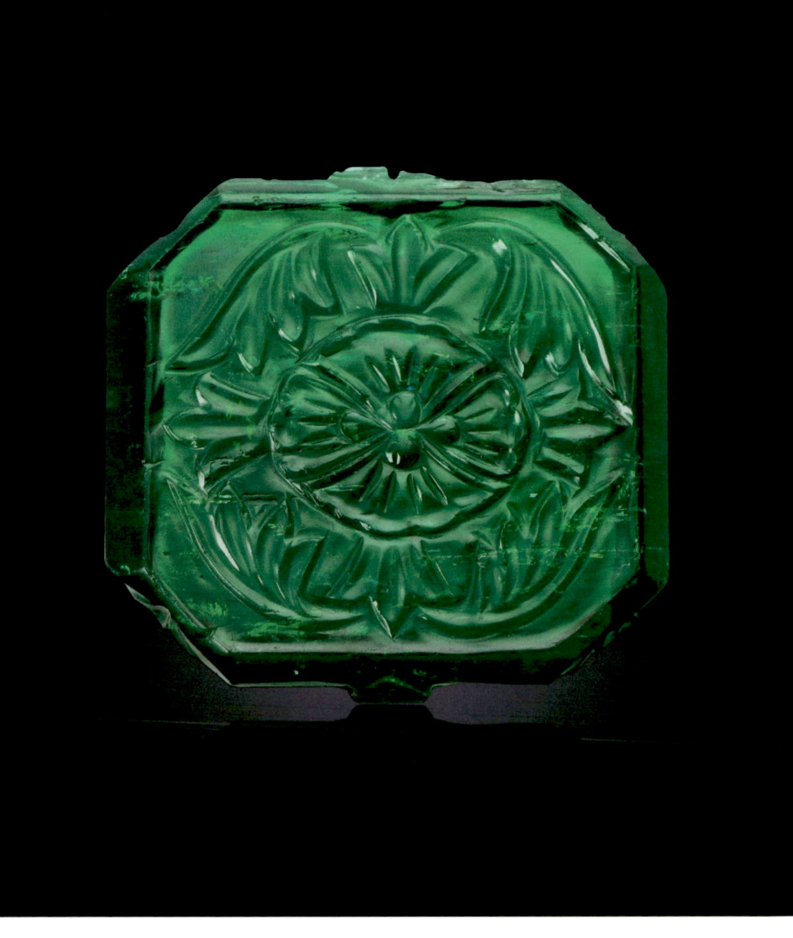

6 *(left)*

Emerald

North India, ca. 1650. Weight 87.8 ct
CAT. 11

The carving on this emerald tablet is in relief, the background cut back around the motifs into the surface with a low rim around the edge. The purity and saturation of the gem combined with the highly desirable color indicate that it belonged to a royal collection, the lugs on opposing sides suggesting that it was strung around the arm or a turban as an ornament.

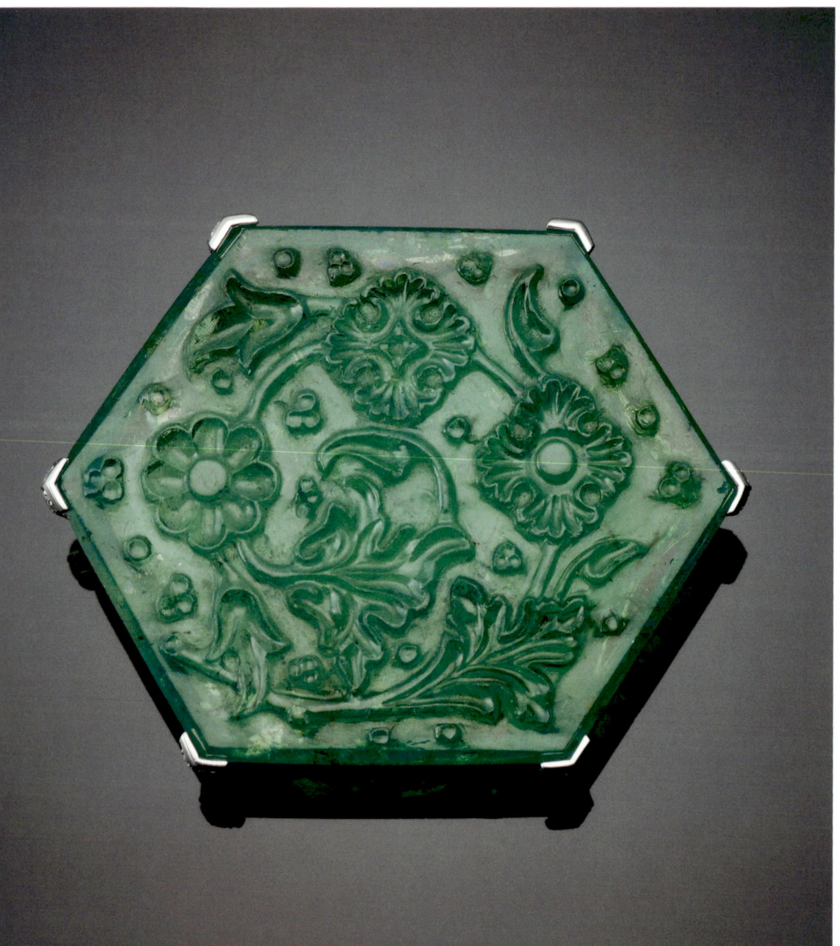

7 *(below left)*

The Taj Mahal Emerald

India, 1650–1700; mount by Cartier, 2012.
Weight 141.13 ct
CAT. 14

This substantial carved gem was one of a group of emeralds mounted in the Collier Bérénice, a spectacular shoulder ornament designed by Cartier and shown at the *Exposition internationale des arts décoratifs et industriels modernes* held in Paris in 1925. It is shown in a photograph of that year along with a diadem, emerald earrings, and a clip brooch (cat. 129), designed as the centerpiece of Cartier's presentation at the fair. Unsold, the dramatic suite of jewelry was broken up and the various pieces remounted. The Taj Mahal emerald was reset by Cartier in 2012 and doubles as the centerpiece for a tiara.

8 *(opposite)*

Necklace

India, eighteenth or early nineteenth century.
Emeralds, pearls, modern stringing
CAT. 22

Emerald beads were worn abundantly by Indian rulers, whether as turban ornaments, earrings, armbands, or necklaces. Around the neck they were usually mounted in multiple strands, alternating with two or three pearls, as seen in many portraits of Mughal emperors and princes from the early seventeenth century onward.

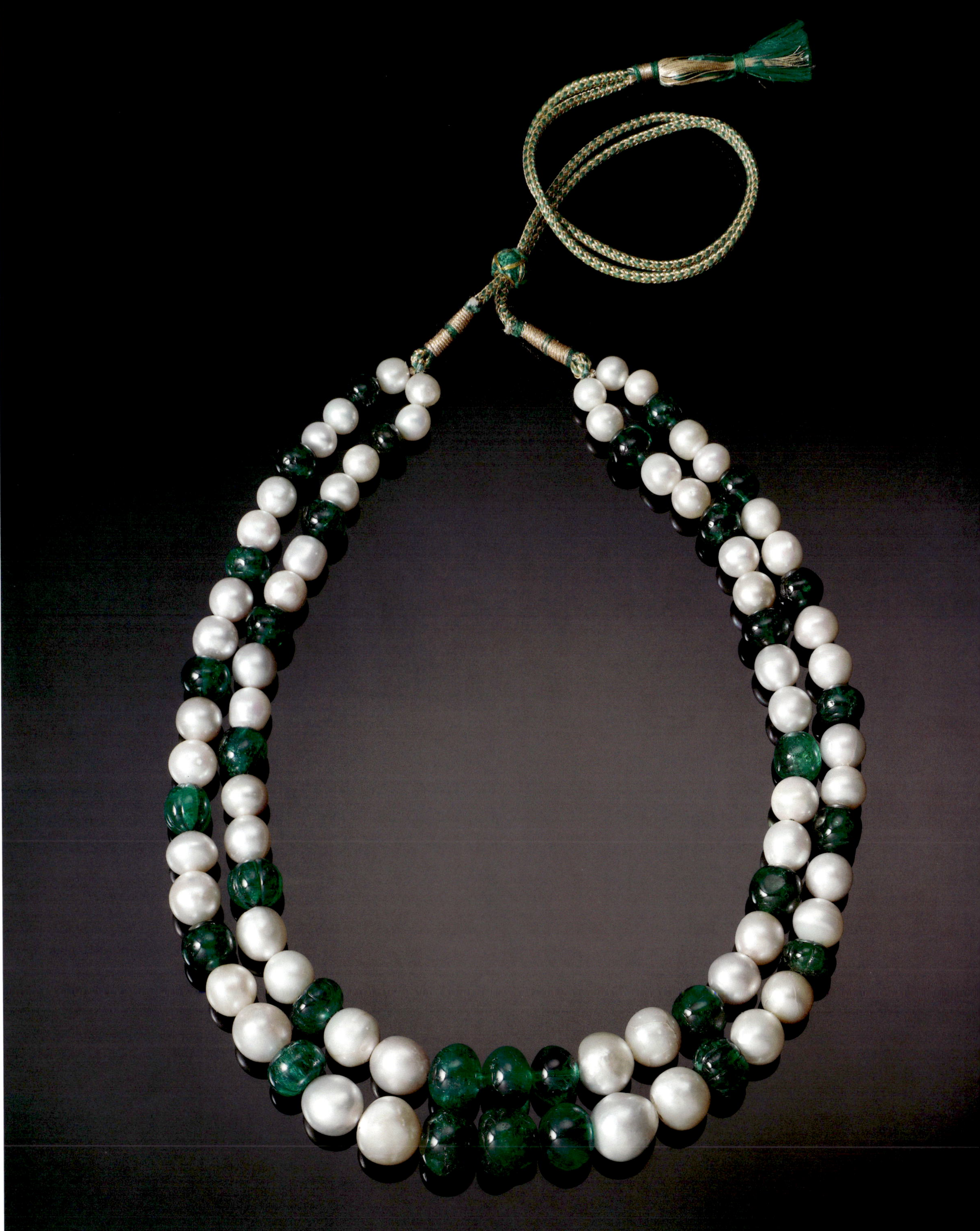

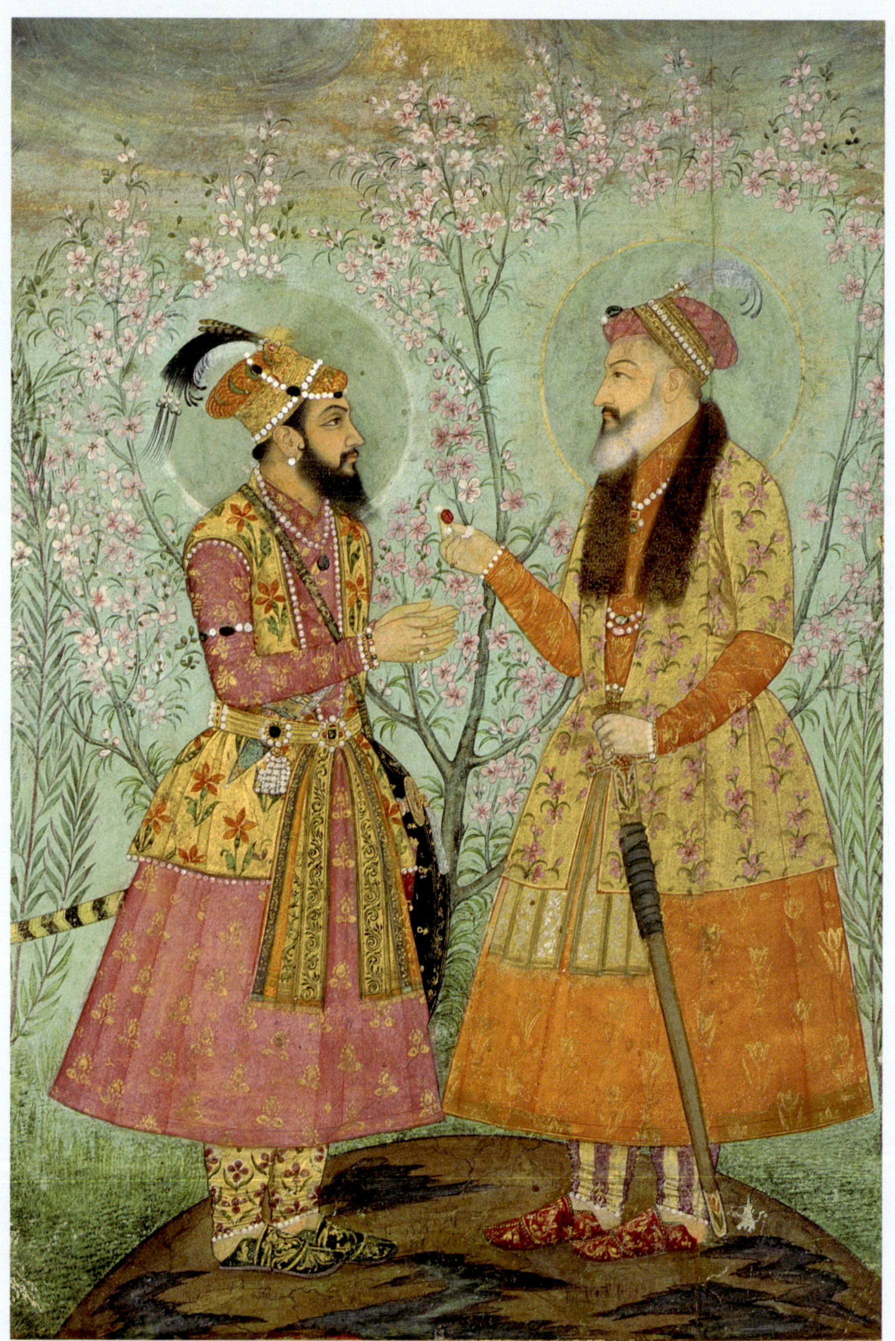

FIG. 22. Shah Jahan offers a spinel to Dara Shikoh, detail of a folio from the Nasir al-Din Shah Album, ca. 1650. Watercolor on paper, with gold, folio: 14⅝ × 9¾ in. (37.3 × 24.9 cm). The Trustees of the Chester Beatty Library, Dublin, CBL In 50.3

RUBIES AND SPINELS

Badashan is a Province inhabited by people who worship Mahommet, and have a peculiar language. It forms a very great kingdom, and the royalty is hereditary . . . It is in this province that those fine and valuable gems the Balas Rubies are found.

Marco Polo (ca. 1254–1324),
Venetian merchant, explorer, and writer

Rubies and spinels were mined in Badakhshan in Afghanistan, as well as in Sri Lanka and Burma. Rubies were prized as the "king of precious stones" in ancient Sanskrit for their dramatic red color. Reputed to protect the wearer in battle, they were often included in precious ceremonial weapons made for the Mughals. Spinels, also called balas rubies, were frequently confused with rubies because of their red coloring. The two gemstones were not identified as separate entities until the nineteenth century. Some famous rubies, such as the Black Prince's Ruby in the British Imperial State Crown, are in fact spinels.

Being the color of blood, spinels in India were associated with vitality, and wearing them was believed to enhance life force and stamina. For the Mughal emperors, spinels were especially significant and ranked above all other gemstones. They were often engraved with dynastic inscriptions, a tradition inherited from the Mughals' Timurid ancestors. Like emeralds and rubies, they were worn as pendants, beads in necklaces and bracelets, and as rings.

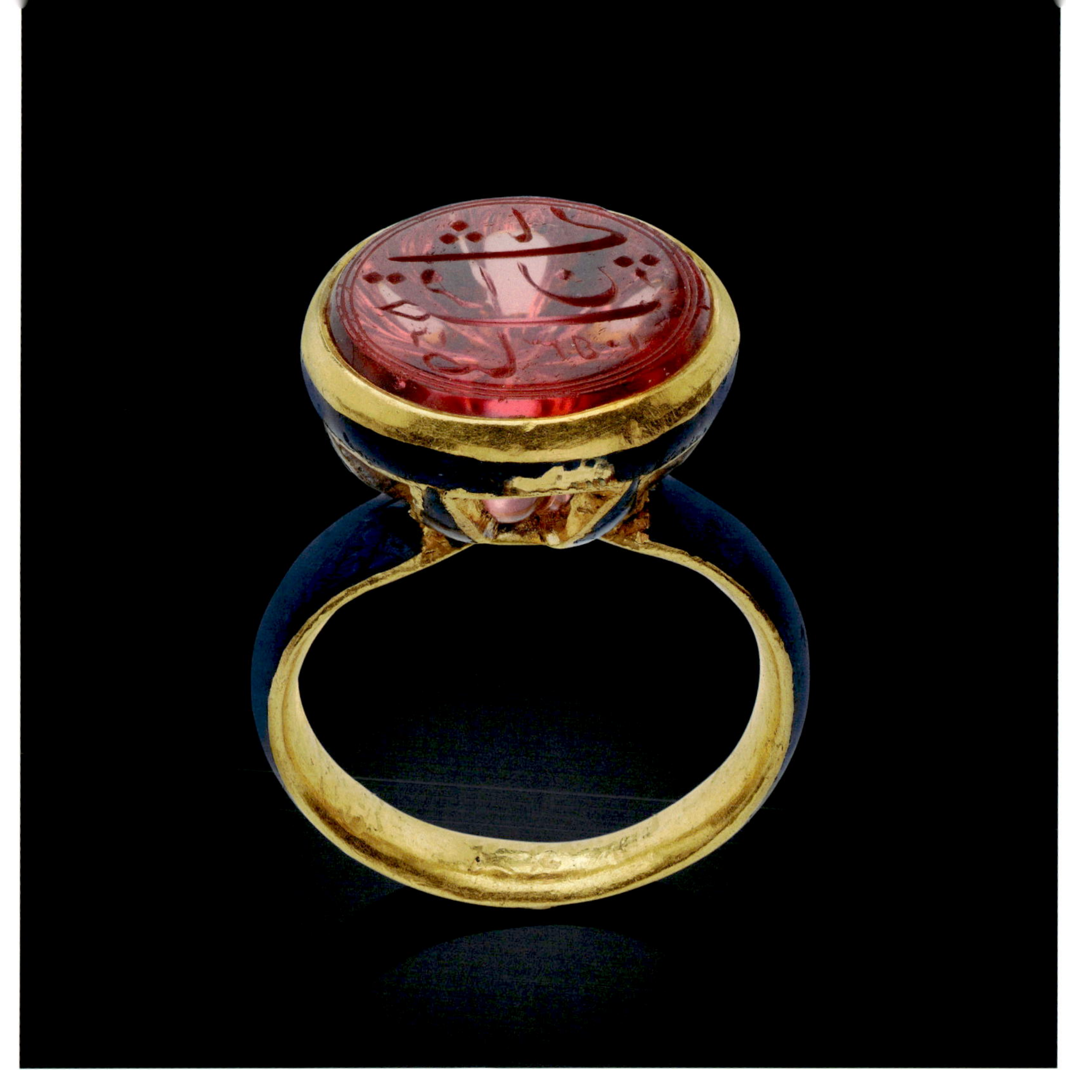

9

Ring with Shah Jahan's spinel

North India, spinel dated to 1643–1644, ring ca. 1900. Gold, enamel. Spinel inscribed in Persian: *Second Lord of the Auspicious Conjunction 1053 16*
CAT. 24

Dating from 1643, this spinel bears the title of Emperor Shah Jahan (r. 1628–1658): *Sahib Qiran-i-Thani*, or "Second Lord of the Auspicious Conjunction." This title was chosen by the ruler in reference to his ancestor Timur (Tamerlane), the founder of the dynasty, who referred to himself as "Lord of the Auspicious Conjunction" as a way of recognizing that his rule was sanctioned by the heavens.

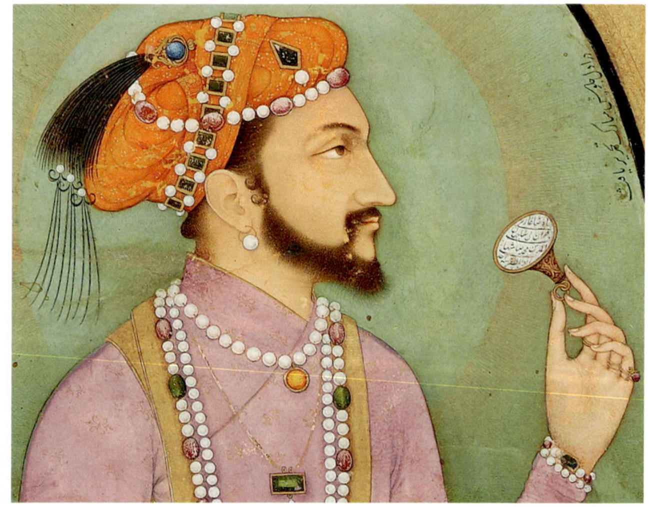

FIG. 23. Abu al-Hasan, detail of *Shah Jahan Holding the Imperial Seal*, North India, 1628. Opaque watercolor on paper, 7⅛ × 5½ in. (18.2 × 13.9 cm). Aga Khan Trust for Culture, AKM135

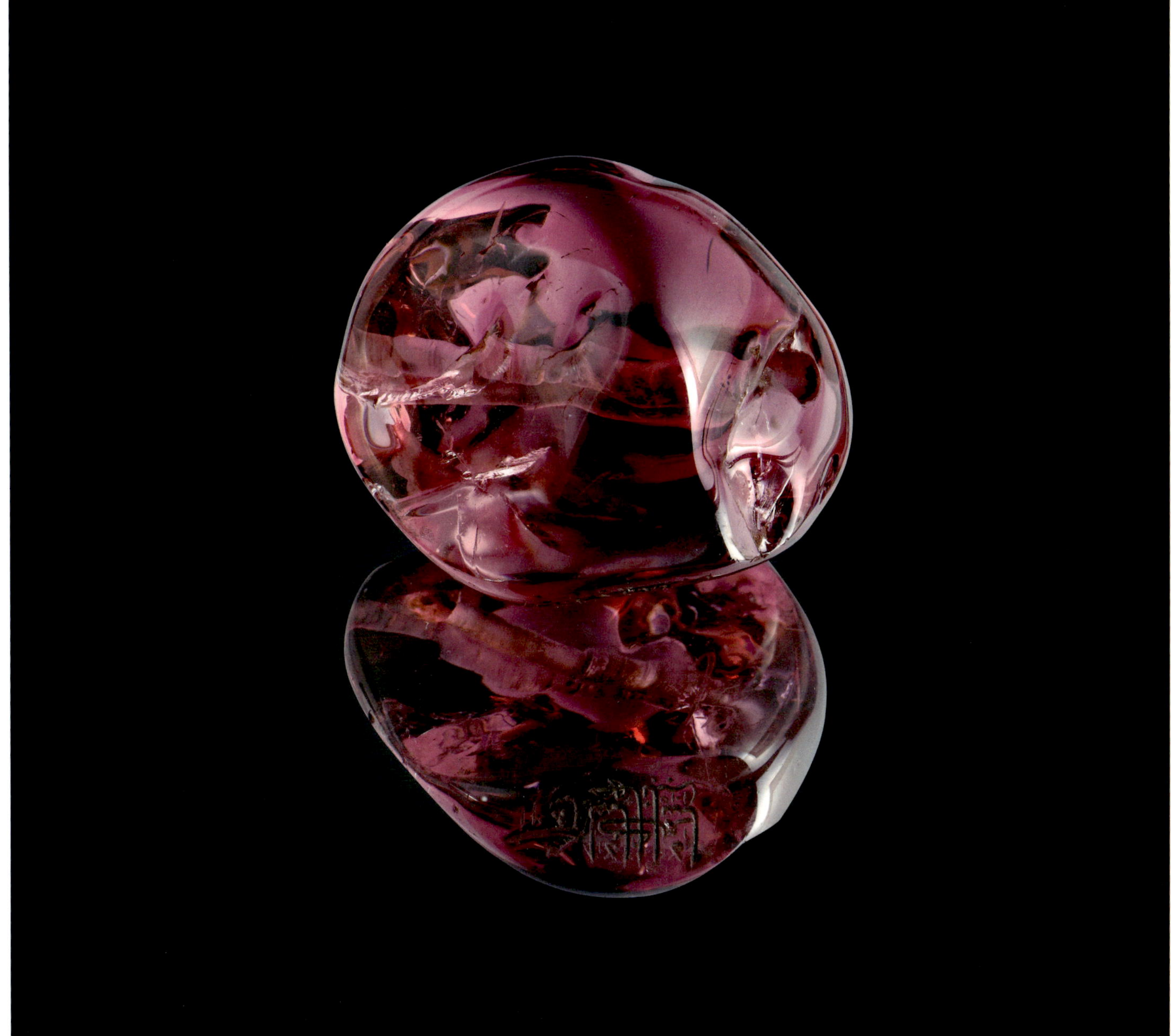

10

Imperial spinel

India, ca. 1606–1607 and 1628–1629. Weight 94.26 ct.
Inscribed in Persian: *Akbar / Jahangir / Shah Jahan*
CAT. 25

This spinel bears the names of three Mughal emperors: Akbar, Jahangir, and Shah Jahan, suggesting that it was passed down from one ruler to the next. Such a stone would have belonged in the Imperial Treasury, which was dispersed following the Sack of Delhi by Nadir Shah in 1739.

11

Imperial spinel necklace

North India, spinels dated to between 1607–1608 and 1754–1755. Spinels, pearls, emerald, modern stringing; 51.8 cm. Seven spinels inscribed in Persian: *Glorious spinel / Shah Jahan son of Jahangir Shah [1]04 . . . / Jahangir Shah [son] of Akbar Shah 1016 / Second Lord of the Auspicious Conjunction 1043 6 / Belonging to Alamgir Shah 1017 1 / Jahangir Shah [son] of Akbar Shah / Alamgir Shah son of Shah Jahan 1071 (?) 4 / Ahmad Shah, Pearl of Pearls, 1168 / Jahangir Shah [son] of Akbar Shah 1017 / Alamgir Shah son of Shah Jahan 10 . . . / Jahangir Shah [son] of Akbar Shah*
CAT. 27

The spinels in this necklace bear multiple inscriptions, including that of *la'l-i jalali* (glorious spinel), which refers to the Emperor Akbar himself. Dynastic gemstones of this size and quality would have originated in the Mughal Imperial Treasury, where they were prized not only for their material value and physical properties but also because of their distinguished provenance.

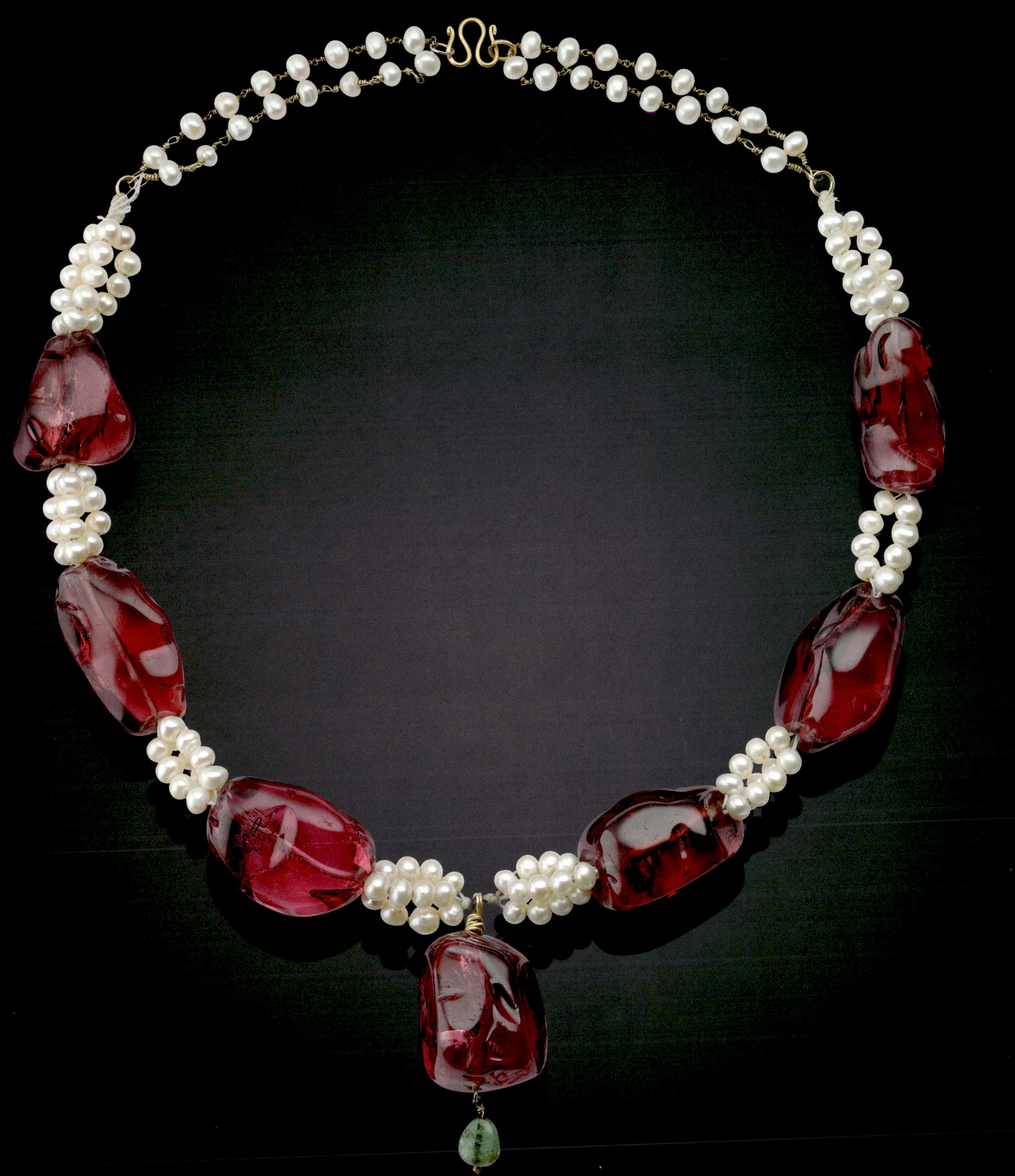

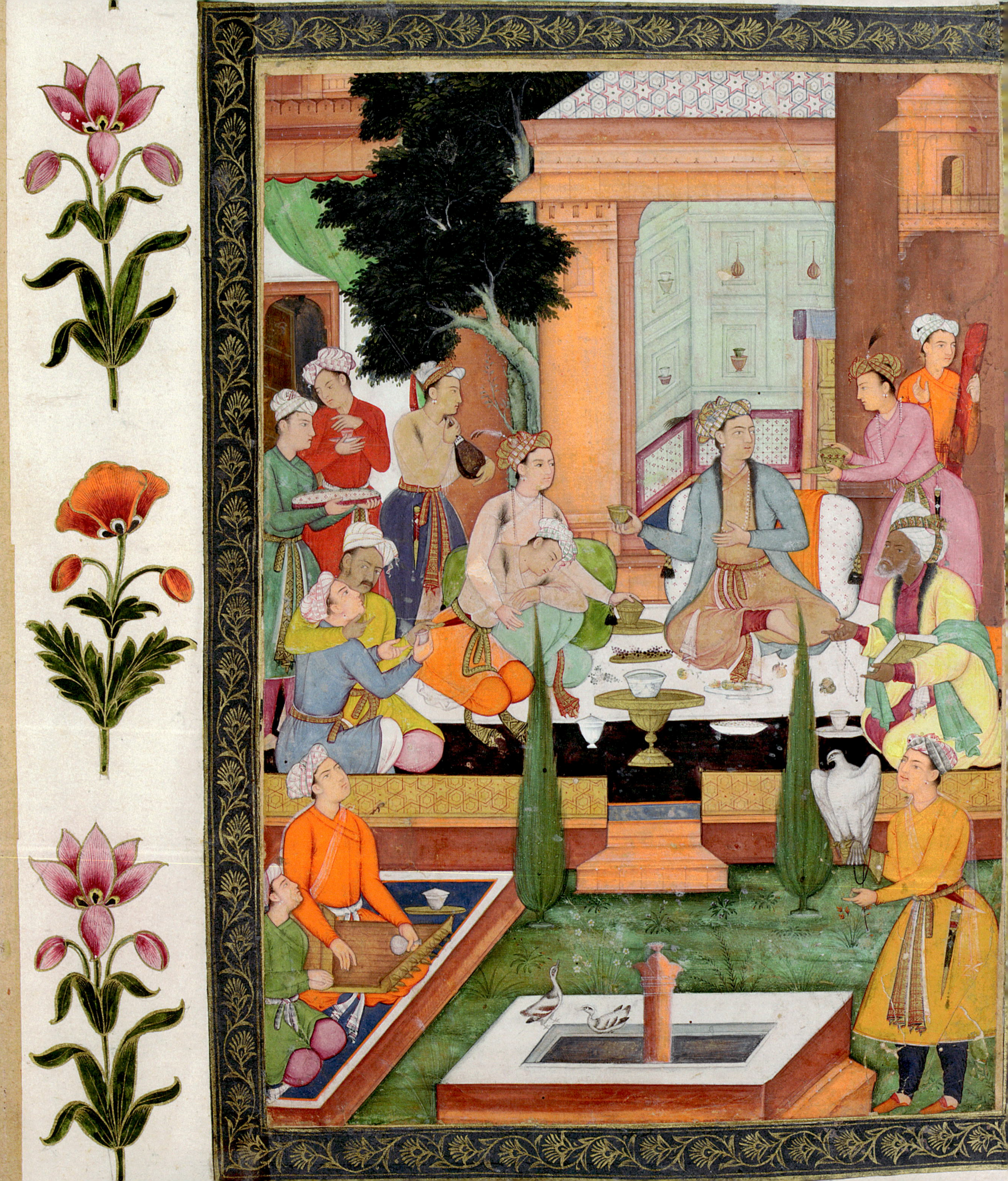

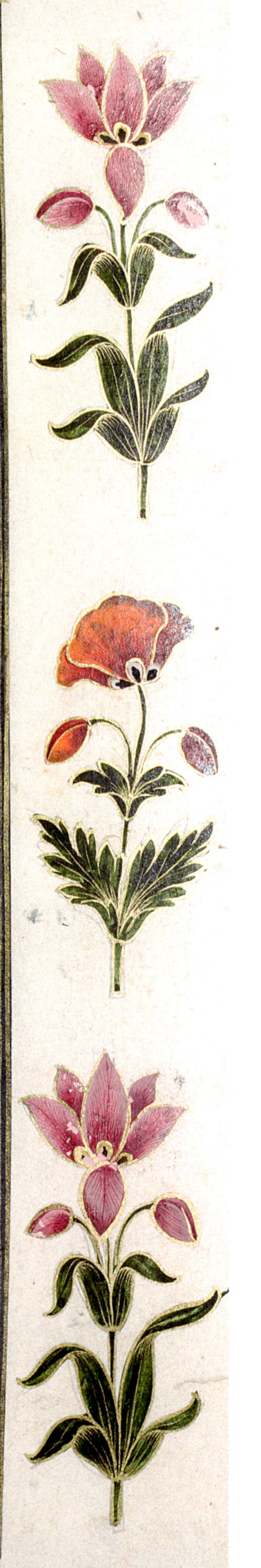

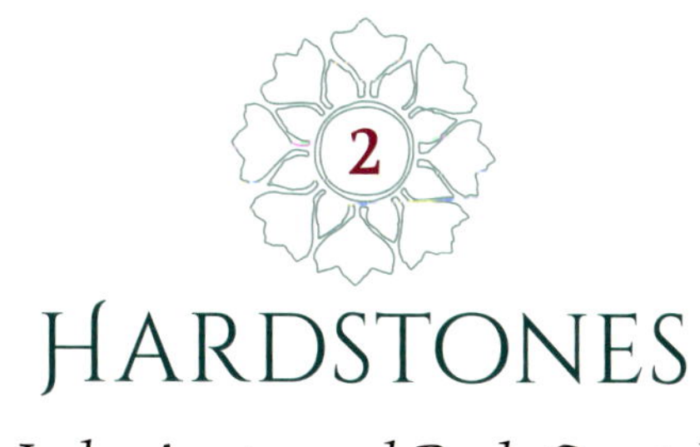

HARDSTONES

Jade, Agate, and Rock Crystal

As among European princes of the period, hardstones were deeply admired by Mughal rulers and came to be used for all kinds of luxury accessories and decoration.

In addition to their intrinsic visual and tactile qualities, these materials were often endowed with a spiritual significance and purpose. In Islamic culture, jade was understood to invoke victory and was especially used in the production of weapons and accessories for warfare or hunting. Jade was also believed to detect and counteract poison, proving to be a practical and useful material for drinking vessels in an environment of courtly intrigue.

The working of agate, onyx, and rock crystal—the colorless variety of quartz—was likewise raised to a high art at the hands of Mughal lapidaries. These materials were sometimes further enhanced by being encrusted with precious stones, creating a dazzling effect that came to characterize the richness of Mughal courtly life.

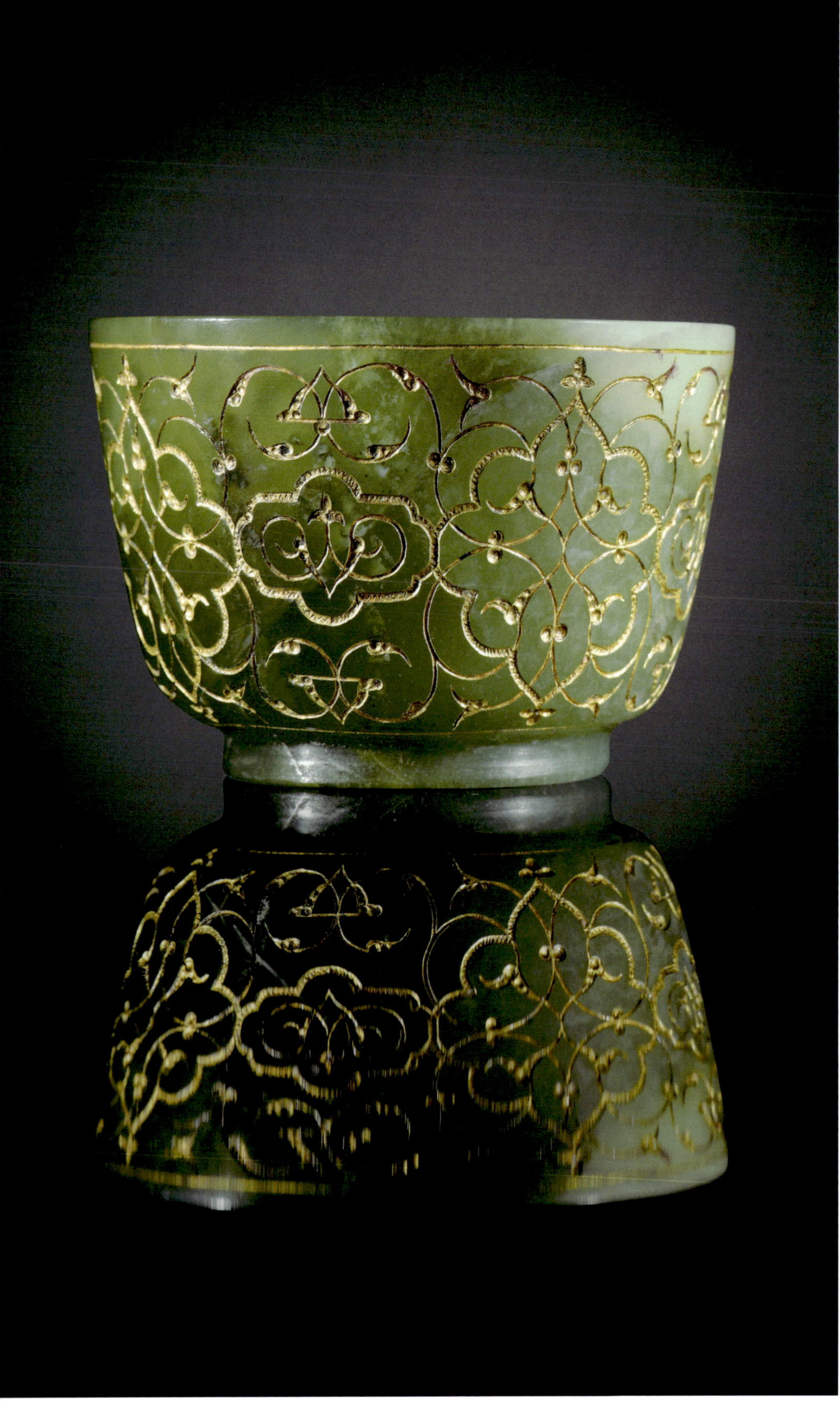

12

Cup

Central Asia, 1450–1500; the decoration possibly later: Central Asia or Iran, sixteenth century. Jade, gold
CAT. 32

The Timurid appreciation of jade inspired the collecting of this material at the Mughal court. This cup is a significant example of the high level that jade carving reached in Central Asia. Its surface is engraved with interlacing arabesques in a complex and highly elaborate gilded design. Gilded jade vessels appear in royal inventories of the period, providing an indication of how highly they were prized.

13

The Wine Cup of Jahangir

North India, ca. 1607–1608. Jade

CAT. 34

Created in 1607–1608, this cup is the earliest securely dated imperial Mughal jade vessel known and was certainly made as a personal commission by Emperor Jahangir. The exterior is decorated with the emperor's name and title along with two quatrains of Persian poetry. The shape of the cup is derived from small Chinese porcelain prototypes dating from the fifteenth century. Similar cups, of gold or other materials, are depicted in Mughal paintings and on coins of the early seventeenth century.

Inscriptions in Persian:

- In the upper band in alternate quatrefoils:
The wine cup / of the Emperor / of the Age / [regnal] year two.

- In the upper band in the larger cartouches:
See this body of a cup, pregnant with life, A jasmine petal, pregnant with the Judas tree [blossom].
No, no, I am wrong! The cup, thanks to its extreme subtlety, Is water pregnant with liquid fire!

- Around the body:
[It] was completed on the order of His Most Exalted Majesty, the Glorified Khaqan, the Lord of the Kings of the World, the Manifestation of Divine Graces, the Pearl of the Casket of Succession and Emperorship, the Sun of the Celestial Sphere of Sultanhood and World Rulership, the Moon of the Heaven of Justice and Prosperity, Abul-Muzaffar Padshah son of Akbar Shah, Nur al-Din Jahangir Muhammad, Warrior Emperor [in] year 1016.

- Around the base:
Your face, from which, because of wine, the anemone grows, Is like the petal of a rose on which dew grows.
If the hand which took the cup from your hand
Were to turn to dust, a cup would grow from it.[1]

NOTE

1. These readings and translations, by Will Kwiatowski, are based on those of A. S. Melikian-Chirvani in Melikian-Chirvani 1999, pp. 83–140. Slightly different translations were offered by Robert Skelton (Skelton et al. 1982, 117) and by A. S. Melikian-Chirvani (Melikian-Chirvani 1999, 92–93).

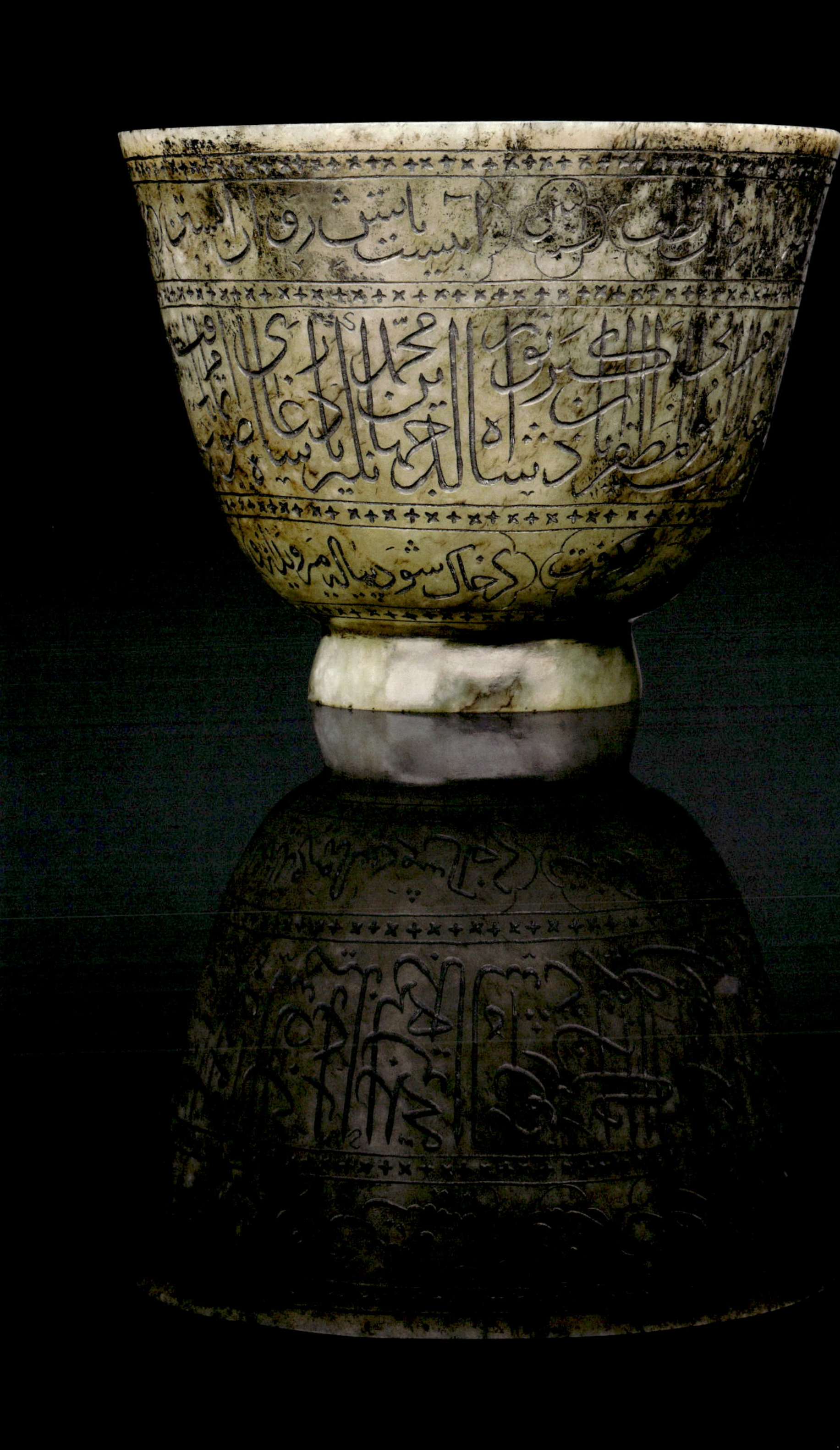

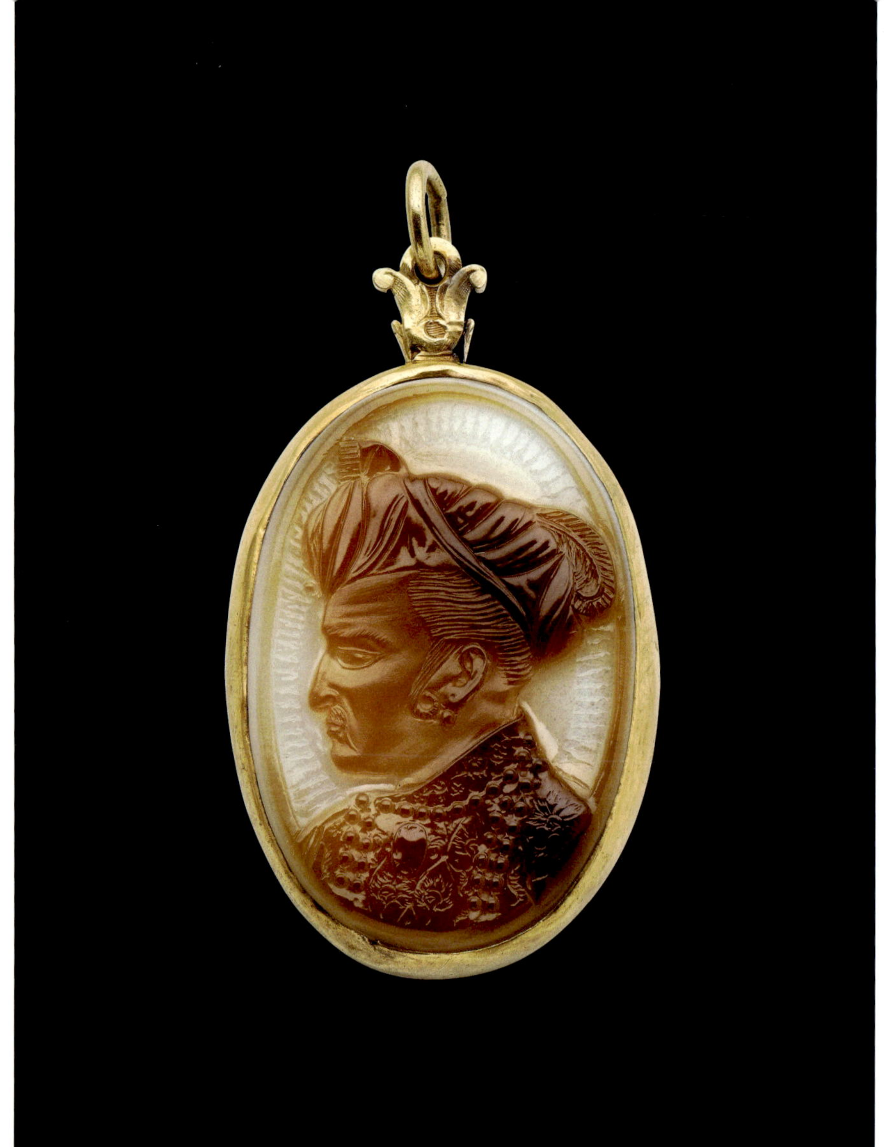

14

Cameo of the Emperor Jahangir
(obverse and reverse)

France or Italy, 1610–1630; mount, France, 1630–1640.
Agate, gold
CAT. 35

At the Mughal court, as in the West, portraits of rulers were worn by courtiers as symbols of homage and allegiance. The portrait cameo was a Western convention that appears to have been introduced to India by European lapidaries. The relatively stiff representation of Emperor Jahangir, evident above all in the rendering of his turban, suggests that this cameo was carved in Europe after an engraving or portrait rather than executed based on a direct likeness of the ruler.

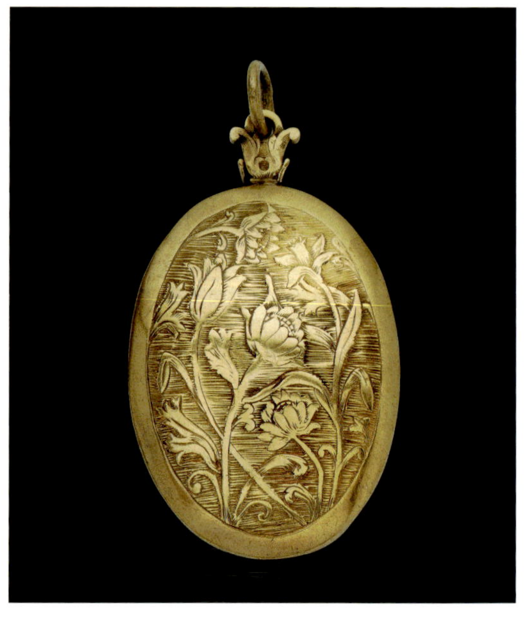

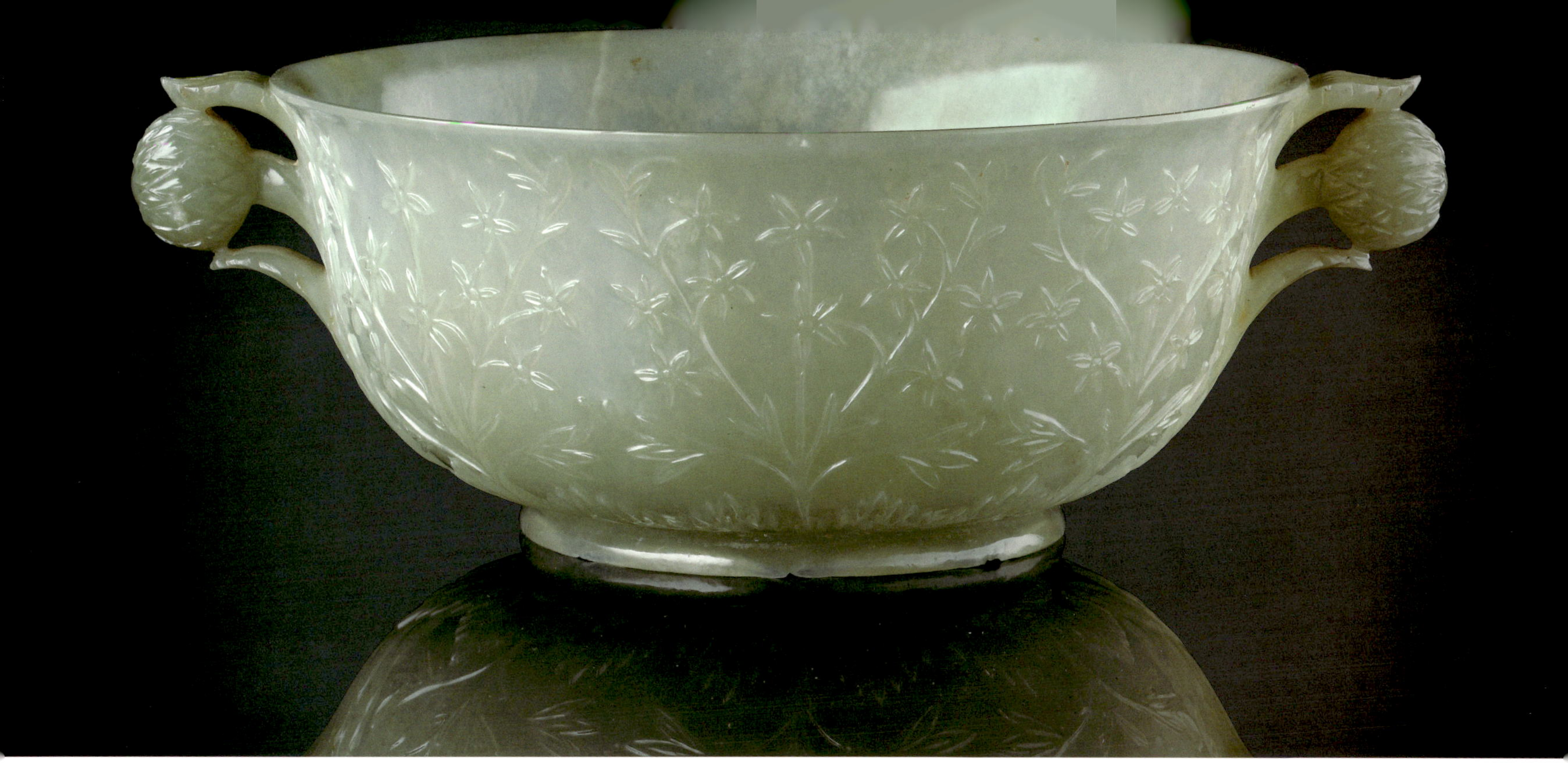

15

Bowl (side and bottom)

North India, 1650–1700. Jade

CAT. 37

The overall shape of this bowl is derived from Chinese ceramic forms and appeared in jade in Iran and Central Asia during the second half of the fifteenth century. The flower in the base is a composite bloom comprising a poppy and a chrysanthemum, with the multi-petal chrysanthemum in the center and the large petals of the poppy forming the outer rim. The distinctive flowers around the sides are similar to the five-petal shapes decorating the margins of mid-seventeenth-century Mughal album pages. The relief-carved flowers can also be compared to the carved marble panels to be found on buildings from the time of Emperor Aurangzeb (r. 1658–1707), such as the Moti Masjid in Delhi, dating from 1663.

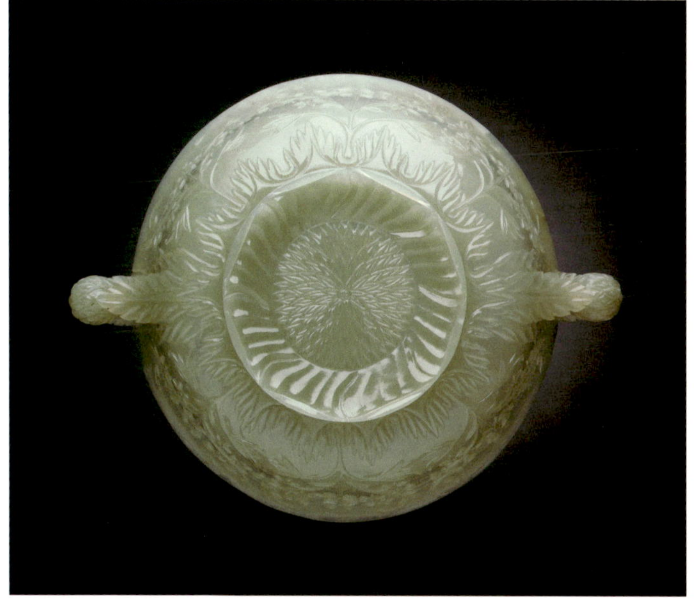

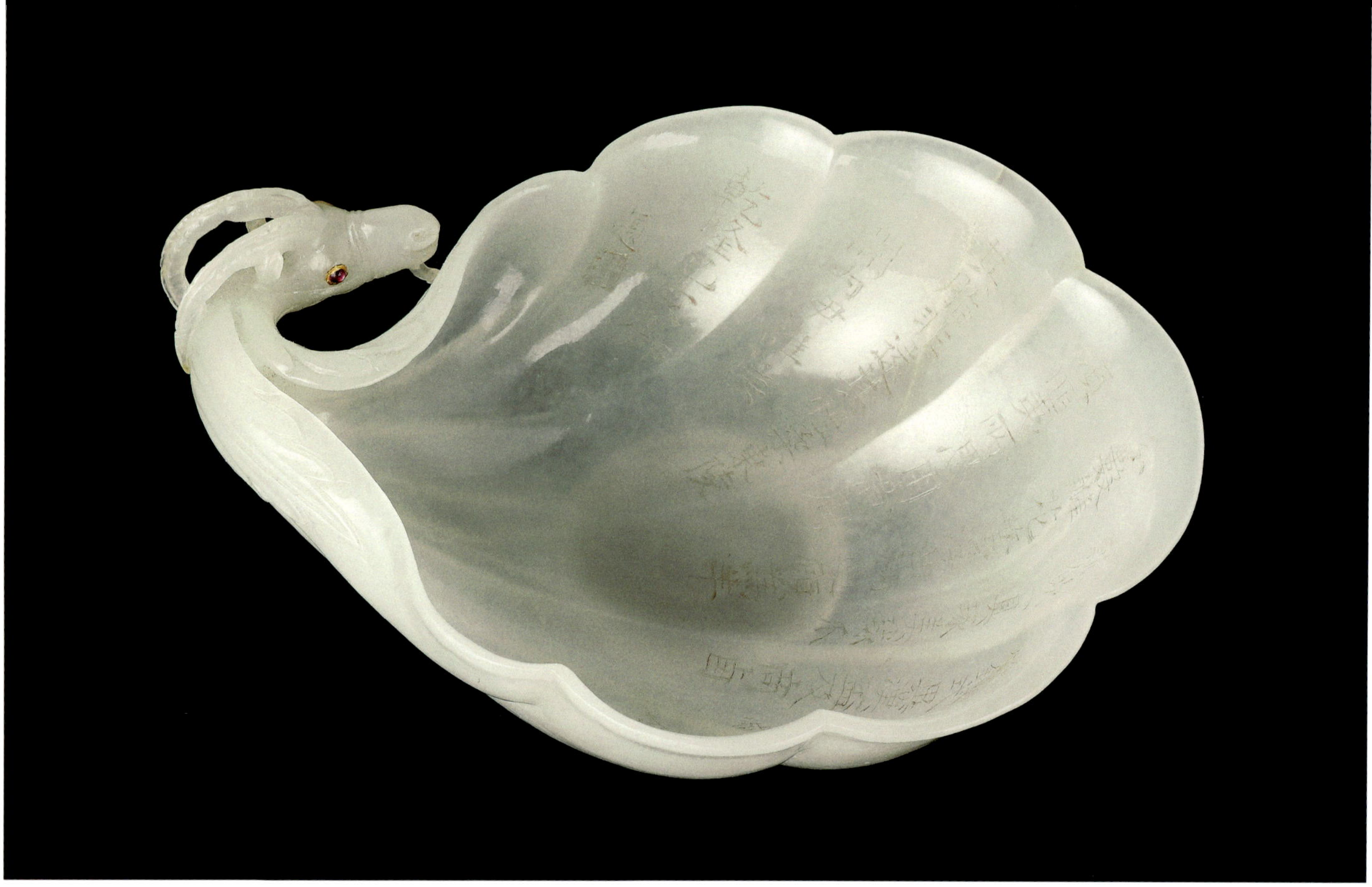

16

Cup (full view and detail)

North India, 1660–1680. Jade, ruby eyes set in gold, silver foot ring

CAT. 40

The Chinese poem inscribed in this bowl is one of a group written by Emperor Qianlong (r. 1736–1795) in which he praises Mughal jades. The emperor formed a substantial collection of these objects, which are now in the National Palace Museum, Taipei.

The present poem is number 51 in the series of the emperor's writings and has not yet been found on any other jade. The animal head on the cup is of a wild goat or an ibex whose horns have been carefully carved.

The poem translates as follows:

The good property in Lutai (Deer Terrace Pavilion) comes from far-off lands where this cup was carefully carved and pierced by fine artisans. The design is different from those cups of the Han dynasty as well as from the you *vessels of the Shang. This ladle cup is carved from exquisite jade.*

The gourd has multiple lobes, and flowers as well as leaves are shown. The crooked handle is turned around to resemble a ram's head. [This design] is fantastic and the concept behind is comprehensive.

The smoothness makes it easy to get close to, and the nature is soft.

Neither the Dongling [jade] (aventurine quartz) nor [the jade from] Guannei is comparable.

Imperially composed in the jihai year of the Qianlong reign (1779, the 44th year of the Qianlong reign).[1]

NOTE

1. An alternative translation reads: *This ram's-head petal cup dedicated to the emperor is a famous product of Lutai. It is engraved by an excellent craftsman. It is a cup with a shape quite different to the han cup and Shang containers. Its body is mainly crafted with exquisite curves while the petals are engraved with leaves and its handle is twisted in the shape of a ram's head. It is crafted with heavenly handiwork, made of the finest material and has a texture such that no one in China can make such a fine cup;* see Forsyth and McElney 1994, 413.

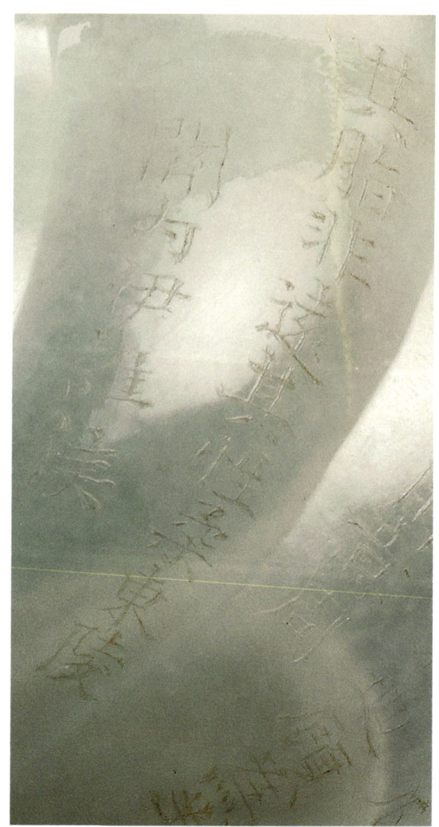

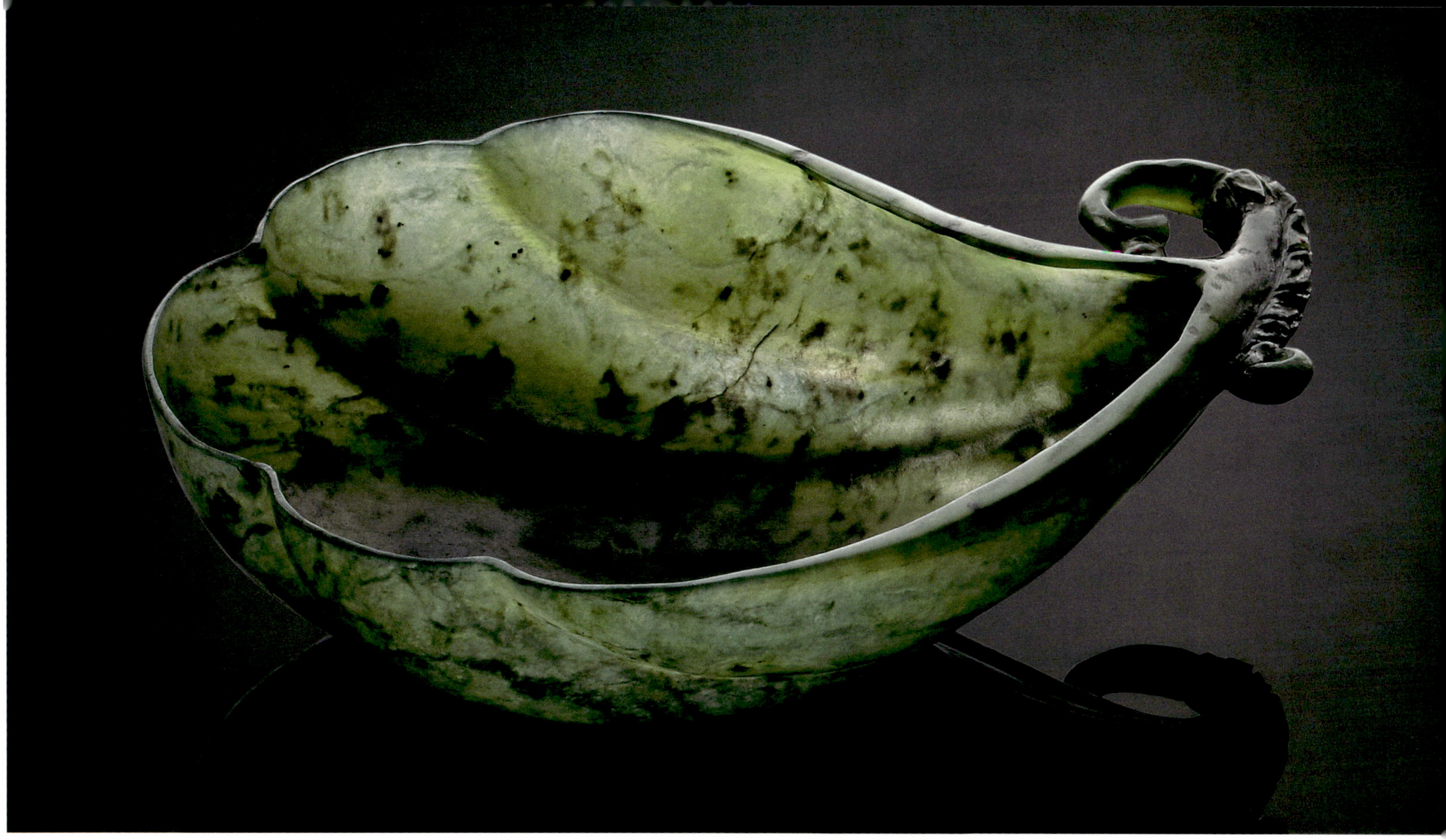

17

Cup (side and bottom)

India, 1675–1725. Jade

CAT. 41

The type of jade used for this cup is unusual, with black flecks in the stone and the polished surface featuring a matte finish. It is possible that this is a rare variety of nephrite, perhaps from Siberia. Its shape is inspired by that of a gourd.

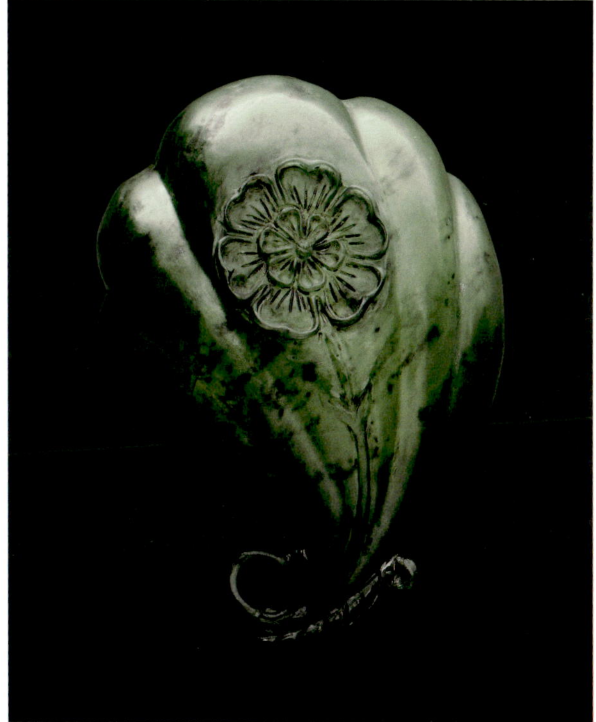

MUGHAL JADES

In the reign of Alamgir (Aurangzeb 1618–1707), access to trade routes leading to Khotan through Kashmir opened up. As a consequence, the supply of nephrite jade to the Mughal court seems to have grown enormously after 1665.

Susan Stronge, ed., *Bejewelled Treasures: The Al Thani Collection*, 2015

The Mughal emperors continued the legacy of their Timurid ancestors, who ruled in Central Asia and Persia, in collecting and prizing jade. Sourced in Khotan in Central Asia, Mughal jade initially followed Chinese porcelain or Islamic metalwork shapes in favored dark-green colors, and was carved with inscriptions reflecting both its importance to the emperors and its rarity. From the time of Emperor Jahangir in the 1600s, Western influences appeared in carved floral decoration based on hardstone artworks from Italy. These highly refined *pietre dure* objects probably made their first appearance as diplomatic gifts to the Mughal court and were subsequently fashioned by European craftspeople seeking work in India. Possibly due to this European influence, there emerged a preference for white jade over the green jade of earlier eras.

The most distinctive treatment of Mughal jade was its decoration with precious stones. Rubies, emeralds, and, to a lesser extent, diamonds were inlaid into the surface, set in gold with stylized floral and animal decoration. In the eighteenth century, the wider availability of jade allowed it to be used for various purposes, from jewelry such as turban ornaments and pendants to hookah bases, boxes, crutches, and flywhisks.

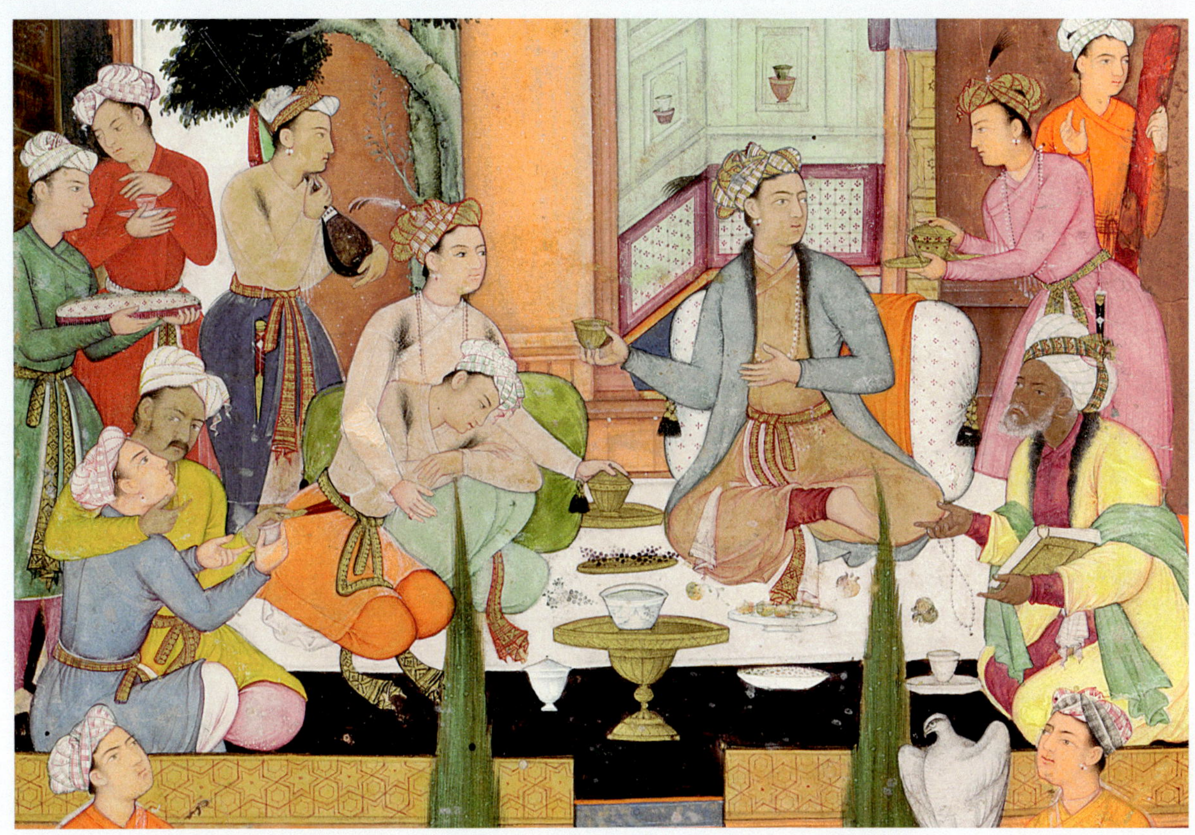

FIG. 24. Detail of a folio from the Small Clive Album representing a convivial gathering, India, ca. 1615–1620. Opaque watercolor and gold on paper, 7⅛ × 5⅛ in. (18.2 × 13.2 cm). Victoria and Albert Museum, London, Gift of Mr. John Goelet, IS.48:53/B-1956

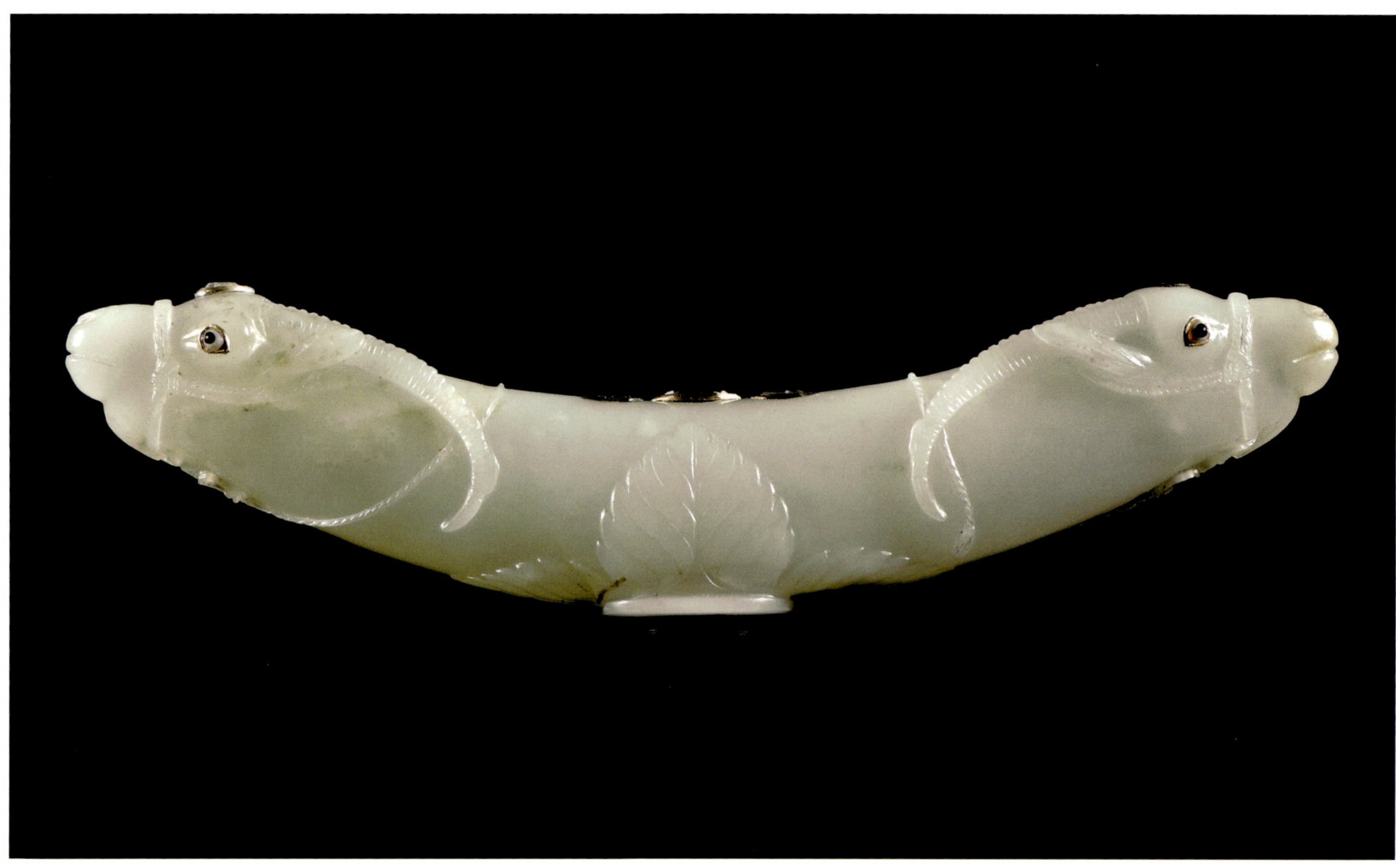

18

Crutch handle

North India, ca. 1650. Jade, agate eyes, diamonds set in gold (added later)
CAT. 45

Crutches with short sticks (see cat. 78) were used for supporting the arm while sitting. They are depicted used by holy men. The Mughal appreciation of flora and fauna is evident in the fine and decorative arts produced for courtly consumption. This crutch handle is carved at either end with the head of what appears to be an ibex (*rang*), a species of wild goat that lives in rocky and mountainous areas.

19

Hookah base

North India, 1740–1780. Jade, inlaid with rubies, diamonds, and emeralds set in gold

CAT. 46

This richly decorated vessel would have been the water reservoir, which made up part of the equipment for smoking tobacco. Having been introduced to Europe from the Americas, this intoxicant first appeared at the Mughal court in the late sixteenth century. Emperor Akbar (r. 1556–1605) was offered tobacco in 1604 by one of his nobles, Asad Beg, who recorded the event and wrote a description of the hookah that was used on the occasion, mentioning a burner, pipe, and mouthpiece. The style of inlay on this spherical hookah base suggests that it was made in the mid-eighteenth century. The piece was displayed at the exhibition of Indian art staged in Delhi in 1902–1903 to celebrate the coronation of Edward VII.

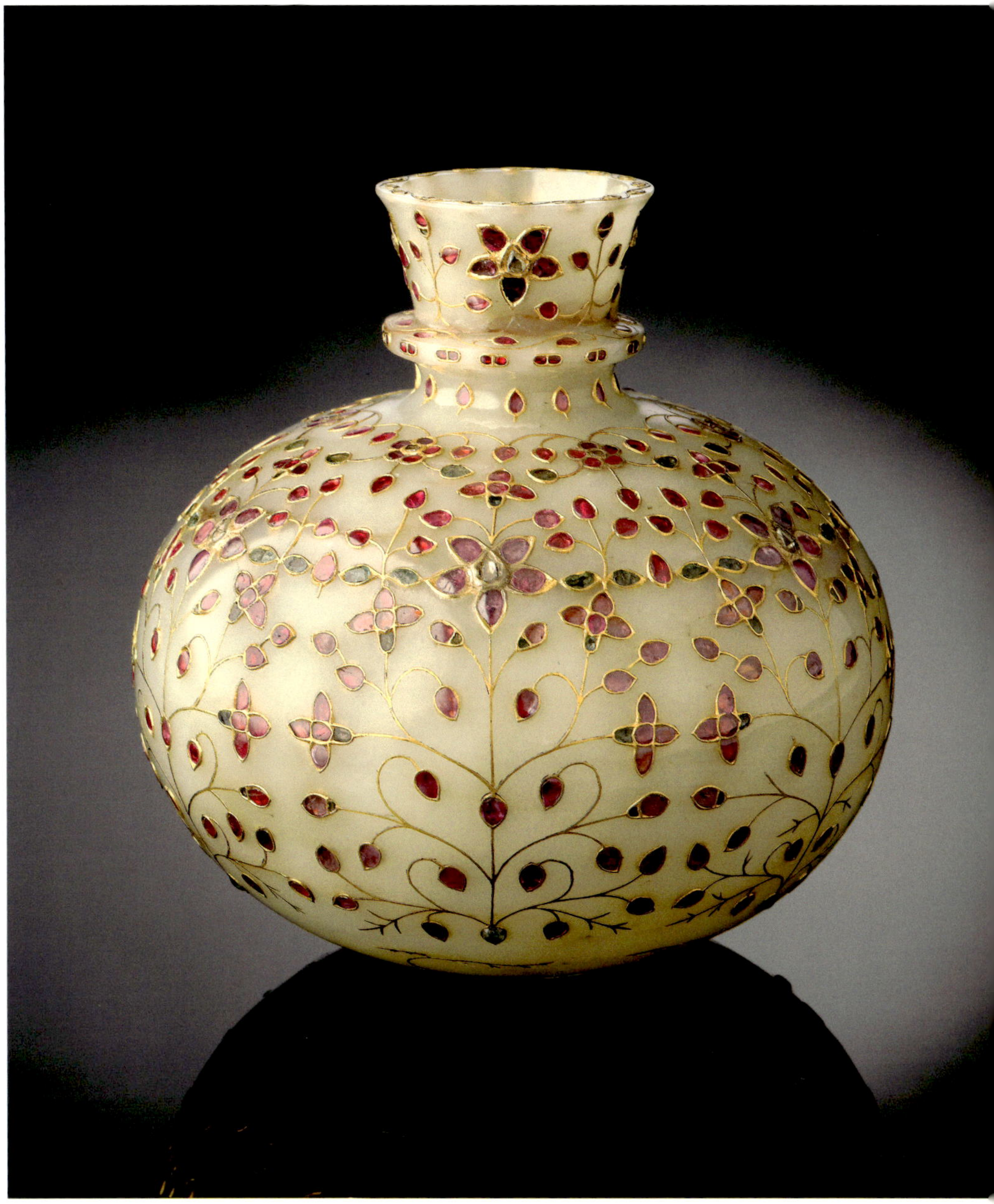

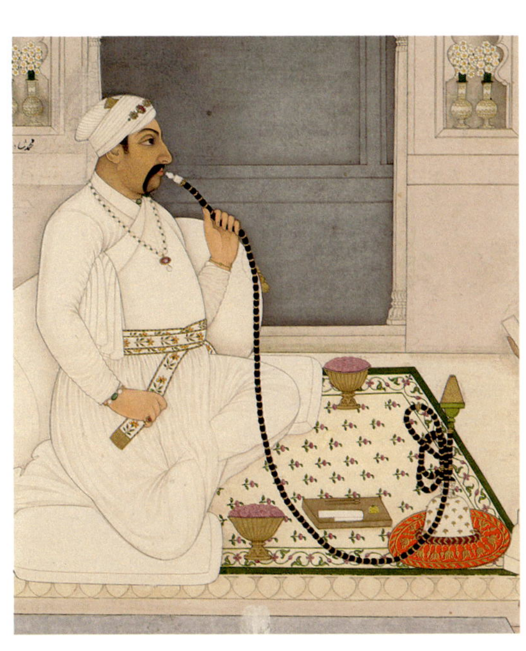

FIG. 25. Attributed to Chitarman, detail of Muhammad Shah with four courtiers, ca. 1730. Gouache on paper, 12¼ × 18⅜ in. (31.2 × 46.8 cm). The Bodleian Libraries, the University of Oxford, Given to the Bodleian by Francis Douce, Ms. Douce Or. a. 3, fol. 14a

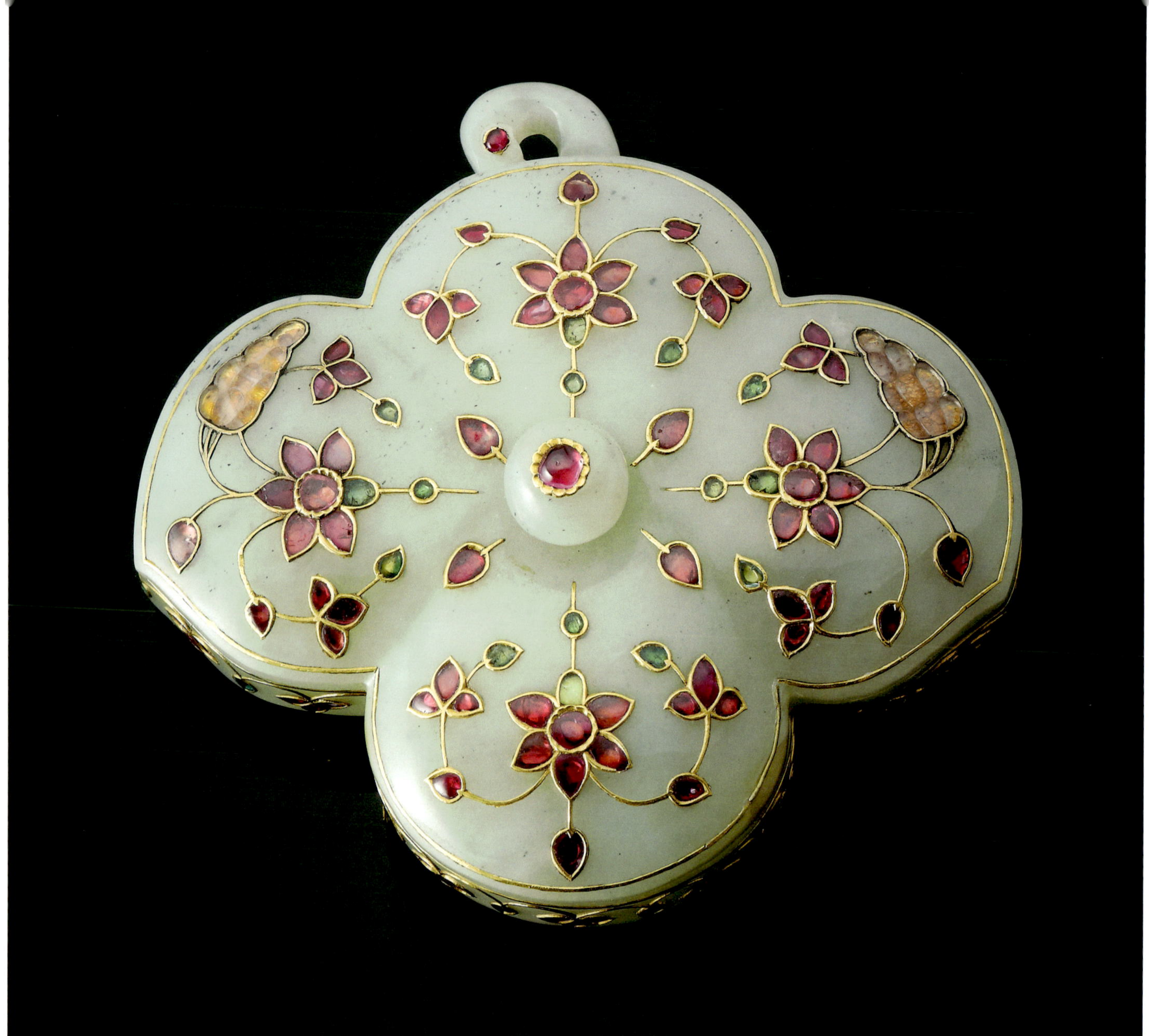

20

Box for *paan*

North India, 1740–1780. Jade with rubies, emeralds, and rock crystal set in gold

CAT. 44

Compartmentalized containers of this type would have been used at court for keeping and presenting ingredients used for *paan*, a delicacy usually containing sliced areca nut, cardamom, clove, and lime paste (*chuna*), wrapped in an areca nut leaf. It was chewed for freshening the breath.

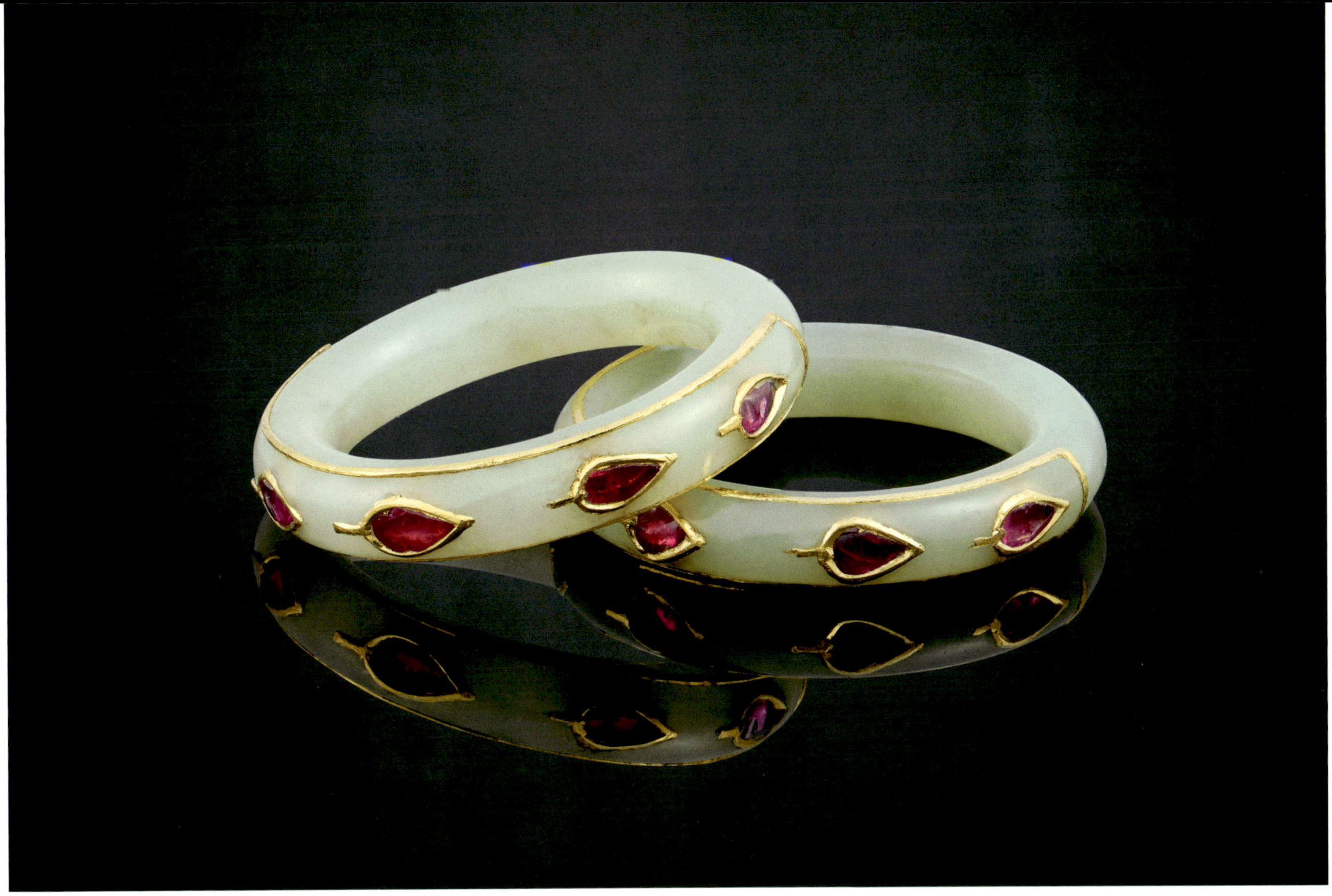

21

Pair of falcon bracelets

North India, ca. 1800. Jade with rubies set in gold
CAT. 47

Even before the Mughal presence in the subcontinent, falconry was a favored pastime among Indian rulers. This art and the development of paraphernalia to adorn falcons reached a high point under imperial rule, as testified by contemporary texts and images. Miniature paintings of falcons show them adorned with fine materials, including jeweled necklaces and bracelets, such as this pair, which are made of jade inlaid with rubies.

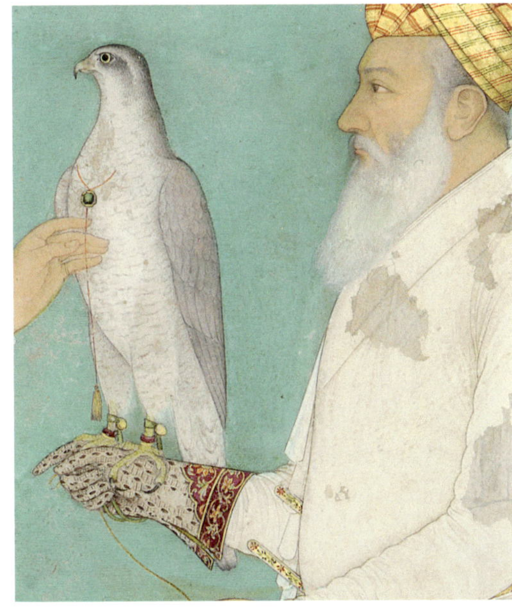

FIG. 26. Hashim, detail of Shah Jahan with an elderly courtier holding a falcon, ca. 1650. Watercolor on paper, with gold, $11\frac{1}{8} \times 7\frac{3}{8}$ in. (28.4 × 18.9 cm). The Trustees of the Chester Beatty Library, Dublin, CBL In 62.4

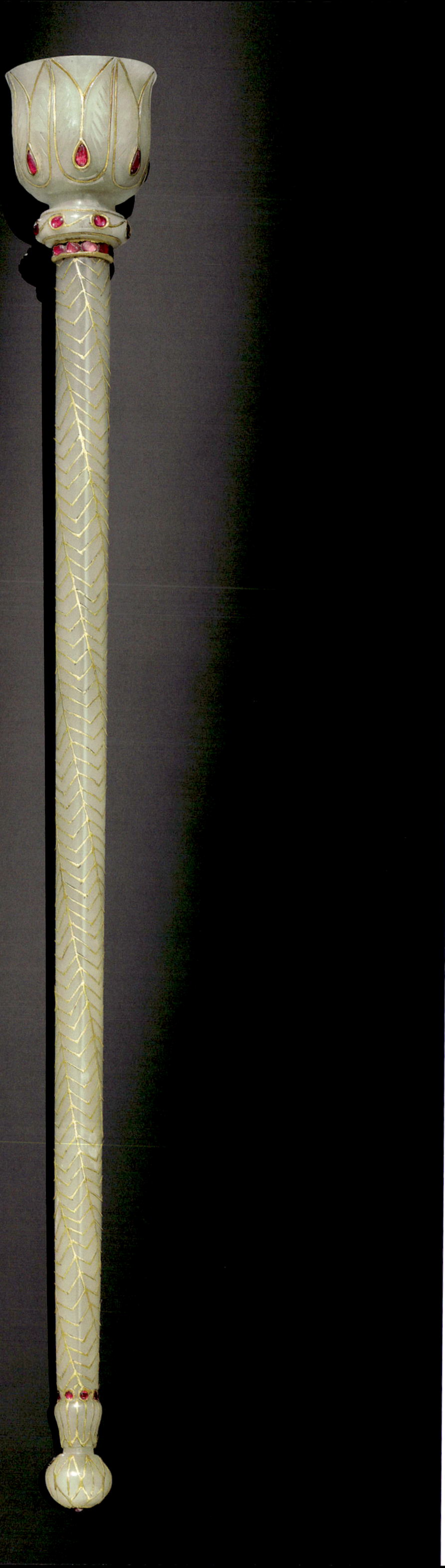

22

Flywhisk

North India, 1675–1725. Jade, gold, rubies
CAT. 49

Since ancient times, depictions of deities and royalty in India show them with trappings of authority, among which are flywhisks (*chauri*). The flywhisk would typically be mounted with a yak's tail that would be waved back and forth in order to keep insects away, reflecting the superior physical conditions to which ruling figures were entitled. This example in jade is particularly sophisticated in that the shaft is inlaid in gold with a chevron design like a spider's web and twisted on a diagonal axis.

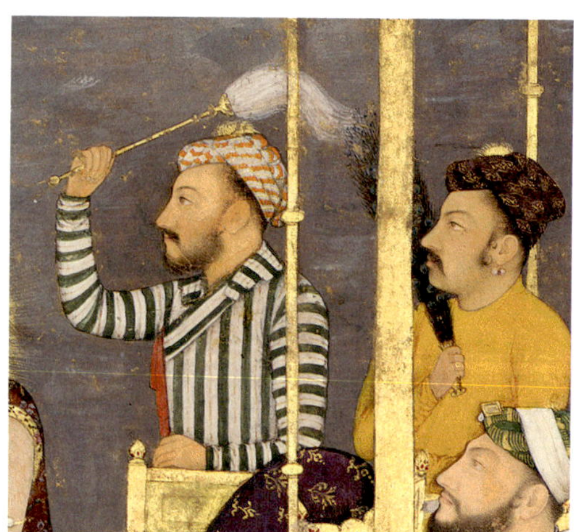

FIG. 27. Lalchand, The submission of Rana Amar Singh of Mewar to Prince Khurram, detail of folio 46b from the *Padshahnama*, ca. 1640. Opaque watercolor and gold on paper, 12¾ × 8½ in. (32.4 × 21.6 cm). Royal Collection Trust

23

Flask

North India or Deccan, 1740–1780. Rock crystal, diamonds, emeralds, and rubies set in gold and silver
CAT. 54

Bottles with an open mouth and tall neck are known as *surahi*, a Persian term that is used poetically to refer to the long neck of a girl. This example is exceptionally rare, since it appears that no other rock crystal bottles of comparable size have survived. The floral designs are similar to those on a jade hookah base in The Al Thani Collection (cat. 46/pl. 19). Although the most likely place of production is within a court in North India, the use of both silver and gold for the gem settings is found in jewelry attributed to Deccani workshops.

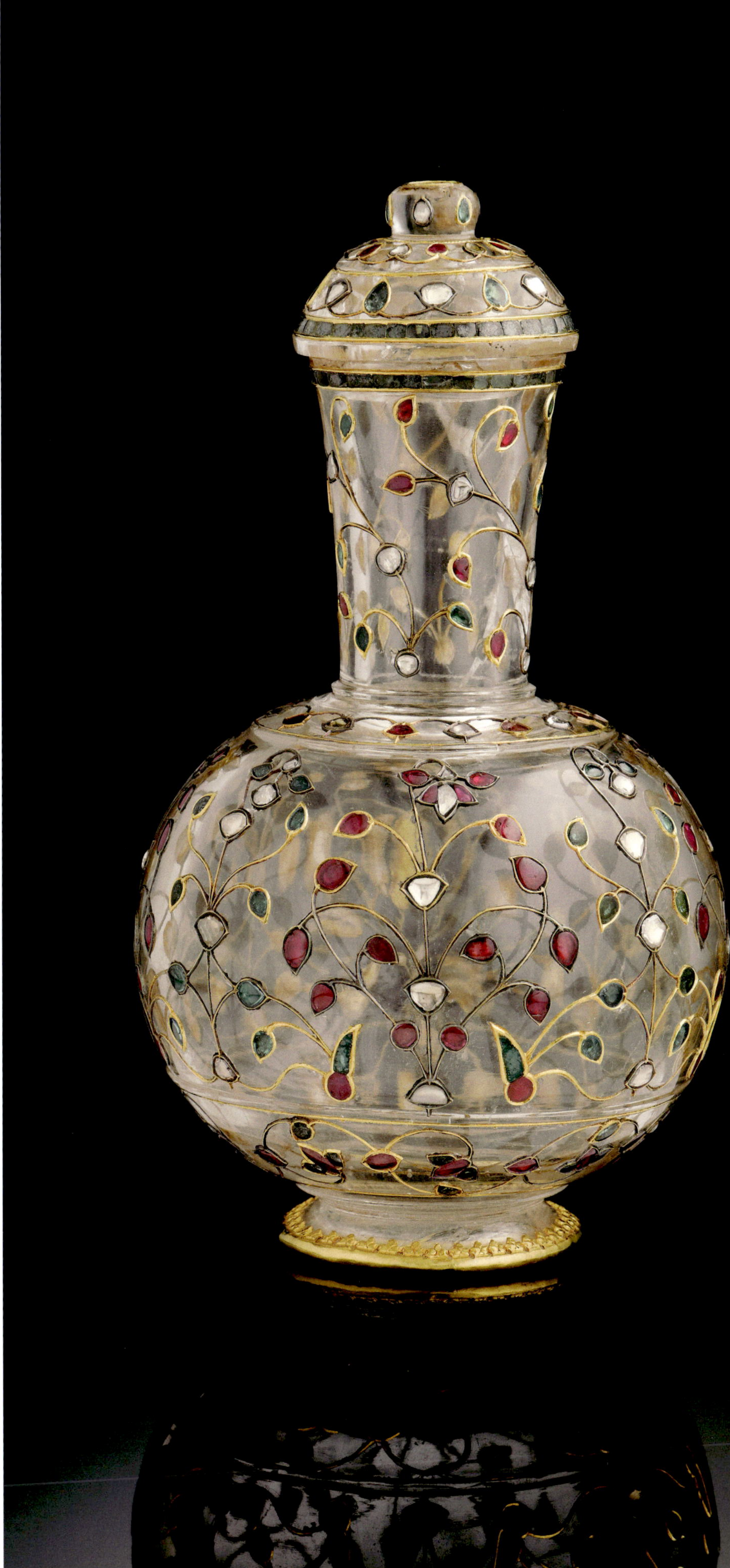

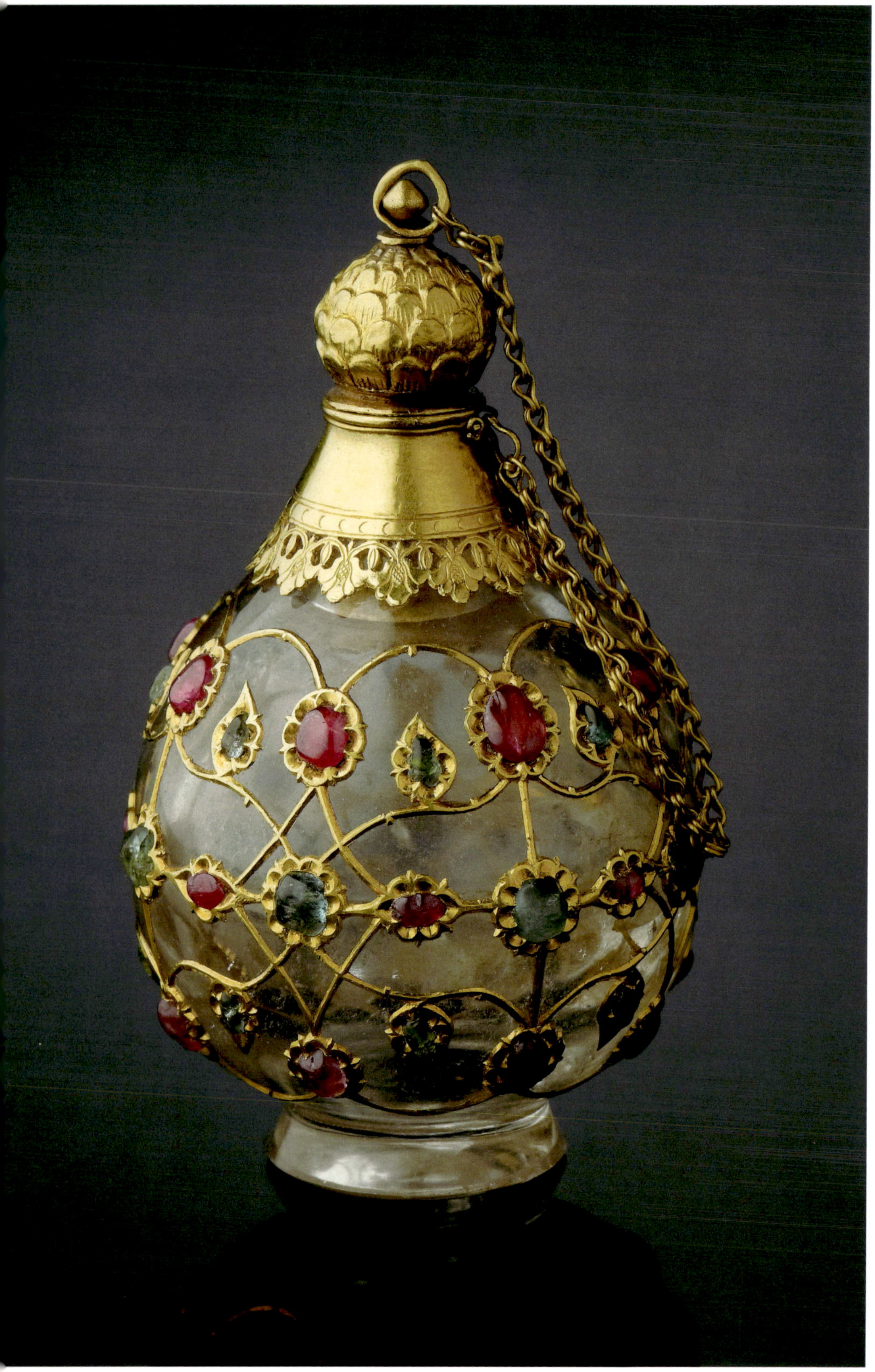

24
Flask

North India, 1650–1700. Rock crystal, gold set with rubies and emeralds
CAT. 53

Objects of rock crystal were highly prized at the Mughal court. Although Indian rulers would have received examples made by lapidaries in the West, they also commissioned pieces locally, such as this example, whose shape suggests that it was used for holding perfume. The surface is covered with arabesques in gold wire and is inset with gemstones with finely articulated mounts. The stopper, shaped like a floral bloom, and the mount around the collar are original and are rare surviving examples of seventeenth-century Indian goldsmiths' work.

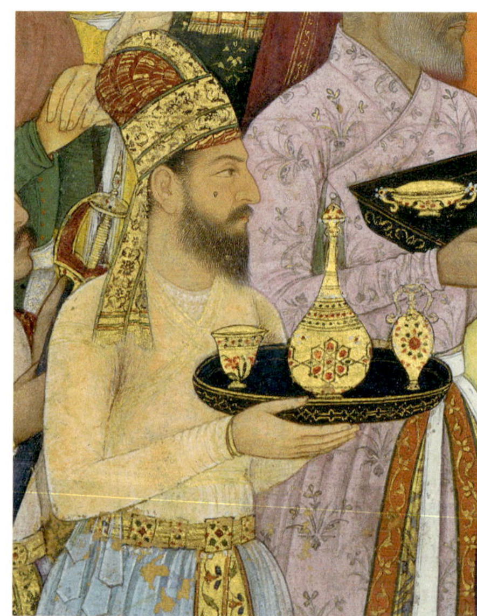

FIG. 28. Murar, Jahangir receives Prince Khurram on his return from the Deccan, detail of folio 49a from the *Padshahnama*, ca. 1640. Opaque watercolor and gold, 12⅛ × 8¼ in. (30.8 × 20.9 cm). Royal Collection Trust

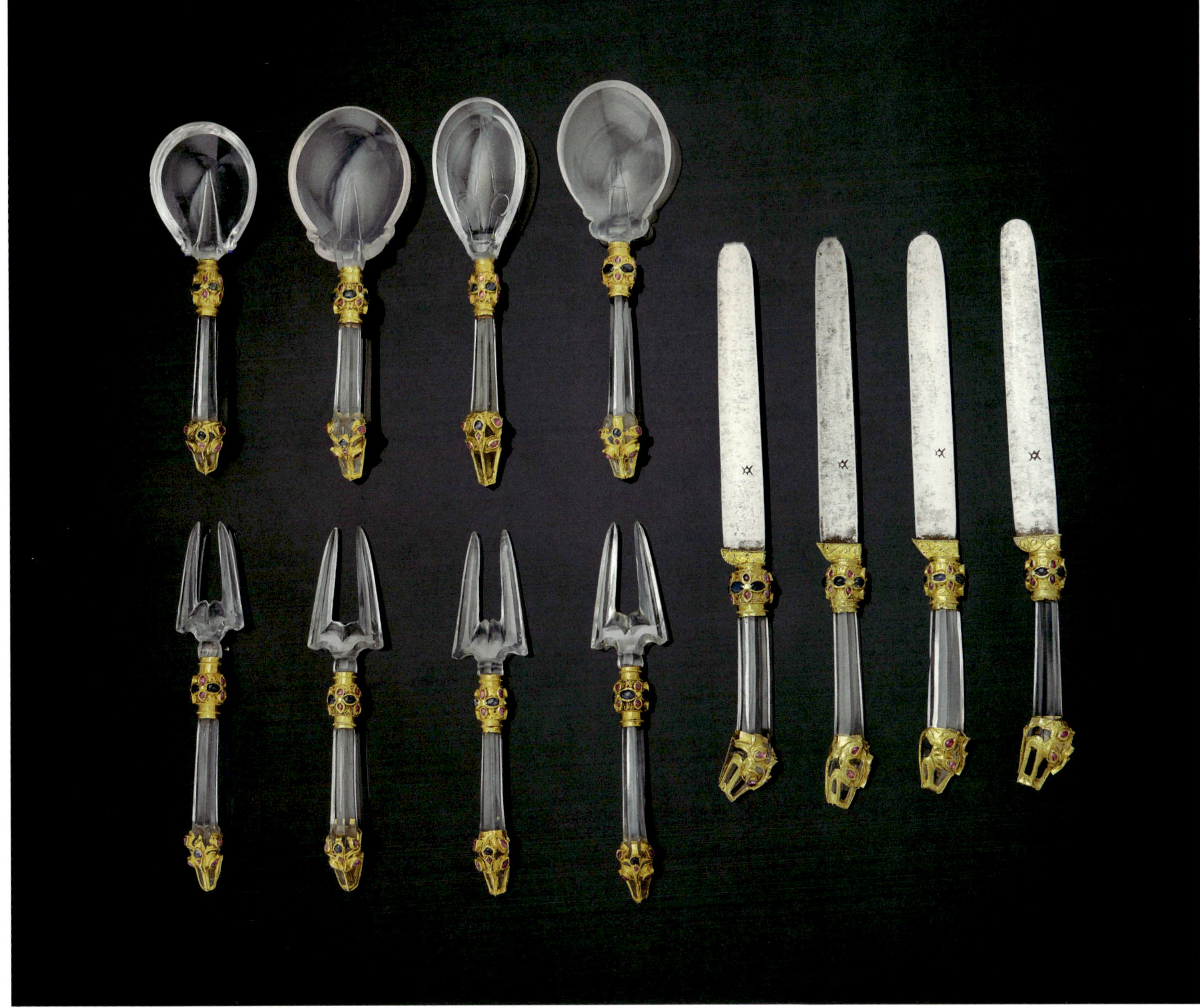

25

Set of flatware

India or Sri Lanka, sixteenth to seventeenth centuries.
Rock crystal, rubies and sapphires set in gold
CAT. 55

This set of flatware comprises four knives, four spoons, and four forks, all made of rock crystal and carved in octagonal sections. Each has a collar of gold, *kundan* set with rubies and sapphires and decorated with small spirals of gold wire. The style of the gold mounts is similar to that found on hardstone objects mounted in Goa and Ceylon under Portuguese patronage in the late sixteenth and early seventeenth centuries.

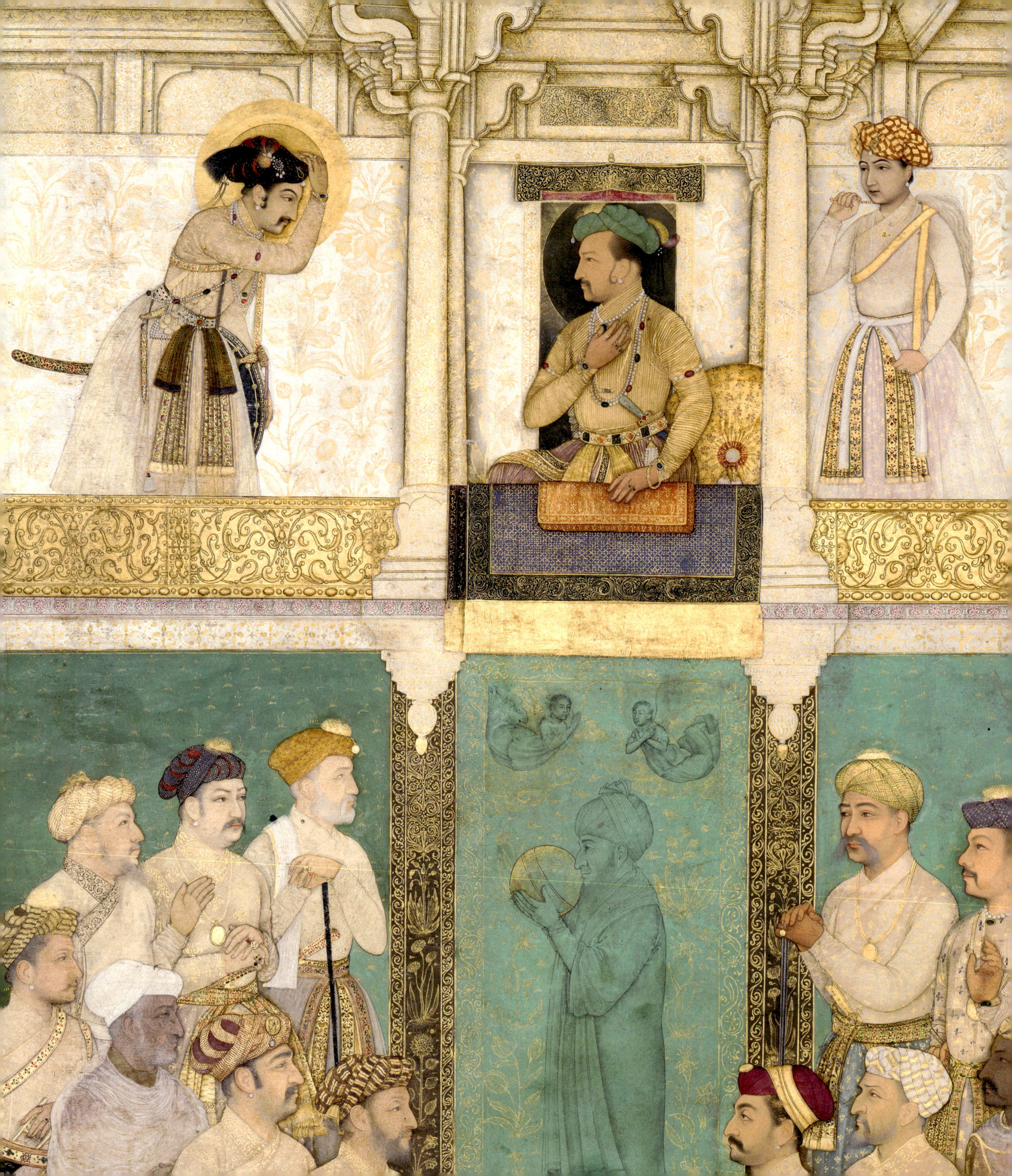

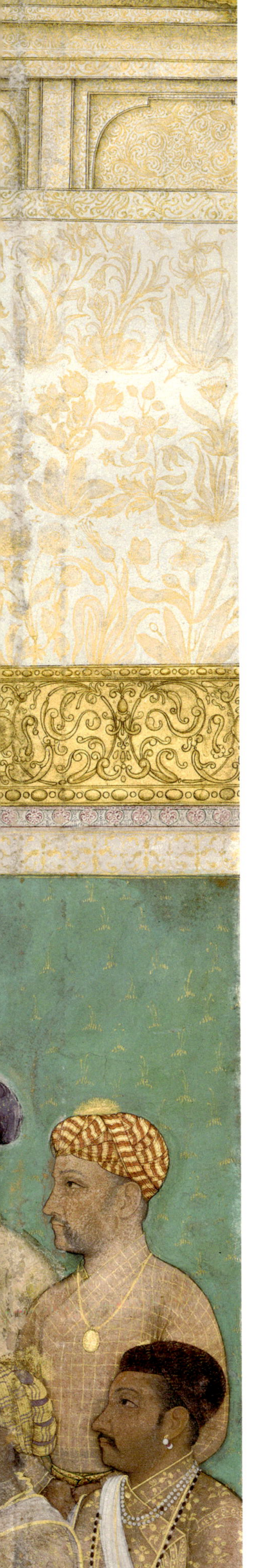

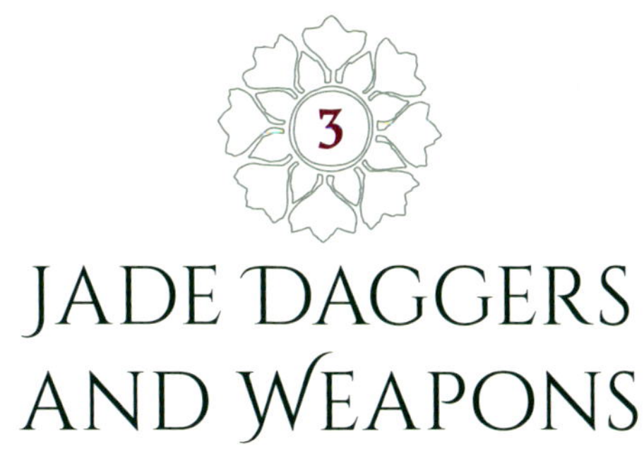

JADE DAGGERS AND WEAPONS

Prized by the Mughal emperors for its purported ability to bring victory in battle, jade was often employed for highly valued ceremonial weapons worn by the emperors and their court. Some were given by the emperor to conquered foes, royal princes, and ambassadors. The most common type was for dagger handles, which were displayed in the sash or waistband, but jade was also used for sword hilts and even powder horns to contain gunpowder for rifles.

A favorite form of the dagger hilt from the 1630s was carved with an animal head for the pommel (or terminal), such as a lion, camel, horse, or ram. These animals were associated with power and, therefore, initially could be worn only by the imperial family. Other types of jade daggers were more abstract in form and would be decorated with ornamental repeating or floral patterns set with precious stones, predominantly rubies, which were also thought to protect the wearer in battle. But emeralds and diamonds were also used, set in gold worked in the *kundan* technique. Each hilt was attached to an elaborately fashioned steel blade, sometimes inlaid with gold inscriptions and decoration. These blades could also be pierced with slots filled with balls, in a manner likewise found in Turkey and Iran in the sixteenth and seventeenth centuries.

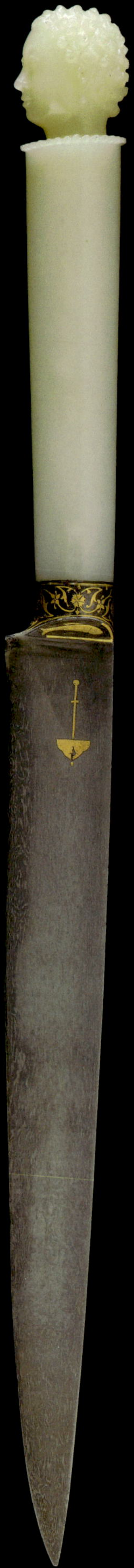

26

The Shah Jahan Dagger

North India, hilt: 1620–1625, blade: 1629–1636.
Jade, watered steel blade inlaid with gold
Inscribed in Persian: *Second Lord of the Auspicious Conjunction 2 or 9*
CAT. 56

The hilt of this dagger represents a high point of Mughal jade carving. The distinctive treatment of the boy's head with a ruff at the neck is clearly influenced by European sculpture, and may have been copied from an Indo-Portuguese head of Christ as the Good Shepherd. The craftsman who carved the handle could have been Indian or European. One of the several European lapidaries working at the Mughal court was probably involved at least in its design. It has been suggested that the curly-headed figure may derive from depictions of cherubs or angels seen on a number of allegorical paintings of the Jahangir period. The blade is inscribed with Shah Jahan's title as well as with an umbrella and fish, both symbols of kingship.

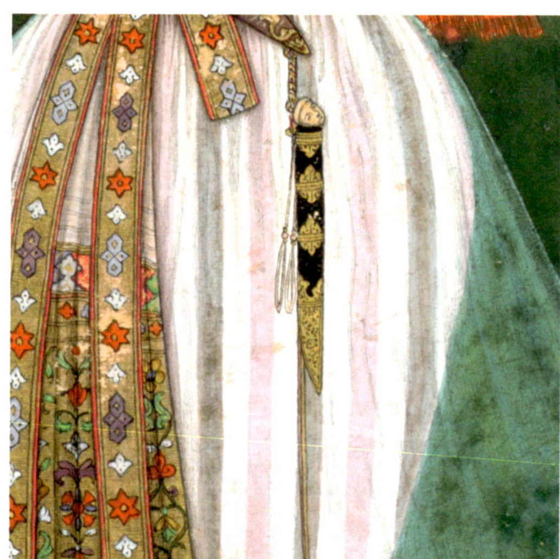

FIG. 29. Bichitr, *Prince Salim*, detail of a folio from the Minto Album, Mughal, India, ca. 1630. Opaque watercolor and gold on paper, 9⅞ × 7⅛ in. (25 × 18.1 cm). Victoria and Albert Museum, London, IM.28-1925

27

Dagger and scabbard

North India, 1620–1640. Jade inlaid with rubies, emeralds, and diamonds set in gold, watered steel blade inlaid with gold

CAT. 57

Such precious daggers are shown in miniatures worn tucked into the belts or sashes of the Mughal rulers. This dagger is exceptional in that its scabbard is made of jade matching the hilt. Both are inlaid with gemstones to compose a design of birds amid intersecting vines. The flexibility of the *kundan* technique has permitted the maker to define each bird individually, giving them a distinctive character.

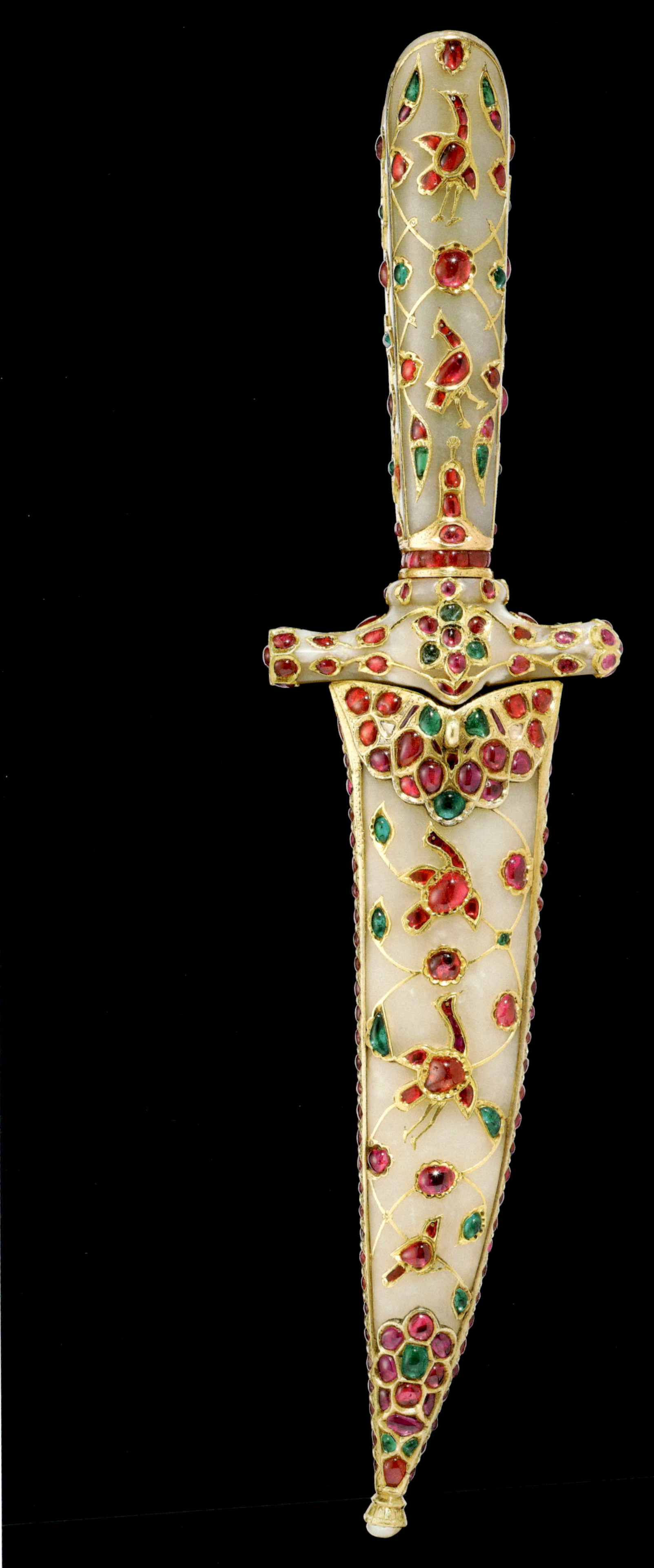

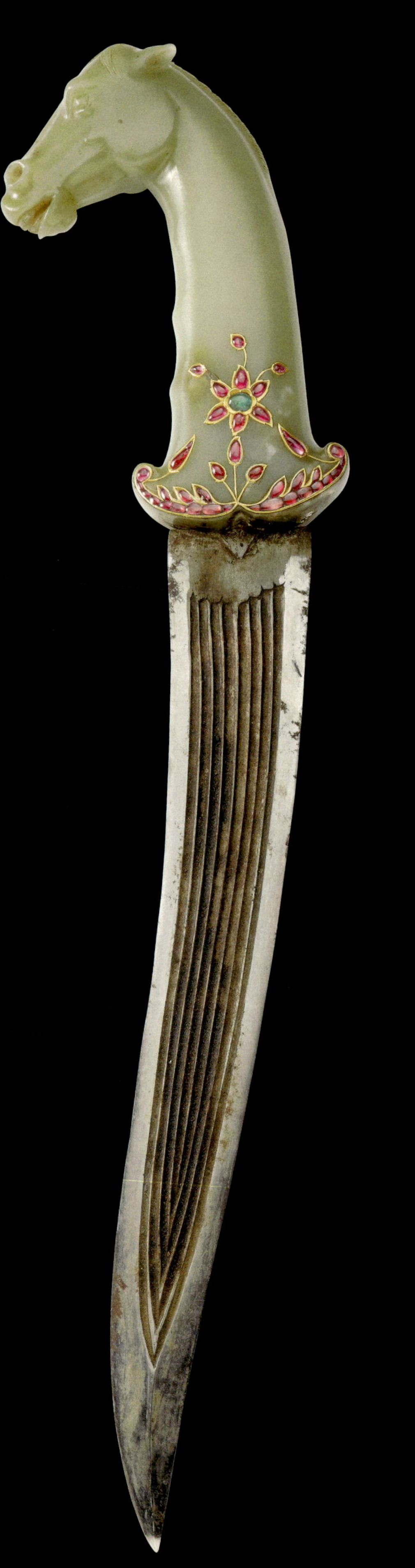

28

Dagger

North India, 1700–1750. Jade inlaid with gold, rubies, and emerald; steel blade
CAT. 61

The origin of Mughal zoomorphic dagger hilts is uncertain; they do not appear on courtly weapons before the second quarter of the seventeenth century. There are a number of possible prototypes based on Indian, Iranian, and European designs. Horse-head dagger hilts are first depicted in folios of the Windsor *Padshahnama* (ca. 1635), including one illustrating the presentation of Dara Shikoh's wedding gifts, in which the prince has a white horse-head dagger in his belt.

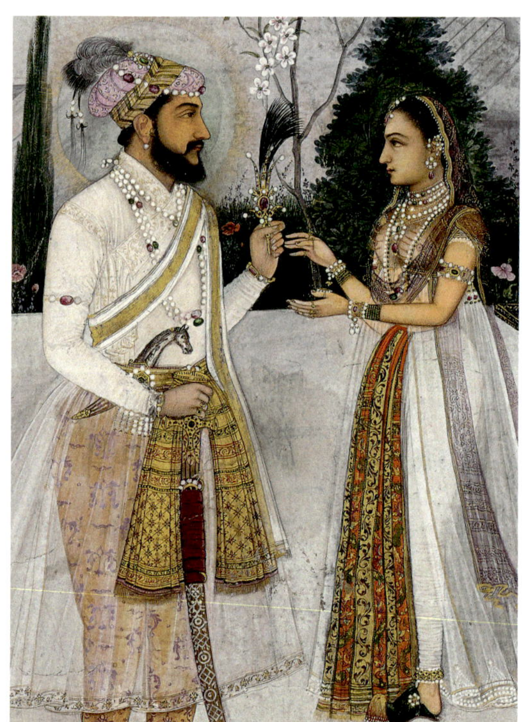

FIG. 30. Shah Jahan presents a *sarpech* to a princess in a garden (detail), ca. 1660–1680. Opaque watercolor with gold on paper, 9½ × 7⅛ in. (24 × 18 cm). The Al Thani Collection

29

Dagger

North India, 1720–1740 (lower section: 19th century). Jade inlaid with rubies set in gold, steel blade inlaid with gold

CAT. 59

The curved tips of the horns identify this animal as a gazelle. Its head is expressive, with careful modeling around the eyes, on the cheeks, and on the ears, while the piercing around the horns creates a three-dimensional sculptural effect. The refined carving of the upper section of the hilt contrasts with the simpler treatment of the cylindrical base, suggesting that this is a composite piece perhaps designed to preserve the high-quality older upper element.

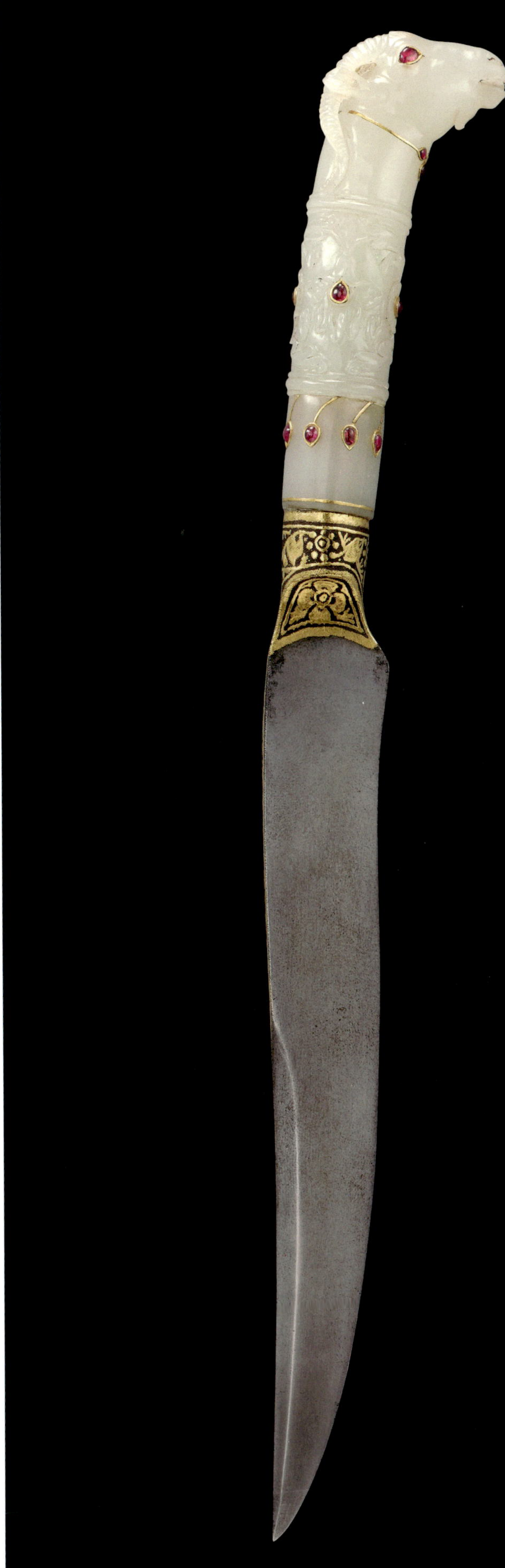

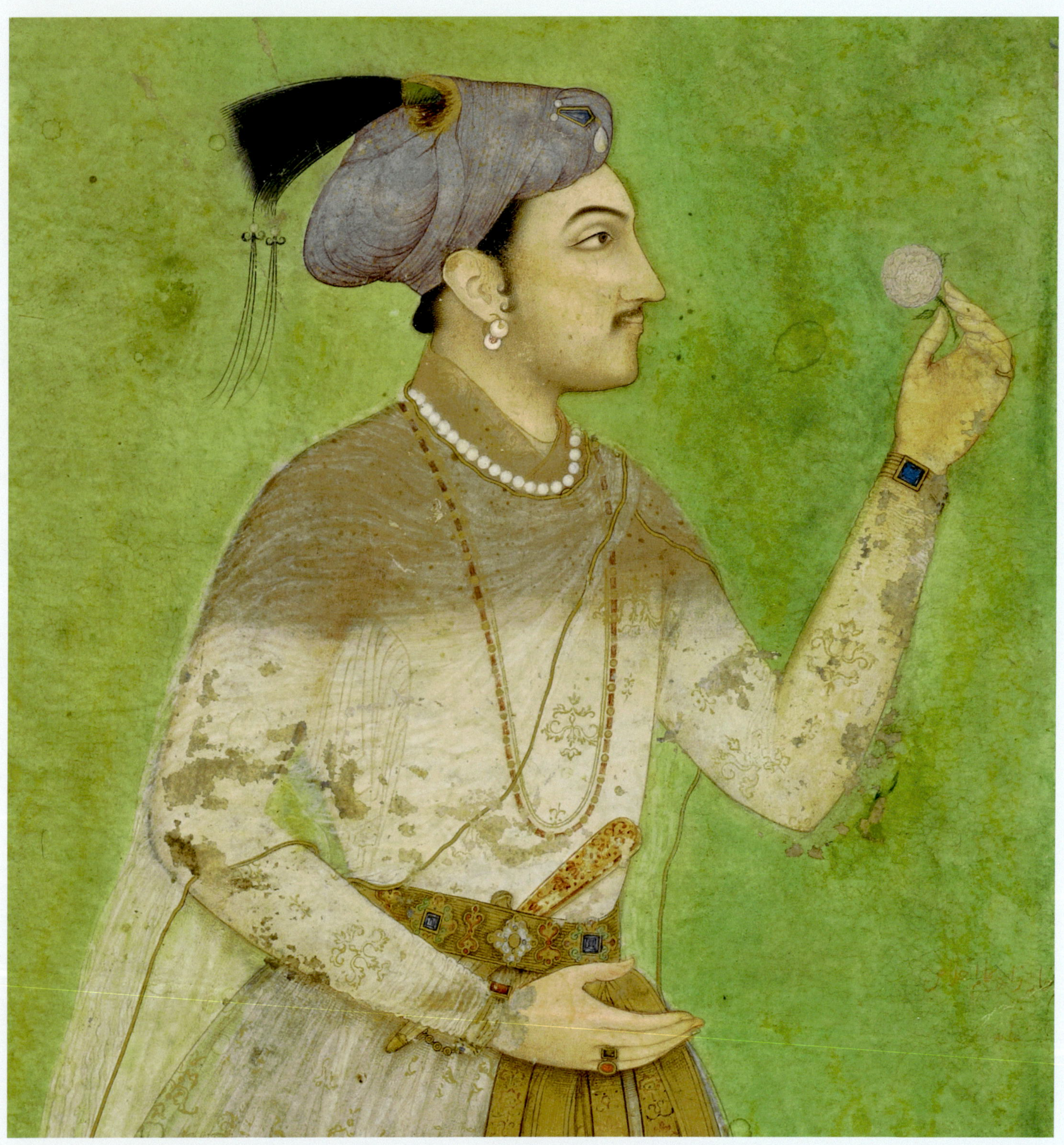

FIG. 31. Detail of Jahangir as a youth holding a pink rose, dressed in diaphanous white with a mauve turban and full gold patka, North India, ca. 1620–1630. Opaque watercolor on paper; 6⅛ × 3⅛ in. (15.8 × 8 cm). British Library, London

THE *KUNDAN* TECHNIQUE OF SETTING GEMSTONES

In other countries, the jewels are secured in the sockets made for them, but in Hindustan, it is effected with kundan.

From Colonel H. S. Jarrett, *The A'in-I Akbari by 'Abu'l Fazl 'Allami*, vol. III, revised 2nd edition corrected and annotated by Sir Jadunath Sarkar[1]

The gemstones set into the jade daggers and weapons for the Mughal court were applied by a technique singular to Indian goldsmiths' work known as *kundan*. Having hollowed out a space for the gem in the jade, or rock crystal, this method of setting the stone involved surrounding the gem with small strips of gold to hold it in place. Using pure 24-carat gold that was consequentially ductile, the soft metal was pushed around the stone with a metal tool to provide a secure setting. It meant that the object being applied with gemstones did not need to be heated—and therefore potentially damaged—as in classical Western jeweler techniques.

Already described in the times of Emperor Akbar (r. 1556–1605), *kundan* became the principal method of setting stones in Indian jewelry, gold objects, jade, and hardstones. For jewelry, a gold frame was fabricated first, then set with gemstones in the *kundan* technique, and often elaborately decorated with enamel, a feature found on much Indian jewelry that was influenced by European examples. Although the adoption of European setting techniques with open backs prevailed in the nineteenth century, *kundan* settings for traditional Indian jewelry survived. The technique is still widely performed today.

NOTE

1. Susan Stronge, ed., *Bejewelled Treasures: The Al Thani Collection*. London: V&A Publishing, 2015.

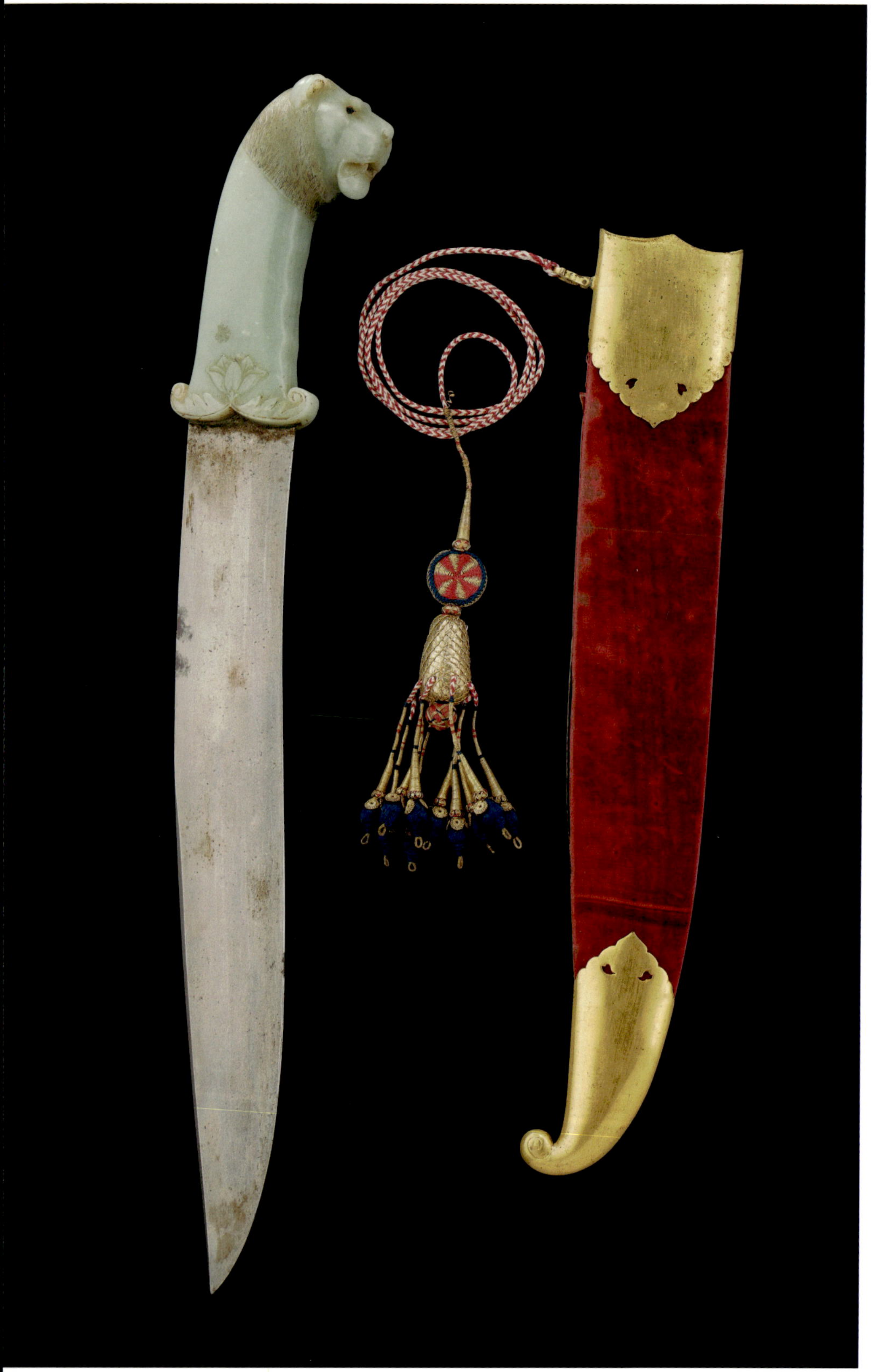

30

Dagger

North India or Deccan, ca. 1750. Jade, steel blade; scabbard: wood, textile, gold, cord
CAT. 60

The lion has been identified as a symbol of royalty across cultures. In India it has played a dominant role in representations of kingship since ancient times, evident in the ornamentation of thrones and other symbols of power. Within an Islamic context, this powerful beast has been associated with the fourth Caliph, Ali, cousin and son-in-law of the Prophet Muhammad, who was known as Asadullah ("Lion of God").

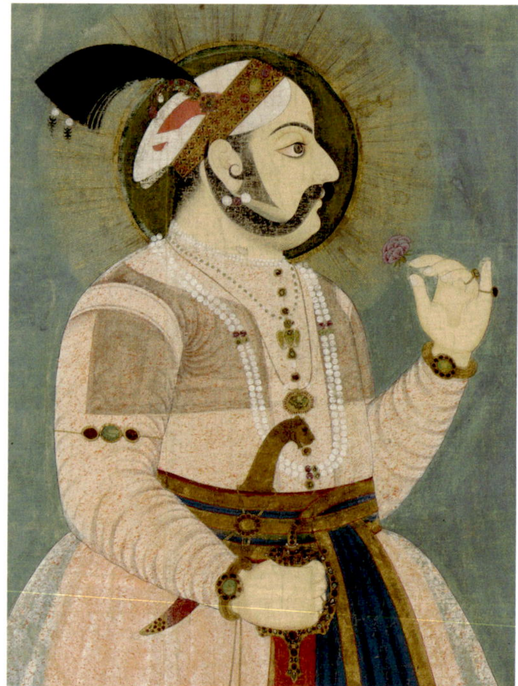

FIG. 32. Detail of *Maharana Amar Singh*, Udaipur, India, ca. 1735–1740. Opaque watercolor on cotton cloth, 83⅞ × 54 in. (213 × 137 cm). Victoria and Albert Museum, London, Purchased with the assistance of The Art Fund, IS.55-1997

31

Dagger

North India or Deccan, 1700–1725. Jade inlaid with rubies and emeralds set in gold, watered steel blade; scabbard: wood, textile, gold, enamel
CAT. 63

The carved scale decoration combined with the rubies gives the hilt of this dagger a strong sculptural effect, which is enhanced by the close fitting and shaping of the flat and pavé-cut rubies and emeralds. The pierced blade is related to examples from sixteenth- or seventeenth-century Turkey and Iran, which also contain small balls in the cut slots.[1]

NOTE

1. Ivanov 1979. A specimen is in the Kahlili Collections, inv. no. MTW 1143; Alexander 1992, 102–103, no. 51, referred by David Alexander to sixteenth-century Ottoman Turkey. See also cat. 71.

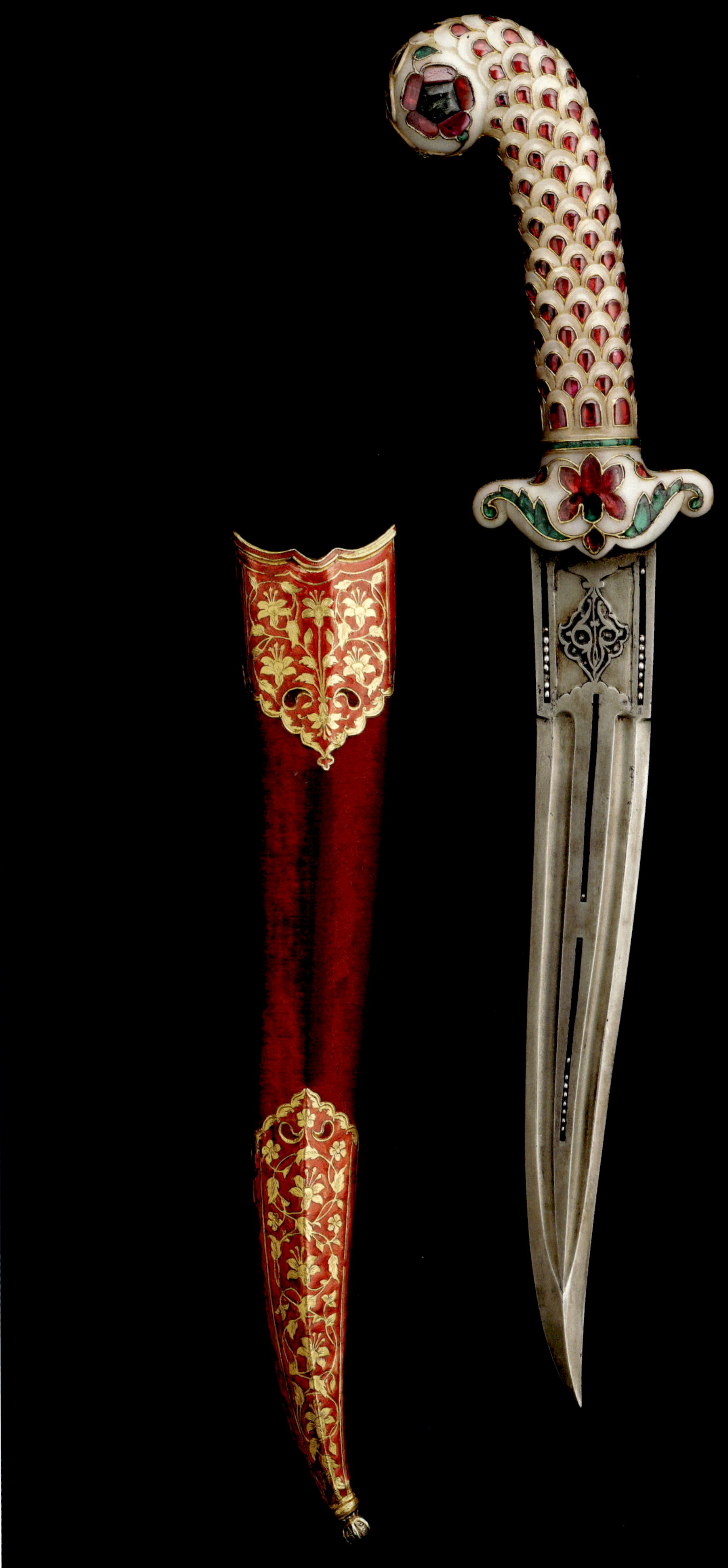

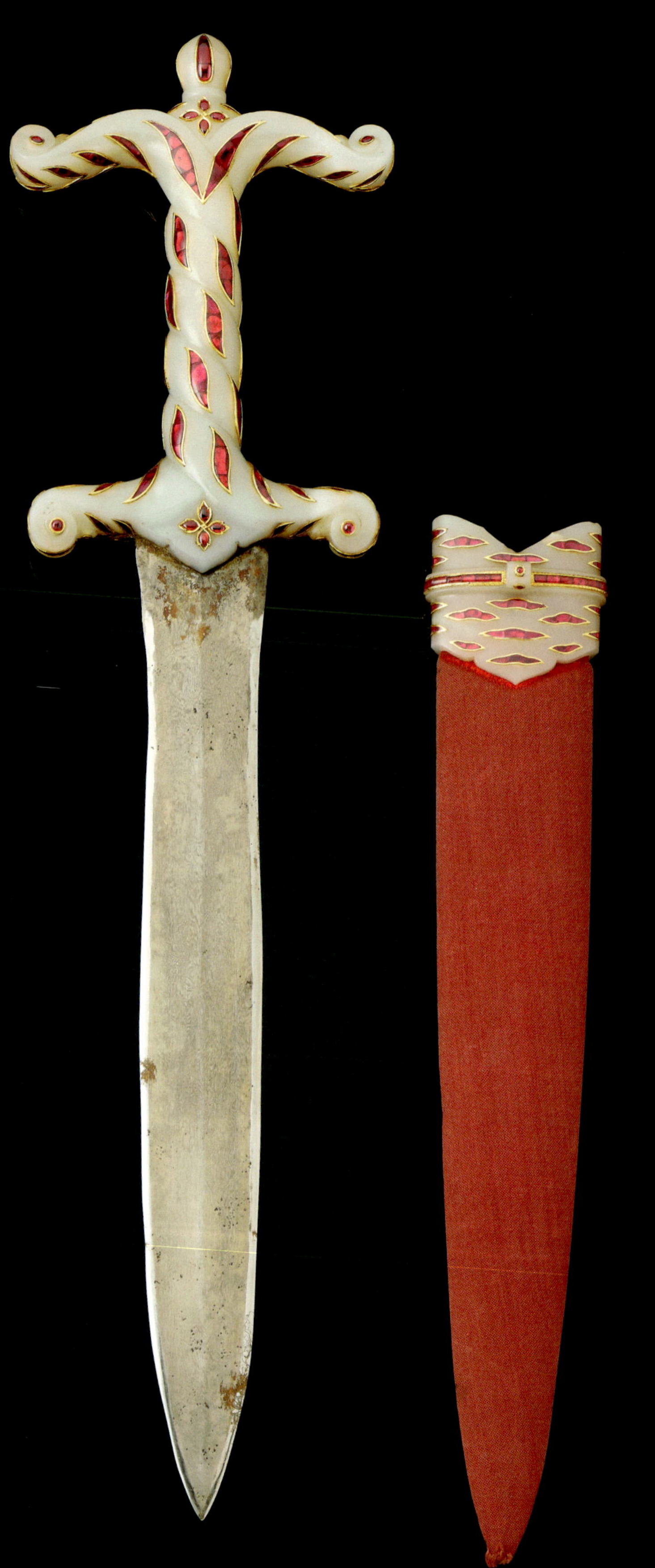

32

Dagger

North India or Deccan, ca. 1675–1700. Jade inlaid with rubies set in gold, steel blade; scabbard: wood, textile
CAT. 64

The abstracted tiger (*bubri*) motif of the inlaid rubies on the present hilt is commonly associated with Tipu Sultan of Mysore (d. 1799), but in fact was used widely in India as an abstracted representation of the animal's power. The inventive spiraled grip form was also adopted in Rajasthan, possibly as a result of gifts from the Mughal court.

33 *(opposite)*

Dagger

North India or Deccan, 1700–1725. Jade inlaid with rubies and diamonds set in gold, watered steel blade inlaid with gold
CAT. 66

This dagger exemplifies the wide range of decorative motifs and techniques used on pistol-shaped hilts. This may indicate that lapidaries and goldsmiths were able to exercise a degree of invention with surface decoration while remaining within a prescribed form. Often used for Timurid and early Mughal jade vessels, dark green jade was employed less frequently in seventeenth- and eighteenth-century India.

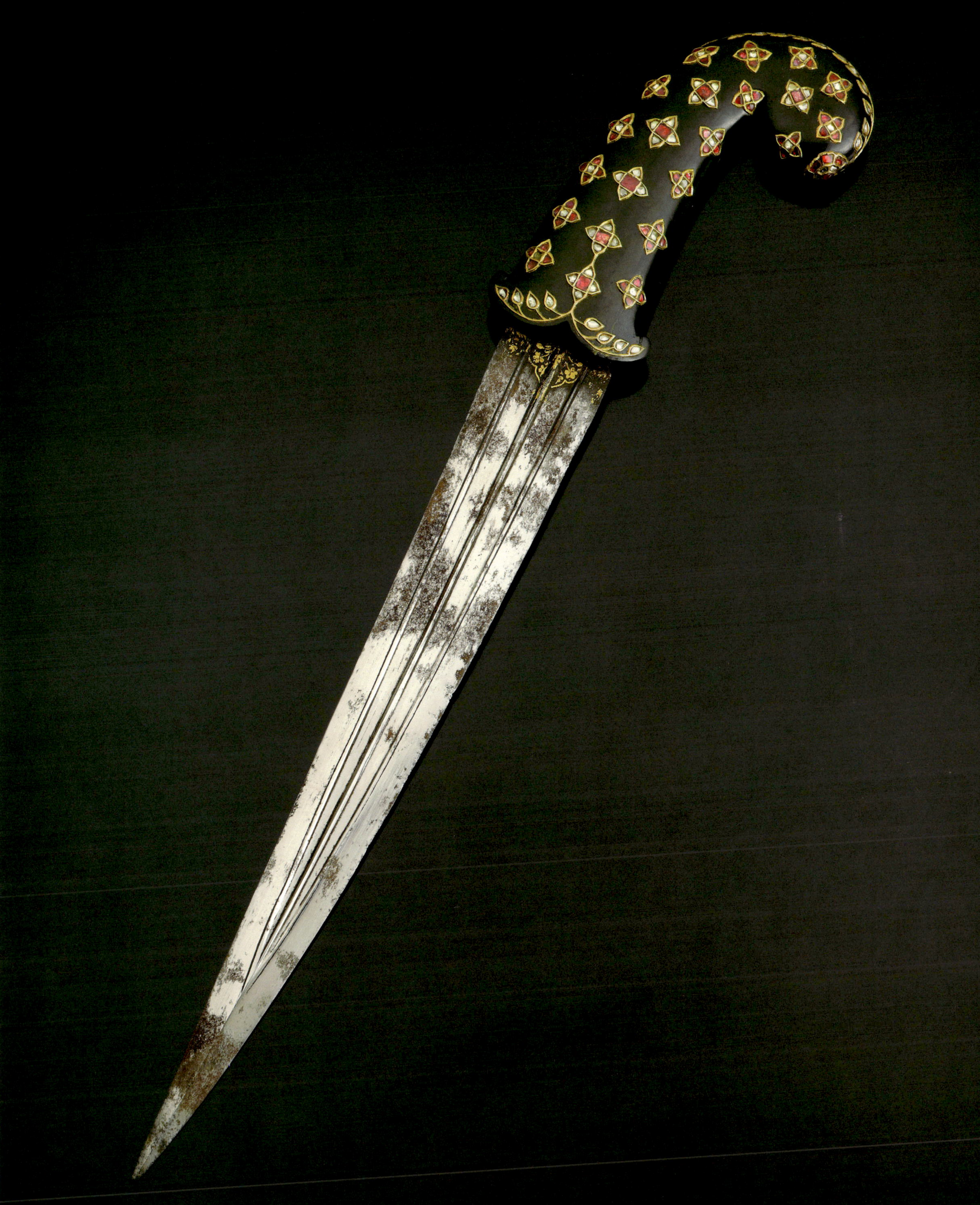

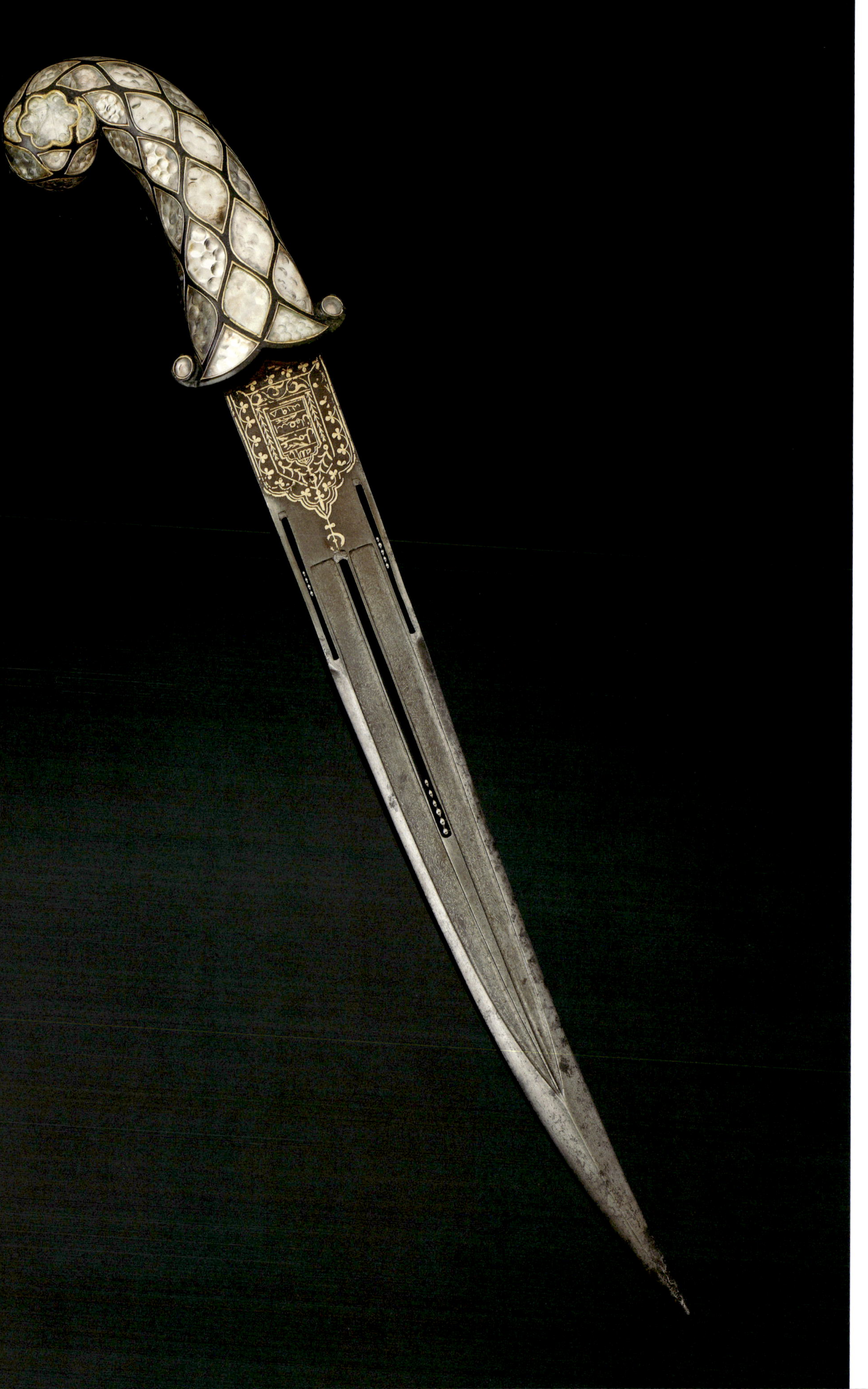

34 *(opposite)*

Dagger

North India, ca. 1725–1750; blade: Iran or India, 1783–1784. Jade inset with rock crystal set in gold, foil backing, watered steel blade inlaid with gold. Inscribed in Persian on both side of the blade: *O Allah! Work of Isfahan 1198*
CAT. 68

The decoration of this dagger hilt is unusual in that it combines two hardstones: rock crystal set into jade. The back of the rock crystals are foiled to give reflection. The highly inventive workmanship can be attributed to Mughal craftsmen, either at an imperial center or in one of the Successor States. Sections of foiled rock crystal or glass were used for the interior decoration of Mughal palaces where a mirrored room (*sheeh mahal*) became a standard feature.

35

Dagger

Lucknow (?), ca. 1775–1790. Jade inlaid with serpentine and rubies set in gold, watered steel blade inlaid with gold
CAT. 71

The workmanship of this pistol-shaped hilt suggests that it was made in Lucknow, North India. The features of interwined gold stems on the pommel, spiky florets, and symmetrical decoration on the lower grip are also found on other pieces made in a Lucknow workshop. The serpentine is carved in relief to give subtle dimension to the leaves and flowers.

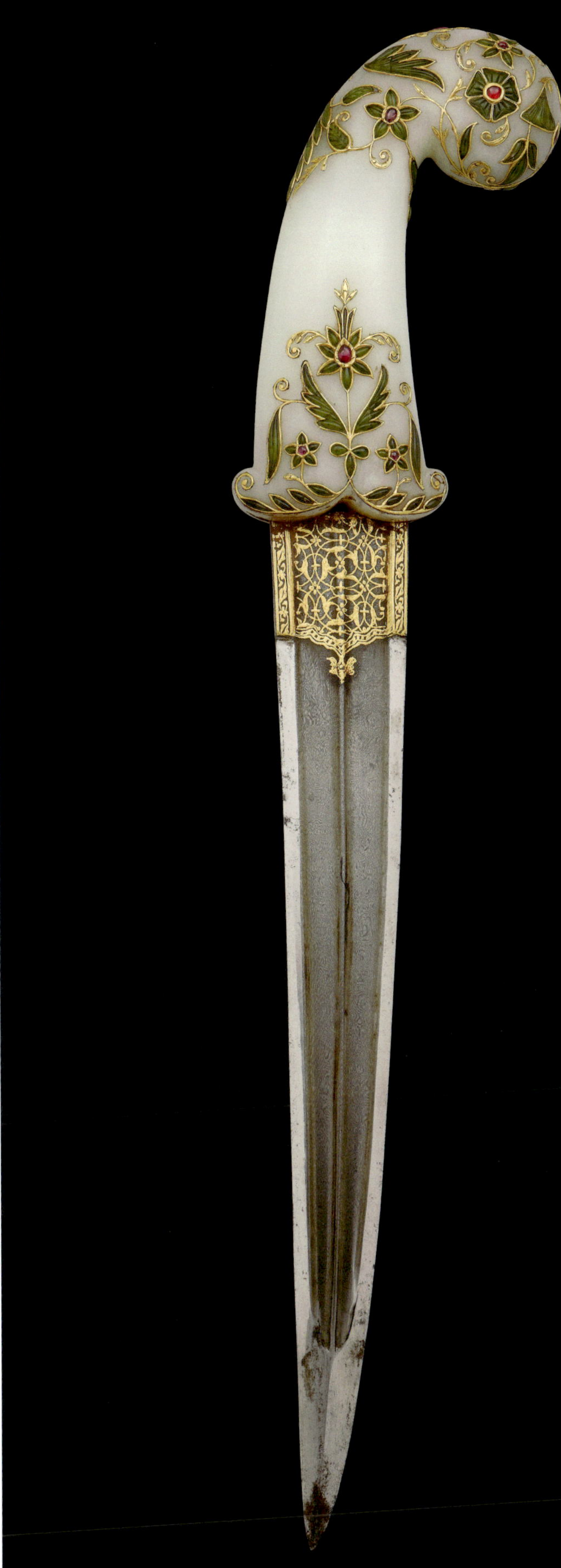

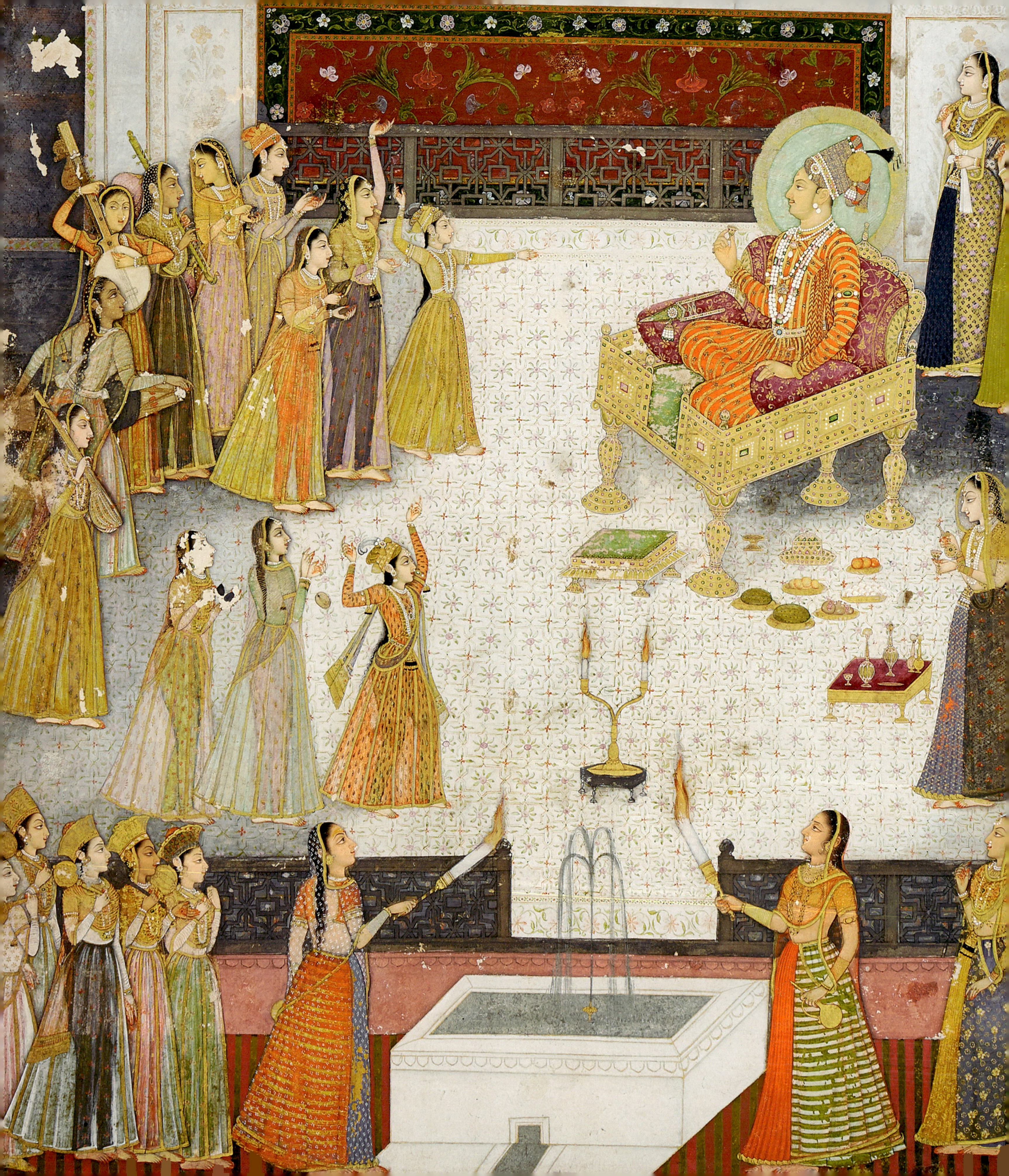

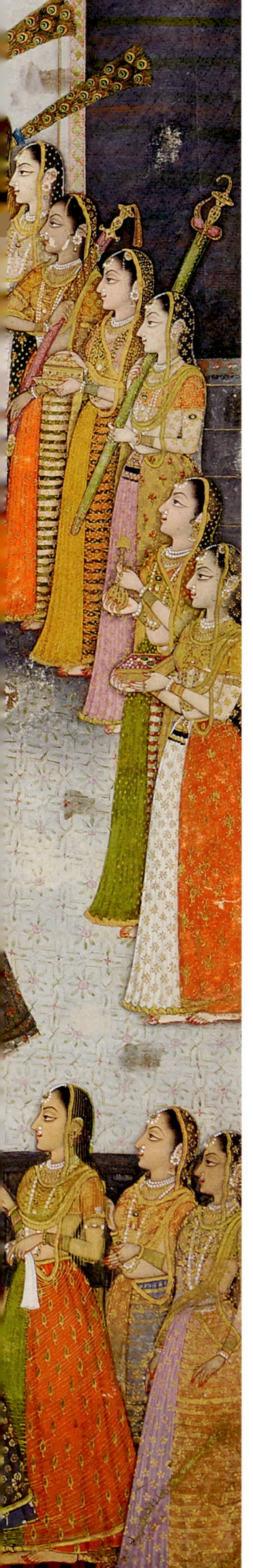

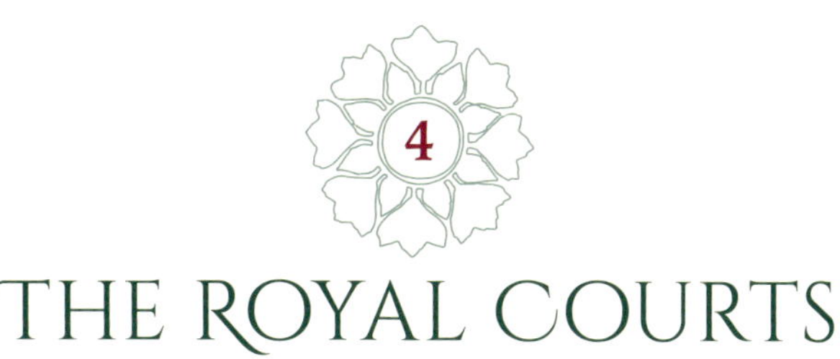

THE ROYAL COURTS

Gold and Enamels

Gold was the favored material for jewelry and the paraphernalia of royal life. While lavish jewels made for the emperors and maharajas were set in gold, many of the ceremonial objects surrounding the rulers as markers of their power were also made of gold. In addition to the extraordinary thrones that were the principal emblems of Mughal power, for courtly objects—such as pen cases, flywhisks, crutches, and the vessels placed in front of the rulers known as durbar sets, which often included cups, rosewater sprinklers, and containers for *paan*—the material of preference was likewise gold. Gold was rarely unadorned, and for these pieces the metal could be decorated in a variety of ways, with gemstones set in the *kundan* technique (see page 87), and with enamel whose rich, deep colors were akin to the gemstones. Sometimes enamel further enhanced the lavish decoration with diamonds, emeralds, and rubies to give an unparalleled sense of opulence.

Enameling is also typical of Indian jewelry, particularly that from the north of the subcontinent. This technique made its first appearance during the Mughal period, probably inspired by an appreciation of the sophisticated enameled jewelry of Renaissance workshops, which arrived at the imperial court as gifts from Western ambassadors. The dominant role that enameling has come to play in India is evidence of the ingenious assimilation of foreign techniques.

The Mughal approach to gold and jewelry shaped tastes throughout the subcontinent, establishing forms and styles that continued even after its collapse in the eighteenth century and the rise of Successor States and new kingdoms.

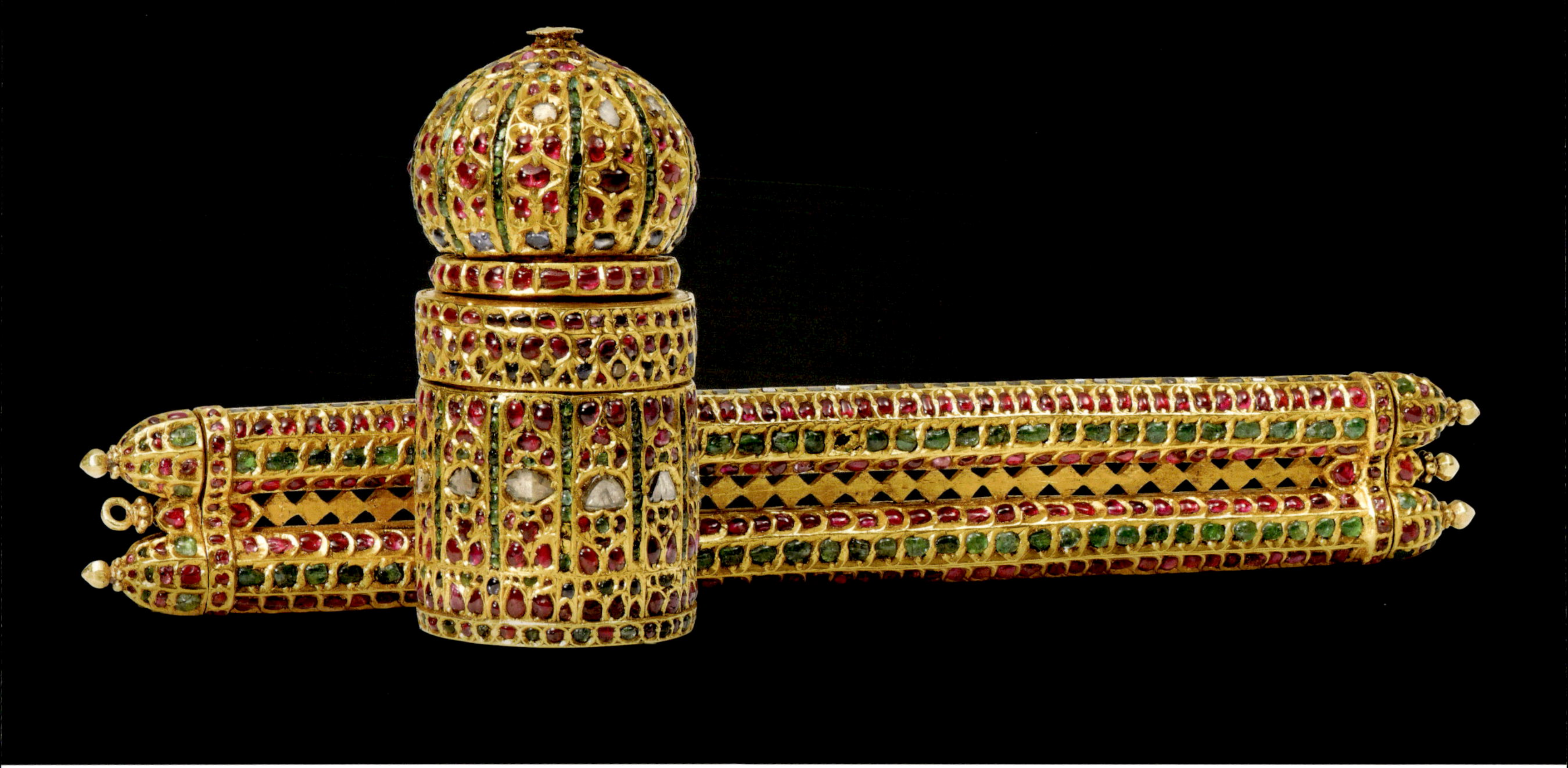

36

Pen case and inkwell

North India or Deccan, 1575–1600. Gold set with rubies, emeralds, diamonds, sapphires, lac
CAT. 72

This spectacular object is a unique surviving example of a gold gem-set State pen case and inkwell (*david-i daulat*). Jeweled pen cases and inkwells were presented as signs of the highest distinction, a practice from the time of Emperor Jahangir (r. 1605–1627) extending into the reign of Emperor Aurangzeb (r. 1658–1707). They were worn in the sashes of these high-ranking courtiers (see fig. 33) The elaborate *kundan* settings feature small claws and cusped rosettes securing gemstones that cover the entire surface. This object reflects the hybrid nature of the Mughal court in that the form of this pen case is based on an Iranian shape known since the early sixteenth century, whereas the decoration of the underside of the inkwell is decorated with the image of a sacred bird (*hamsa*), a symbol of learning and the vehicle of the Hindu deity Sarasvati, the goddess of writers and poets.

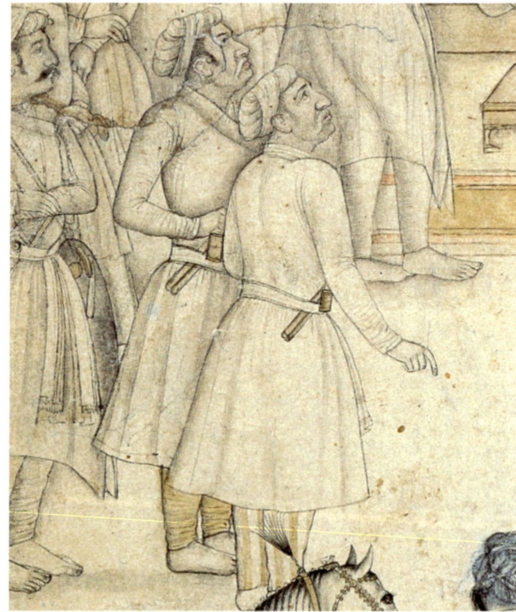

FIG. 33. Detail of The submission of Rana Amar Singh of Mewar to Prince Khurram, India, 1620–1628. Tinted brush and ink drawing on paper, 11 × 7⅜ in. (28.1 × 18.7 cm). The Trustees of the Chester Beatty Library, Dublin, CBL In 60.6

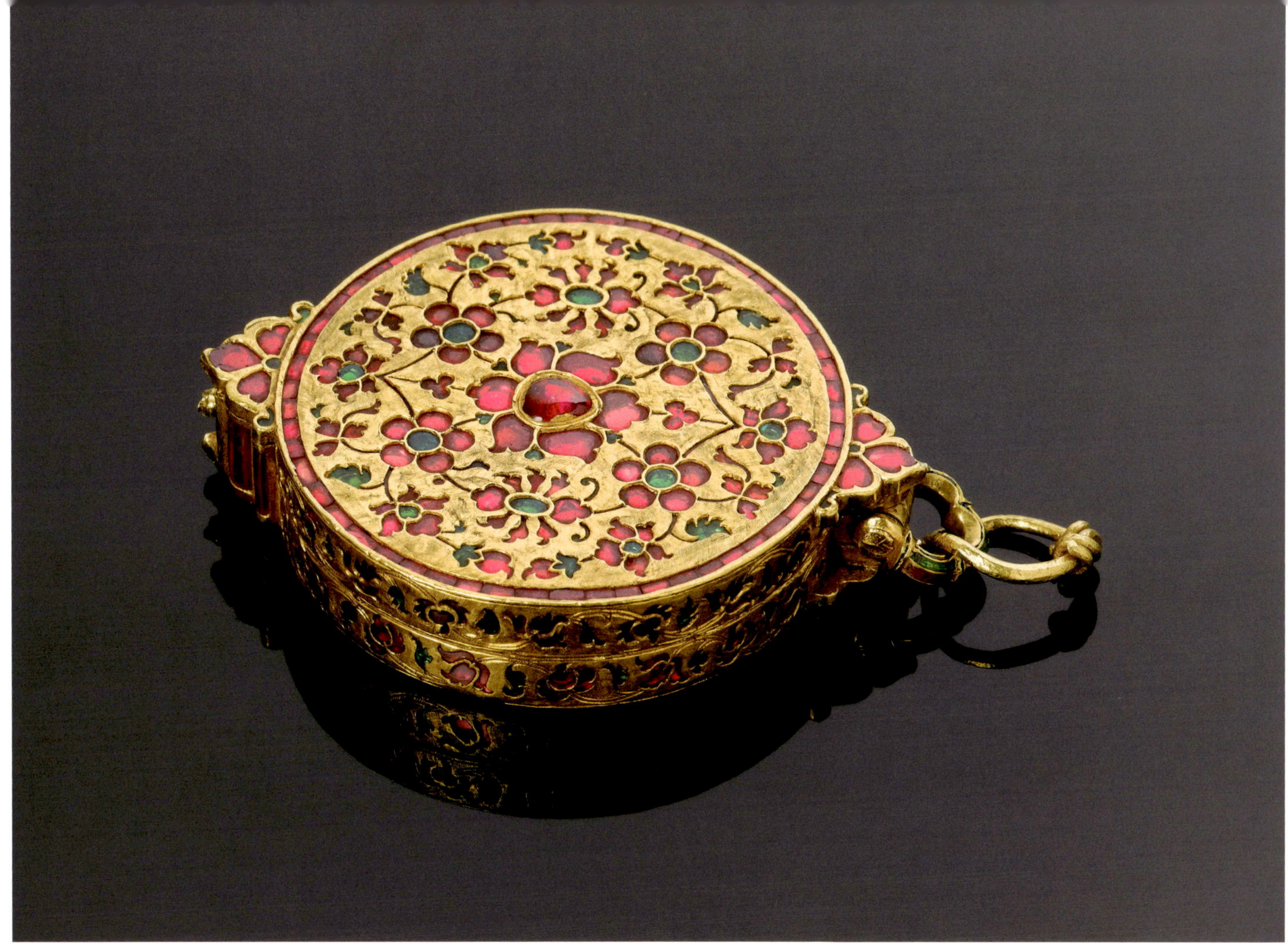

37

Locket pendant

North India or Deccan, 1575–1625. Gold with rubies, emeralds, enamel. Inscribed in Persian inside with the weight: *9 tola, 6 masha (?) ya*

CAT. 73

The decoration on this locket can be compared to floral designs on early seventeenth-century buildings, including the gateway of the tomb of Akbar at Sikandra, which was completed in 1614. The inscription gives the weight of the piece, suggesting that it was originally in the Mughal Imperial Treasury. This provenance is supported by the high quality of the goldsmiths' work, in which sheets of gold are laid over the gems and cut to the shape of each stone.

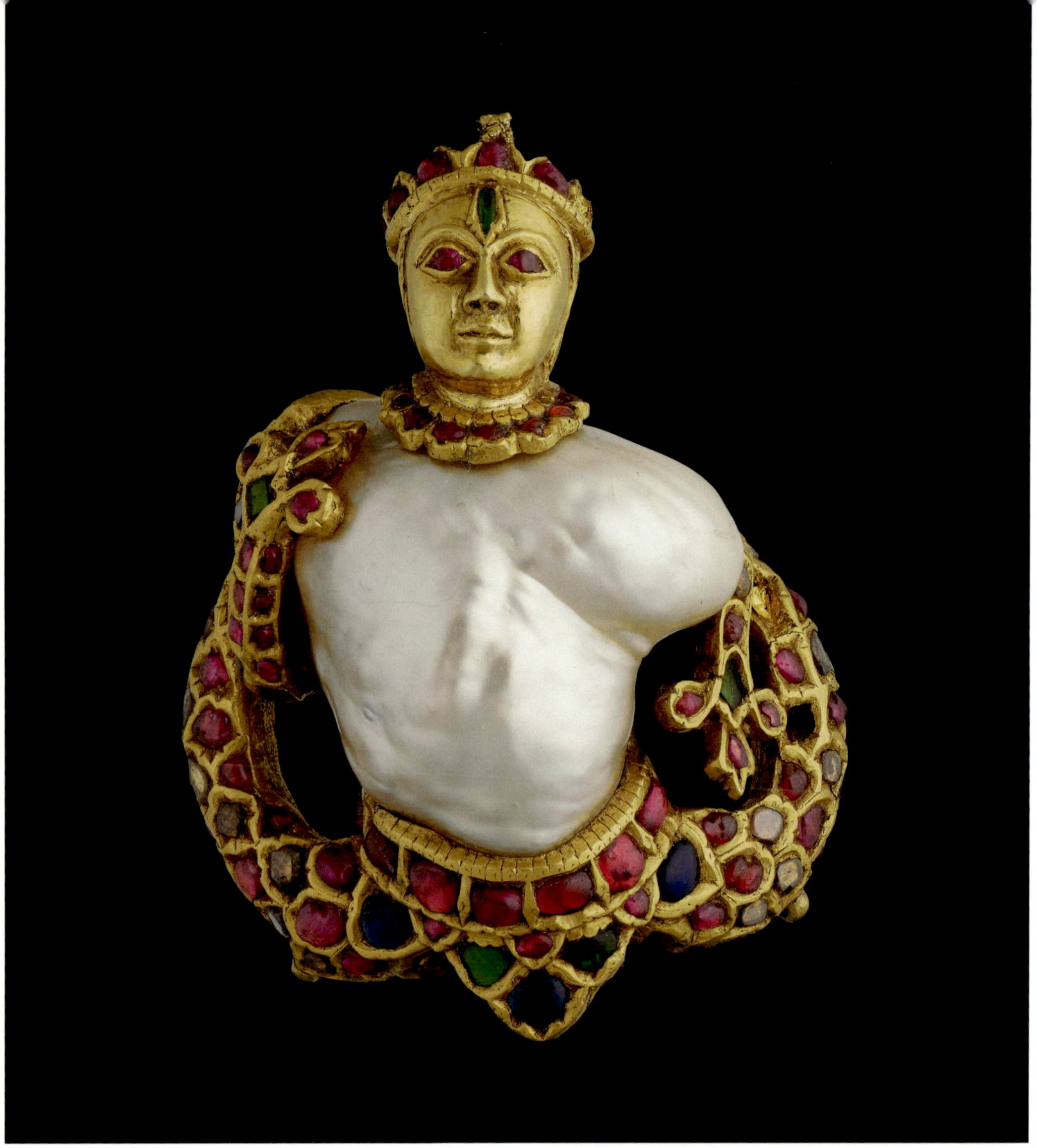

38

Pendant (obverse and reverse)

India, ca. 1575–1625. Baroque pearl, gold set with rubies, emeralds, sapphires, glass, enamel, on a lac core

CAT. 74

Although made in India, this rare pendant is inspired by European Renaissance jewelry, in which baroque pearls were used as the body or torso for figurative compositions often depicting mythical creatures. In this hybrid piece, a substantial lustrous pearl has been combined with gems, gold, and glass in typical Indian *kundan* settings. With its intertwining tail, the figure itself is likely to be a snake god, or *Nagadevata*.

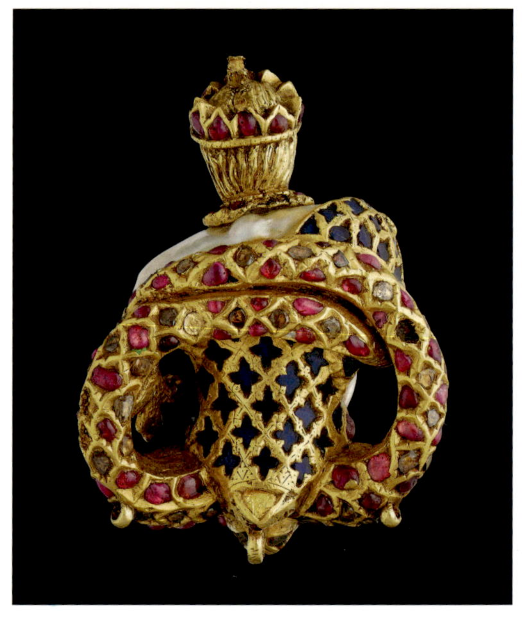

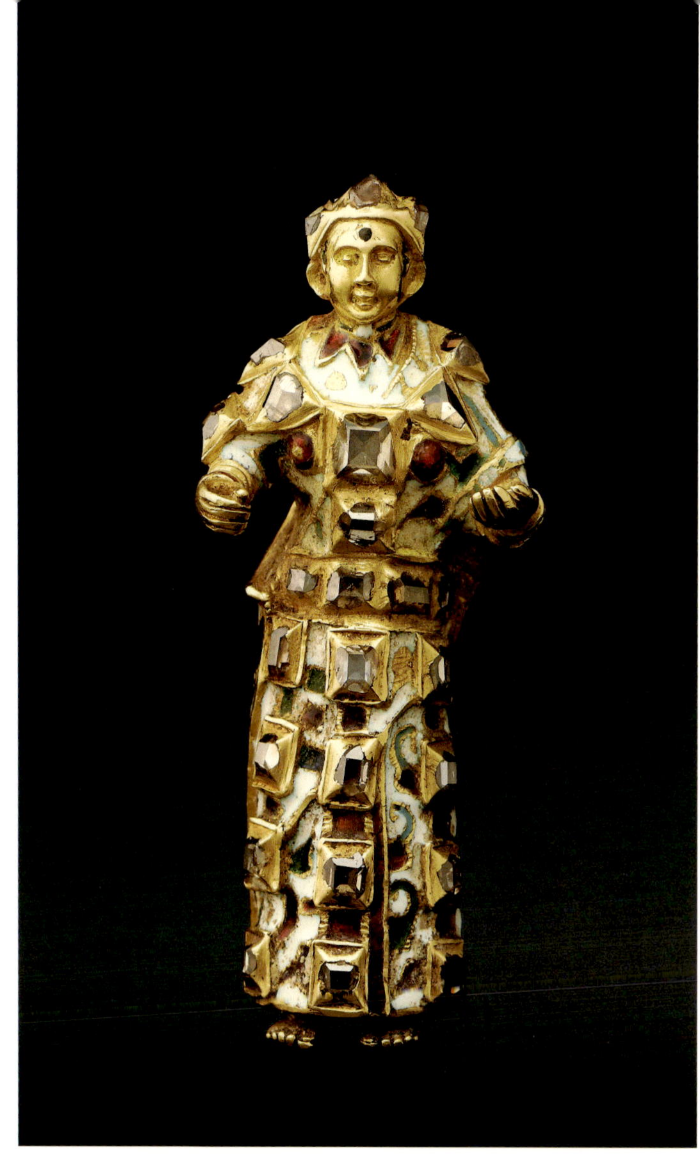

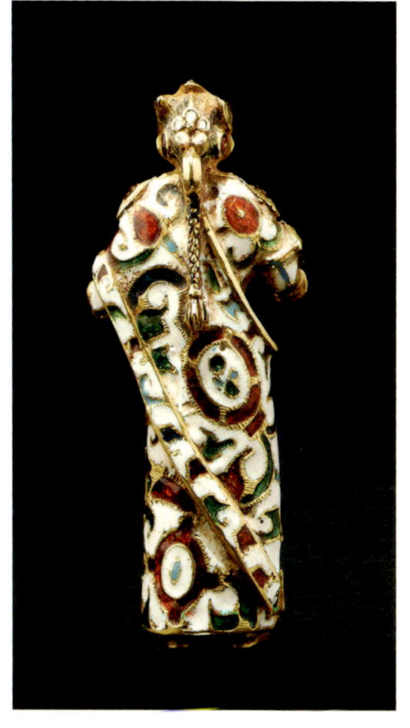

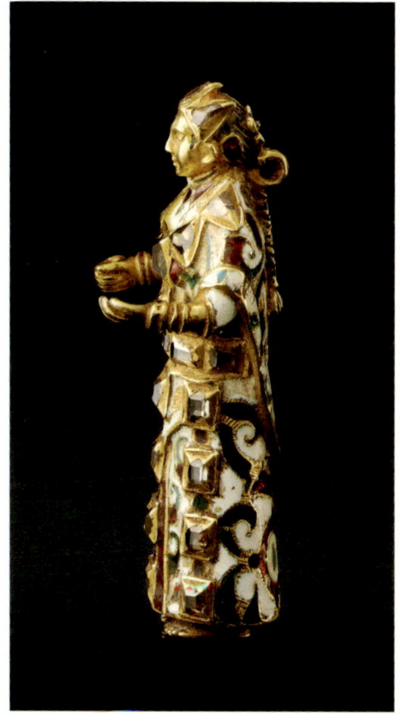

39

Figure of a female saint (obverse, reverse, and side)
Goa or North India, 1625–1660. Gold set with diamonds, decorated with enamel around a lac core. Inscribed in Persian: *2 tola, 7 masha*
CAT. 75

This *kundan*-set gold figure of an unidentified female saint reveals European influence, while the gem settings confirm that it was made in India. Emperor Akbar showed considerable interest in Christian iconography, and under imperial patronage works of art were created in which Indian techniques were sometimes married with objects made in Western styles or forms. The open-armed posture of this figure derives from Christian devotional sculpture, while the garment and hairstyle are typically Indian.

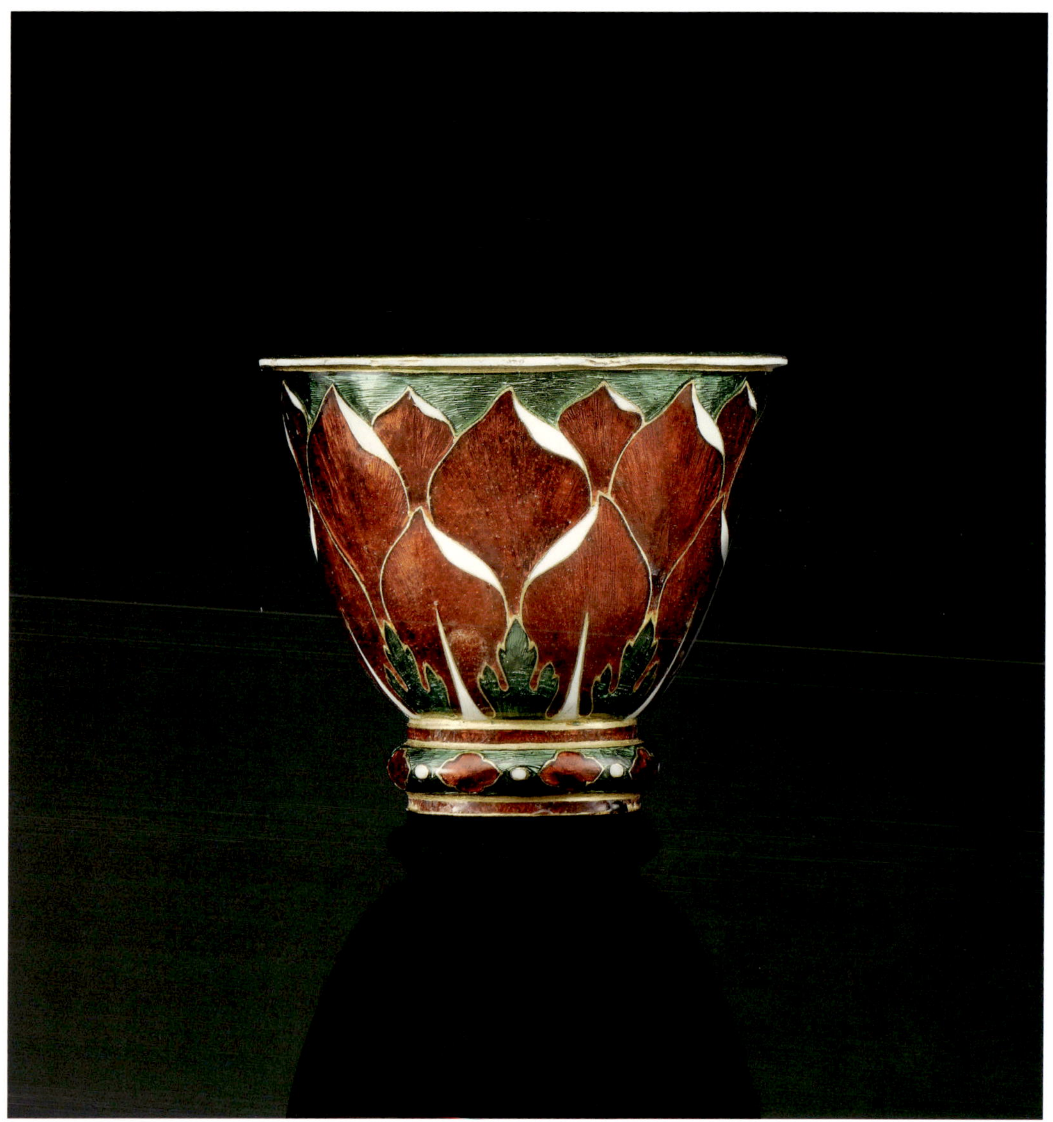

40

Cup

North India, ca. 1635–1640. Gold, enamel

CAT. 76

Cups of similar small size and form appear in seventeenth-century miniature paintings and seem to have been made in gold, jade, and ceramic, as well as carved out of single pieces of gemstone. Such vessels were used for drinks, including a liquor of opium mixed with fruit. This cup is an outstanding example of Mughal enamel work, the design of overlapping petals framed by fine fillets around the rim and foot.

41

Wand fittings

North India, ca. 1650. Gold, enamel around a lac core
CAT. 77

These two enameled gold fittings were originally mounted on a wand or staff of office, the central section of which is missing. Wands of this type were held by senior officials at the Mughal court. The finial is in the form of a parrot's head. The confident depiction of flowers and cloud bands can be compared to the architectural decoration dating from the first half of the seventeenth century, as well as to other gold and enameled objects of the period.

42

Durbar set

North India, 1750–1775. Silver gilt

CAT. 84

When presented at gatherings, this durbar set would have looked magnificent as part of the formalities of hospitality at eighteenth-century Indian courts. It comprises trays and vessels for offering delicacies and *paan*, rosewater sprinklers, stands for perfume, and components of a hookah. Close examination reveals that the pieces were assembled from multiple parts rather than made from single ingots of silver.

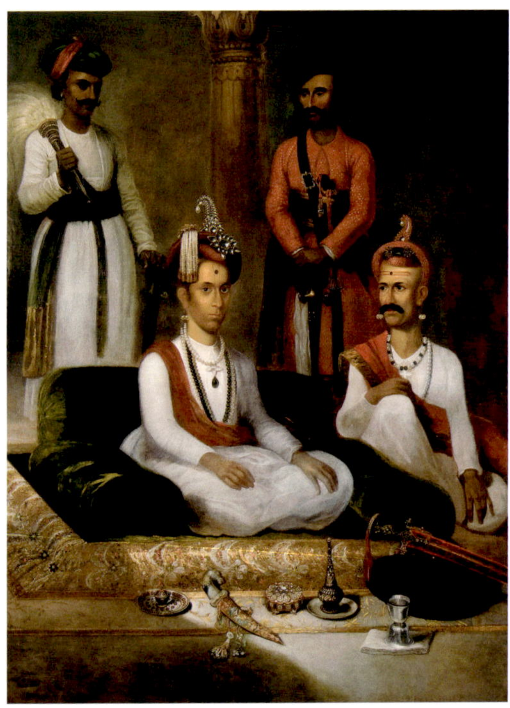

FIG. 34. James Wales, detail of *Madhu Rao Narayan, the Maratha Peshwa with Nana Fadnavis and Attendants, Poona*, 1792. Oil on canvas, 90⅛ × 74¾ in. (229 × 190 cm). Royal Asiatic Society of Great Britain and Ireland, London, RAS 01.014

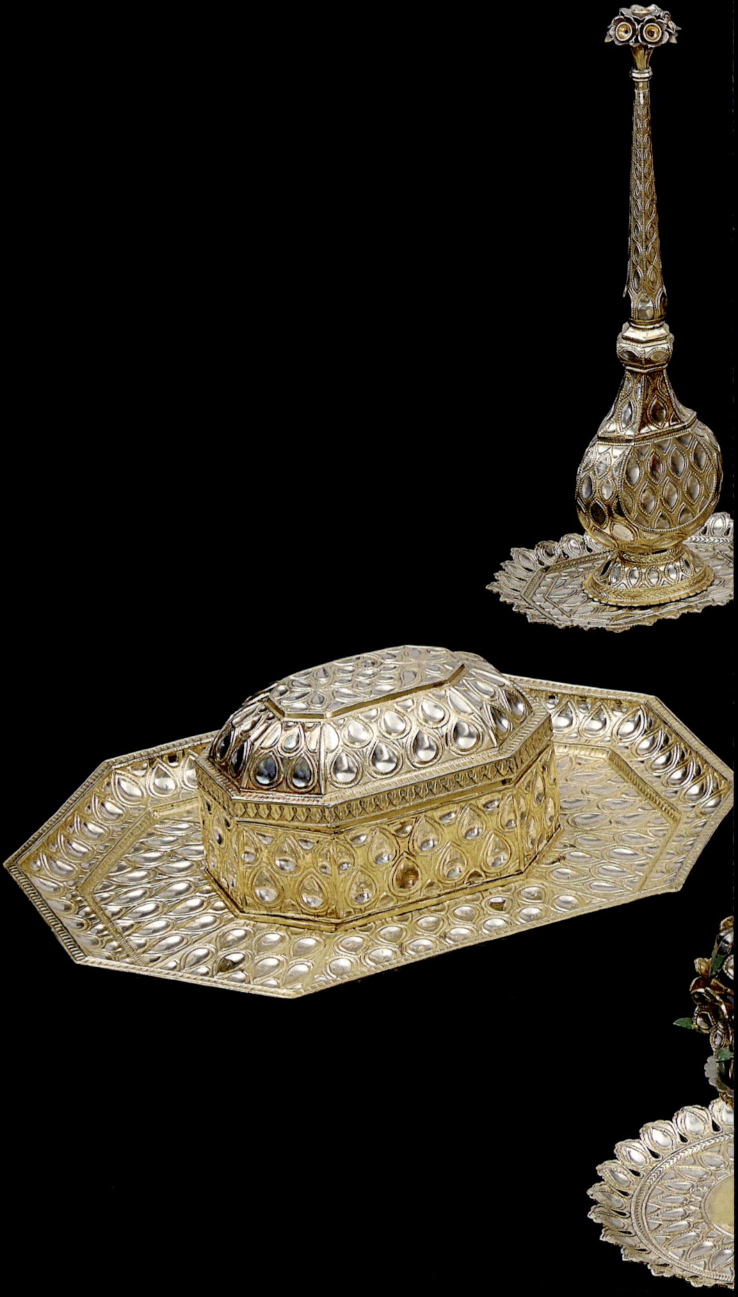

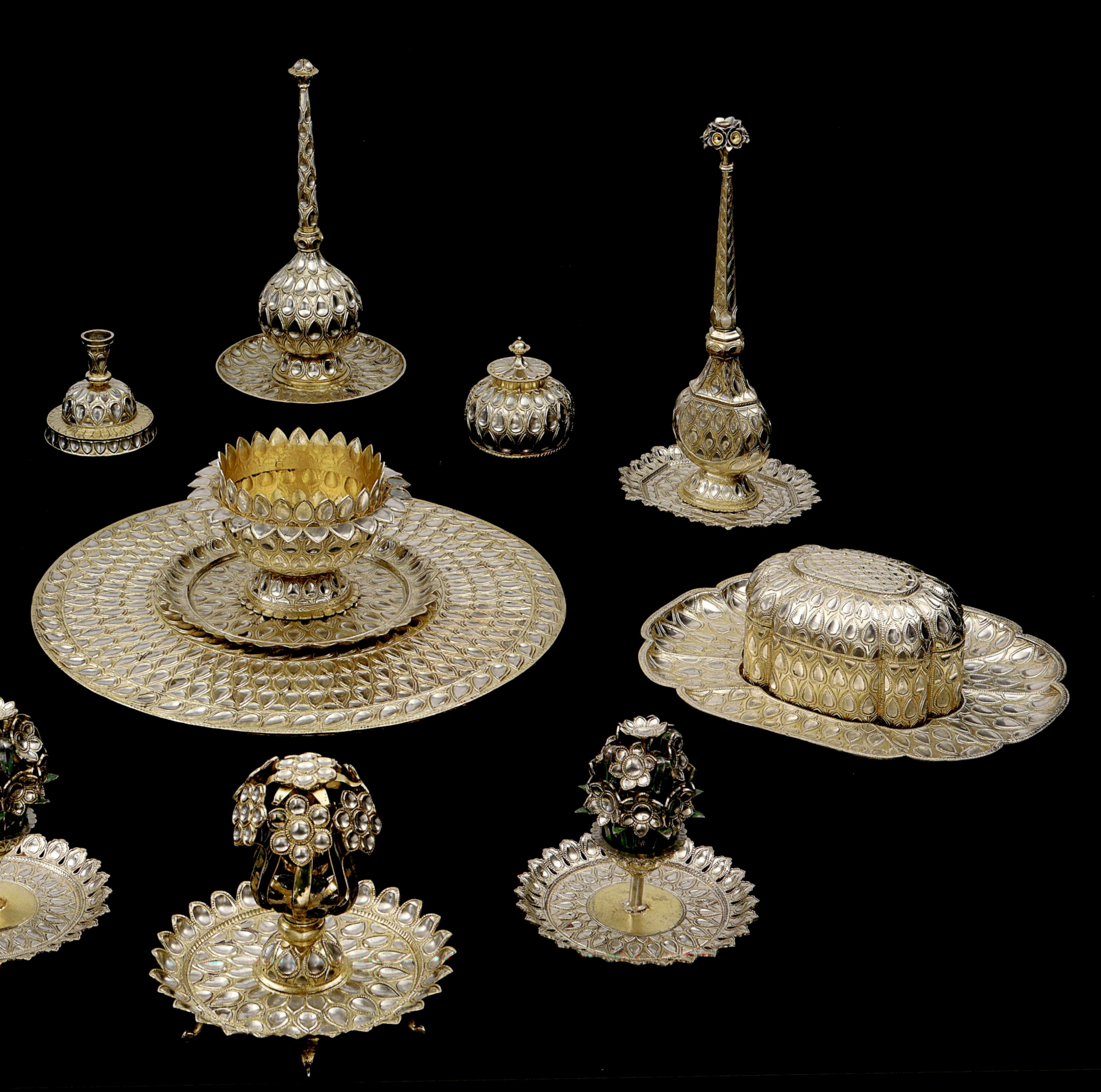

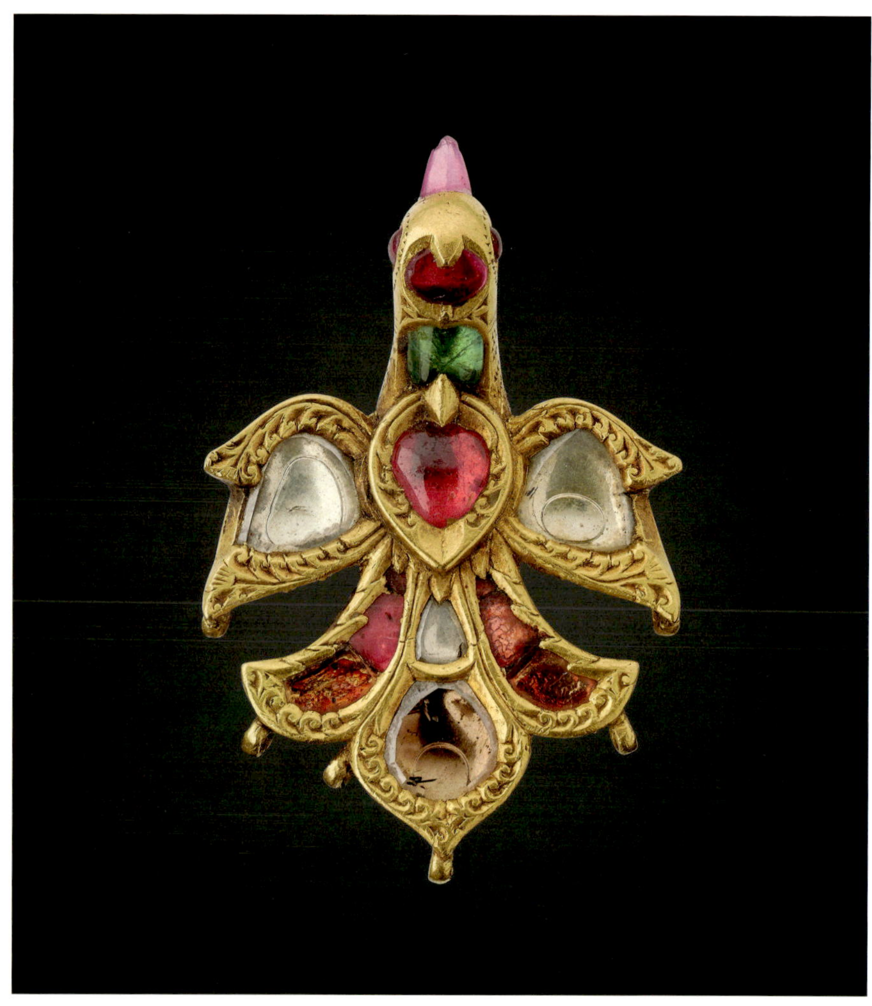

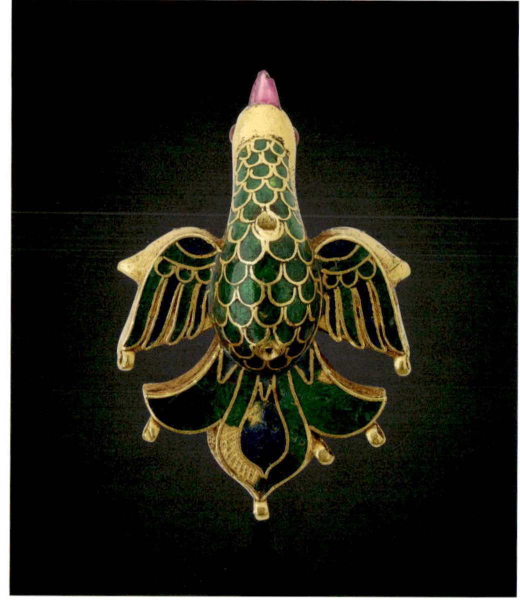

43

Bird pendant (obverse and reverse)

Deccan (?), ca. 1700. Gold, diamonds, rubies, emeralds, enamel, lac core

CAT. 83

This bird pendant would have been worn on the chest, hanging from a gold or pearl chain or a suspension cord. While the front is inset with precious stones, the back is decorated with an unusual cloisonné technique seldom seen in Indian enamel work. The green-and-blue palette combined with the carved *kundan* setting suggests that it was made in the Deccan.

44

Rosewater sprinkler

North India, 1675–1725. Gold set with rubies, emeralds, pearls. Inscribed in Persian on the base: *64 tola, 4 masha / 64 tola, 2 masha*
CAT. 81

In an Indian courtly context, rosewater was sprinkled over guests at the end of a meal or a visit as a sign of favor and hospitality. This gem-encrusted bottle was probably made in the Mughal imperial workshops; the inscription of the bottle's weight on its foot suggests that it was a Treasury object. A related bottle was taken from the Mughal Treasury by the Iranian warrior Nadir Shah when he plundered Delhi in 1739.

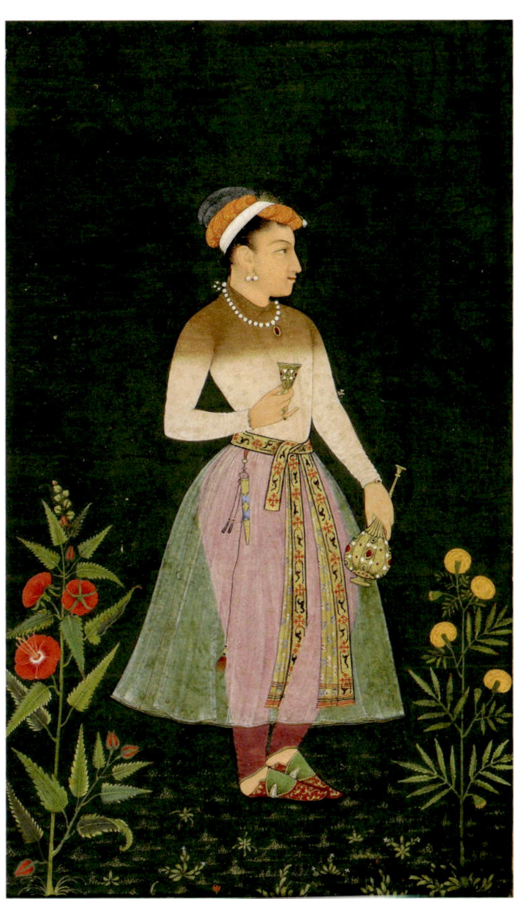

FIG. 35. Portrait of a youth standing between flowers holding a jeweled bottle and cup, detail of a folio from the Dara Shikoh Album, North India, 1630–1640. Opaque watercolor, 5⅞ × 3½ in. (14.9 × 8.9 cm). British Library, London

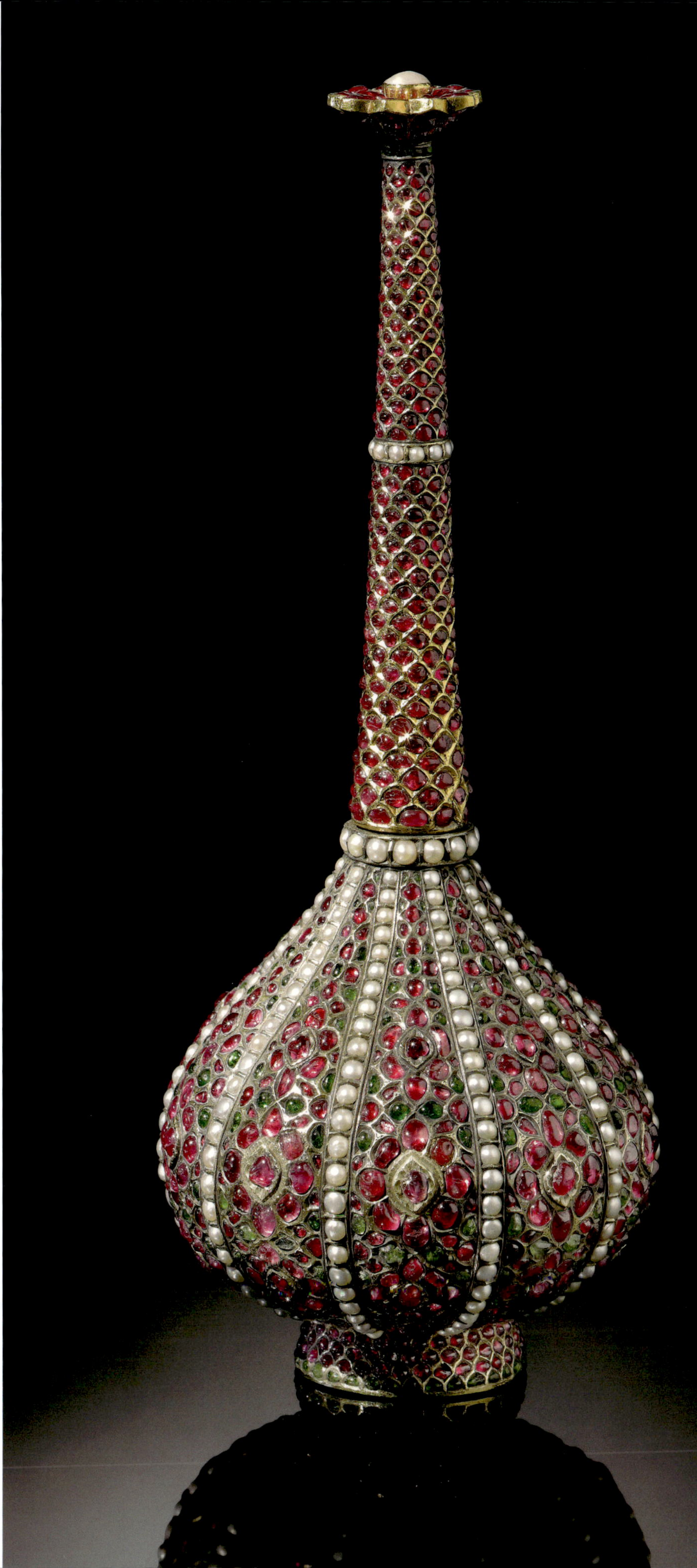

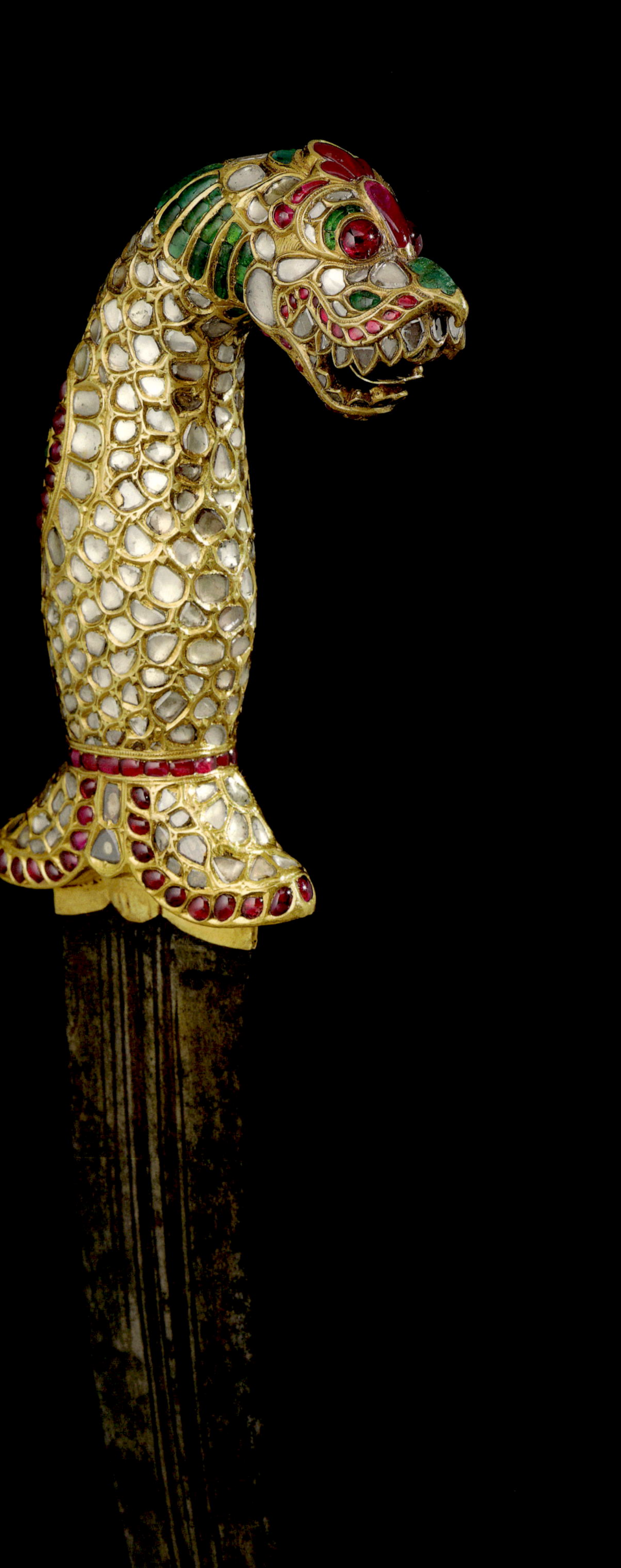

45
Dagger

Tanjore or Mysore, 1790–1810. Gold set with diamonds, rubies, and emeralds on a lac core, steel blade
CAT. 93

The hilt of this dagger is in the form of a *yali*, a terrifying mythical beast with bulging eyes and long sharp teeth. Massive *yalis* carved from stone often form brackets that support the roof of temples in South India. The motif is also used for smaller furniture fittings in ivory and wood as well as for the hilts of weapons.

46

Punch dagger

North India or Deccan, 1680–1720.
Gold, diamonds, rubies, emeralds,
steel blade. 16½ × 3⅝ (42.1 × 9.4 cm)
CAT. 82

This punch dagger (*katar*) is characterized by parallel side bars, horizontal grips, and a triangular blade. Its form is first mentioned in Indian literature in the mid-eleventh century and is illustrated in a Deccani manuscript dated 1570. Mughal emperors gave jeweled *katars* as symbols of honor to favored courtiers; in addition, the gems on this particular punch dagger suggest it was a presentation piece, made in the late seventeenth or early eighteenth century.

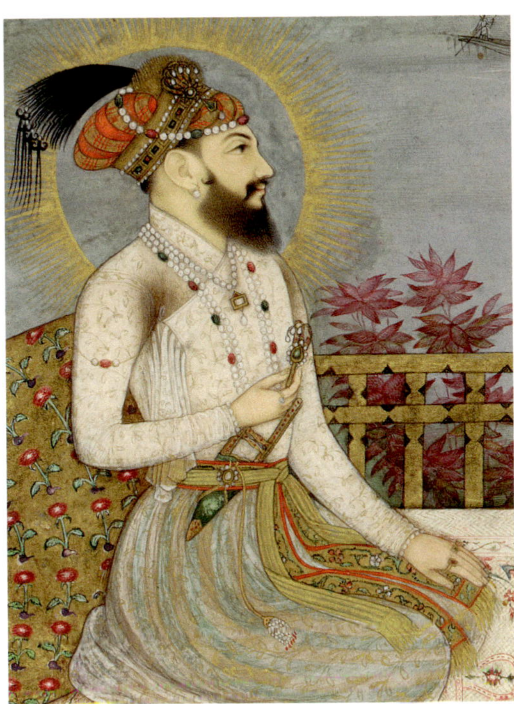

FIG. 36. Emperor Shah Jahan examines jewels by the Dal Lake, Kashmir (detail), ca. 1645–1650. Gouache on paper, 7⅞ × 5 in. (20.1 × 12.8 cm). Bodleian Libraries, the University of Oxford, Given to the Bodleian by Francis Douce, MS. Douce Or. a. 1, fol. 23a

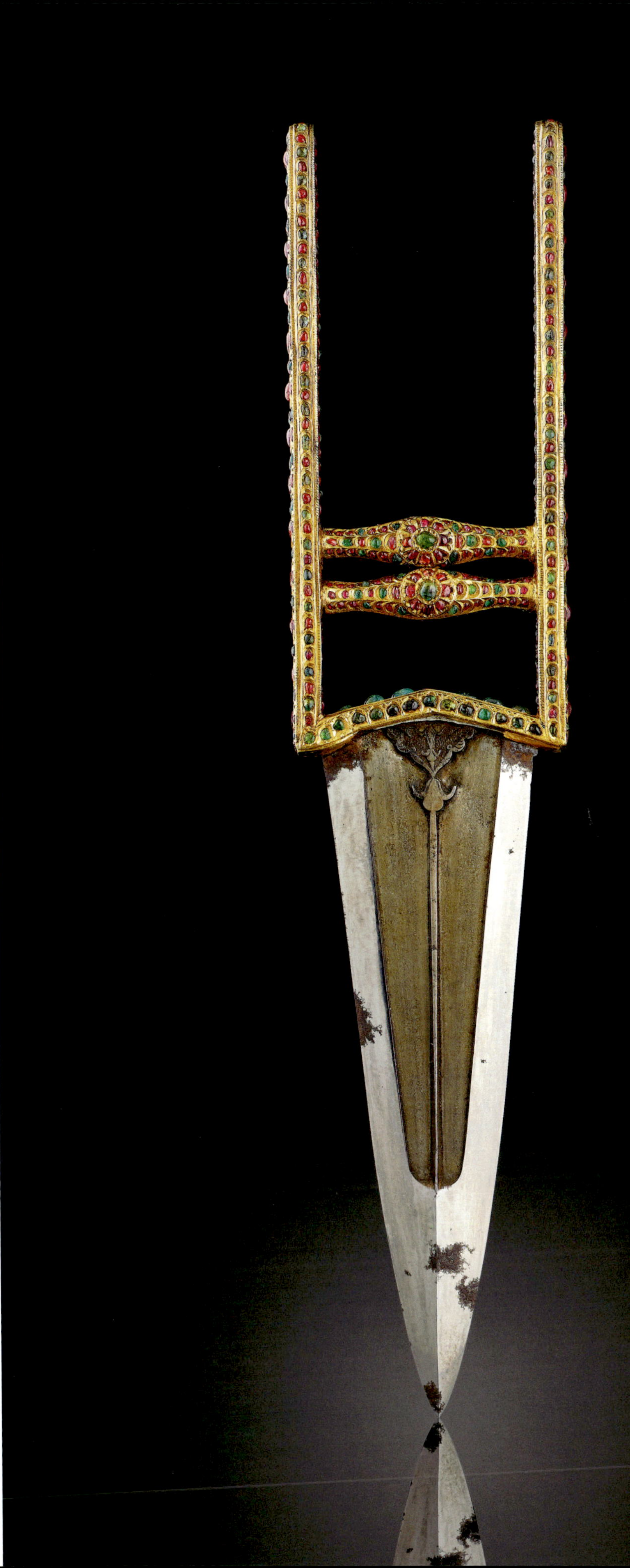

THE PEACOCK THRONE

It should be stated that the Great Mogul has seven magnificent thrones, one wholly covered with diamonds, the others with rubies, emeralds, or pearls.

Jean-Baptiste Tavernier, *Les Six Voyages de Jean-Baptiste Tavernier*, 1676

The Peacock Throne was the most splendid (and legendary) of a series of gold and jeweled thrones created for the Mughal court. These thrones were made for the rulers of India as a mark of prestige and an outward demonstration of divine right in the golden age of the Mughal Empire. Emperor Jahangir (r. 1605–1627), who was fascinated by European art and technology, employed a French goldsmith at his court, Augustin Hiriart (1585–1632) from Bordeaux. Hiriart, who traveled to India in search of new patrons, designed Jahangir's throne and also provided the design for a jeweled throne for Emperor Shah Jahan (r. 1628–1658) that was unrealized prior to Hiriart's sudden death in 1632.[1]

The new jeweled throne for Shah Jahan was supplied by Sa'ida-ye (Said) Gilani, an Iranian poet and calligrapher turned goldsmith. Seven years in the making, the Peacock Throne utilized such vast amounts of gold and gemstones that it was reportedly the most magnificent example of a jeweled goldsmith's work ever created. It was inaugurated in 1635 for the emperor, who was famously the builder of the Taj Mahal. With references to the Throne of Solomon—and, correspondingly, good kingship—through its jeweled gold decoration, the throne was placed under a jeweled canopy surrounded by a fringe of pearls and was supported by twelve enameled columns. Set on the roof were two enameled and jeweled peacocks, from which the throne's name was later taken. According to varying accounts, one of the peacocks was set with the enormous Koh-i-Noor diamond, the greatest jewel from the Imperial Treasury. Celebrated as one of the greatest Mughal treasures, the Peacock Throne was looted by the ruler of Persia, Nadir Shah (1688–1747), after he invaded India and sacked Delhi in 1739. Shah took the throne back with him to Iran, where it disappeared. The Peacock Throne is presumed to have been dismantled for its precious materials by the time of the assassination of Nadir Shah in 1747, fomenting a legend of spectacular opulence that survives to the present day.

NOTE

1. Susan Stronge, "The Sublime Thrones of the Mughal Emperors of Hindustan," *Jewellery Studies* 10 (2004): 52–62.

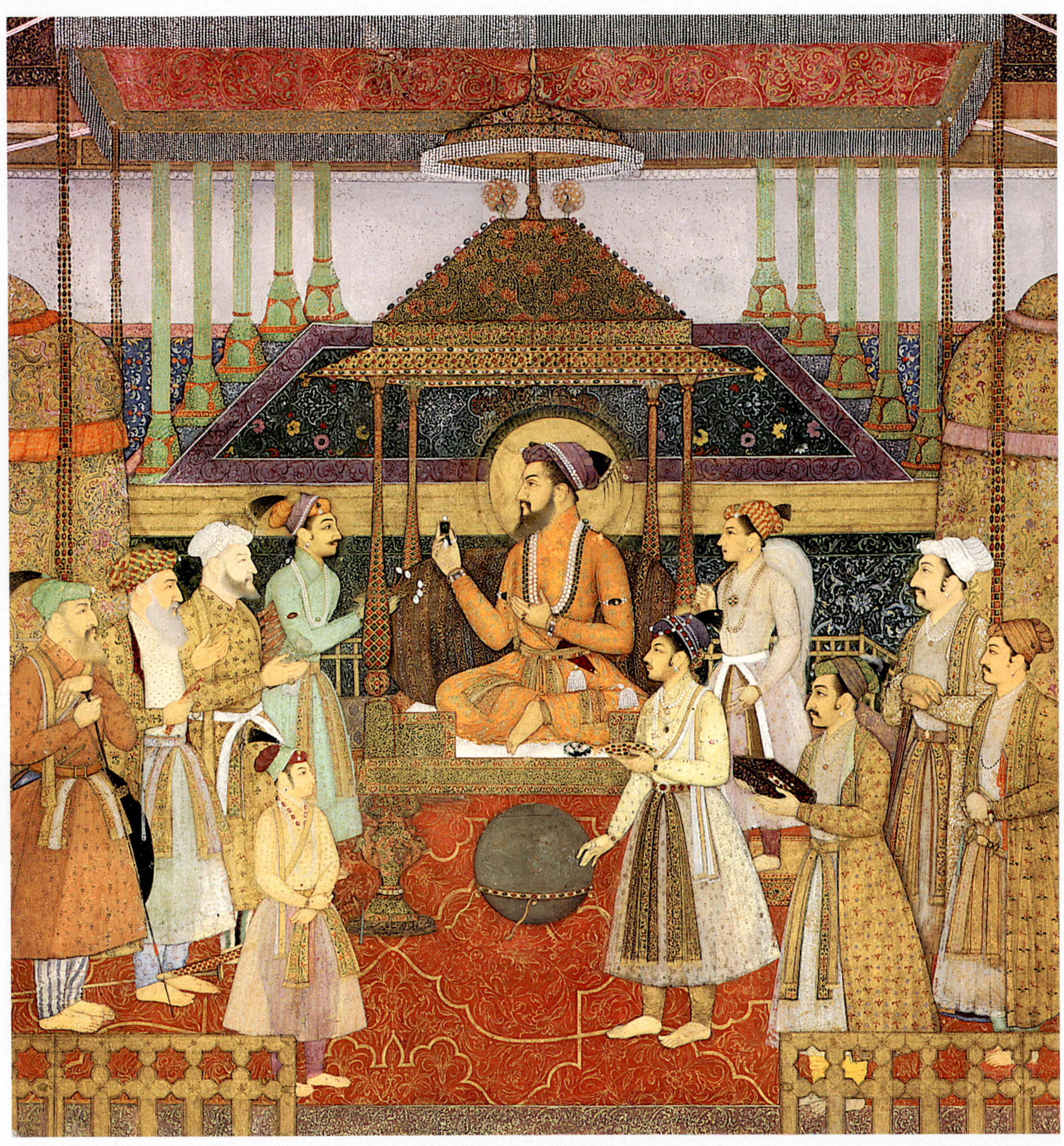

FIG. 37. Abid, son of Aqa Reza, The Emperor Shah Jahan on the Peacock Throne, detail of a folio from the *Padshahnama* (*Histories of the Reign of the King of the World*), 1640. Opaque watercolor and gold on paper, mounted as an album page, 14⅜ × 9¾ in. (36.7 × 25 cm). San Diego Museum of Art, USA, Edwin Binney 3rd Collection, 1990.352

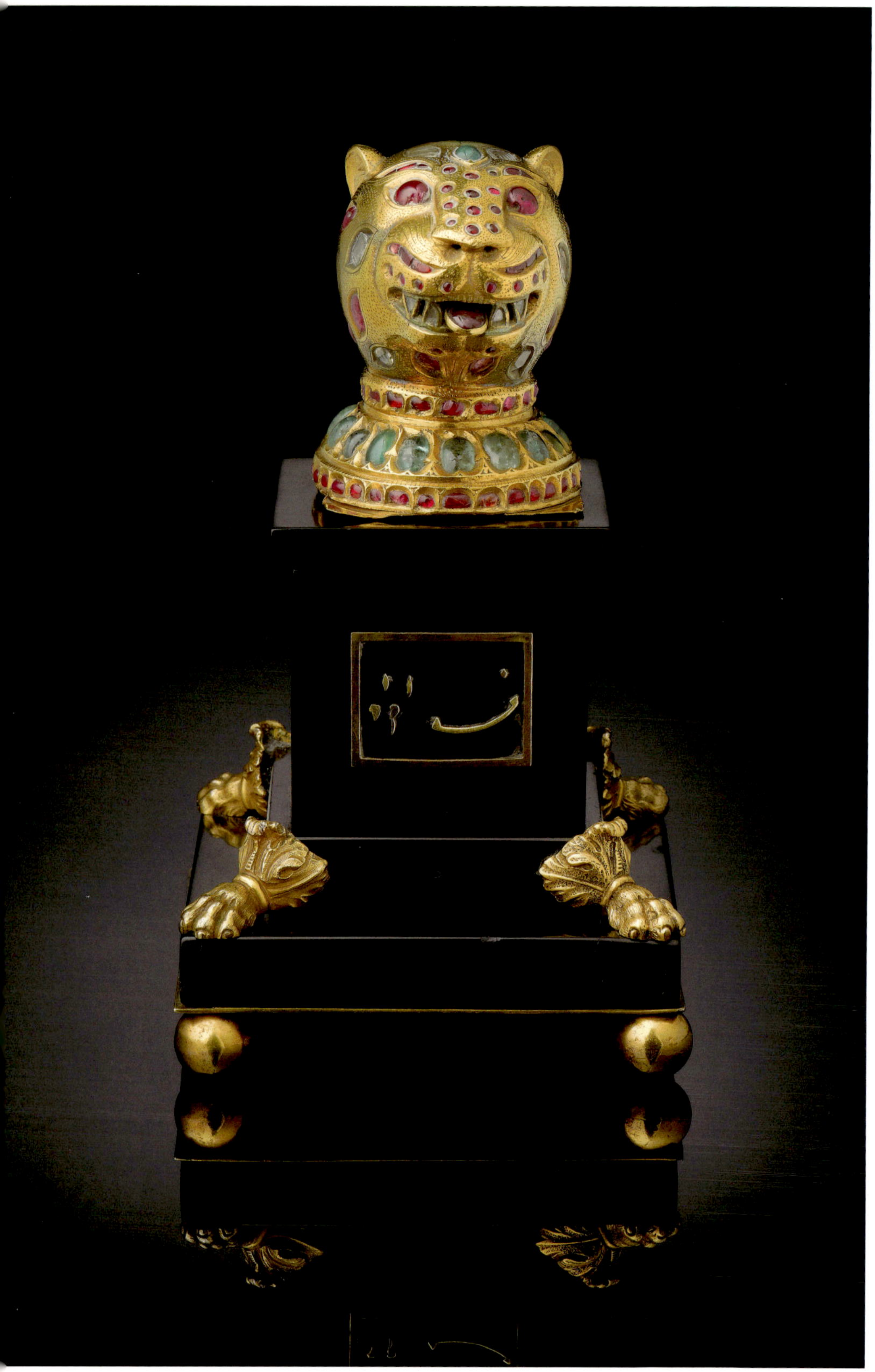

47

Finial from Tipu Sultan's throne

Mysore, ca. 1787–1793; plinth: ca. 1800.
Gold set with rubies, emeralds, and diamonds, lac, black marble plinth, with gilt metal
CAT. 85

This is one of eight tiger's-head finials from a gold throne commissioned by Tipu Sultan, ruler of Mysore, a fierce enemy of the British in their efforts to exercise control over South India. Accounts of its appearance vary (see fig. 38), but contemporary chroniclers agree that the throne featured the tiger motif, which is the hallmark of the ruler's possessions. It consisted of a polygonal base on tiger supports surrounded by railings and mounted by a canopy with a jeweled huma bird. Completed in 1793, the throne was broken up following Tipu's defeat by British forces at the Battle of Seringapatam only six years later. Two throne components—an encrusted bird finial and a gold tiger head—entered the British Royal Collection, while the finials were dispersed into different collections.

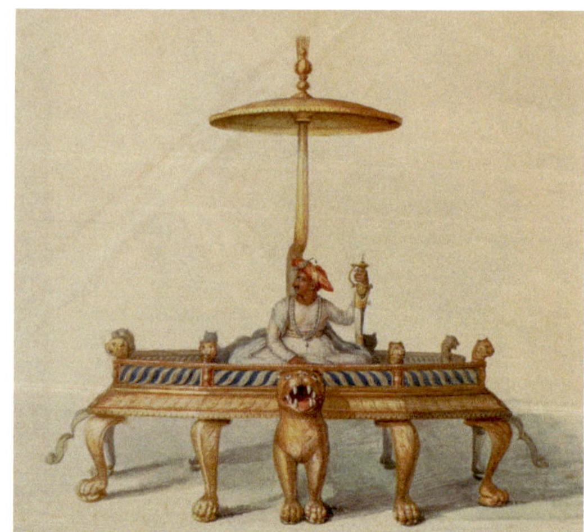

FIG. 38. Anna Tonelli, detail of *Tipu Sahib, Sultan of Mysore (1749–1799), Enthroned*, 1800. Watercolor on paper, 14¼ × 21 in. (35.5 × 53.2 cm). Clive Museum at Powis Castle and Garden, Powys, Wales (POW.D.67)

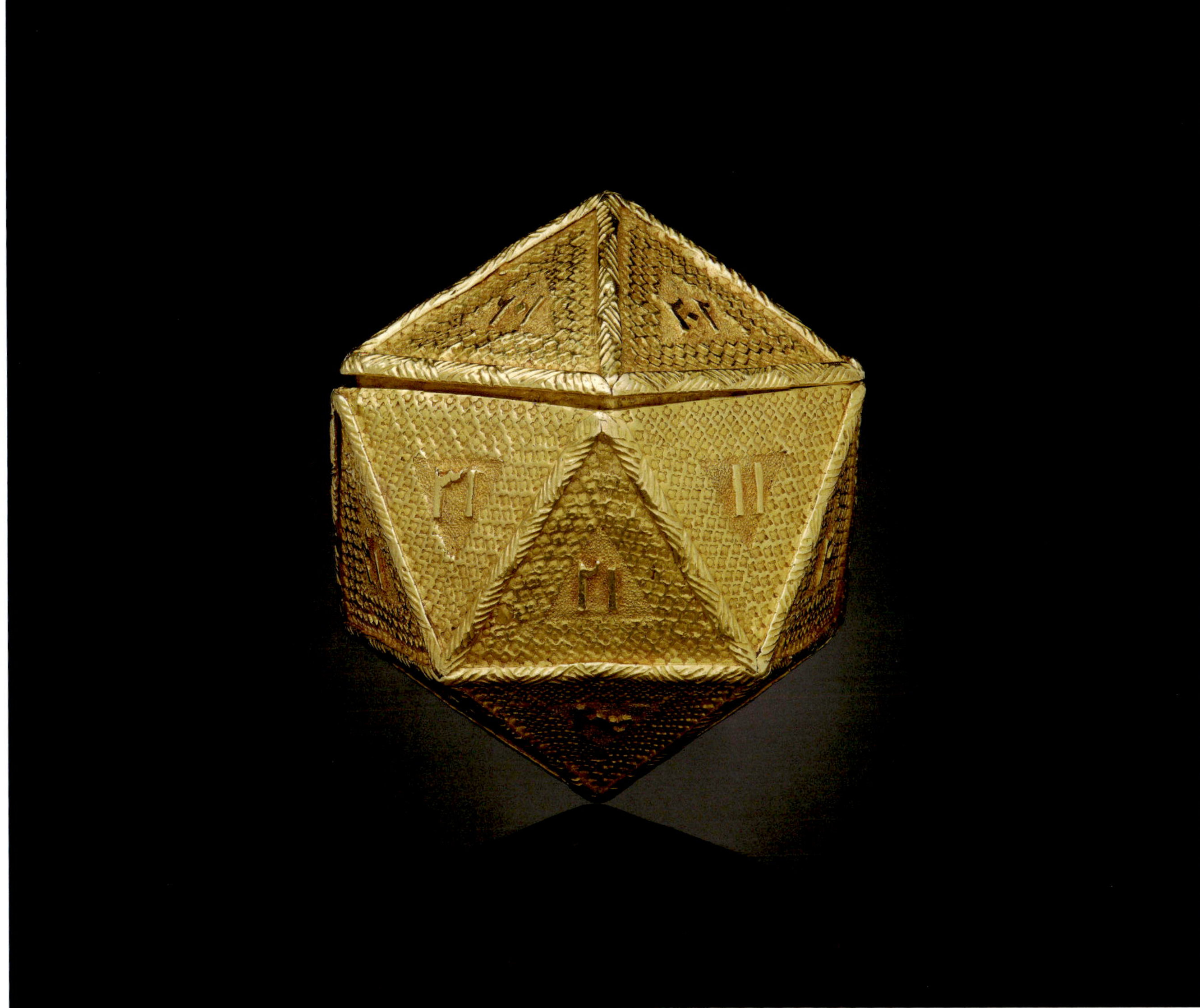

48

Tipu Sultan's magic box

Mysore, 1780–1790. Gold. Inscribed: *11 | 20 | 21 | 32 | 42 | 51 | 61 | 71 | 81 | 101 | 201 | 301 | 401 | 601 | 701 | 801 | 901 | 202*
CAT. 86

Each of the twenty faces of this icosahedron is decorated with a numeral. The twenty numbers appear to be unrelated to one another, although recent research has suggested that they represented mathematical calculations known to the ancient Greeks. Tipu owned a large library that included a number of scientific texts on mathematics and astronomy. The box originally contained two manuscript notes, one with a diagram of the twenty sides and the other indicating that "this twenty-sided golden box was found in the treasury of Tippoo Sahib at the taking of Seringapatam on 4 May 1799."

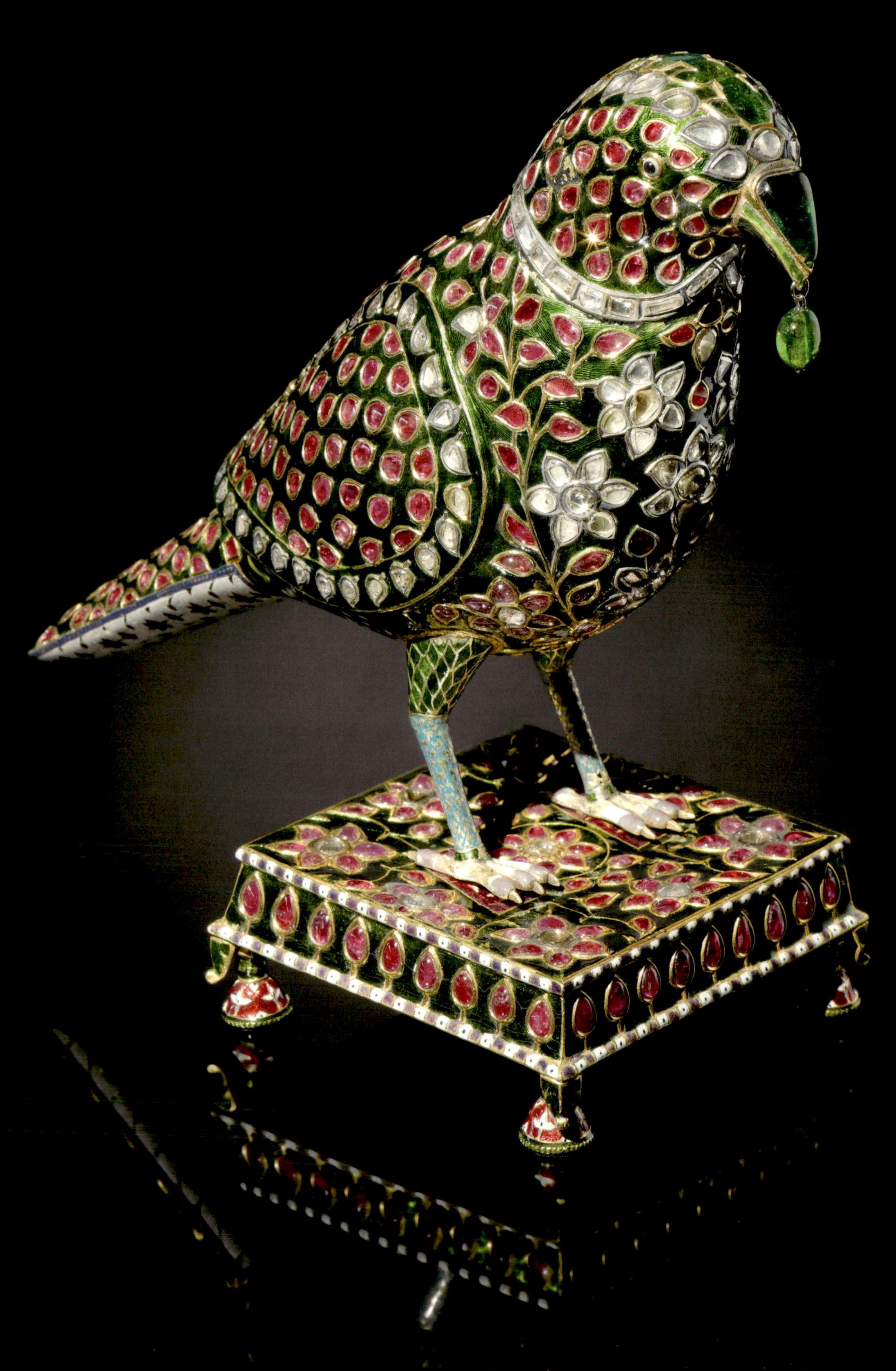

49 *(opposite)*

Parrot

Parrot: Hyderabad, 1775–1825; base: North India, 1700–1750. Gold, rubies, diamonds, emeralds, lac
CAT. 88

The mythical huma bird is an Iranian symbol, and according to legend, anyone on whom its shadow falls would become the ruler. Drawing on Iranian tradition at the Mughal court and its Successor States, birds were considered symbols of royalty. This example and cat. 89 are both believed to have been used as adornments around the throne of the Nizams of Hyderabad. The differences between the bird and the base shown here suggest that they were not conceived together: the former was made in the Deccan, the latter earlier in North India.

50

Rosewater sprinkler

North India or Deccan, 1755–1825. Gold, rubies, diamonds, emeralds, enamel
CAT. 90

The translucent green enamel suggests that this rosewater sprinkler was made in North India or the Deccan, while the floral panels and the settings indicate a late eighteenth- or early nineteenth-century date. It would have formed part of a group of ritual objects used at formal court durbar assemblies, during which honored guests would be sprinkled with rosewater and offered *paan*. Other items would have included containers for offerings, dishes, and a spittoon.

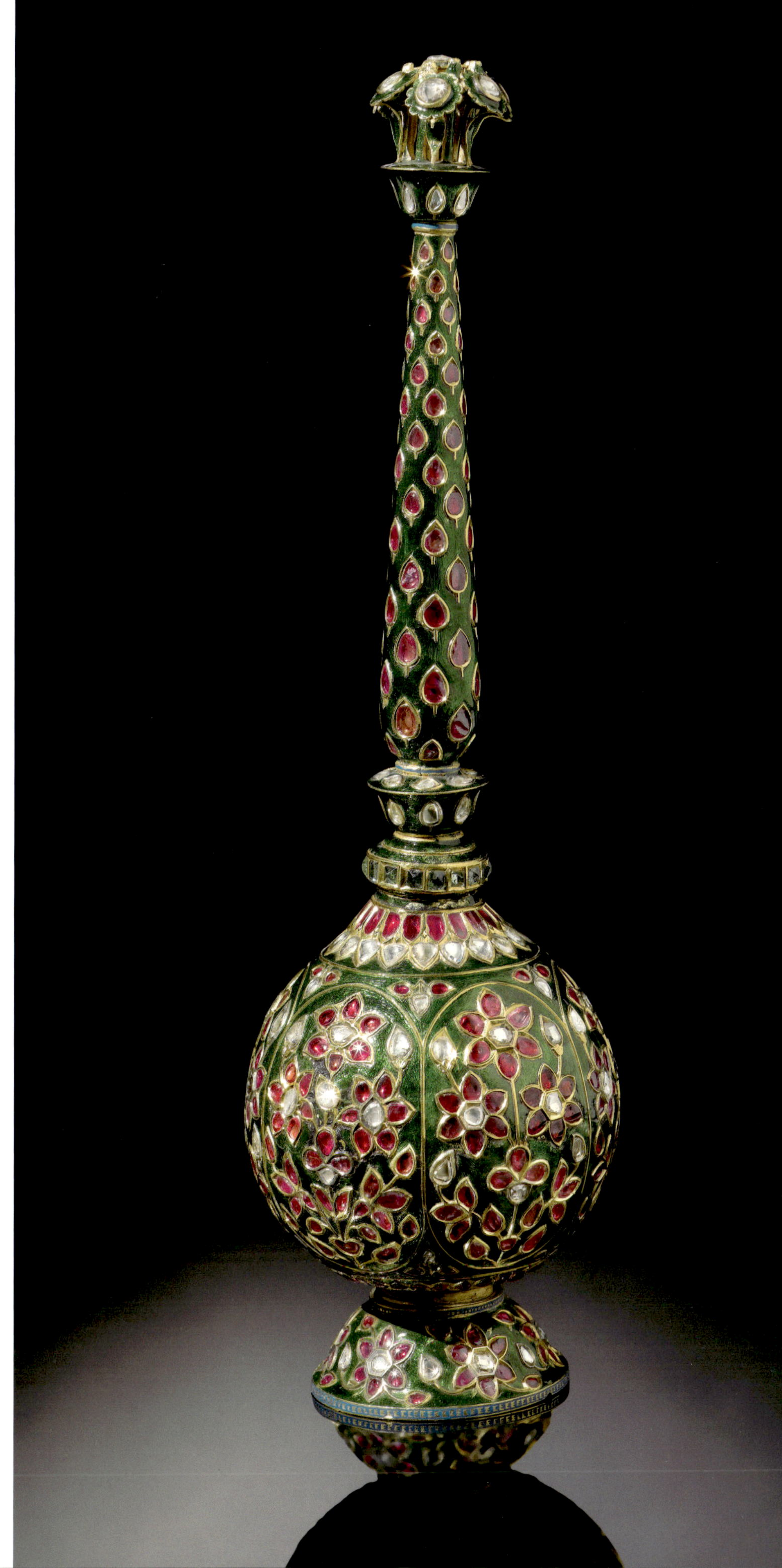

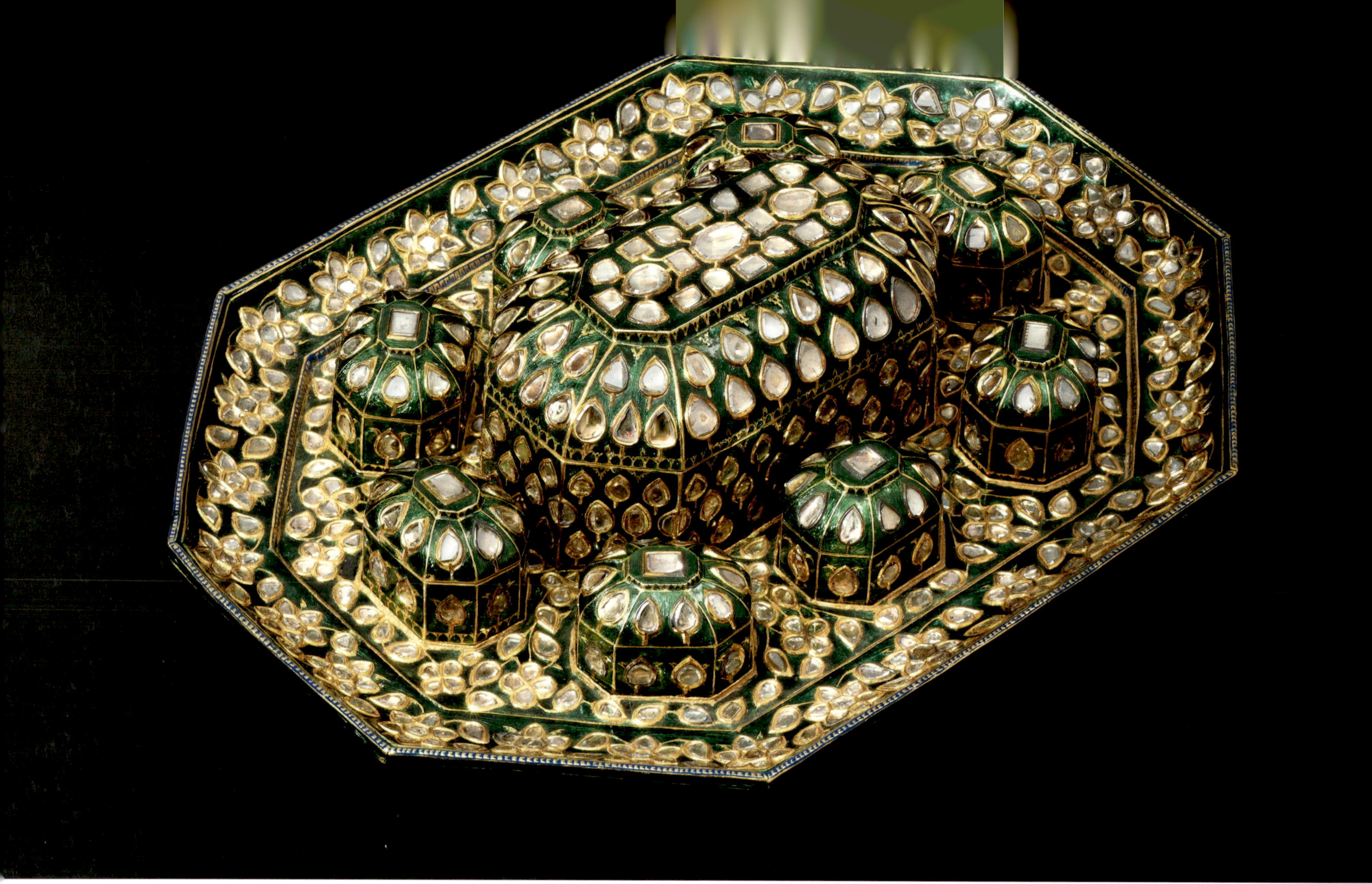

51

Container for *paan*

Hyderabad, 1760–1780. Gold, silver, diamonds, enamel, lac

CAT. 91

This set of boxes was used for containing *paan*, a digestive and mild stimulant composed of sliced areca nut, lime, and various spices, rolled together into an areca nut leaf. Eighteenth- and early nineteenth-century observers noted that the *paan* was always offered to guests as part of the ceremonies at a formal durbar assembly. Richly decorated containers such as these were especially meant for ritual purposes. The translucent green enamel, florets, and gem settings on this example suggest that it was made in Hyderabad.

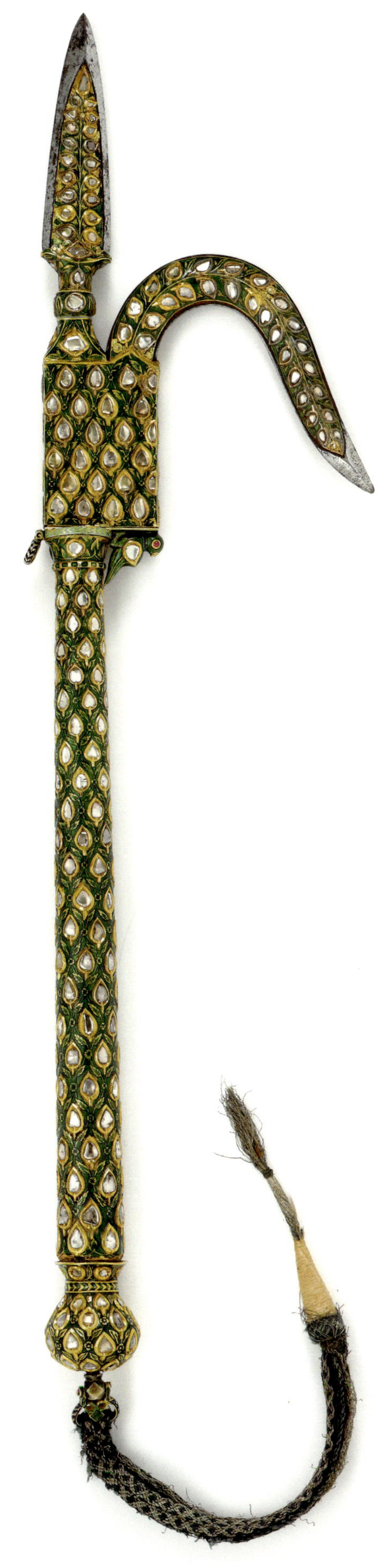

52

Elephant goad

North India, 1880–1900. Gold, steel, diamonds, rubies, enamel, silk, metal thread
CAT. 94

The practical function of the goad (*ankus*) was for the driver (*mahout*) to control the elephant. However, it also had a symbolic importance as an attribute of various Hindu deities, including the elephant-headed god Ganesh. Richly decorated examples such as this were used in formal royal processions, in which the elephant played a central role. This goad is assembled from six pieces: spear point, hook, plate between hook and shaft, shaft, pommel, and swivel; it is constructed strongly enough for practical use, but its rich decoration also made it suitable for ceremonial procession.

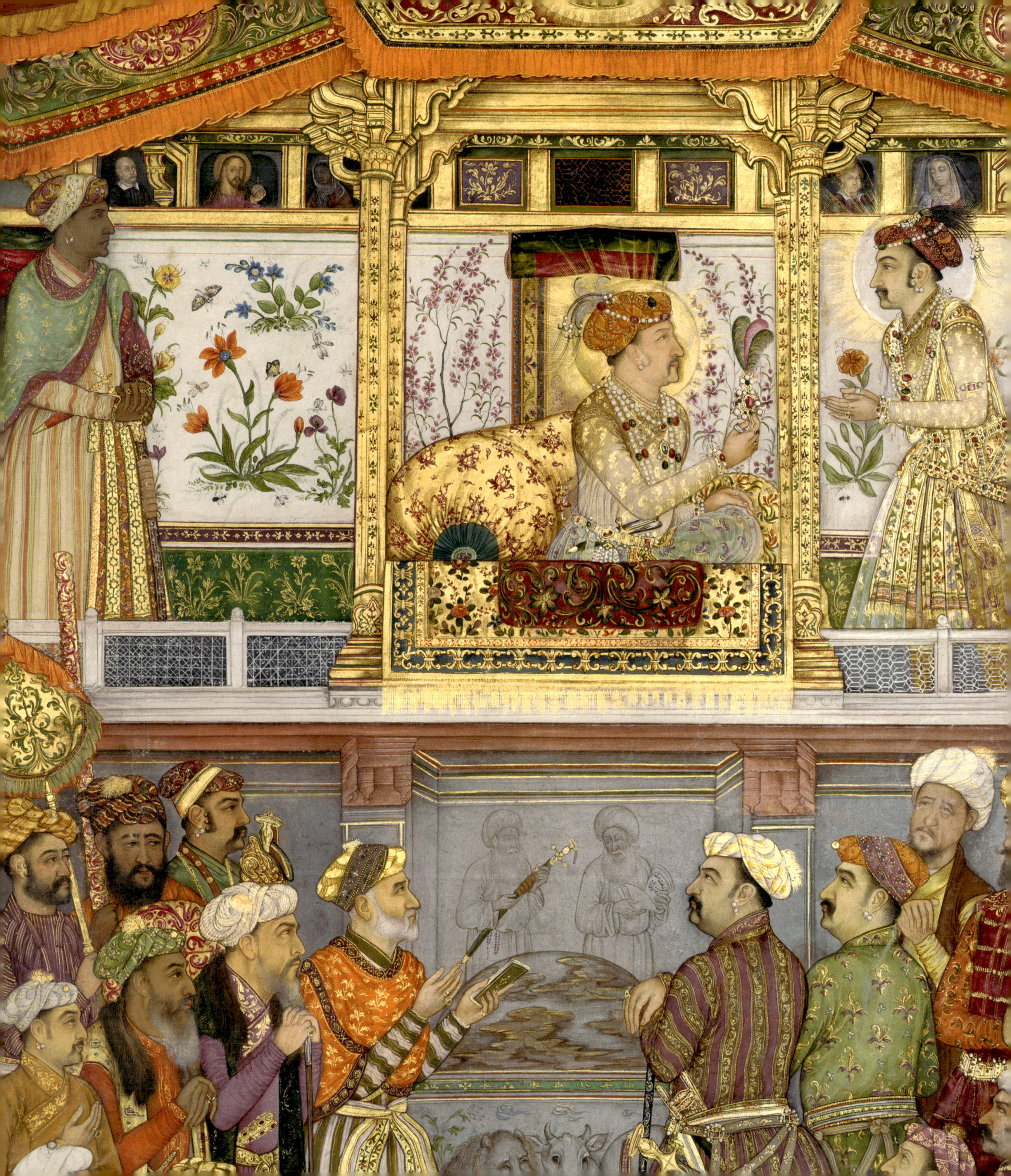

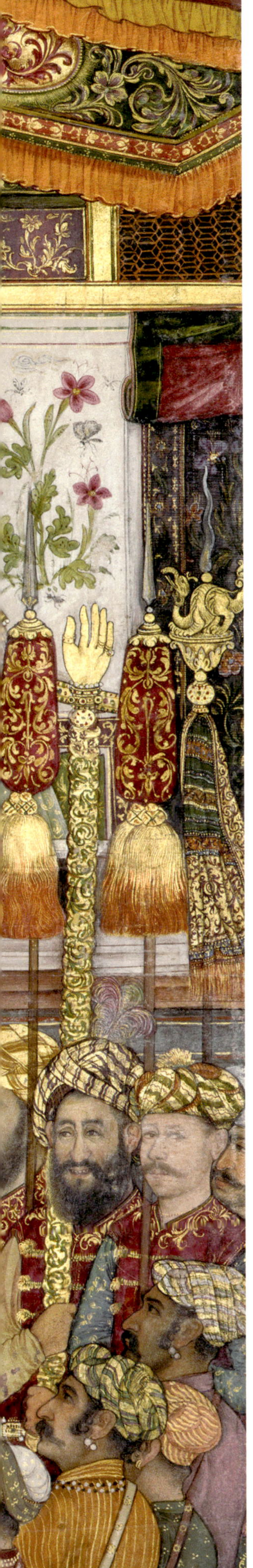

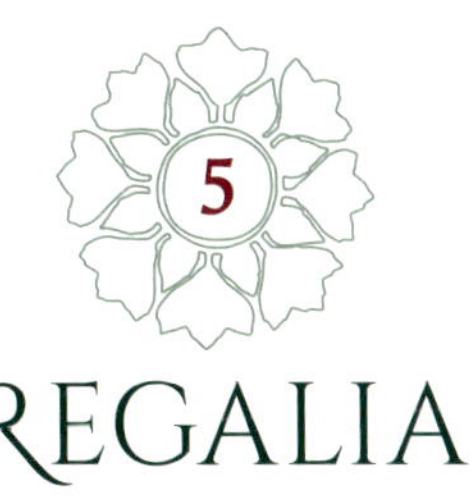

REGALIA

The Mughal Empire, the Maharajas, and the British Raj

In India, the ownership of great jewels was considered an intrinsic aspect of kingship. The finest gems were worn not by women but by men, as a reflection of the wealth and power of the State. The adornment considered appropriate for a ruler extended from turban ornaments or crowns to necklaces, earrings, armbands, bracelets, rings, belts, and anklets.

Although these jewelry types remained constant from the Mughal period onward, their style and the technique used in their production changed over time. In the nineteenth century—especially after the establishment of British rule in 1858—fashionable Indian jewelry was increasingly shaped by Western influence.

This was evident in design, in the faceting of gems and in their setting, as the closed-back *kundan* mount indigenous to India gradually gave way to open, Western-style claw settings for holding precious stones. Protected by Pax Britannica, Indian princes of the later nineteenth and twentieth centuries were actually deprived of any true military and political purpose. In such an environment, power and status were increasingly articulated through the wearing of more and more extravagant jewelry. From the late nineteenth century onward, the princes who constituted India's ruling class began to replace gold with platinum as the favored setting for their most important gems, eventually having their pieces remounted in Europe in the latest Western styles.

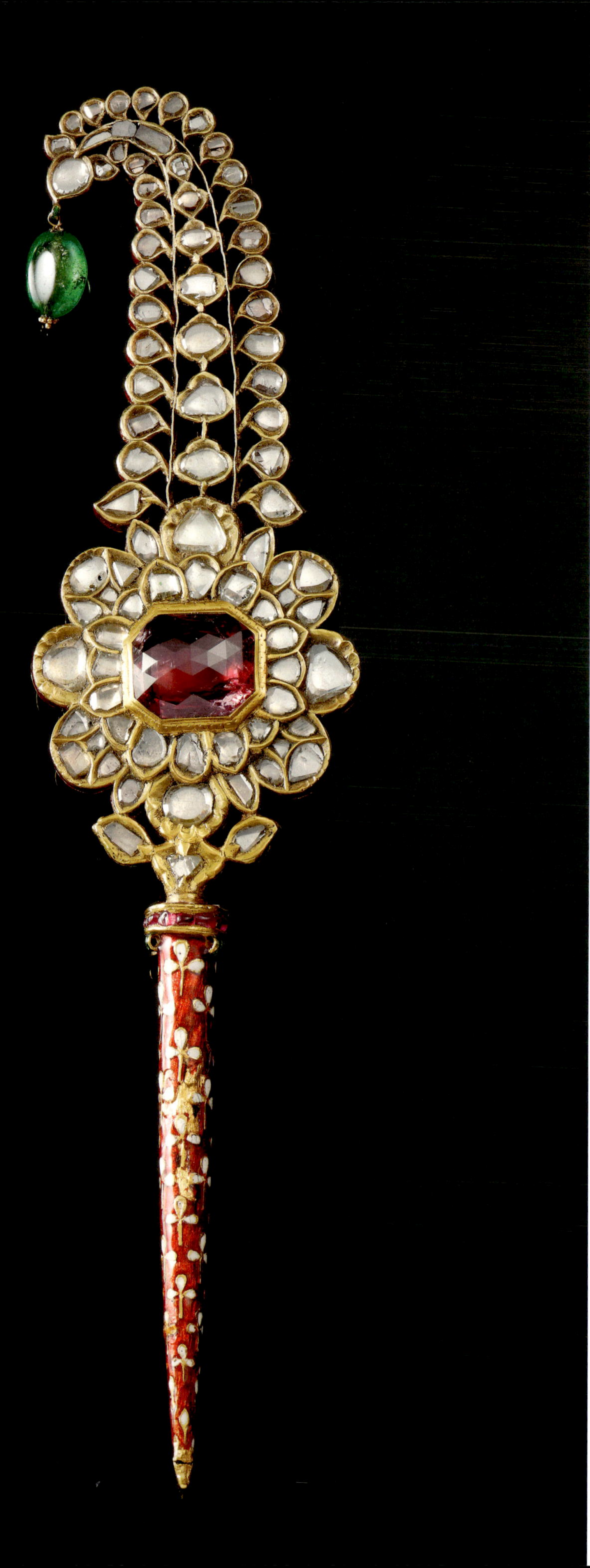

53

Turban ornament (obverse and reverse)

North India, 1675–1750. Gold, spinel, diamonds, rubies, emerald, enamel
CAT. 96

At the Mughal court, the use of turban ornaments was restricted to members of the ruling family and those upon whom the emperor bestowed great favor at court. This form, based on a stylized feather, was popularized by Jahangir and is a visible feature in some of his portraits. The deep-red translucent enamel on this piece is characteristic of the late seventeenth and early eighteenth centuries, relating to objects taken by Nadir Shah when he plundered Delhi in 1739. The reverse is designed with a plume holder into which an actual feather would have been inserted when the turban ornament was worn.

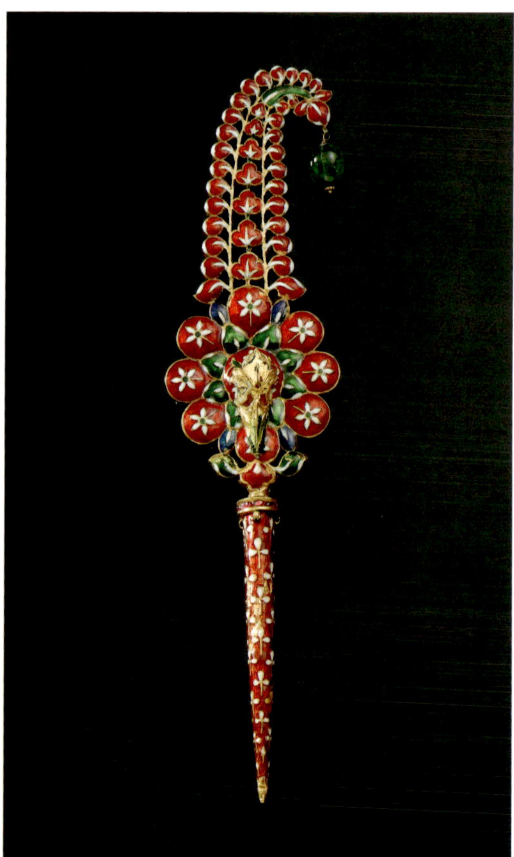

54

Turban ornament

South India, 1775–1825. Gold, diamonds, rubies, emeralds

CAT. 98

Typically South Indian in style and technique, this turban ornament follows the basic form of a *jigah*, but instead of featuring a drop pearl or emerald, the top extends to the left in the form of an abstracted elephant's trunk. The use of this motif enhances the royal symbolism of the turban ornament; in India, the elephant was the traditional mount of a king and was therefore intrinsically associated with royalty.

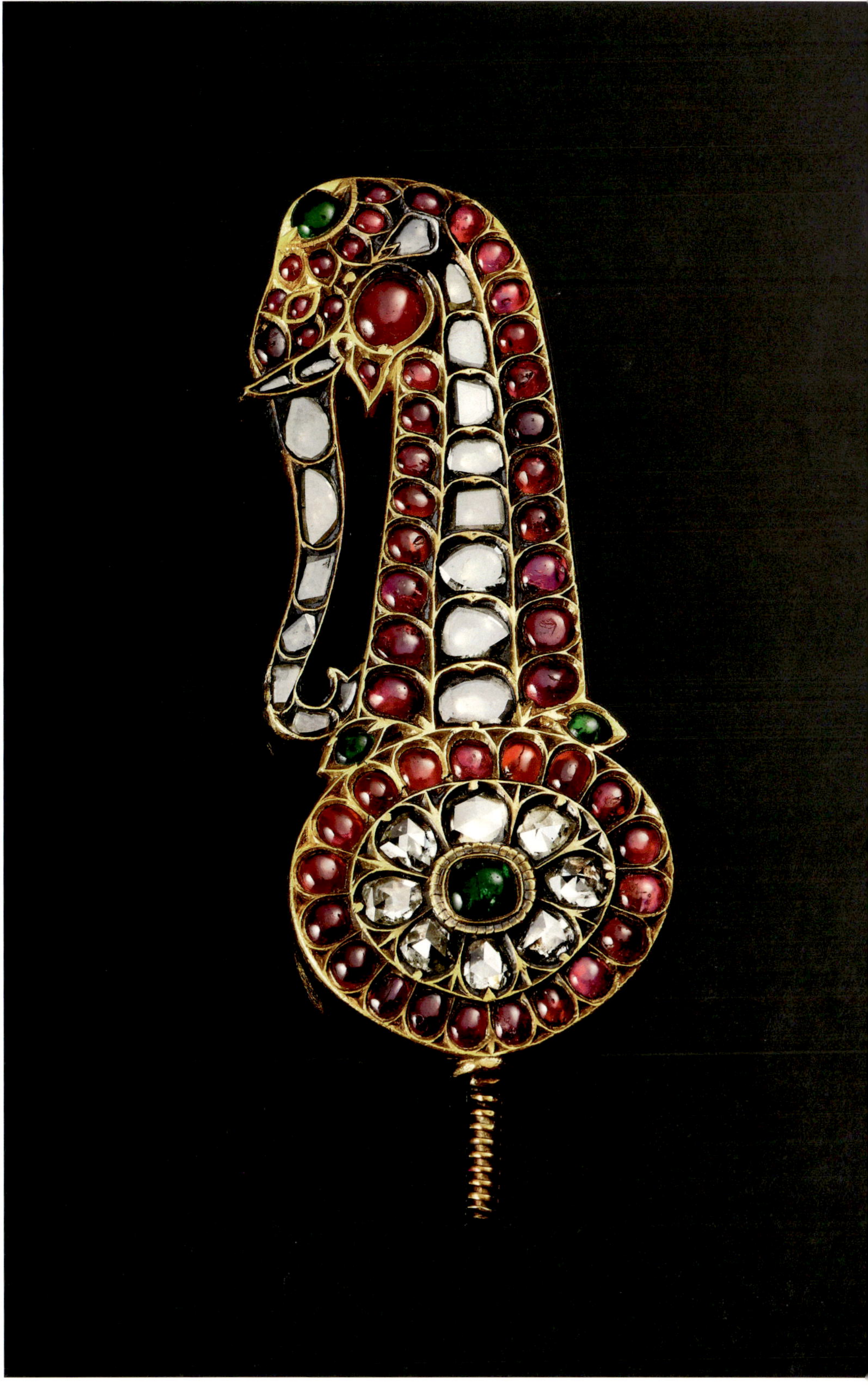

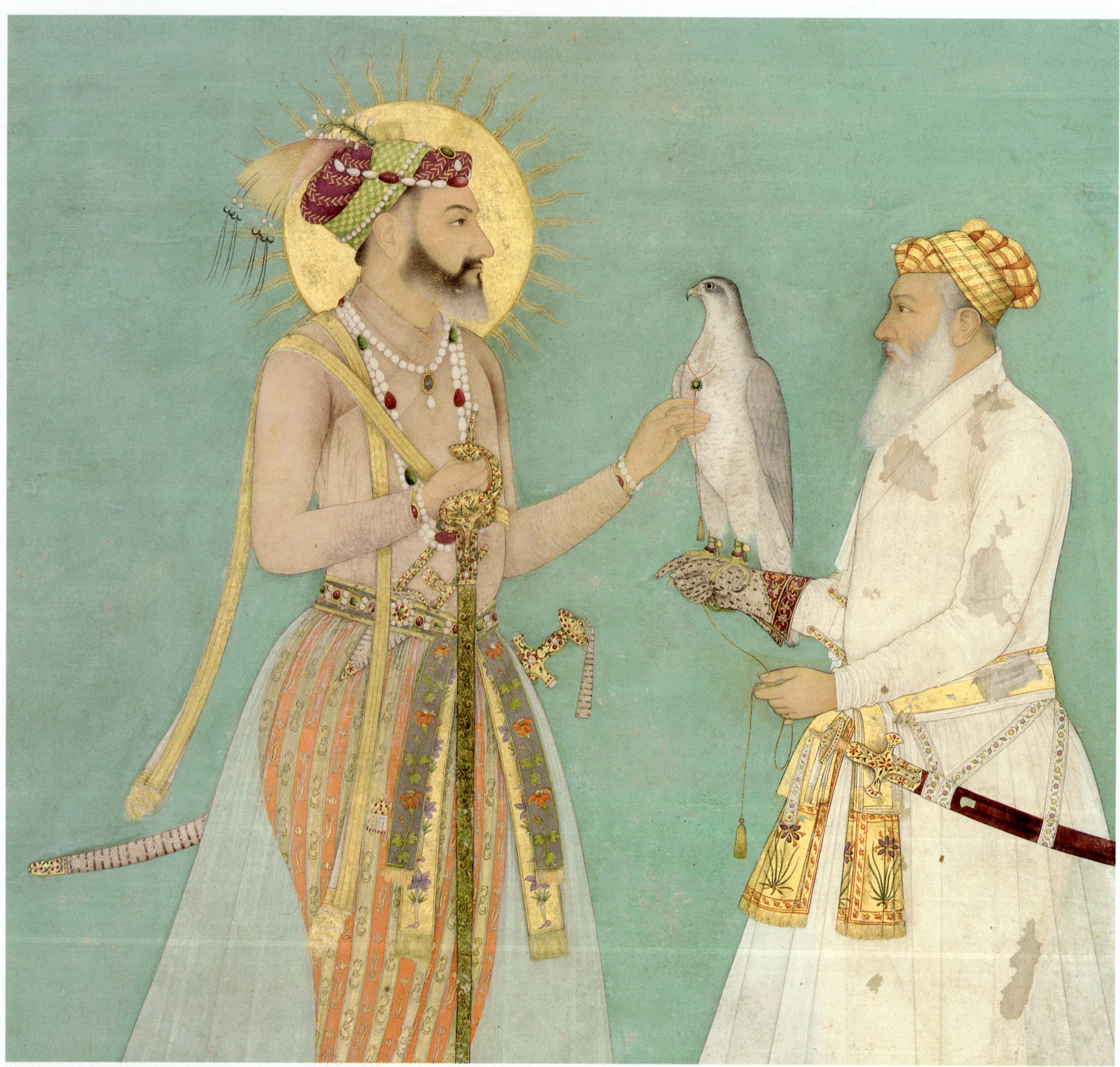

FIG. 39. Hashim, detail of Shah Jahan with an elderly courtier holding a falcon, ca. 1650. Watercolor on paper, with gold, 11⅛ × 7⅜ in. (28.4 × 18.9 cm). The Trustees of the Chester Beatty Library, Dublin, CBL In 62.4

TURBAN ORNAMENTS

Composed of Diamonds of an extraordinary size and value, beside an oriental topaz, which may be pronounced unparalleled, exhibiting a lustre like the sun.

François Bernier, French physician and traveler, on Emperor Aurangzeb's turban ornament, *Travels in the Mogul Empire A.D. 1656–1668* (cited in Amin Jaffer, ed., *Beyond Extravagance*, 2013: 102, n. 287)

Mughal emperors and rulers of the Successor States wore turban ornaments as a sign of their rank. Often designed as large jeweled brooches and backed by plumes of feathers, these objects represented an opportunity to show off large gemstones. Usually worn only by the emperor, turban ornaments were given as presents to favored princes and courtiers in exceptional circumstances. In the 1603–1613 account of his sojourn in India, English visitor William Hawkins mentions more than two thousand superb examples in the treasury of Emperor Jahangir.

The form of the turban ornament may have originated with Iranian types of plumed devices worn by Emperor Akbar in the 1590s. European aigrettes, which were hat jewels set with heron or egret feathers, were also a possible influence from the early seventeenth century. Displayed by both men and women in Europe, diamond-set aigrettes with feathers were worn by the ruling elites, from James I of England to Marie Antoinette of France.

Amid the waning of the Mughal Empire in the eighteenth century, regulations governing the wearing of turban ornaments were relaxed. New forms could reflect the curved feathers they contained or even the heads of prized elephants. In the nineteenth century, the jeweled turban ornament became more elaborate, spreading horizontally in the manner of a European tiara, and could be complemented by strings of gemstone beads encircling the turban.

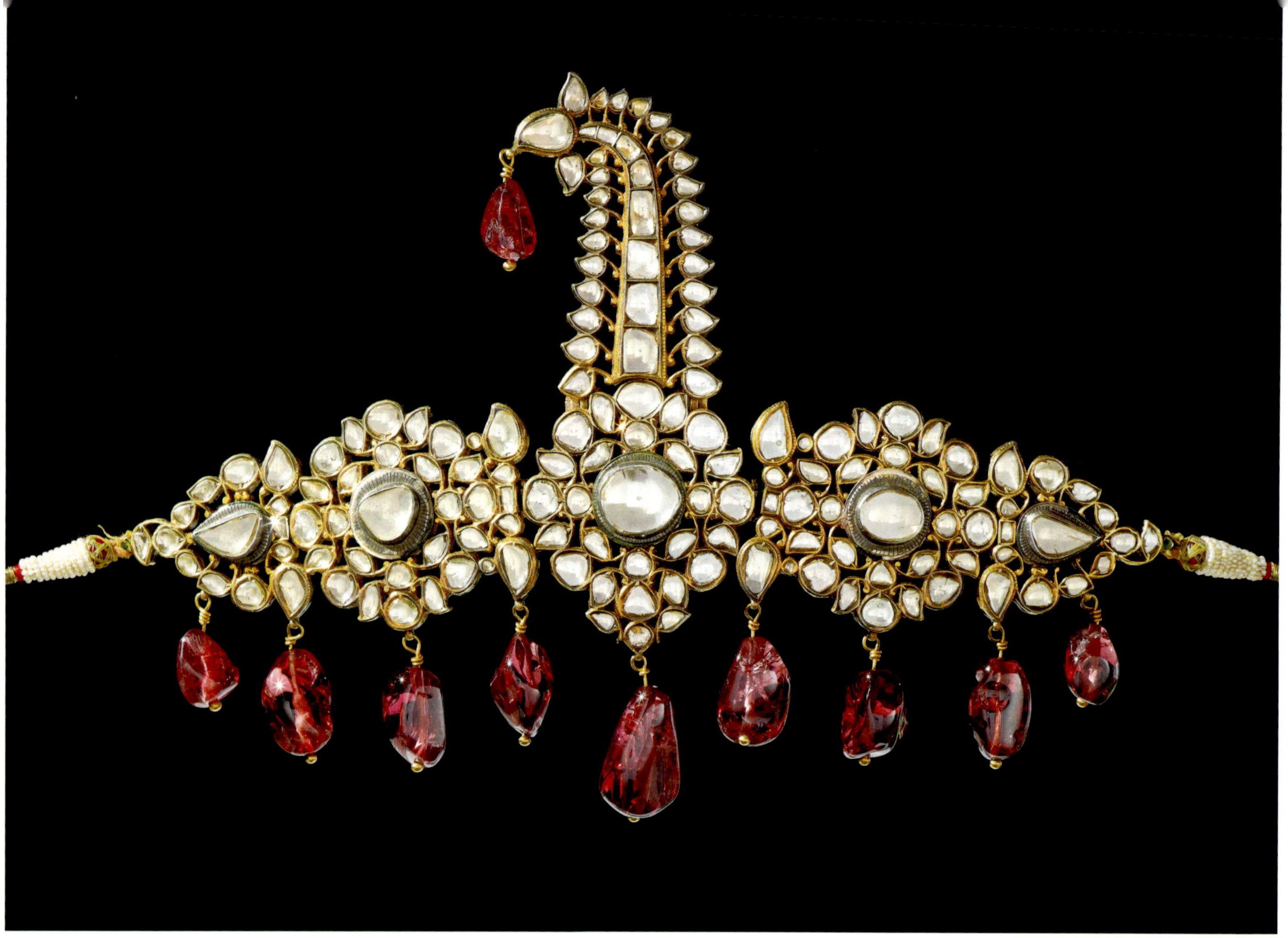

55

Turban ornament

Hyderabad, 1800–1850. Lower left spinel dated to 1607–1608 and 1633–1634. Gold, diamonds, spinels, pearls, enamel, modern stringing
CAT. 100

Nineteenth-century turban ornaments assumed increasingly substantial proportions, completely spanning the front of the headdress. The silver mounts for the central diamonds on this example suggest that it was made in Hyderabad, whose rulers emerged as India's leading princes after the Mughal Empire collapsed. The piece is suspended with historic spinels, one of which bears inscriptions referring to the Mughal rulers Jahangir and Shah Jahan—an example of how dynastic Mughal gems were reused as trophies by Successor States.

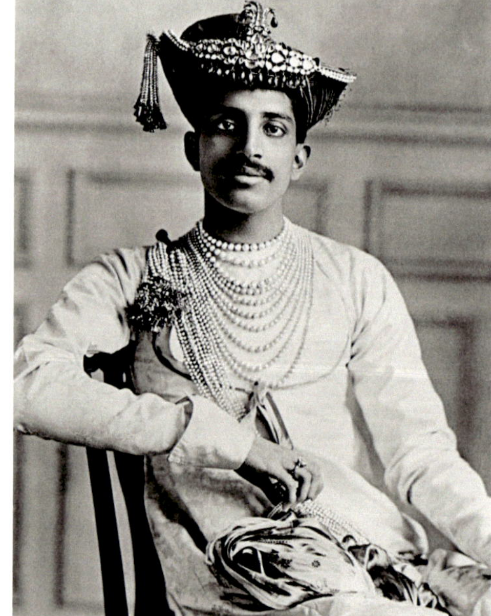

FIG. 40. Maharaja Tukoji Rao III of Indore, ca. 1916. John Fasal Collection

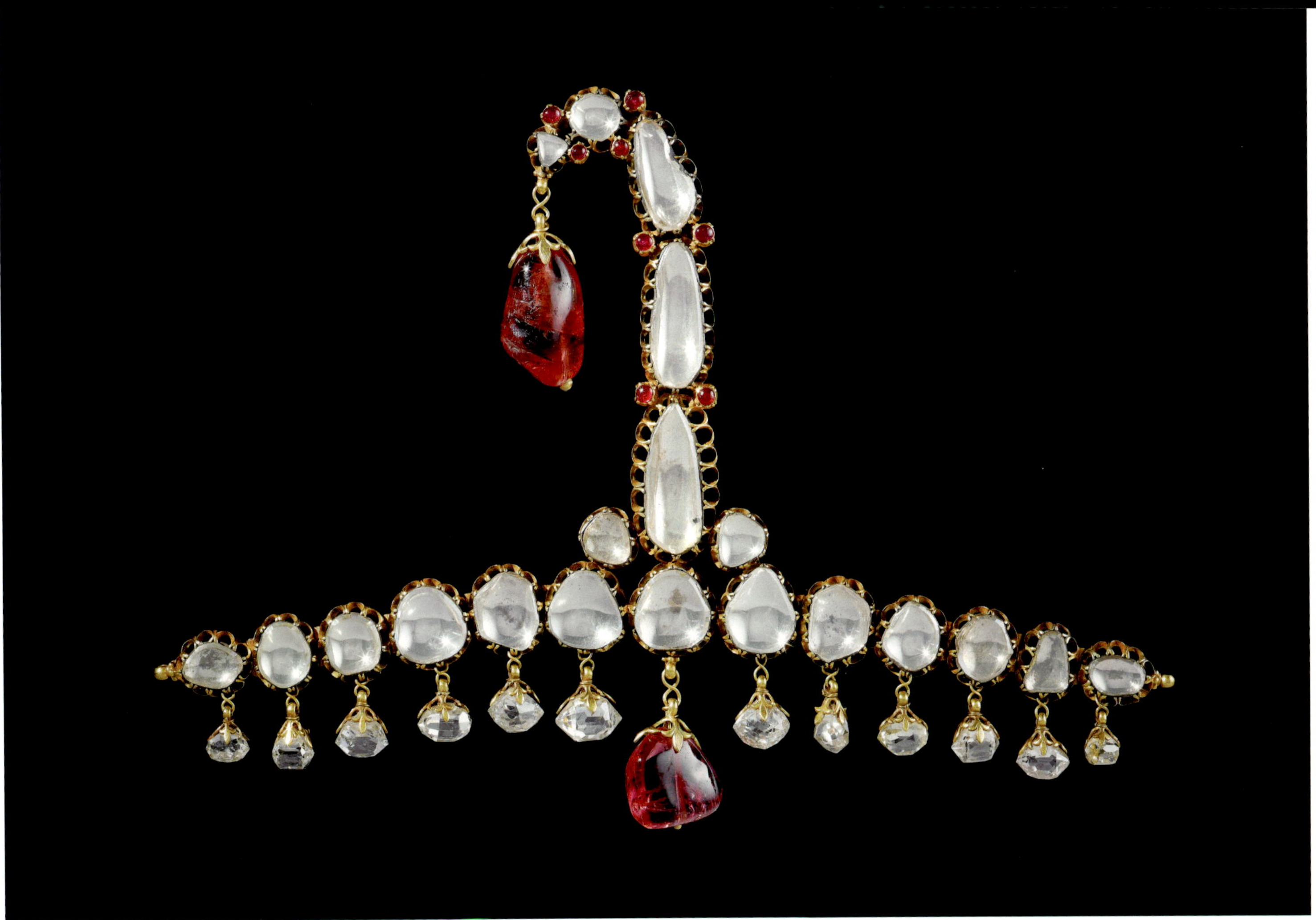

56

Turban ornament

North India, 1875–1900. Spinels dated to 1639–1640. Gold, diamonds, rubies, spinels. Inscribed in Persian on the spinels: *12 Shah Jahan [son] of Jahangir Shah 1049*

CAT. 102

The conspicuous Western-style claw settings on this turban ornament illustrate the shift away from traditional *kundan* mounts in the later nineteenth century. In spite of the seemingly modern technique, the diamonds in this turban ornament are foiled in silver in a traditional manner, bringing additional depth and brilliance to the stones. The shape and cutting of the gems in this piece predate the *sarpech*, suggesting that they were reused from older pieces of jewelry. Both pendant spinels have Mughal inscriptions, testifying to the status these stones continued to enjoy long after they had been removed from the Imperial Treasury.

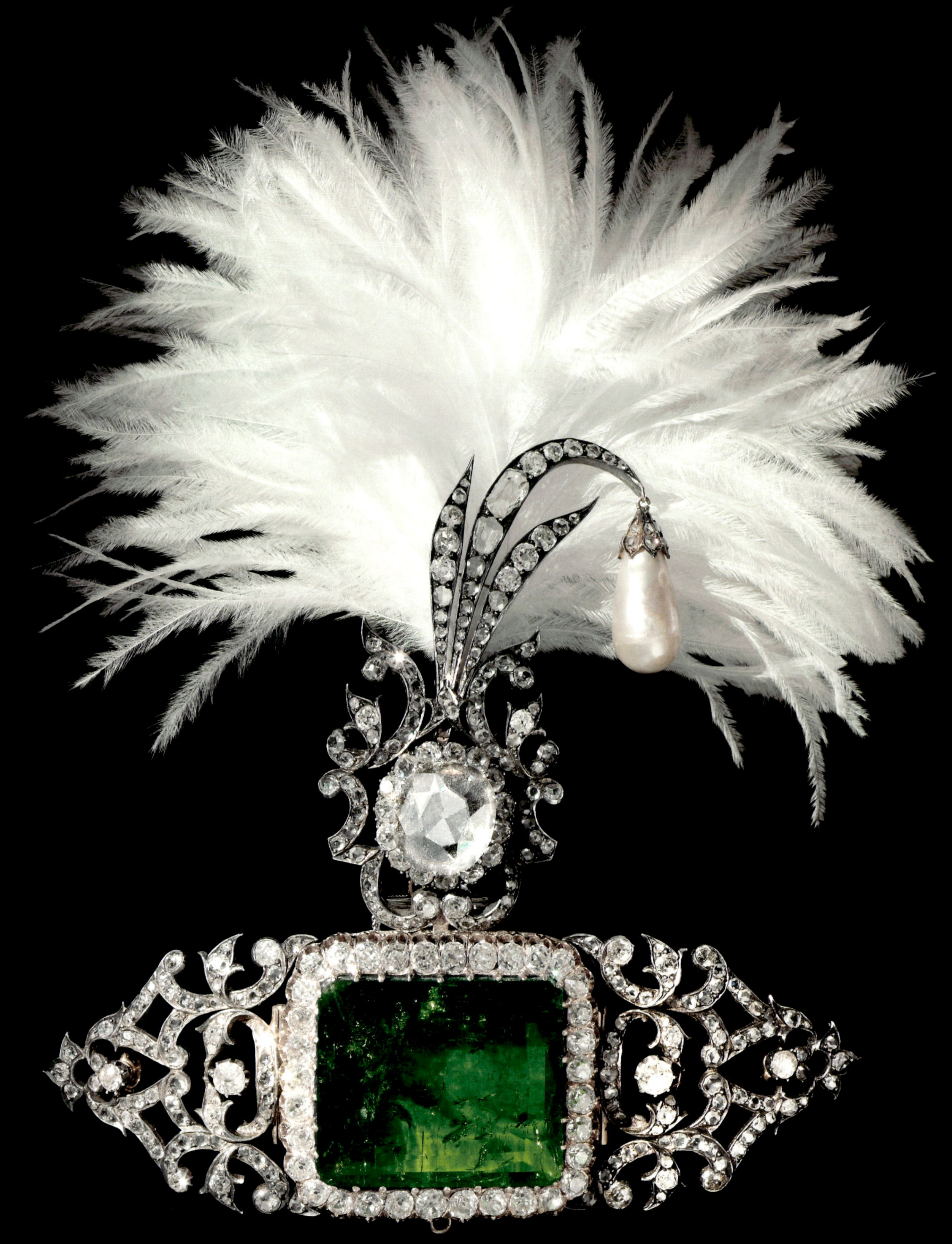

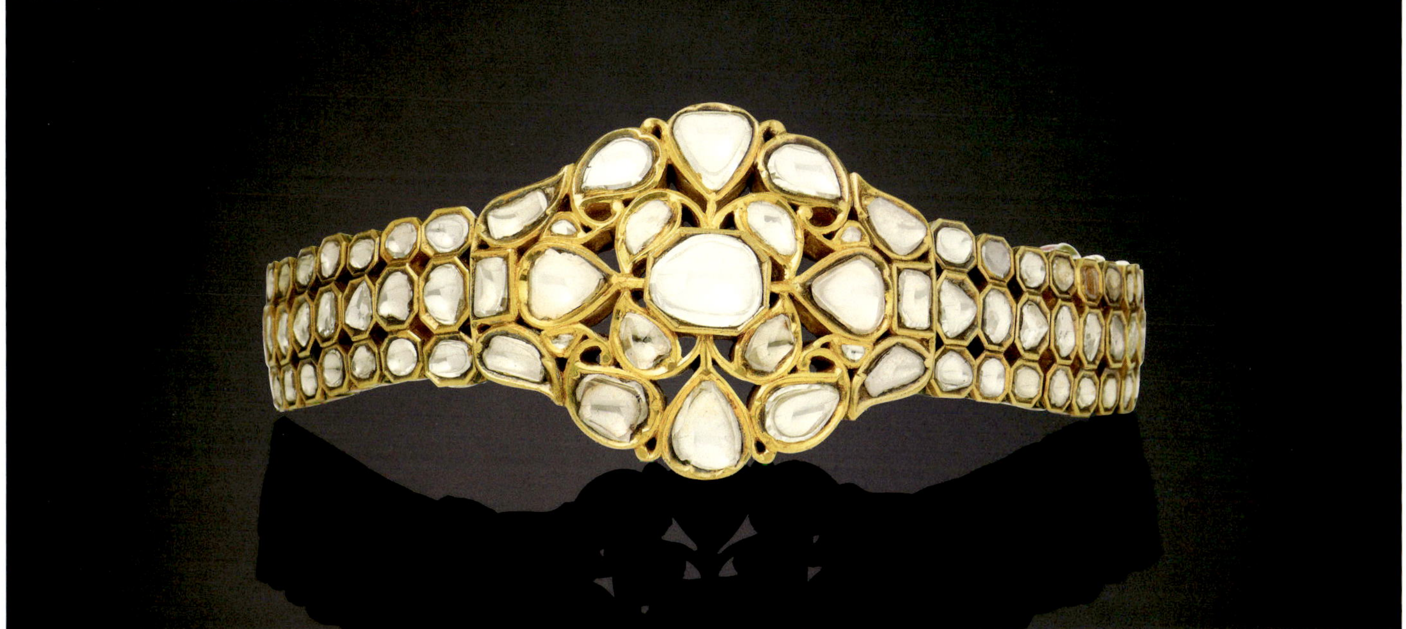

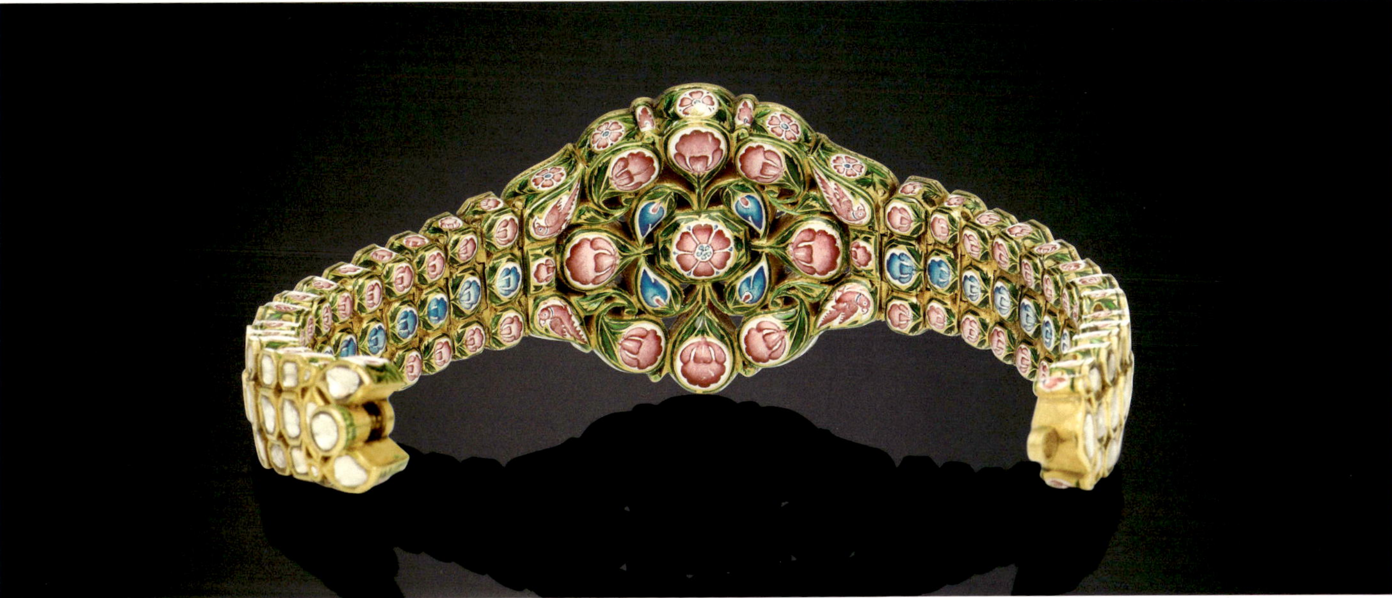

57 *(opposite)*

Turban ornament

India, ca. 1900; clip: Cartier Paris, 2012. Gold, silver, emerald, diamonds, pearls, feathers
CAT. 103

Framed within a border of brilliant-cut diamonds, the setting for the substantial emerald in this turban ornament echoes European jewelry designs of the period. The setting technology likewise shows growing Western influence; the gems are neither foiled nor encased in closed settings typical of Indian jewelry. The ornament has a dual purpose: when the top section is removed, it can double as an armband (*bazuband*).

58

Pair of bracelets

Benares, India, 1800–1825. Gold, diamonds, enamel
CAT. 105

Designed to be worn by a man, these bracelets are set with diamonds and decorated on the reverse in the distinctive pink enamel (*gulabi minakari*) for which Benares (Varanasi) was so renowned. The articulated form was of a type fashionable throughout much of India in the late eighteenth and early nineteenth century.

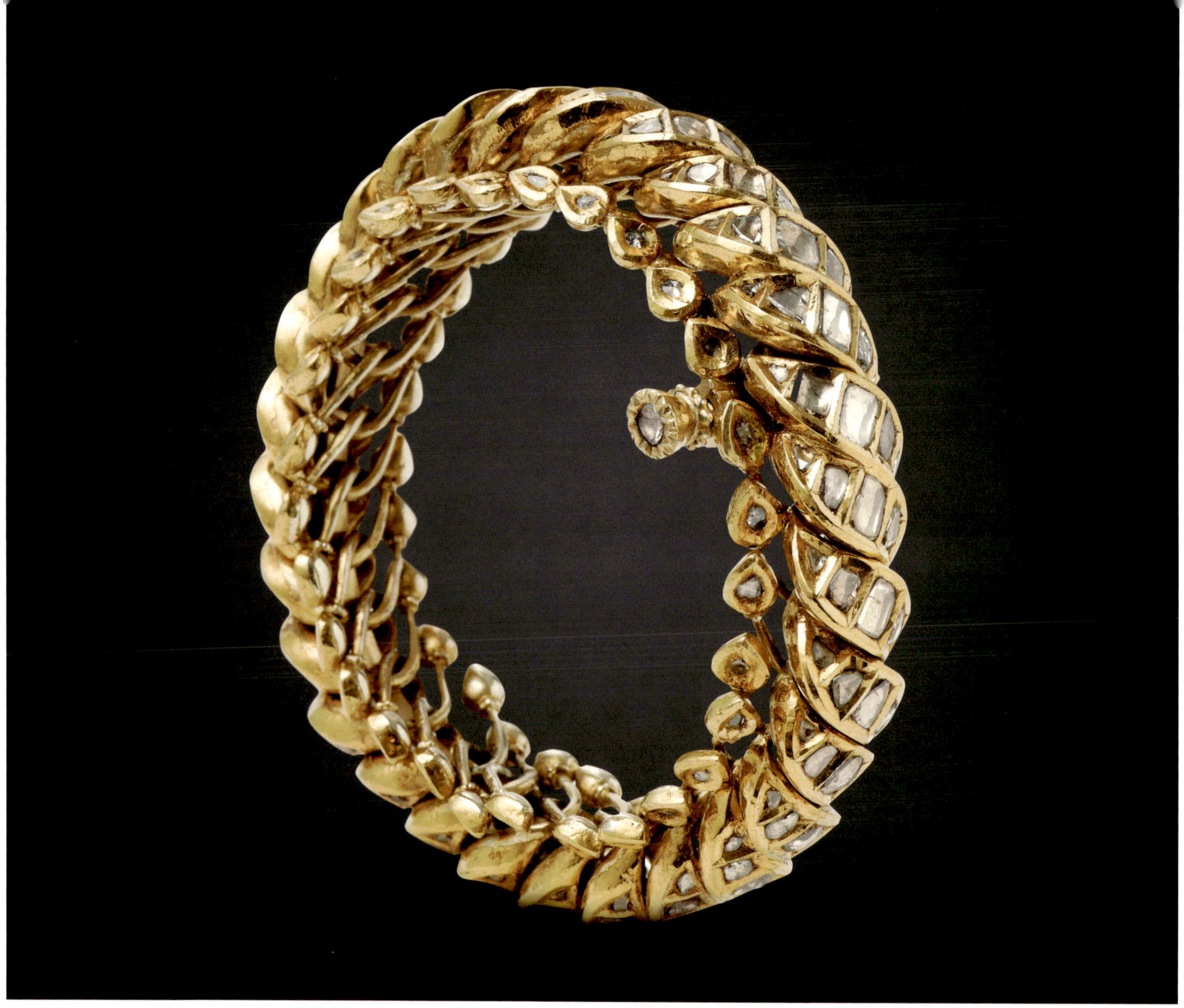

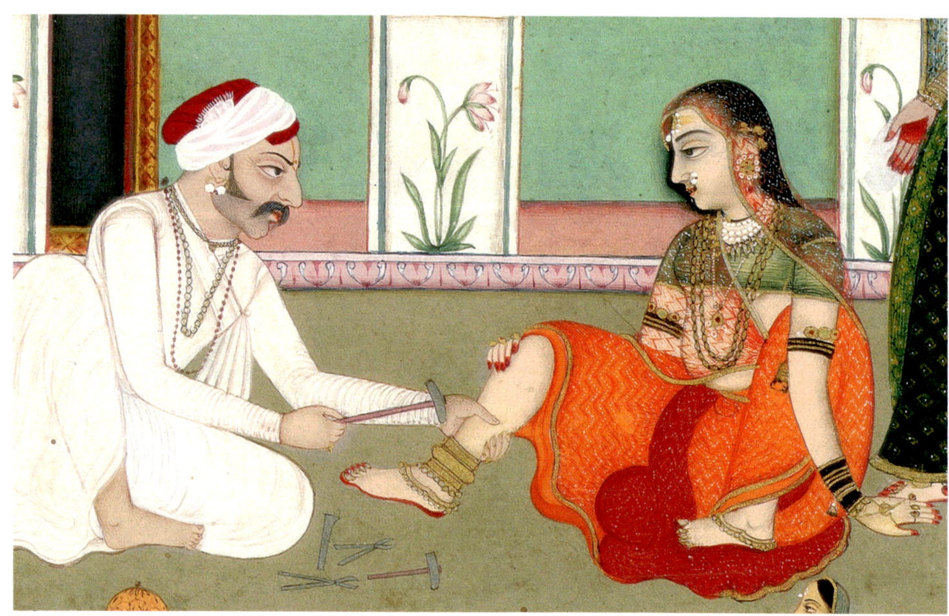

FIG. 41. In a goldsmith's workshop, Bundi, India (detail), ca. 1760. Ink, opaque watercolor, gold on paper, 9¾ × 6½ in. (24.5 × 16.3 cm). The David Collection, Copenhagen, 17/1981

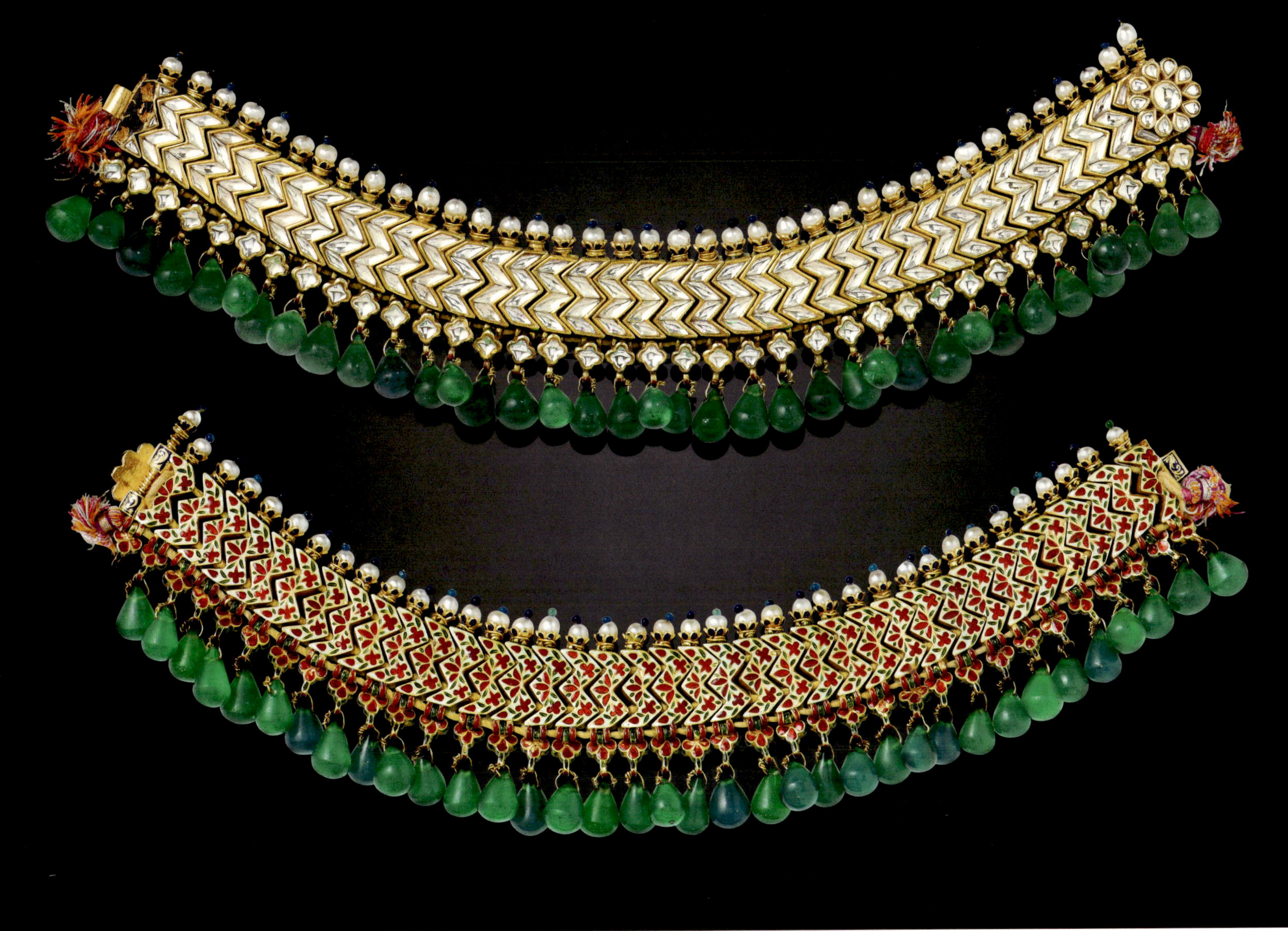

59 *(opposite)*

Anklet

Hyderabad or Rajasthan, 1800–1850. Gold, diamonds
CAT. 106

Across India, the bestowal of a gold anklet was a great honor (*tazim*) conferred by a ruler upon a vassal of subject in recognition of status and achievements. Flexible gold anklets like this one, set with table-cut diamonds, are also seen in the collection of the Nizams of Hyderabad and could probably indicate their origin, although similar forms are also known in Rajasthan.

60

Pair of anklets

Jaipur or Bikaner, 1800–1850. Gold, white sapphires, pearls, glass beads, enamel
CAT. 107

Adorning the feet with gold was considered a mark of status for men and women across the subcontinent. The ingenuity of Indian jewelers allowed for tremendous flexibility and movement in the design of anklets. On this pair it was achieved by the use of interlocking double-chevron bars fastened together by invisible threads. The fine enamel work on the reverse suggests that they were made in Rajasthan, probably in Jaipur or Bikaner.

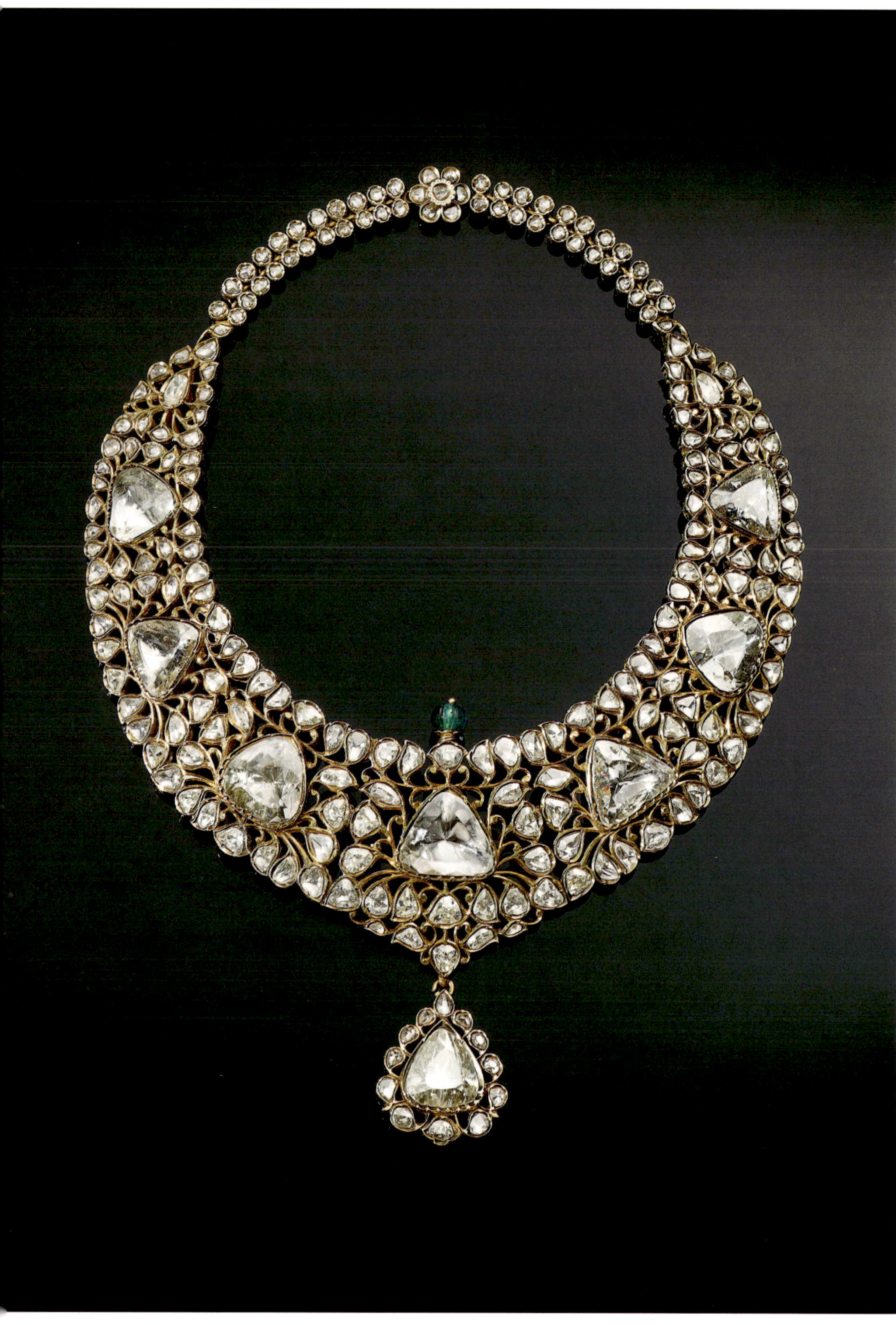

61

The Nizam of Hyderabad Necklace

India, 1850–1875. Gold, diamonds, emerald, enamel
CAT. 113

The relative peace that accompanied the establishment of British rule over India witnessed a period in which court ceremony and hierarchy enjoyed tremendous importance. In particular, the Delhi durbars of 1877, 1903, and 1911 provided an opportunity for Indian princes to meet and compete in the splendor of their apparel and jewels. This necklace is a tour de force of Indian princely jewelry, designed to express the power and wealth of the owner in such an arena. The eight large diamonds are modified brilliant cuts, each with an estimated weight of 10 to 15 carats, and represent an advance in gem-faceting technology in India. Although the diamonds are backed by foil and encased in closed settings in traditional Indian style, the openwork design and the symmetrical arrangement of the gems and the central pendant reveal Western influence.

62

Necklace

India, 1850–1900. Gold, silver, emeralds, diamonds, pearls, modern stringing
CAT. 114

The large emeralds and the diamond spacers are all foiled to enhance their brilliance and set in closed mounts, the former in gold and the latter in silver. While the arrangement of the gems and the absence of ornamentation on the reverse point to Western influence, the necklace retains the traditional Indian method of fastening by an adjustable cord. The brilliant cut of the diamonds and the overall aesthetics of the piece suggest a late nineteenth-century date of production.

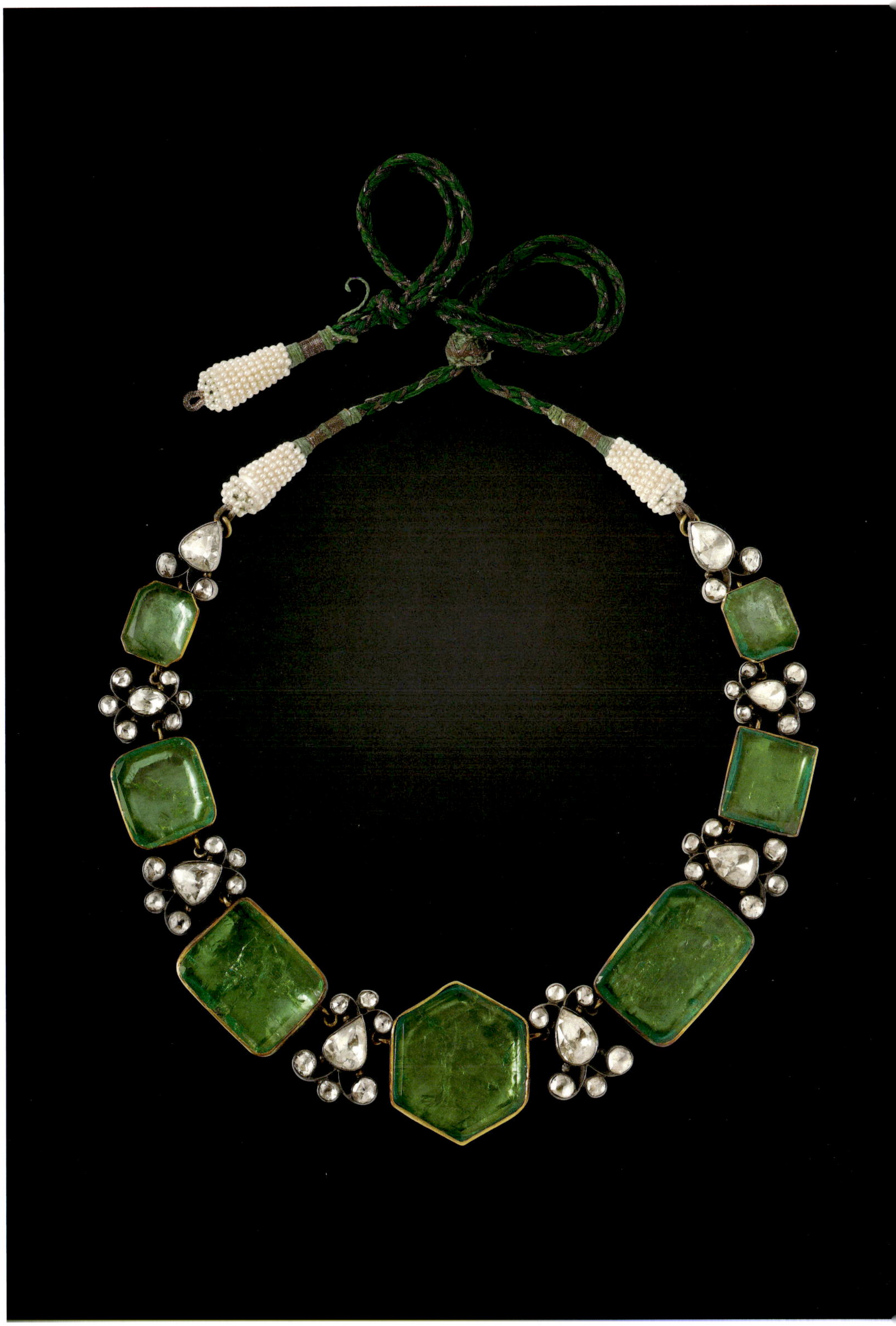

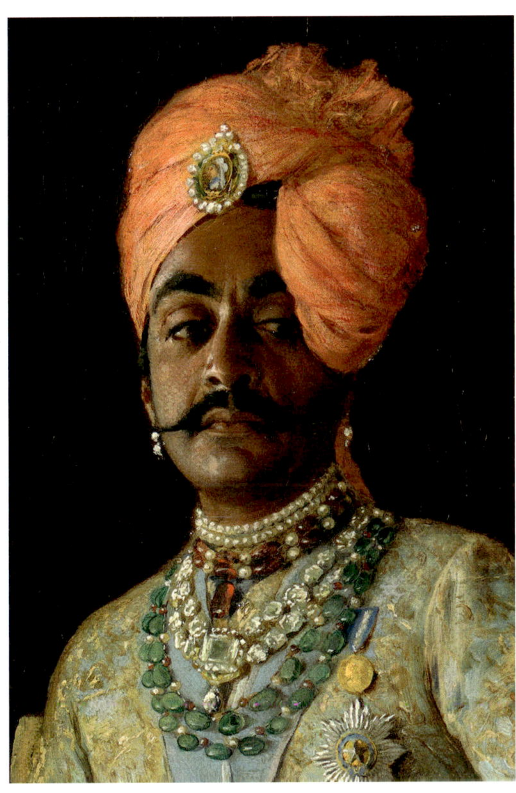

FIG. 42. Rudolf Swoboda, detail of *Sir Pratap Singh (1845–1922)*, 1888. Oil on canvas, 22½ × 15⅝ in. (57.2 × 39.5 cm). Royal Collection Trust

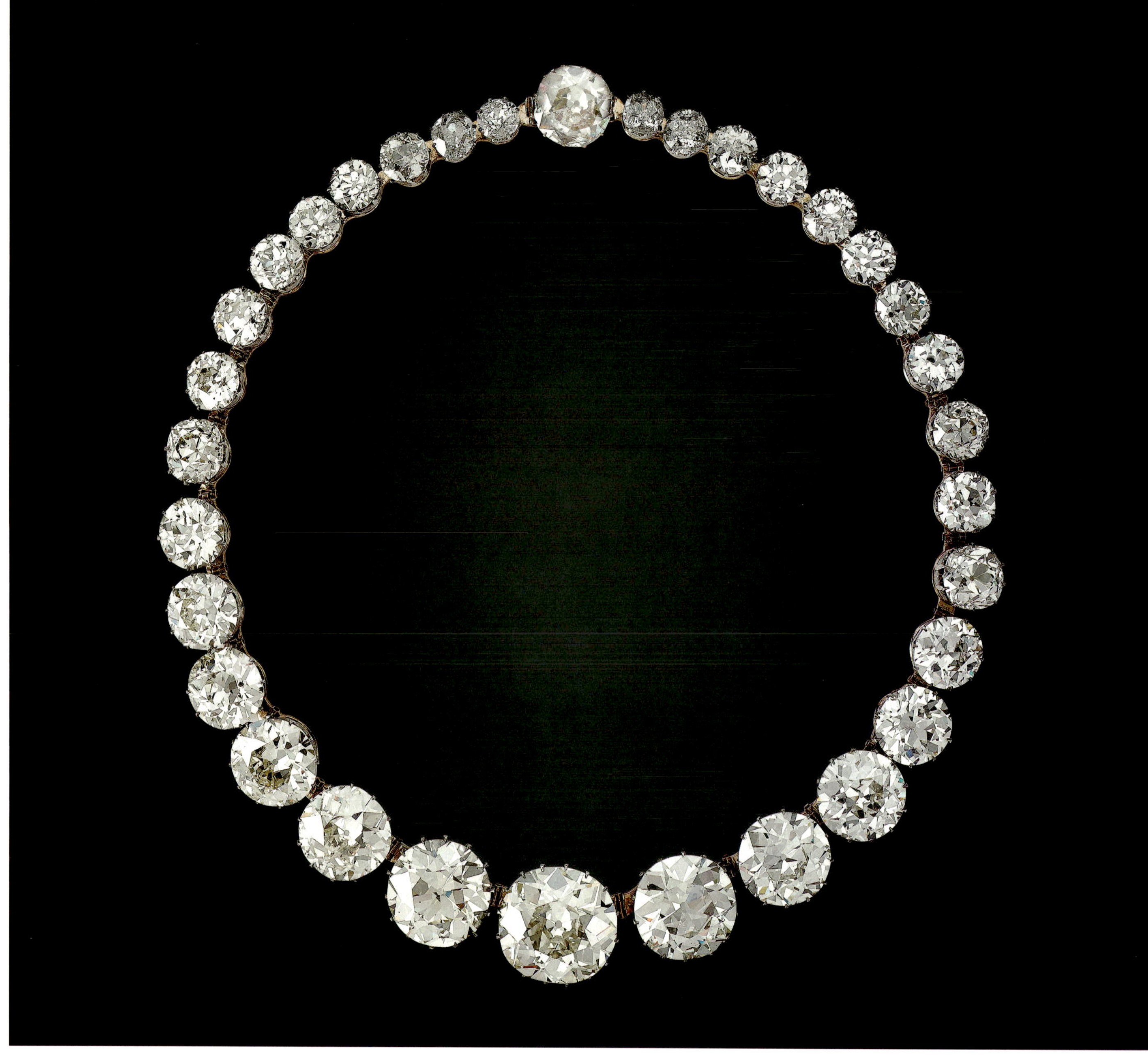

63

Necklace

Hyderabad, ca. 1890. Gold, diamonds

CAT. 115

This necklace of graduated brilliant-cut diamonds—or rivière—was made in India but is closely based on European prototypes. Whereas in the West such a piece of jewelry would have been worn by a woman, in India it certainly adorned the neck of a prince, reflecting the wealth and power of his state. The rare grouping of substantial old-mine Golconda gems suggests that this necklace was commissioned by a leading family such as the Asaf Jahi dynasty of Hyderabad.

64

Ceremonial sword of the Nizam of Hyderabad

Hyderabad, 1880–1900. Gold, silver, diamonds, rubies, emeralds, steel blade

CAT. 120

In both India and the West, a State sword signified royal authority, accompanying a ruler at formal occasions and representing him when absent. This spectacular example is a hybrid of East and West in that it follows the Mughal type of an encrusted sword hilt but is influenced by European models in the setting of the diamonds in the grip, which is similar to that of Napoleon's consular sword (fig. 43). Based on style and production, the sword was likely to have been made during the reign of Nizam Mahbub Ali Khan of Hyderabad (r. 1869–1911).

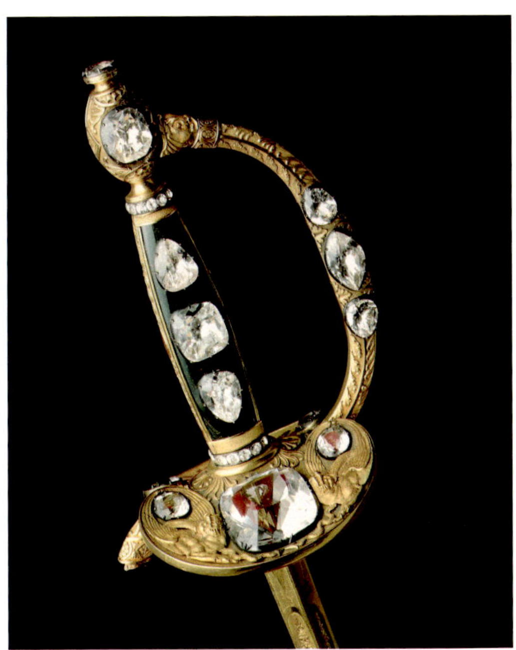

FIG. 43. Nicolas-Noël Boutet, François-Regnault Nitot, and Jean-Baptiste-Claude Odiot, detail of Napoleon's coronation sword, 18th century. Damascened steel, shell, jasper, gold, precious stone, 37¾ in. (96 cm). Château de Fontainebleau, France, N204

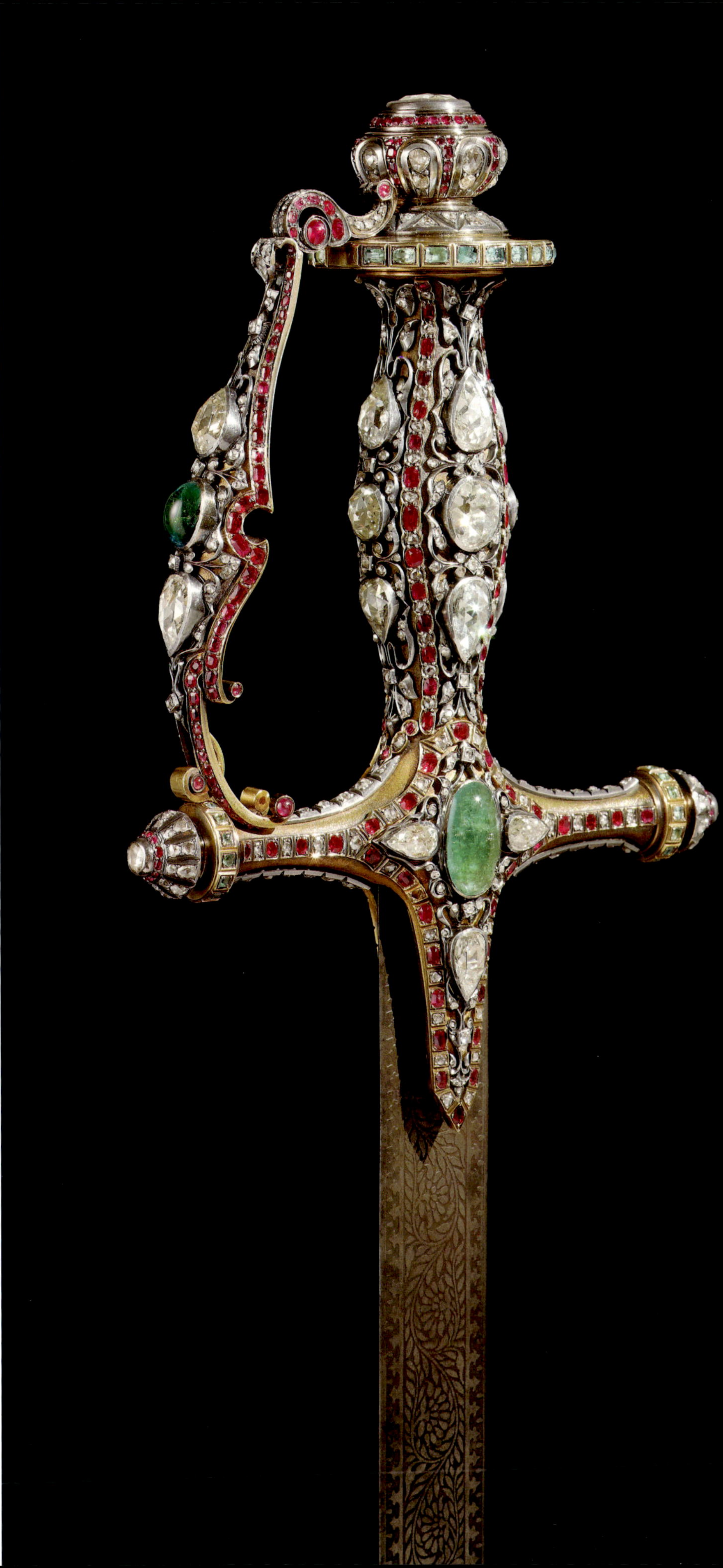

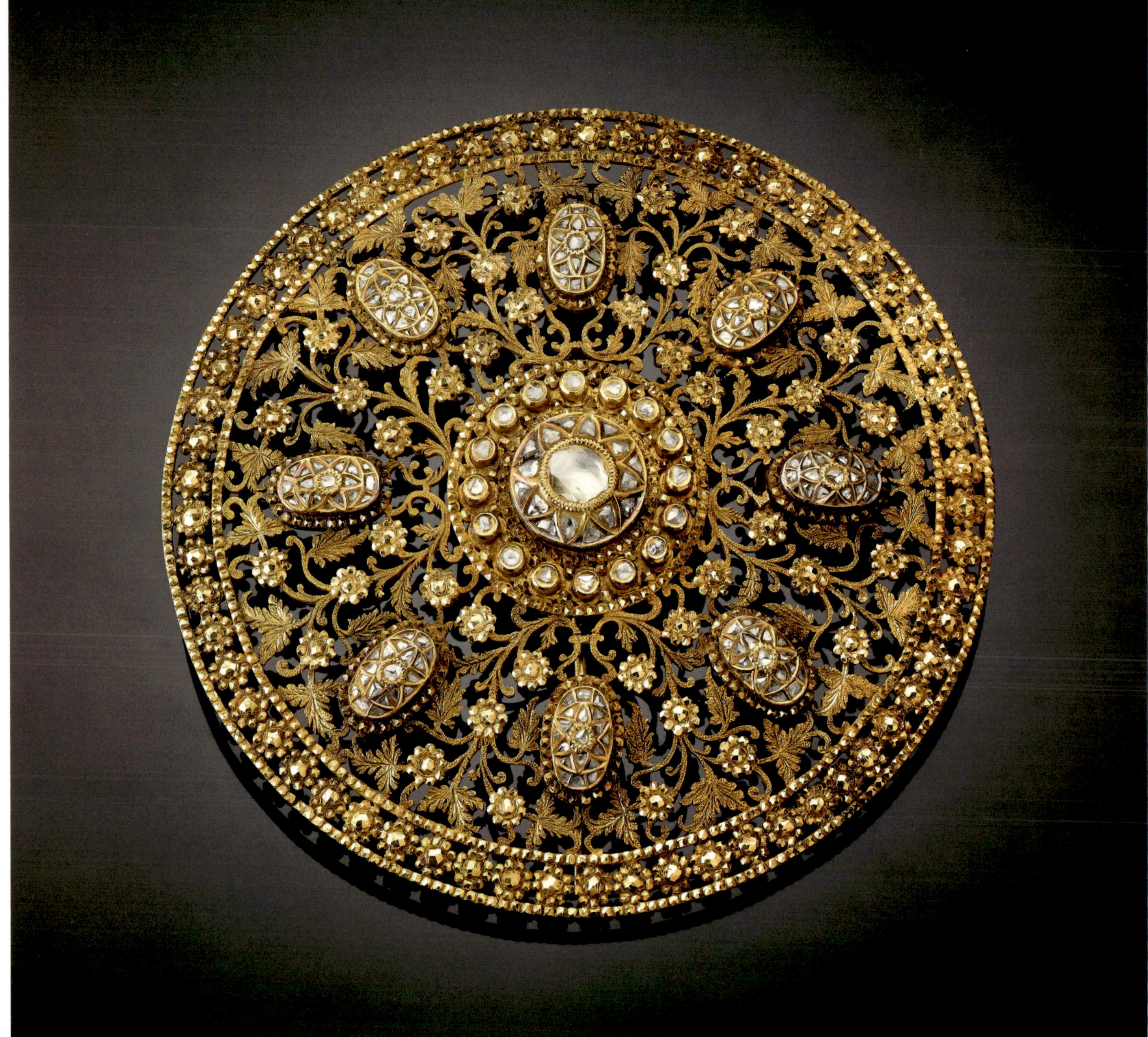

65

Hair ornament

Western India, ca. 1900. Gold, diamonds

CAT. 119

This round ornament would have been worn by a woman at the back of her head, over a braid or chignon. The circular shape is meant to evoke the sun while the central lotus motif symbolizes purity. The openwork decoration is influenced both by traditional filigree and by the nineteenth-century taste for lace. The gold flower heads are faceted in a manner similar to Western cut-steel jewelry to give added sparkle to the piece.

66

Plait ornament

South India, 1890–1910. Silver, diamonds, rubies, pearls
CAT. 116

Indian jewelry features a variety of distinctive forms specifically intended to adorn a woman's hair, such as this piece, which would have been suspended over a single long plait. Its name, *jadanagam*, comes from the Sanskrit *naga* (cobra), a reference to the long tapering form of the ornament as well as to the imagery of the uppermost section, which is an abstract representation of a hooded serpent. In Hinduism, the worship of snakes was associated with fertility, hence their appearance on jewelry for women. The setting of the diamond-leaf sections is influenced by French jewelry.

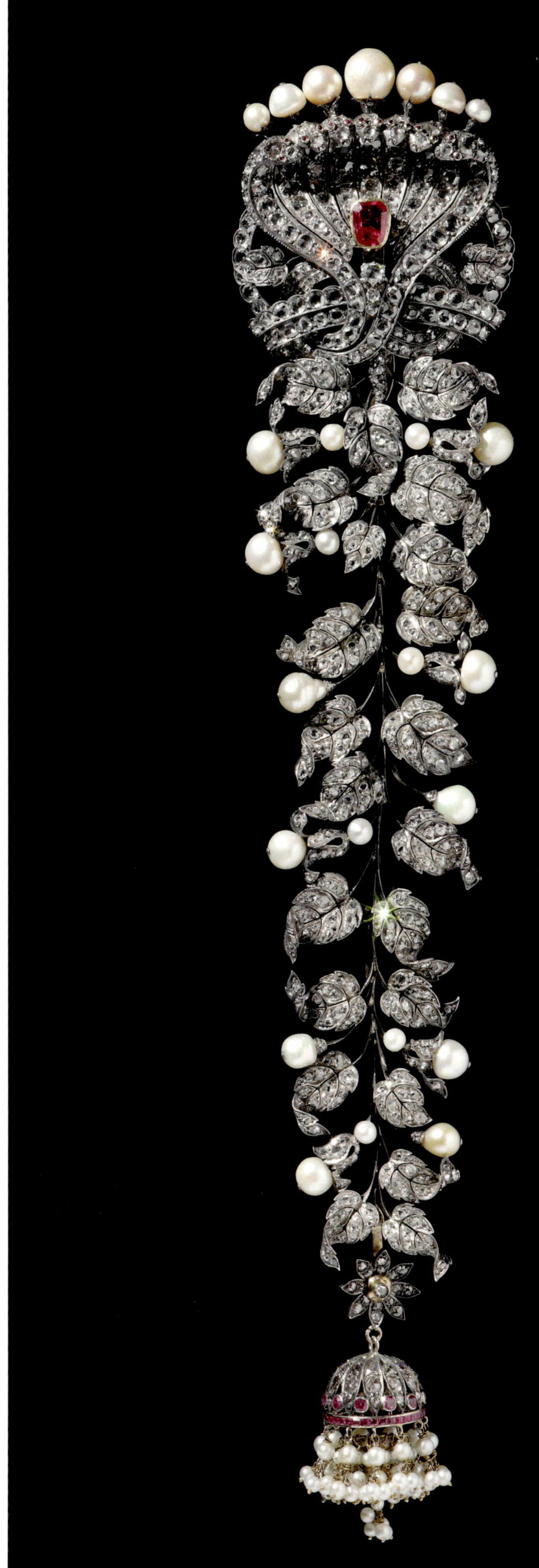

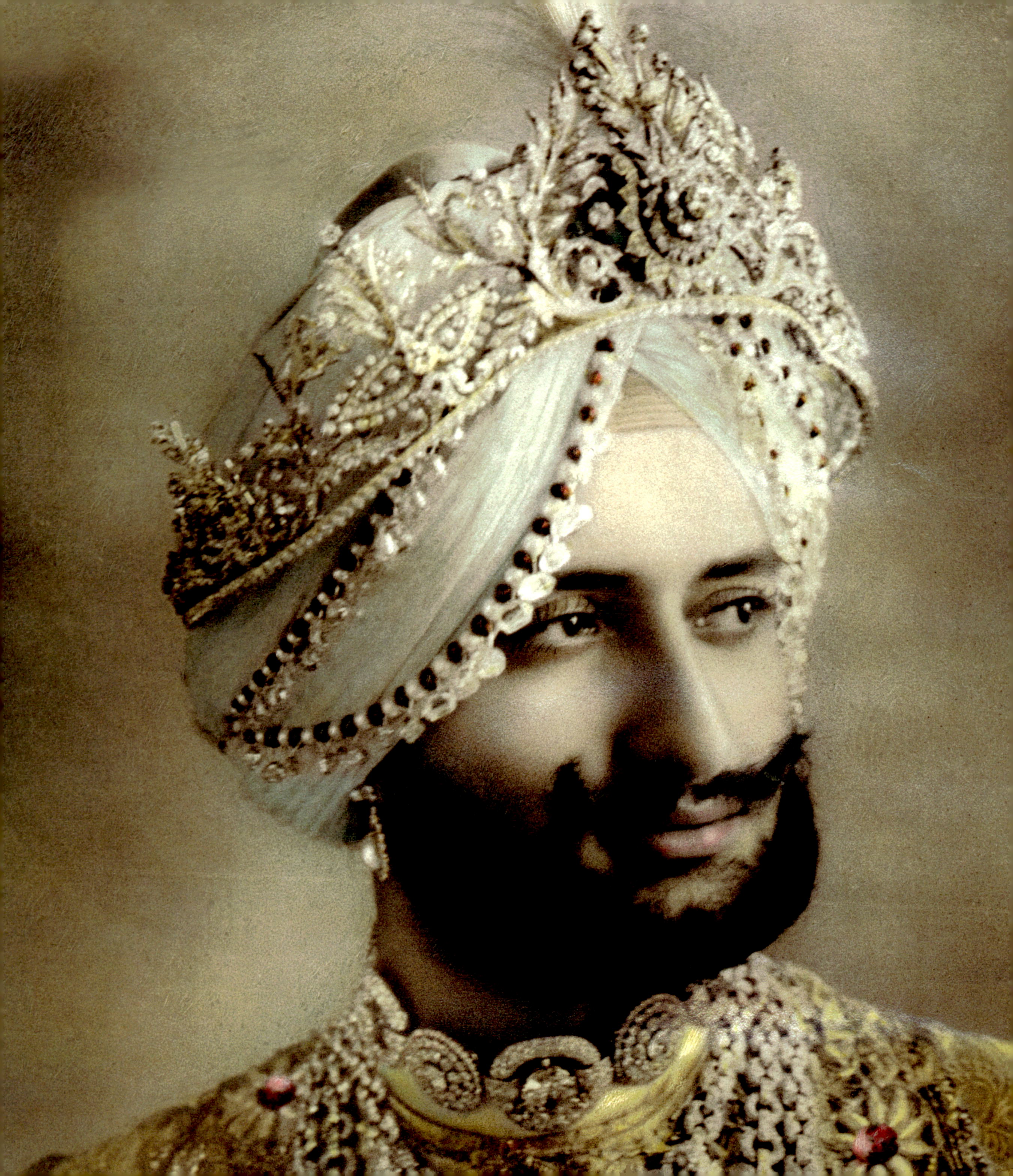

THE TWENTIETH CENTURY

Jewelry Made for the Maharajas

Jewelry for the maharajas witnessed dramatic changes in the early twentieth century. European methods of manufacture, such as the use of open settings and the employment of platinum, influenced the making of jewelry in India. Furthermore, Indian maharajas started to patronize European jewelry houses directly for resetting their jewelry, as well as using the prodigious amounts of precious stones in their treasuries for the production of new pieces. The Maharaja of Patiala had much of his ceremonial jewelry recast by the Parisian houses of Cartier and Boucheron in the late 1920s, while the Maharaja of Nawanagar had his pieces made by Cartier London in the 1930s.

Objects such as turban ornaments created for the Indian maharajas for state occasions retained traditional forms, but jewelry for the maharajas also used fashionable Art Deco European styles originally applied to jewelry for women in the West. And for the first time ever, prominent pieces of jewelry were made for the wives of maharajas, signifying a major shift more in line with Western notions of gender in the wearing of jewelry. By the time of Indian independence in 1947 and the maharajas' accompanying loss of their ruling status, the tradition of making major pieces of jewelry for men dwindled to the point that significant items would now be supplied only to elite Indian women.

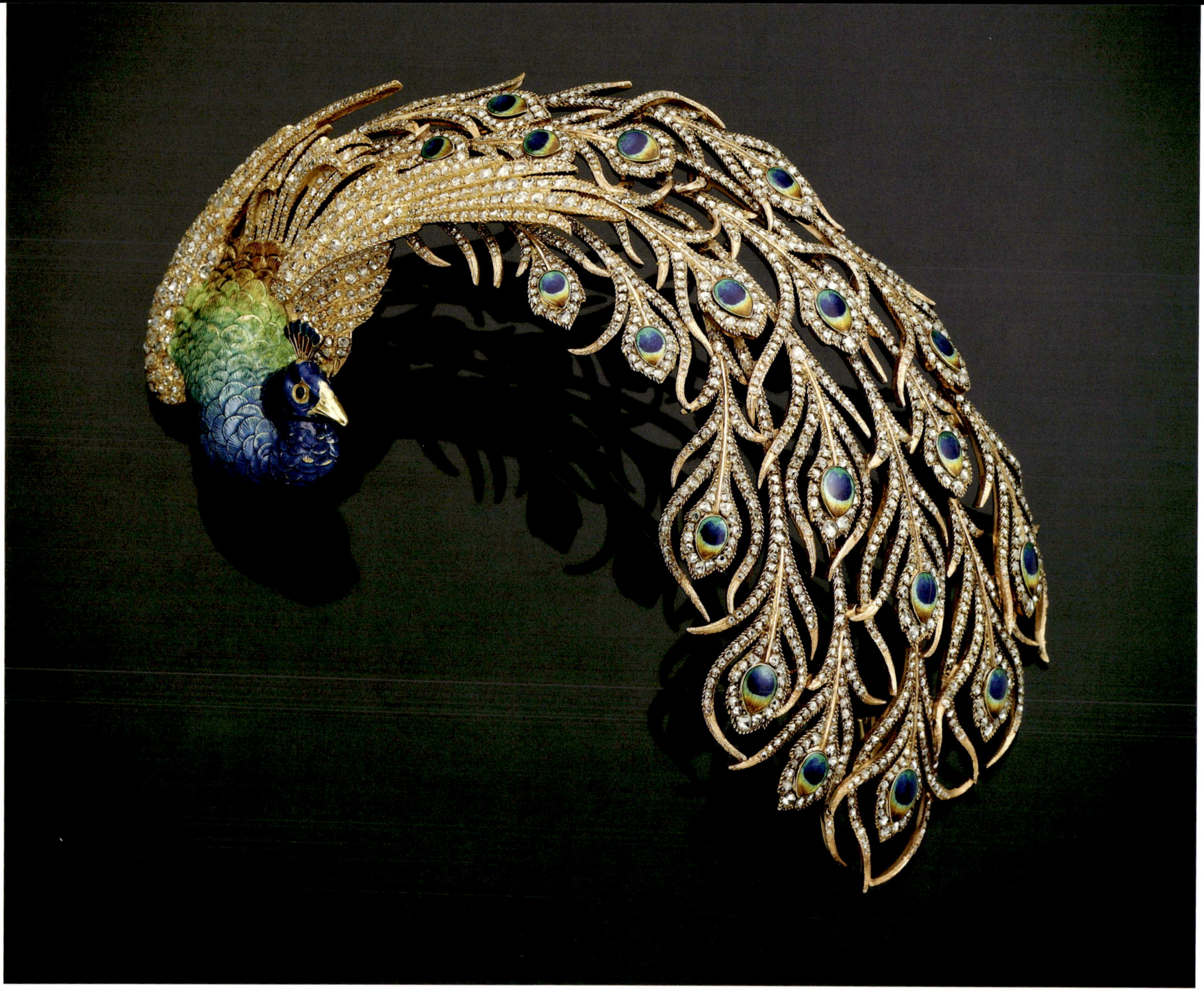

67

Aigrette

Mellerio dits Meller (Mellerio, known as Meller), Paris, ca. 1905. Gold, platinum, diamonds, enamel
CAT. 123

The peacock motif signified the exotic in European jewelry. This aigrette was made by the long-established Parisian jewelers, Mellerio dits Meller, who had made peacock feather jewelry as far back as 1867; 1,742 graduated rose diamonds are set into the wings and tail. An ardent Francophile, Maharaja Jagatjit Singh of Kapurthala bought this aigrette while in Paris in 1905 and gave it to his young Spanish wife, Anita Delgado, whom the ruler met in 1906 when he went to Madrid for the wedding of King Alfonso XIII to Princess Victoria Eugenie of Great Britain.

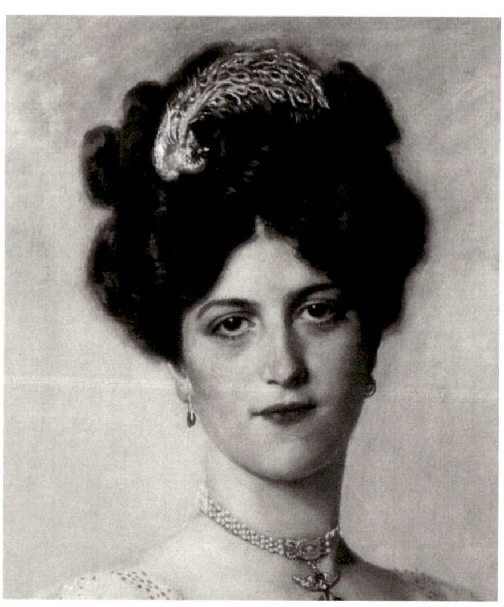

FIG. 44. Edward Patry, detail of *Anita Delgado, Maharani of Kapurthala*, 1907. Oil on canvas, 63 × 39⅜ in. (160 × 100 cm). Collection of Elisa Vázquez de Gey

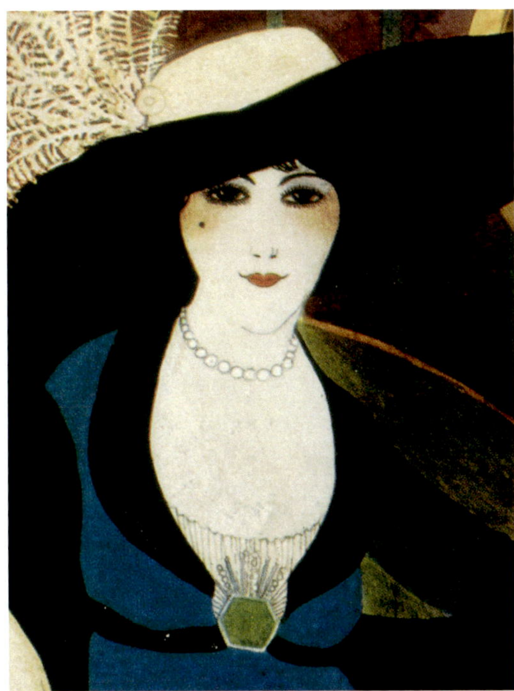

FIG. 45. Detail of cover of *Comoedia Illustré*, 1 March 1911, showing Jeanne Dirys in *Le Cadet de Coutras* wearing the Paul Iribe aigrette as a *plaque de corsage*. Bibliothèque nationale de France

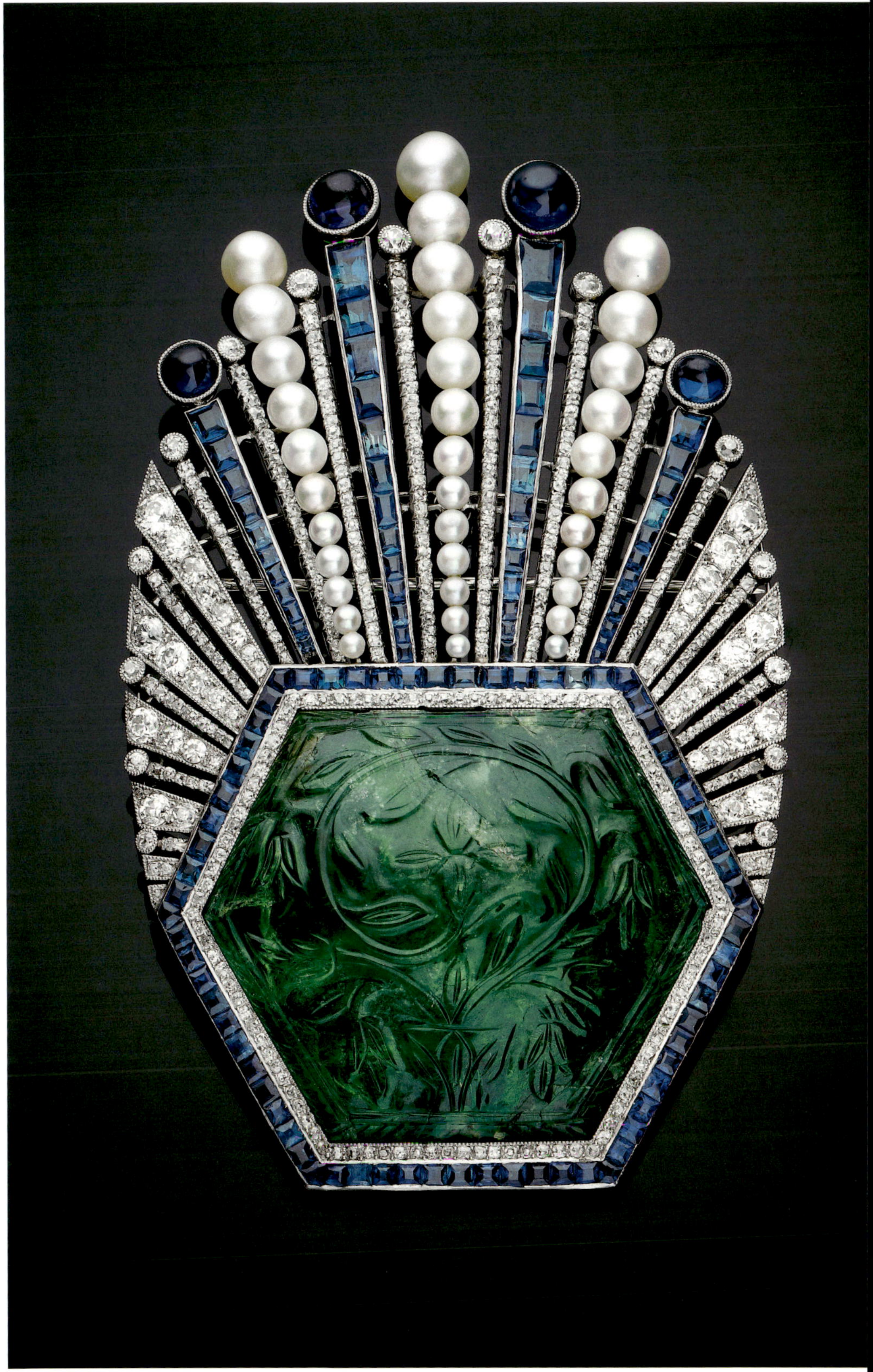

68

Aigrette

Designed by Paul Iribe; made by Robert Linzeler, Paris, 1910. Emerald: India, 1850–1900. Platinum, emerald, sapphires, diamonds, pearls
CAT. 126

This spectacular aigrette is perhaps the first recorded example of a carved Indian emerald being mounted in modern Western jewelry, providing inspiration for the future work of the Cartier brothers, who later owned it. The piece was executed by goldsmith Robert Linzeler to a design by Paul Iribe, a leading cultural figure in early twentieth-century Paris, who presented it to his wife, the actress Jeanne Dirys. The combination of blue and green would have been seen as a radical innovation in European jewelry of the time.

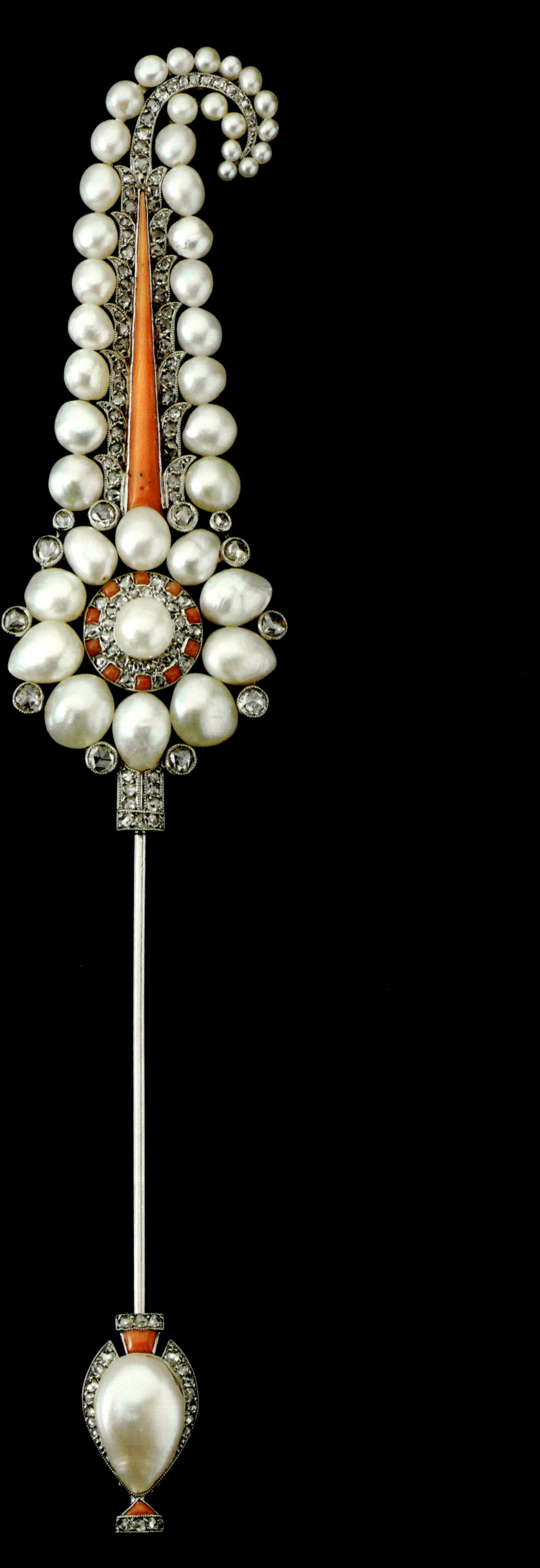

69

Brooch

Cartier Paris, 1922. Platinum, pearls, coral, diamonds
CAT. 127

The design of this *cliquet* brooch draws direct inspiration from a seventeenth- or eighteenth-century turban ornament, or *jigah*. The influence of India on Cartier's designs dates back to Jacques Cartier's visit there in 1911. Aside from building relationships with prospective clients and suppliers of gemstones, Cartier began purchasing pieces of Indian jewelry, which the firm sometimes remounted into more fashionable European forms (see cat. 136).

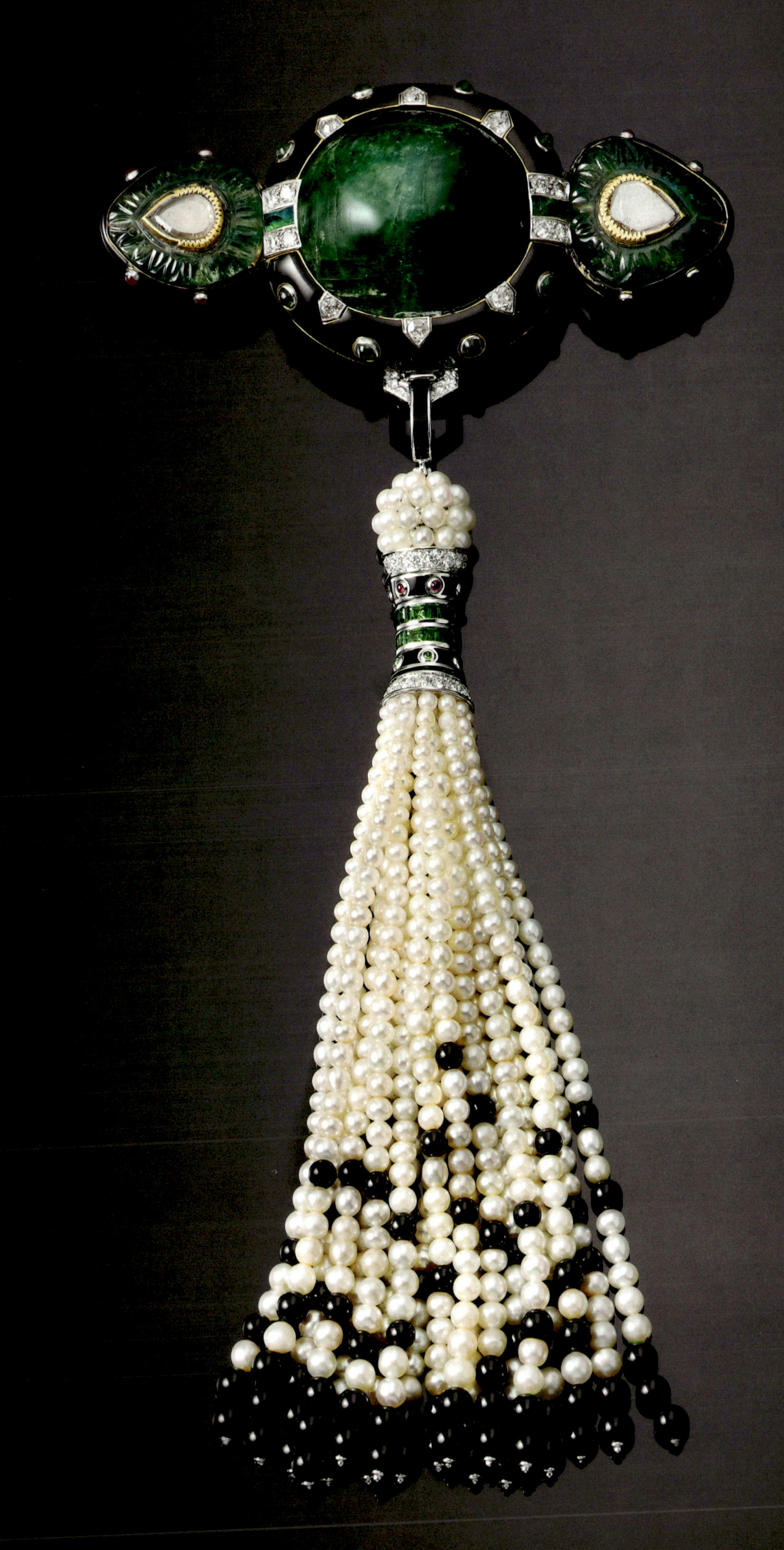

70

Shoulder brooch

Cartier London, 1924; pendant tassel re-created from original records by Cartier workshops, Paris, 2012. Brooch: platinum, emeralds, rubies, diamonds, enamel, gold; tassel: pearls, onyx
CAT. 128

Throughout the 1920s, much of Cartier designers' work reveals the strong influence of Indian jewelry, pieces of which were sometimes remounted by the firm in their own creations. The two extremities of the upper part of this brooch are made of old Indian carved emeralds set with Indian cut diamonds possibly from an armband (*bazuband*). They were almost certainly acquired by Cartier in India and incorporated into a new high-style Art Deco brooch with a platinum, diamond, and onyx setting and hung with a stylish black-and-white tassel.

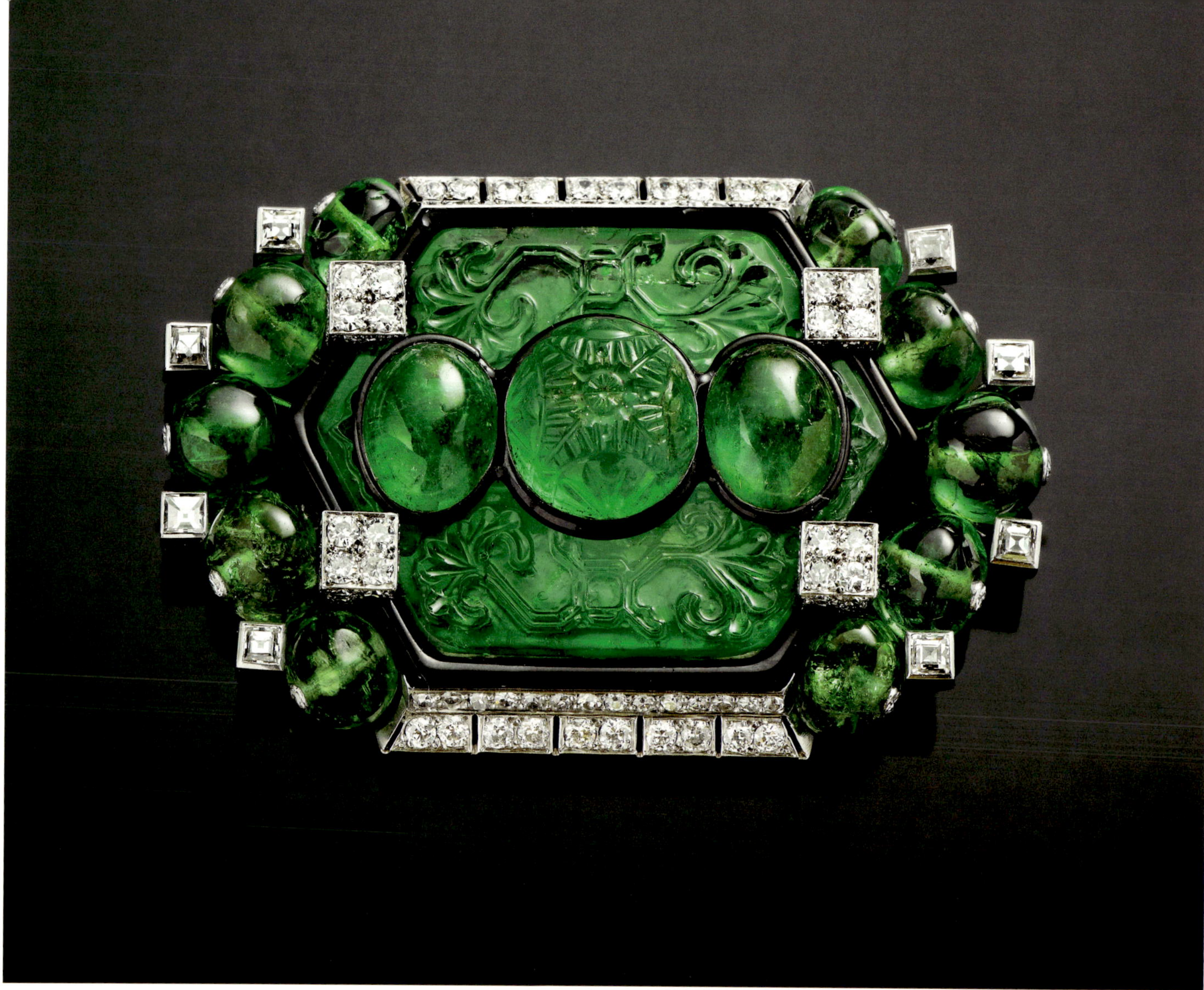

71

Clip brooch

Cartier Paris, 1925; modified by Cartier in 1927.
Platinum, emeralds, diamonds, enamel
CAT. 129

Like the Taj Mahal Emerald (cat. 14/pl. 7), this brooch once formed part of a spectacular presentation of emerald jewelry, including a diadem, a pair of earrings, and a shoulder ornament, designed by Cartier for the 1925 Paris international exposition. Still, the avant-garde ensemble remained unsold and was broken up. Perhaps at the request of a prospective buyer, in 1927 the brooch's features were altered, leading to its present appearance.

72 *(opposite)*

Pair of Manchette bracelets

Van Cleef & Arpels, Paris, 1926 and 1928.
Platinum, diamonds, emeralds. Private collection
CAT. 137

This pair of bracelets with their fringe of emerald beads are inspired by Indian anklets such as the pair shown as cat. 107/pl. 60. They were designed for Daisy Fellowes, who was the international fashion icon of the 1920s and 1930s, incorporating Indian emerald beads mounted on to highly stylized Art Deco bracelets made up of a complex abstract assemblage of geometric-cut diamonds. The bracelets can be transformed into a necklace by joining them together.

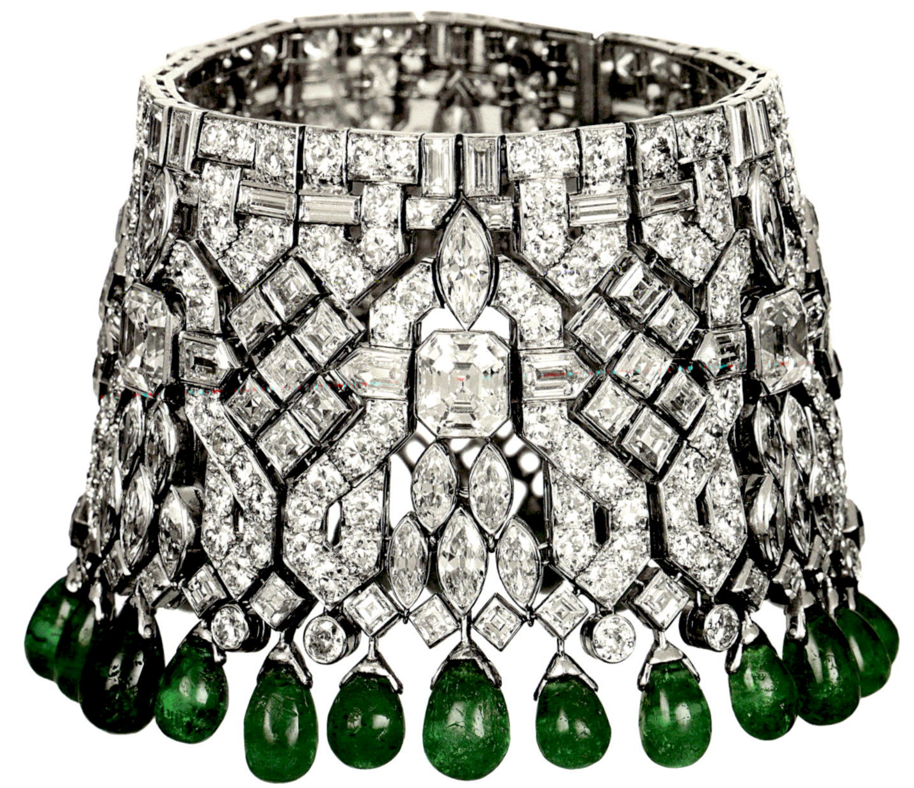

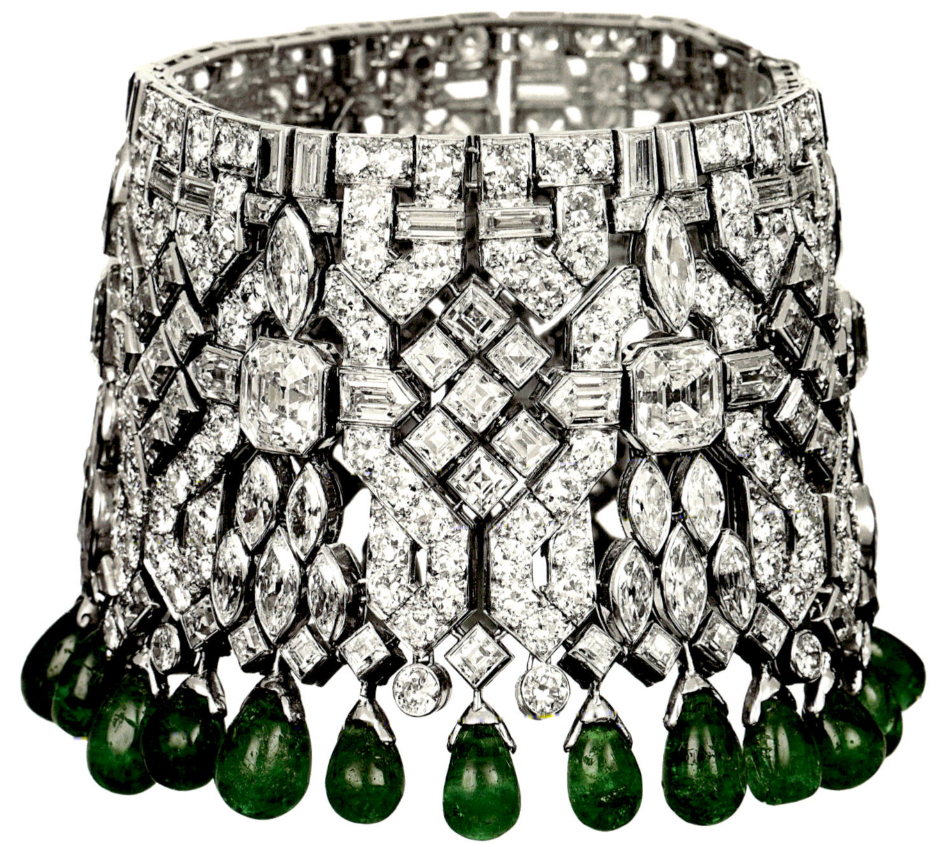

CARTIER AND INDIA

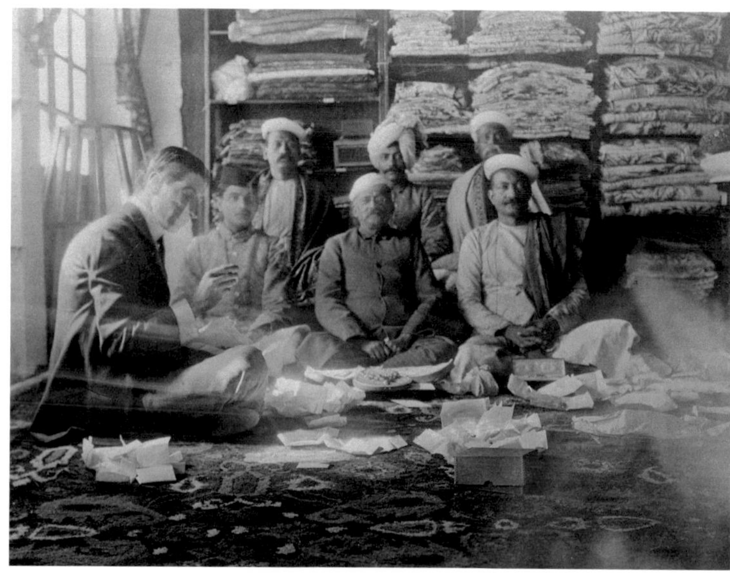

FIG. 46. Jacques Cartier with Indian gemstone dealers, 1911. Photograph from Jacques Cartier's album recording his voyage to India in 1911, Cartier Archives

In the first half of the twentieth century, India was the most persistent exotic influence on Western jewelry. Of all the non-Western cultural styles brought to bear on fine jewelry made by the major European houses—among them ancient Egyptian, Persian, Chinese, and Japanese—that of India remained the most stalwart. The Parisian jewelry firm of Cartier started to take its keynotes from India in 1911, following Jacques Cartier's visit to that year's Delhi Durbar. Cartier was so impressed by the magnificence of the jewelry worn by the maharajas at the ceremonies marking the coronation of King George V and Queen Mary that he started to include Indian stones and designs in his jewelry. The firm now incorporated carved Indian colored gemstones, particularly carved Mughal emeralds, into a new type of highly colored jewelry, while adopting forms based on Indian traditional jewelry, such as the armband, anklet, or bangle.

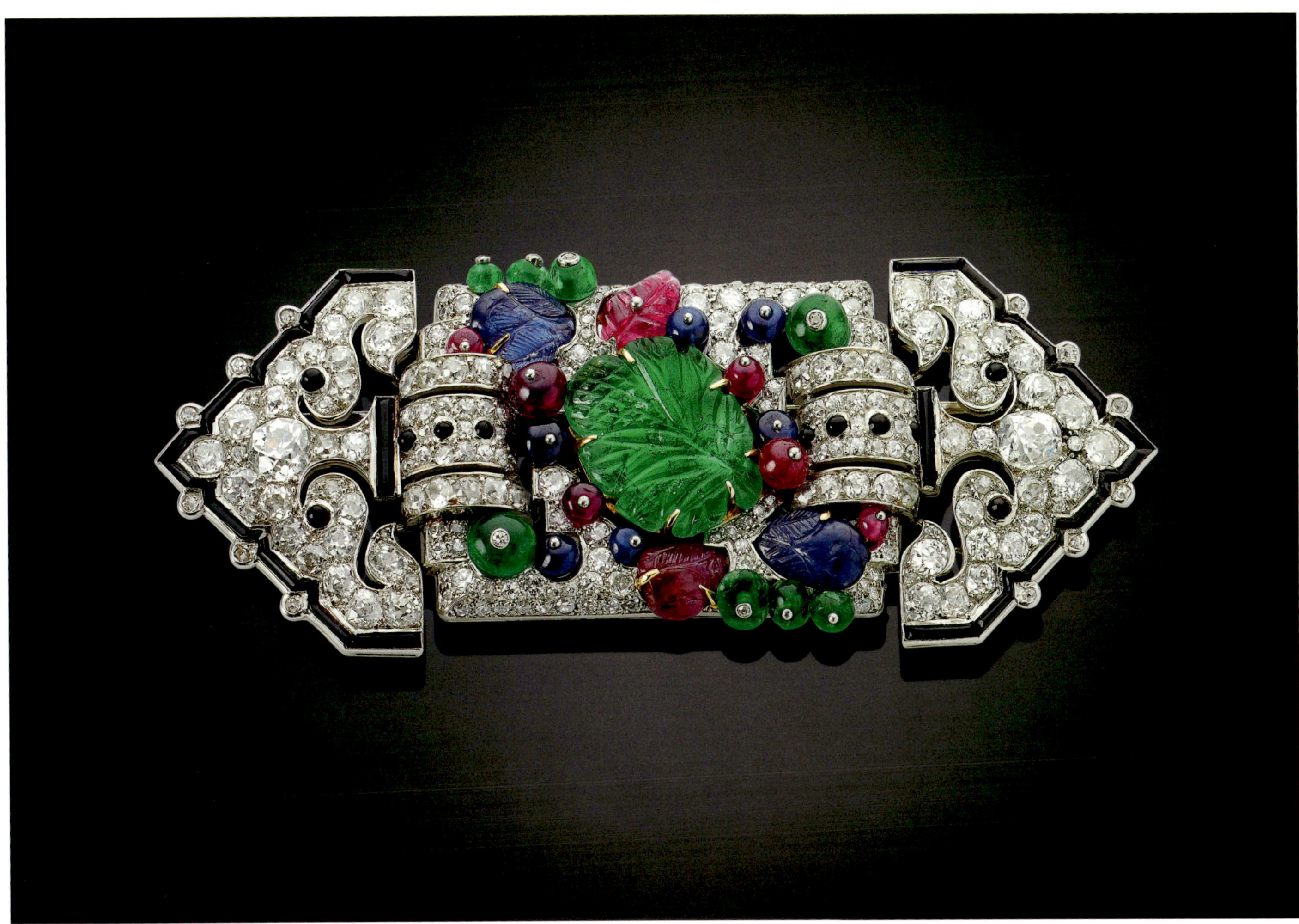

73

Brooch

Cartier Paris, 1929. Platinum, diamonds, sapphires, rubies, onyx, emeralds
CAT. 135

This brooch epitomizes Cartier's exotic creations of the period. The happy mixture of multicolored carved gems and beads is typical of the Tutti Frutti style, so named because of the gemstones' resemblance to fruit and foliage. The profusion of color and the asymmetrical arrangement of the carved gemstones contrasts with the more severe background palette of black and silver and severely geometric frame.

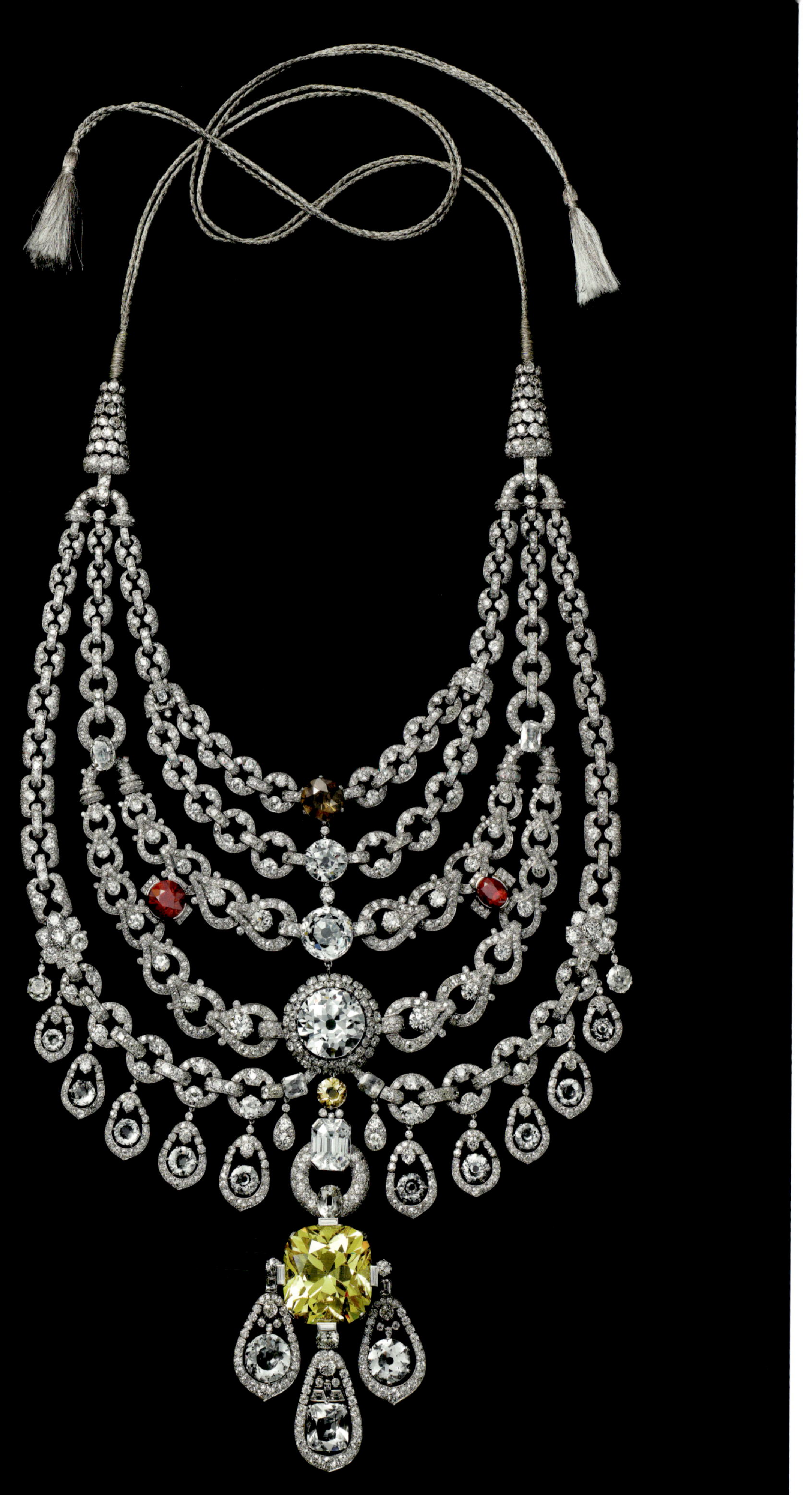

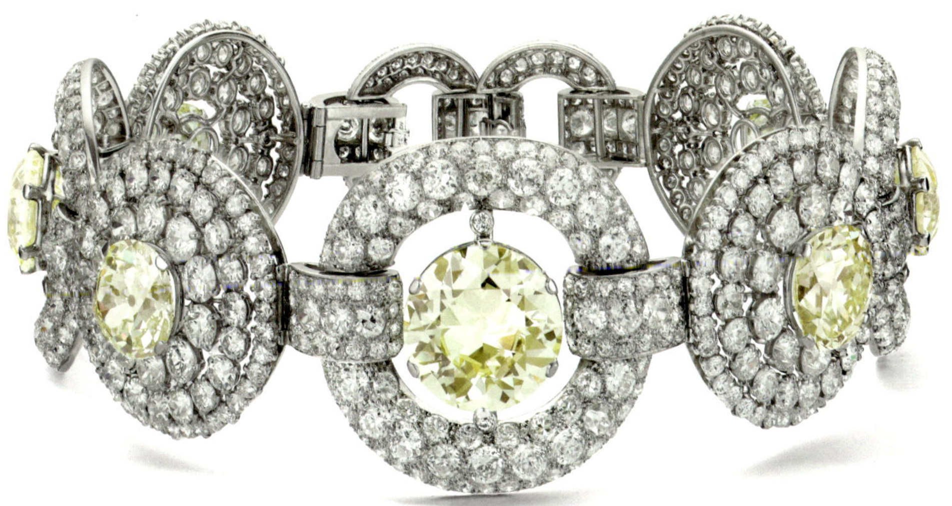

74 *(opposite)*

The Maharaja of Patiala Necklace

Cartier Collection, Paris, 1928. Platinum, diamonds, synthetic ruby, smoky quartz, citrine
CAT. 139

This lavish order placed by Maharaja Bhupinder Singh of Patiala, completed in 1928, was the largest ever made by Cartier. The ceremonial necklace was constructed around a 234.65-carat yellow diamond, the famous De Beers diamond. Composed of nearly three thousand diamonds and other precious stones set in chains, it was large enough to cover the breast of the prince. Dismantled after 1948, the necklace's remains minus the large gemstones were rediscovered in 1998. The necklace was reconstituted in Cartier's workshops using traditional techniques and synthetic stones. It represents the zenith of the exchange between East and West in jewelry, through its use of meticulous European methods of manufacture to make a newly envisioned concept of traditional Indian ceremonial jewelry. It achieved a level of magnificence during the twilight years of the Indian maharajas that was never surpassed.

75

Patiala diamond choker

Cartier Collection, Paris, 1928. Platinum, diamonds
CAT. 138

Also known as a dog collar, this choker necklace complements the great ceremonial necklace created by Cartier for the Maharaja of Patiala in 1928. Indian tradition required that, during major events, several necklaces be superimposed to create an image of splendor and power for the maharajas. In the West, necklaces of this design would be worn only by women.

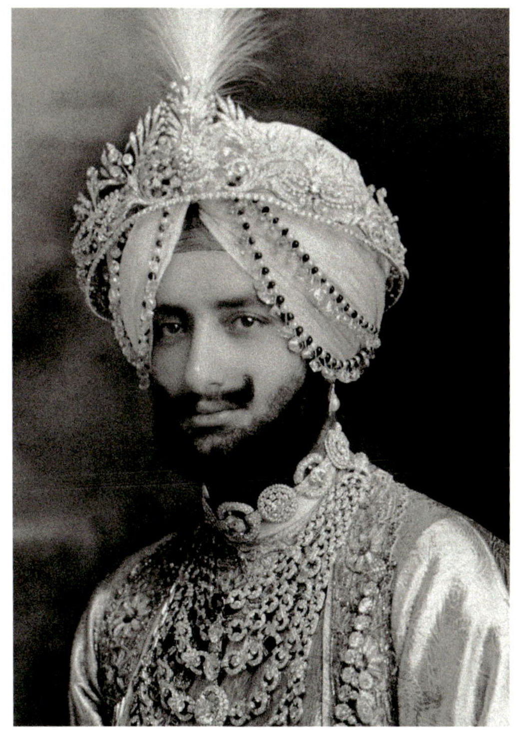

FIG. 47. Detail of Maharaja Yadavindra Singh of Patiala wearing the diamond-and-platinum necklace created by Cartier in 1928 for his father, Maharaja Bhupinder Singh, ca. 1940. John Fasal Collection

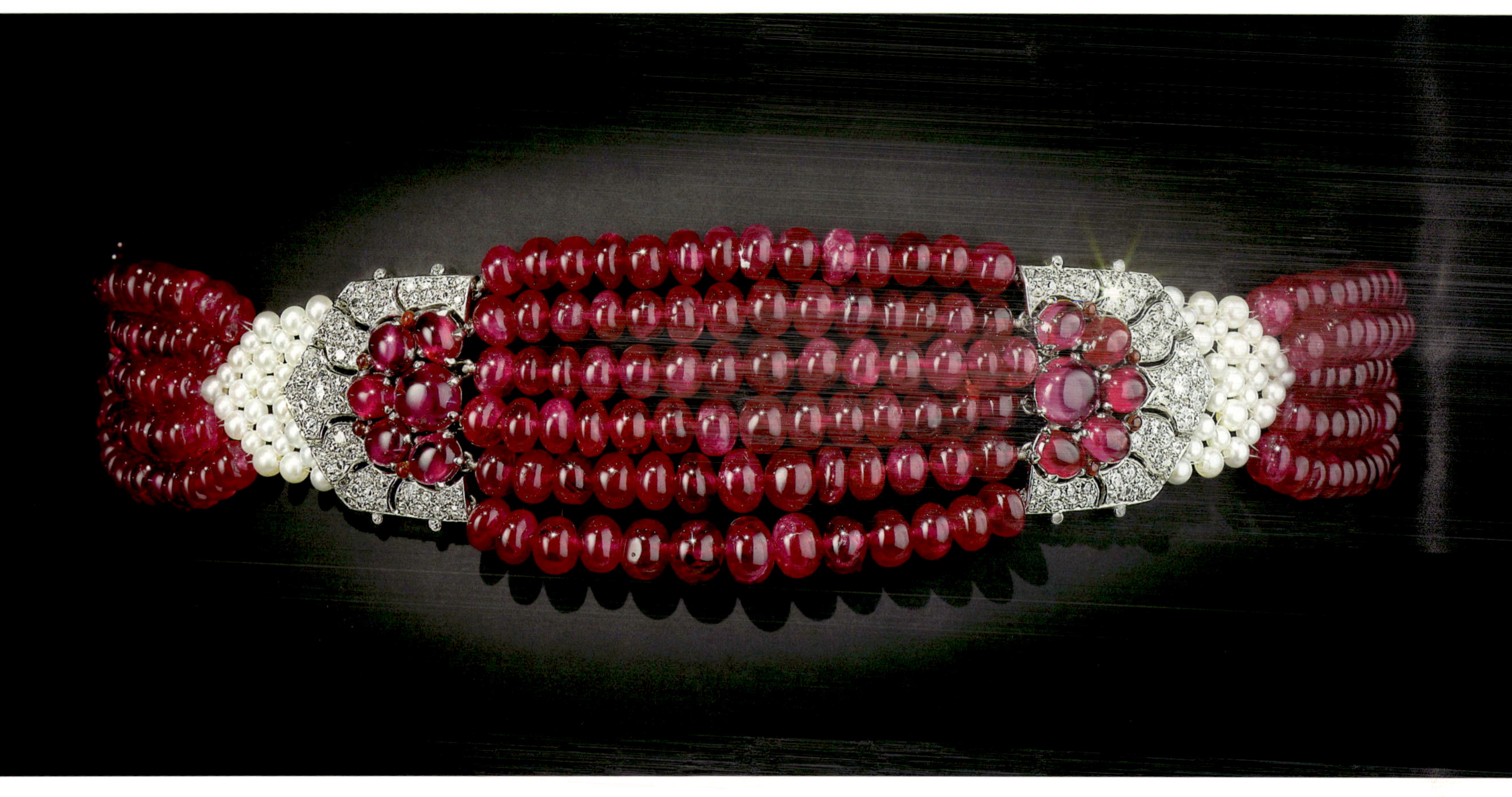

76

Patiala ruby choker

Cartier Paris, 1931; restored and restrung by Cartier Tradition, Geneva, 2012. Rubies, diamonds, pearls, platinum

CAT. 140

Maharaja Bhupinder Singh of Patiala's extensive commissions from European masters were principally for male jewelry. However, in 1931 he asked Cartier to make a series of pieces for the women of his family. This choker is the uppermost section of a spectacular triple-tier necklace executed in a high Art Deco taste.

77
Nawanagar turban ornament

India, 1907, with later modifications ca. 1935.
White gold, diamonds, feathers
CAT. 144

Maharaja Ranjitsinhji of Nawanagar, a great connoisseur of precious gems and jewelry, wore this turban ornament. Although made in India, its styling is thoroughly Western—evident, for instance, in the use of white gold and open-set brilliant-cut diamonds rather than the traditional yellow gold and closed-set gems. Originally the sprays of diamonds on the upper section were more spread out, a design that was remodeled into a tighter composition during the reign of Ranjitsinhji's nephew and successor, Maharaja Digvijaysinhji.

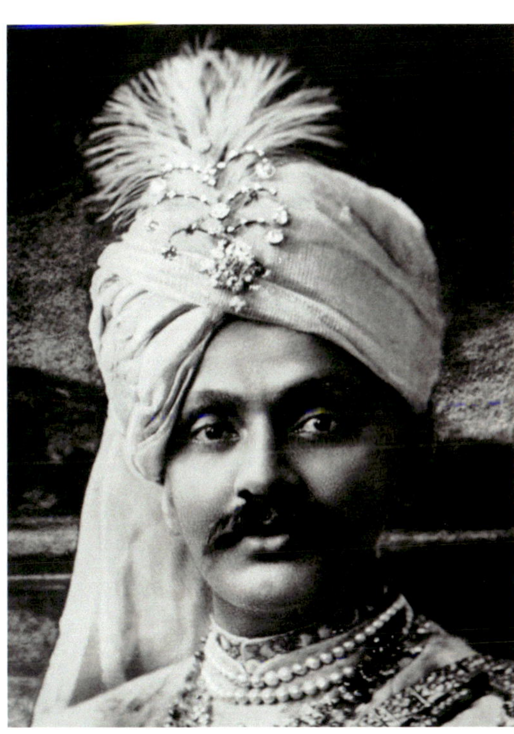

FIG. 48. Detail of Maharaja Ranjitsinhji Vibhaji, Jam Sahib of Nawanagar, ca. 1911. John Fasal Collection

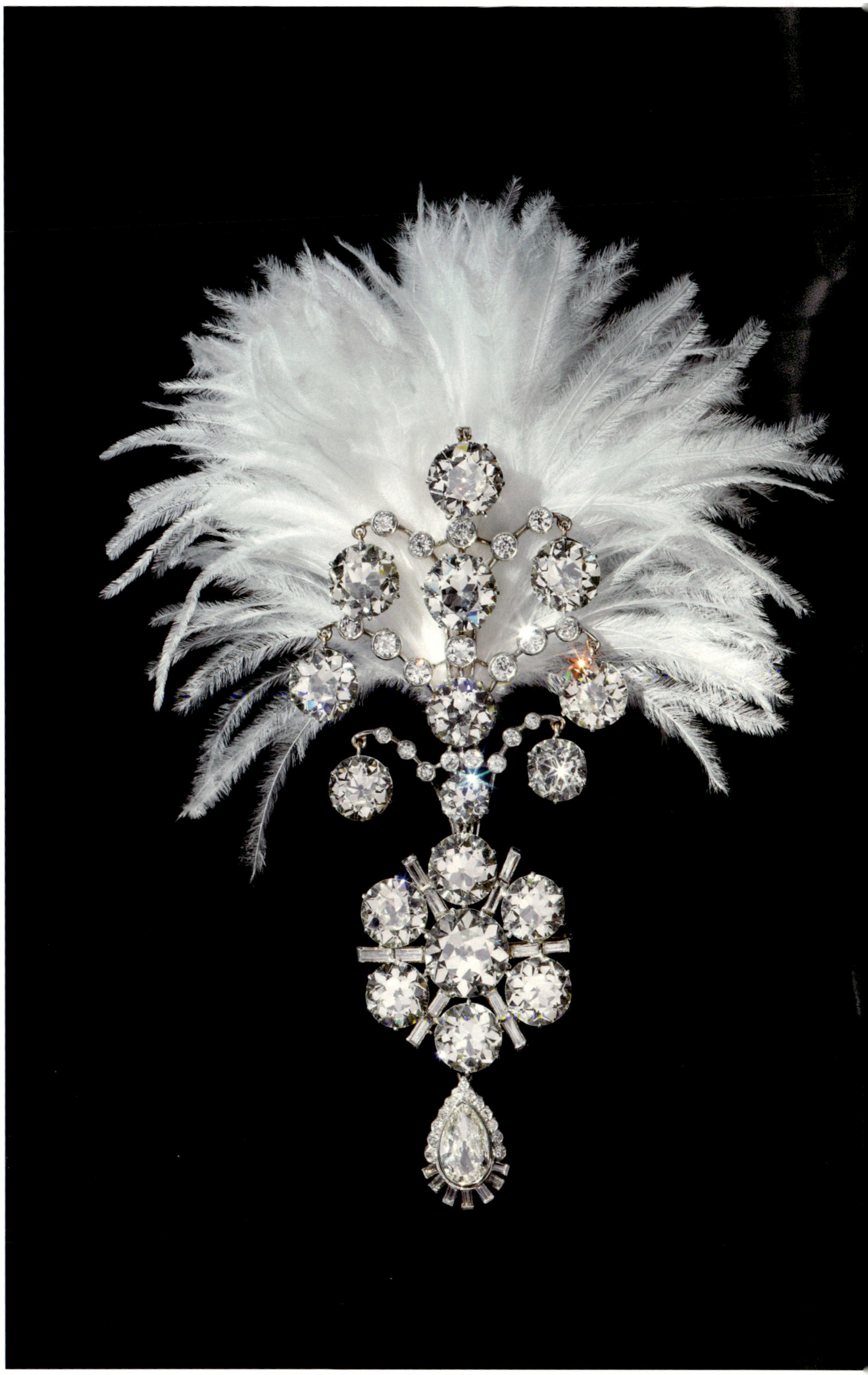

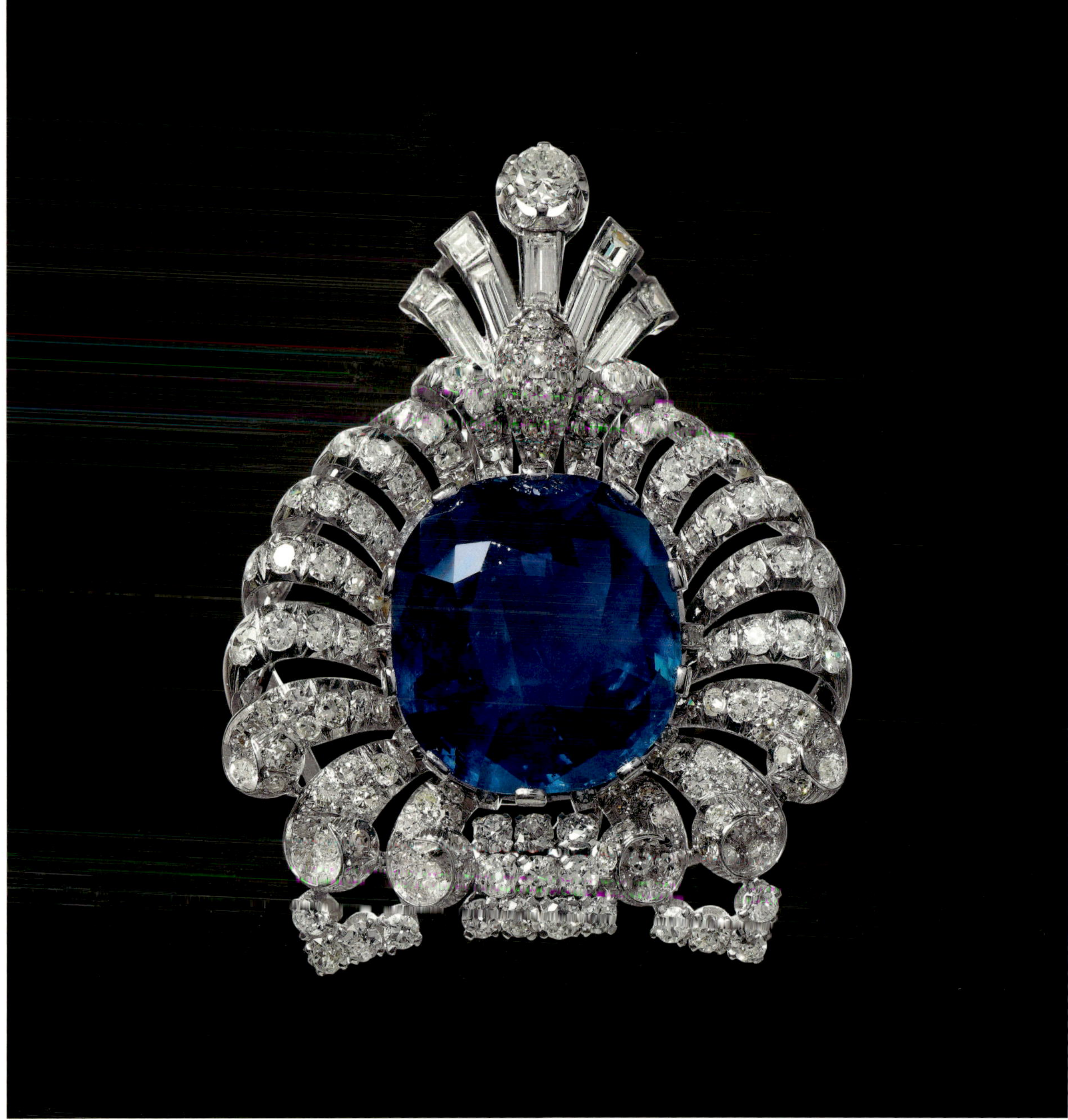

78

Nawanagar turban ornament

India, ca. 1920; modified ca. 1925–1935.
Diamonds and a large sapphire in platinum
CAT. 145

Showcasing an exceptional 109.5-carat sapphire, this piece was designed for Maharaja Ranjitsinhji of Nawanagar. Although made in India, it is strongly influenced by European taste, particularly in the choice of platinum for the setting. Initially made as a brooch or pendant, it was later embellished with additional diamonds to convert it into a turban ornament.

79

Nawanagar Tiger's Eye turban ornament

Cartier London, 1937. Platinum, diamonds

CAT. 146

The creative dialogue between Indian princes and European jewelry houses in the early twentieth century is evident in this magnificent turban ornament. It was made in 1937 for Maharaja Digvijaysinhji of Nawanagar using an exceptional 61.5-carat golden hue diamond acquired a few years earlier from Cartier by his predecessor, Maharaja Ranjitsinhji of Nawanagar. The use of baguette-cut diamonds transformed the traditional Indian shape into a masterpiece of Art Deco design. Notwithstanding its impressive effect, this turban ornament was designed for multiple purposes: the upper section can be removed, transforming the piece into a brooch. In addition, the central diamond was designed to detach from the mount so that the maharaja could have the pleasure of handling the gem.

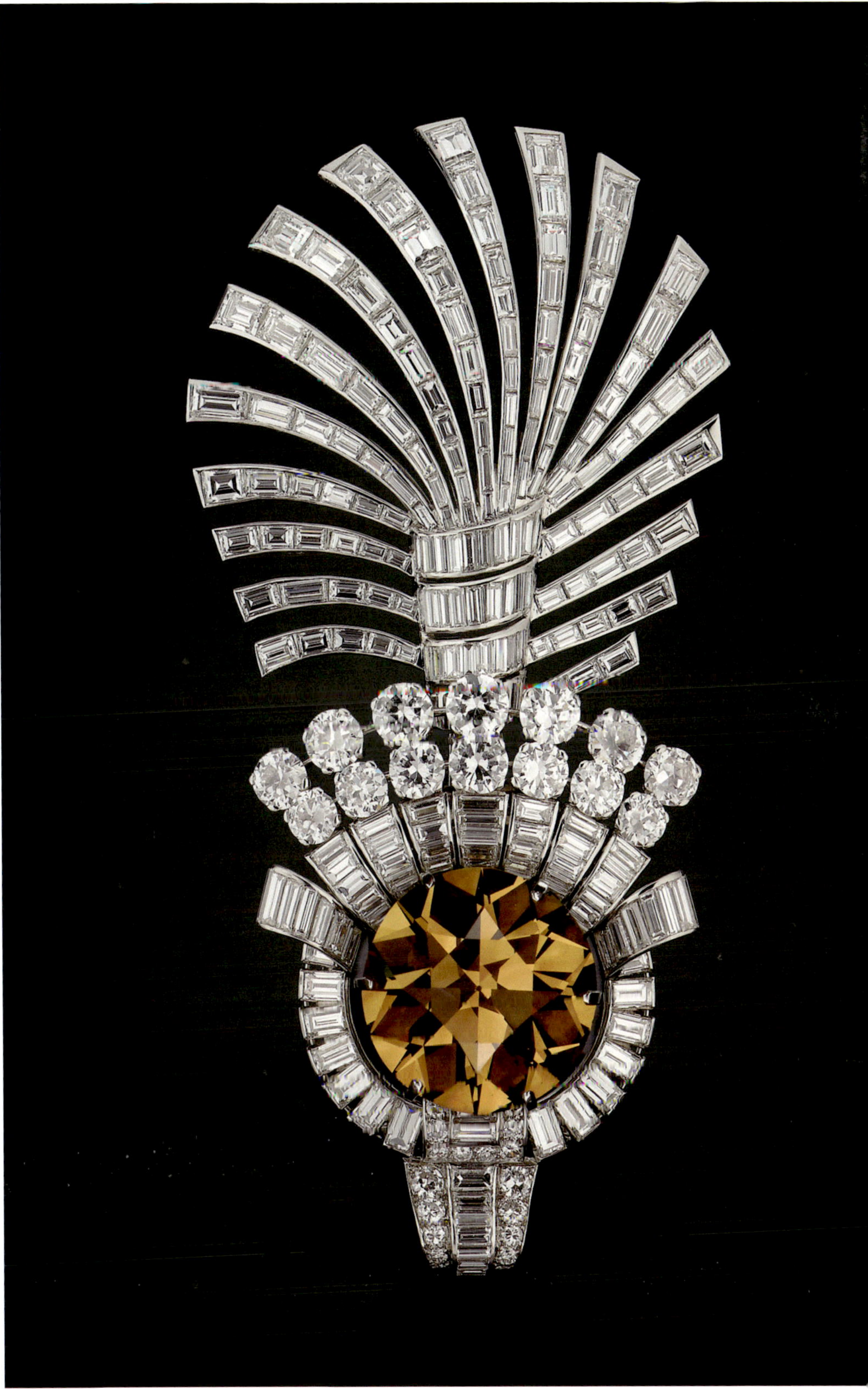

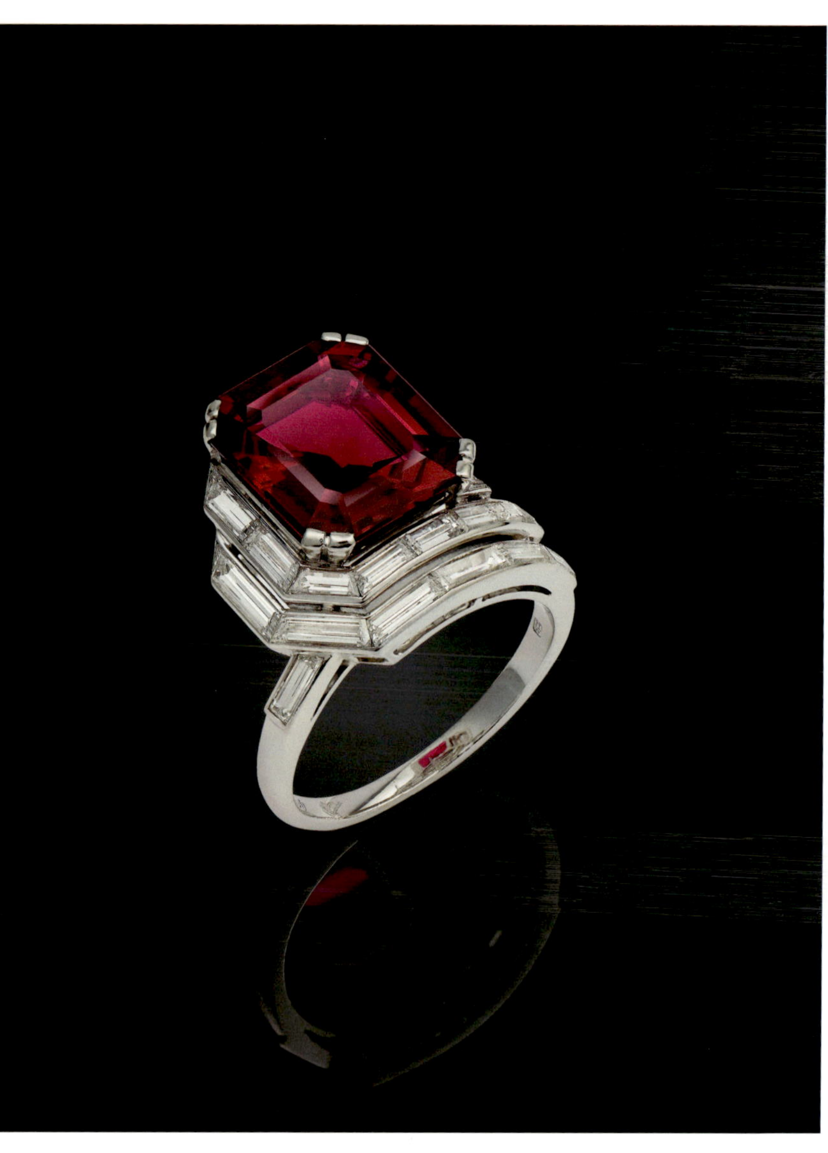

80

Indore ruby ring

Mauboussin, 1930s; altered by Harry Winston, ca. 1940–1945. Ruby, diamonds, platinum
CAT. 141

Designed by Mauboussin, the setting for this exceptional ruby reflects the taste for asymmetric design in the period. Maharaja Yeshwant Rao Holkar II of Indore was a loyal client of the firm, partly due to his friendship with Jean Goulet, a member of the Mauboussin family with whom he shared an interest in Indian religions. Goulet was invited to Indore to catalogue the gems in the Royal Treasury, some of which the firm remounted. It is probably the ring shown worn in the portrait of the maharaja on page 30.

81 *(opposite)*

Nawanagar ruby necklace

Cartier, 1937. Platinum, rubies, diamonds
CAT. 147

The stylistic encounter between Cartier and princely India reaches a high point in this necklace. It was designed for Maharaja Digvijaysinhji of Nawanagar in 1937 using an exceptional group of oval and cushion-cut Burmese rubies collected by his predecessor Maharaja Ranjitsinhji, a renowned connoisseur of gems and a friend of Jacques Cartier. Following Indian independence, the necklace was returned to Cartier for resale. The original design, meant for an Indian prince, was altered to suit a woman's physique, the line of single rubies to the rear having been substantially reduced. This ruby necklace was worn in its modified shape by Mrs. Loel Guinness at Truman Capote's Black and White Ball in 1966.

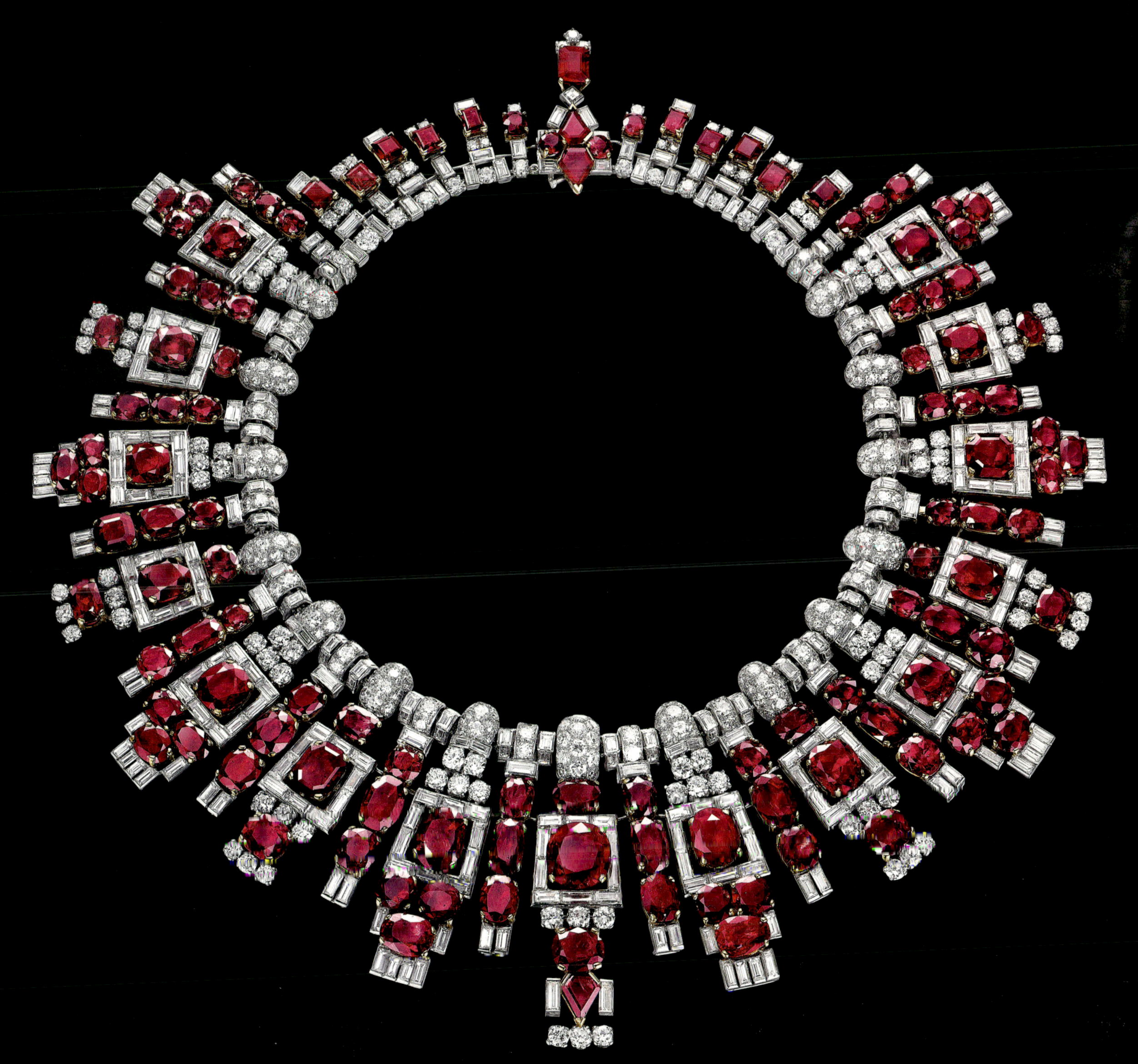

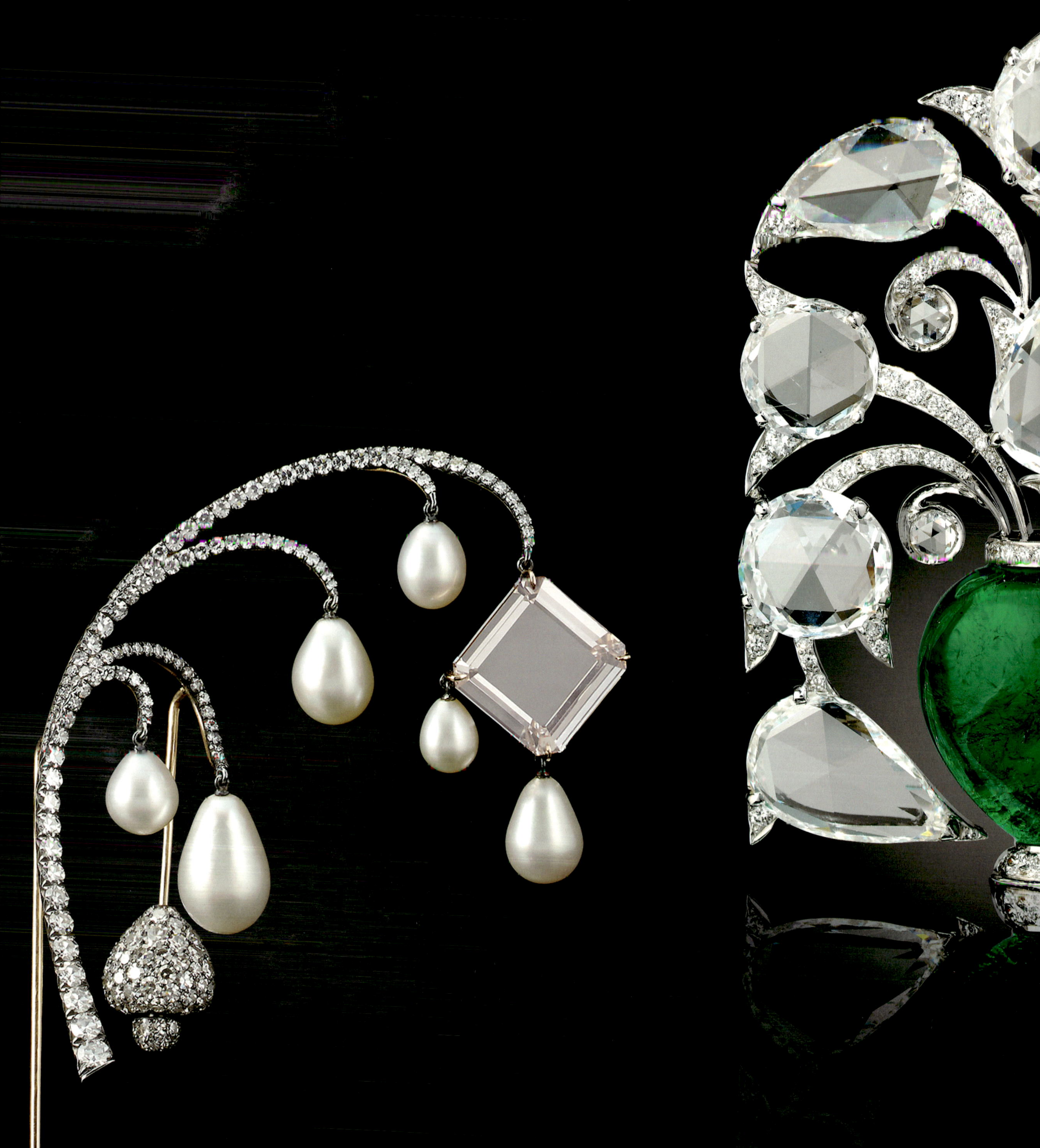

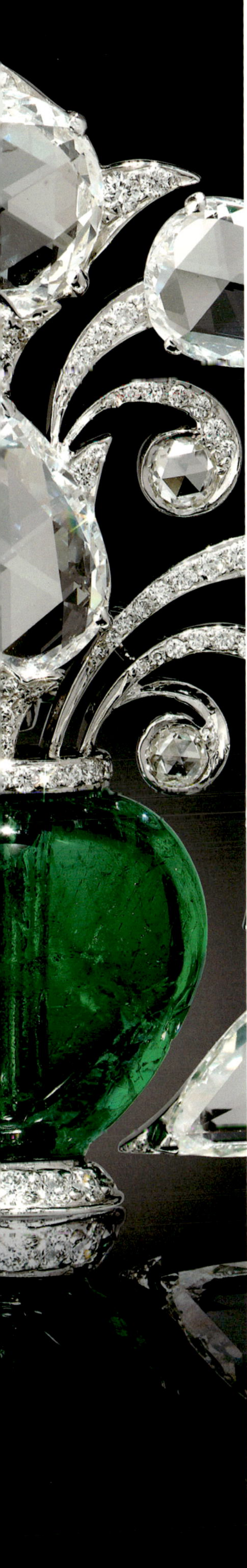

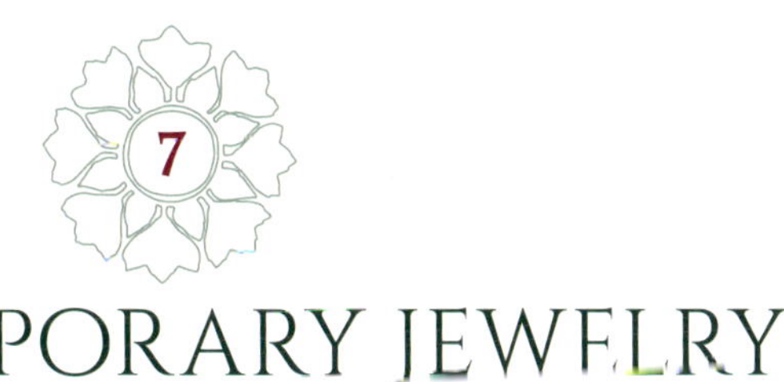

CONTEMPORARY JEWELRY

Bhagat and JAR

The work of leading contemporary jewelers, East and West, continues to reflect the influence of India in a variety of expressions. Renowned Parisian jeweler JAR has incorporated historic Indian stones into his work, appreciating their distinctive shapes and cuts that stand out against the geometrically faceted gems that dominate Western jewelry today. At times his creations also draw on Indian motifs, as is apparent in the group of his objects included here.

JAR's jewels can be contrasted with the pieces created by the Mumbai-based jeweler Bhagat, whose work is characterized by the use of custom-cut flat diamonds and natural pearls in almost invisible platinum settings. These pieces often echo traditional Indian jewelry forms, but they are executed with a sensibility that reflects the precision of the great European jewelry houses, with a fresh minimalist approach. Through these works, these two jewelers reflect the ongoing cross-cultural exchange between India and the West.

82

Pearl necklace

Bhagat, Mumbai, 2012. Pearls, diamonds, platinum
CAT. 150

Necklaces with multiple rows of pearls are typical items of Indian royal male jewelry. Through the nineteenth and early twentieth centuries, the wearing of pearls by Indian rulers became increasingly profuse, reflecting the overall growth in the scale of jewelry during the British Raj. The greater part of the pearls worn at Indian courts were fished in the waters of the Persian Gulf and taken to India through trade channels. The splendor of the five rows in this necklace, featuring 377 natural pearls of the finest quality, reflects former Indian traditions, although now intended for a woman.

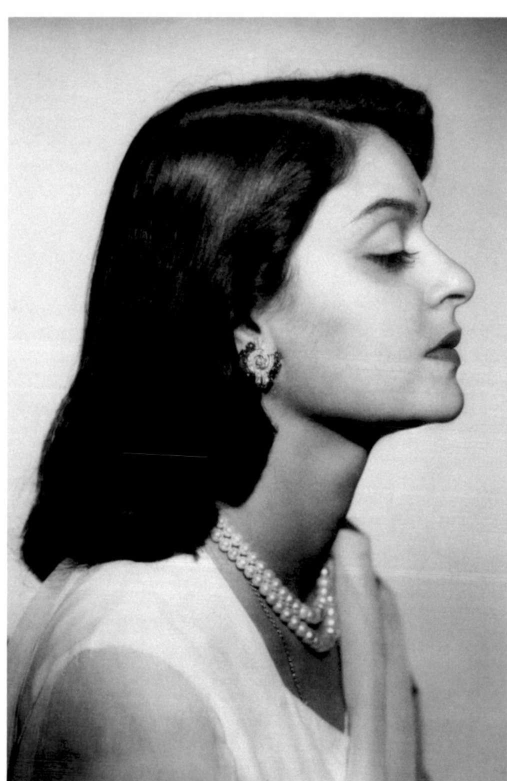

FIG. 49. Detail of Maharani Gayatri Devi of Jaipur, aged 21, 1940. John Fasal Collection

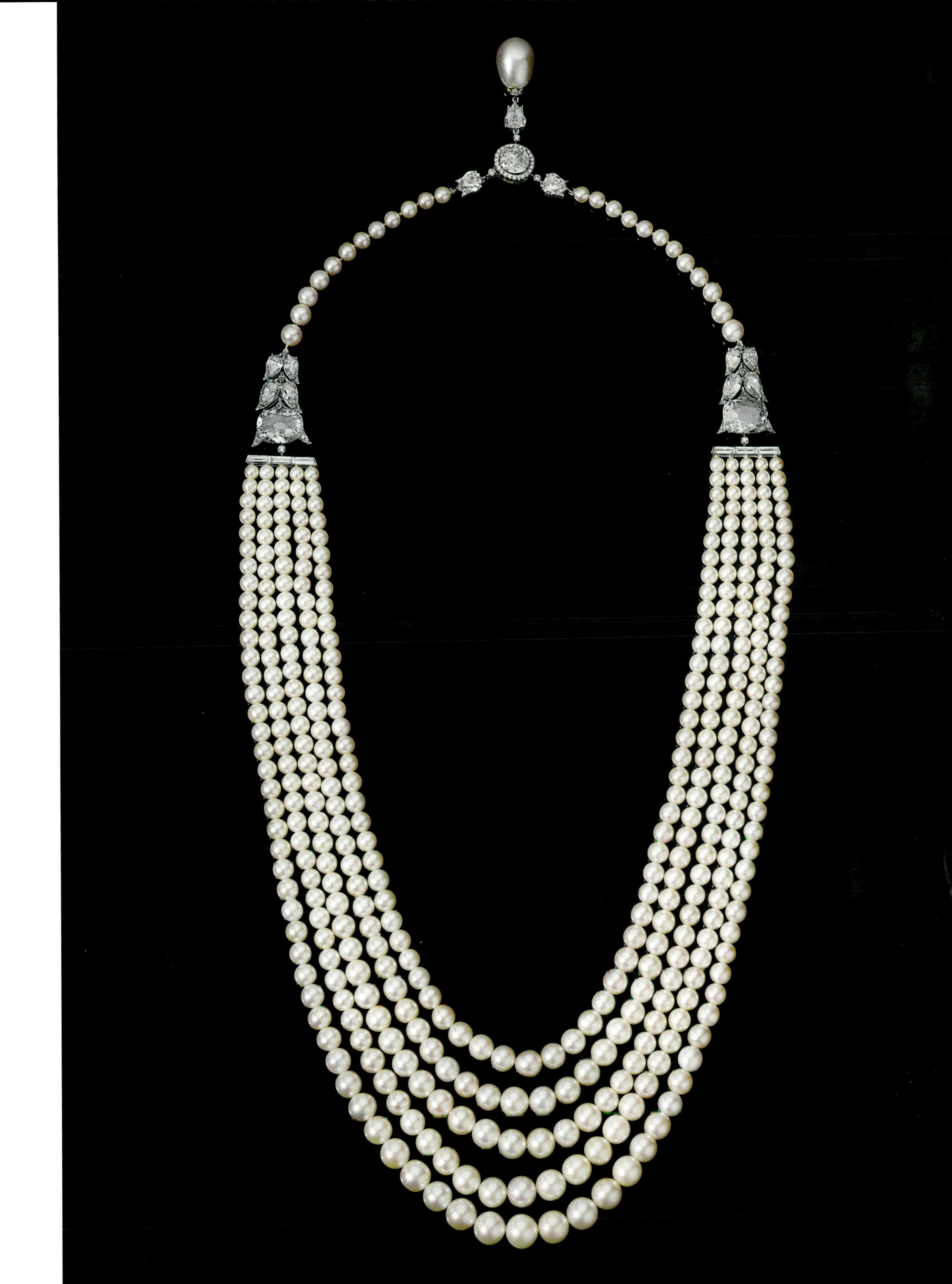

83

Pair of bangles

Bhagat, Mumbai, 2012. Platinum, diamonds, pearls
CAT. 151

In this pair of bangles, Bhagat reinterprets the traditional Indian bangle (*kada*), a form that is ubiquitous among all classes of women throughout India. With a profile of alternating drop-shaped natural pearls and an exterior face of round diamonds, the classic shape is transformed into a slender minimal contemporary form.

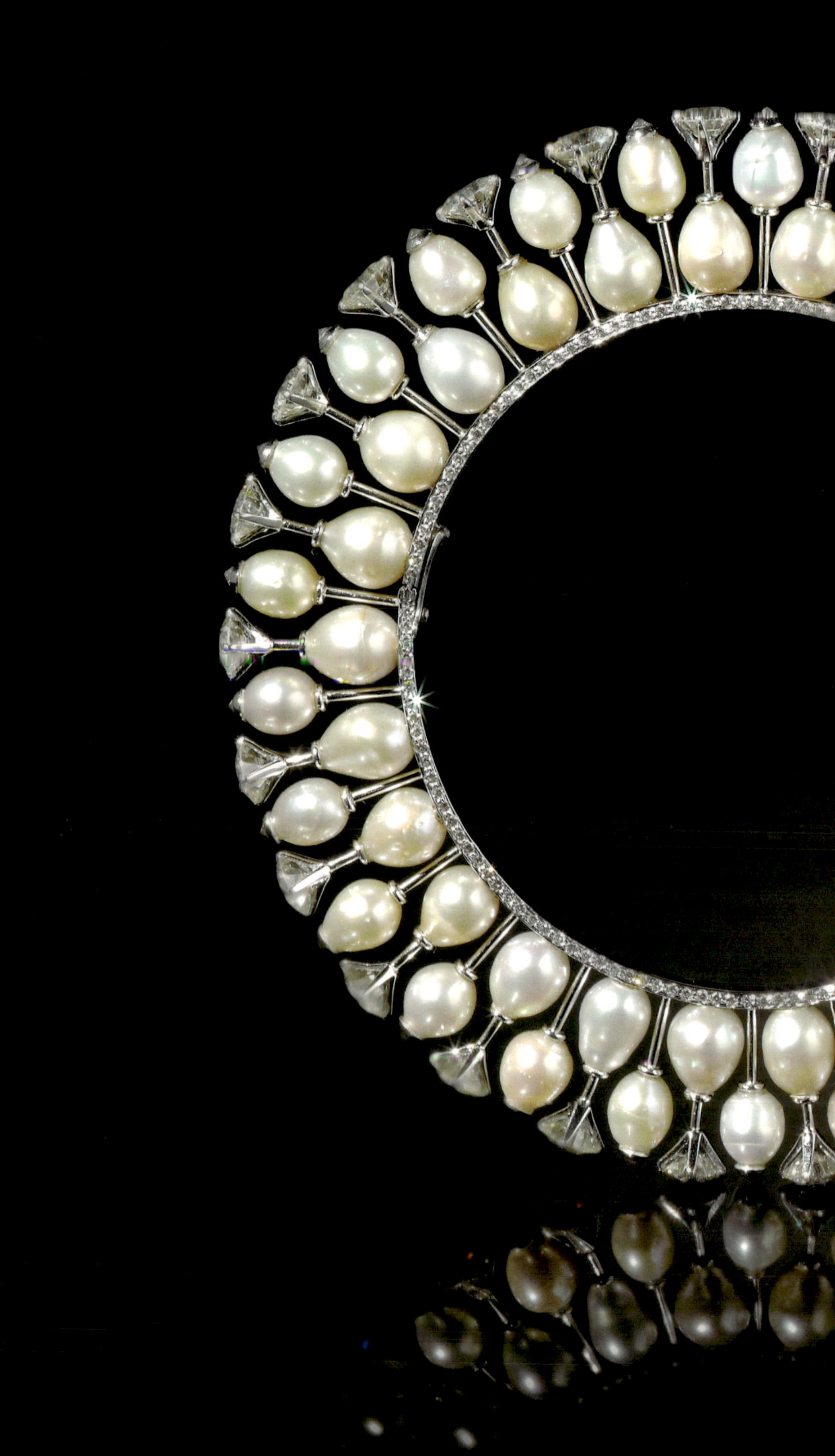

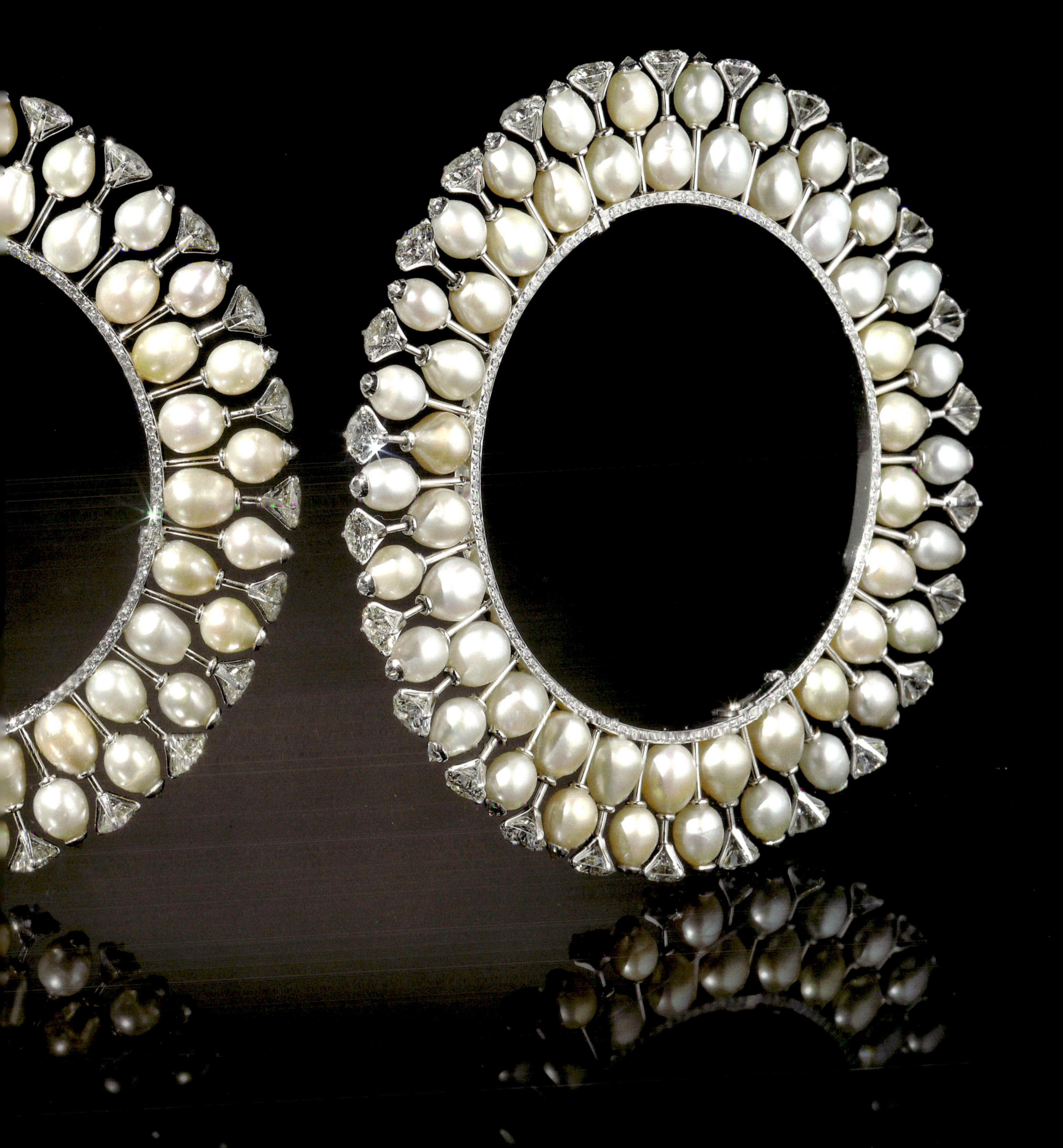

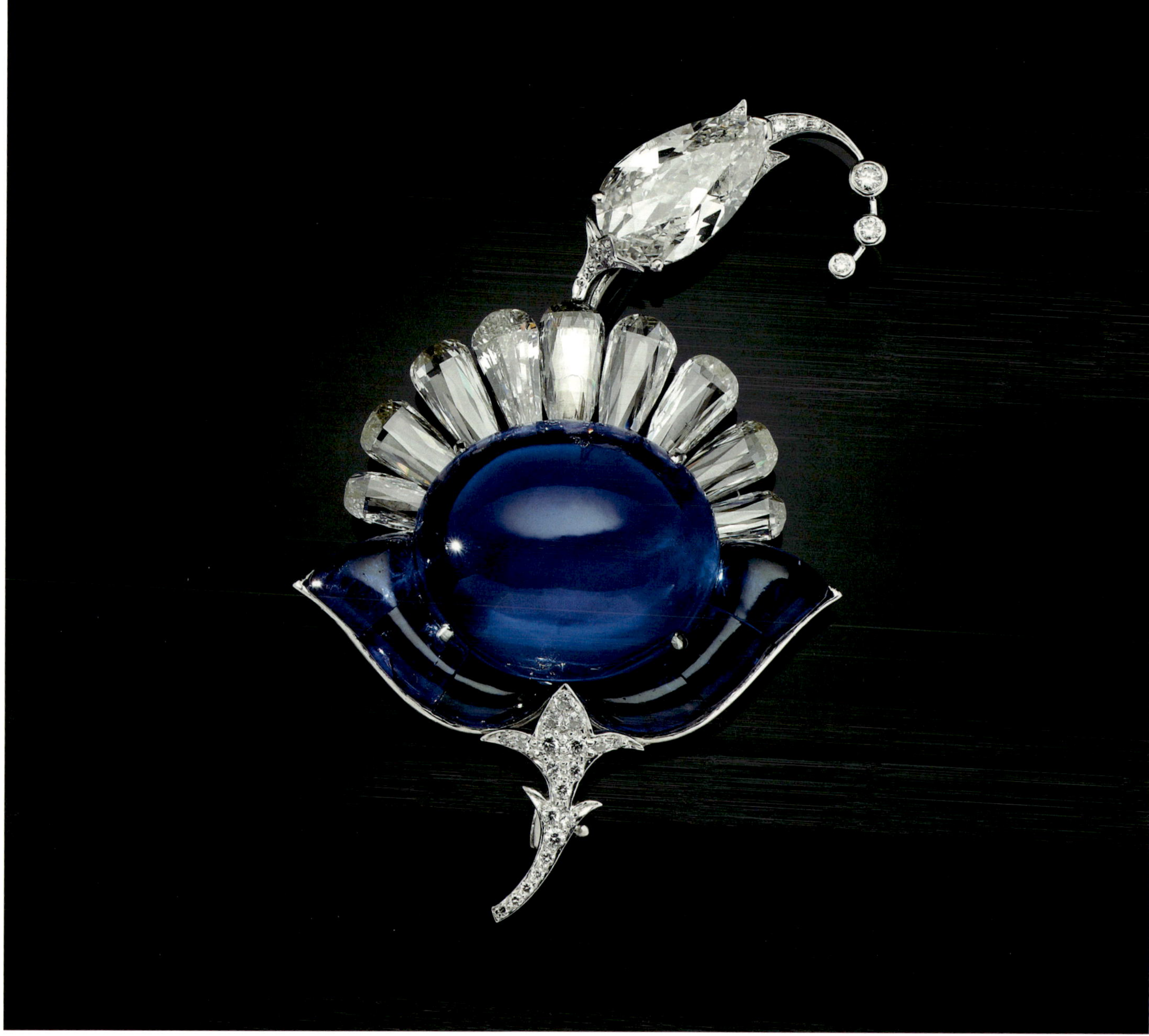

84
Brooch
Bhagat, Mumbai, 2012. Sapphires, diamonds, platinum
CAT. 154

Here Bhagat has reconceived the turban ornament in a diminutive form as a woman's brooch. The tilting pear-shaped diamond simulates the effect of the curve of a feather, while the central cabochon sapphire evokes the single large gemstone that usually defines a turban ornament. The sapphire leaves and the diamond petals are custom-cut, a specialty of Bhagat's workshop.

85 *(opposite)*
Brooch
Bhagat, Mumbai, 2014. Platinum, diamonds, pearls
CAT. 152

Mughal ornament provides a continuous source of inspiration for Bhagat's jewelry. In this innovative pendant brooch, the dominant motif is a floral spray taken from Mughal architecture, specifically the inlaid floor designs at the Mausoleum of Itimad al-Daula, Agra, built in 1622–1628. Typical of Bhagat's jewelry, the diamond petals have been custom-cut for this design.

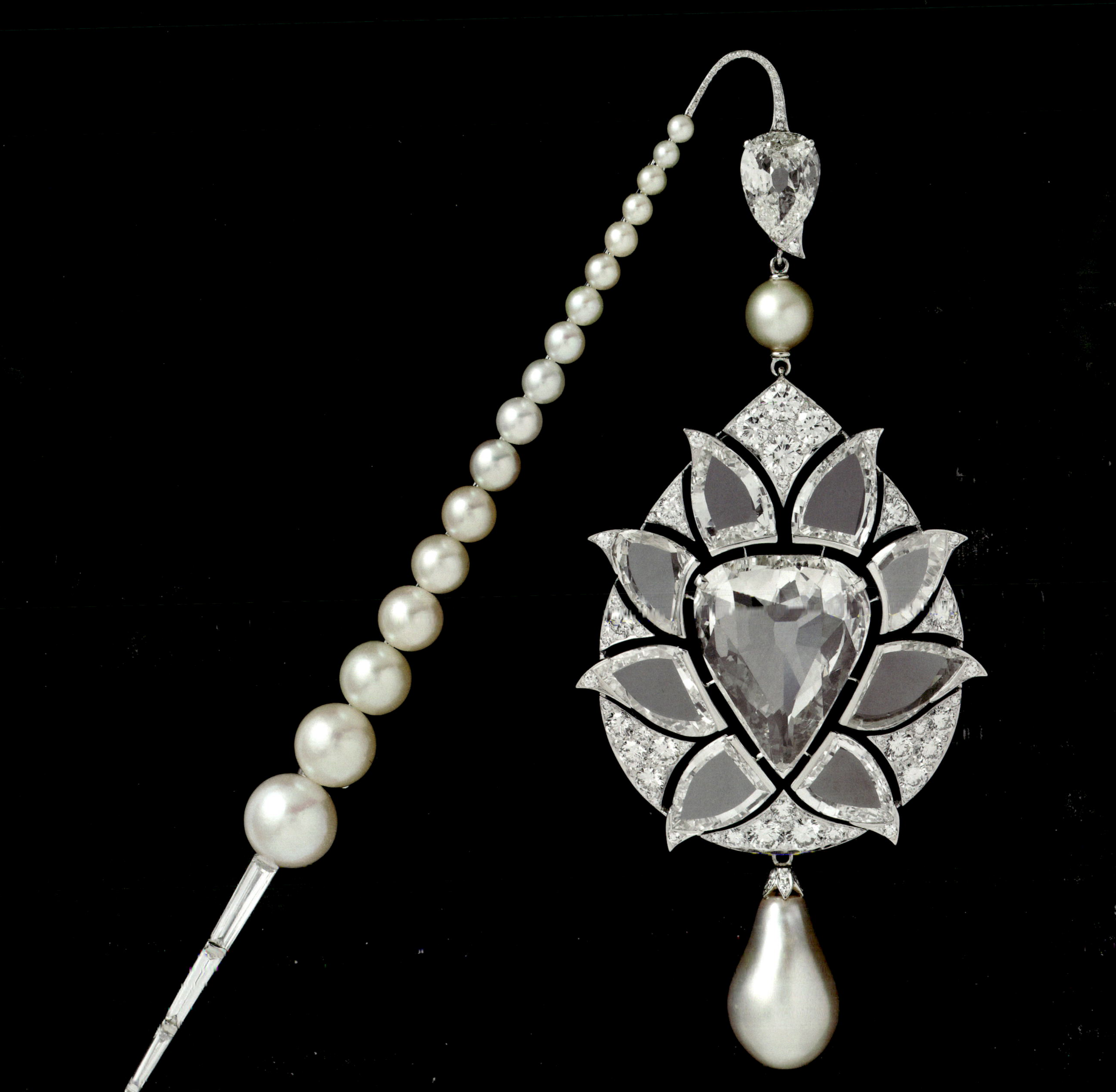

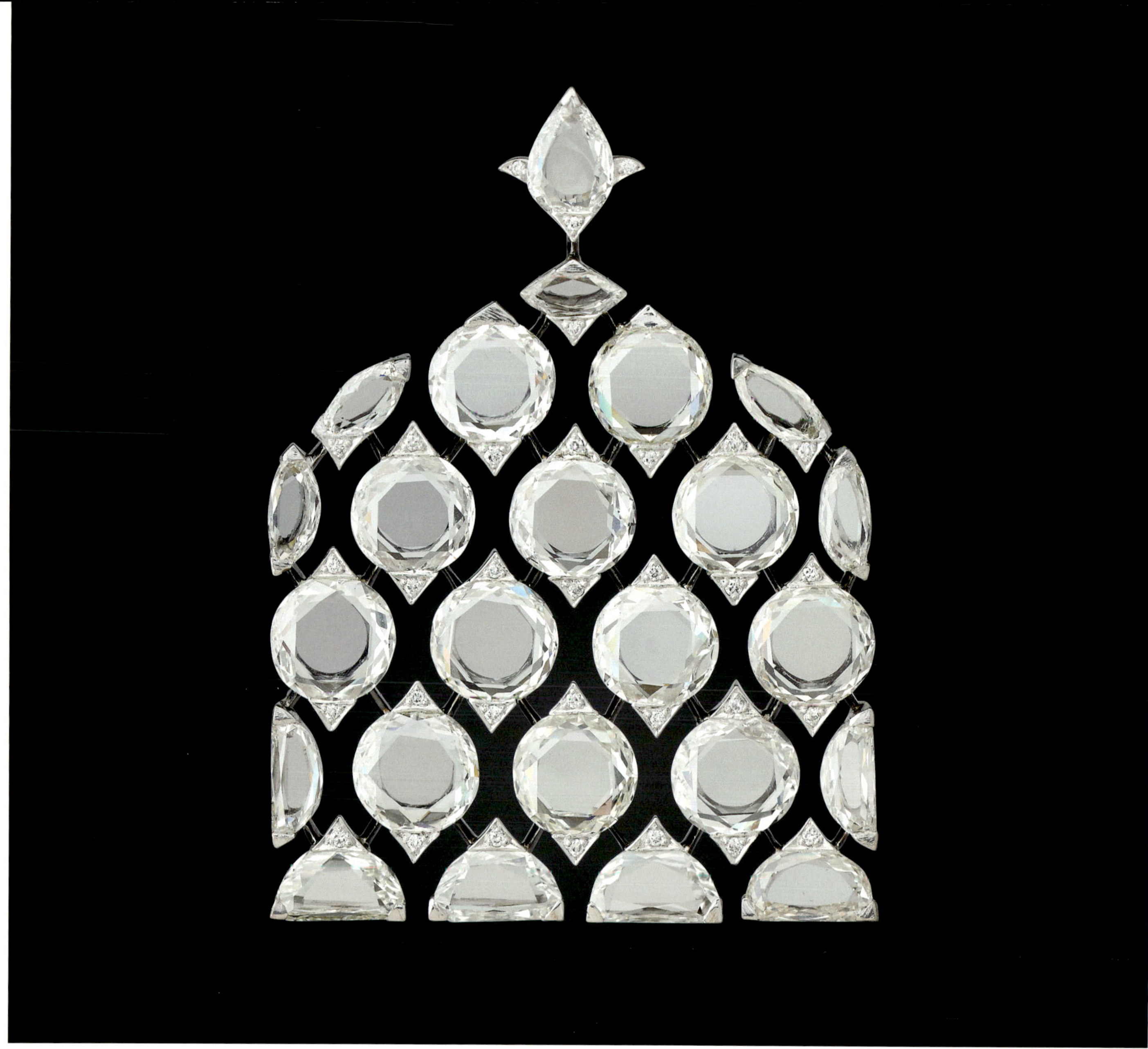

86

Brooch

Bhagat, Mumbai, 2015. Platinum, diamonds

CAT. 153

This brooch is inspired by the Indian pierced screen (*jali*) featured in traditional architecture to admit air while restricting sight. Bhagat uses specially cut diamonds in a variety of shapes and forms. Linked with minimal mounts, they create the illusion that the gems are freely floating in space, leaving the impression that the design is created by the voids.

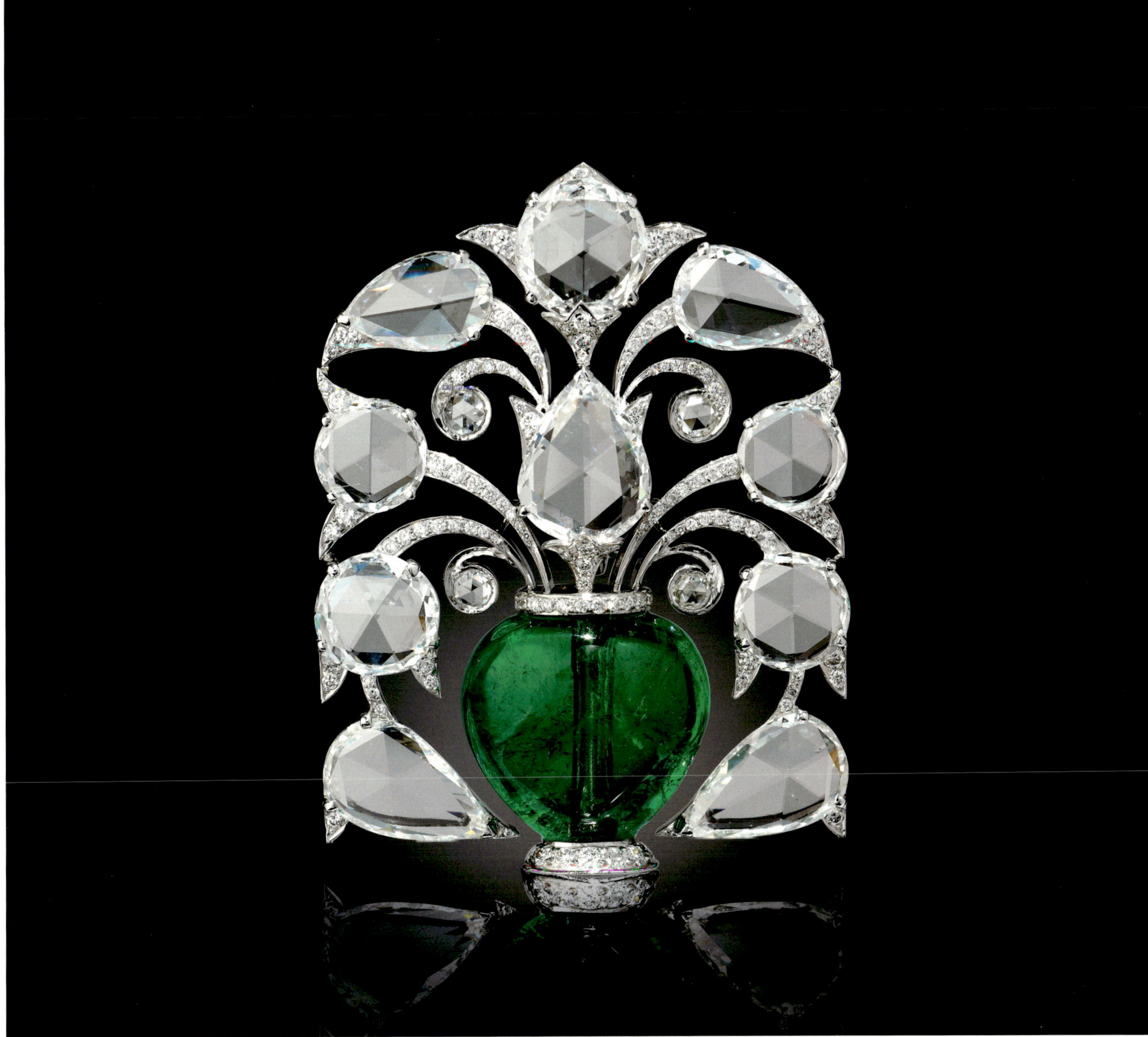

87

Brooch

Bhagat, Mumbai, 2014. Emerald, diamonds, platinum
CAT. 155

The flowering plant is a central motif in the Mughal fine and decorative arts. Bhagat's brooch draws on that tradition while equally recalling Cartier's jardinière creations in which gemstones—normally of different colors—are configured to represent diverse flowers. Bhagat, however, retains his more minimal palette, the translucency of the stones evoking the purity of nature.

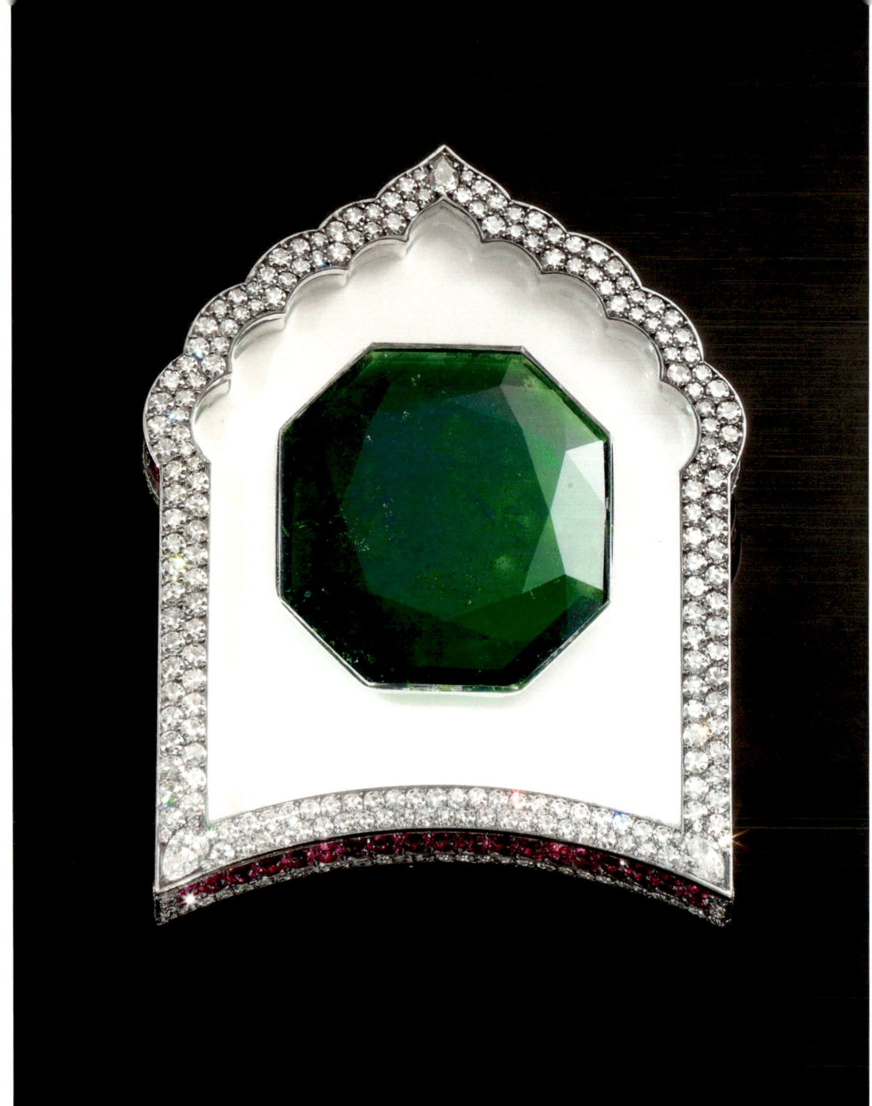

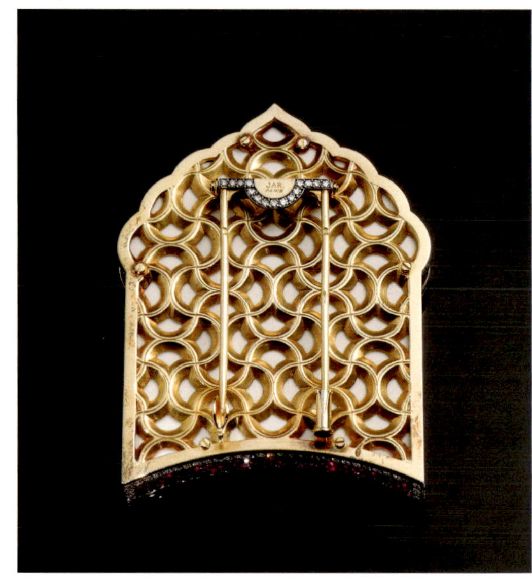

88

Brooch (obverse and reverse)

JAR, Paris, 2002. Emerald, rock crystal, white agate, diamonds, rubies, gold

CAT. 156

Shaped like a cusped arch, this brooch reflects JAR's long-standing passion for the art and architecture of the Indian subcontinent. The central octagonal emerald rests in a setting of rock crystal posited over a layer of white agate. The reverse is carved in the manner of a pierced screen, a traditional feature of Indian architecture that permitted the free flow of air while maintaining privacy by restricting the gaze.

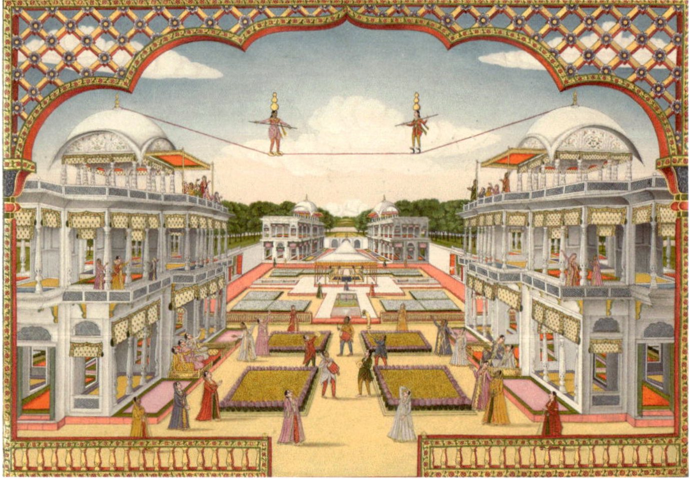

FIG. 50. Attributed to Mihr Chand, Acrobats performing on a tightrope for a women's dancing party, detail of a folio from the Lady Coote Album, ca. 1780. Ink, watercolor, gold on paper, 10 × 14¾ in. (25.5 × 37.6 cm). Fine Arts Museums of San Francisco, Gift of Dr. and Mrs. William K. Ehrenfeld, 1983.2.12

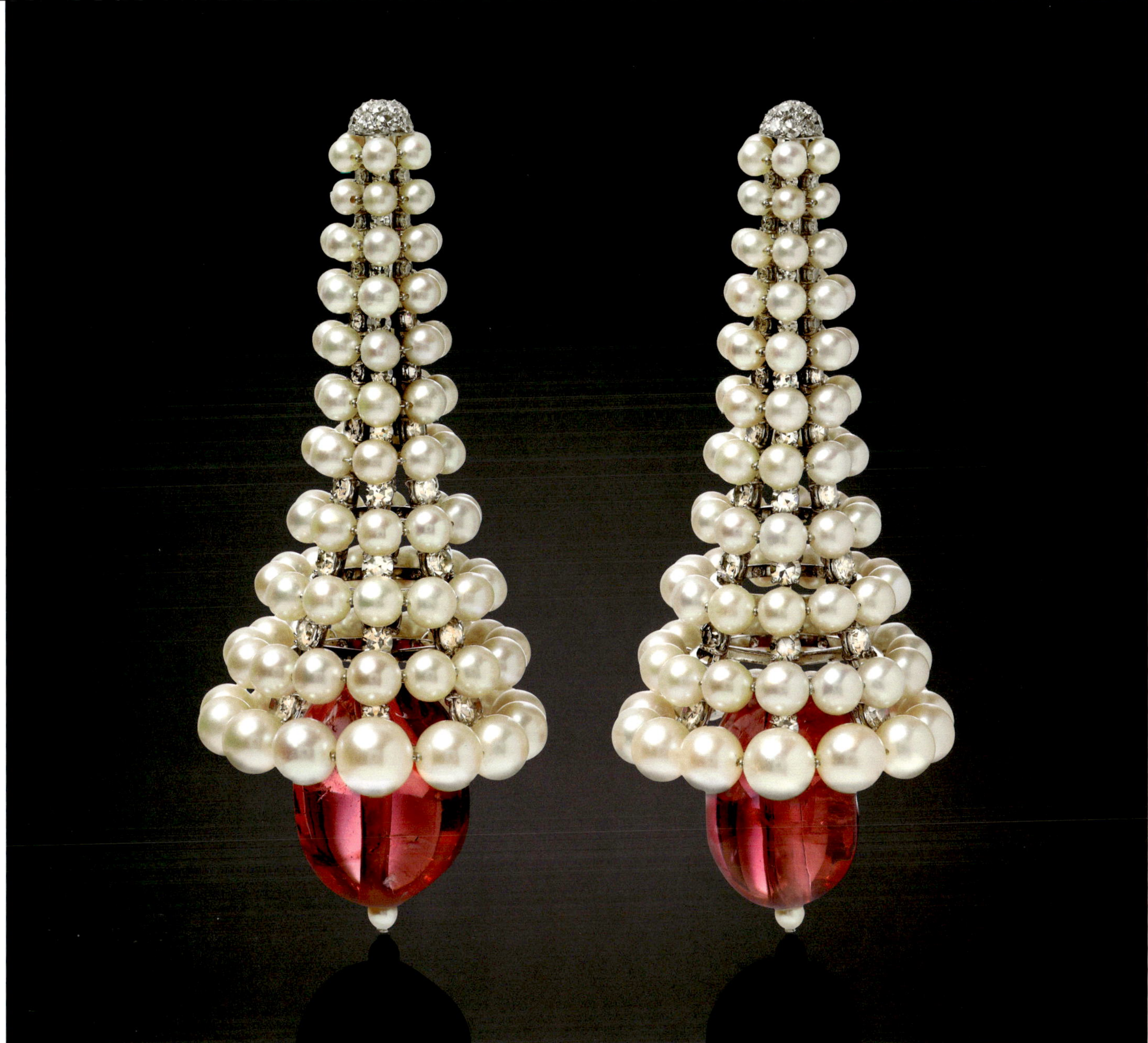

89

Pair of earrings

JAR, Paris, 2010. Pearls, spinels, diamonds, silver, gold, seed pearls

CAT. 157

In this pair of spectacular bell-shaped earrings, JAR combines natural pearls with spinels, both gemstones characterizing imperial Mughal taste. The concentric rings of pearls follow the shape of a bell, each encasing a spinel suspended in the manner of a clapper.

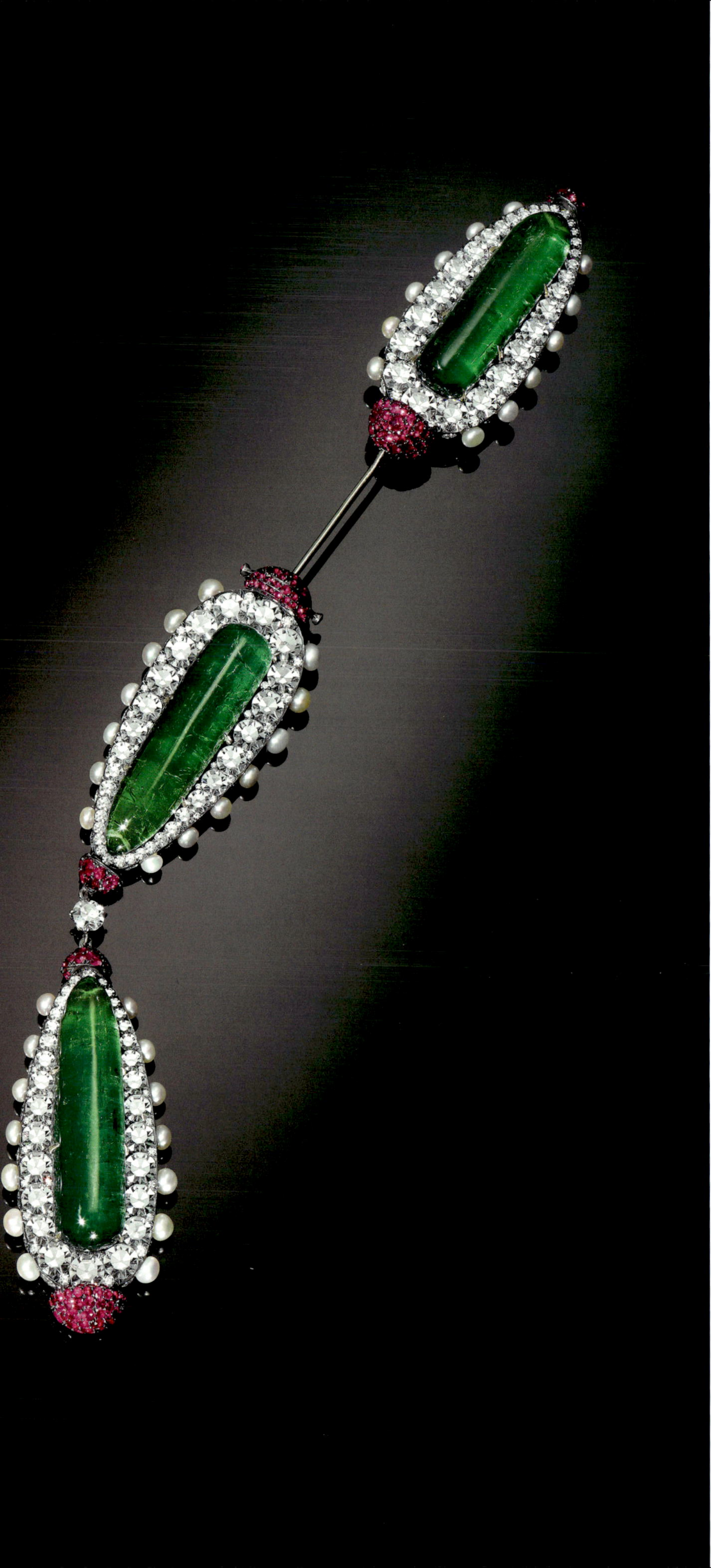

90

Jabot or *cliquet* brooch

JAR, Paris, 2013. Emeralds, diamonds, pearls, rubies, gold

CAT. 159

Three elongated emeralds originating in the mines of northern Afghanistan's Panjshir Valley compose the main part of this brooch. Examples of the distinctive gem formation are evident in the headgear worn by Maharaja Sher Singh of Punjab as immortalized in a painting by August Theodor Schoefft (fig. 51).

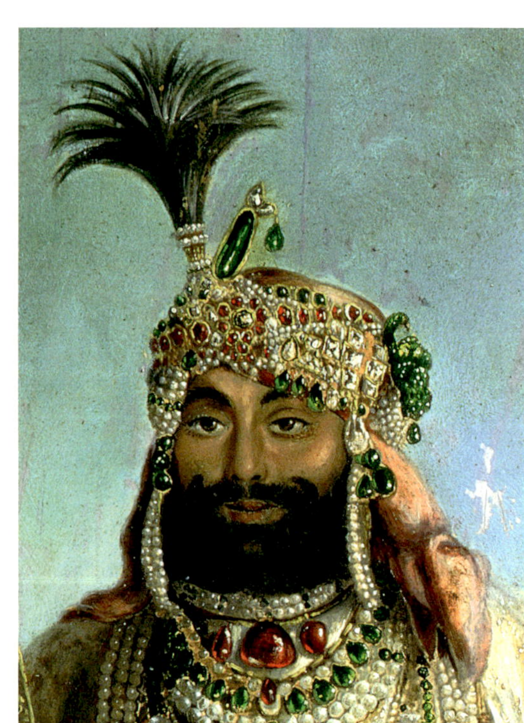

FIG. 51. August Theodor Schoefft, detail of *Portrait of Maharaja Sher Singh, in Regal Dress*, ca. 1850. Oil on panel, 18⅝ × 14 in. (47.3 × 35.5 cm). Private collection

91

Necklace (obverse and clasp)

JAR, Paris, 2014. Pearls, diamonds, gold

CAT. 160

This spectacular necklace evokes the Indian princely manner of wearing profuse ropes of pearls to cover the entire chest. This fashion translated into royal jewelry in the West, the multiple rows of pearls characterizing the apparel of Queen Alexandra and Queen Mary, both empresses of India. The ownership of rare gems was an intrinsic aspect of kingship across cultures. Before the development of the cultured-pearl technique, it required a true miracle of nature to find a row of pearls of identical size, shape, color, and luster.

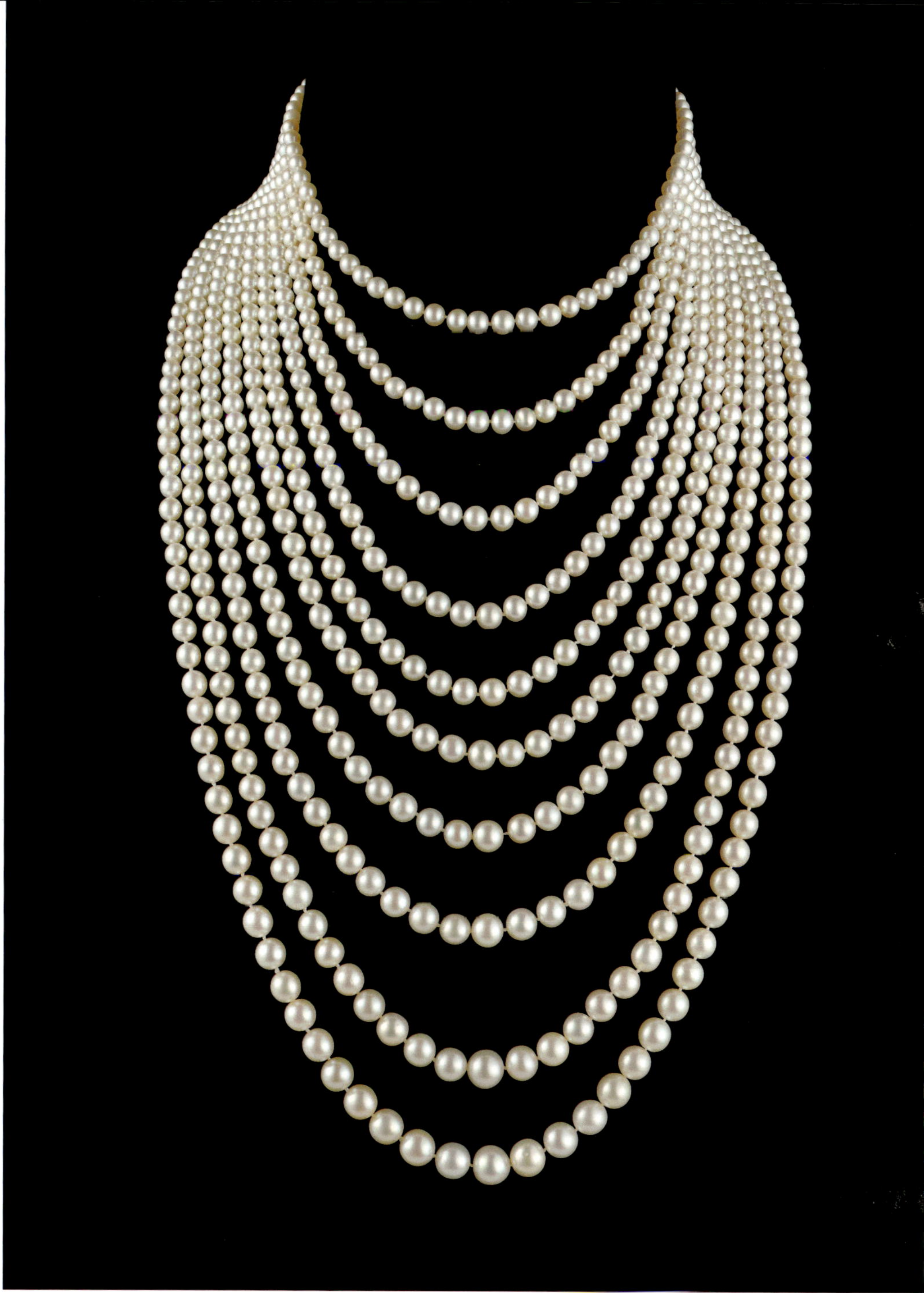

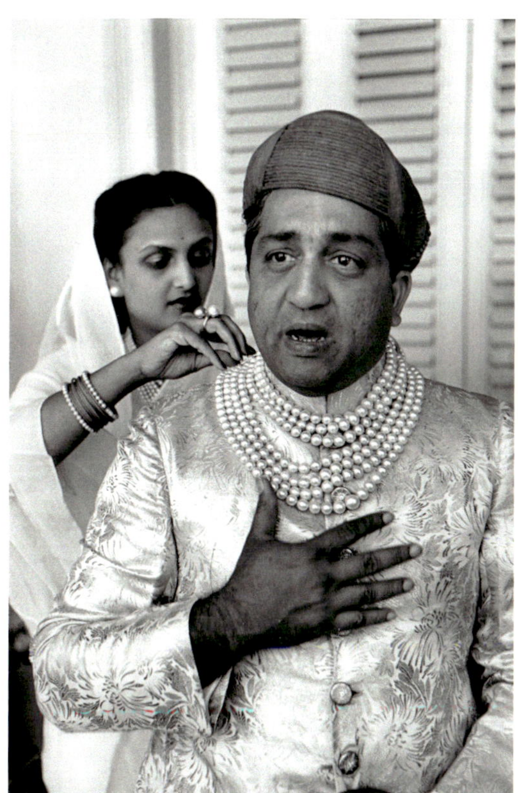

FIG. 52. Henri Cartier-Bresson, Gaekwad of Baroda wearing pearls, 1948

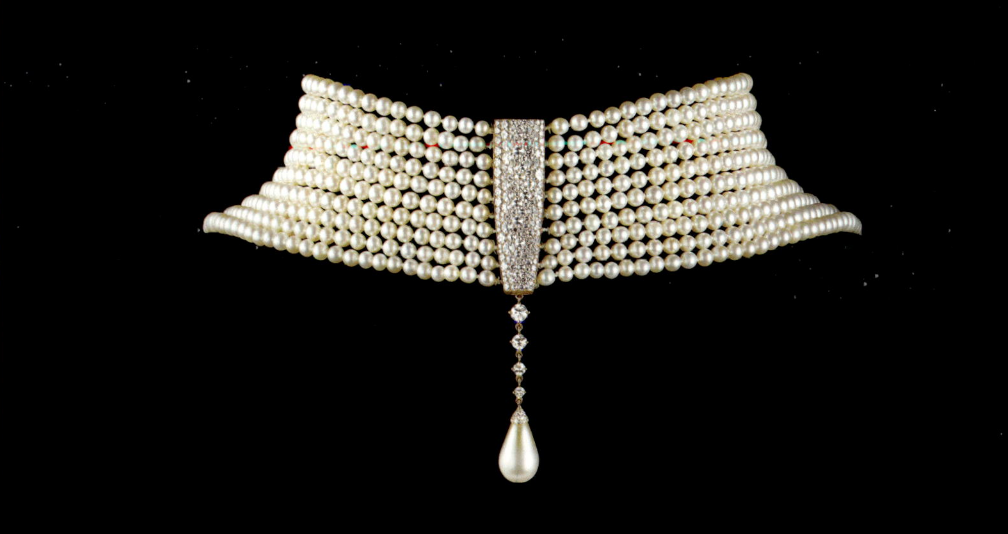

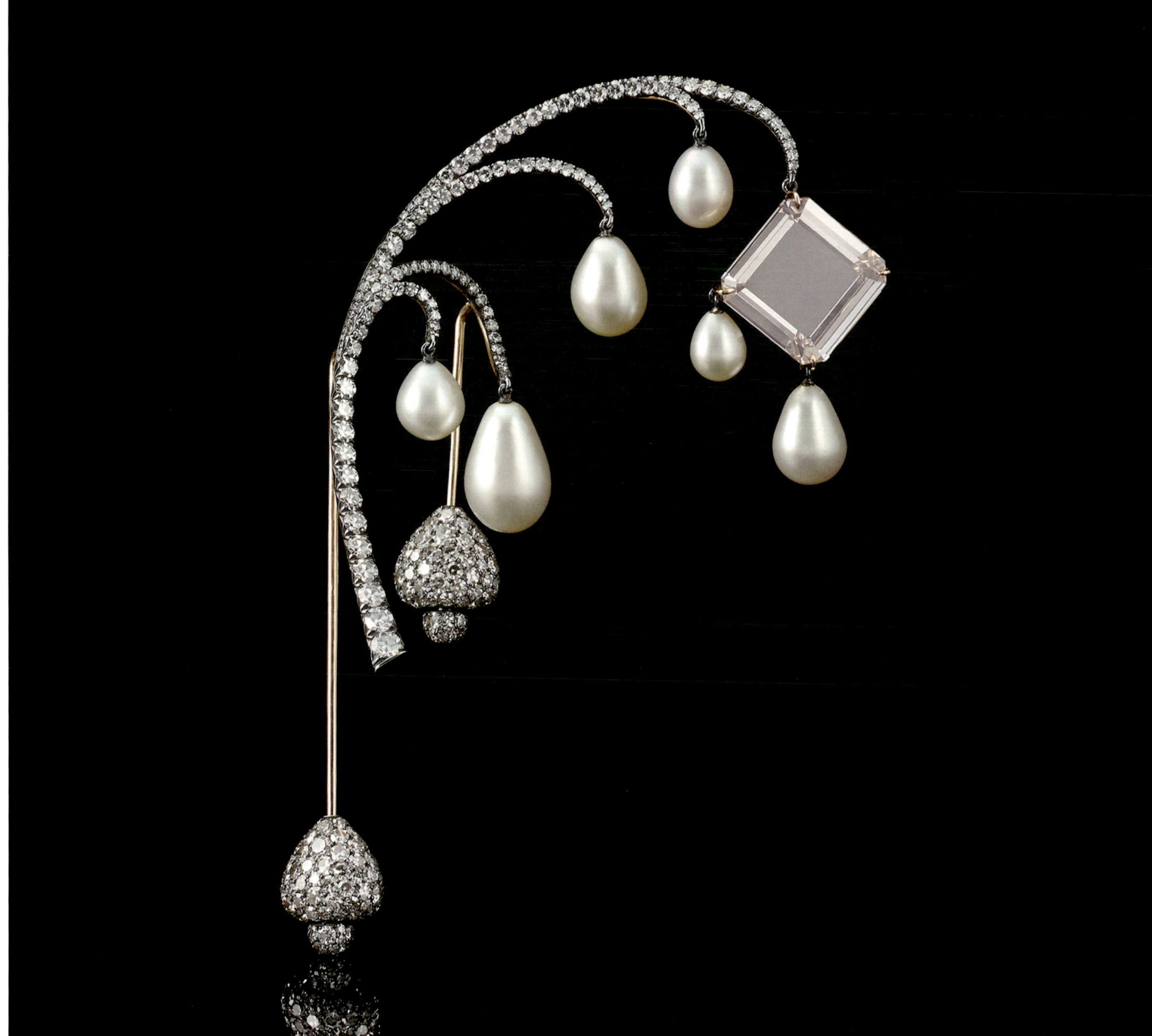

92

Turban ornament

JAR, Paris, 2016. Pearls, diamonds, gold, silver, platinum

CAT. 161

JAR's contemporary turban ornament follows the shape of a classic Mughal *jigah*, itself inspired by the gentle curve of a feather. Since antiquity, the wearing of rare plumage on the head was regarded as a symbol of authority. This jewel captures the sense of movement of a feature, the multiple natural pearl drops and the rare square pink diamond all designed to be *en tremblant*.

93 *(opposite)*

Elephant brooch

JAR, Paris, 2016. Titanium, diamonds, white cacholong, sapphires, gold, platinum

CAT. 163

This sculptural brooch by JAR draws on the Indian tradition of adorning royal animals with jewelry. Modeled in titanium, this brooch is patinated to resemble the skin of an elephant and mounted with an aigrette in the form of a spray of diamonds such as was fashionable during the Belle Époque.

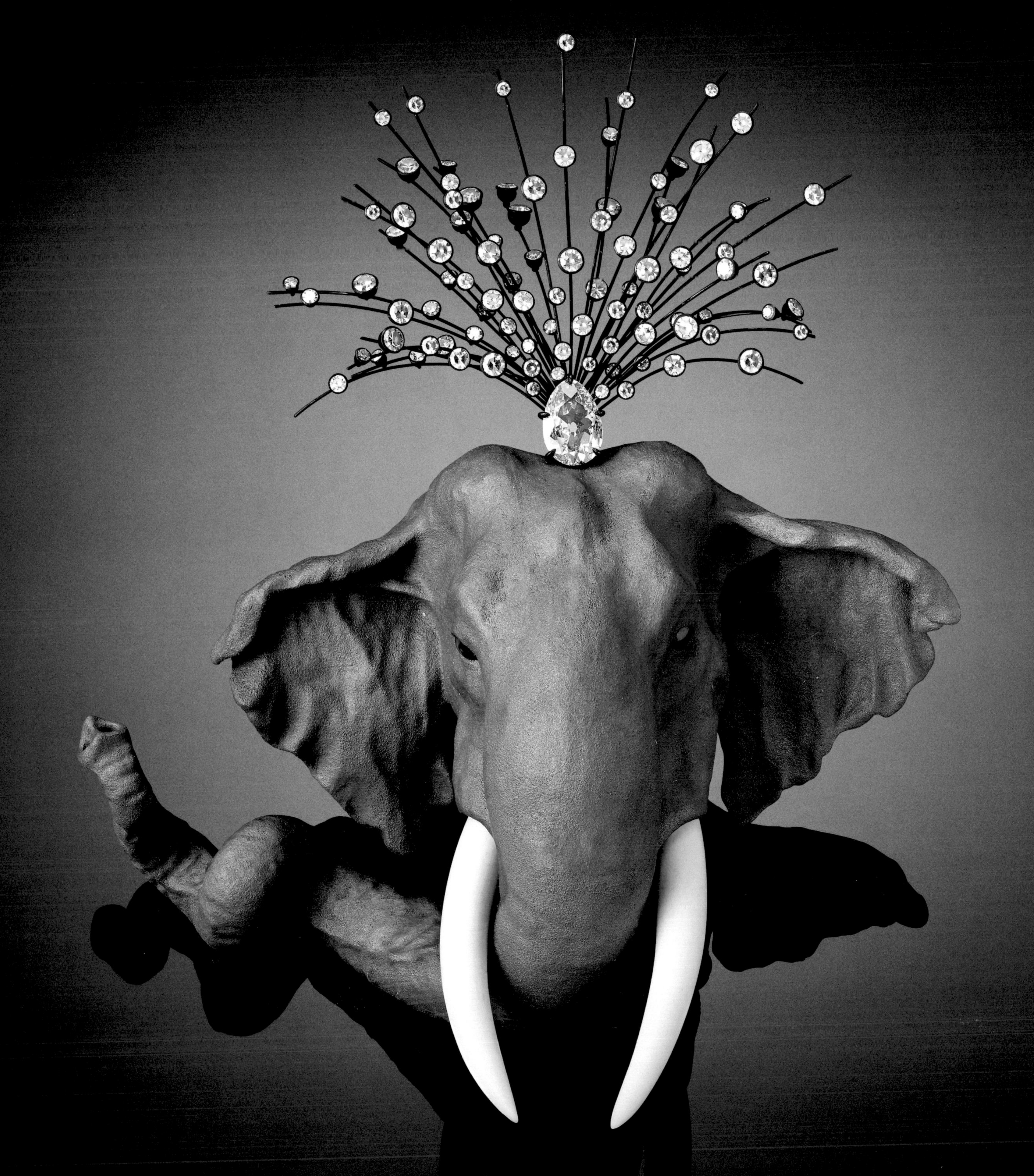

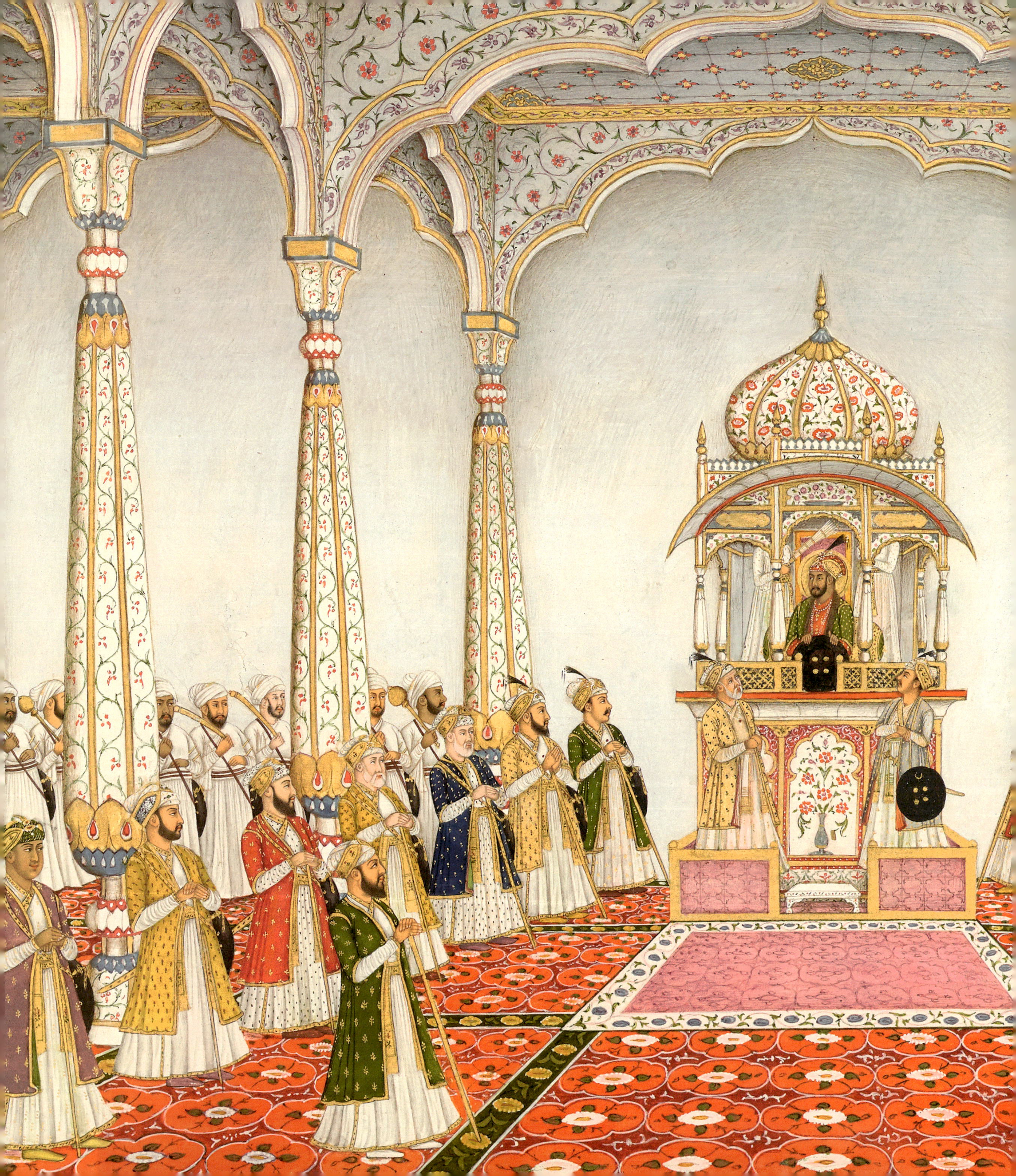

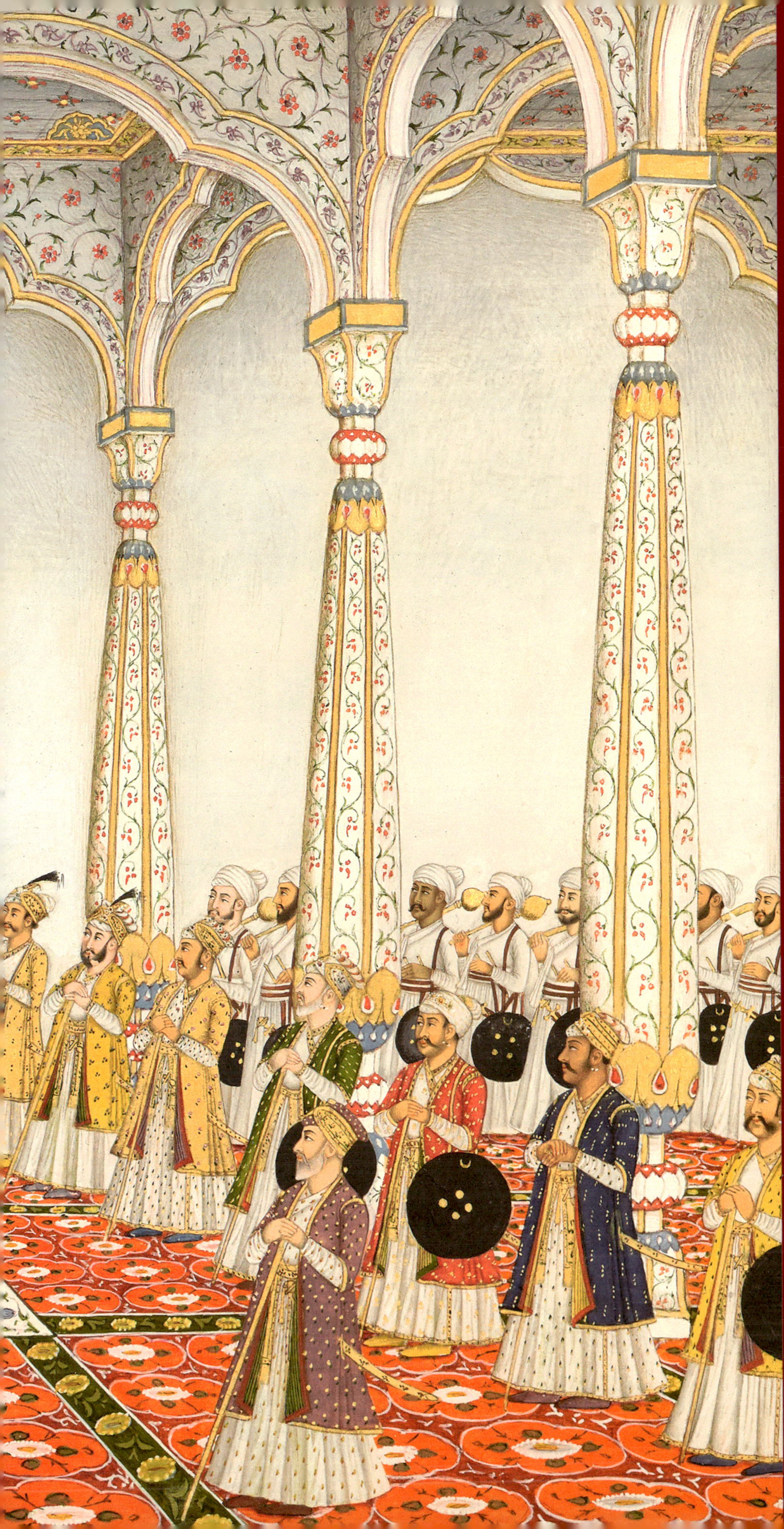

APPENDICES

CATALOGUE OF THE EXHIBITION

This list is arranged chronologically where possible and reflects the most complete information available at time of publication. Dimensions are provided in centimeters.

1
THE MUGHAL COURT
Gemstones and Jewelry

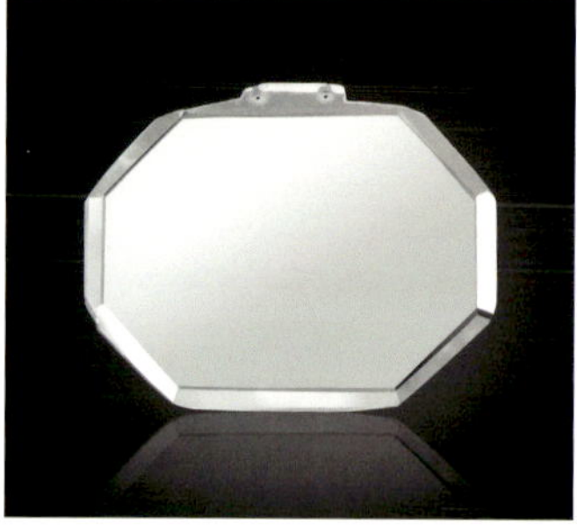

1. Portrait-cut Diamond
India, 1650–1700
Cut-cornered, rectangular portrait-cut, grade J, type IIa
2.5 × 3.3 × 0.18 cm
Weight 20.22 ct
PL. 1

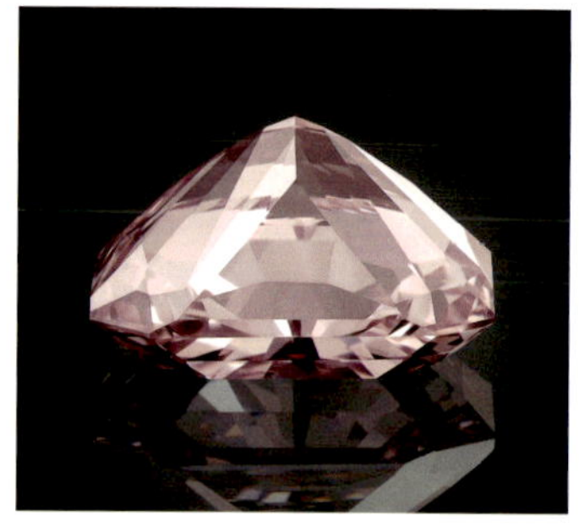

2. The Agra Diamond
India, before 1526; reworked 1880 and 1990
Cut-cornered, rectangular mixed-cut, fancy intense pink
1.8 × 1.7 cm
Weight 28.15 ct
PL. 3

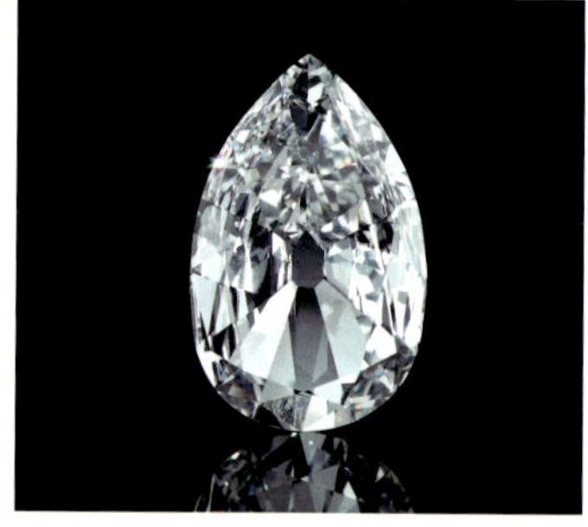

3. The Arcot II Diamond
India, ca. 1760; modified 1959 and 2011
Brilliant-cut, pear-shaped, grade D, internally flawless, type IIa
2.7 × 1.6 × 0.5 cm
Weight 17.21 ct
PL. 2

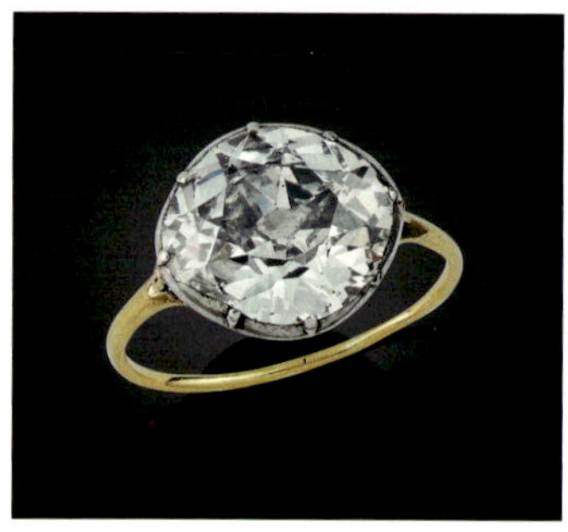

4. Ring
England, ca. 1764
Diamond, gold
2.4 × 2 × 1.2 cm
Weight of diamond 5.5 ct

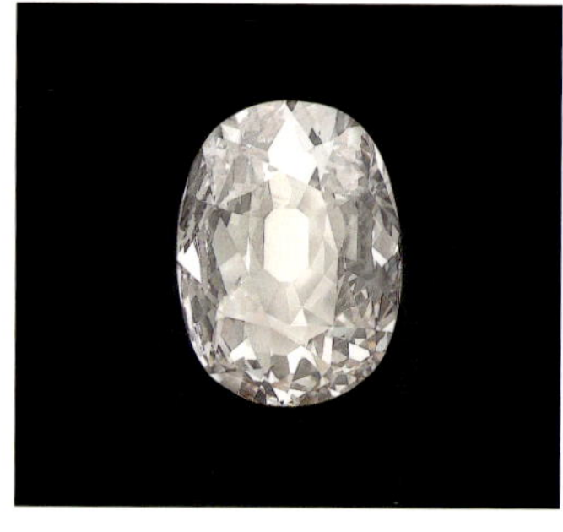

5. The Pink Golconda Diamond
Light pink, internally flawless
1.8 × 1.4 × 0.5 cm
Weight 10.46 ct

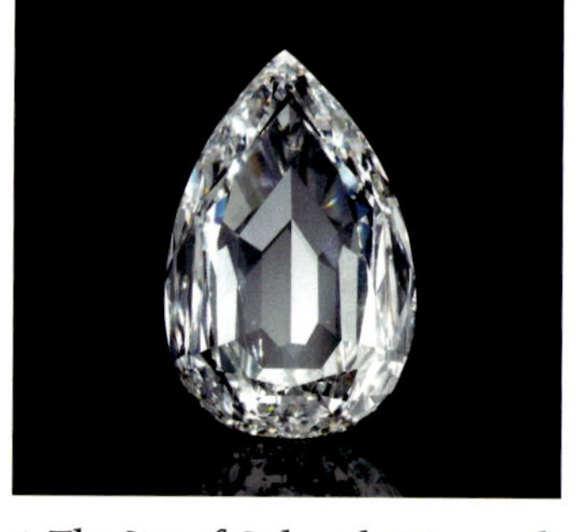

6. The Star of Golconda Diamond
Grade H, internally flawless
3.8 × 2.4 × 0.7 cm
Weight 57.31 ct

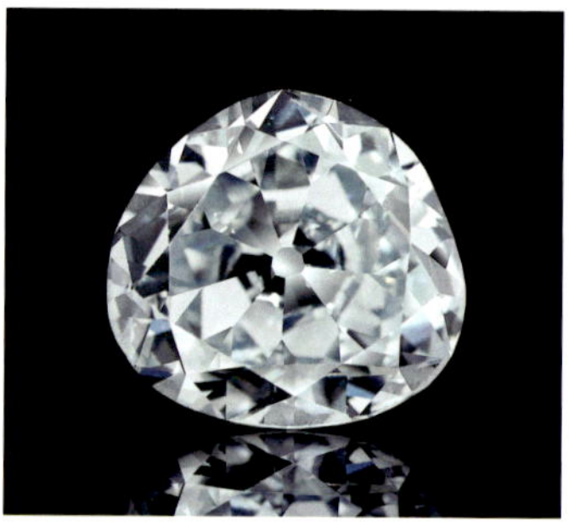

7. The Idol's Eye Diamond
India. Modified brilliant-cut light blue, VVS2 clarity
2.6 × 2.8 × 1.3 cm
Weight 70.21 ct
PL. 4

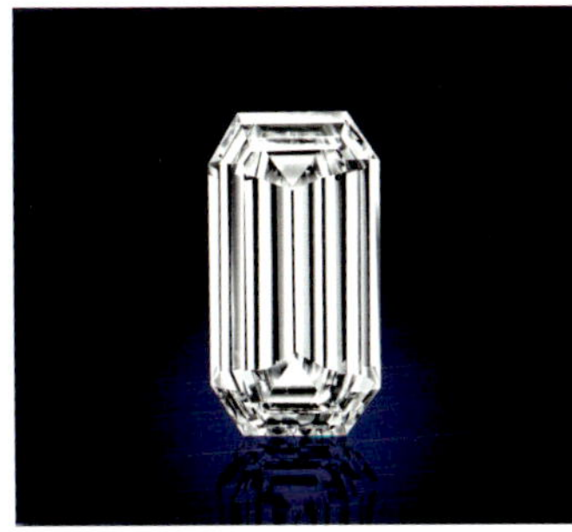

8. The Mirror of Paradise Diamond
Grade D, internally flawless
3.5 × 1.9 × 0.9 cm
Weight 52.58 ct

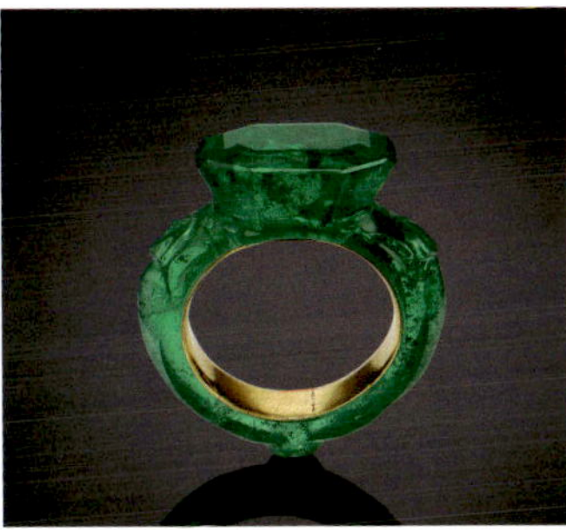

9. Ring
India, 16th century
Emerald, gold
2.8 × 1.5 × 0.9 cm

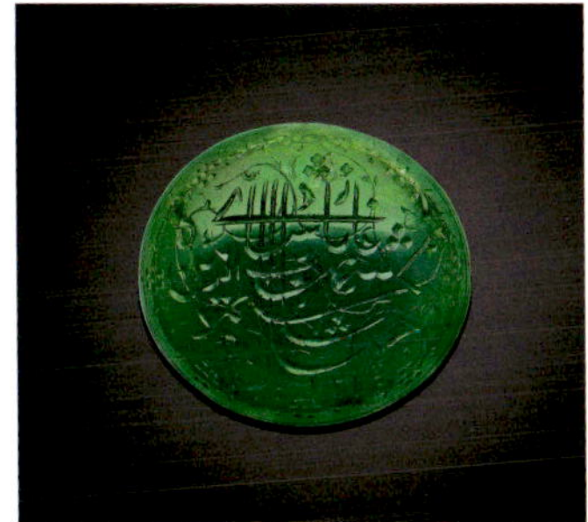

10. The Shah Jahan Emerald
North India or Deccan, 1621–1622
2.2 × 2.4 × 0.7 cm
Weight 30.31 ct
PL. 5

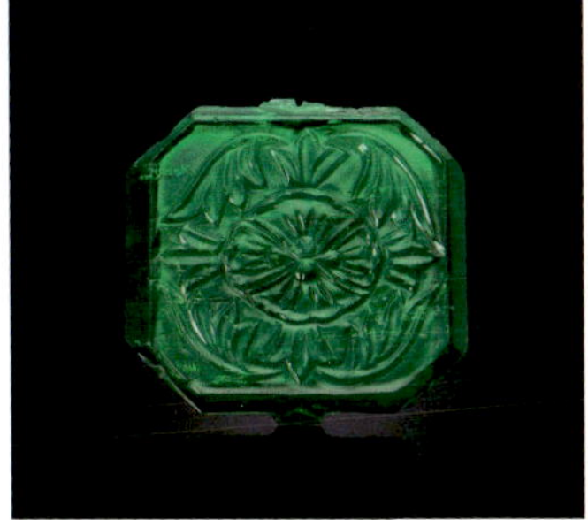

11. Emerald
North India, ca. 1650
3.8 × 3.2 × 0.8 cm
Weight 87.8 ct
PL. 6

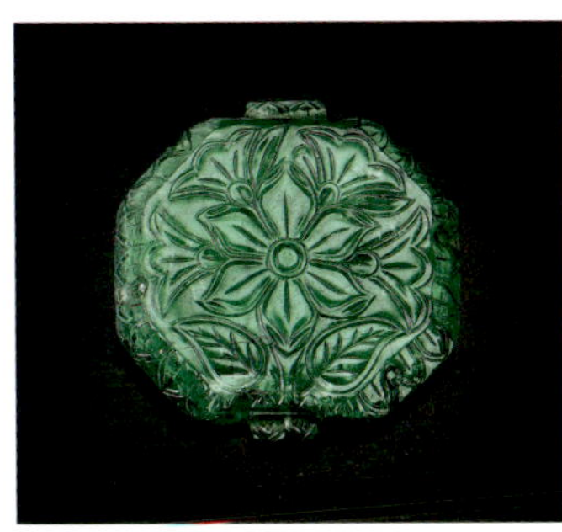

12. Emerald
North India, 1650–1700
3.5 × 3.5 × 0.8 cm
Weight 79.78 ct

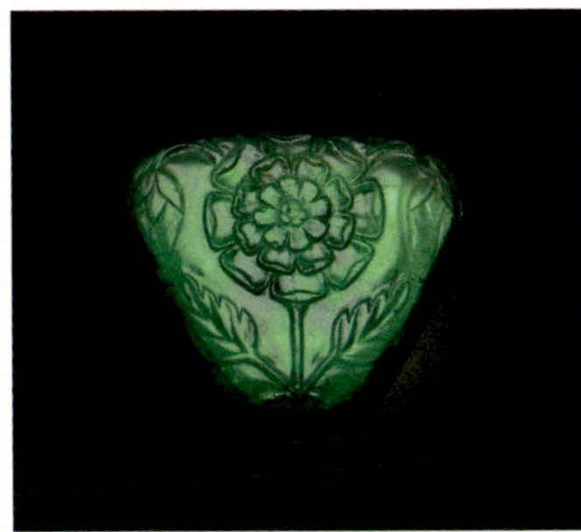

13. Emerald
India, 1650–1700
2.3 × 2.8 × 0.5 cm
Weight 26 ct

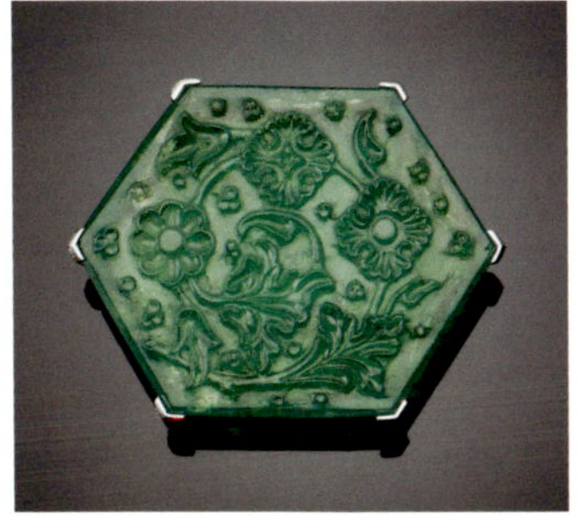

14. The Taj Mahal Emerald
India, 1650–1700; mount by Cartier, 2012
5.3 × 4 cm
Weight 141.13 ct
PL. 7

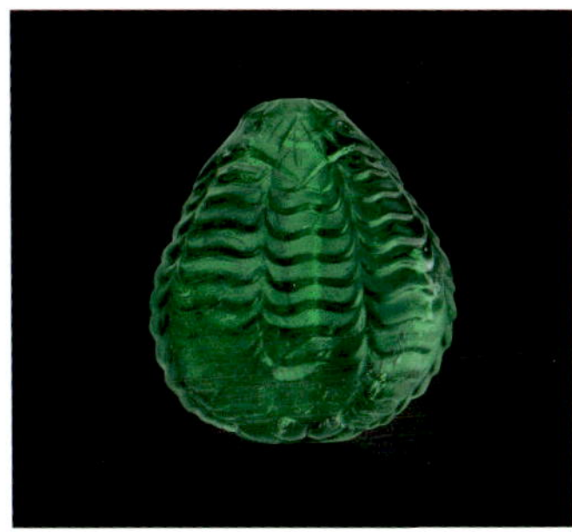

15. Emerald
North India, 1650–1700
2.7 × 2.5 × 1.7 cm
Weight 52.15 ct

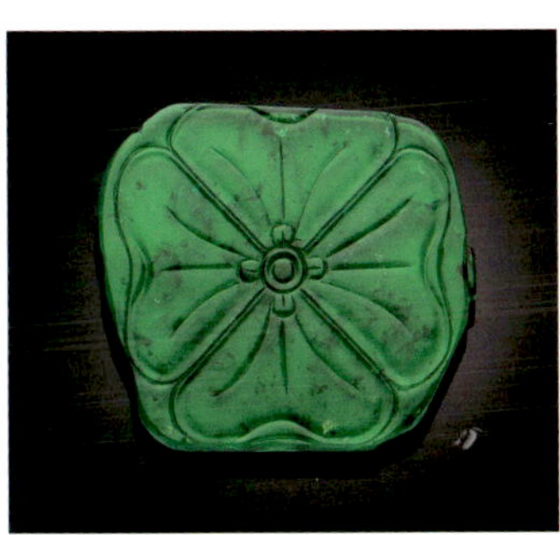

16. Emerald
India, 1650–1750
5.6 × 6.4 × 0.5 cm
Weight 211.7 ct

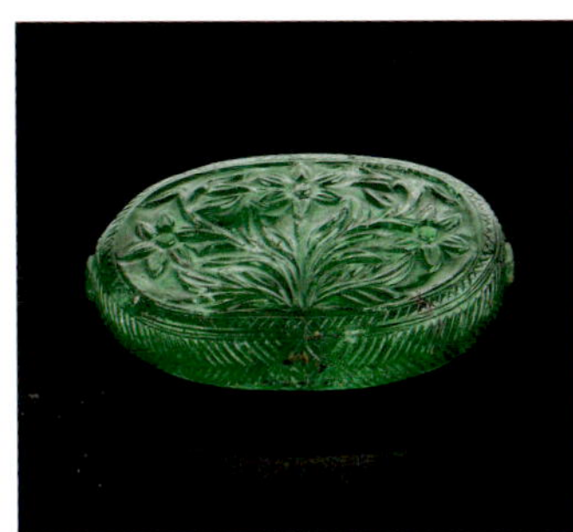

17. Emerald
India, 1675–1725
3.6 × 5.4 × 1.3 cm
Weight 218.22 ct

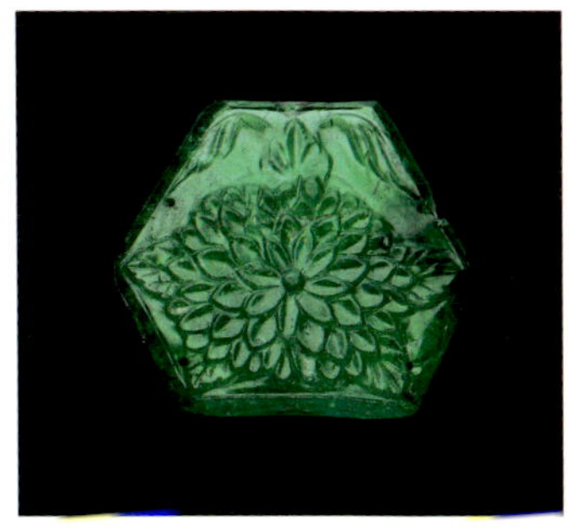

18. Emerald
India, 1680–1720
2.8 × 3.3 × 0.8 cm
Weight 52.2 ct

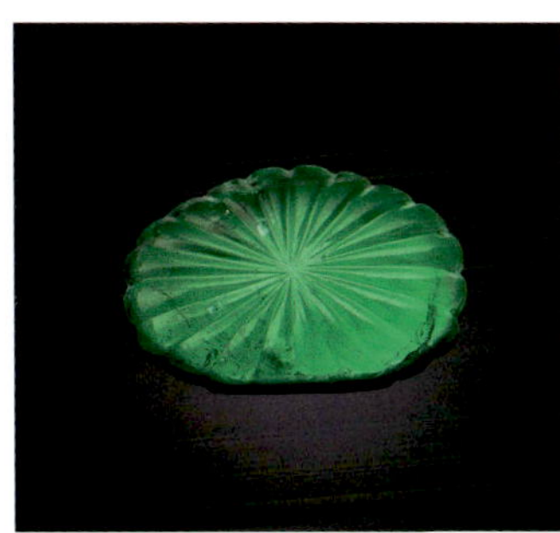

19. Emerald
India
1.2 × 1.9 × 0.5 cm
Weight 10 ct

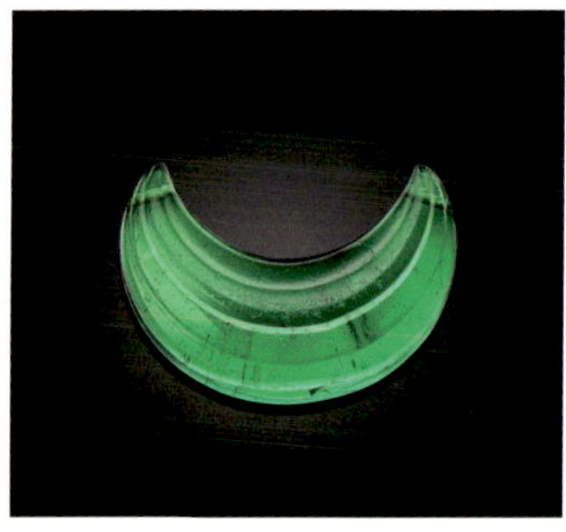

20. Emerald
India
1.7 × 2.1 × 0.5 cm
Weight 10.8 ct

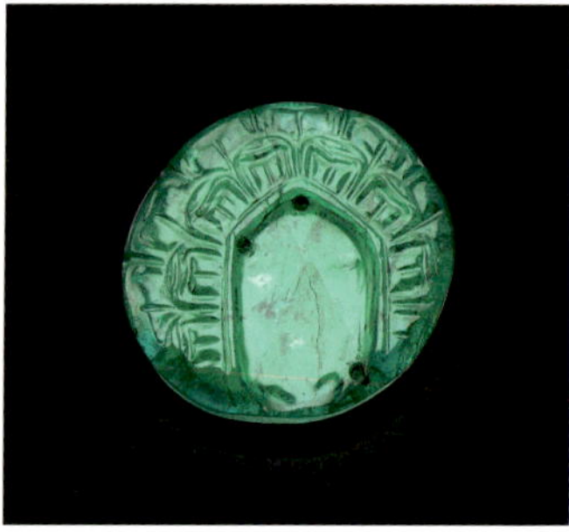

21. Emerald
India
2.6 × 2.4 × 2.4 cm
Weight 52.15 ct

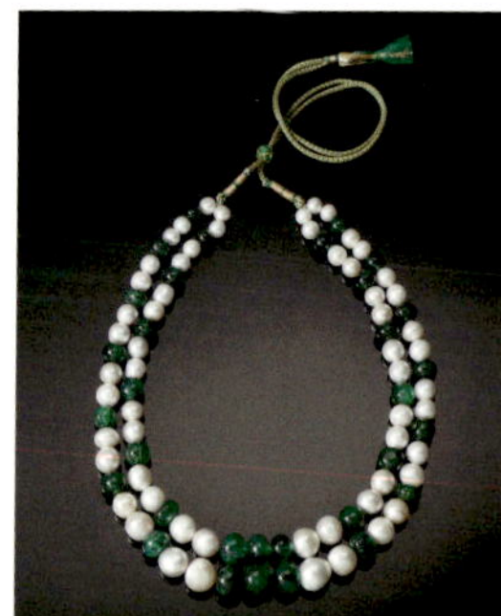

22. Necklace
India, 18th or early 19th century
Emeralds, pearls, modern stringing
48 cm (including cord)
PL. 8

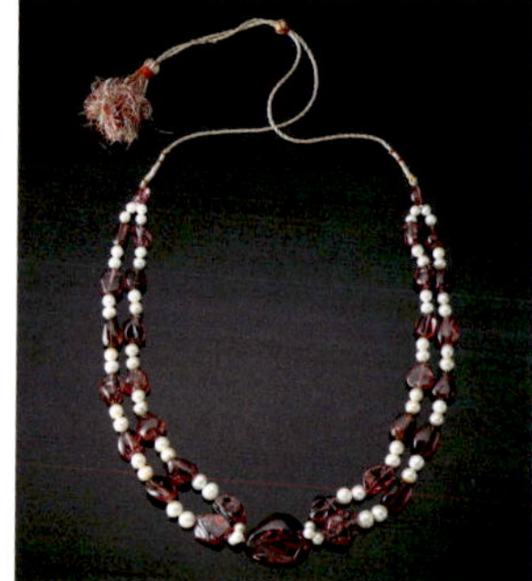

23. Imperial spinel necklace
North India, 1600–1650. Four spinels dated to 1609–1635
Spinels, pearls, gold, modern stringing
54.7 cm (excluding cord)
Weight of central spinel 162 ct
Weight of other spinels 790 ct

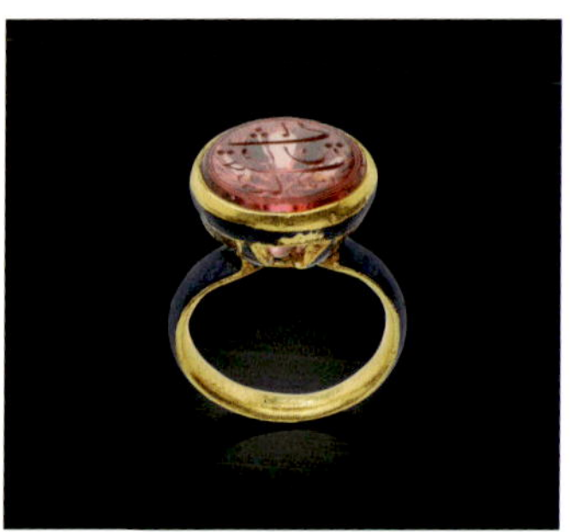

24. Ring with Shah Jahan's spinel
North India, spinel dated to 1643–1644, ring: ca. 1900
Gold, enamel
2.8 × 2.1 × 1.6 cm
Spinel inscribed in Persian: *Second Lord of the Auspicious Conjunction 1053 16*
PL. 9

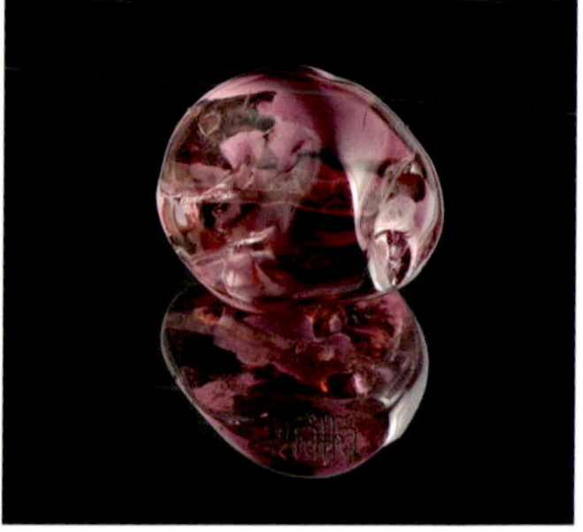

25. Imperial spinel
India, ca. 1606–1607 and 1628–1629
2.2 × 2.7 × 1.8 cm
Weight 94.26 ct
Inscribed in Persian: *Akbar | Jahangir | Shah Jahan*
PL. 10

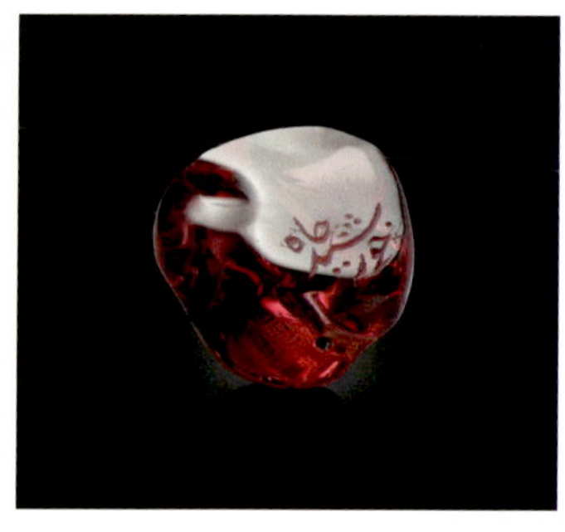

26. Imperial spinel
India, ca. 1610–1611
2.1 × 2.2 × 1.1 cm
Weight 55.9 ct

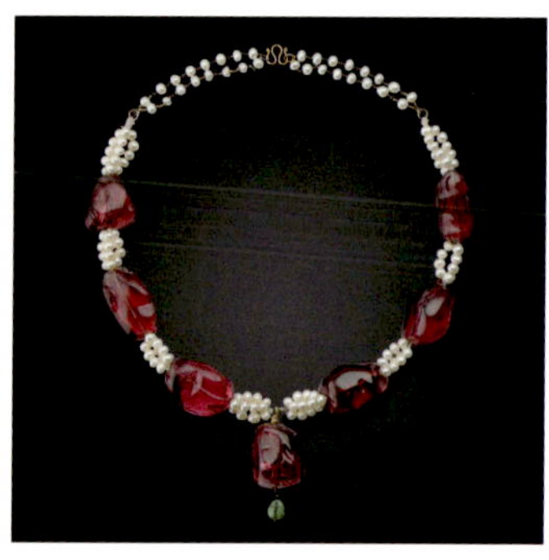

27. Imperial spinel necklace
North India, spinels dated to between 1607–1608 and 1754–1755
Spinels, pearls, emerald, modern stringing
51.8 cm
PL. 11

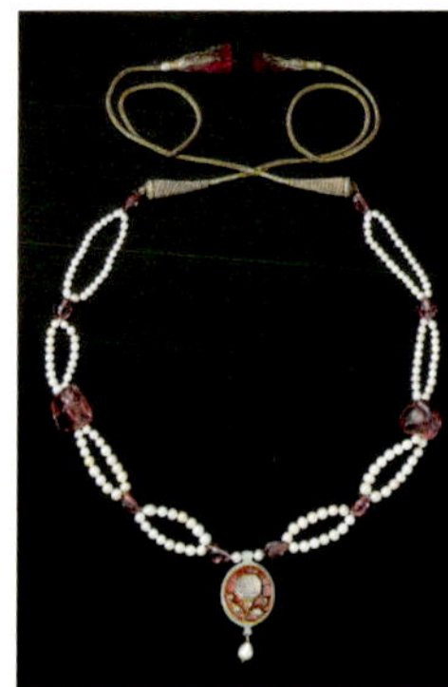

28. The Shah Jahan Necklace
North India, 17th century.
Spinel ca. 1609–1610
Spinels, pearls, jade, rubies, diamond, gold, modern stringing
26.6 cm (excluding cord)
Inscribed in Persian on the diamond: *Shah Jahan Warrior Emperor*
Inscribed in Persian on the largest spinel on the left side: *Jahangir [son] of Akbar Shah 1018*

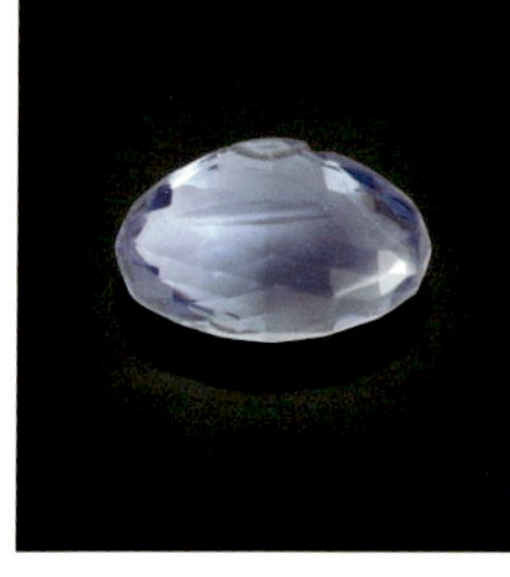

29. The Indore sapphire *taweez* pendant
India, 18th century
1.9 × 2.1 × 1.5 cm
Weight 23.2 ct

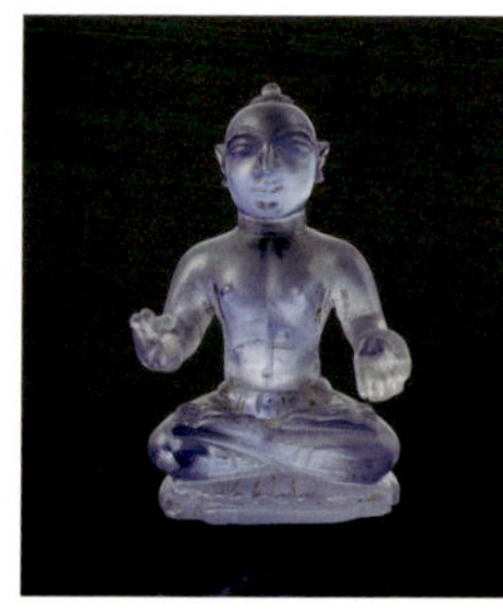

30. Hindu saint
South India (?), 1650–1750
Sapphire
3 × 2 × 1 cm
Weight 37.8 ct

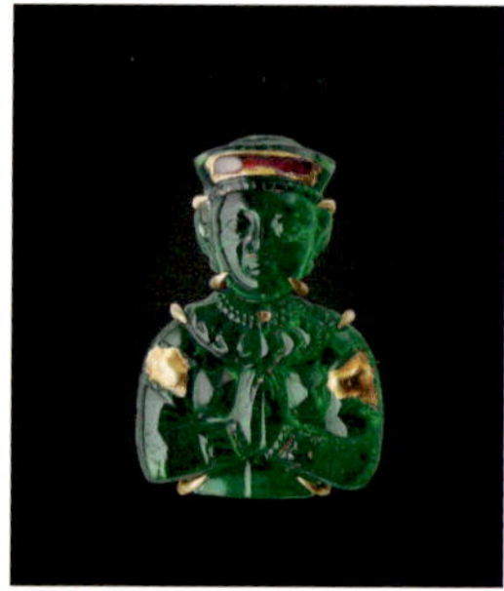

31. Hindu saint
South India (?), 1650–1750
Modern mount, emerald, ruby, gold
1.9 × 1.3 × 0.3 cm
Weight of emeralds 2 ct (head), 6.6 ct (torso)

2
HARDSTONES
Jade, Agate, and Rock Crystal

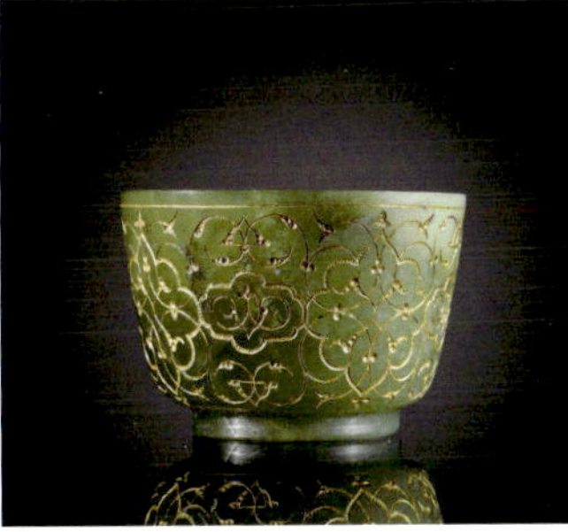

32. Cup
Central Asia, 1450–1500;
the decoration possibly later:
Central Asia or Iran, 16th century
Jade, gold
5.5 × 8 cm
PL. 12

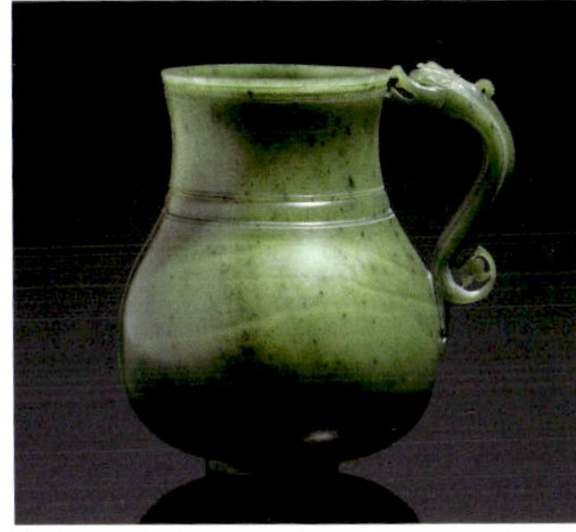

33. Jug
Central Asia, 1500–1550
Jade
11.7 × 12.2 cm

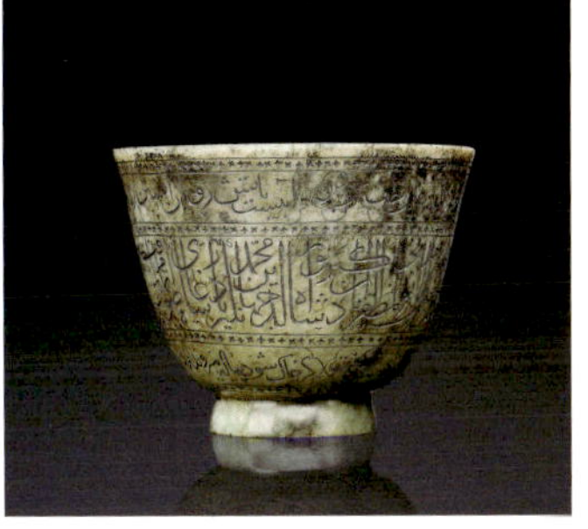

34. The Wine Cup of Jahangir
North India, ca. 1607–1608
Jade
5.5 × 7.4 cm
Inscribed
PL. 13

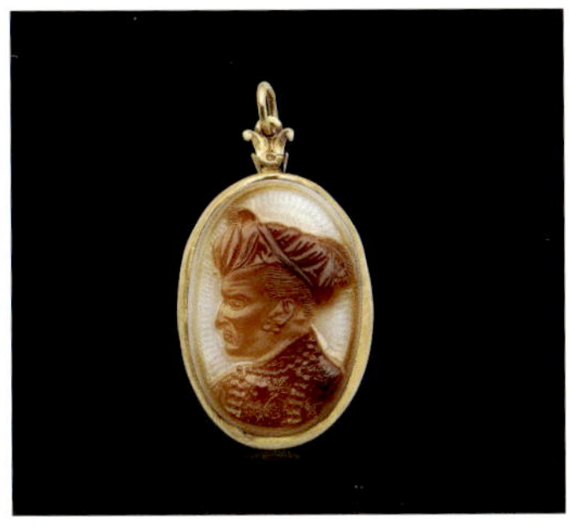

35. Cameo of the Emperor Jahangir (obverse)
France or Italy, 1610–1630; mount, France, 1630–1640
Agate, gold
5.1 × 3.1 cm
PL. 14

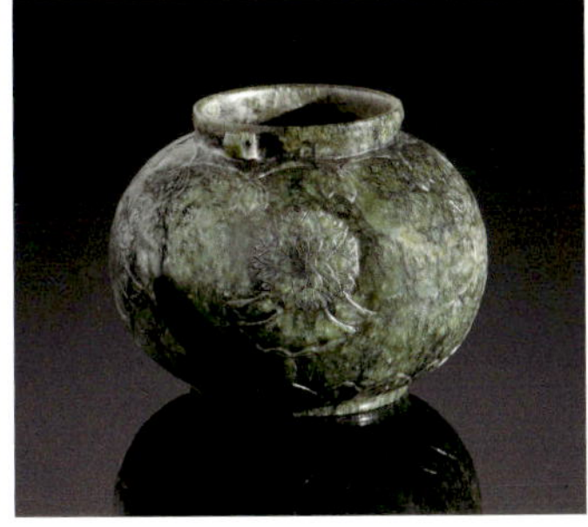

36. Inkwell
North India, 1600–1625
Jade
6.2 × 8.2 cm; diam. at mouth: 4.6 cm

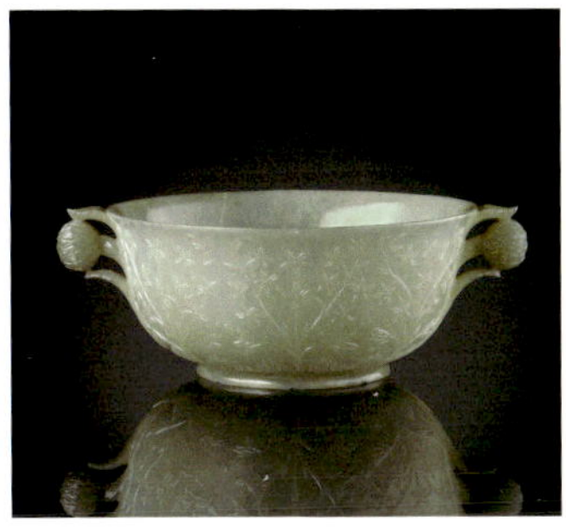

37. Bowl
North India, 1650–1700
Jade
5.2 × 15.7 cm
PL. 15

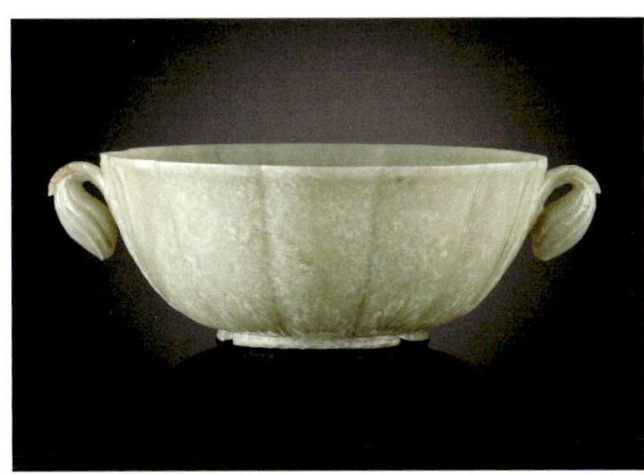

38. Wine bowl
North India, 1700–1750
Jade
7 × 51.6 × 17.1 cm

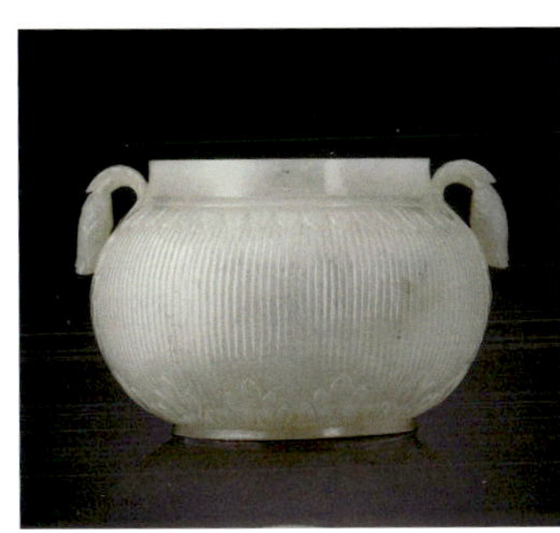

39. Double-handled jar
North India or Deccan, 1740–1780
Jade
7 × 11.5 × 10.6 cm

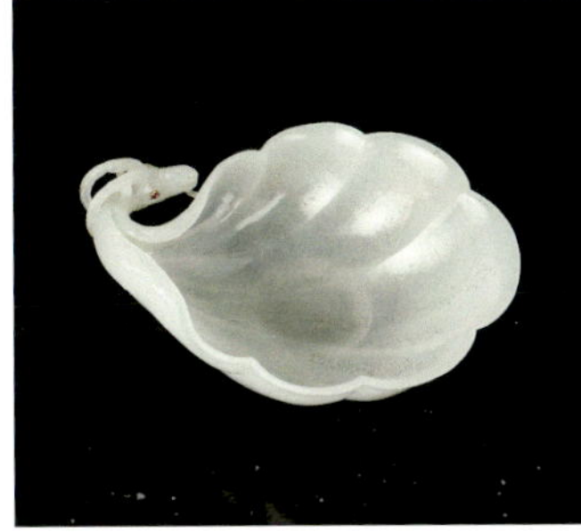

40. Cup
North India, 1660–1680
Jade, ruby eyes set in gold,
silver foot ring
2.5 × 6.1 × 8.4 cm
Inscribed in Chinese with a poem written by Emperor Qianlong between 1756 and 1794
PL. 16

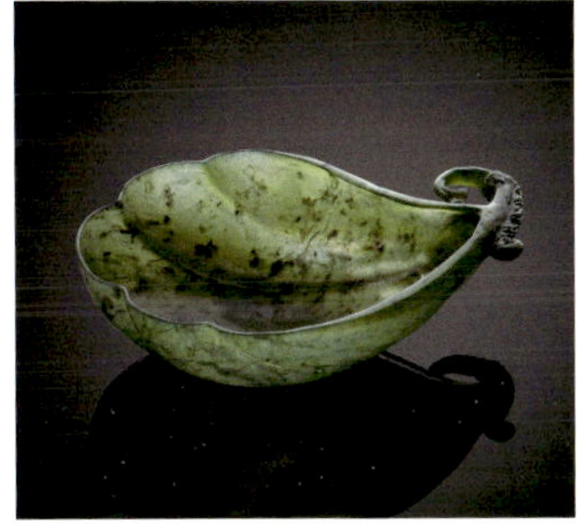

41. Cup
India, 1675–1725
Jade
2.6 × 9.9 × 7 cm
PL. 17

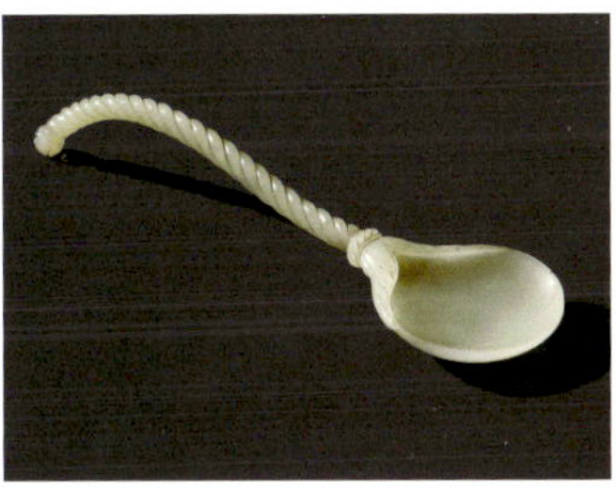

42. Spoon
India, 1650–1700
Jade
13.1 cm, bowl: 3.7 cm

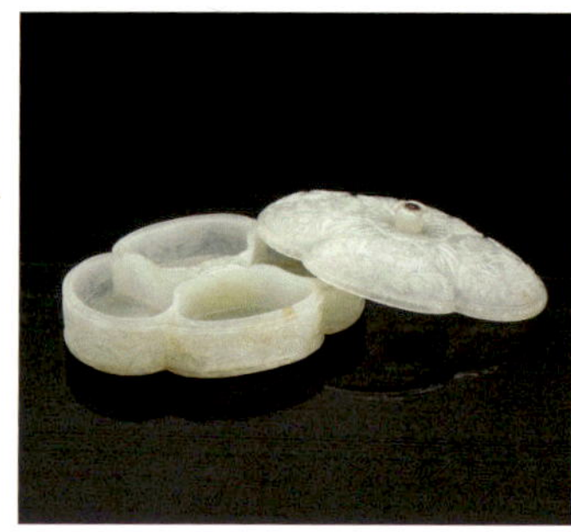

43. Box
North India, ca. 1740–1800
Jade, ruby
2.8 (1.4 without lid) × 8.2 × 6.1 cm

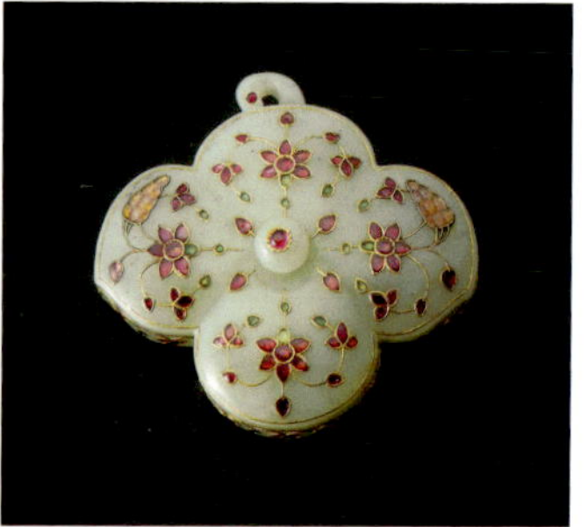

44. Box for *paan*
North India, 1740–1780
Jade with rubies, emeralds, and rock crystal set in gold
4.2 × 10.8 × 10.2 cm
PL. 20

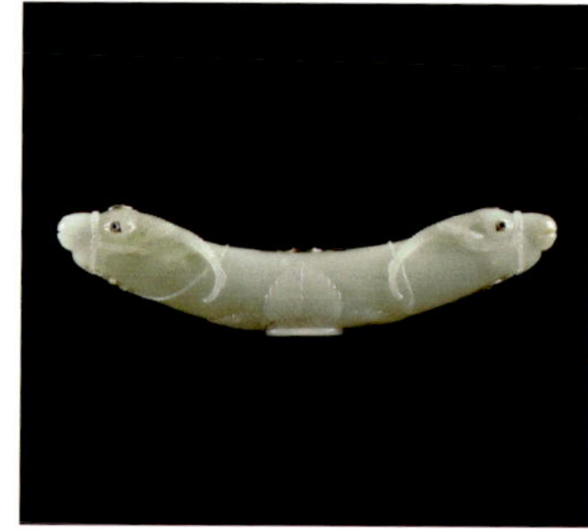

45. Crutch handle
North India, ca. 1650
Jade, agate eyes, diamonds set in gold (added later)
3.2 × 12.8 cm
PL. 18

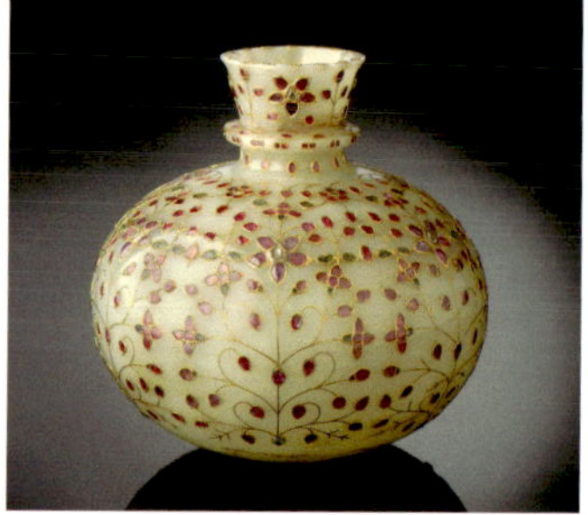

46. Hookah base
North India, 1740–1780
Jade, inlaid with rubies, diamonds, and emeralds set in gold
16.2 × 16 cm
PL. 19

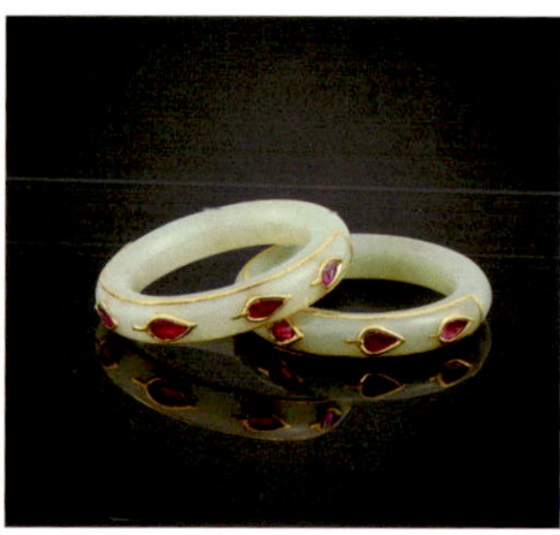

47. Pair of falcon bracelets
North India, ca. 1800
Jade with rubies set in gold
4.1 cm each
PL. 21

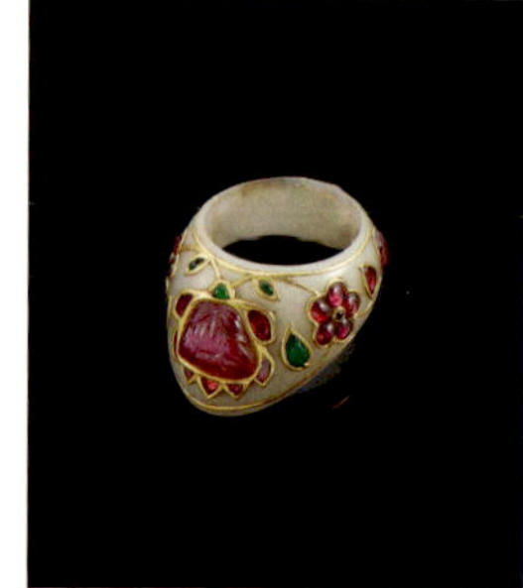

48. Archer's ring
North India, 1630–1650
Nephrite jade with rubies and emeralds set in gold
1.9 × 2.9 × 3.7 cm

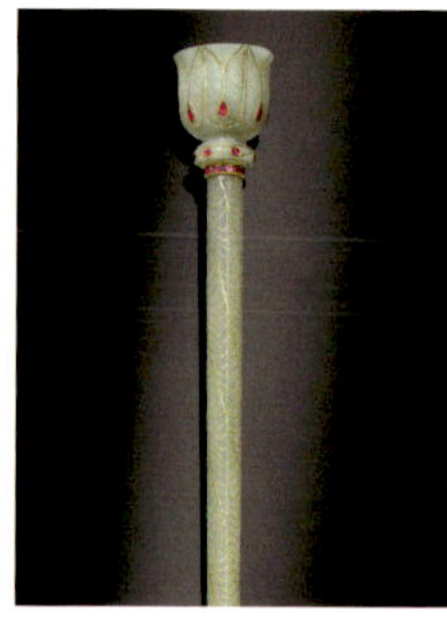

49. Flywhisk (detail)
North India, 1675–1725
Jade, gold, rubies
29.8 × 3.5 cm
PL. 22

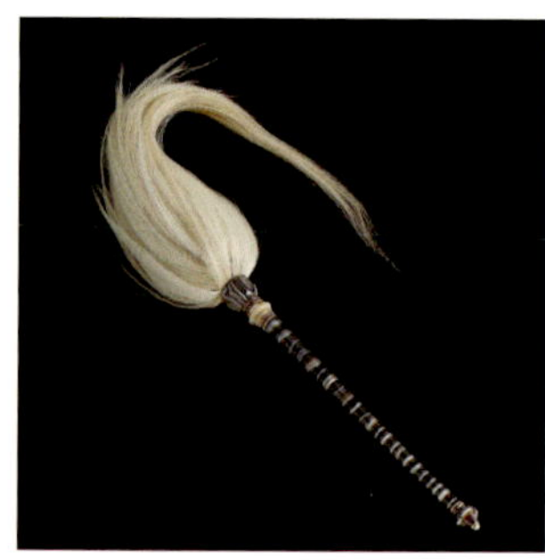

50. Flywhisk
North India, 1750–1760
Banded agate, carnelian, sard, rubies, emeralds, pearls, gold, silver gilt
23.5 (excluding tail) × 2.2 cm

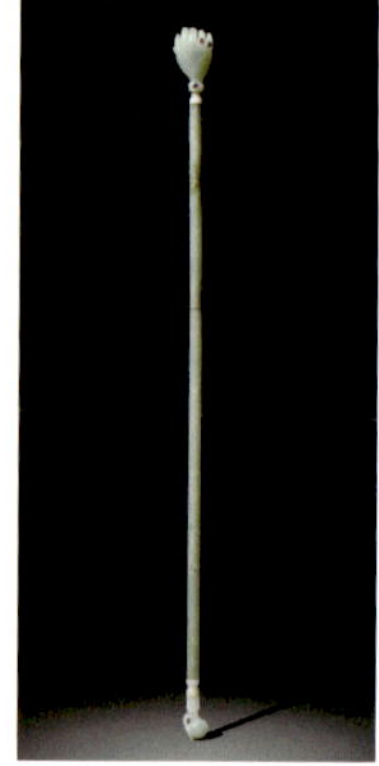

51. Back scratcher
North India, 1750–1760
Gold, jade, ruby, emerald
47.5 × 2.8 cm

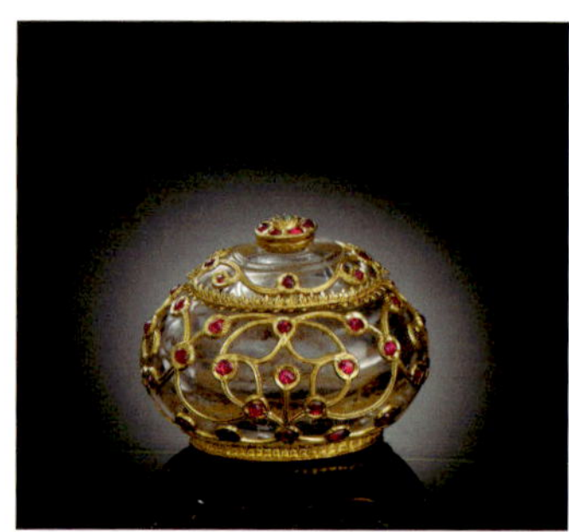

52. Box
Goa, Deccan or North India, 1575–1625
Rock crystal, gold, rubies, emeralds
4.8 × 5.9 × 4.8 cm

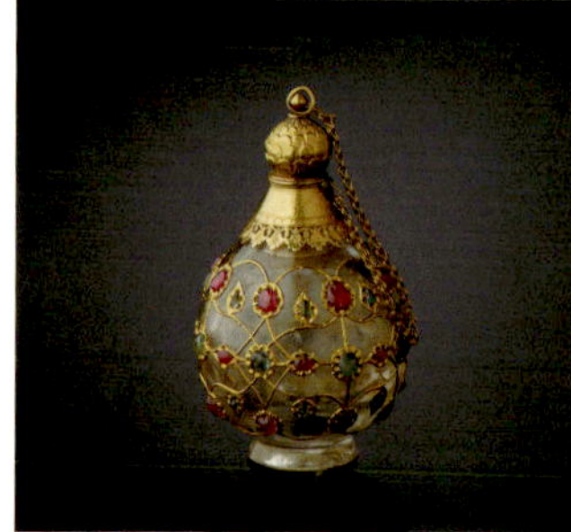

53. Flask
North India, 1650–1700
Rock crystal, gold set with rubies and emeralds
9.2 × 5.5 cm
PL. 24

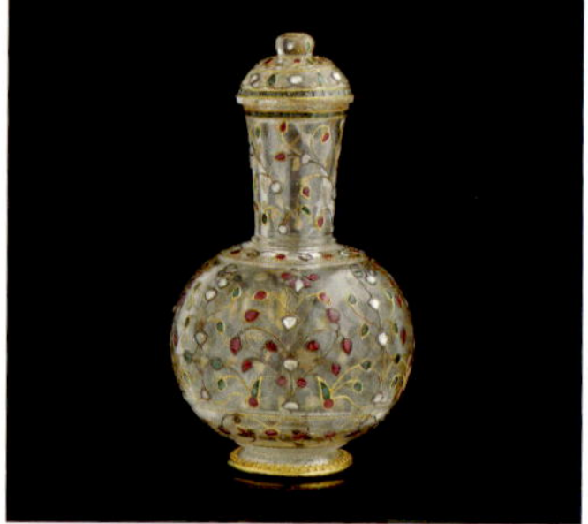

54. Flask
North India or Deccan, 1740–1780
Rock crystal, diamonds, emeralds, and rubies set in gold and silver
19.2 × 11.3 cm
PL. 23

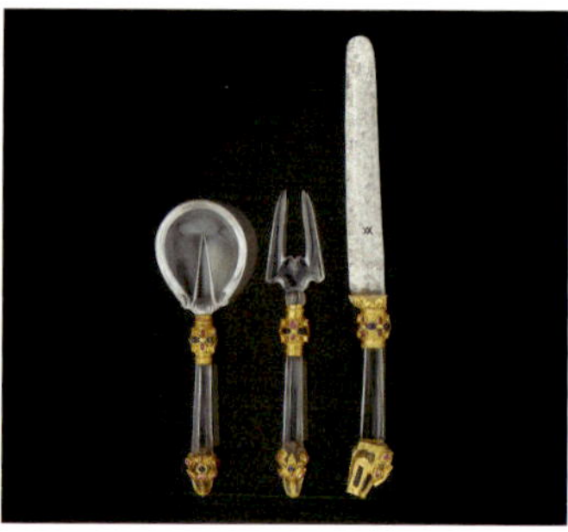

55. Set of flatware
India or Sri Lanka, 16th–17th centuries
Rock crystal, rubies and sapphires set in gold
(knife: 21.8 × 1.7 cm; fork: 14.3 × 2.9 cm; spoon: 15.5 × 5 cm)
PL. 25

3
JADE DAGGERS AND WEAPONS

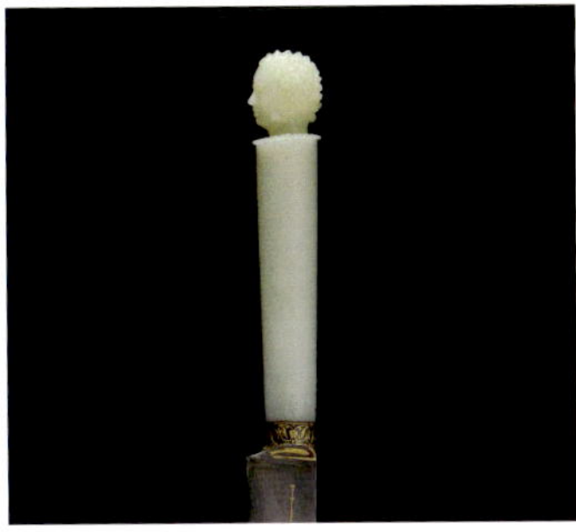

56. The Shah Jahan Dagger (detail)
North India, hilt: 1620–1625;
blade: 1629–1636
Jade, watered steel blade inlaid with gold
29.7 cm; hilt 11.1 cm; head 2.4 cm
Inscribed in Persian: *Second Lord of the Auspicious Conjunction* 2 or 9
PL. 26

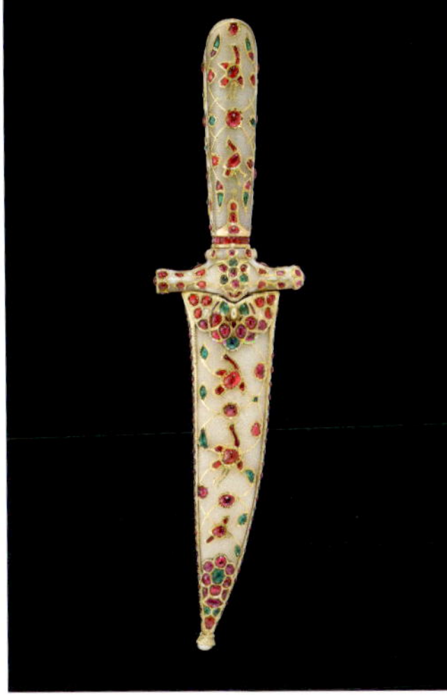

57. Dagger and scabbard
North India, 1620–1640
Jade inlaid with rubies, emeralds, and diamonds set in gold, watered steel blade inlaid with gold
26 × 6.6 cm (dagger: 24 cm)
PL. 27

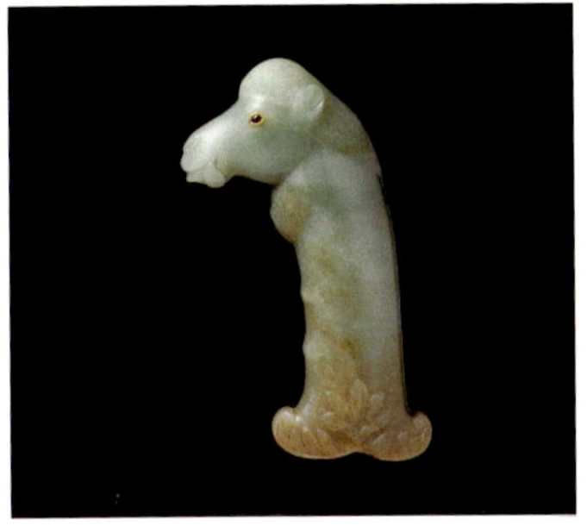

58. Hilt
India, 17th century
Jade, rubies
13.2 cm

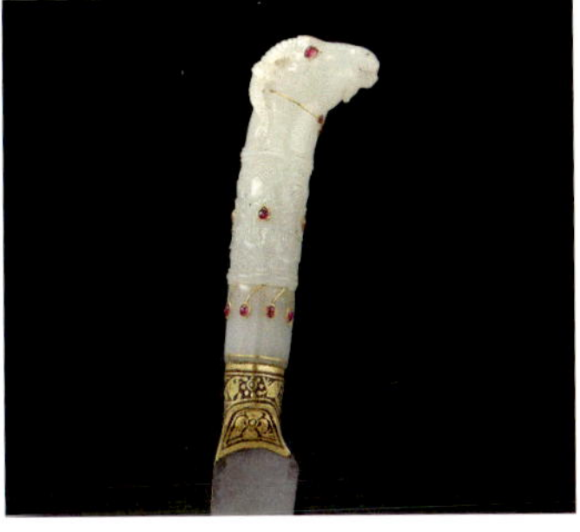

59. Dagger (detail)
North India, 1720–1740 (lower section: 19th century)
Jade inlaid with rubies set in gold, steel blade inlaid with gold
27.3 × 1.4 cm (hilt: 8.9 cm; blade: 18.4 cm)
PL. 29

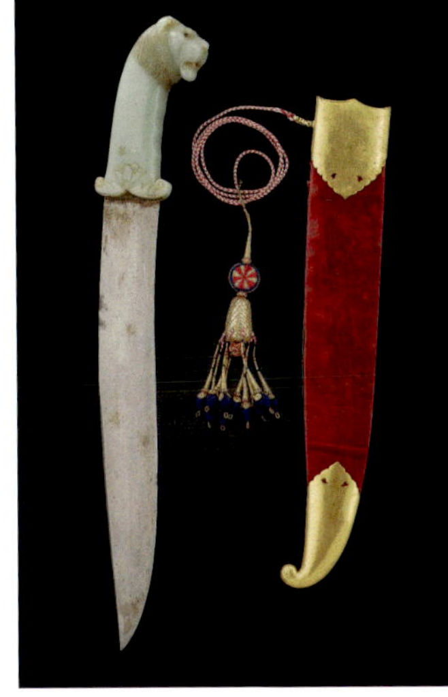

60. Dagger
North India or Deccan, ca. 1750
Jade, steel blade; scabbard: wood, textile, gold, cord
45.5 × 6.1 cm (scabbard: 35.5 × 6.3 cm)
PL. 30

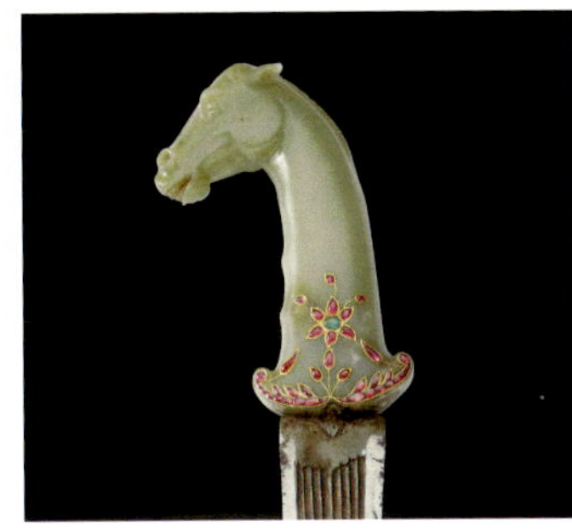

61. Dagger (detail)
North India, 1700–1750
Jade inlaid with gold, rubies, and emerald; steel blade
38.6 × 7.3 cm
PL. 28

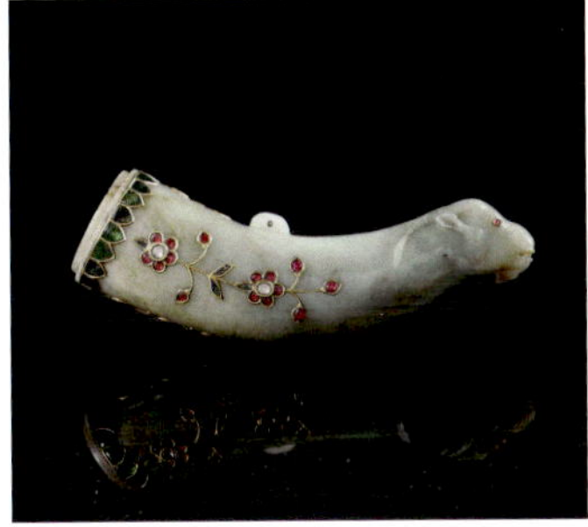

62. Powder horn
India, 1725–1775
Jade, diamonds, rubies, emeralds
4.9 × 18 × 4.9 cm

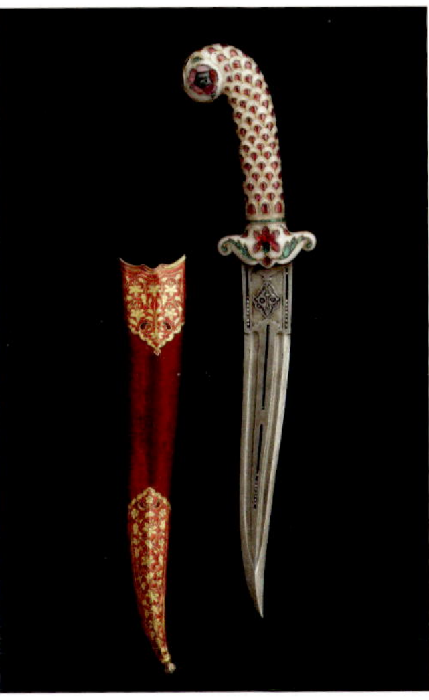

63. Dagger
North India or Deccan, 1700–1725
Jade inlaid with rubies and emeralds set in gold, watered steel blade; scabbard: wood, textile, gold, enamel
35.8 × 6.4 cm (scabbard: 25.5 × 4.4 cm)
PL. 31

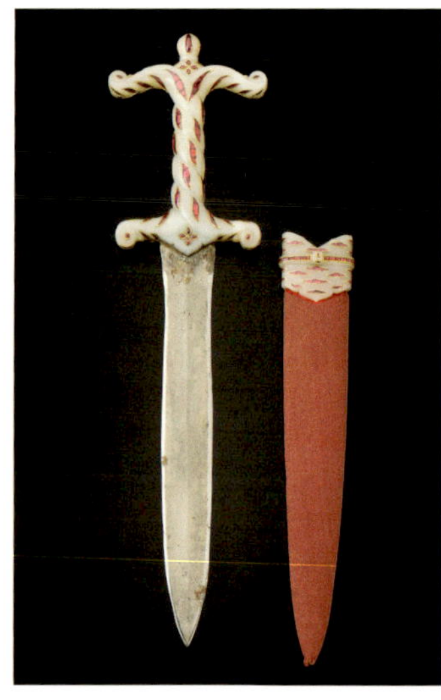

64. Dagger
North India or Deccan, ca. 1675–1700
Jade inlaid with rubies set in gold, steel blade; scabbard: wood, textile
36.3 × 9.6 cm (scabbard: 25 × 4.7 cm; medallion: 4.1 × 4.7 cm)
PL. 32

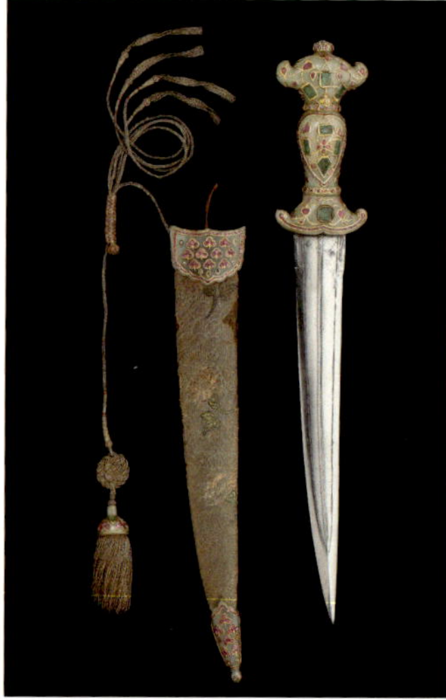

65. Dagger
North India or Deccan, 1700–1750; scabbard silk: India or Iran, ca. 1650
Gold, jade, rubies, emeralds, diamonds, watered steel blade; scabbard: wood, silk; locket and chape: jade, gold, rubies, diamonds
39 × 6.4 cm (scabbard: 34.1 × 4.5 cm)

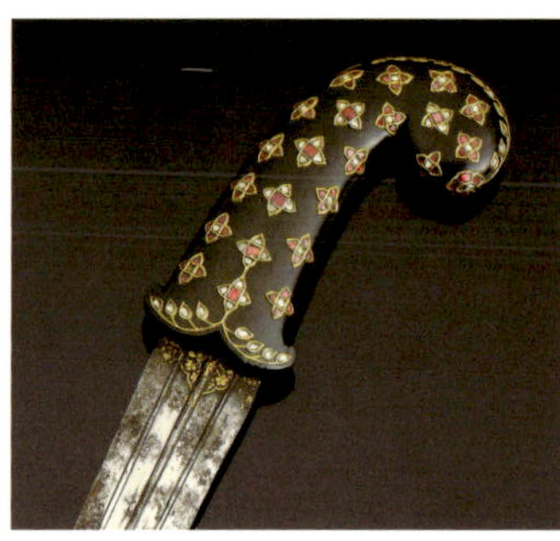

66. Dagger (detail)
North India or Deccan, 1700–1725
Jade inlaid with rubies and diamonds set in gold, watered steel blade inlaid with gold
43 × 6.5 cm
PL. 33

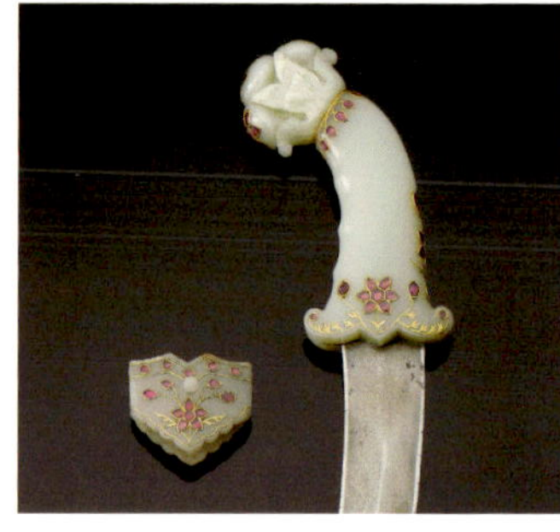

67. Dagger (detail)
Deccan, 1675–1725
Jade inlaid with gold, rubies, and emeralds, watered steel blade
39.5 × 6.2 cm (locket: 4.1 × 5.1 cm)

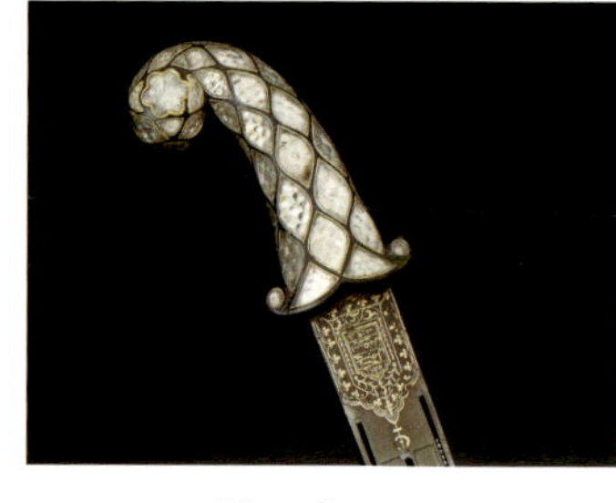

68. Dagger (detail)
North India, ca. 1725–1750; blade: Iran or India, 1783–1784
Jade inset with rock crystal set in gold, foil backing, watered steel blade inlaid with gold
47.5 × 6.5 cm
Inscribed in Persian on both sides of the blade: *O Allah! Work of Isfahan 1198*
PL. 34

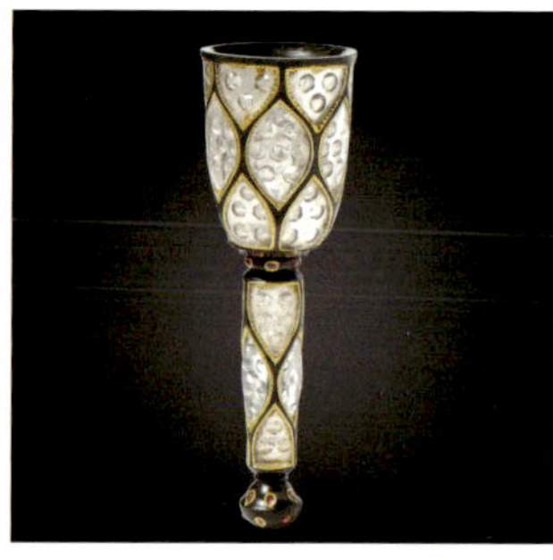

69. Flywhisk
India, 1725–1750
Jade, gold, rock crystal, rubies, foil
18.2 × 5.9 cm

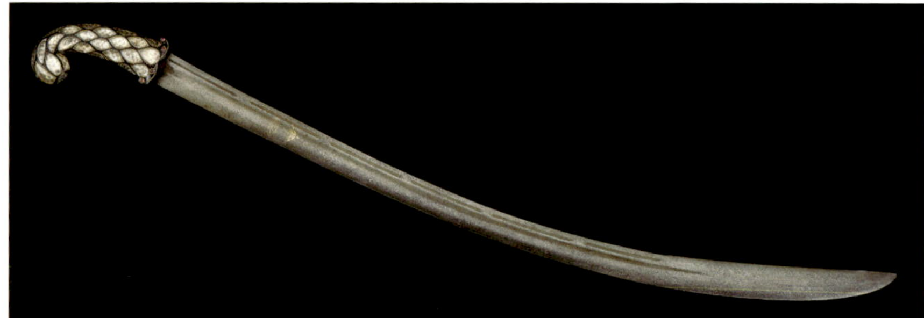

70. Sword
India, 1725–1750 (blade: 1750–1800)
Hilt: jade, gold, rock crystal foil; blade: watered steel, gold
92 × 7 cm (hilt: 13 cm)
Inscribed in gold in Arabic on the blade: *Help from God and near victory*

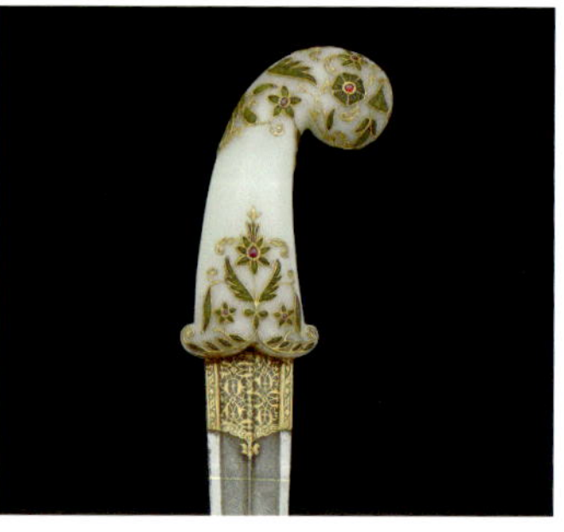

71. Dagger (detail)
Lucknow (?), ca. 1775–1790
Jade inlaid with serpentine and rubies set in gold, watered steel blade inlaid with gold
39.2 cm
PL. 35

4
THE ROYAL COURTS
Gold and Enamels

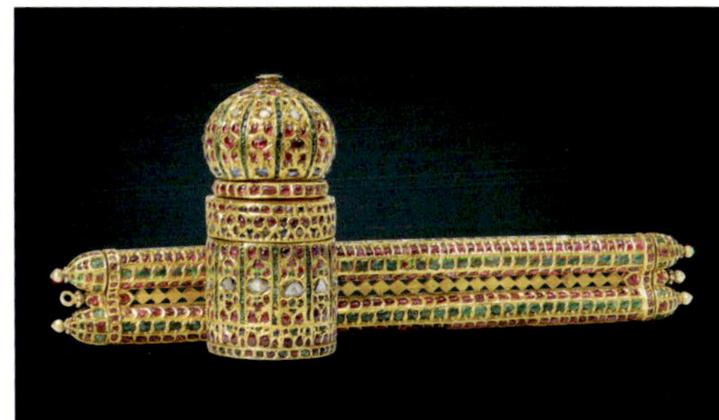

72. Pen case and inkwell
North India or Deccan, 1575–1600
Gold set with rubies, emeralds, diamonds, sapphires, lac
4 × 30.6 cm (inkwell: 11.4 × 5.4 cm)
PL. 36

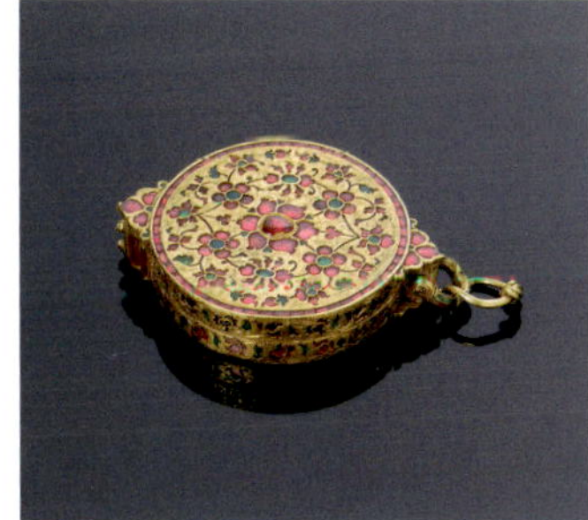

73. Locket pendant
North India or Deccan, 1575–1625
Gold with rubies, emeralds, enamel
6.9 × 5 × 1.2 cm
Inscribed in Persian inside:
9 tola 6 masha (?) ya
PL. 37

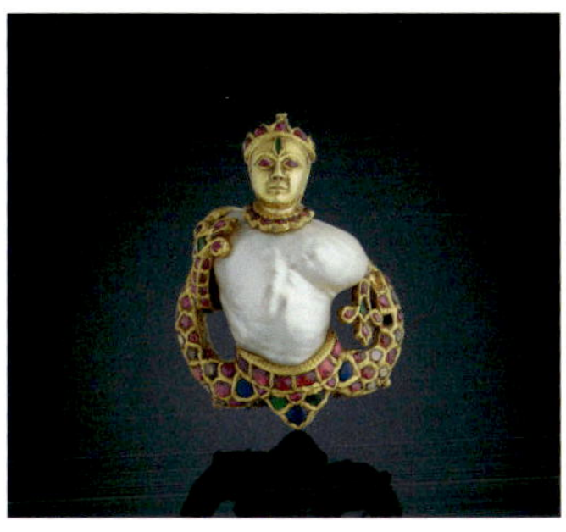

74. Pendant (obverse)
India, ca. 1575–1625
Baroque pearl, gold set with rubies, emeralds, sapphires, glass, enamel, on a lac core
6.6 × 5.2 × 3 cm
PL. 38

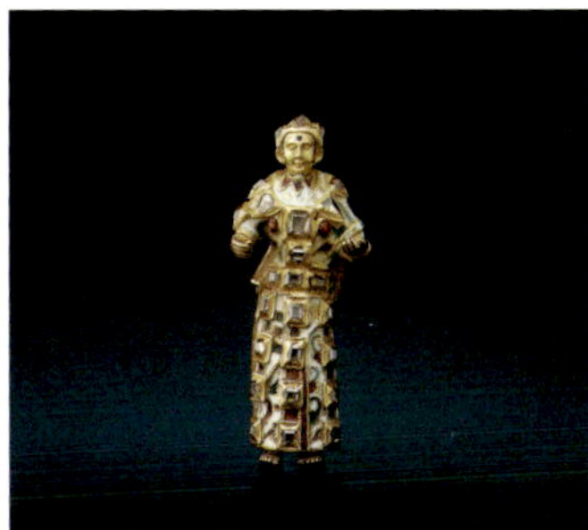

75. Figure of a female saint (obverse)
Goa or North India, 1625–1660
Gold set with diamonds, decorated with enamel around a lac core
5.4 × 2.2 × 2.2 cm
Inscribed in Persian: *2 tola, 7 masha*
PL. 39

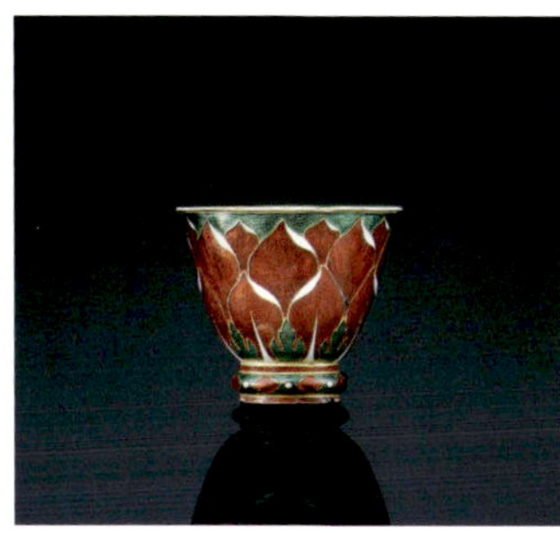

76. Cup
North India, ca. 1635–1640
Gold, enamel
3 × 3.7 cm
PL. 40

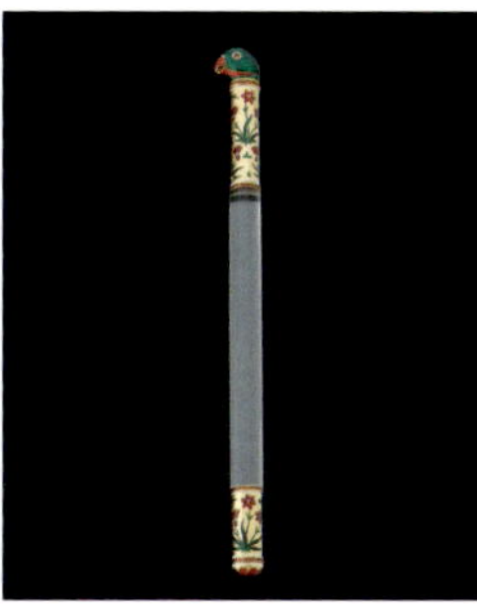

77. Wand fittings
North India, ca. 1650
Gold, enamel around a lac core
Upper section: 8.3 × 2.6 cm; lower section: 4.5 × 1.75 cm
PL. 41

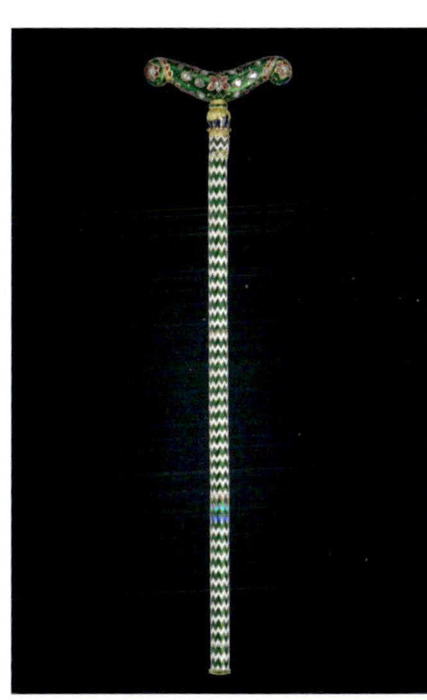

78. Armrest crutch
North India, 1650–1700
Gold, diamonds, rubies, enamel, lacquer
52.8 × 15.6 × 2.9 cm

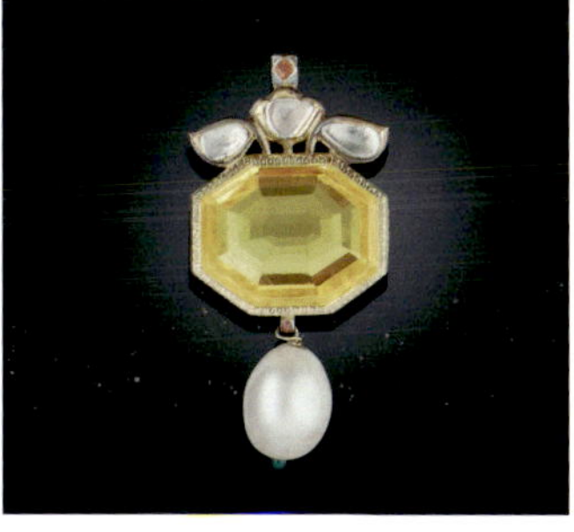

79. Pendant (obverse)
Deccan, ca. 1650–1700
Gold, yellow sapphire, diamonds, pearl, enamel
5.9 (4 without pearl) × 2.9 × 0.9 cm

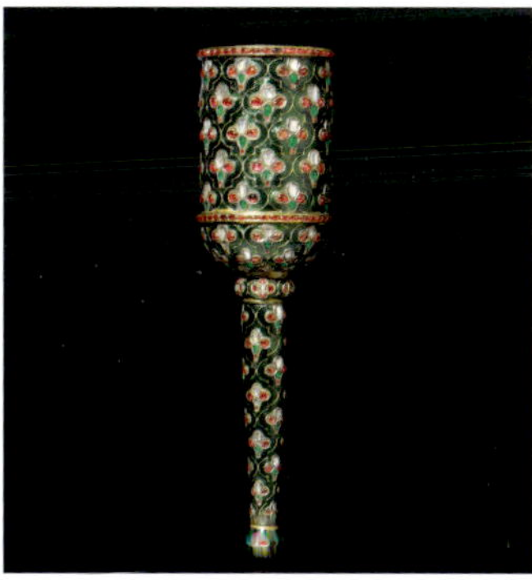

80. Flywhisk
North India or Deccan, 1675–1725
Gold, diamonds, rubies, emeralds, enamel, lac
12.2 × 6.1 cm

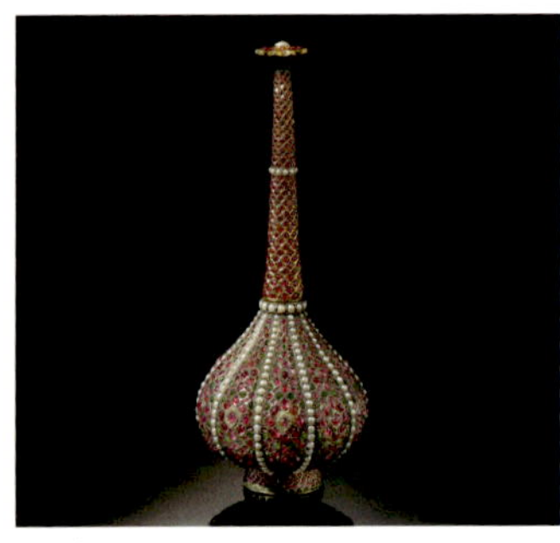

81. Rosewater sprinkler
North India, 1675–1725
Gold set with rubies, emeralds, pearls
25.7 cm
Inscribed in Persian on the base:
64 tola, 4 masha / 64 tola, 2 masha
PL. 44

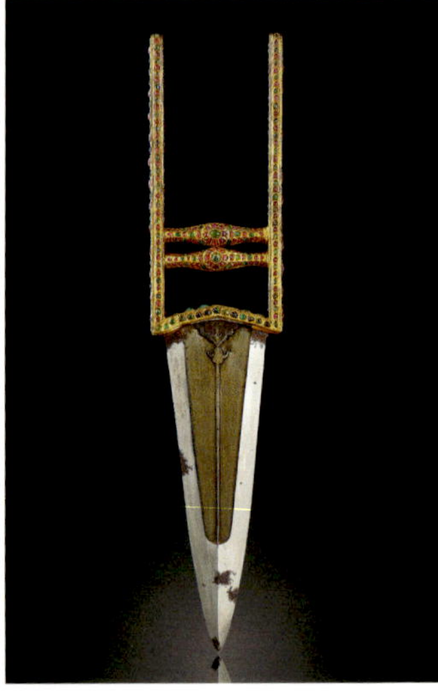

82. Punch dagger
North India or Deccan, ca. 1680–1720
Gold, diamonds, rubies, emeralds, steel blade
42.1 × 9.4 × 1.7 cm
PL. 46

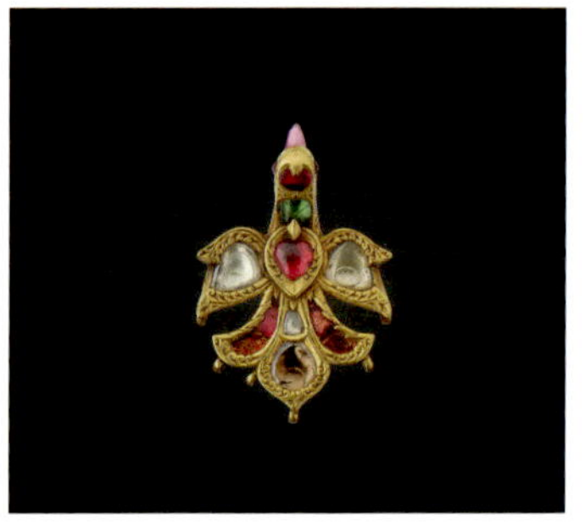

83. Bird pendant (obverse)
Deccan (?), ca. 1700
Gold, diamonds, rubies, emeralds, enamel, lac core
(3.4 × 2.2 × 1.2 cm)
PL. 43

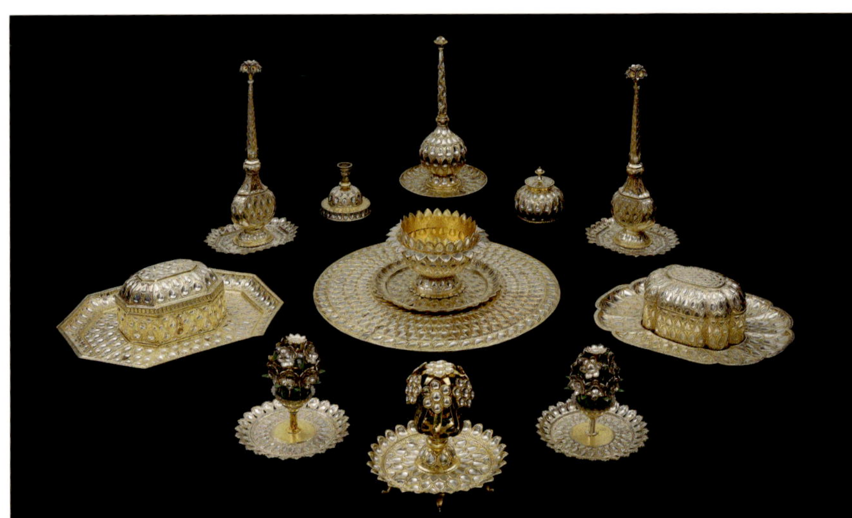

84. Durbar set
North India, 1750–1775
Silver gilt
Clockwise from top center:
A) Vessel: 25.4 × 8.2 cm; tray: 1.1 × 15.2 cm
B) 28.5 cm
C) Vessel: 1 × 14.9 × 1.9 cm; tray: 28.5 cm
D) Vessel: 8.4 × 14.6 × 10.4 cm; tray: 2 × 28.2 × 22 cm
E) 11.4 × 14 cm (tray)
F) 14 cm (tray only: 5.5 cm) × 16.5 cm (tray)
G) 12.5 × 14 cm (tray)
H) Vessel: 8.5 × 14.3 × 10.2 cm; tray: 2 × 29.9 × 24 cm
I) Vessel: 28.5 cm; tray: 1.5 × 14.8 × 11.5 cm
J) 7.7 × 8.6 cm
K) Vessel: 9.6 × 15.2 cm; smaller tray: 1.4 × 19.2 cm; larger tray: 1 × 36.3 cm
PL. 42

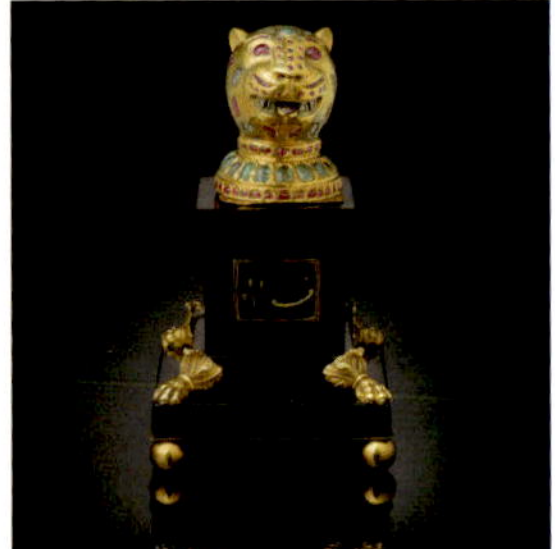

85. Finial from Tipu Sultan's throne
Mysore, ca. 1787–1793; plinth: ca. 1800
Gold set with rubies, emeralds, and diamonds, lac, black marble plinth, with gilt metal
17.1 cm (finial: 6.8 × 5.4 × 5.5 cm; plinth: 10.3 × 10 × 10 cm)
PL. 47

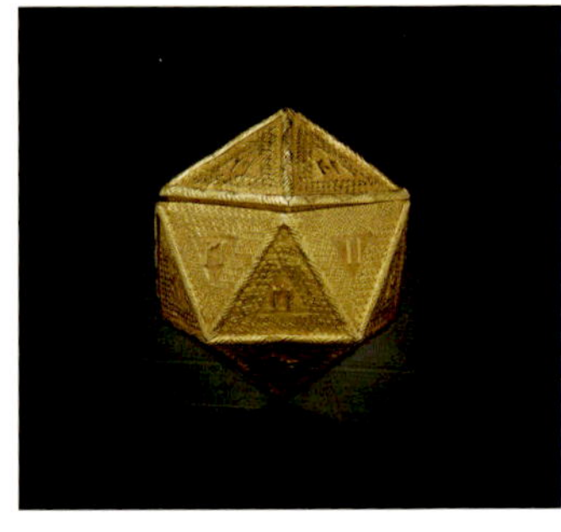

86. Tipu Sultan's magic box
Mysore, 1780–1790
Gold
5.5 × 5.8 × 4.7 cm
Inscribed: *11 / 20 / 21 / 32 / 42 / 51 / 61 / 71 / 81 / 101 / 201 / 301 / 401 / 601 / 701 / 801 / 901 / 202*
PL. 48

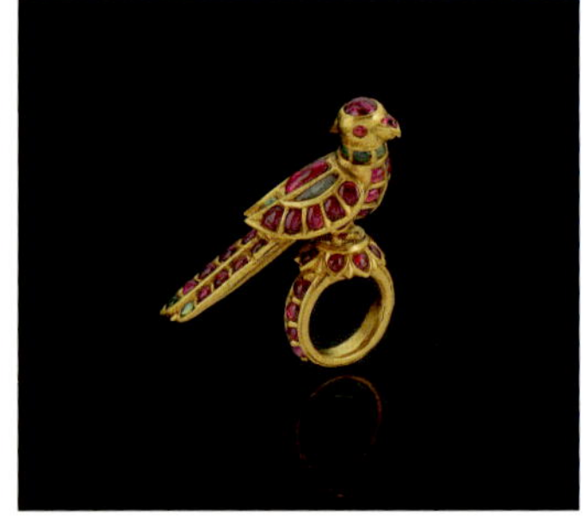

87. Tipu Sultan's hawking ring
Mysore, 1775–1799
Gold, rubies, emeralds
5.7 × 2.7 × 5 cm

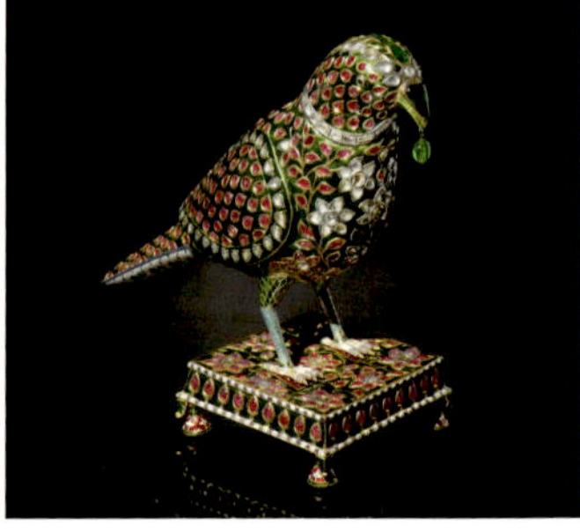

88. Parrot
Parrot: Hyderabad, 1775–1825; base: North India, 1700–1750
Gold, rubies, diamonds, emeralds, lac
20.1 × 9.5 × 22.6 cm (base: 9.5 × 9.5 cm)
PL. 49

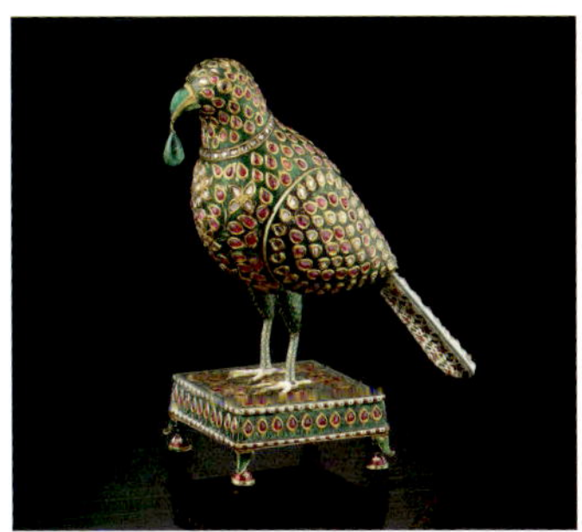

89. Parrot
Hyderabad, 1775–1825
Gold, diamonds, rubies, emeralds, enamel, lac
21.6 cm (parrot: 17.9 × 19.3 cm; base: 4.3 × 9.7 × 9.7 cm)

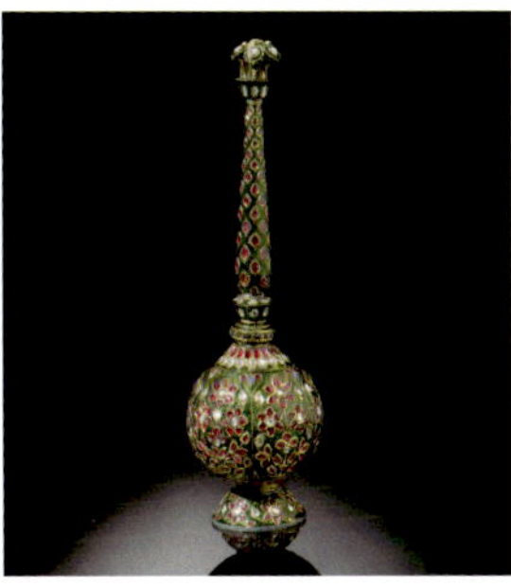

90. Rosewater sprinkler
North India or Deccan, 1755–1825
Gold, rubies, diamonds, emeralds, enamel
28.6 × 8 cm
PL. 50

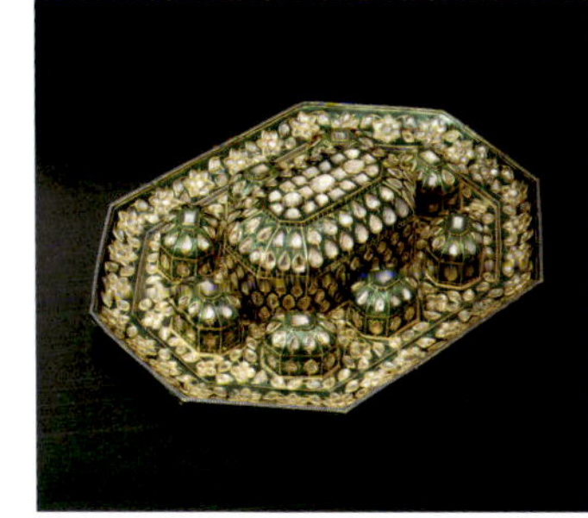

91. Container for *paan*
Hyderabad, 1760–1780
Gold, silver, diamonds, enamel, lac
6.1 × 35 × 29 cm (tray: 1.5 × 35 × 29 cm; large box: 5.3 × 11.2 × 6.2 cm; small boxes: 2.7 × 3.7 × 2.8 cm each)
PL. 51

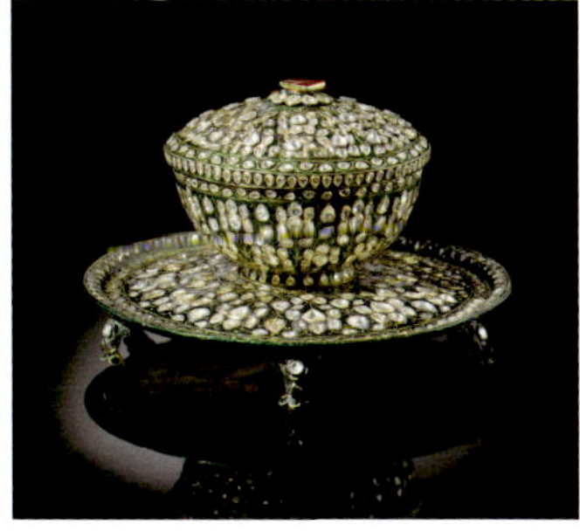

92. Covered bowl and tray
Hyderabad, 1790–1810
Gold, diamonds, rubies, emeralds
12.5 cm (tray: 3.1 × 12.8 cm; bowl: 9.4 × 12.3 cm)

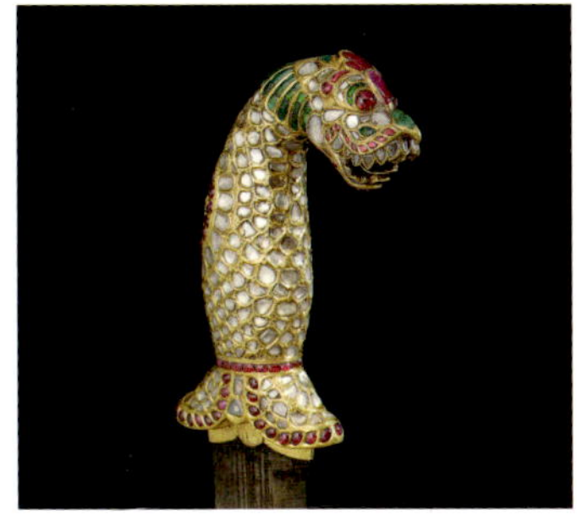

93. Dagger (detail)
Tanjore or Mysore, 1790–1810
Gold set with diamonds, rubies, and emeralds on a lac core, steel blade
34.1 cm (hilt: 11.6 cm; blade: 22 cm)
PL. 45

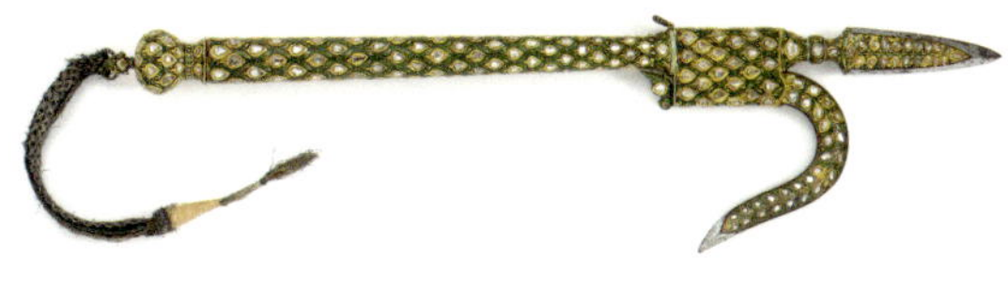

94. Elephant goad
North India, 1880–1900
Gold, steel, diamonds, rubies, enamel, silk, metal thread
46 × 11.2 cm
PL. 52

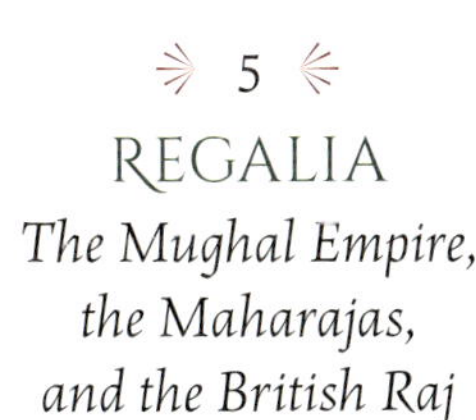

5
REGALIA
The Mughal Empire, the Maharajas, and the British Raj

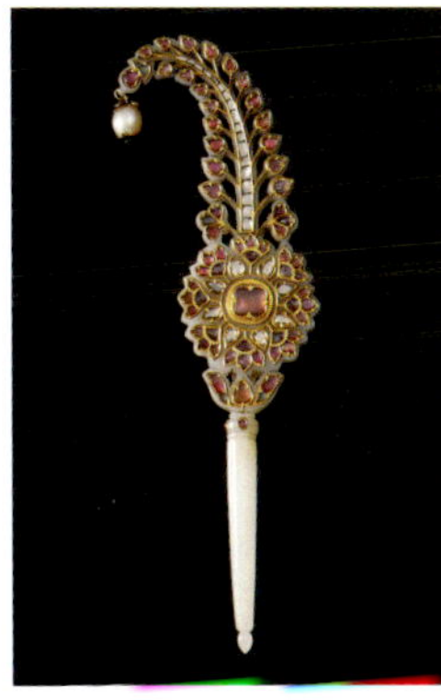

95. Turban ornament
North India or Deccan, 1675–1725
Jade, diamonds, rubies, emeralds, pearl
19.6 × 4.5 cm

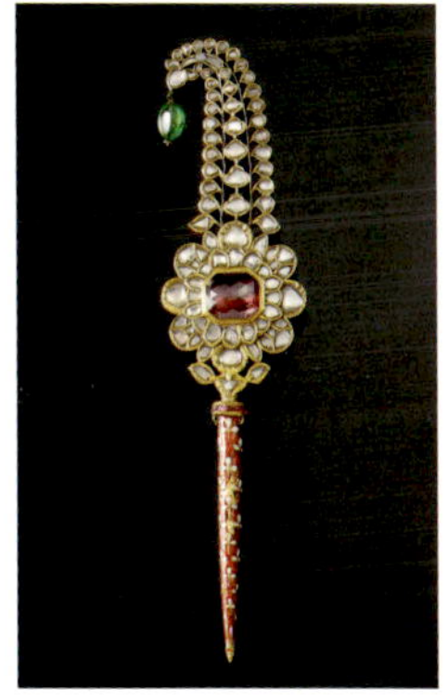

96. Turban ornament (obverse)
North India, 1675–1750
Gold, spinel, diamonds, rubies, emerald, enamel
22.5 × 5.4 cm
PL. 53

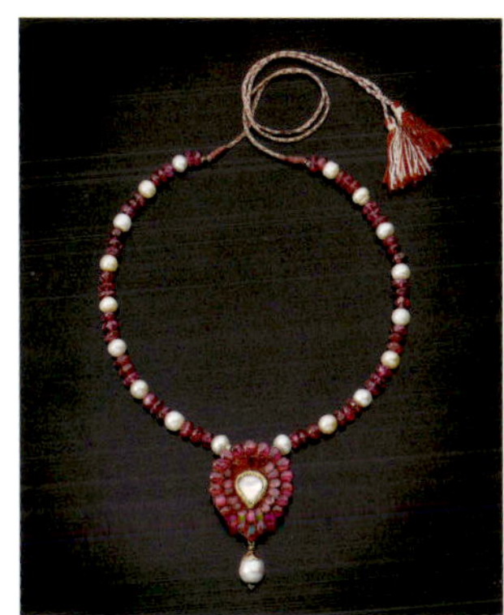

97. Turban ornament
Hyderabad, 1750–1800
Gold, diamond, rubies, pearls, enamel
21.5 cm (excluding cord; pendant: 5.7 [4 without pearl] × 3.5 cm)

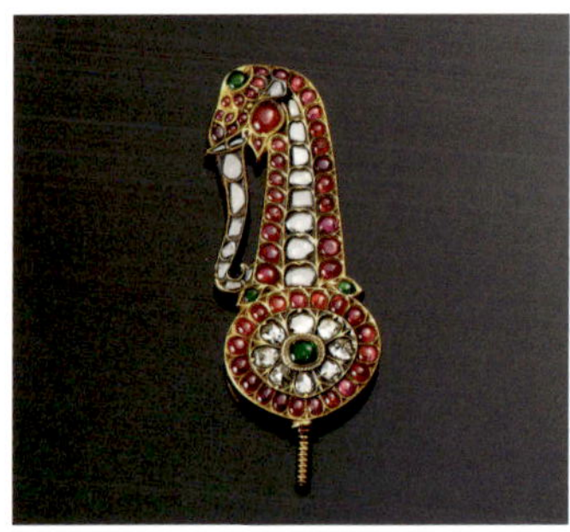

98. Turban ornament
South India, 1775–1825
Gold, diamonds, rubies, emeralds
8.2 × 2.9 cm
PL. 54

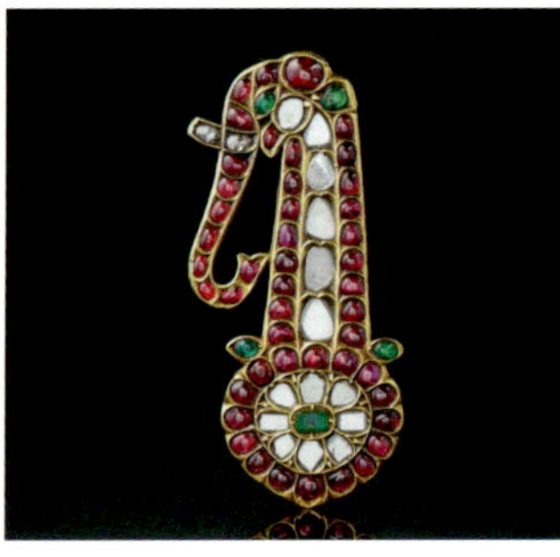

99. Turban ornament
South India, 1775–1825
Gold, diamonds, rubies, emeralds
8.5 × 2.8 cm

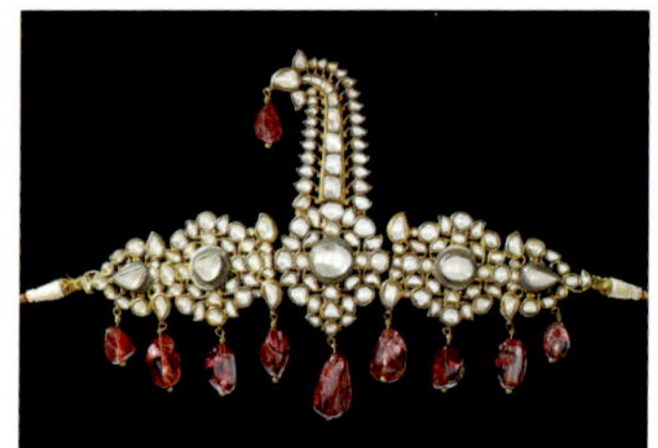

100. Turban ornament
Hyderabad, 1800–1850. Lower left spinel dated to 1607–1608 and 1633–1634. Gold, diamonds, spinels, pearls, enamel, modern stringing
18.5 × 27.2 cm (excluding cord)
Inscribed in Persian on the lower-left spinel: *1043 Second Lord of the Auspicious Conjunction 6 | Jahangir Shah [son] of Akbar Shah 1016*
PL. 55

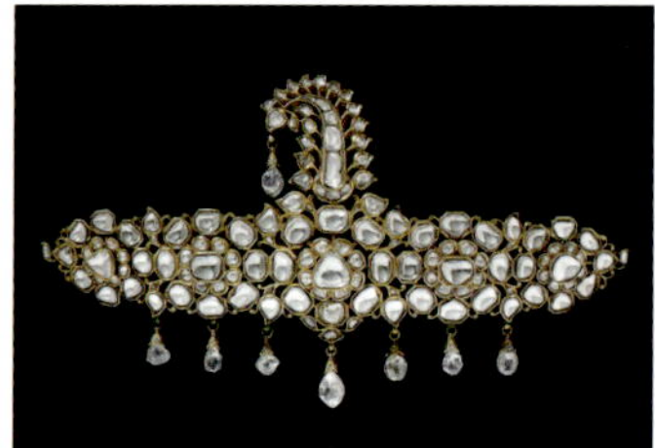

101. Turban ornament
Jaipur, 1825–1875
Gold, diamonds, enamel
10.5 × 19.2 cm

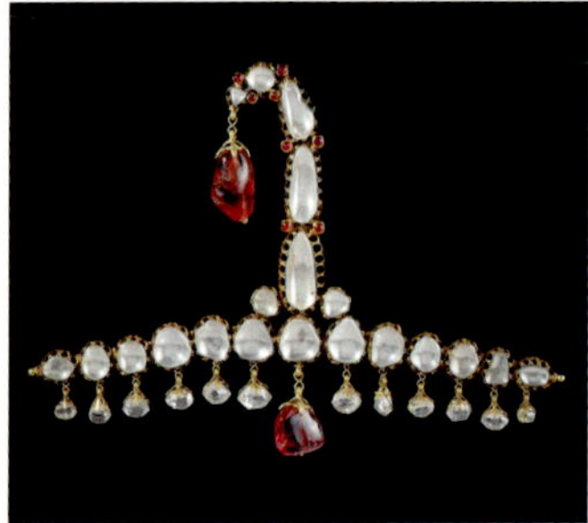

102. Turban ornament
North India, 1875–1900. Spinels dated to 1639–1640.
Gold, diamond, rubies, spinels
13.7 × 19.8 cm
Inscribed in Persian on the spinels: *12 Shah Jahan [son] of Jahangir Shah 1049*
PL. 56

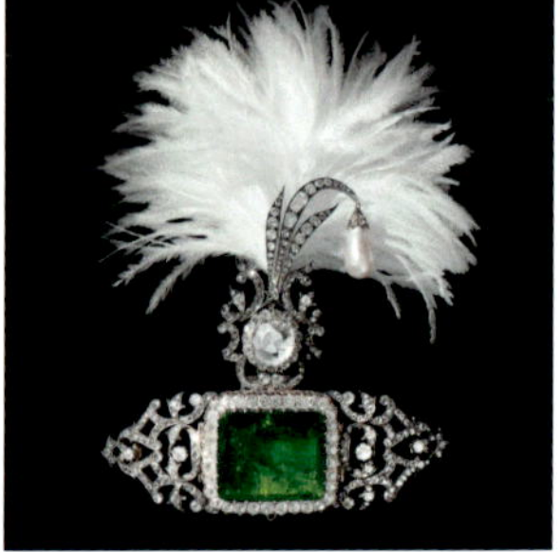

103. Turban ornament
India, ca. 1900 (clip: Cartier Paris, 2012)
Gold, silver, emerald, diamonds, pearl
11.7 × 12.8 cm
PL. 57

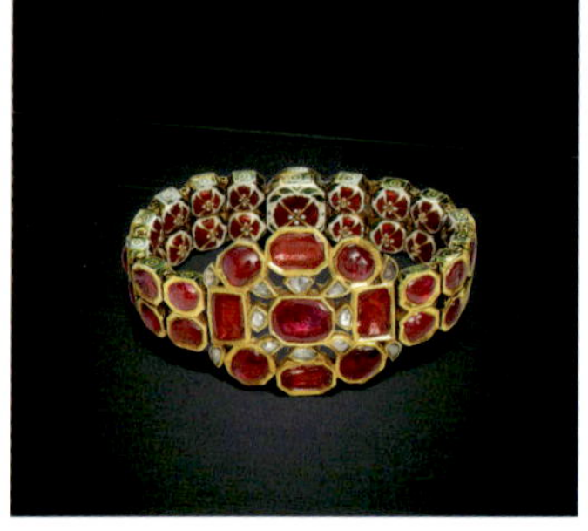

104. Bracelet
Jaipur, 1750–1800
Gold, rubies, spinels, diamonds, enamel
22.4 × 4.7 cm

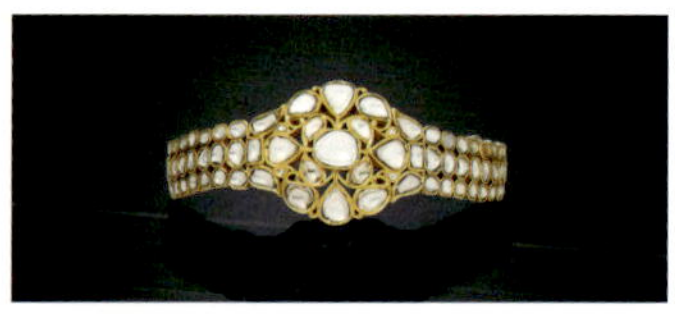

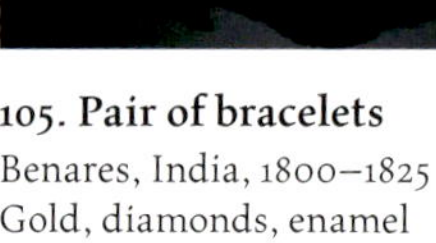

105. Pair of bracelets
Benares, India, 1800–1825
Gold, diamonds, enamel
24 × 4.3 cm; 24 × 4.4 cm
PL. 58

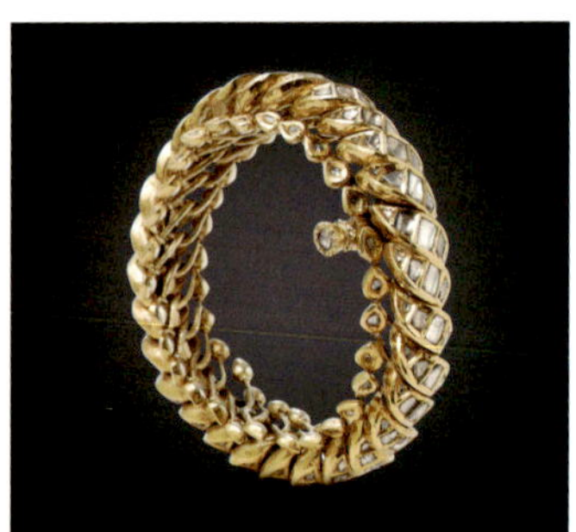

106. Anklet
Hyderabad or Rajasthan, 1800–1850
Gold, diamonds
10 cm wide
PL. 59

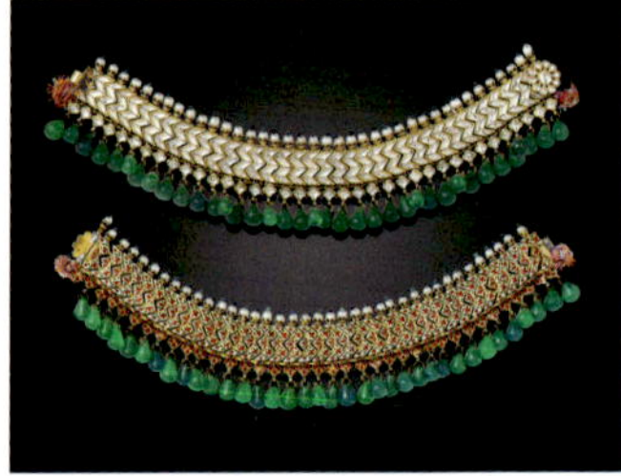

107. Pair of anklets
Jaipur or Bikaner, 1800–1850
Gold, white sapphires, pearls, glass beads, enamel
5 × 26 cm; 5 × 26.2 cm
PL. 60

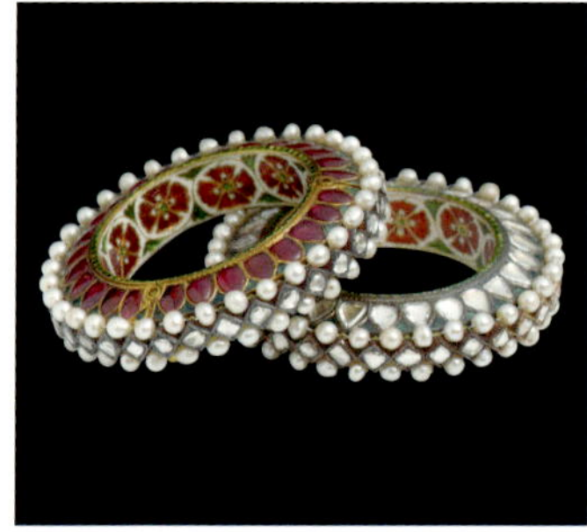

108. Pair of bangles
Jaipur, 1775–1825
Gold, rubies, diamonds, enamel
Each 7.2 cm wide

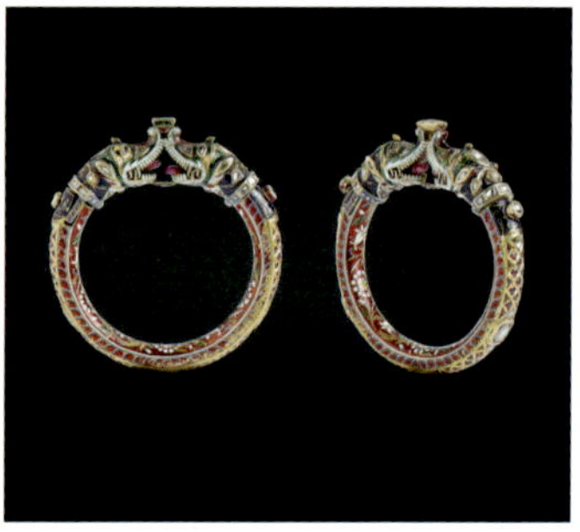

109. Pair of bangles
Jaipur or Dholpur, 1850–1880
Gold, diamonds, rubies, enamel
Each 7.1 cm wide

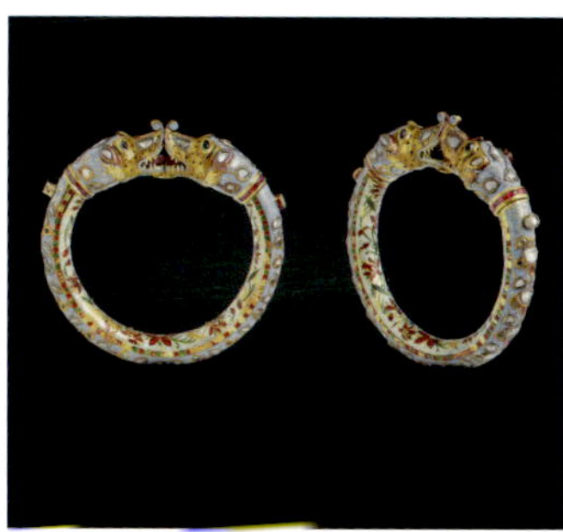

110. Pair of bangles
Jaipur, 1880–1900
Gold, diamonds, rubies, enamel
8.4 and 8.8 cm wide

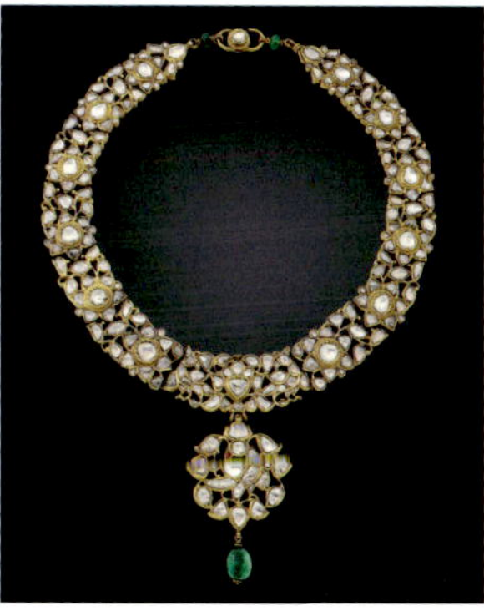

111. Necklace (obverse)
India, 1750–1800
Gold, diamonds, rubies, emeralds
26.6 × 18.5 cm (pendant: 5.5 cm)

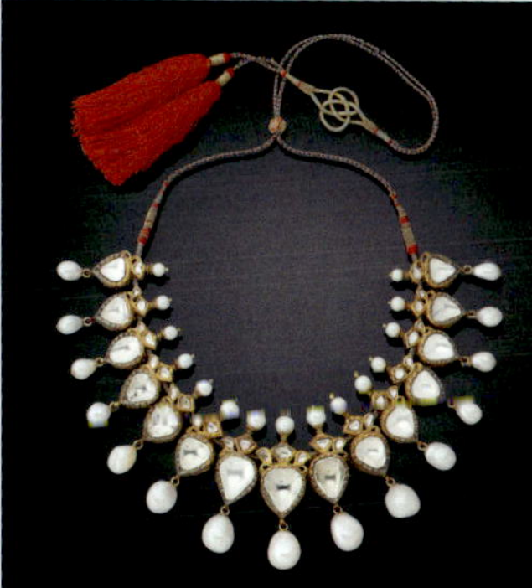

112. Necklace
India, 1800–1850
Gold, diamonds, pearls, enamel, modern stringing
26.5 cm

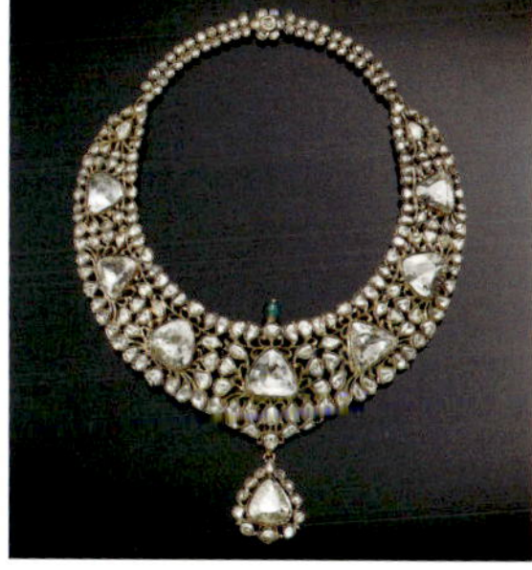

113. The Nizam of Hyderabad Necklace
India, 1850–1875
Gold, diamonds, emerald, enamel
26 × 19.6 cm
PL. 61

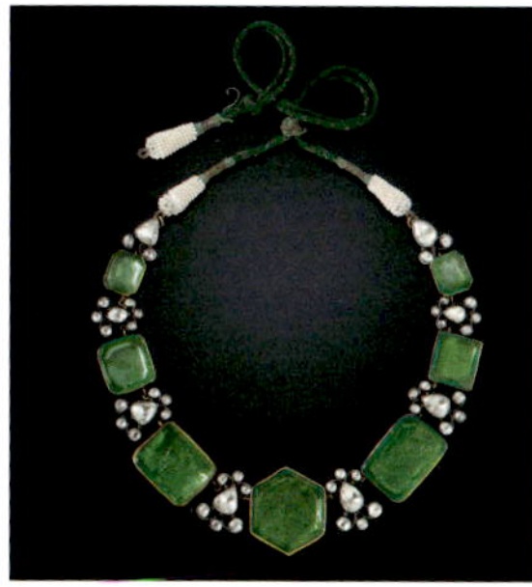

114. Necklace
India, 1850–1900
Gold, silver, emeralds, diamonds, pearls, modern stringing
31 cm (excluding cord)
PL. 62

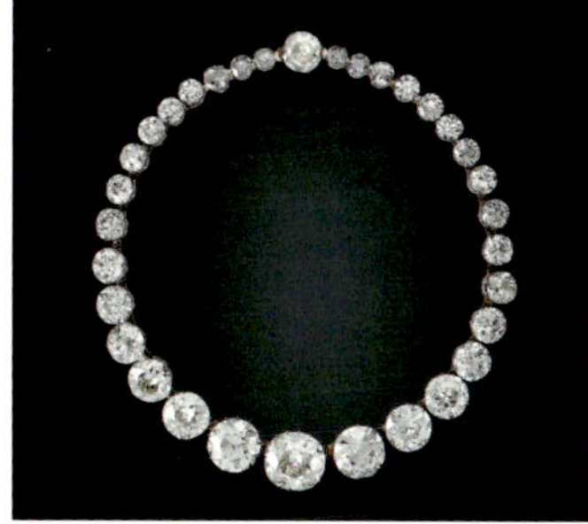

115. Necklace
Hyderabad, ca. 1890
Gold, diamonds
35.5 cm
PL. 63

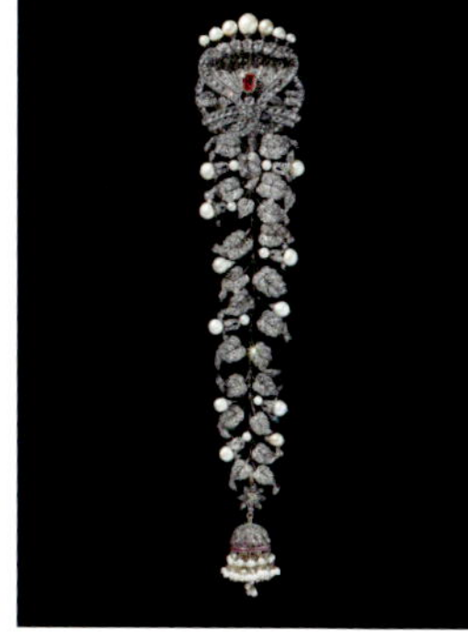

116. Plait ornament
South India, 1890–1910
Silver, diamonds, rubies, pearls
31 × 6.6 cm
PL. 66

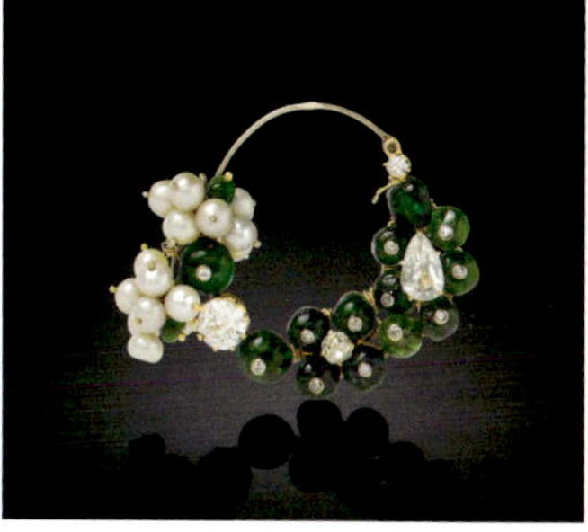

117. Nose ring
Western India, 1925–1950
Gold, diamonds, pearls, emeralds
3.5 × 3.4 cm

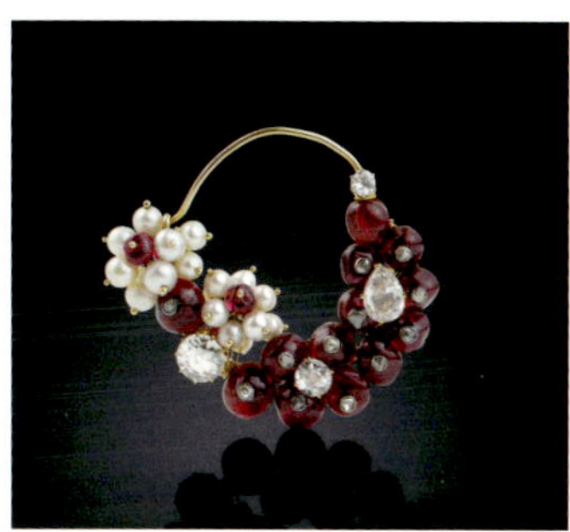

118. Nose ring
Western India, 1925–1950
Gold, diamonds, pearls, rubies
4.2 × 3.7 cm

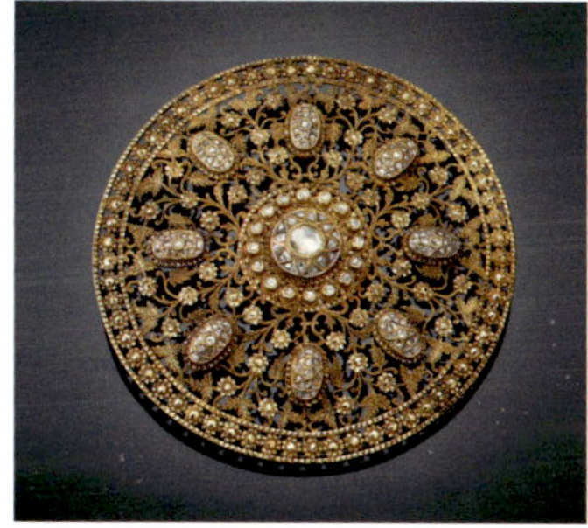

119. Hair ornament
Western India, ca. 1900
Gold, diamonds
13.7 cm
PL. 65

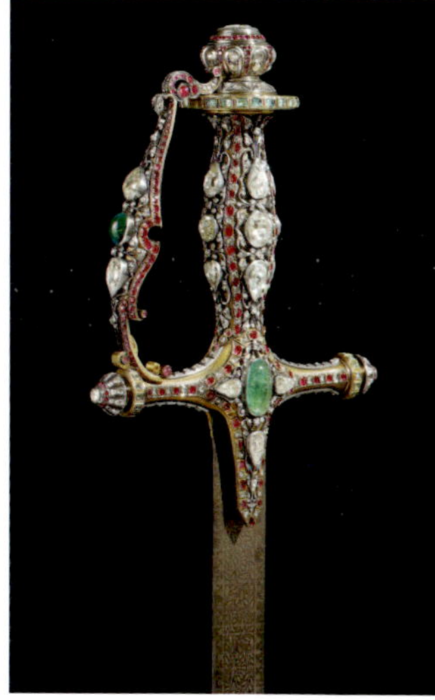

120. Ceremonial sword of the Nizam of Hyderabad
Hyderabad, 1880–1900
Gold, silver, diamonds, rubies, emeralds, steel blade
98 cm (hilt: 23.5 cm)
PL. 64

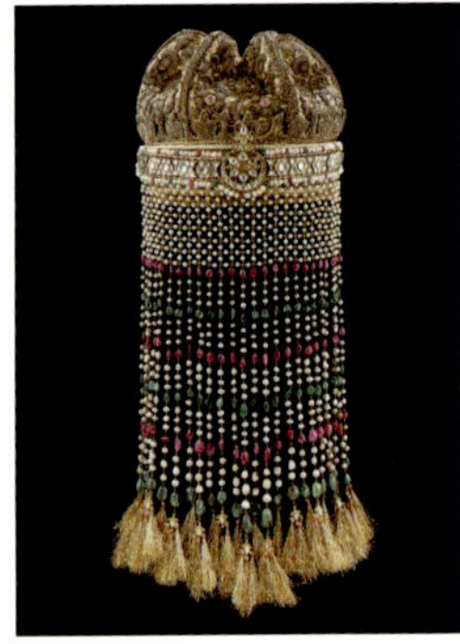

121. *Topi* and *sehra*
Tonk, 1875–1900
Gold, diamond, ruby, emerald, pearl; textile, gold and gold wire, emeralds, diamonds, rubies, pearls
Topi: 14 × 15 cm; *sehra*: 42 × 25.5 cm

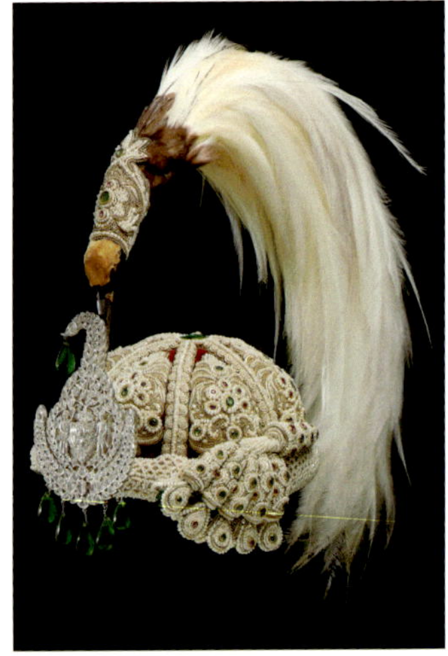

122. Crown
Nepal, ca. 1900
Cloth, pearls, colored glass, diamonds, emeralds, rubies; silver badge; mounted with bird-of-paradise plumes
41 × 21 × 28 cm (cap: 15.8 × 24 cm; badge: 18 × 10.5 cm)
Inscribed in Nepali on the silver badge: *Honourable Government of Nepal* and *Mother and land of birth are greater than Heaven*

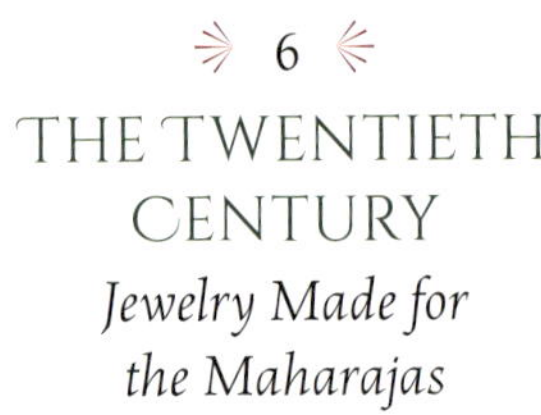

6

THE TWENTIETH CENTURY

Jewelry Made for the Maharajas

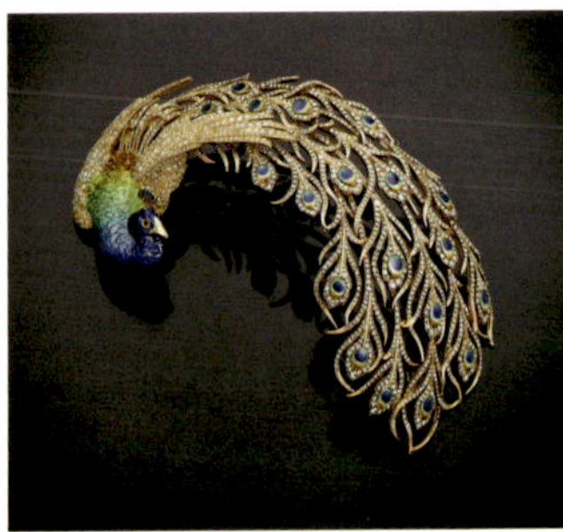

123. Aigrette
Mellerio dits Meller (Mellerio, known as Meller), Paris, ca. 1905
Gold, platinum, diamonds, enamel
15.5 × 6 cm
PL. 67

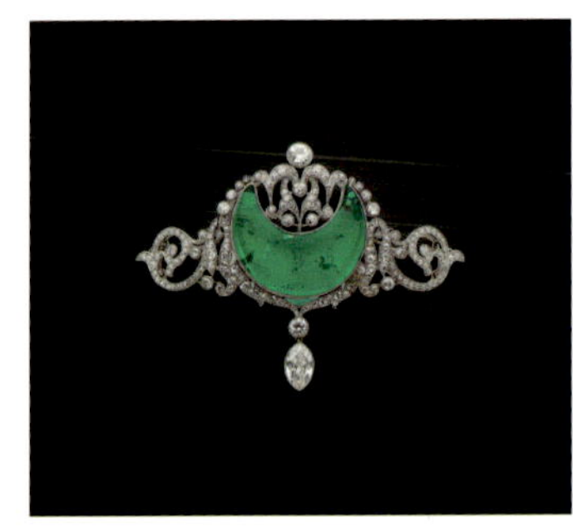

124. Anita Delgado's brooch
France, ca. 1910
Emerald set in platinum with diamonds
7 (5.5 excluding the drop) × 10 cm

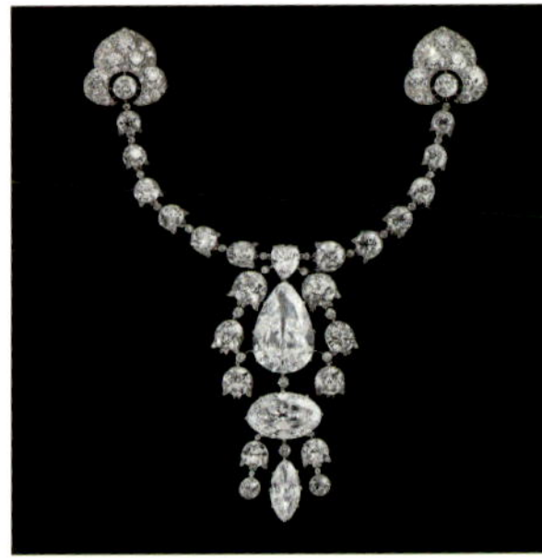

125. Brooch
Cartier Paris, with maker's mark for the Henri Picq workshop, 1912
Platinum, diamonds
20.8 cm
Weight of pear-shaped diamond 34 ct
Weight of oval diamond 23.55 ct
Weight of marquise-shaped diamond 6.5 ct

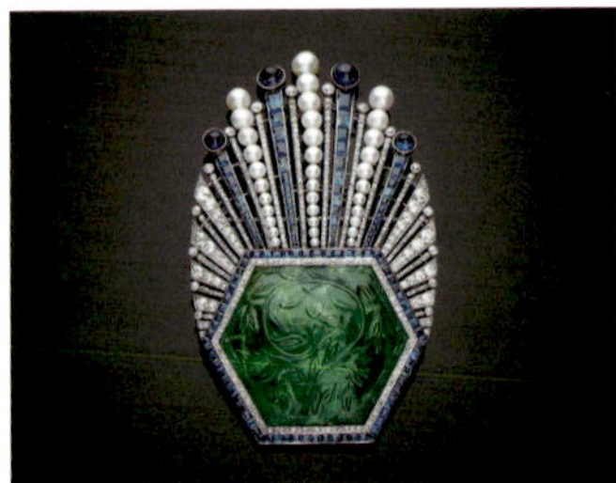

126. Aigrette
Designed by Paul Iribe; made by Robert Linzeler, Paris, 1910
Emerald: India, 1850–1900
Platinum, emerald, sapphires, diamonds, pearls
9 × 5.8 × 1.5 cm
PL. 68

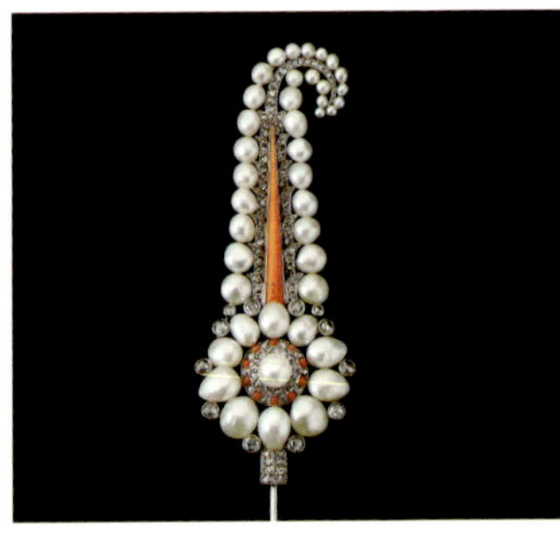

127. Brooch
Cartier Paris, 1922
Platinum, pearls, coral, diamonds
15.3 × 3.1 cm
PL. 69

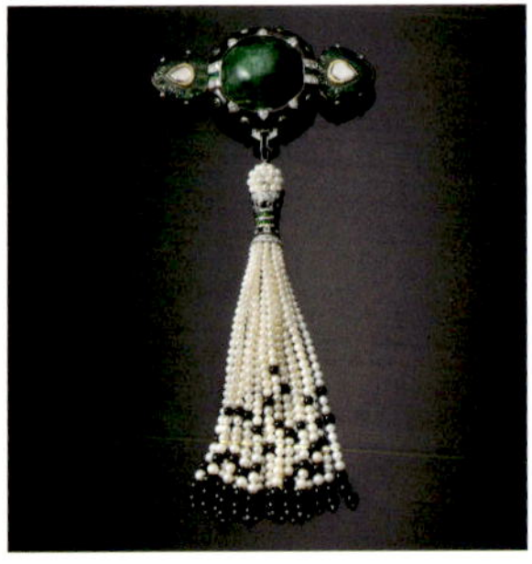

128. Shoulder brooch
Cartier London, 1924; pendant tassel re-created from original records by Cartier workshops, Paris, 2012
Brooch: platinum, emeralds, rubies, diamonds, enamel, gold; tassel: pearls, onyx
15.3 × 7 cm
PL. 70

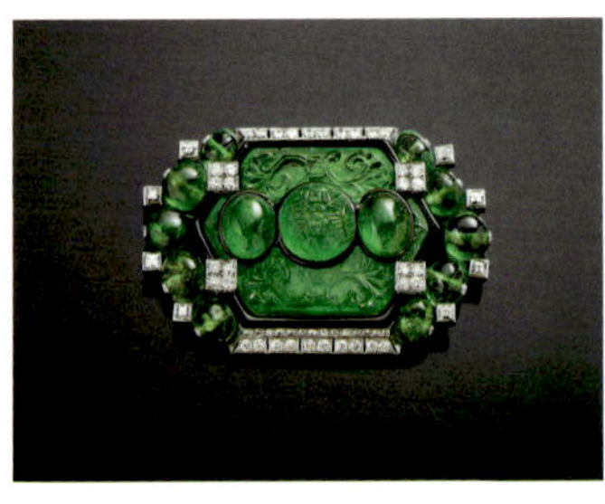

129. Clip brooch
Cartier Paris, 1925; modified by Cartier in 1927
Hexagonal emerald: India, ca. 1700; central cabochon emerald: India, 1675–1725
Platinum, emeralds, diamonds, enamel
4.4 × 6.7 cm
Weight of hexagonal emerald ca. 88.03 ct
Weight of carved cabochon emerald ca. 15.65 ct
PL. 71

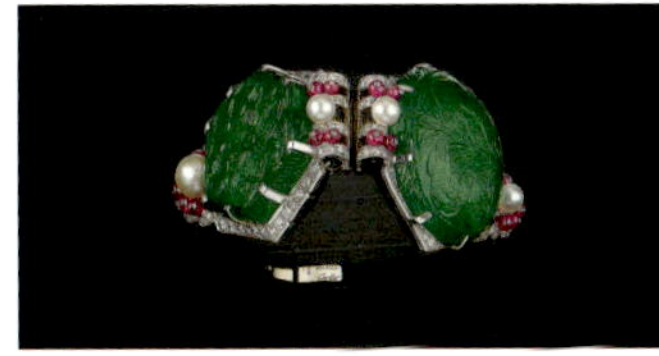

130. Bracelet with brooch clips
Cartier, 1938
Hexagonal emerald: 19th century;
oval emerald: 19th century or later
Modern bracelet reproduction of original design
Brooches: platinum, carved emeralds, pearls, rubies, diamonds
Bracelet: blackened white gold
Hexagonal clip: 5 × 4 cm; oval clip: 5 × 4 cm; bracelet frame: 6 cm
Weight of hexagonal emerald 56.5 ct
Weight of oval emerald 93.9 ct

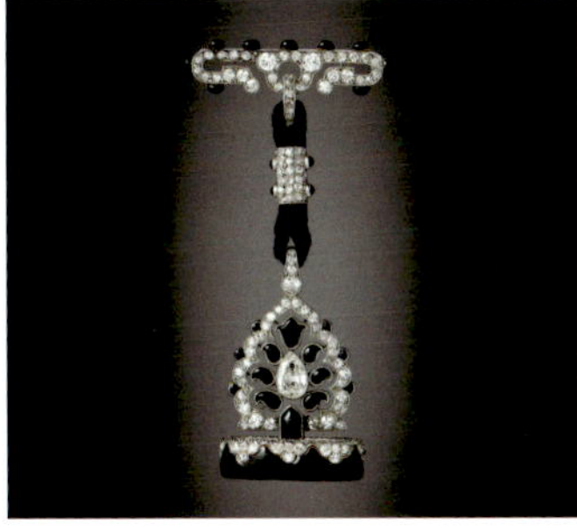

131. Lapel watch
Unknown maker, French assay marks; movement by Agassiz & Compagnie (No. 300010), France and Switzerland, ca. 1924–1926
Platinum, gold, diamond, black onyx, modern stringing
6.7 × 3.4 cm (watchcase 1.4 × 2.2 cm)

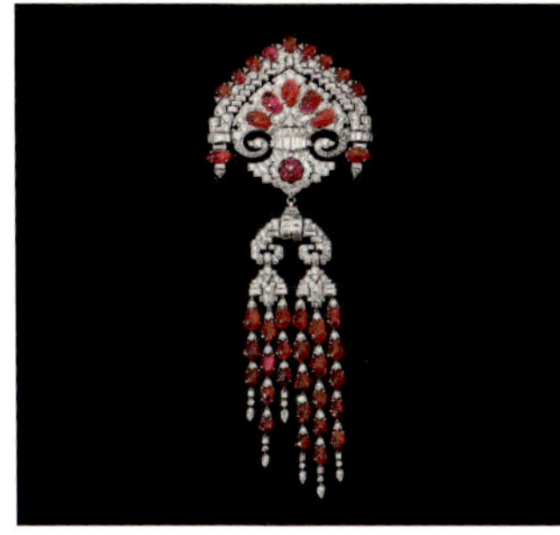

132. Brooch
Lacloche Frères, Paris, ca. 1930
Platinum, diamonds, rubies
16.9 × 6.1 cm

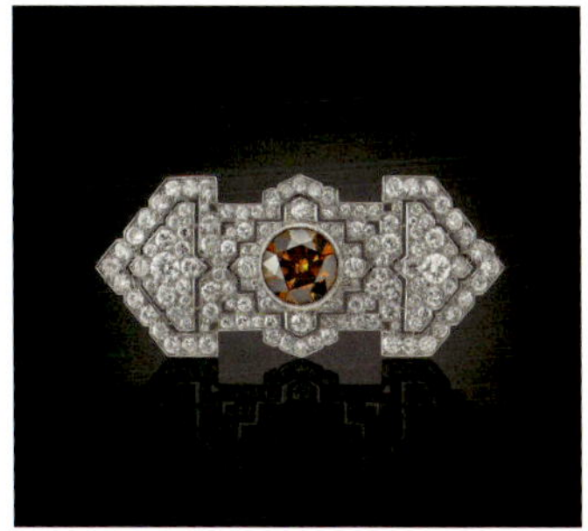

133. Brooch
Cartier Paris, ca. 1920
Platinum, diamonds, golden brown diamond
2.6 × 6.2 cm

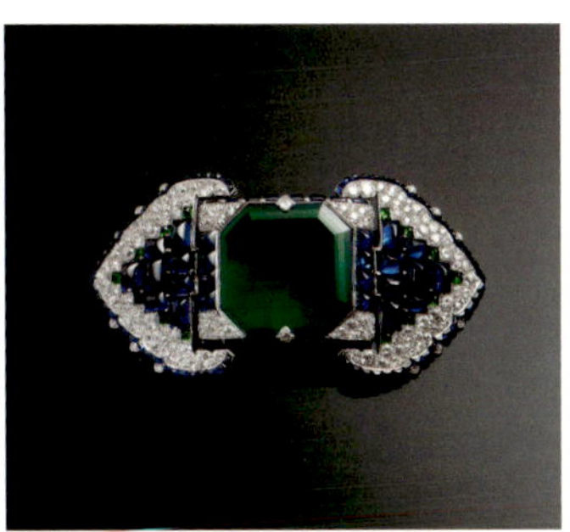

134. Belt brooch
Cartier Paris, 1922
Platinum, emeralds, sapphires, diamonds
4.2 × 8.5 cm

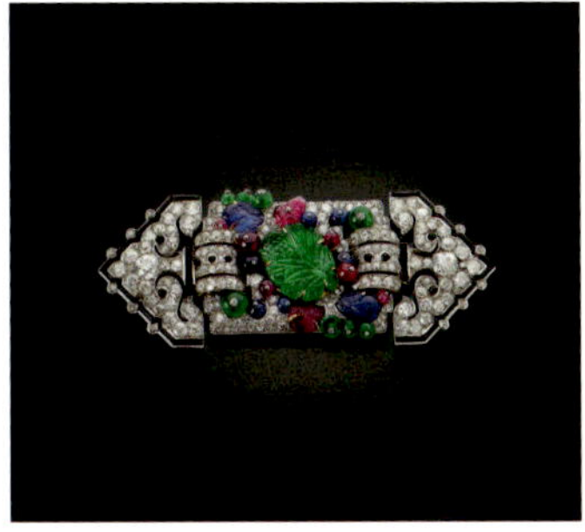

135. Brooch
Cartier Paris, 1929
Platinum, diamonds, sapphires, rubies, onyx, emeralds
3.5 × 8.7 cm
PL. 73

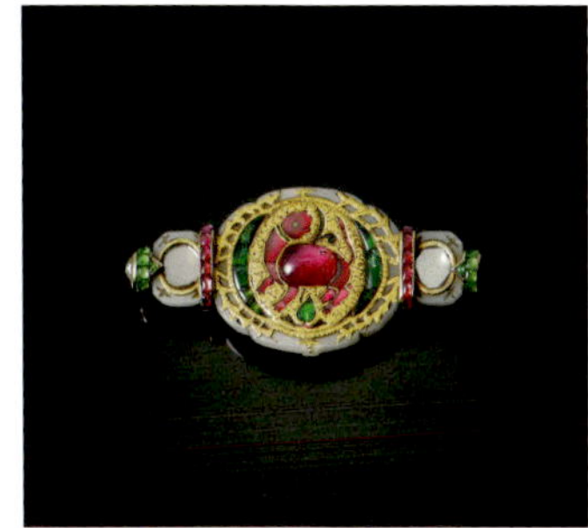

136. Brooch
Cartier, ca. 1930; *bazuband*: North India, 1650–1750
Jade, gold, rubies, emeralds, diamonds
2.5 × 5.7 cm

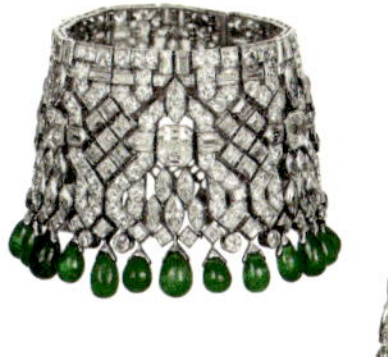

137. Pair of Manchette bracelets
Van Cleef & Arpels, 1926 and 1928
Platinum, diamonds, emeralds
Private collection
PL. 72

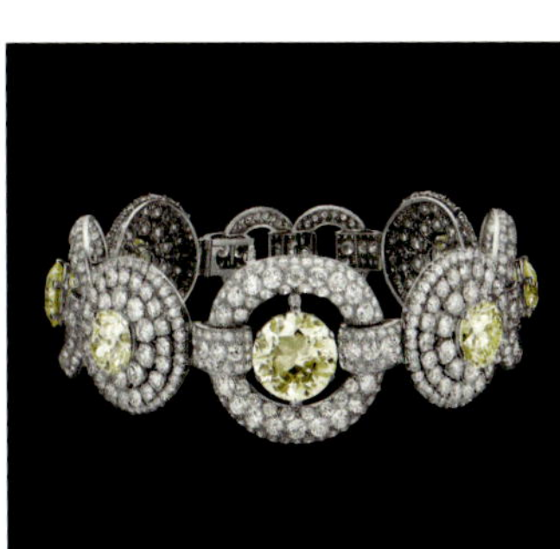

138. Patiala diamond choker
Cartier Collection, Paris, 1928
Platinum, diamonds
4.1 × 31.5 cm
PL. 75

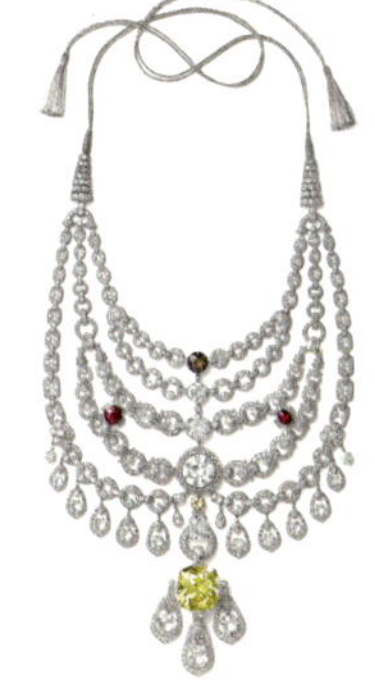

139. Maharaja of Patiala Necklace
Cartier Collection, Paris, 1928
Platinum, diamonds, synthetic ruby, smoky quartz, citrine
27 cm
Weight of yellow diamond 234.65 ct
PL. 74

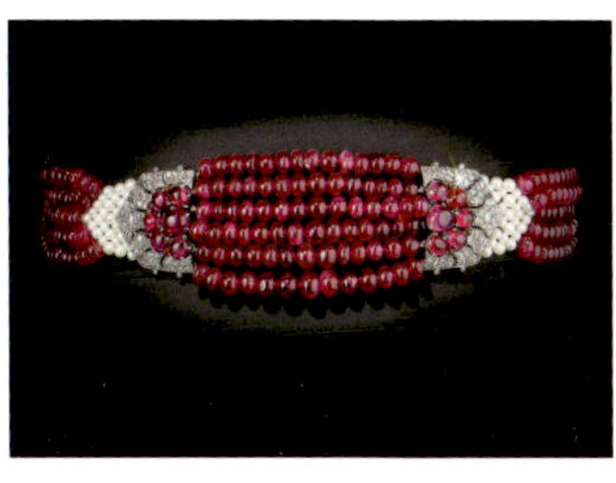

140. Patiala ruby choker
Cartier Paris, 1931; restored and restrung by Cartier Tradition, Geneva, 2012
Rubies, diamonds, pearls, platinum
2.2 × 33.3 cm
PL. 76

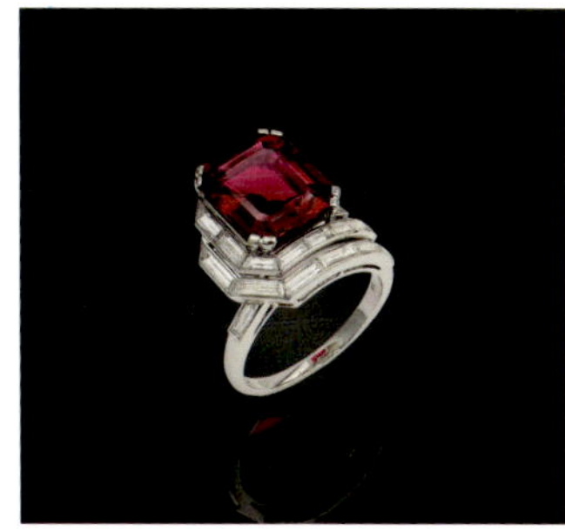

141. Indore ruby ring
Mauboussin, 1930s; altered by Harry Winston, ca. 1940–1945
Ruby, diamonds, platinum
2.5 × 2.1 × 2.4 cm
Weight of ruby 8.01 ct
PL. 80

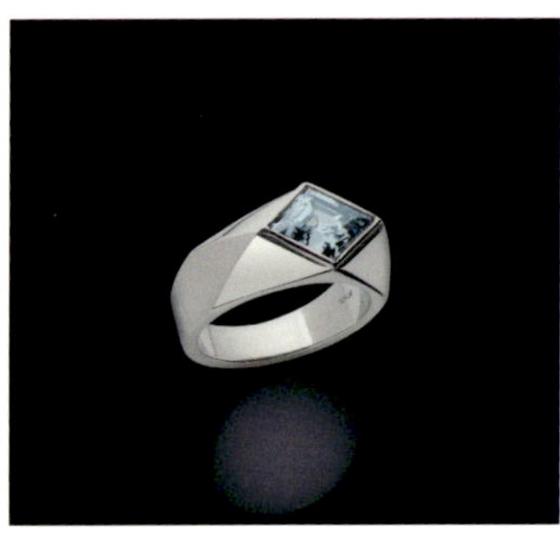

142. Ring
Harry Winston, New York, ca. 1943
Lozenge-shaped, step-cut diamond
2.5 × 2.1 cm (aperture 1.8 cm)
Weight of diamond 2.5 ct

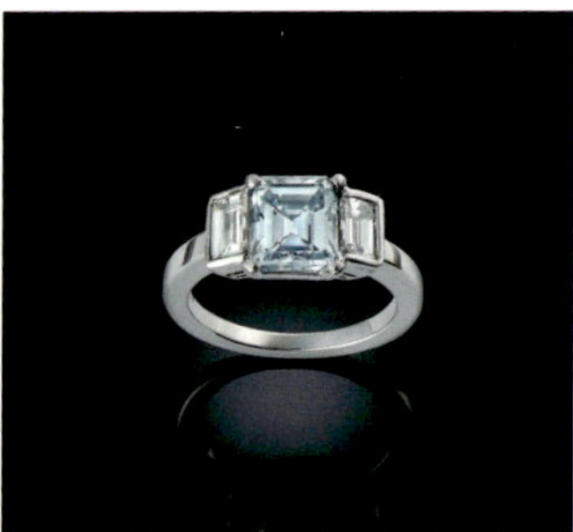

143. Ring
Harry Winston, New York, ca. 1943
Diamonds in platinum
2.4 × 2.1 cm (aperture 1.7 cm)
Weight of blue diamond 2.3 ct

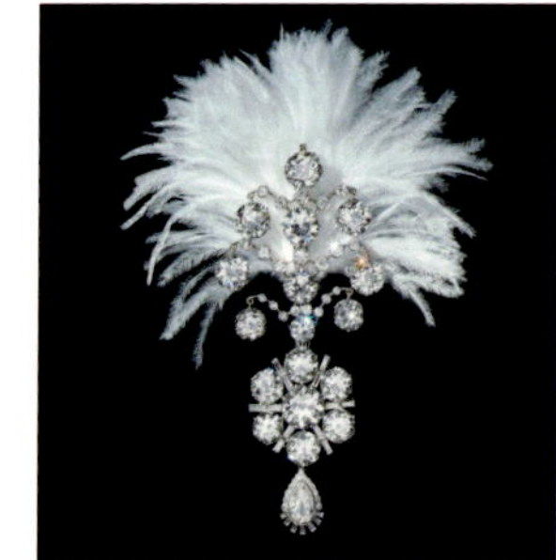

144. Nawanagar turban ornament
India, 1907, with later modifications ca. 1935
White gold, diamonds
15 × 6.5 cm
Weight of diamonds 152.6 ct
PL. 77

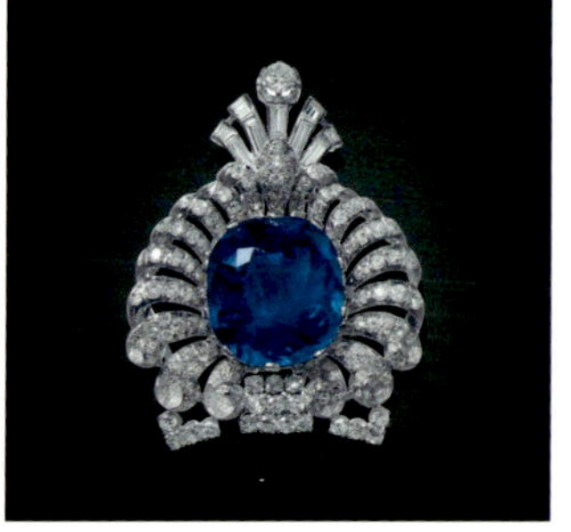

145. Nawanagar turban ornament
India, ca. 1920; modified ca. 1925–1935
Diamonds and a large sapphire in platinum
7.5 × 6 cm
Weight of sapphire 109.5 ct
PL. 78

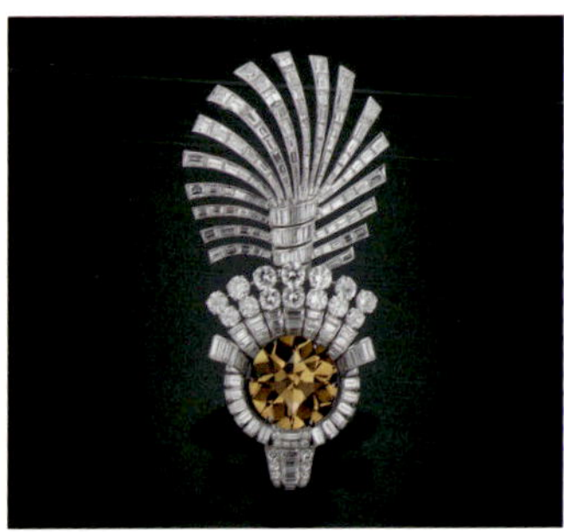

146. Nawanagar Tiger's Eye turban ornament
Cartier London, 1937
Platinum, diamonds
12.7 × 6 cm
Tiger's Eye diamond weight 61.5 ct
PL. 79

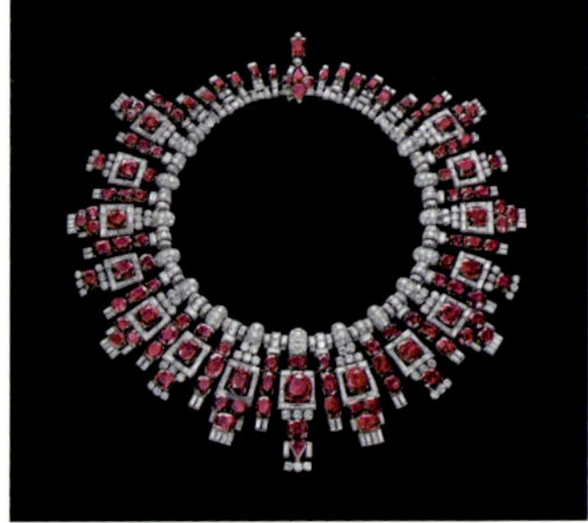

147. Nawanagar ruby necklace
Cartier, 1937
Platinum, rubies, diamonds
20.5 × 19.5 cm
PL. 81

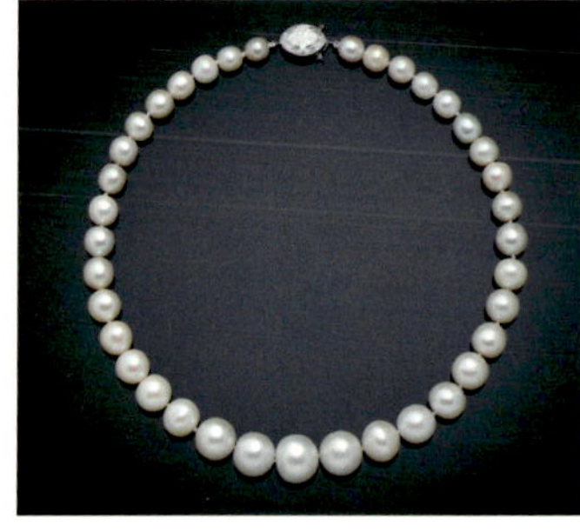

148. Pearl necklace
1940–1950
Pearls, platinum, diamond
40.8 cm (including clasp)
Weight of pearls 53.7 g

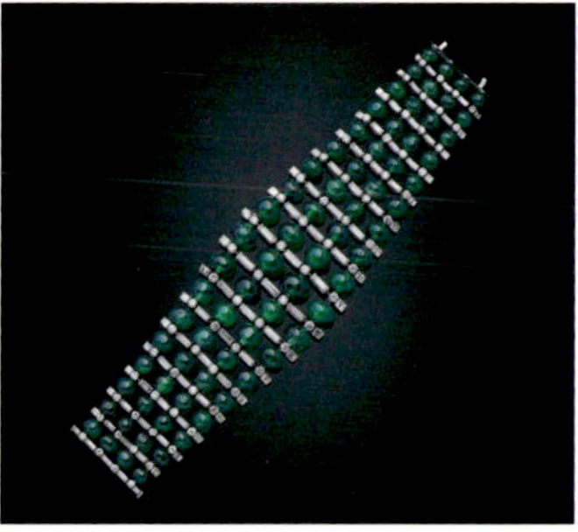

149. Maharani Sita Devi of Baroda's bracelet
France, 1950–1960
Platinum, emeralds, diamonds
18 × 4.7 cm

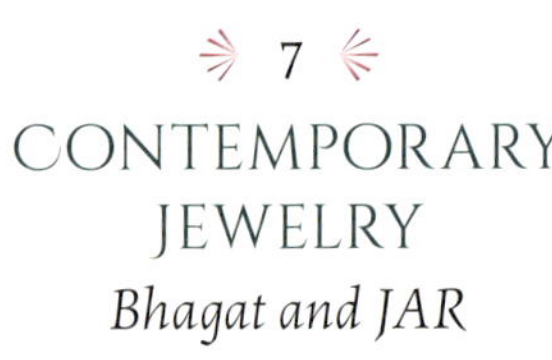

7 CONTEMPORARY JEWELRY *Bhagat and JAR*

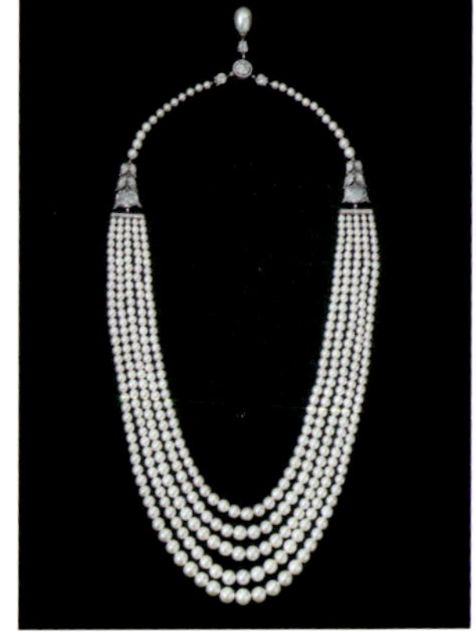

150. Pearl necklace
Bhagat, Mumbai, 2012
Pearls, diamonds, platinum
35 cm
Weight of pearls 640 ct
PL. 82

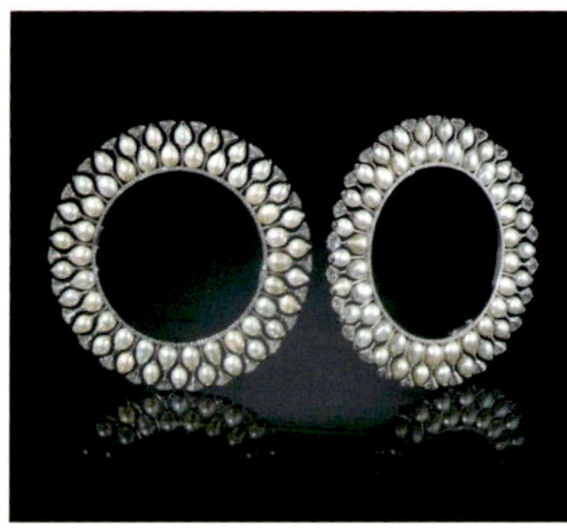

151. Pair of bangles
Bhagat, Mumbai, 2012
Platinum, diamonds, pearls
Each 8.6 cm wide
PL. 83

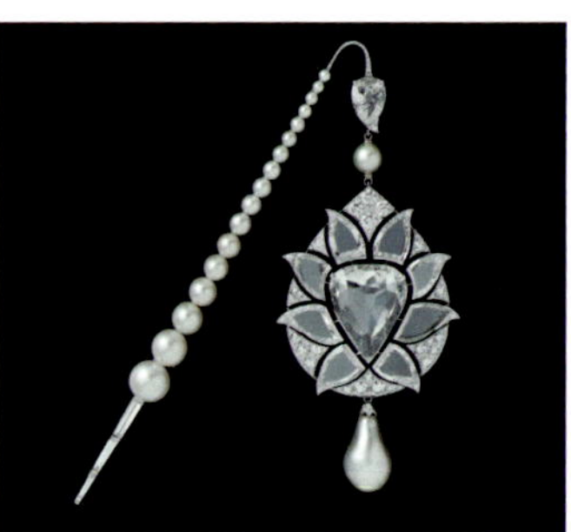

152. Brooch
Bhagat, Mumbai, 2014
Platinum, diamonds, pearls
9.3 × 4 cm
Weight of diamonds 31.4 ct (including central diamond 13 ct)
Weight of pearls 40 ct (including drop pearl 15.4 ct)
PL. 85

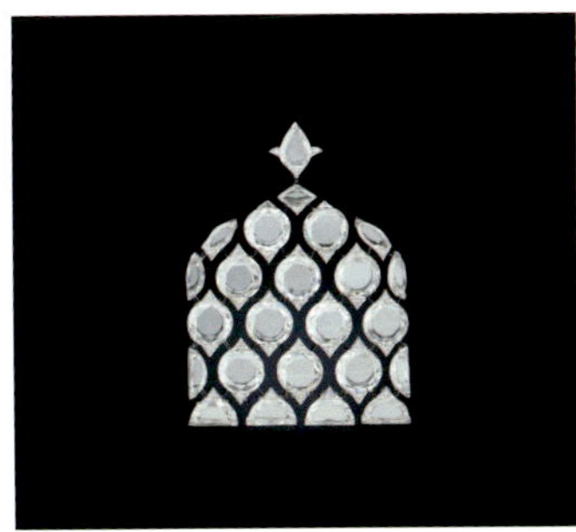

153. Brooch
Bhagat, Mumbai, 2015
Platinum, diamonds
5.2 × 4 cm
PL. 86

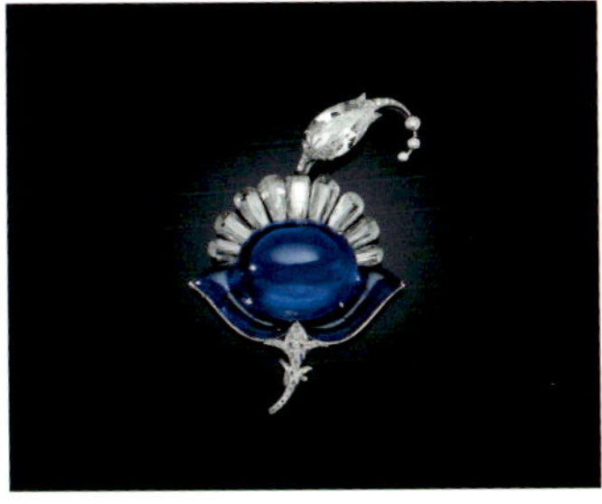

154. Brooch
Bhagat, Mumbai, 2012
Sapphires, diamonds, platinum
5.9 × 3.7 cm
Weight of sapphires 54.6 ct (including central cabochon 45 ct)
Weight of diamonds 9.1 ct (including pear-shaped diamond 3 ct)
PL. 84

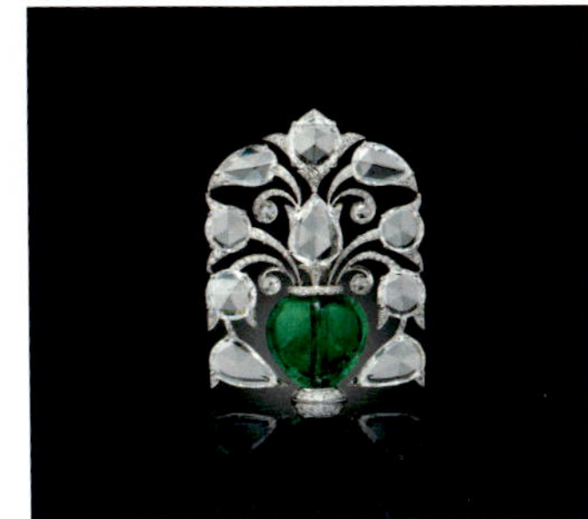

155. Brooch
Bhagat, Mumbai, 2014
Emerald, diamonds, platinum
4.7 × 3.5 cm
Weight of emerald 20 ct
Weight of diamonds 12.5 ct
PL. 87

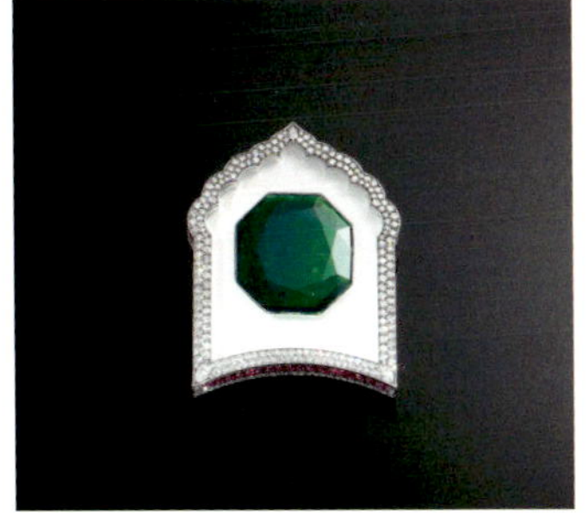

156. Brooch (obverse)
JAR, Paris, 2002
Emerald, rock crystal, white agate, diamonds, rubies, gold
6.2 × 4.9 × 0.9 cm
Weight of emerald 35.4 ct
PL. 88

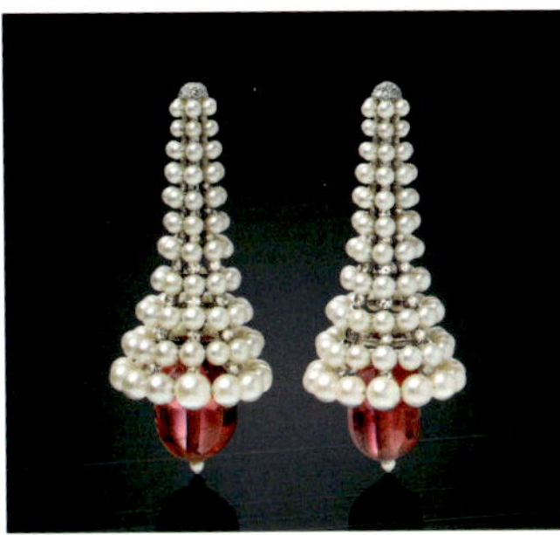

157. Pair of earrings
JAR, Paris, 2010
Pearls, spinels, diamonds, silver, gold, seed pearls
Each 8.4 × 4.1 cm
Weight of spinels 66.1 ct, 62.5 ct
PL. 89

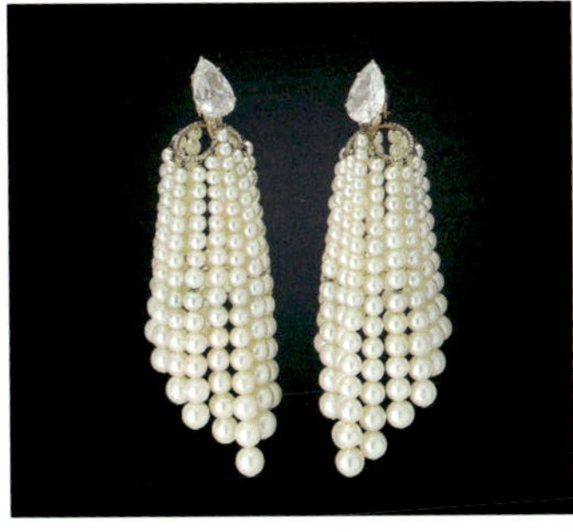

158. Pair of earrings
JAR, Paris, 2012
Pearls, diamonds, gold
Each 11 × 3 cm
Weight of pear-shaped diamonds 4.1 ct, 4.6 ct

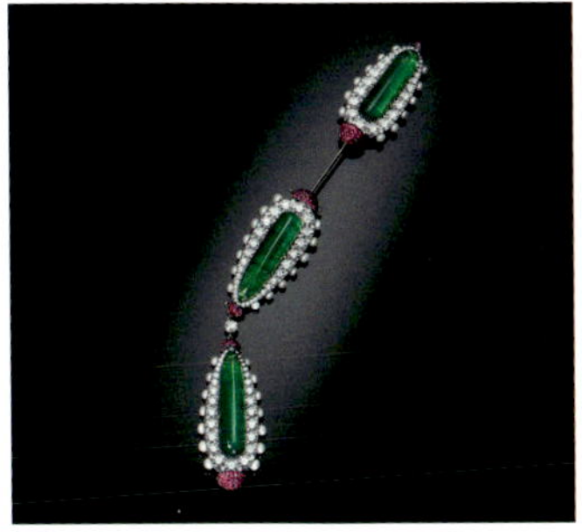

159. Jabot or *cliquet* brooch
JAR, Paris, 2013
Emeralds, diamonds, pearls, rubies, gold
19.7 × 3 cm
Weight of emeralds 33.3 ct, 27.9 ct, 27.34 ct
PL. 90

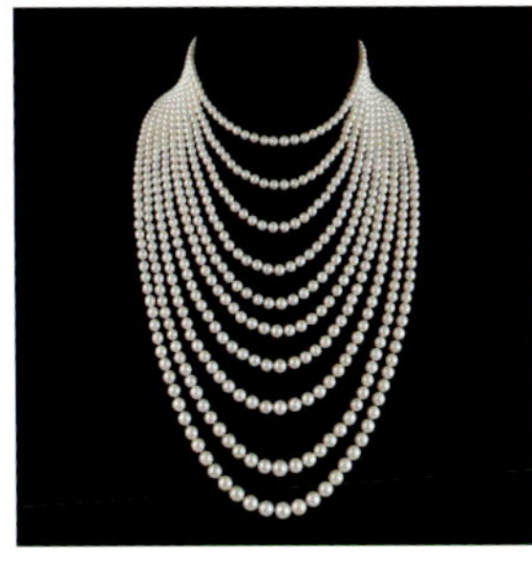

160. Necklace (obverse)
JAR, Paris, 2014
Pearls, diamonds, gold
Shortest pearl strand: 36.5 cm; longest pearl strand: 80.5 cm; clasp: 8.5 cm, including drop
Weight of pearls 1,322.8 ct (including drop pearl 9.8 ct)
PL. 91

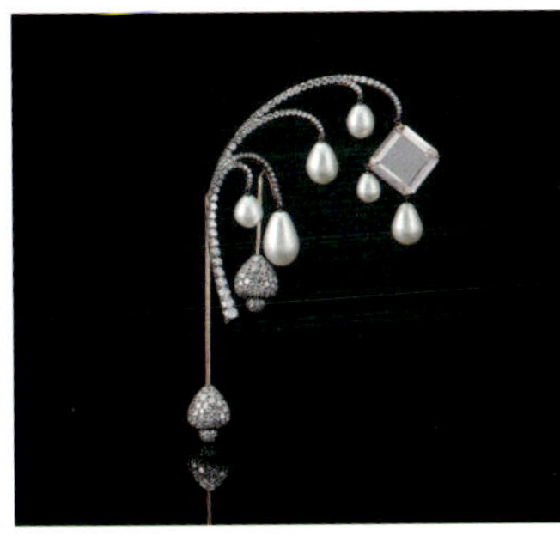

161. Turban ornament
JAR, Paris, 2016
Pearls, diamonds, gold, silver, platinum
12.2 × 6.9 cm
Weight of pink diamond 18.38 ct
PL. 92

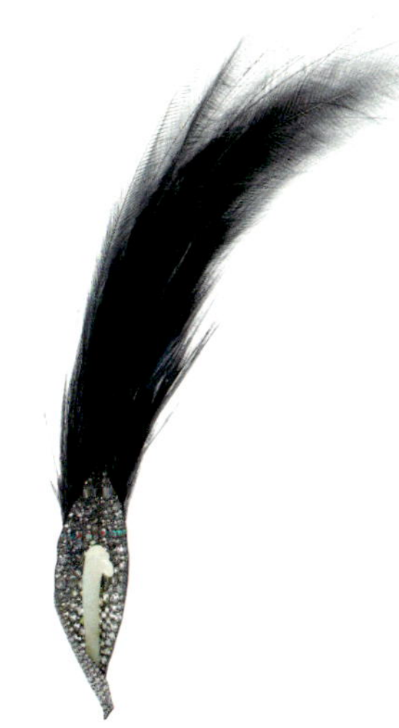

162. Brooch
JAR, Paris, 2016
Hilt: North India, 18th century
Blackened silver, gold, diamonds, chrysoberyls, green tourmalines, green sapphires, nephrite jade, feathers
12.5 (50 including feathers) × 4 cm
Weight of diamonds 8.1 ct
Weight of chrysoberyls 77.9 ct
Weight of tourmalines 1.8 ct
Weight of sapphires 0.98 ct

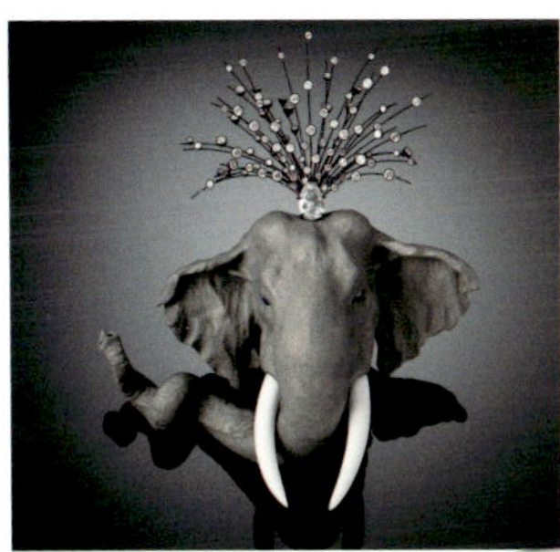

163. Elephant brooch
JAR, Paris, 2016
Titanium, diamonds, white cacholong, sapphires, gold, platinum
16 × 13 cm
Weight of diamonds 9.8 ct (including pear-shaped diamond 2.3 ct)
Weight of sapphires 4.6 ct
PL. 93

MATERIALS AND TECHNIQUES

GOLD

Although naturally endowed with only limited deposits of gold, India has nevertheless traditionally been a store of this precious metal, which was most often acquired as bullion in payment for exports, including textiles and spices.

The French physician François Bernier in the later seventeenth century observed that gold and silver, after circulating elsewhere in the world, came to be "swallowed up, lost in some measure" in India. Italian traveler Giovanni Francesco Gemelli Careri, writing at the same period, also was of the opinion that gold and silver were drawn into India as a result of trade.

Gold had to be refined and purified before it could be used for jewelry; if it had too many impurities, it would become brittle and difficult to work. Conversely, when it is too pure, it cannot be successfully beaten, soldered, or drawn as wire, and it also distorts under pressure. Indian jewelry is notable for its use of pure gold in certain instances, including gold leaf, and the gold used in the *kundan* technique, which is "hyper-purified." In this, the Indian goldsmith's practice differs from his fellows' practices elsewhere in the world.

Because *kundan* work requires the gold to be extremely pure, a further cementation process could be used. The gold was coated with salt and cow dung, wrapped in cloth, covered with clay, and placed in a fire of cow dung. This process could be repeated three or more times before the gold was considered sufficiently pure. It would then be boiled in an acid made of fruit juice, following which it was cleaned and wound around a cane for storage for future use.

SILVER

Silver was refined with methods similar to those used for gold.

LAC

One of the distinguishing characteristics of Indian jeweled objects made of sheet gold is the use of lac as a backing or support. Lac is derived from resin secreted by the *Coccus lacca* insect and gathered from trees on which the female insects lay their eggs. The resin would be purified and used for various purposes including varnish and sealing wax in addition to jewelry. Lac was also used as a glue to secure an object onto a support held by the goldsmith while it was being made.

GOLDSMITHS AND CRAFTSMEN

There are several terms used to describe jewelers and goldsmiths, including *soona*, *sonar*, or *sunar* (goldsmith), who were members of the Hindu goldsmith caste.

In small villages, gem setting might be carried out by the local goldsmith. In larger centers, it was a skill specific to gem setters known as *jaria*, *murassa-kar*, and *kundansaz*. The importance of the gem setter can be judged by the fact that he was paid more than other craftsmen, according to the *A'in-I Akbari*. The role of the *zarnishan*, who cut metal and hardstones for inlay with gold, is described in the *A'in-i Akbari*. The difficulty of this work is also emphasized by the high rate of pay the craftsman received.

Enamel designs were prepared by the *chitera*, who worked for the master jeweler and who also kept pattern books. The object to be enameled was made by the goldsmith, then passed to the *gharai*, or engraver. Both these craftsmen were from Hindu goldsmith or carpenter subcastes. The design was created using a steel stylus and then polished using steel and agate tools.

TOOLS

Implements include hammers, tongs, files, draw plates, and blocks with recesses for making beaded wire. A traveling goldsmith and jeweler's workshop can be seen in a Bundi painting dateable to ca. 1760, now in the David Collection, Copenhagen (fig. 41 and page 205). In this, the craftsman is fastening an anklet onto a lady's leg, using a variety of hammers and pincers, while his assistant uses a blowpipe (*nal, banknal,* or *banqual*).

KUNDAN

Kundan is a uniquely Indian goldsmithing technique that allowed jewelers a great degree of latitude in creating settings for gems set on metals, hardstones, and other materials. Once raised to 100 percent purity, gold was cut into small strips and pressed into place with an iron stylus. The extreme purity allowed the strips of gold to bond molecularly at room temperature, enabling fine settings to be created on surfaces that could not normally be heated. The gold strips were often applied over a malleable lac base; once a sufficient number of layers of gold had been laid so as to create a mount, a carefully predetermined gem was inset and the mount sealed.

FOILING AND GEM SETTING

In Indian jewelry, gold or silver foil is often placed behind gemstones to create a reflective effect.

ENAMELING

Still popular today, enameling was one of the characteristic methods of decorating metal surfaces in the Mughal period. Enamel is powdered glass that is applied to recesses in a sheet metal background (champlevé) or to an area outlined by wire or strips of metal (cloisonné) and then fired. The powdered enamel melts, flows into the recessed or enclosed area, and fuses to the background. Enamels can also be painted onto a background and fired. The vast majority of Indian enameling, on gold, silver, and copper alloy, was carried out using the champlevé technique, while the cloisonné technique was effectively not used in India at all. Further enhancement of the decoration was achieved with the basse-taille technique, in which the underlying metal background was chased and carved with decoration visible through a layer of translucent enamel.

Painted enamel involves the firing of a design applied over a previously fired enamel ground, usually opaque white. Overpainting of enamel colors onto an opaque white enamel ground was used on copper alloy objects in the seventeenth and eighteenth centuries. Examples of enamel painted on gold include a group of weapon hilts, such as a *katar* and a dagger in the al-Sabah Collection that can be dated to the mid-seventeenth century. The technique is also found on later eighteenth- and nineteenth-century enameling from Benares and Sind, both influenced by the painted enamels of the late Zand and Qajar periods in Iran.

HARDSTONE CARVING

Early Indian hardstone carving was usually on chalcedony and other locally available materials.

Jades carved for the Mughals are from the nephrite variety of the stone. Although early Mughal jades, particularly those previously owned by the Timurids, were made in dark green nephrite, in the seventeenth century there was a preference for lighter shades, including white and pale green.

In the nineteenth century, jade substitutes and jade simulants were used for objects such as Qur'an stands. Jade was relatively scarce for the Mughals in the late sixteenth and early seventeenth centuries: William Hawkins, an English sea captain, described jade and jade vessels he saw in the Mughal treasury in 1608–1613, recording that Jahangir had one *battman* (55 pounds/25 kg) of jade. This is substantially less than the weight of diamonds, rubies, and emeralds in the treasury. The availability of jade improved later in the century: François Bernier, writing of his travels in India between 1656 and 1668, noted the importation of jade from Central Asia through Kashmir, and describes inlaid vessels made of the material. Larger quantities may have become available as a result of the reopening of access to Greater Tibet (Ladakh) under Aurangzeb (r. 1658–1707). In the reigns of Jahangir (r. 1605–1627) and Shah Jahan (r. 1628–1658), it is probable that jade carving was centered around the court in Agra.

CASTING

The manufacture of copper-alloy chains used for anklets, in which the links are all made at once in a single casting, was a specialty of Sawai Madhopur at Ranthambore Fort in Rajasthan, although it may have been more widespread. A resin model was encased in a mixture of clay and cow dung and attached with a vent to a crucible containing the metal to be used. It was placed in a furnace, and when the metal was molten the crucible was inverted and the metal flowed into the mold, melting the resin. This is a version of lost-wax casting, using a one-time-only mold. It is possible that the resin models were made as antetypes, cast from a reusable mold.

CHASING, ENGRAVING, AND STAMPING

Sheet gold can be worked in a number of ways. It can be embellished with repoussé decoration, which involves working on the metal from the back, creating a design in relief that can then be enhanced by chasing in details from the front. Chasing involves using punches of various shapes and a hammer to decorate or work the surface of an object without the loss of any material.

Engraving is a form of decoration that involves the removal of material using hammer and chisel. This is impractical when working with the very thin gold sheet found on most Indian jewelry, and is encountered less often than chasing or repoussé work. Gold and silver sheet could also be decorated using a stamp that had been worked with a design, allowing a number of identical objects to be decorated quickly, rather than laboriously decorating each individually using chisels and punches.

NIELLO

Niello is a black-colored metallic sulfide made by heating various combinations of silver, copper, and lead with sulfur. It was widely used in medieval Iran as an inlay to decorate silver, and the technique was probably transmitted from there to India.

GOLD-INLAID STEEL

The metal was heated to blue, then hatched with a knife, and the design drawn on the hatching with a bodkin. Gold wire was applied along the drawn pattern, and sunk into the metal using a copper tool. In some cases, gold or silver leaf was applied using an adhesive. Such work could be exceptionally fine.

SOLDER

Solder is a metal alloy melted to bond two pieces of metal together. It is usually a mixture of the metal to be joined and one or more other metals to lower the melting point, so that the solder can be melted and applied without adversely affecting the main metal.

The solder is heated using a flame and directed at the point to be soldered using a blowpipe, while the object itself is supported on a charcoal block or mica sheet. Fine soldering is required for the assembly of filigree.

Adapted from Michael Spink and Robert Skelton, "Materials and Techniques in Indian Jewelry." In Amin Jaffer, ed., Beyond Extravagance: A Royal Collection of Gems and Jewels, *2013*

SELECTED BIBLIOGRAPHY

Alexander, David. *The Arts of War: Arms and Armour of the 7th to 19th Centuries*, The Nasser D. Khalili Collection of Islamic Art, vol. 21. London: Nour Foundation and Azimuth Editions, 1992.

Allan, James W. *The Art and Architecture of Twelver Shi'ism: Iraq, Iran and the Indian Sub-Continent.* London: Azimuth Editions, 2012.

Al-Tifashi, Ahmad Ibn Yusuf. *Arab Roots of Gemology: Ahmad Ibn Yusuf al-Tifaschi's Best Thoughts on the Best of Stones.* Translated and with commentary by S. N. Abul Huda. Lanham, MD, and Folkestone, UK: Scarecrow Press, 1998.

Archer, Mildred, Christopher Rowell, and Robert Skelton. *Treasures from India: The Clive Collection of Powis Castle.* London: Herbert Press, The National Trust, 1987.

Bachollet, Raymond, Daniel Bordet, and Anne-Claude Lelieur. *Paul Iribe.* Paris: Éditions Denvël, 1982.

Bala Krishnan, Usha R. *Jewels of the Nizams.* New Delhi: India Book House, 2001.

______, and Meera Sushil Kumar. *Dance of the Peacock: Jewellery Traditions of India.* Mumbai: India Book House, 1999. Reprinted 2001, 2004.

Balfour, Ian. *Famous Diamonds*, 2nd ed. Santa Monica, CA: GIA, 1992; 4th ed. London: Christie's, 2000.

Bari, Hubert, Caterina Cardona, and Giancarlo Parodi, eds. *Diamanti: Arte, storia, scienza.* Exhibition catalogue. Rome: De Luca Editori d'Arte, 2002.

Bari, Hubert, and Violaine Sautter. *Diamants: Au coeur de la terre, au coeur des* étoiles, *au coeur du pouvoir.* Exhibition catalogue. Paris: Adam Biro; Jeddah, Saudi Arabia: Mouawad, 2001. Translated by Michael Hing as *Diamonds: In the Heart of the Earth, in the Heart of the Stars.*

Beach, Milo. *The Grand Moghul: Imperial Painting in India, 1600–1800.* Williamstown, MA: Sterling and Francine Clark Art Institute, 1978.

______. *The Imperial Image: Paintings for the Mughal Court*, 2nd ed. Washington, DC: Freer Gallery of Art and Mapin Publishing, 2012.

______, Ebba Koch, and Wheeler Thackston. *King of the World.* London: Arthur M. Sackler Gallery and the Royal Library, Windsor, 1997.

Bernier, François. *Travels in the Mogul Empire A.D. 1656–1668.* Translated and annotated by Archibald Constable and revised by Vincent A. Smith, 2nd ed. London: Humphrey Milford and Oxford University Press, 1916. Reprint. New Delhi: Low Price Publications, 2011.

Birdwood, George C. M. *The Industrial Arts of India*. 2 vols. London: Chapman & Hall, 1884, new ed. London: South Kensington Art Museum Handbooks.

______. *Paris Universal Exhibition of 1878: Handbook to the British Indian Section*, 2nd ed. London: Offices of the Royal Commission, 1878.

Boucheron, Alain. "Boucheron." In *The Master Jewelers*, edited by A. Kenneth Snowman, 89. London: Thames & Hudson, 1990.

Buddle, Anne, Pauline Rohatgi, and Ian G. Brown, eds. *The Tiger and the Thistle: Tipu Sultan and the Scots in India*. Exhibition catalogue. Edinburgh: National Gallery of Scotland, 1999.

Calza, Gian Carlo. *Akbar: The Emperor of India.* Exhibition catalogue. Milan: Skira, 2012.

______. *I nababbi: L'India nella società inglese del Settecento.* Pavia, Italy: Centro Studi per I Popoi Extra-Europei dell'Università di Pavia, 1972.

Carsix, Robert. "Bijoux dessinés par Pierre Iribe," *Art et décoration* (January 1911).

Chapman, Martin. *Cartier and America*. Exhibition catalogue. Munich, Berlin, London, New York: Fine Arts Museums of San Francisco and DelMonico · Prestel, 2009.

Comoedia illustré, March 1, 1911; February 1, 1912.

Crill, Rosemary. *Marwar Painting: A History of the Jodhpur Style*. Mumbai and Jodhpur: India Book House and Mehrangarh Publishers, 2000.

______, and Kapil Jariwala, eds. *The Indian Portrait, 1560–1860.* Exhibition catalogue. London: National Portrait Gallery, 2010.

Dundek, Marijan. *Diamonds*. Exhibition catalogue. London: National Portrait Gallery, 2010.

Elgood, Robert. *Hindu Arms and Ritual: Arms and Armour from India, 1400–1865*. London: Eburon, 2004.

______. *Islamic Arms and Armour.* London: Scholar Press, 1979.

Exhibition of Arms and Armour and Associated Works of Art. London: Howard Ricketts, 1973.

Falk, Toby, and Mildred Archer. *Indian Miniatures in the India Office Library*. London: Sotheby Parke Bernet, 1981.

Fallon, S. W. *New Hindustani English Dictionary.* Benares: E. J. Lazarus; London: Trübner, 1879. Reprint. New Delhi: Asian Educational Services, 1989.

Fane, Diana, and Amy G. Poster. *The Guennol Collection: Cabinet of Wonders*. Exhibition catalogue. Brooklyn: Brooklyn Museum of Art, 2000.

Forbes, Rosita. *India of the Princes*. London: Travel Book Club, 1939.

Forsyth, Angus, and Brian McElney. *Jades from China*. Exhibition catalogue. Bath, UK: Museum of East Asian Art, 1994.

González-Palacios, Alvar, ed. *Objects for a Wunderkammer*. London: P&D Colnaghi & Co., 1981.

The Guennol Collection. Vol. 2. New York: Metropolitan Museum of Art, 1982.

Haidar, Navina Najat, and Courtney Ann Stewart. *Treasures from India: Jewels from the Al-Thani Collection*. Exhibition catalogue. New York: Metropolitan Museum of Art, 2014.

Haidar, Syed Zafar. *Islamic Arms and Armour of Muslim India*. Lahore, Pakistan: Bahadur Publishers, 1991.

Hales, Robert. *Islamic and Oriental Arms and Armour: A Lifetime's Passion*. London: Robert Hales C. I., 2013.

Hue-Williams, Sarah, and Raymond Sancroft-Baker. *Hidden Gems: Jewellery Stories from the Saleroom*. London: Unicorn Press, 2016.

Hughes, Graham. *Modern Jewellery: An International Survey, 1890–1967.* London: Studio Vista, 1963.

Ivanov, Anatoly. "A Group of Iranian Daggers of the Period from the Fifteenth Century to the Beginning of the Seventeenth with Persian Inscriptions." In Robert Elgood. *Islamic Arms and Armour.* London: Scholar Press, 1979.

Jackson, Anna, and Amir Jaffer, eds. *Maharaja:*

The Splendour of India's Royal Courts. Exhibition catalogue. London: Victoria and Albert Museum, 2009.

Jackson, Anna, Amin Jaffer, and Christina Lange. *Maharaja: Pracht der indischen Führstenhöfe.* Exhibition catalogue. Munich: Hirmer, 2010.

Jaffer, Amin. *Made for Maharajas.* New York: Vendome Press, 2006.

______, ed. *Beyond Extravagance: A Royal Collection of Gems and Jewels.* New York: Assouline, 2013.

______, ed. *Jewels of the Mughal Emperors and Maharajas: Treasures from The Al Thani Collection.* Exhibition catalogue. Miho, Japan: Miho Museum, 2016.

______, and Gian Carlo Calza, eds. *Treasures of the Mughals and the Maharajas: The Al Thani Collection.* Exhibition catalogue. Milan: Skira editore S.p.A., 2017.

______, and Amina Taha-Hussein Okada, eds. *From the Great Mughals to the Maharajas: Jewels from The Al Thani Collection.* Exhibition catalogue. Paris: Réunion des musées nationaux, 2017.

Jahangir. *The Jahangirnama: Memoirs of Jahangir, Emperor of India.* Translated, edited, and annotated by Wheeler M. Thackston. Washington, DC: Freer Gallery of Art and Arthur M. Sackler Gallery; Oxford: Oxford University Press, 1999.

______. *The Tuzuk-i-Jahangiri or Memoirs of Jahangir.* Translated by Alexander Rogers and Henry Beveridge. 2 vols. London: Royal Asiatic Society, 1909–1914. Reprint. New Delhi: Atlantic Publishers, 1989.

Keverne, Roger, ed. *Jade.* London: Anness Publishing, 1991.

Khalidi, Omar. *Romance of the Golconda Diamonds.* Ahmedabad, India: Mapin Publishing; Middletown, CT: Grantha, 1999.

Komaroff, Linda. *Gifts of the Sultan: The Arts of Giving at the Islamic Courts.* Exhibition catalogue. Los Angeles: Los Angeles County Museum of Art, 2011.

Krahl, Regina. *The Emperor's Broken China: Reconstructing Chenghua Porcelain.* London: Sotheby's, 1995.

Kunz, George F., and Charles H. Stevenson. *The Book of the Pearl: The History, Art, Science and Industry of the Queen of Gems.* New York: Century, 1908.

Lane, Kris. *Colour of Paradise: The Emerald in the Age of Gunpowder Empires.* New Haven, CT: Yale University Press, 2010.

Lentz, Thomas W., and Glenn D. Lowry. *Timur and the Princely Vision: Persian Art and Culture in the Fifteenth Century.* Exhibition catalogue. Los Angeles: Los Angeles County Museum of Art, 1989.

London, Robert, ed. *The Indian Heritage: Court Life and Arts under Mughal Rule.* Exhibition catalogue. London: Victoria and Albert Museum, 1982.

Losty, Jeremiah P., and Malini Roy. *Mughal India: Art, Culture and Empire.* London: British Library, 2012.

Markel, Stephen. "Fit for an Emperor: Inscribed Works of Decorative Art Acquired by the Great Mughals." *Orientations* 21, no. 8 (August 1990): 22–36.

Melikian-Chirvani, Assadullah Souren. "From the Royal Boat to the Beggar's Bowl." *Islamic Art* 4 (1991): 3–112.

______. "*Rekab*: The Polylobed Wine Boat from Sasanian to Saljuq Times." *Au Carrefour des religions: Mélanges offerts à Philippe Gignoux; Res Orientales* 7 (1995): 187–204.

______. "Sa'ida-ye Gilani and the Iranian Style Jades of Hindustan." *Bulletin of the Asia Institute*, new series, 13 (1999): 83–140.

Meylan, Vincent. *Van Cleef & Arpels: Treasures and Legends.* Woodbridge, UK: Antique Collectors' Club, 2012.

Michell, George. *The Majesty of Mughal Decoration.* London: Thames & Hudson, 2007.

Morel, Bernard. *The French Crown Jewels.* Antwerp: Fonds Mercator, 1988.

Pal, Pratapaditya. *Indian Painting, Vol. 1: 1000–1700, A Catalogue of the Los Angeles County Museum of Art Collection.* Los Angeles: Los Angeles County Museum of Art, 1993.

______, et al. *Romance of the Taj Mahal.* Exhibition catalogue. London: Thames & Hudson, 1989.

Papi, Stefano, and Alexandra Rhodes. *20th Century Jewellery and the Icons of Style*. London: Thames & Hudson, 2013.

Prior, Katherine. "Twentieth-Century Encounters between Indian and European Jewellery." In *Beyond Extravagance*, edited by Amin Jaffer. New York: Assouline, 2013.

______, and John Adamson. *Maharajas' Jewels.* New York: Vendome Press, 2000. Reprint. Ahmedabad, India: Mapin Publishing, 2004.

Ray, Simon. *Indian and Islamic Works of Art, November 2009*. London: Simon Ray, 2009.

Ricketts, Howard, and Philippe Missillier, eds. *Splendeur des armes orientales*. Exhibition catalogue. Paris: Acte-Expo, 1988.

Rivett-Carnac, J. H. "Specimens of Indian Metal Work." *Journal of Indian Art and Industry* 9, no. 77 (January 1902): 33–39; (April 1902): 67–70.

Rudoe, Judy. *Cartier, 1900–1939*. Exhibition catalogue. London: British Museum Press, 1997.

Salomé, Laurent, and Laure Dalon, eds. *Cartier: Le style et l'histoire*. Exhibition catalogue. Paris: Somogy and MNAAG, 2016.

Sarkar, Sir Jadu Nath, trans. *Maas-ir-i-'Alamgiri of Saqi Must'ad Khan*. Calcutta, India: Asiatic Society, 1947.

Sastri, Alladi Jagannatha. *A Family History of the Venkatagiri Rajas*. Madras, India: Addison Press, 1922.

Scherbina, Ekaterina, ed. *India: Jewels That Enchanted the World*. Exhibition catalogue. Moscow: Indo-Russian Jewelry Foundation and the Moscow State Historical and Cultural Museum and Heritage Site, 2014.

Schimmel, Annemarie. *A Two-Colored Brocade: The Imagery of Persian Poetry.* Chapel Hill and London: University of North Carolina Press, 1992.

Sergeant, Philip W. *The Ruler of Baroda: An Account of the Life and Work of the Maharaja Gaekwar.* London: John Murray, 1928.

Skelton, Robert. "A Decorative Motif in Indian Art." In *Aspects of Indian Art: Papers Presented at a Symposium at the Los Angeles County Museum of Art*, edited by Pratapaditya Pal, 147–152. Leiden, Netherlands: Brill, 1972.

______. "Islamic and Mughal Jades: The Jade-Carving Tradition in Turkestan, Persia, Turkey and India." In *Jade*, edited by Roger Keverne. London: Anness Publishing, 1991.

______. "The Shah Jahan Cup." *Victoria and Albert Museum Bulletin* 2/3 (July 1966). Revised and reprinted in *Victoria and Albert Museum Bulletin Reprints* 5 (1969): 104–111.

______, et al. *The Indian Heritage: Court Life and Arts under Mughal Rule.* Exhibition catalogue. London: Victoria and Albert Museum, 1982.

Spink, Michael, ed. *Islamic and Hindu Jewellery.* London: Spink & Son, 1988.

Stronge, Susan. "Jade at the Mughal Court in the 17th Century." *Transactions of the Oriental Ceramic Society* 76 (2012): 71–84.

______. "Jewels for the Mughal Court." *V&A Album* 5 (1986): 308–317.

______. *Painting for the Mughal Emperor: The Art of the Book, 1560–1660*. Exhibition catalogue. London: Victoria and Albert Museum, 2002.

______, ed. *Bejewelled Treasures: The Al Thani Collection*. Exhibition catalogue. London: V&A Publishing, 2015.

Sultans of Deccan India, 1500–1700: Opulence and Fantasy. Exhibition catalogue. New York: Metropolitan Museum of Art; New Haven, CT: Yale University Press, 2015.

Tavernier, Jean-Baptiste. *Travels in India by Jean-Baptiste Tavernier, Baron of Aubonne*. Translated by V. Ball. 2 vols. London and New York: Macmillan, 1889.

Teng, Shu-p'ing. *Catalogue of a Special Exhibition of Hindustan Jade in the National Palace Museum*. Translated by David M. Kamen. Taipei, Taiwan: National Palace Museum, 1983.

______. *Exquisite Beauty: Islamic Jades*. Taipei, Taiwan: National Palace Museum, 2012.

Tillander, Herbert. *Diamond Cuts in Historic Jewellery, 1381–1910*. London: Art Books Publishing, 1995.

Tottenham, Edith L. *Highnesses of Hindostan.* London: Grayson & Grayson, 1934.

Treasures of the Courts. Exhibition catalogue. London: Spink & Son, 1994.

Trnek, Helmut, and Nuno Vassallo e Silva. *Exotica*. Lisbon: Calouste Gulbenkian Foundation, 2001.

Untracht, Oppi. *Traditional Jewelry of India*. New York: Harry N. Abrams; London: Thames & Hudson, 1997. Reprinted 2008.

Vassallo e Silva, Nuno. "Precious Stones, Jewels and Cameos: Jacques de Coutre's Journey to Goa and Agra." In *Goa and the Great Mughal*. Exhibition catalogue. Lisbon: Calouste Gulbenkian Foundation, 2004.

Watt, George. *Indian Art at Delhi, 1903: Being the Official Catalogue of the Delhi Exhibition, 1902–1903*. Calcutta, India: Superintendent of Government Printing, 1903.

Weeden, Edward St. Clair. *A Year with the Gaekwar of Baroda*. Boston: Dana Estes, 1911.

Welch, Stuart Cary. *India: Art and Culture, 1300–1900*. Exhibition catalogue. New York: Metropolitan Museum of Art and Holt, Rinehart & Winston, 1985.

______, et al. *The Emperor's Album: Images of Mughal India*. Exhibition catalogue. New York: Metropolitan Museum of Art, 1987.

Wright, Elaine. *Muraqqa': Imperial Mughal Albums from the Chester Beatty Library, Dublin*. Alexandria, VA: Art Services International, 2008.

Young-Sánchez, Margaret, et al. *Cartier in the 20th Century*. Exhibition catalogue. New York: Denver Art Museum and Vendome Press, 2014.

PICTURE GALLERY

MARTIN CHAPMAN

This Picture Gallery features full reproductions of works of art shown decoratively or in detail elsewhere in this volume.

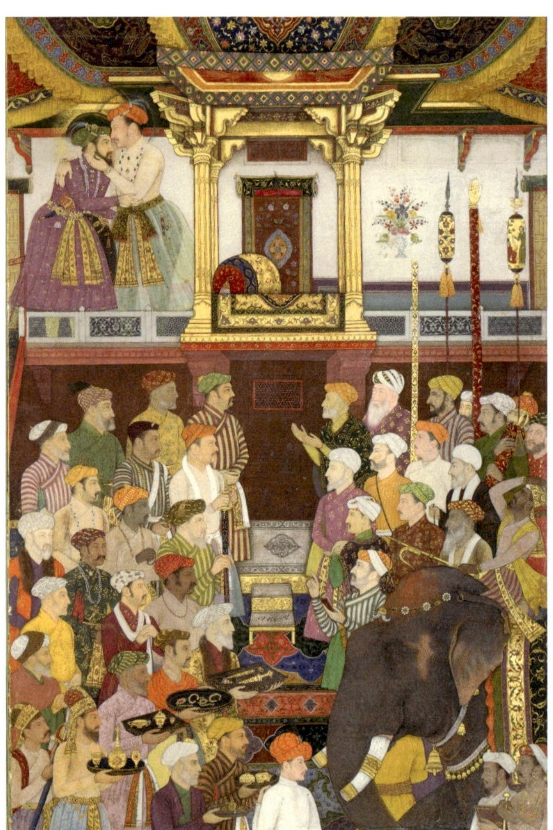

1

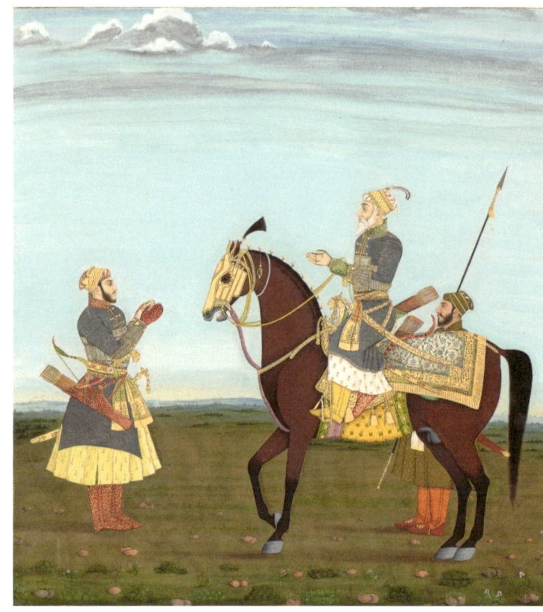

2

1 (*pages 4–5, 12–13*). Murar, Jahangir receives Prince Khurram on his return from the Deccan, folio 49a from the *Padshahnama*, ca. 1640. Opaque watercolor and gold on paper; 12⅛ × 8¼ in. (30.8 × 20.9 cm). Royal Collection Trust.
Many aspects of the sumptuousness of the Mughal court are shown here from the program of jewels worn by the emperor, Prince Khurram (later Shah Jahan), and members of their court, through the jewelry and precious jeweled vessels presented on trays, to the gold elephant goad wielded by the Mahout (see cat. 94/pl. 52).

2 (*pages 6–7*). Attributed to Mihr Chand, Portrait of Assadkhan Alamgir, folio from the Lady Coote Album, ca. 1780. Ink, transparent and opaque watercolor, gold paint on paper, 17¾ × 24¾ in. (45.2 × 62.7 cm). Fine Arts Museums of San Francisco, Museum purchase, Achenbach Foundation for Graphic Arts Endowment Fund, 1982.2.70.2.
A later portrait of the Mughal emperor Aurangzeb (1618–1707) on horseback, under whom the empire grew to its largest extent, overcoming China as the world's largest economy by 1700. Aurangzeb was less inclined to showy demonstrations of jewels than his predecessors.

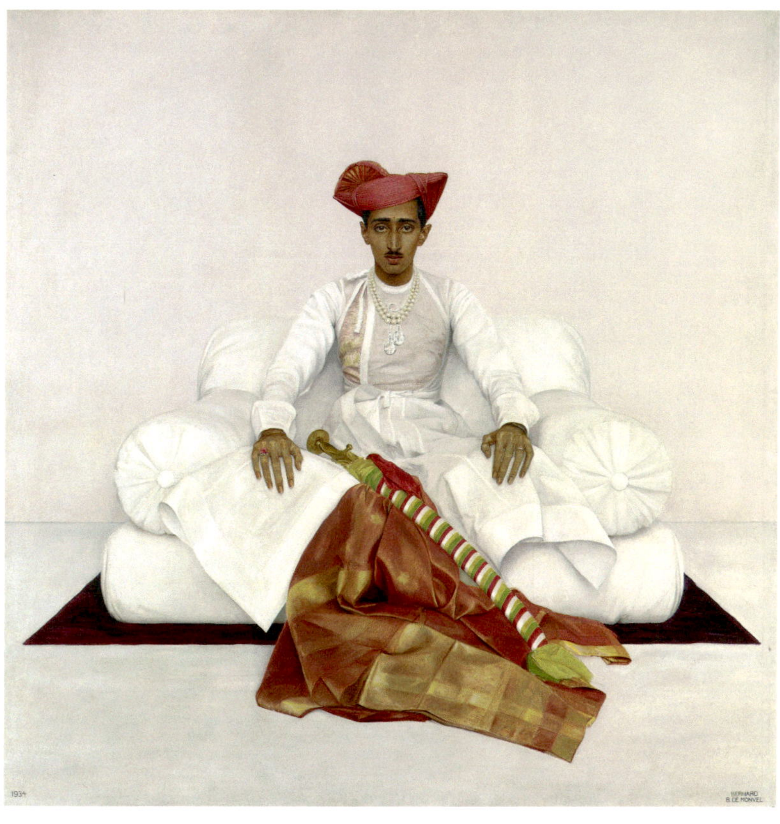

3

4

3 (*pages 8–9*). Bernard Boutet de Monvel, *Maharaja Yeshwant Rao Holkar II of Indore in Indian Dress*, 1934. Oil on canvas, 70⅞ × 70⅞ in. (180 × 180 cm). The Al Thani Collection.
The Maharaja of Indore is depicted in traditional Indian dress on a white throne wearing the famous Indore Pear diamonds around his neck on a pearl necklace made by Chaumet. He also wears a ruby ring, probably cat. 141/pl. 80.

4 (*pages 14–15*). Attributed to Bishandas, Jahangir entertains Shah Abbas I of Persia, folio from the St. Petersburg Album, ca. 1620. Opaque watercolor, gold, ink on paper, 9⅞ × 7¼ in. (25 × 18.3 cm). Freer Gallery of Art and Arthur M. Sackler Gallery, Smithsonian Institution, Washington, DC, Purchase, Charles Lang Freer Endowment, F1942.16a.
The encounter between Emperor Jahangir and Shah Abbas I of Persia includes an array of precious objects assembled in front of the two rulers to mark the significance of the occasion. It includes ornate European works of art of the type that were acquired by Jahangir, a Mannerist ewer, a possibly Venetian table, and a German silver gilt automaton figure of Diana on a stag cradled by the Mughal ambassador to the Persian court on the right.

5 (*page 19*). René-Antoine Houasse, *Equestrian Portrait of Louis XIV Wearing His Diamonds*, ca. 1679. Oil on canvas, 100 × 78¾ in. (255 × 200 cm). Chateaux de Versailles et de Trianon, Versailles, France, MV2109.
Louis XIV is shown at the height of his prowess as a war-waging monarch on horseback wearing an array of diamonds and gemstones. Jewels are worn on his coat, in his hat, and set into his sword, on the horse harness, the stirrups, and sewn onto the saddlecloth.

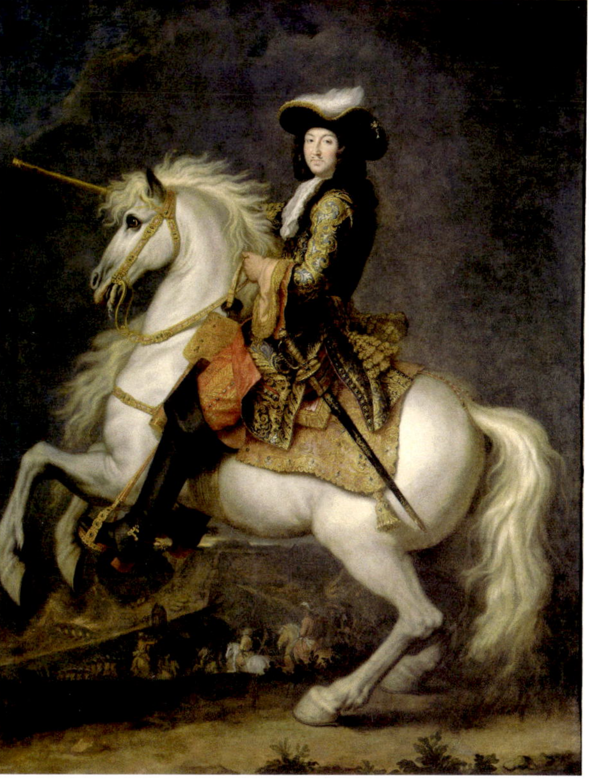

5

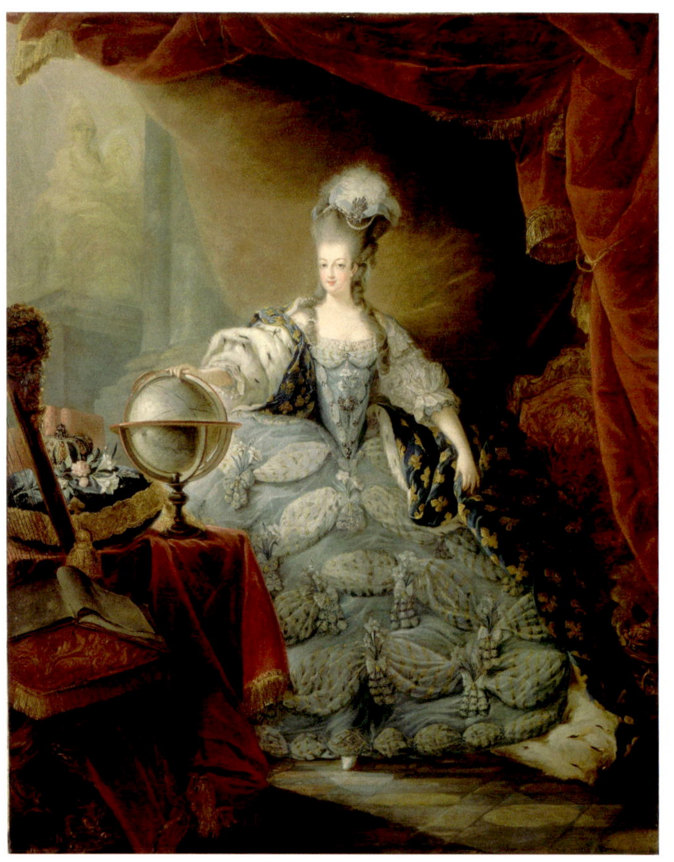

6

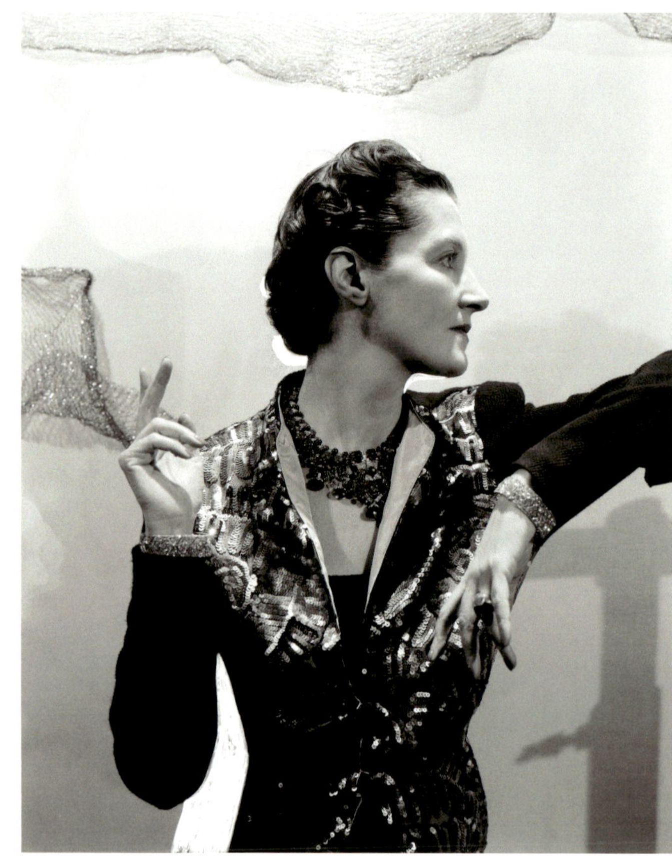

7

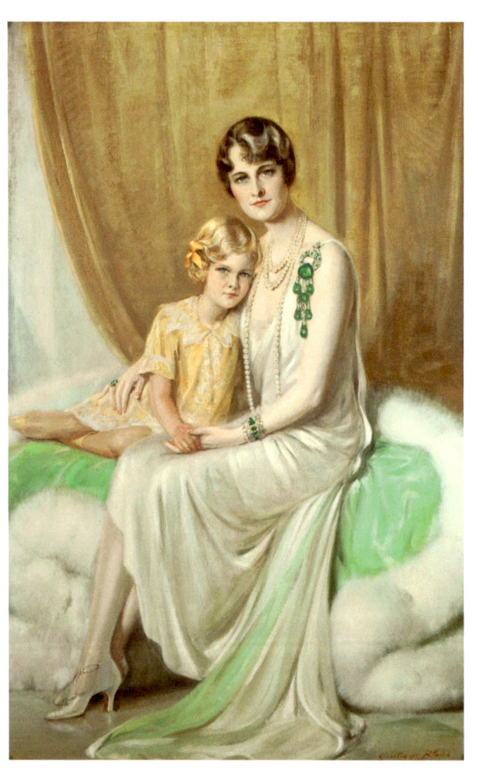

8

6 (*page 20*). Jean-Baptiste Gautier-Dagoty, *Marie Antoinette in court dress*, 1775. Oil on canvas, 63 × 50⅜ in. (160 × 128 cm). Chateaux de Versailles et de Trianon, Versailles, France, MV8061. *Queen Marie Antoinette is portrayed wearing many jewels on her dress with a diamond aigrette in her hair or wig. The aigrette functioned similarly to the Indian turban ornament in that it was intended to hold a feather.*

7 (*page 25*). Cecil Beaton, The Hon. Mrs. Reginald Fellowes wearing the Cartier Tutti Frutti necklace, 1936. *Daisy Fellowes wears her famous Cartier necklace made in 1936 from carved Indian emeralds, rubies, and sapphires.*

8 (*page 27*). Giulio de Blaas, *Portrait of Mrs. Hutton and Nedenia Hutton*, 1929. Oil on canvas, 59⅛ × 39⅛ in. (150 × 99 cm). Hillwood Estate, Museum & Gardens, Washington, DC, Bequest of Marjorie Merriweather Post, 1973, 51.146. *Marjorie Merriweather Post is portrayed wearing her Cartier shoulder brooch set with large carved Mughal emeralds.*

9 (*pages 30–31*). Bernard Boutet de Monvel, *Maharaja Yeshwant Rao Holkar II of Indore in Western Dress*, 1929. Oil on canvas, 74¾ × 47¼ in. (190 × 120 cm). The Al Thani Collection.
In contrast to the portrait of the Maharaja of Indore in traditional dress (see pages 8–9), this shows Indore in Western white-tie evening dress of the late 1920s and posed in a fashionable Parisian apartment.

10 (*page 32*). A Mughal prince, probably Shah Shuja', folio from the Late Shah Jahan Album, India, ca. 1650. [Reverse with panel of calligraphy by (Mir) 'Ali al-Katib, Heart or Bukhara, 1500–1550]. Paper, opaque pigments, 8⅝ × 5 in. (21.9 × 12.7 cm). The Al Thani Collection.
The prince wears the jeweled emblems of his royal position at the Mughal court, jeweled turban ornaments, pearl necklaces, bracelets with single gemstones (probably spinels and emeralds), upper-arm bracelets, rings, a jeweled punch dagger, and a sword.

11 (*page 35*). Portrait of Asaf Khan holding a jeweled turban, India, ca. 1640. Paper, opaque pigments, gold, 5½ × 3¼ in. (14.2 × 8.4 cm). The Al Thani Collection.
The grand vizier (prime minister) of Emperor Shah Jahan, Asaf Khan (ca. 1569–1641) was father to Mumtaz Mahal, for whom the Taj Mahal was built as a mausoleum. He holds a jeweled turban and wears pearl earrings, bracelets, and a jeweled sash.

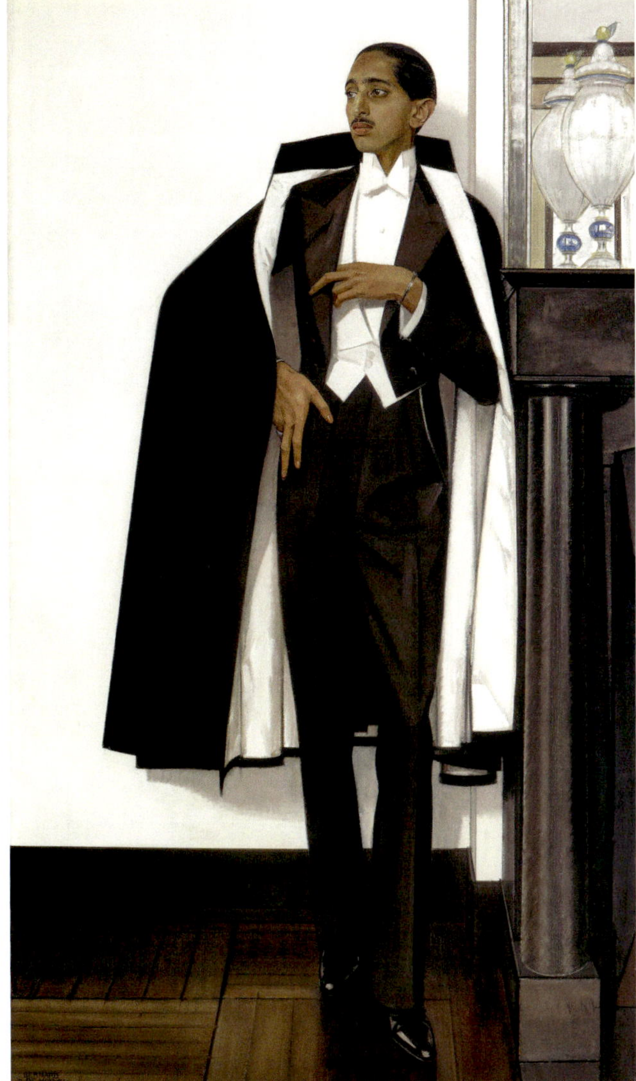

9

10

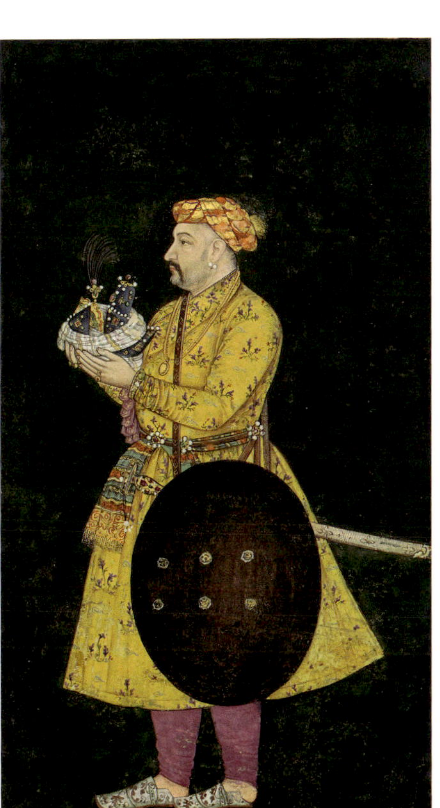

11

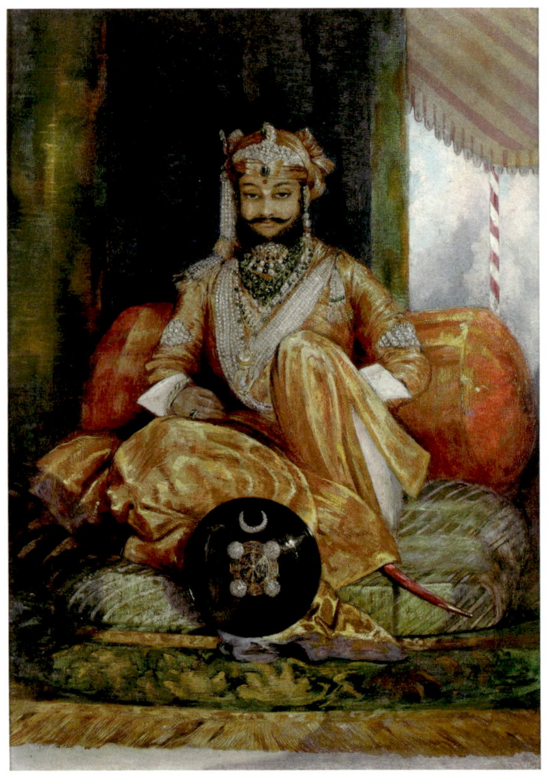

12

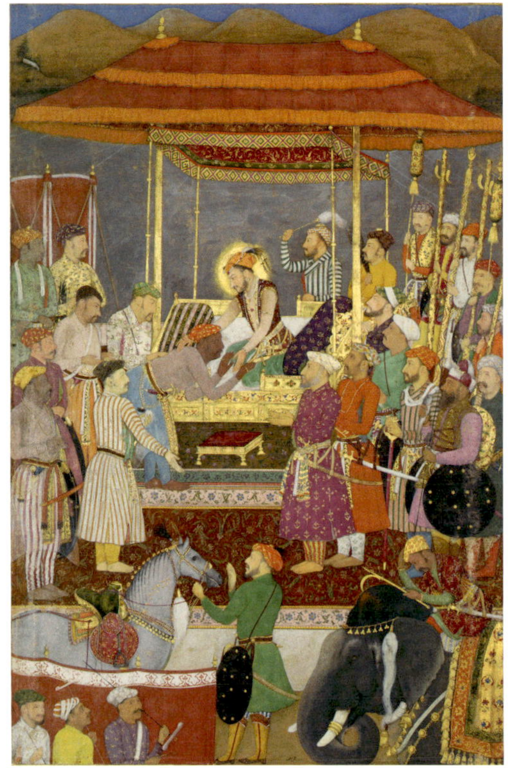

13

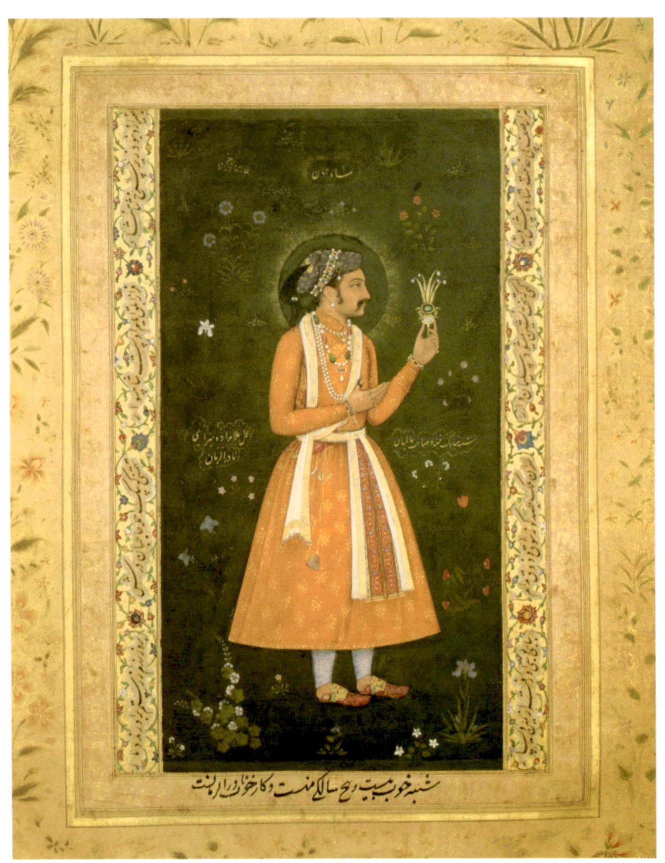

14

12 (*page 38*). George Landseer, *Maharaja Tukoji Rao II of Indore*, 1861. Oil on canvas, 23⅜ × 17 in. (59.4 × 43.2 cm). The Al Thani Collection.
The Maharaja of Indore is painted wearing a sumptuous array of jeweled necklaces, bracelets, and turban ornaments.

13 (*pages 42–43, 76*). Lalchand, The submission of Rana Amar Singh of Mewar to Prince Khurram, folio 46b from the *Padshahnama*, ca. 1640. Opaque watercolor and gold on paper, 12¾ × 8½ in. (32.4 × 21.6 cm). Royal Collection Trust.
The full panoply of Prince Khurram (later Shah Jahan)'s court is depicted here with the canopied throne, the program of wearing jewels, flywhisk, swords, and jewel-decorated caparisoned horse and elephant with a mahout *(driver) holding an elephant goad.*

14 (*pages 45–46*). Abu'l-Hasan Nader al-Zaman, *The Prince Khurram, later Shah Jahan*, folio from the Minto Album, ca. 1616–1617. Opaque watercolor and gold on paper, folio: 15¼ × 10½ in. (38.7 × 26.6 cm), painting: 8⅛ × 4½ in. (20.6 × 11.5 cm). Victoria and Albert Museum, London, IM.14-925.
The prince is portrayed wearing the range of jewels denoting his status: necklaces, bracelets, rings, turban jewels, and earrings of pearls and gemstones. He holds a turban ornament set with a large emerald and a large diamond with stylized gold feathers similar to contemporary European examples.

15 (*pages 46–47*). Tilly Kettle, *Muhammad Ali Wallajah, Nawab of Arcot*, 1772–1776. Oil on canvas, 94 × 58¼ in. (239 × 148 cm). Victoria and Albert Museum, London, IM.124-1911.
The Nawab of Arcot ruled over the lucrative Golconda diamond mines. He is depicted in his finest jewels, with ropes of pearl necklaces, turban ornament, and bracelets—many set with diamonds, including a pendant to one of the pearl necklaces that is a large flat diamond of a type similar to cat. 1/pl. 1.

16 (*page 52*). Hashim, Shah Jahan standing on a globe, folio from the Shah Jahan Album, ca. 1630–1640. Opaque watercolor, ink, gold on paper, 9⅞ × 6¼ in. (25.1 × 15.8 cm). Freer Gallery of Art, Smithsonian Institution, Washington, DC, Purchase F1939.49a.
Shah Jahan is shown holding a large jewel and wears the customary program of jewels for a Mughal emperor: a turban ornament, pearls, and gem-set necklaces, including emeralds, bracelets, a punch dagger, and a sword.

17 (*page 56*). Shah Jahan offers a spinel to Dara Shikoh, folio from the Nasir al-Din Shah Album, ca. 1650. Watercolor on paper, with gold, folio: 14⅝ × 9¾ in. (37.3 × 24.9 cm). The Trustees of the Chester Beatty Library, Dublin, CBL In 50.3.
Dara Shikoh was the eldest son of Shah Jahan and was favored as his successor. The emperor presents a spinel that was probably of imperial dynastic significance similar to cat. 25/pl. 10 and cat. 27/pl. 11.

18 (*page 58*). Abu al-Hasan, *Shah Jahan Holding the Imperial Seal*, North India, 1628. Opaque watercolor on paper, 7⅛ × 5½ in. (18.2 × 13.9 cm). Aga Khan Trust for Culture, AKM135.
Shah Jahan holds the imperial seal engraved in a similar manner to the emerald in cat. 10/pl. 5. Visible in his pearl necklaces, bracelets, and turban ornaments are emeralds plus spinels or rubies.

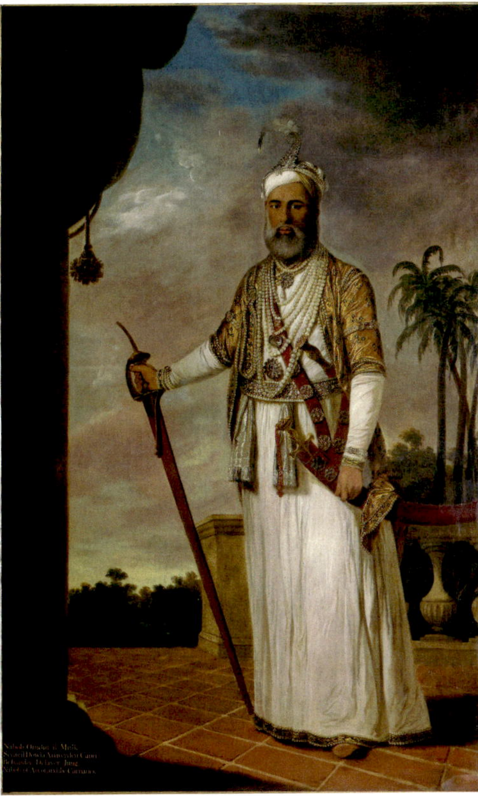

15

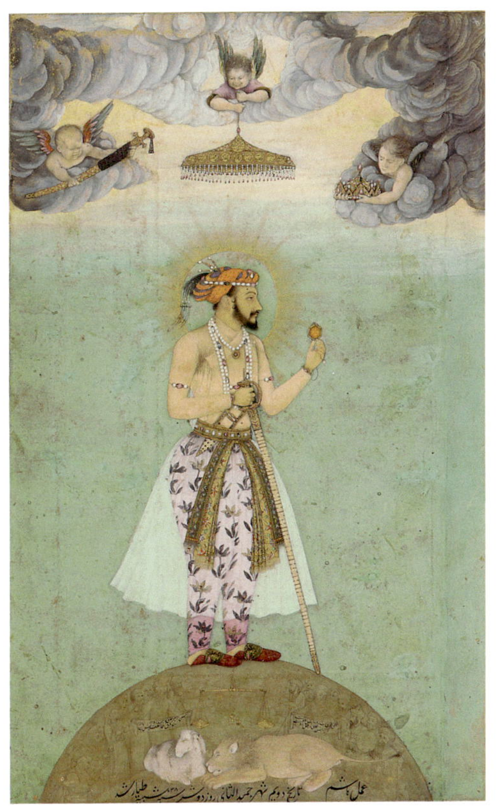

16

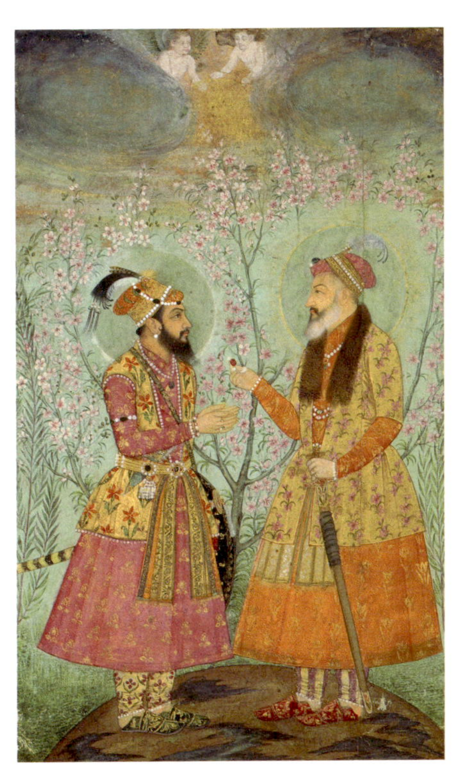

17

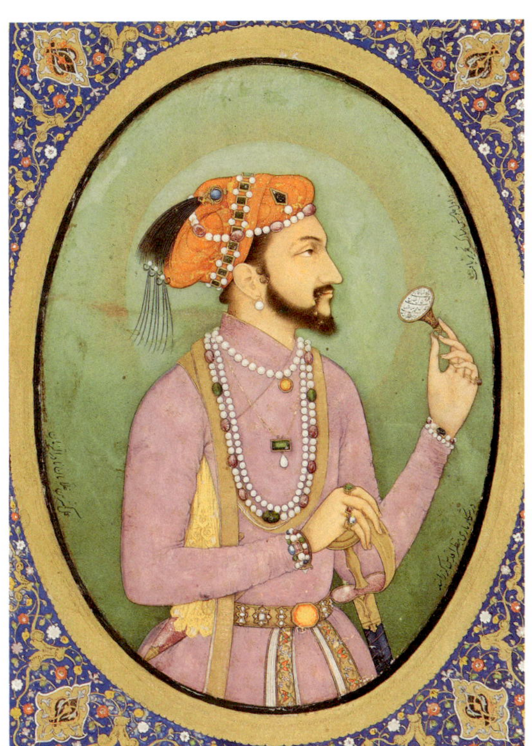

18

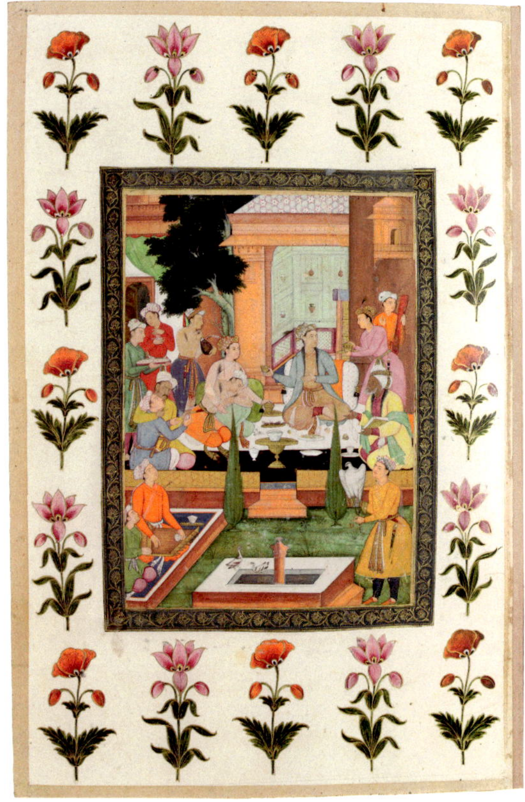

19

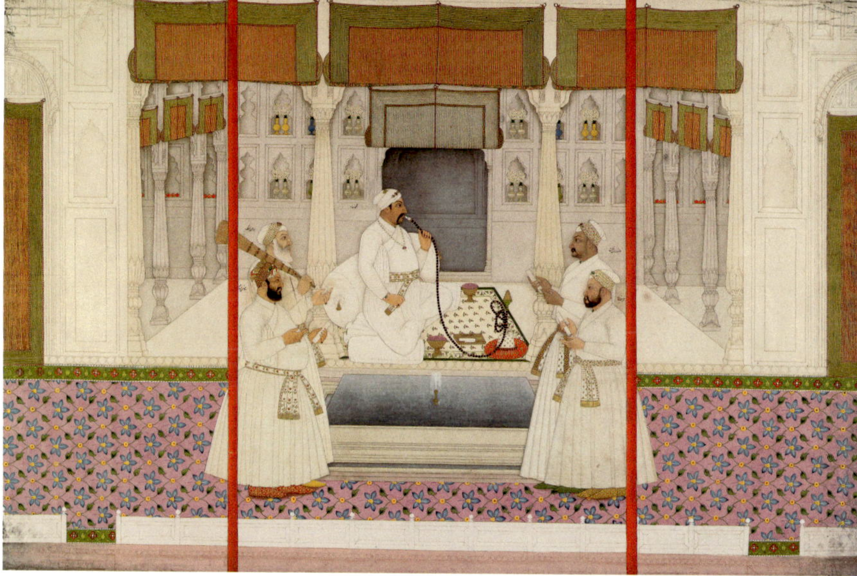

20

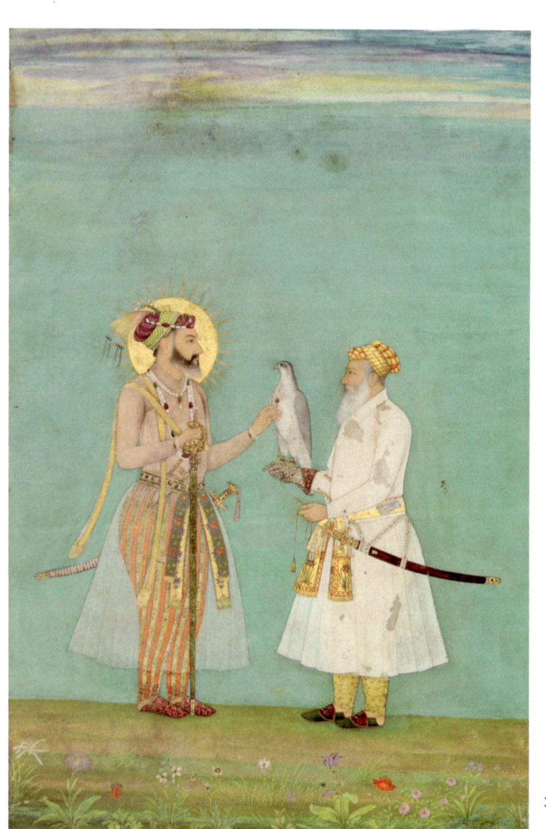

21

19 (*pages 62–63, 71*). Folio from the Small Clive Album representing a convivial gathering, India, ca. 1615–1620. Opaque watercolor and gold on paper, 7⅛ × 5⅛ in. (18.2 × 13.2 cm). Victoria and Albert Museum, London, Gift of Mr. John Goelet, IS.48:53/B-1956. *This court event shows the use of precious vessels, some of which may have been jade or hardstone.*

20 (*page 73*). Attributed to Chitarman, Muhammad Shah with four courtiers, ca. 1730. Gouache on paper, 12¼ × 18⅜ in. (31.2 × 46.8 cm). The Bodleian Libraries, the University of Oxford, Given to the Bodleian by Francis Douce, Ms. Douce Or. a. 3, fol. 14a. *Mughal emperor Muhammad Shah (r. 1719–1748) is smoking tobacco through a water pipe with a hookah base similar to cat. 46/pl. 19.*

21 (*pages 75, 124*). Hashim, Shah Jahan with an elderly courtier holding a falcon, ca. 1650. Watercolor on paper, with gold, 11⅛ × 7⅜ in. (28.4 × 18.9 cm). The Trustees of the Chester Beatty Library, Dublin, CBL In 62.4. *Falconry was one of the noble pursuits that the Mughal emperors adopted from Persian court traditions. As a signifier of its imperial status, the falcon is wearing a jeweled necklace and jeweled bracelets.*

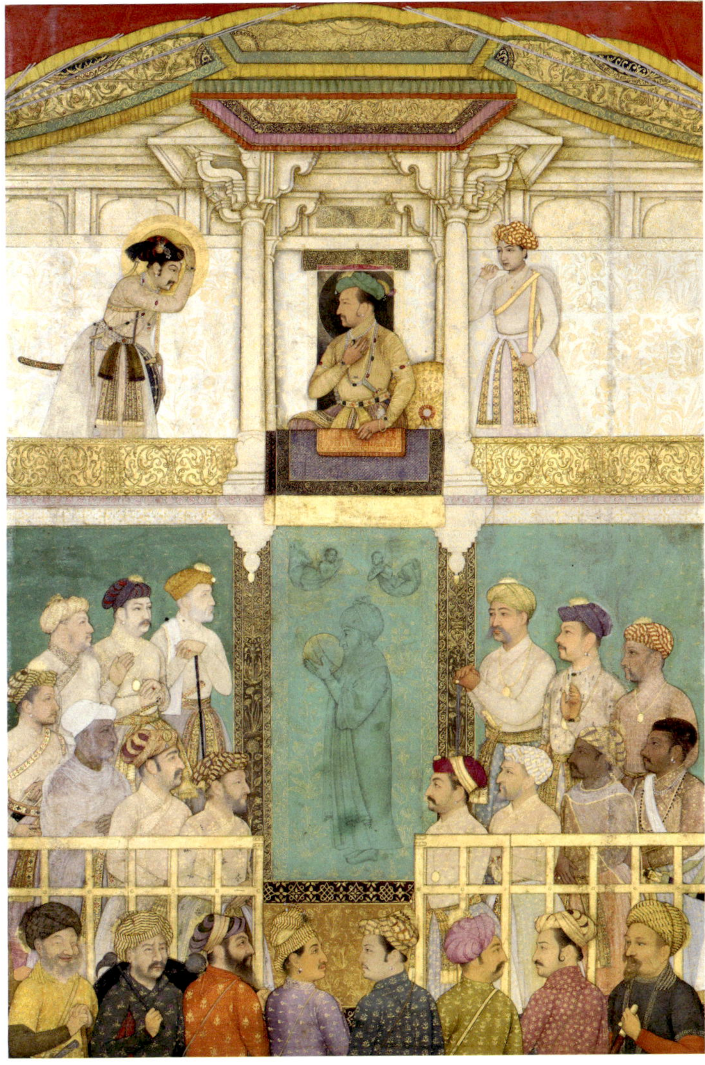

22

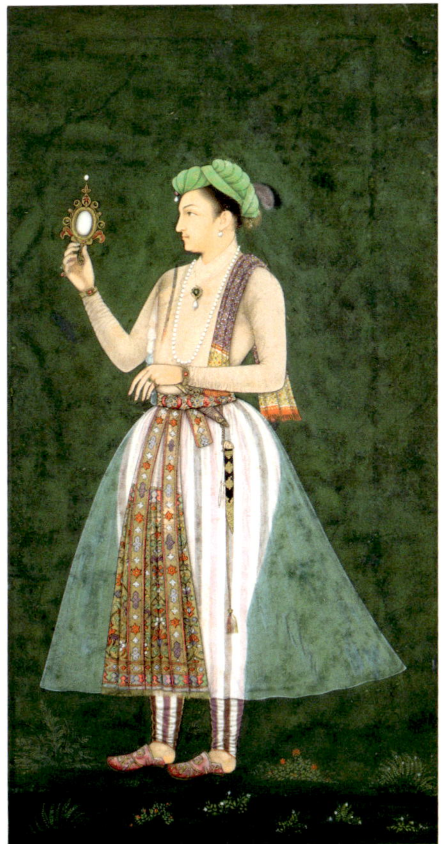

23

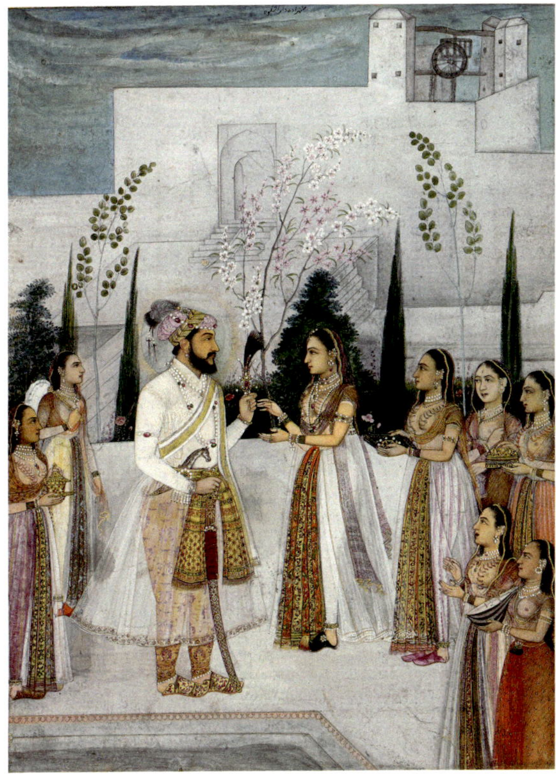

24

22 (*pages 80–81*). Attributed to Abid, Jahangir receives Prince Khurram, folio 192b from the *Padshahnama*, ca. 1635. Opaque watercolor and gold on paper, painting: 14 × 9½ in. (35.8 × 24.2 cm). Royal Collection Trust.
Emperor Jahangir's court is depicted with the members of the imperial family and their attendants wearing jewels in amounts according to rank.

23 (*page 82*). Bichitr, *Prince Salim*, folio from the Minto Album, Mughal, India, ca. 1630. Opaque watercolor and gold on paper, 9⅞ × 7⅛ in. (25 × 18.1 cm). Victoria and Albert Museum, London, IM.28-1925.
Prince Salim (later Jahangir) has a dagger suspended from his sash carved with a human head similar to cat. 56/pl. 26. He also holds what looks like an elaborate jewel or jeweled mirror.

24 (*page 84*). Shah Jahan presents a *sarpech* to a princess in a garden, ca. 1660–1680. Opaque watercolor with gold on paper, 9½ × 7⅛ in. (24 × 18 cm). The Al Thani Collection.
Shah Jahan presents a sarpech *or turban ornament with a large black feather as a mark of favor to a princess. He wears a horse-head dagger similar to cat. 61/pl. 28. This is also an unusual depiction of royal women wearing jewels.*

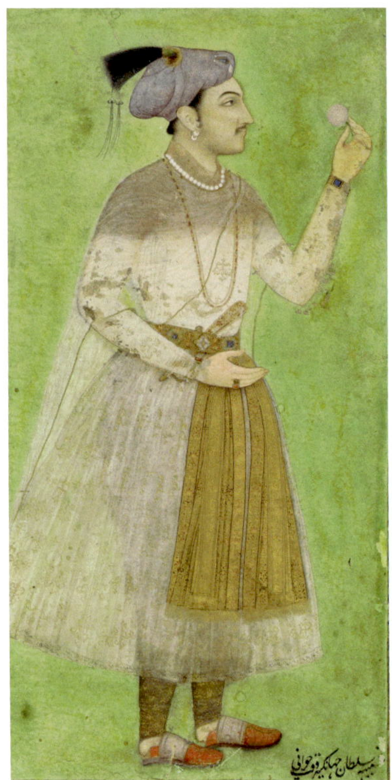

25

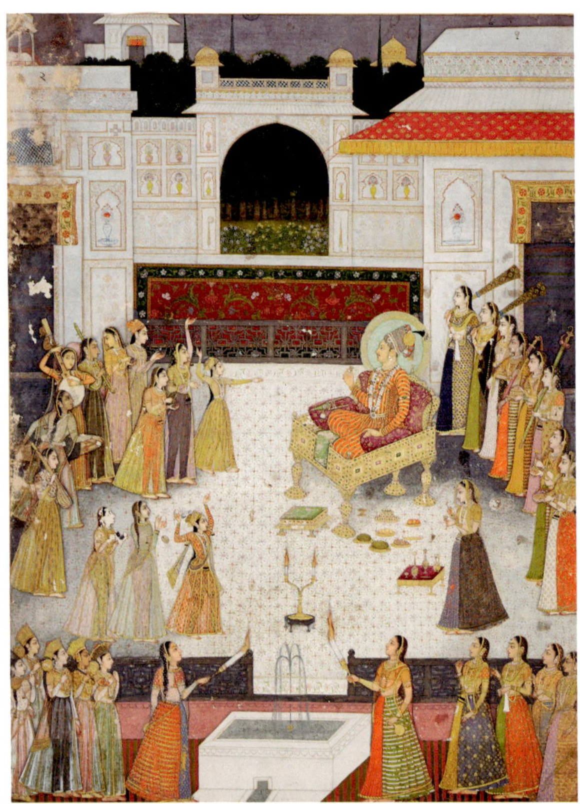

27

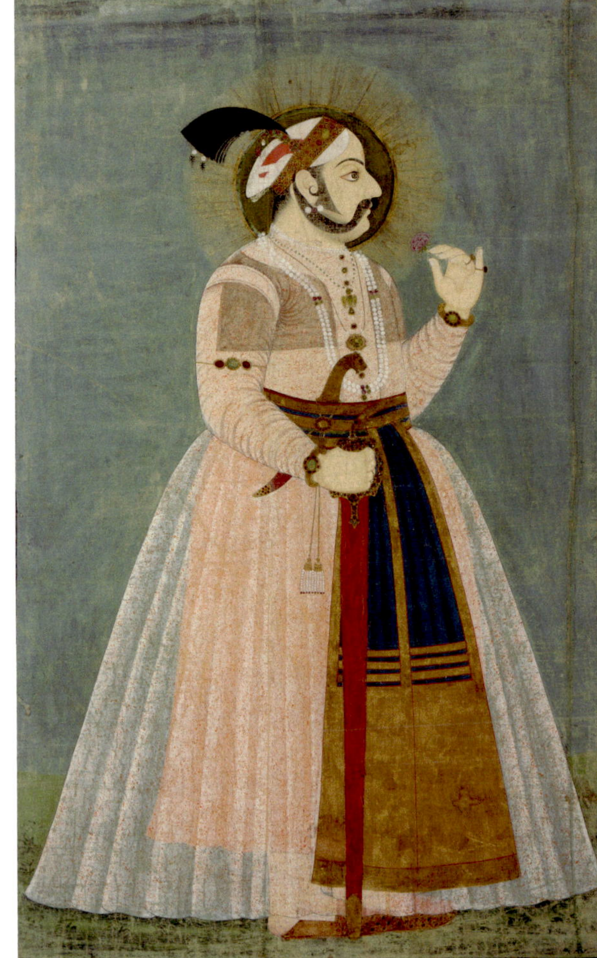

26

25 (*page 86*). Jahangir as a youth holding a pink rose, dressed in diaphanous white with a mauve turban and full gold *patka*, North India, ca. 1620–1630. Opaque watercolor on paper, 6⅛ × 3⅛ in. (15.8 × 8 cm). British Library, London.
Jahangir has a jade dagger in his sash that resembles cat. 57/pl. 27 with its setting of gemstones in the kundan *technique.*

26 (*page 88*). *Maharana Amar Singh*, Udaipur, India, ca. 1735–1740. Opaque watercolor on cotton cloth, 83⅞ × 54 in. (213 × 137 cm). Victoria and Albert Museum, London, Purchased with the assistance of The Art Fund, IS.55-1997.
The maharana *wears a lion-headed dagger in his sash similar to cat. 60/pl. 30.*

27 (*pages 94–95*). Dalchand, Maharaja Abhai Singh watching a dance performance, ca. 1725. Opaque watercolor on paper, 21⅝ × 16⅛ in. (55 × 41 cm). Mehrangarh Museum Trust, Jodhpur, and His Highness Maharaja Gaj Singh of Jodhpur.
Maharaja Singh's court is depicted with emblems of his authority: the jeweled gold throne, the maharaja's jewelry, the jeweled gold vessels, and the jeweled swords held by court ladies.

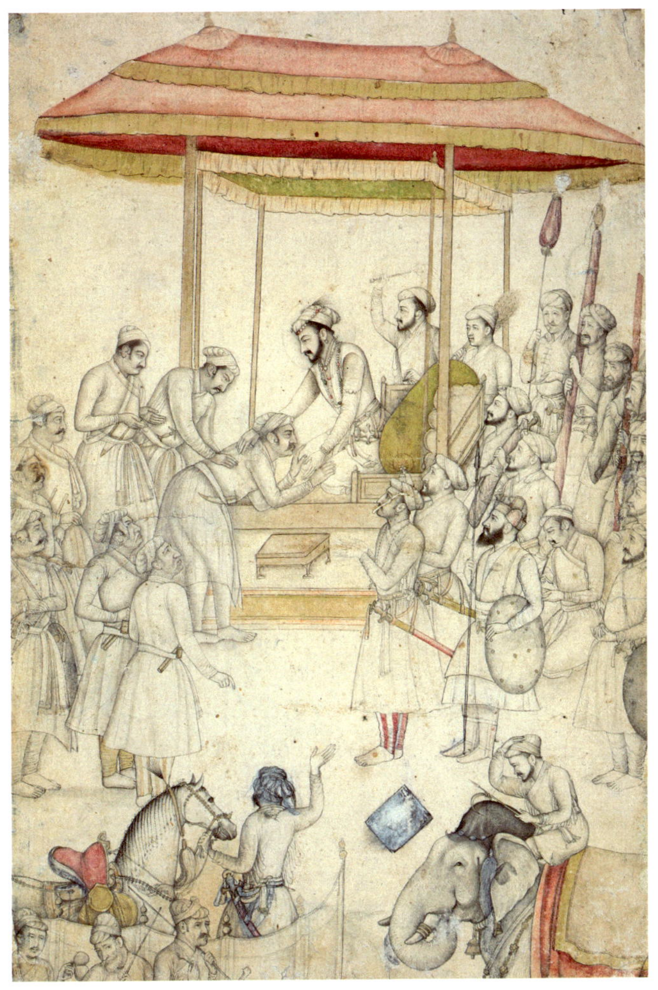

28

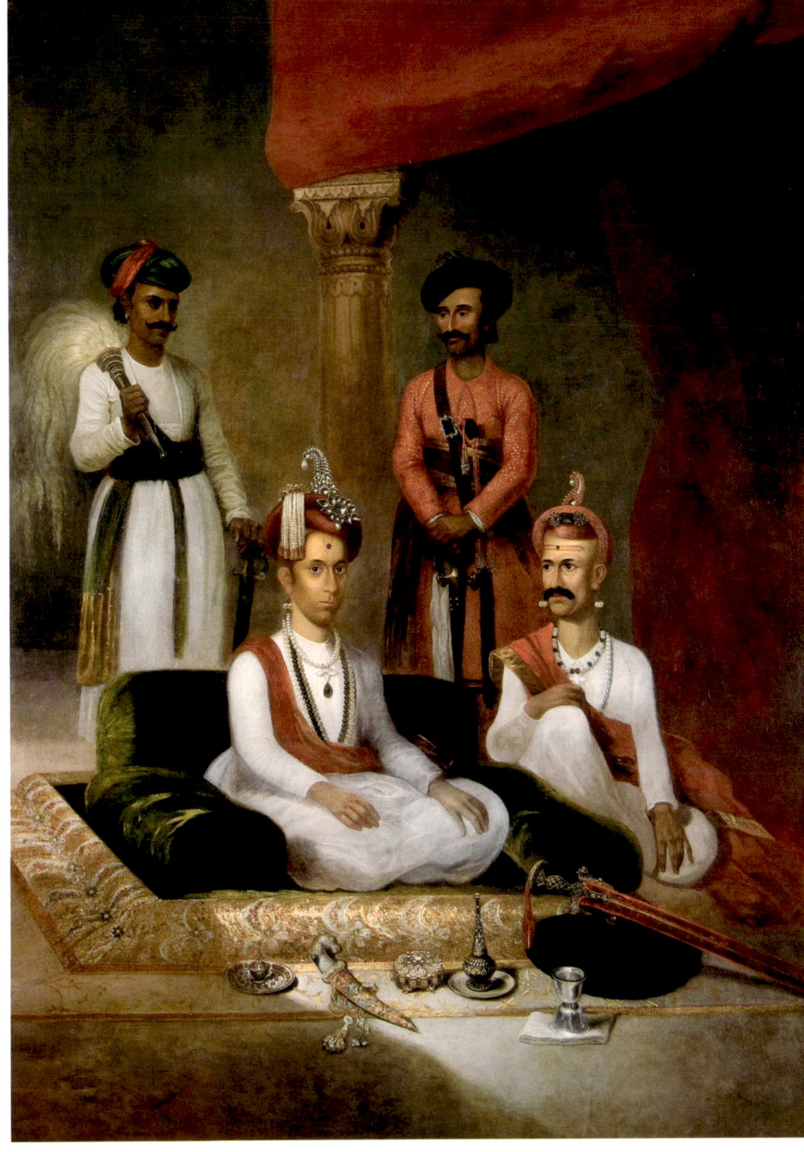

29

28 (*page 96*). Tinted brush and ink drawing on paper, 11 × 7⅜ in. (28.1 × 18.7 cm). The Trustees of the Chester Beatty Library, Dublin, CBL In 60.6.
The courtiers of Prince Khurram (later Shah Jahan) are wearing pen cases in their sashes. The submission of Rana Amar Singh of Mewar to Prince Khurram, India, 1620–1628.

29 (*page 102*). James Wales, *Madhu Rao Narayan, the Maratha Peshwa with Nana Fadnavis and Attendants, Poona*, 1792. Oil on canvas, 90⅛ × 74¾ in. (229 × 190 cm). Royal Asiatic Society of Great Britain and Ireland, London, RAS 01.014.
The emblems of the royal life are shown in front of the princes; a rosewater sprinkler, beaker, paan *boxes, and a dagger are made of precious metals.*

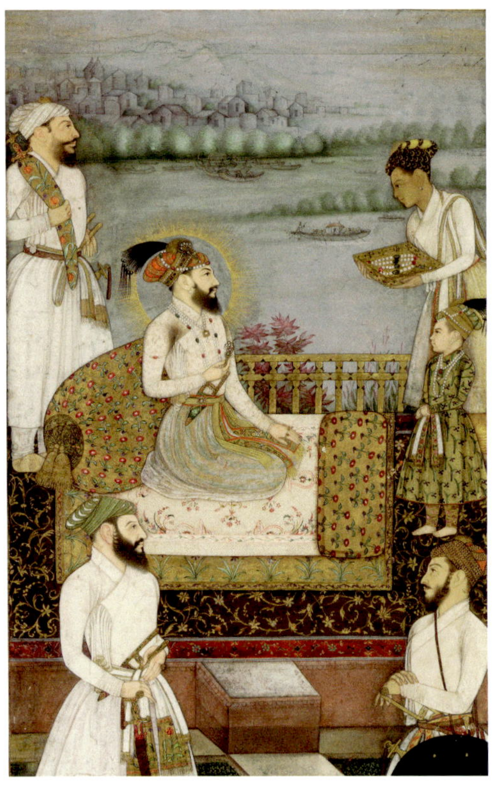

30

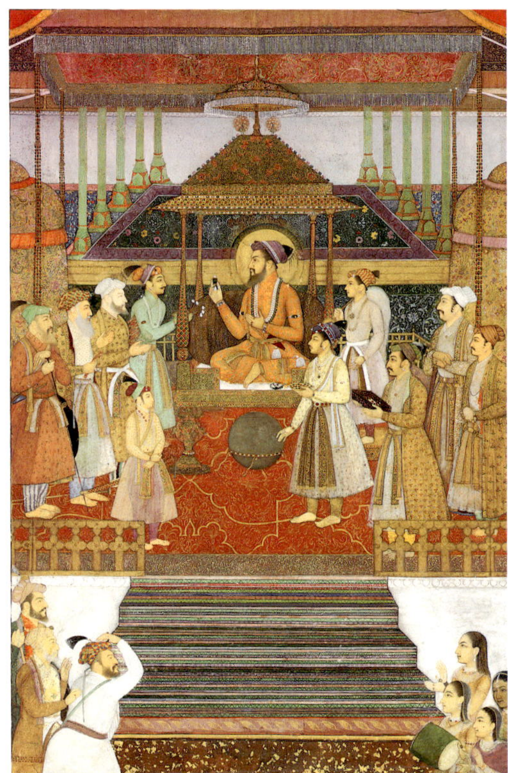

31

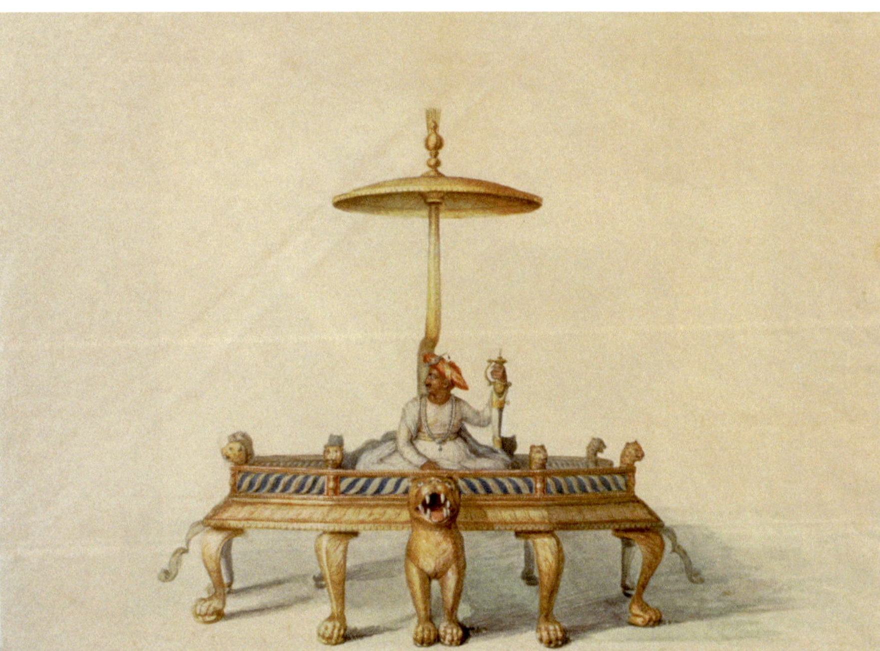

32

30 (*page 107*). Emperor Shah Jahan examines jewels by the Dal Lake, Kashmir, ca. 1645–1650. Gouache on paper, 7⅞ × 5 in. (20.1 × 12.8 cm). The Bodleian Libraries, the University of Oxford, Given to the Bodleian by Francis Douce, Ms. Douce Or. a. 1, fol. 23a. *The Emperor Shah Jahan wears a jeweled punch dagger similar to cat. 82/pl. 46 in his sash.*

31 (*page 109*). Abid, son of Aqa Reza, The Emperor Shah Jahan on the Peacock Throne, folio from the *Padshahnama (Histories of the Reign of the King of the World)*, 1640. Opaque watercolor and gold on paper, mounted as an album page, 14⅜ × 9¾ in. (36.7 × 25 cm). San Diego Museum of Art, USA, Edwin Binney 3rd Collection, 1990.352. *Shah Jahan sits on the jeweled throne he commissioned in 1628. It was made of gold set with jewels and with a canopy supported by enameled gold columns. On the canopy sat two enameled gold peacocks, which gave the throne its (later) name.*

32 (*page 110*). Anna Tonelli, *Tipu Sahib, Sultan of Mysore (1749–1799), Enthroned*, 1800. Watercolor on paper, 14¼ × 21 in. (35.5 × 53.2 cm). Clive Museum at Powis Castle and Garden, Powys, Wales (POW.D.67). *Tipu Sultan is sitting on his octagonal gold throne and under a canopy on which sits a Huma bird (bird of paradise). The finials from each of the angles were modeled as gold tigers' heads set with rubies and emeralds (see cat. 85/pl. 47).*

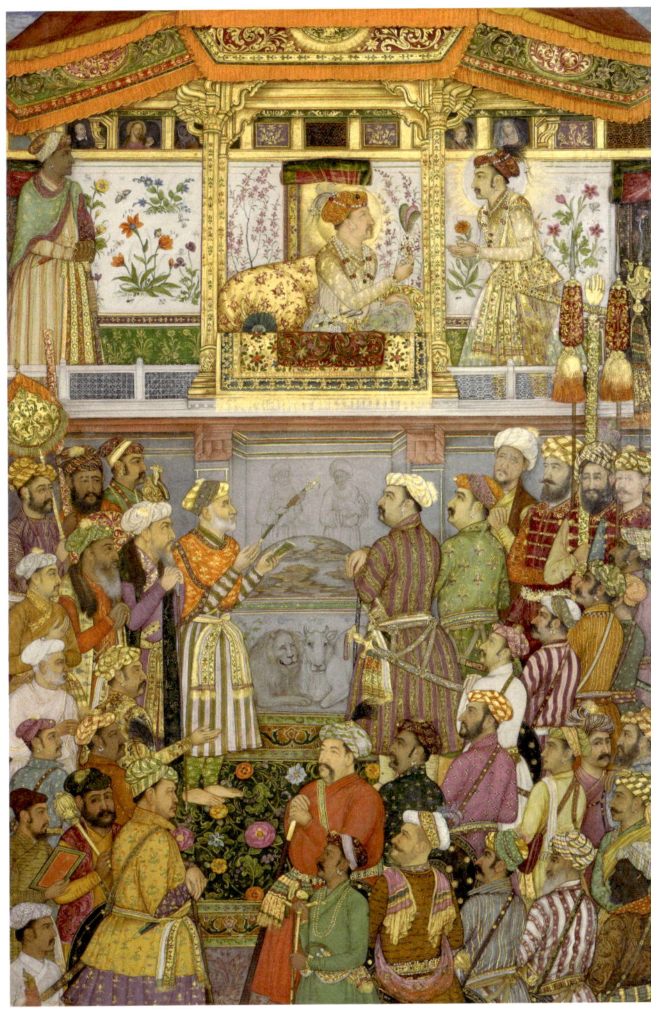

33

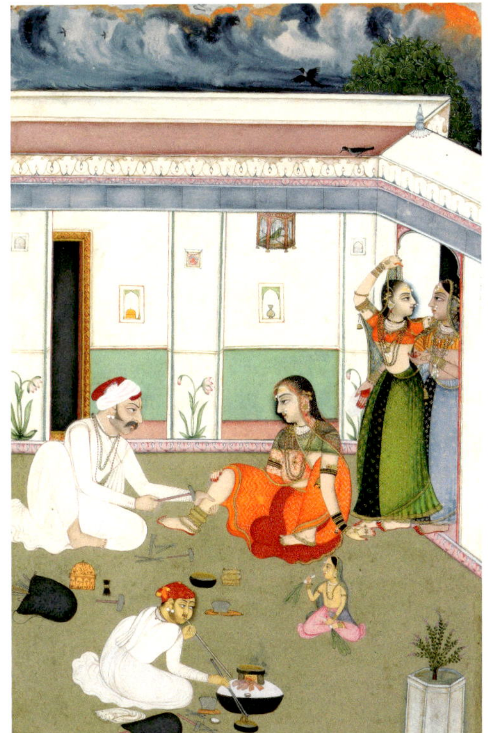

34

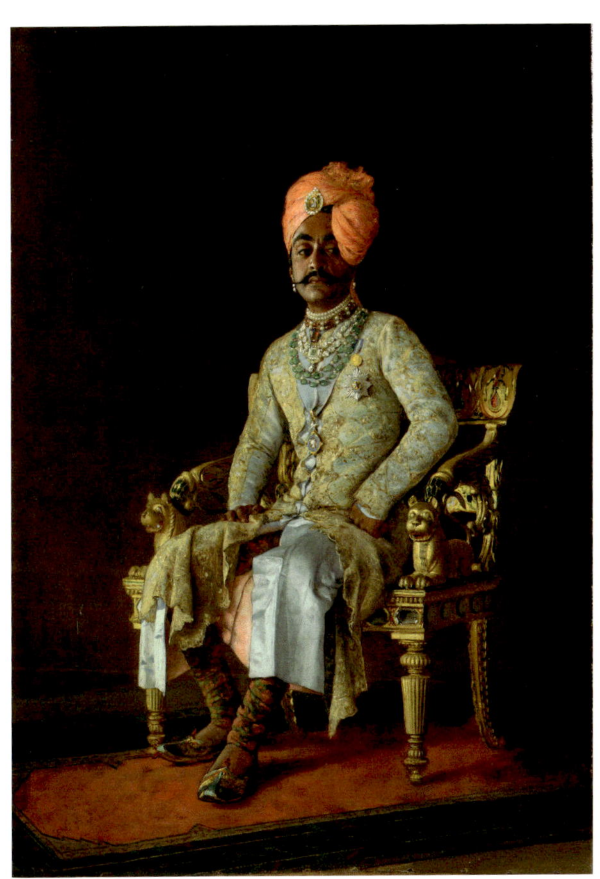

35

33 (*pages 116–117*). Payag, Jahangir presents Prince Khurram with a turban ornament, folio 195a from the *Padshahnama*, ca. 1640. Opaque watercolor and gold on paper, 12 × 8 in. (30.6 × 21.1 cm). Royal Collection Trust.
The magnificence of the court of Emperor Jahangir is shown in this miniature. The emperor presents a jeweled turban ornament to his son, later Emperor Shah Jahan, while members of the court dressed in their finery look on.

34 (*page 126*). In a goldsmith's workshop, Bundi, India, ca. 1760. Ink, opaque watercolor, gold on paper, 9¾ × 6½ in. (24.5 × 16.3 cm). The David Collection, Copenhagen, 17/1981.
The goldsmith is fitting a gold anklet to a woman similar to that in cat. 106/ pl. 59.

35 (*page 129*). Rudolf Swoboda, *Sir Pratap Singh (1845–1922)*, 1888. Oil on canvas, 22½ × 15⅝ in. (57.2 × 39.5 cm). Royal Collection Trust.
Pratap Singh, later Maharaja of Idar, was a career officer in the Indian army. He served his father, the Maharaja of Jodhpur, and brother as chief minister of the state and as aide-de-camp to King Edward VII from 1887 to 1910. He is portrayed in traditional Indian dress with gemstone necklaces, including one of emeralds similar to cat. 114/pl. 62.

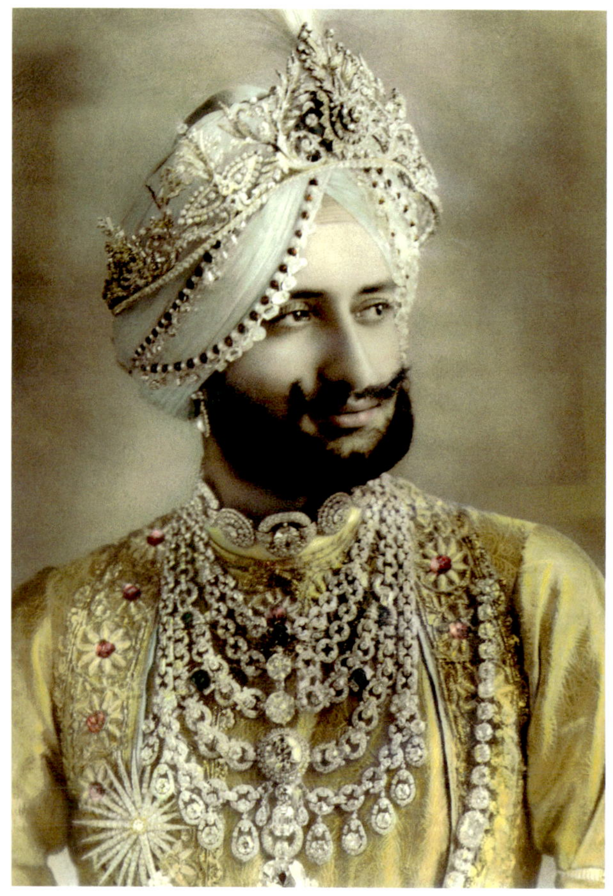

36

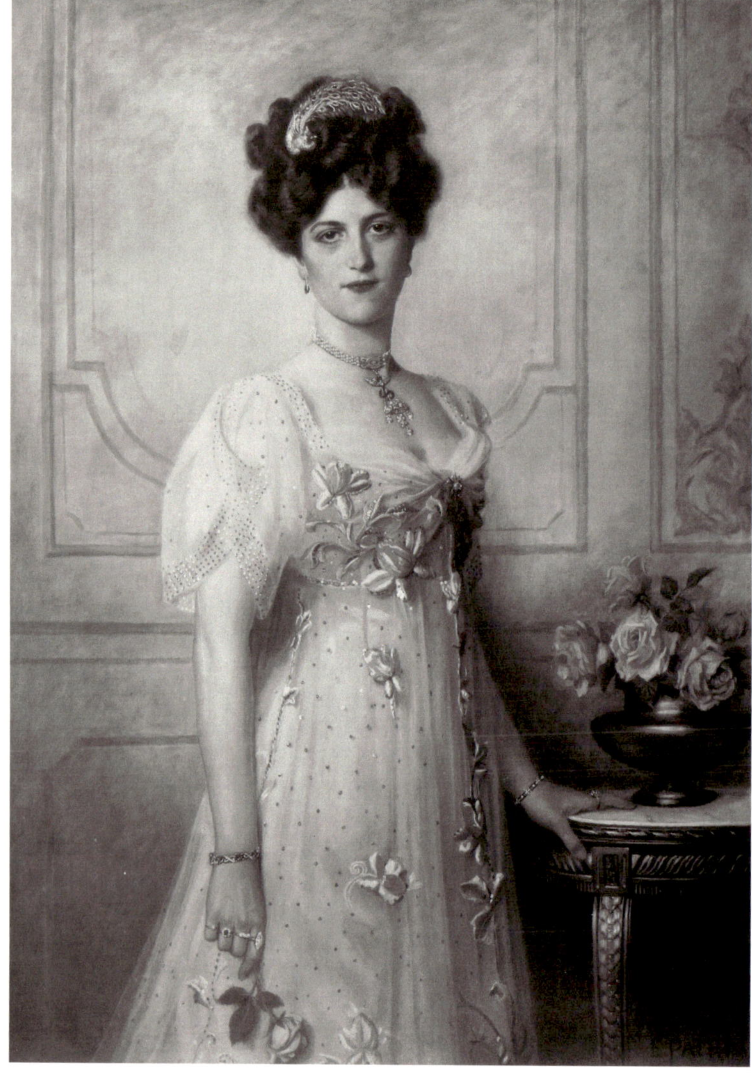

37

36 (*pages 134–135*). Sir Yadavindra Singh, Maharaja of Patiala, wearing the two diamond necklaces created for his father, Sir Bhupinder Singh in 1928, ca. 1940. Cartier Archives. *Colored photograph of the Maharaja of Patiala wearing his ceremonial jewelry, including the large Cartier bib necklace and choker (cat. 139/pl. 74 and cat. 138/pl. 75) made for his father in 1928, and the enormous diamond-set turban ornament.*

37 (*page 136*). Edward Patry, *Anita Delgado, Maharani of Kapurthala*, 1907. Oil on canvas, 63 × 39⅜ in. (160 × 100 cm). Collection of Elisa Vázquez de Gey. *The beautiful Spanish dancer Anita Delgado (1890–1962) met the Maharaja of Kapurthala at the 1906 wedding of King Alfonso of Spain to Princess Victoria of Battenburg. Delgado is portrayed wearing the French peacock aigrette (cat. 123/pl. 67) given to her by the maharaja.*

38 (*page 137*). Cover of *Comoedia Illustré*, 1 March 1911, showing Jeanne Dirys in *Le Cadet de Coutras* wearing the Paul Iribe aigrette as a *plaque de corsage*. Bibliothèque nationale de France, Paris.
The actress Jeanne Dirys is shown in the play Le Cadet de Coutras *wearing the Paul Iribe aigrette (cat. 126/pl. 68) as a* plaque de corsage.

39 (*page 164*). August Theodor Schoefft, *Portrait of Maharaja Sher Singh, in Regal Dress*, ca. 1850. Oil on panel, 18⅝ × 14 in. (47.3 × 35.5 cm). Private collection.
Sher Singh was maharaja of the Sikh empire and the Punjab. He is depicted during his short reign from 1841 to 1843 in his full program of ceremonial jewels set with rubies, emeralds, and pearls. He wears several layers of necklaces, upper-arm bracelets, and turban ornaments—including a pin made of an elongated emerald (see cat. 159/pl. 90).

40 (*pages 168–169*). The royal chamber in the public audience hall in the middle of Yazdah Darreh, with the ruler, Alam Bahador Badshah, and the great commanders, folio from the Lady Coote Album, ca. 1780. Ink, transparent and opaque watercolor, and gold paint on paper, 11¾ × 16⅜ in. (30 × 41.5 cm). Fine Arts Museums of San Francisco, Museum purchase, partial gift of Mr. and Mrs. John D. MacDonald and Achenbach Foundation for Graphic Arts Endowment Fund 1982.2.70.3.
Shah Alam II (r. 1769–1806) was one of the last Mughal emperors. He ruled over a crumbling empire yet still commanded respect. He is depicted presiding here at a court gathering in the palace.

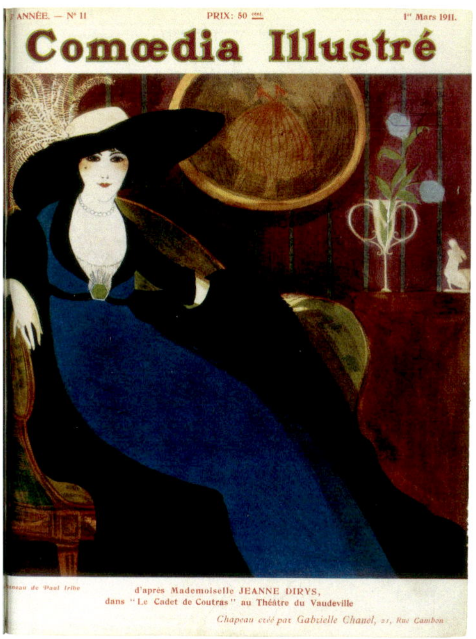

38

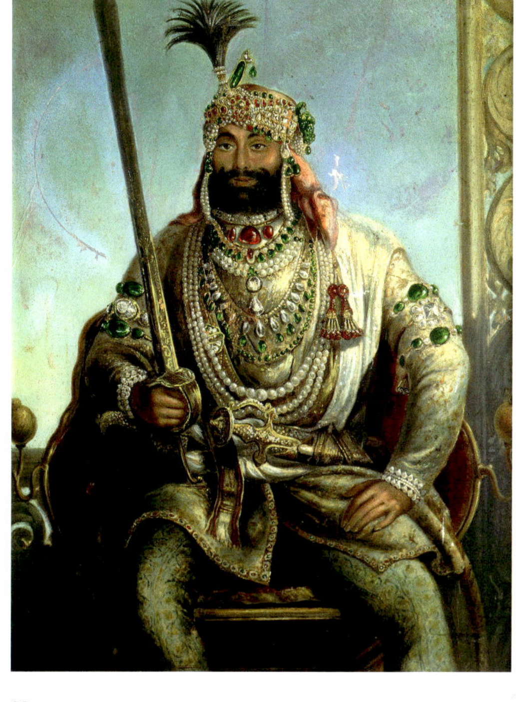

39

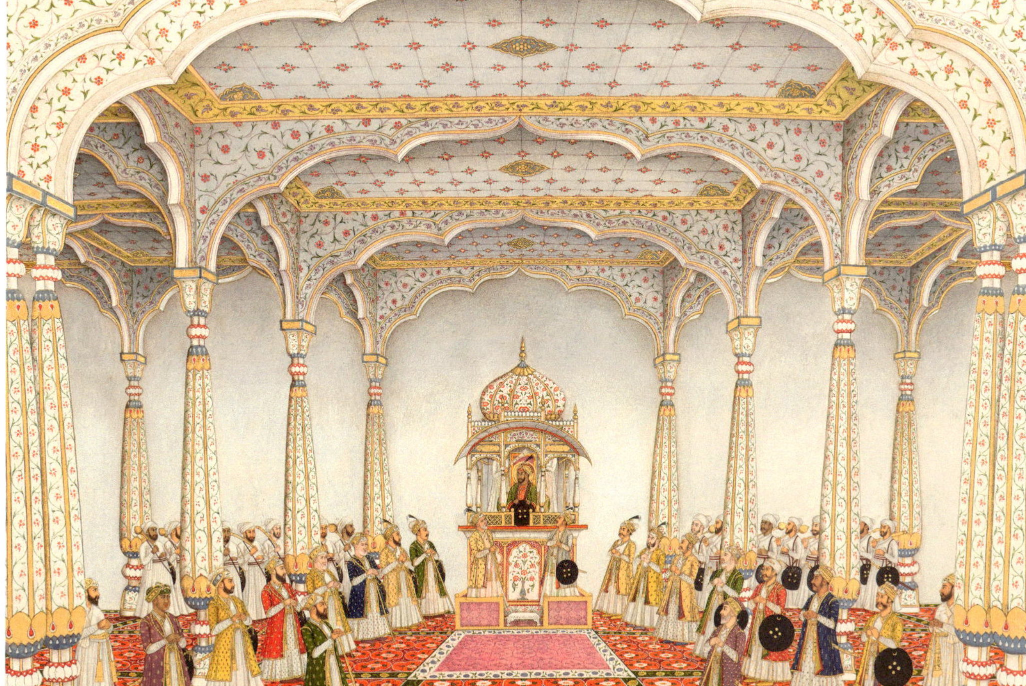

40

Published in 2018 by the Fine Arts Museums of San Francisco and DelMonico Books • Prestel on the occasion of the exhibition

East Meets West

Jewels of the Maharajas from The Al Thani Collection

at the Legion of Honor, San Francisco, from November 3, 2018, to February 24, 2019.

This exhibition is organized by the Fine Arts Museums of San Francisco.

Education and outreach programs have been made possible by the generosity of Diane B. Wilsey. Additional support has been provided by Jamie and Philip Bowles.

An earlier version of Amin Jaffer's essay was previously published in *Treasures of the Mughals and the Maharajas: The Al Thani Collection* (Milan: Skira Editore S.p.A., 2017), edited by Amin Jaffer. Parts of the Catalogue were derived from *Treasures of the Mughals and the Maharajas* and *Beyond Extravagance: A Royal Collection of Gems and Jewels* (New York: Assouline Publishing, 2013), edited by Amin Jaffer. The "Materials and Techniques" glossary was adapted from Michael Spink and Robert Skelton's essay, "Materials and Techniques in Indian Jewelry," in *Beyond Extravagance*. The bibliography was adapted from *Treasures of the Mughals and the Maharajas*.

LIBRARY OF CONGRESS CATALOGING-IN-PUBLICATION DATA

Names: Chapman, Martin (Curator), editor. | Jaffer, Amin, editor. | Legion of Honor (San Francisco, Calif.), host institution.
Title: East meets West: jewels of the maharajas from the Al Thani Collection / edited by Martin Chapman and Amin Jaffer. Other titles: East meets West (Al Thani Collection)
Description: San Francisco and New York: Fine Arts Museums of San Francisco and DelMonico Books • Prestel, 2018. | Issued in connection with an exhibition held November 3, 2018–February 24, 2019, Fine Arts Museums of San Francisco, Legion of Honor. | Includes bibliographical references.
Identifiers: LCCN 2018029521| ISBN 9783791357836 (hardback) | ISBN 3791357832
Subjects: LCSH: Jewelry—India—Exhibitions. | Jewelry—Europe—Exhibitions. | East and West—Exhibitions. | Al Thani, Hamad bin Abdullah, Sheikh—Art collections—Exhibitions. | Al Thani Collection—Exhibitions. | Jewelry—Private collections—Qatar—Exhibitions. | BISAC: ART / Collections, Catalogs, Exhibitions / General.
Classification: LCC NK7376.A1 E26 2018 | DDC 739.270954—dc23
LC record available at https://lccn.loc.gov/2018029521

A CIP catalogue record for this book is available from the British Library.

ISBN (hardback): 978-3-7913-5783-6
ISBN (Indian edition): 978-3-7913-6920-4

Fine Arts Museums of San Francisco
Golden Gate Park
50 Hagiwara Tea Garden Drive
San Francisco, CA 94118-4502
famsf.org

Leslie Dutcher, Director of Publications
Danica Michels Hodge, Managing Editor
Victoria Gannon, Editor
Trina Enriquez, Associate Editor
José Jovel, Publications Assistant

Project managed by Trina Enriquez
Edited by Trina Enriquez and Jane Friedman
Designed and typeset by Yvonne Tsang
Proofread by Susan Richmond with Jane Friedman
Production management by Karen Farquhar, DelMonico Books • Prestel
Printed in China

DelMonico Books, an imprint of Prestel, a member of Verlagsgruppe Random House GmbH

Prestel Verlag
Neumarkter Strasse 28
81673 Munich

Prestel Publishing Ltd.
14-17 Wells Street
London W1T 3PD

Prestel Publishing
900 Broadway, Suite 603
New York, NY 10003

www.prestel.com

PICTURE CREDITS

PLATES All photographs except pls. 74 and 75: © The Al Thani Collection. All rights reserved. Photographs by Prudence Cuming Associates, Matt Pia, and Laziz Hamani; pl. 74: Vincent Wulveryck, Cartier Collection © Cartier; pl. 75: Marian Gérard, Cartier Collection © Cartier. FIGURES 1: © Trustees of the British Museum; 2: © Herzog Anton Ulrich-Museum, Braunschweig, Kunstmuseum des Landes Niedersachsen, photograph by Museumsfotograf; 3: © The Metropolitan Museum of Art / Art Resource, NY; 4, 20, 45: © Bibliothèque nationale de France, Paris; 5, 6: Gérard Blot, © RMN–Grand Palais / Art Resource, NY; 7: © W. and D. Downey / Getty Images, Hulton Royals Collection; 8: © National Portrait Gallery, London; 9: Photograph by Nils Herrmann, Cartier Collection © Cartier; 10: Courtesy of Sotheby's Picture Library, © The Cecil Beaton Studio Archive at Sotheby's; 11: © Hillwood Estate, Museum, and Gardens, photograph by Edward Owen; 12: © Hillwood Estate, Museum, and Gardens, photograph by Brian Searby; 13, 14: © The Al Thani Collection 2018. All rights reserved. Photograph by Matt Pia; 15: © Sotheby's Picture Library; 16: © The Al Thani Collection 2017. All rights reserved. Photograph by Matt Pia; 17, 50: © Fine Arts Museums of San Francisco, photograph by Randy Dodson; 18, 52: © Henri Cartier-Bresson / Magnum Photos; 19, 24, 29, 32: © Victoria and Albert Museum, London; 21: © Freer Gallery of Art, Smithsonian Institution, Washington, DC, Purchase F1939.49a; 22, 26, 33, 39: © The Trustees of the Chester Beatty Library, Dublin; 23: Courtesy of the Aga Khan Trust for Culture, AKM135; 25: © The Bodleian Libraries, the University of Oxford, Ms. Douce Or. a.3, fol. 14a; 27, 28, 42: © Royal Collection Trust / Her Majesty Queen Elizabeth II 2018; 30: © The Al Thani Collection 2018. All rights reserved. Photograph by Prudence Cuming Associates; 31, 35: © The British Library Board / The Image Works; 34: Courtesy of Royal Asiatic Society of Great Britain and Ireland; 36: © The Bodleian Libraries, the University of Oxford, Ms. Douce Or. a. 1, fol. 23a; 37: © San Diego Museum of Art, USA / Edwin Binney 3rd Collection / Bridgeman Images; 38: © National Trust Images / Erik Pelham; 40, 47, 48, 49: © John Fasal Collection, photograph by Prudence Cuming Associates; 41: © The David Collection, Copenhagen, photograph by Pernille Klemp; 43: © RMN–Grand Palais / Art Resource, NY, photograph by Christian Jean; 44: Courtesy of Elisa Vázquez de Gey; 46: Cartier Archives © Cartier; 51: © Christie's Images / Bridgeman Images. PICTURE GALLERY 1, 13, 22, 33: Royal Collection Trust / © Her Majesty Queen Elizabeth II 2018; 2: © Fine Arts Museums of San Francisco, photograph by Joseph McDonald; 3: © The Al Thani Collection 2015. All rights reserved. Photograph by Prudence Cuming Associates; 9: © The Al Thani Collection 2017. All rights reserved. Photograph by Prudence Cuming Associates; 14, 19: © Victoria and Albert Museum, London; 27: © Mehrangarh Museum Trust, Jodhpur, Rajasthan, India, and His Highness Maharaja Gaj Singh of Jodhpur.